W9-AAO-842

DB2 Universal Database v7.1 for UNIX, Linux®, Windows®, and OS/2

Database Administration Certification Guide, 4th Edition

ISBN 0-13-091366-9

90000

9 780130 913661

IBM DB2 Certification Guide Series

DB2 Universal Database v7.1 for UNIX, Linux®, Windows®, and OS/2

Database Administration Certification Guide, 4th Edition

GEORGE BAKLARZ ■ BILL WONG

PRENTICE HALL PTR, UPPER SADDLE RIVER, NEW JERSEY 07458
www.phptr.com

Editorial/production supervision: *Nicholas Radhuber*
Cover design director: *Jerry Votta*
Cover designer: *Bruce Kenselaar*
Manufacturing manager: *Maura Zaldivar*
Marketing manager: *Debby vanDijk*
Acquisitions editor: *Michael Meehan*
Editorial assistant: *Linda Ramagnano*

IBM Corporation:
Consulting Editor: *Sheila Richardson*
Manager, DB2 UDB Certification Program: *Susan Visser*

Published by Prentice Hall PTR
Prentice-Hall, Inc.
Upper Saddle River, NJ 07458

Prentice Hall books are widely used by corporations and government agencies for training, marketing, and resale.
The publisher offers discounts on this book when ordered in bulk quantities.
For more information, contact
    Corporate Sales Department,
    Phone 800-382-3419; FAX: 201-236-7141
    E-mail: corpsales@prenhall.com
Or write: Prentice Hall PTR
    Corporate Sales Department
    One Lake Street
    Upper Saddle River, NJ 07458

Printed in the United States of America
10 9 8 7 6 5 4 3 2

ISBN 0-13-091366-9

Prentice-Hall International (UK) Limited, *London*
Prentice-Hall of Australia Pty. Limited, *Sydney*
Prentice-Hall Canada Inc., *Toronto*
Prentice-Hall Hispanoamericana, S.A., *Mexico*
Prentice-Hall of India Private Limited, *New Delhi*
Prentice-Hall of Japan, Inc., *Tokyo*
Pearson Education Asia Pte. Ltd.
Editora Prentice-Hall do Brasil, Ltda., *Rio de Janeiro*

Table of Contents

PART FOUR - Developing Applications.............. 673

Chapter 13 - Application Development Overview 675

Foreword

One of the biggest challenges that computer professionals face today is finding and taking the time to develop new skills to keep up with the changes in technology. Our value as professionals is increased by learning new technologies and developing skills in the use of industry-leading products. We're in the fastest paced industry in the world and the skills shortage has placed a premium on our time. This book provides a fast and easy way to help your career with DB2.

Relational database technology was invented by IBM Research over two decades ago, and IBM delivered the first commercially available relational database, DB2, in the early 1980s. The promise of relational technology was the ability to represent data in a simple tabular form, access it through the expressive yet easy-to-learn SQL query language and put that power in the hands of business analysts and other decision makers. Over the last 20 years, many businesses have realized the value of this promise. Today, tens of thousands of businesses, large and small, all over the world, rely on DB2 databases to store their key corporate data assets and run their business both traditionally and over the Web.

As companies move into an Internet age of broad-band communications, databases must be able to store and serve huge multimedia files, manage ever-increasing volumes of data, handle the tremendous growth in the number of users, deliver steadily improved performance, and support the next generation of applications. With its virtually unlimited ability to scale, its multimedia extensibility, its industry-leading performance and reliability, and its platform openness, DB2 Universal Database has helped lead this evolution. DB2 Universal Database is the first multimedia, Web-ready relational database management system, strong enough to meet the demands of large corporations yet flexible enough to serve medium-sized and small businesses.

Managing this new generation of databases requires a new set of skills. Performance optimization, scalability, data layout, and recovery strategy are simply a starting list of topics that must be dealt with effectively. Mission critical databases are the norm now, and the role of the administrator in this realm is demanding. Keep the system going at peak performance 7 days a week, 24 hours a day. DB2 is designed to be the database for this environment and provides the tools required to meet these expectations.

This Certification Guide is an excellent way to learn about DB2, to develop new skills, and to provide new opportunities for yourself in the computer industry. The included trial copy of DB2 will let you get started quickly and give you hands-on experience that is so helpful to learning. You'll find the self-study design lets you proceed at your own pace, while learning material necessary to complete the formal DB2 UDB certification exams for DB2 UDB Database Administrator. Enjoy the Certification Guide, enjoy using DB2, and enjoy the benefits of being a certified DB2 professional.

Brett MacIntyre
Director, Database Technology
IBM Data Management Division

Preface

This book is a complete guide to the IBM's relational database servers, known as DB2 Universal Database Version 7.1. DB2 Universal Database (DB2 UDB) Version 7.1 is available on many operating systems, and the book has been written with this in mind. Any significant differences in the implementation of DB2 UDB on various operating systems are highlighted. If you are planning to become certified, or you would simply like to understand the powerful new DB2 UDB database servers from IBM, then read on. Those interested in becoming an IBM Certified Professional will want to review the sample questions at the end of this book.

The book is divided into four parts:

- Part 1 - Introduction to DB2 UDB (Chapters 1–4).

  Installing and configuring DB2 UDB servers and clients are covered in Chapters 1, 2, 3, and 4.
- Part 2 - Using SQL (Chapters 5–8).

  The Structured Query Language (SQL) is discussed in Chapter 5, 6 and 7. Database concurrency is discussed in Chapter 8.
- Part 3 - DB2 UDB Database Administration (Chapters 9–12).

  Creating a DB2 UDB database and its related table spaces is covered in Chapter 9. The common administration tasks are discussed in Chapters 10 and 11. Database monitoring and performance considerations are discussed in Chapter 12.
- Part 4 - Developing Applications with DB2 UDB (Chapters 13–14).

  An introduction to application development for DBAs is given in Chapter 13. Chapter 14 deals with some of the DBA activities that are related to application development. SQL used in a programming environment is discussed in chapter 15.

This book can be used as a self-study guide to help you prepare for the DB2 Universal Database V7.1 certification exams or as a guide to DB2 Universal Database V7.1.

The path to certification involves successfully completing these exams:

The test objectives are provided in Appendix A. These should be used as a guide to ensure that you are fully prepared to take the DB2 UDB V7.1 exams.

Experience with DB2 Universal Database Version 7.1 is the best way to prepare for any of these DB2 UDB V7.1 certification exams. Use this Certification Guide in conjunction with your day-to-day use of DB2 UDB V7.1 to assist you in preparing for exams 512 and 513. A companion book, *DB2 Universal Database Version 7.1 Application Development Certification Guide,* will help you prepare for exam 514.

The DB2 Family Fundamentals (512) exam covers these skills:

- Understanding DB2 products and components
- Creating database objects
- Understanding various DB2 data types
- Using SQL to manipulate database objects
- Describing DB2 concurrency

For more details on the test objectives of this exam, see "DB2 Family Fundamentals (512)" on page 744.

The DB2 for OS/2, Windows, UNIX, and Linux Database Adminstration (513) exam covers these skills:

- Managing DB2 instances
- Creating and maintaining database objects
- Managing table spaces
- Using utilities: IMPORT, LOAD, REORG, RUNSTATS
- Managing recovery procedures (BACKUP/RESTORE)
- Analyzing resource problems

For more details on the test objectives of this exam, see "DB2 for OS/2, Windows, and UNIX Database Administration (513)" on page 746.

Note: More information about DB2 UDB certification can be found at http://www.ibm.com/certify.

Conventions

Many examples of SQL statements, DB2 commands, and operating system commands are included throughout the book. SQL statements are usually displayed within a shaded box, and any of the mandatory sections of the statements are shown in uppercase letters. An example of an SQL statement is shown:

```
SELECT lname, fname
FROM candidate
WHERE lname = 'WONG' OR
lname = 'BAKLARZ'
```

SQL is not a case-sensitive language, so the above query would provide the same result regardless of the case of the SQL keywords or the database object (table names or column names). Of course, the data in the database is stored *exactly* as it was entered (including case). Therefore, the above query would only find the candidates with the last name of "WONG" or "BAKLARZ." If the data were stored as 'Wong', it would not be part of the result table.

If SQL keywords are referred to in the text portion of the book, they will be shown as a monospaced font. For example, the SELECT statement is used to retrieve data from a DB2 database.

DB2 commands will be shown using the same method as SQL keywords. For example, the CREATE DATABASE command allows you to define the initial location of database objects. DB2 commands are issued from the Command Line Processor (CLP) utility. This utility will accept the commands in upper- and lowercase letters. The CLP program itself is an executable called db2. In some operating systems, such as AIX, the program names are case sensitive. Therefore, be careful to enter the program name using the proper case.

There are a few operating-system-specific commands in this book. If the commands must be in lowercase they will be shown as such. For example, the UNIX command to create a user is the mkuser command.

Occasionally, notes are provided to highlight a particular point or features that are new to DB2 UDB Version 7.1:

Note: A note may be used to explain a minor operating system difference or it may be used to summarize a concept.

DB2 Version 7.1-specific features are highlighted with this note format.

There are a few syntax diagrams shown in the book. We recommend that the Command Line Processor or the *DB2 UDB V7.1 Command Reference* be used to verify the syntax of DB2 UDB commands. The *DB2 UDB V7.1 SQL Reference* should be used to verify the syntax of SQL statements. To emphasize a term or concept, the term is shown in **bold** type or emphasized with *italics*.

Contributions

The DB2 Universal Database Certification Guide was updated for Version 7.1, making this the fourth edition. Many people from all over the world assisted with the previous versions of this book, and we would like to thank them for their efforts.

For this version of the book, we would like to thank the many customers, colleagues, and technical support personnel we have worked with throughout the years and for their help in creating a better database.

In particular, we would like to thank:

- Susan Visser, for her encouragement and guidance in updating this book
- Bob Harbus, Juliana Hsu, and Rick Swagerman for technical insights into DB2 (that we didn't already know!)
- Bert Nicol for scheduling us to be in the office for more than a day
- Sheila Richardson and Terry McElroy for help in working through the publication process
- Nick Radhuber at Prentice Hall for his publishing expertise and patience
- Mike Babin for management support of this effort
- The DB2 development team for their continued support of this book

Acknowledgments

I'm always thankful that I have an understanding family that could deal with the late nights and busy weekends when I was updating this book. Needless to say, I couldn't have done this without their help and patience! Thanks, Katrina, Geoff and Andrew!

George

I'm taking this opportunity to thank my family; Shirley, Dana, and Austin. Since I've been in the database industry, I've seen the demand for our products increase dramatically as well as the demands for my time away from home. I would not have accomplished any measure of success without their support and understanding. I also owe them a vacation without me working on a book.

Bill

PART 1

Introduction to DB2 UDB

Product Overview

- ◆ DB2 UNIVERSAL DATABASE
- ◆ DB2 CONNECTIVITY
- ◆ DB2 APPLICATION DEVELOPMENT
- ◆ DB2 ADMINISTRATION

*I*n this chapter, you will be introduced to the DB2 Universal Database (DB2 UDB) family of products for UNIX and Intel platforms. DB2 has the ability to store all kinds of electronic information. This includes traditional relational data as well as structured and unstructured binary information, documents and text in many languages, graphics, images, multimedia (audio and video), information specific to operations like engineering drawings, maps, insurance claims forms, numerical control streams, or any type of electronic information. This chapter will illustrate some of the ways to access data in a DB2 database using some of the interfaces provided with the products. A description of each of the DB2 products will be provided to illustrate some of the features and functions.

The DB2 database is an important part of IBM's e-business software portfolio. The e-business Application Framework provides an open blueprint on how to build e-business applications. Popular IBM e-business tools include Visual Age for Java for developing Java programs or components and Tivioli software for distributed systems management. As for application server software, IBM offers several types of servers depending on the business requirement, from Message Queuing (MQ) software to Java-based transaction processing with Websphere Application Server.

The most popular IBM software servers are its database servers, specifically the DB2 Family.

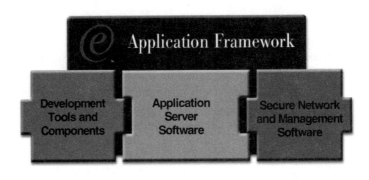

Fig. 1–1 *The e-business Application Framework*

The DB2 Family executes on pervasive devices, Intel, UNIX, AS/400, and mainframe platforms. Supported operating environments include: OS/2, Windows 95/98/2000/NT, Linux, AIX, HP-UX, Sun Solaris, NUMA-Q, OS/400, VSE/VM, and OS/390. The DB2 code base is optimized for each platform to ensure maximum performance. The SQL API is common to all platforms, which allows applications written on one platform to access data on any platform. Internally, the OS/400, VM/VSE, and OS/390 differ from DB2 on the UNIX and Intel platforms, but it is the common SQL API that enables applications to work together. The DB2 code base on Intel and UNIX platforms are identical.

DB2 V7.1 for UNIX, Linux, Windows, and OS/2, provides seamless database connectivity using the most popular network communications protocols, including NetBIOS, TCP/IP, IPX/SPX, Named Pipes, and APPC.

DB2 and e-business

As a core component of IBM's e-business cycle, DB2 is a catalyst for deliving applications that transform a company's operations. Transform is the process that takes a business to an e-business, common applications in this area include: electronic commerce, Enterprise Resource Planning (ERP), Customer Relationship Management (CRM), and Supply Chain Management (SCM). Build is the process of exploiting the integrated Java and multimedia features of DB2. Run is the part of the e-business cycle that ensures performance and scalability; this is especially important with the new Internet-based companies. Finally, with respect to leveraging the data assests, DB2 offers a variety of business intelligence tools to enable end-users makers to make more effective business decisions.

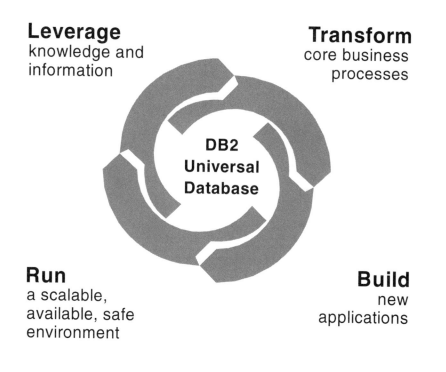

Leverage knowledge and information

Transform core business processes

DB2 Universal Database

Run a scalable, available, safe environment

Build new applications

Fig. 1–2 *The e-business cycle*

In leveraging information in an e-business environment, IBM's Enterprise Information Portal (EIP) provides a secure foundation for a single pont of access to diverse information, business processes, and expertise. Today's high demand for complete and correlated information requires portal access not only to structured transactional and warehouse data, but also to a broader range of content, including XML, HTML, host computer-generated output, images, and audio/video. The IBM Enterprise Information Portal offers access to business data from sources such as spreadsheets, document libraries, company literature, databases, data warehouses, and unstructured information from Web pages. The information can also be searched using parametric or contextual search technologies, with results aggregated across multiple sources and relevant information presented in a context tailored to the user's needs.

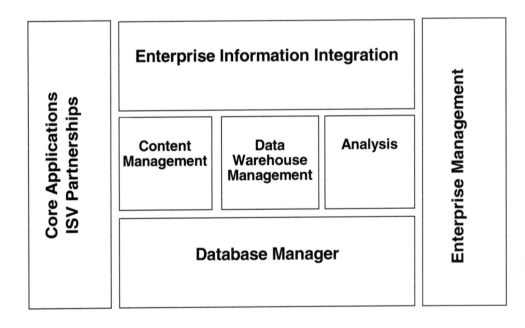

Fig. 1–3 *IBM's Enterprise Information Portal*

DB2 Universal Database

In the distributed environment, DB2 offers several packaging options:

- **Enterprise Edition** - This offering is often used to build e-business applications and to support large departmental applications. It offers the most connectivity options and can share data with third-party databases and DB2 on heterogeneous platforms.

- **Workgroup Edition** - This offering is often used smaller departmental applications or for applications that do not need access to remote databases on the OS/400, VM/VSE, or OS/390 platform.

- **Enterprise Extended Edition -** This offering is used most often to support very large databases. Popular applications include supporting large data warehouses. By providing intra- and interquery parallelism, databases can scale to multiple terabytes. DB2 UDB EEE can exploit clusters or massively parallel hardware architectures.

- **Personal Edition** - This full-function database offering is for single-users and will not accept remote database requests. This offering is available on Windows, OS/2, and Linux.

- **Satellite Edition** - This offering is for single-users and has a smaller footprint than Personal Edition. It will not accept remote database requests. This offering is available on the Windows platform.

- **Everyplace** - This is a mobile computing offering that gives mobile workers access to DB2 data sources in the enterprise through handheld devices such as personal digital assistants (PDAs) and handheld personal computers (HPCs).

 The new DB2 Everyplace executes on a number of pervasive operating environments, including: Palm OS, Windows CE, and EPOC.

DB2 Enterprise Edition

DB2 Enterprise Edition is a relational database management system that is the foundation of many mission-critical systems and the primary focus of this certification guide. It is fully Web enabled, scalable from single processors to symmetric multiprocessors and to massively parallel clusters; and supports unstructured data such as image, audio, video, text, spatial, and XML with its object relational capabilities.

Applications for DB2 Enterprise Edition can scale upward and execute on massively parallel clusters or can scale downward with applications executing on single-user database systems.

DB2 Enterprise Edition is available on the Windows, OS/2, Linux, and UNIX platforms.

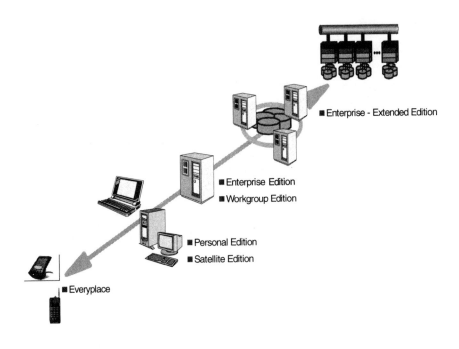

Fig. 1–4 *DB2 Universal Database*

DB2 Workgroup Edition

DB2 Workgroup Edition is designed for use in a LAN environment. It provides support for both remote and local clients. A server with DB2 Workgroup Edition installed can be connected to a network and participate in a distributed environment as show in Figure 1–5.

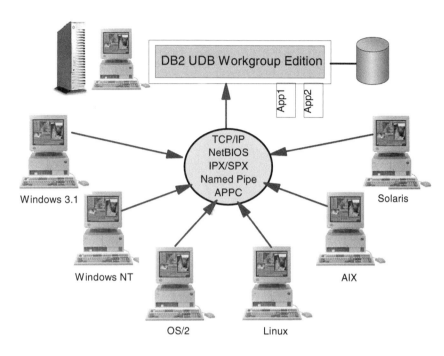

Fig. 1–5 *DB2 Workgroup Edition with remote clients*

In Fig. 1–5, App1 and App2 are local database applications. Remote clients can also execute App1 and App2 if the necessary setup has been performed. A DB2 application does not contain any specific information regarding the physical location of the database. DB2 client applications communicate with DB2 Workgroup Edition using a supported distributed protocol. Depending on the client and server operating systems involved, DB2 Workgroup Edition supports the TCP/IP, NetBIOS, IPX/SPX, Named Pipes, and APPC protocols.

DB2 Workgroup Edition includes DB2 Extenders and Net.Data, a product that allows you to build Internet-ready applications that store data in DB2 databases.

DB2 Workgroup is available on the Windows, OS/2, AIX, Solaris, HP-UX, and Linux platforms.

DB2 Enterprise - Extended Edition

DB2 Enterprise-Extended Edition (or DB2 EEE) is the scalability option that enables DB2 to partition data across clusters or massively parallel computers. To the end-user or application developer, the database appears to be on a single computer. All SQL statements are processed in parallel, thus increasing the execution speed for any given query.

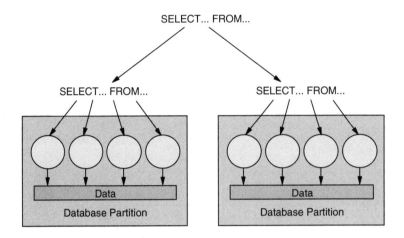

Fig. 1–6 *DB2 processing a query in parallel*

DB2 Enterprise-Extended Edition is available on the Windows, AIX, Solaris, HP-UX, and NUMA-Q platforms. This product is covered in detail in the *DB2 Cluster Certification Guide*.

DB2 Personal Edition

DB2 Personal Edition is a full-function database that enables a single-user to create databases on the workstation on which it was installed. It can be used as a remote client to a DB2 server, since it also contains the DB2 client components. Applications written to execute on the Personal Edition offering can also be used to access a DB2 Server, with no programming changes.

The DB2 Personal Edition product is often used by end-users requiring access to local and remote DB2 databases or developers prototyping applications that will be accessing other DB2 databases.

Fig. 1–7 shows an example of a DB2 Personal Edition installation. In this example, the user can access a local database on his or her desktop machine and access remote databases located on the database server. From the desktop, the user can make changes to the database throughout the day and replicate those changes as a client to the remote database on the DB2 server.

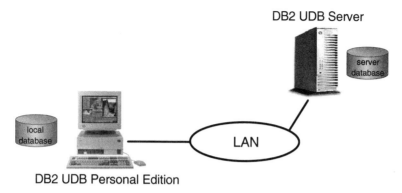

Fig. 1–7 *DB2 Personal Edition*

DB2 Personal Edition includes graphical tools (via the DB2 Administration Client component) that enable a user to administer, tune for performance, access remote DB2 servers, process SQL queries, and manage other servers from a single workstation.

This product is available on Windows, OS/2, and Linux.

DB2 Satellite Edition

DB2 Satellite Edition forms part of a DB2 solution to support systems that operate disconnected from the corporate system the majority of the time and connect occasionally to the corporations central database to exchange data.

DB2 Satellite Edition is a full-function, high-performance DB2 database specially designed for occasionally connected workers using systems running Windows operating systems. The satellite system itself does not require the user to manage the database. This means the end-user is free to focus on business results - the user does not even need to know a database is installed.

The application areas that can benefit from this solution include contract management, insurance application automation, securities marketing, and automobile insurance claims processing. In addition, large-scale branch office deployments are being used to provide automation to franchise stores, insurance agents, and regional offices of large corporations. In these kinds of environments, the applications are custom built, purchased, or a combination.

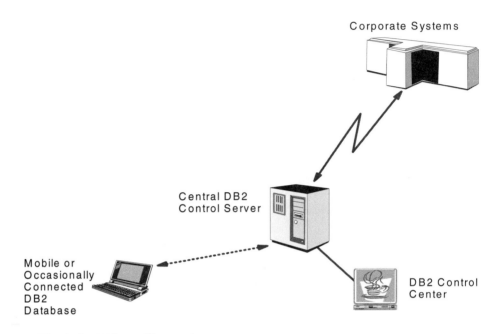

Corporate Systems

Central DB2
Control Server

Mobile or
Occasionally
Connected
DB2
Database

DB2 Control
Center

Fig. 1–8 *DB2 satellite environment*

The satellite environment administration model minimizes the cost of administering a large number of systems by administering collections of systems running the same application and database in groups. Scripts stored at a central administration control point are used to accomplish administrative tasks on the systems in a group. This model also allows for centralized problem determination.

Replication administration uses the same model. Replication subscription definitions are stored in a central control server as scripts. When executed at the satellite system, the scripts set up each satellite for replication with a corporate data store.

 DB2 V7.1 can centrally manage DB2 Workgroup and Enterprise Edition database servers using script-based administration.

DB2 Satellite Edition's small footprint and application compatibility with the rest of the DB2 family make it an ideal candidate for the delivery of distributed applications on systems that will occasionally connect with corporate data stores to exchange data.

This product is only available on the Windows platform.

DB2 Everyplace

DB2 Everyplace is a tiny "fingerprint" database of about 100K. It is designed for low-cost, low-power, small form-factor devices such as personal digital assistants (PDAs), handheld personal computers (HPCs), or embedded devices. DB2 Everyplace runs on devices that use the Palm Computing® Platform, Windows CE, the EPOC operating system, and the QNX Neutrino. DB2 Everyplace provides a local data store on the mobile or embedded device for storing relational data from elsewhere in the enterprise. Relational data can be synchronized to the handheld device from other DB2 data sources such as DB2 Universal Database for UNIX, OS/2 and Windows NT, DB2 for OS/390, and DB2 for AS/400. DB2 Everyplace with IBM Mobile Connect will also synchronize data from other ODBC-compliant data sources such as Oracle and Microsoft.

The DB2 Everyplace Sync Server mobilizes professionals with e-business information anywhere, anytime. It extends the power of DB2 to a wide range of handheld devices, such as those running the Palm Pilot.

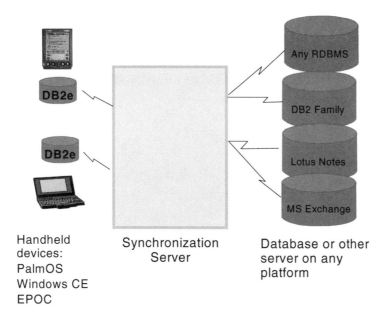

Handheld
devices:
PalmOS
Windows CE
EPOC

Synchronization
Server

Database or other
server on any
platform

Fig. 1–9 *DB2 Everyplace*

Product Overview

The DB2 Everyplace Personal Application Builder supports building applications for small handheld devices that access DB2 Everyplace databases. Some of its capabilities include:

- Supports visual construction of forms for different devices
- Supports the lightweight DB2 Everywhere database on the device
- Provides scripting capabilities for user-defined logic
- Integrates with other tools for application testing and debugging

DB2 Connectivity

DB2 is a very open database and provides a variety of options for connecting to DB2 and non-DB2 databases.

- **DB2 Clients** - Client code is required on workstations for remote users to access a DB2 database.

- **DB2 Connect** - This product provides support for applications executing on UNIX and Intel platforms to transparently access DB2 databases on the OS/400, VM/VSE, and OS/390 environments. Note that DB2 Connect is not required to access DB2 for any of the UNIX or Intel platforms.

- **DB2 DataPropagator** - This product provides replication capabilities for DB2 databases and is integrated in DB2 on the UNIX and Intel platforms.

- **DB2 Net.Data** - Provides the ability for a Web browser to access relational or non-relational data. This middleware provides an easy way to embed database calls into a macro language.

- **DB2 DataJoiner** - This product allows DB2 clients to access, join, and update tables from heterogeneous databases, such as Sybase, Informix, and Microsoft SQL Server.

- **DB2 Relational Connect** - This product allows DB2 clients to access and join tables from Oracle databases, such as Sybase, Informix, and Microsoft SQL Server.

- **WebSphere Application Server** - This Application Server is shipped with DB2 Enterprise Edition and allows developers to use Java as platform in a transaction processing environment.

The *DB2 UDB Quick Beginnings* manual for each platform provides operating system requirements for implementing DB2 distributed configurations.

DB2 Universal Database Clients

A DB2 client can be configured to establish communications with a DB2 server using various communication protocols. The supported protocols vary according to operating system:

Product Overview

- TCP/IP - used in all environments
- NetBIOS - used in OS/2 and Windows environments
- APPC - used in IBM operating environments
- IPX/SPX - used in Novell NetWare LANs
- Named Pipe - used in Windows NT environments

A DB2 client has a number of options for what client code needs to be installed, which will be depend on the requirements of the client. The options include:

- DB2 Runtime Client
- DB2 Administration Client
- DB2 Application Development Client
- DB2 Thin Client

Once a DB2 application has been developed, the DB2 Runtime Client component must be installed on each workstation executing the application. Fig. 1–10 shows the relationship between the application, DB2 Runtime Client, and the DB2 database server. If the application and database are installed on the same system, the application is known as a *local client*. If the application is installed on a system other than the DB2 server, the application is known as a *remote client*.

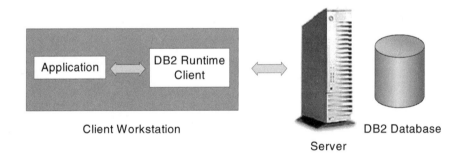

Fig. 1–10 *DB2 Universal Database - Runtime Client*

The Runtime Client provides functions other than the ability to communicate with a DB2 server or DB2 Connect server machine. For example, you can do any of the following:

- Issue an interactive SQL statement on a remote client to access data on a DB2 server or DB2 Connect server.
- Run applications that were developed to comply with the Open Database Connectivity (ODBC) standard or OLE DB.
- Run Java applications that access and manipulate data in DB2 databases using Java Database Connectivity (JDBC) or SQLJ.

Product Overview

If you need to graphically administer and monitor a DB2 database server, then you should install the DB2 Administration Client. It includes all the graphical DB2 administration tools in addition to all of the functionality of the DB2 Runtime Client.

If you need to develop applications, then you should install the DB2 Application Development Client (previously known as the DB2 Software Development Kit). This is a collection of developer's tools that are designed to meet the needs of database application developers. The DB2 Application Development Client includes all of the graphical DB2 administration tools and the DB2 Runtime Client functionality.

The DB2 client product that you should install depends on your requirements and the operating system on the client machine. For example, if you have a database application developed for AIX, and you do not require the DB2 administration or application development tools, you should install the DB2 Runtime Client for AIX.

Some installations prefer having the DB2 Runtime Client reside remotely on another server. Remote workstations then need to access the DB2 Runtime Client code remotely, before getting access to DB2.

DB2 V7.1 supports a federated database environment, where applications see a single database, but they may be located on multiple different DB2 servers.

DB2 V7.1 client support includes: Windows, OS/2, Linux, UNIX, and SGI-IRIX.

DB2 Connect

The DB2 Connect product allows clients to access data stored on database servers that implement the Distributed Relational Database Architecture (DRDA). The target database server for a DB2 Connect installation is known as a *DRDA Application Server.*

Note: The most commonly accessed DRDA application server is DB2 for OS/390.

DB2 Connect supports both the TCP/IP and APPC DRDA communication protocols. The protocol supported depends on the DRDA application server being connected to and the version of the host software being run. For instance, a DB2 Connect server acting as a DRDA Application Requester to a host DRDA

Application Server can connect to DB2 for OS/390 at version 5.1 and higher. Any of the supported network protocols can be used for a DB2 client to establish a connection to the DB2 Connect server.

Some of the major capabilities provided by DB2 Connect include:

- Support for ODBC, OLE DB, CLI, JDBC, and SQLJ applications
- Distributed Join across all DB2 databases
- Distributed Join with Oracle (via Relational Connect)
- Connection Pooling
- S/390 Sysplex Exploitation for failover and load balancing

Some of the common uses of DB2 Connect are:

- Web-enabling DB2 OS/390 by providing browsers direct access
- Leveraging Microsoft applications written using ADO, ODBC, or OLE DB can transparently access DB2 on mainframe platforms
- Offloading mainframe development cycles

The database application must request the data from a DRDA Application Server through a DRDA Application Requester.

> **Note:** The DB2 Connect product provides the *DRDA Application Requester* functionality.

The DRDA Application Server accessed using DB2 Connect could be any DB2 Server on OS/390, VM, VSE, or OS/400. If TCP/IP is the protocol of choice, then the following are prerequisites:

- DB2 for OS/390. Only version DB2 5.1 or higher supports TCP/IP in a DRDA environment.
- DB2 for OS/400. Only OS/400 version 4.3 or higher supports TCP/IP.
- DB2 Server for VSE/VM. Only version DB2 6.1 or higher for VM supports TCP/IP.

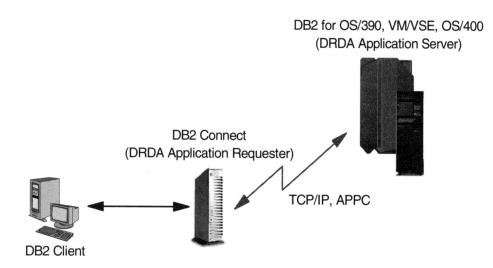

Fig. 1–11 *DRDA application flow*

DB2 Connect is available as a server (Enterprise Edition) and a single-user package (Personal Edition). The DB2 Connect Enterprise Edition product provides the ability for multiple clients to access host data. A DB2 Connect server routes each database request from the DB2 clients to the appropriate DRDA Application Server (Figure 1–11). The remote client communicates with the DB2 Connect server using any of the supported communication protocols. DB2 Connect Personal Edition is available on the following platforms: Windows, OS/2, and Linux. It provides access to host databases from the system where it is installed.

DB2 Replication

DB2 replication (DB2 DataPropagator) allows for data to be propagated from one location to another. It supports a wide variety of databases including DB2, Oracle, Microsoft, Sybase, Informix, IMS, Lotus Notes, and flat files. Replication is also a core technology that enables mobile users to keep their data synchronized with corporate data residing on a DB2 server.

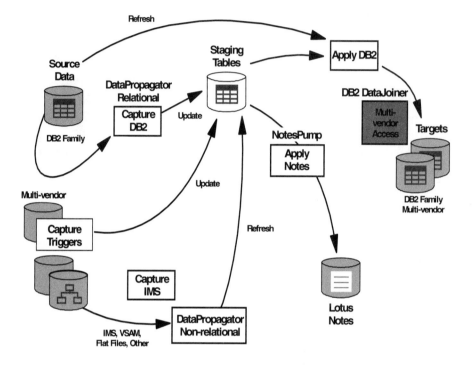

Fig. 1–12 *DB2 replication environment*

DB2 Net.Data

Net.Data provides high-performance Web applications with robust application development function. Net.Data exploits Web server interfaces (APIs), providing higher performance than common gateway interface (CGI) applications. Net.Data supports client-side processing as well as server-side processing with languages such as Java, REXX, Perl, and C++. Net.Data provides conditional logic and a rich macro language, support for Java, JavaScripts, and XML.

In a Net.Data environment, users connected to the Internet or an Intranet can access database applications. Users can either select automated queries or define new ones that retrieve specified information directly from a variety of data sources. The results are returned to the Web browser in HTML format. The Net.Data diagram illustrates how Net.Data allows not only access to DB2 data but also offers native access to Oracle and Sybase, flat files, and other data sources that support ODBC.

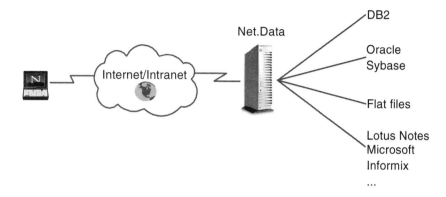

DB2

Net.Data

Oracle
Sybase

Internet/Intranet

Flat files

Lotus Notes
Microsoft
Informix
...

Fig. 1–13 *DB2 Net.Data*

DB2 Relational Connect

DB2 Relational Connect provides applications access to both DB2 and Oracle.
This is particularly useful if there is a heterogeneous database environment where
DB2 and Oracle coexist.

DB2 Relational Connect is targeted for environments where DB2 and
Oracle need to share data.

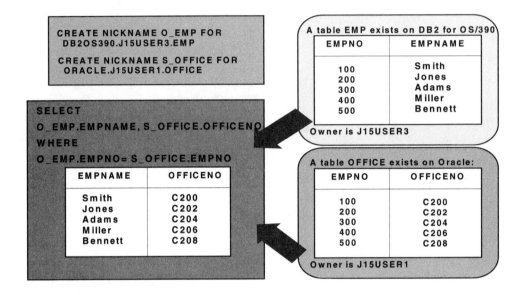

Fig. 1–14 *DB2 Relational Connect*

DB2 DataJoiner

DB2 DataJoiner provides applications to both DB2 and multi-vendor relational databases such as Microsoft, Sybase, and Informix. With a single SQL statement an application can transparently access, join, and update data located across multiple data sources.

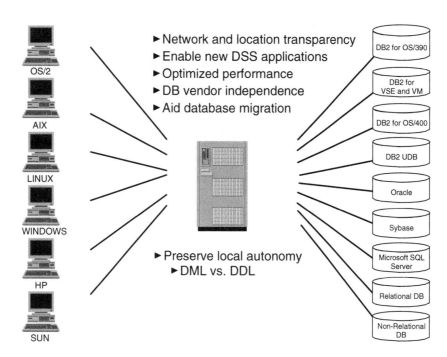

Fig. 1–15 *DB2 DataJoiner*

IBM WebSphere Application Server

IBM WebSphere Application Server is built on an open Java-based platform that enables applications to leverage existing application resources and access various databases, including DB2. Some of the capabilities of WebSphere Application Server include the use of Java servlets, Java Server Pages, and XML to quickly transform static Web sites into vital sources of dynamic Web content. Enterprise Java Beans (EJB) can also be used for implementing EJB components that incorporate business logic. WebSphere Application Server is packaged with DB2.

DB2 Application Development

DB2 offers a rich application development environment that allows the developer to build databases supporting requirements from e-business and business intelligence applications. Many of these tools are integrated with the database; the major tools will be reviewed.

- **DB2 Universal Developer's Edition** - provides the tools for developers to build database applications

- **Stored Procedure Builder** - enables the creation, testing, and debugging of stored procedures on local and remote DB2 servers

- **DB2 Relational Extenders** - enables the SQL API to access unstructured data types including: text, image, audio, video, XML, and spatial data

- **DB2 OLAP Server Starter Kit** - provides the ability to build OLAP cubes using DB2 as the relational data store; a higher-end version, DB2 OLAP Server, is available when there are more users

- **DB2 Data Warehouse Center** - provides the ability to build data marts/warehouses by automating the processes involved in managing, refreshing, moving, and transforming data, including the ability to define star schema model

- **DB2 Data Warehouse Manager** - provides all the capabilities of the Data Warehouse Center, but includes support more data sources and includes the Information Catalog, Query Patroller, and QMF for Windows

DB2 offers support for all popular programming languages and supports the latest Java-based application programming APIs, including: JDBC, SQLJ, ODBC, OLE DB, and CLI.

DB2 Universal Developer's Edition

The DB2 development environment can be installed either on a DB2 server or on a DB2 client. The installation provides all of the necessary data access tools for developing database applications. There are two offerings:

- DB2 Personal Developer's Edition (PDE) - for Windows, OS/2, and Linux platforms.
- DB2 Universal Developer's Edition (UDE) - for all server platforms

The application development environment provided with both product packages allows application developers to write programs using the following methods:

- Embedded SQL
- Call Level Interface or CLI (compatible with the Microsoft ODBC standard)
- DB2 Application Programming Interfaces (APIs)
- DB2 data access through the World Wide Web
- Java applets or applications using JDBC or SQLJ.

The programming environment also includes the necessary programming libraries, header files, code samples, and precompilers for the supported programming languages. Several programming languages, including COBOL, FORTRAN, C, C++, and Java are supported by DB2.

An application developed using the Developer's Edition can be executed on any system with the same operating system that has the DB2 Runtime Client installed. To run the application on another operating system requires the application be rebuilt on the target operating system.

DB2 Personal Developer's Edition (PDE) includes:

- DB2 Personal Edition
- DB2 Connect Personal Edition
- DB2 Extenders

PDE allows a single application developer to develop and test a database application. It is available for Windows, OS/2, and Linux.

DB2 Universal Developer's Edition (UDE) includes all the components in the PDE and:

- DB2 Enterprise Edition
- DB2 Connect Enterprise Edition
- DB2 Workgroup Edition
- Net.Data
- DB2 Application Development Client Pack
- DB2 Administration Client Pack
- DB2 Runtime Client Pack

The Client Packs include the Application Development Client and Administration and Runtime clients for all supported platforms. You can use these to build and run applications on all platforms that DB2 supports.

DB2 Universal Developer's Edition is supported on all platforms that support DB2 Enterprise Edition. It is intended for application development and testing only. The database server can be on a platform that is different from the platform on which the application is developed.

DB2 Stored Procedure Builder

The DB2 Stored Procedure Builder is a graphical application that supports the rapid development of DB2 stored procedures written in Java or SQL. The builder can be launched as a separate application from the DB2 program group or from the integrated development environments such as VisualAge for Java or Microsoft VisualStudio. The Stored Procedure Builder can be used to create stored procedures on local and remote DB2 servers and test, execute, and debug stored procedures.

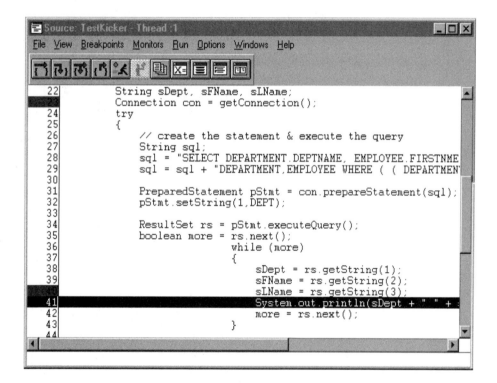

Fig. 1–16 *DB2 Stored Procedure Builder*

 The DB2 Stored Procedure has been enhanced to build stored procedures written in SQL.

DB2 Relational Extenders

DB2 Relational Extenders offer the ability to manipulate data outside of conventional rows and columns to include the manipulation these types of data: text, image, audio, video, and XML. The DB2 Relational Extenders encapsulates the attributes, structure, and behavior of these unstructured data types and stores this information in DB2. From the developer's perspective, the DB2 Relational Extenders appear as seamless extensions to the database and enable the development of multimedia-based applications. The following DB2 Relational Extenders are provided by IBM:

- Text Extender
- Image Extender
- Audio Extender
- Video Extender
- Spatial Extender
- XML Extender
- Net.Search Extender

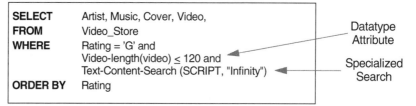

SOLD	ONHAND	RATING	ARTIST	TITLE	COVER	VIDEO	MUSIC	SCRIPT
1212	64	G	Shirley	Inner Light				
39	60	R	Bill	Relics				
73	95	PG-13	Dana	All Good Things				
286	97	PG-13	Austin	Generations				

Mix traditional relational data with unstructured data

```
SELECT      Artist, Music, Cover, Video,
FROM        Video_Store
WHERE       Rating = 'G' and
            Video-length(video) ≤ 120 and
            Text-Content-Search (SCRIPT, "Infinity")
ORDER BY    Rating
```

Datatype Attribute

Specialized Search

Fig. 1–17 *DB2 Relational Extenders*

The purpose of the DB2 Relational Extenders is to provide for the management of unstructured data through the SQL API. By preserving the current investment in relational applications, new nontraditional applications can be introduced by leveraging existing skills. This open environment enables developers and independent software vendors to develop and introduce their own extenders as extensions to DB2.

With DB2 V7.1, the XML Extender is provided with DB2 and allows you to store eXtensible Markup Language (XML) documents as a new column datatype. You also have the ability to decompose and store XML in its component parts as columns in multiple tables. In either case, indexes can be defined over the element or attribute of an XML document for fast retrieval. Furthermore, text search and section search can be enabled on the XML column or its decomposed part via DB2 Text Extender. You can also formulate an XML document from existing DB2 tables for data interchange in business-to-business environments.

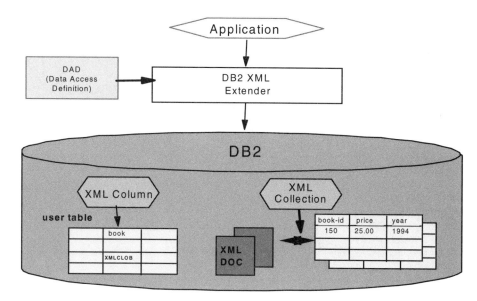

Fig. 1–18 *XML Extender*

 The new XML Extender allows the storage and retrieval of XML documents using the SQL API.

The DB2 Net Search Extender combines in-memory database technology with text search semantics for high-speed text search in DB2 databases. Searching with it can be particularly advantageous in Internet applications where performance is an important factor. Net Search Extender can add the power of fast full-text retrieval to Net.Data, Java, and CLI applications. Its features let you store unstructured text documents of up to 2 gigabytes in databases. It offers application developers a fast, versatile, and intelligent method of searching through such documents.

 The new Net Search Extender was designed to manage heavy text search demands from Internet users querying the Website.

DB2 OLAP Server Starter Kit

The DB2 OLAP Server Starter Kit is a scalable, industrial-strength Online Analytical Processing (OLAP) software that enables you to build sophisticated decision support, planning, and analysis applications for your enterprise. DB2 OLAP Server Starter Kit provides a fast path to turn your warehouse data into business insight. It delivers "speed of thought" query performance to a large set of online users. It is built for e-business with tools to help you quickly deploy Web-based analytical applications.

DB2 OLAP Starter Kit provides DB2 integrated OLAP capabilities. Also, included to build OLAP solutions are: Integration Server to pull data from DB2, an OLAP spreadsheet plug-in for Excel and Lotus 1-2-3, and an Administration Manager.

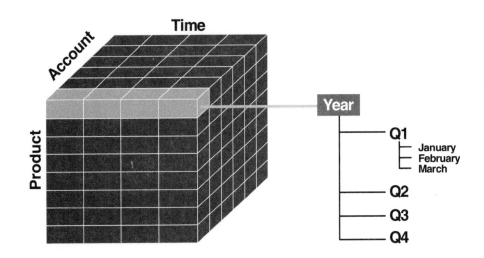

Fig. 1–19 *Multidimensional cube*

DB2 OLAP Server Starter Kit Version 7.1, based on Hyperion Essbase 6.0, provides significant improvements, in the areas of functionality, scalability, performance, and usability, over the previous release, DB2 OLAP Server Version 1.1.

- Attributes, such as colors and sizes can now be defined and analyzed easily. It lets you do detail analysis without increasing the size of your cube.

- Overall performance of system is improved. A reduction of 20% of combined Load and Calculation time has been observed in internal benchmarks based on a mixture of customer applications.

Flexibility in storage is extended to the application level. Depending on individual application needs, the cube can be stored in either DB2 for added flexibility of SQL access or multidimensional storage for optimal performance.

Improved scalability enables analysis at much finer levels of detail with:

- Support of large outlines
- Enhanced concurrent operations
- Optimized I/O operations
- Large data export capability
- Richer calculation functions, including statistical, allocation and forecasting, and member set functions, are added to extend application capabilities
- New features in Spreadsheet Add-in include the new Essbase Query Designer and support of attributes to enhance your usability and productivity

As the number of users grows, the DB2 OLAP Server is available to service greater work demands.

DB2 Data Warehouse Center

This new offering brings together the tools to build, manage, govern, and access DB2 data warehouses. The DB2 Warehouse Center simplifies and speeds warehouse prototyping, development, and deployment. It gives the data center the control for governing queries, analyzing costs, managing resources, and tracking usage. It helps satisfy user requirements for finding, accessing, and understanding information. It provides flexible tools and techniques for building, managing, and accessing the warehouse. And it meets the most common reporting needs for enterprises of any size.

The Data Warehouse Center is integrated with DB2 UDB V7.1 and provides the basic extraction, transformation, and load capabilities to build data warehouses. This tool also provides a star schema builder and a process modeler for automating the steps of transforming data for end-users.

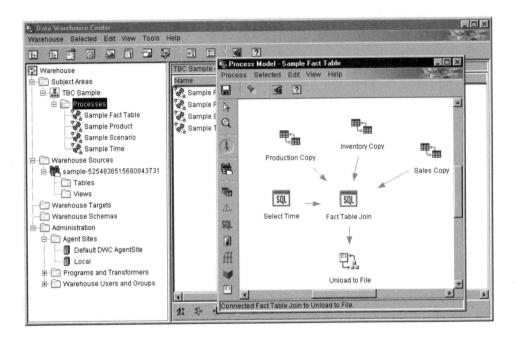

Fig. 1–20 *Data Warehouse Center*

DB2 Warehouse Manager

The DB2 Warehouse Manager adds to basic warehouse and analytical functions available in DB2 Universal Database by providing:

- Additional warehouse scalability through warehouse agents co-located with the database. Warehouse agents manage the flow of data between warehouse sources and warehouse targets.
- Advanced transformations using Java stored procedures and user-defined functions including cleaning data, pivoting tables, and generating keys
- An integrated business information catalog to guide users to relevant information that they can use for decision making.
- Sophisticated query governing and workload distribution (DB2 Query Patroller).
- Query report that satisfies the common reporting needs of most enterprises.
- An integrated business information catalog to guide users to relevant information that they can use for decision making.

The Data Warehouse Manager extends the functions of the Data Warehouse Center by providing support for additional data sources, additional warehouse and statistical transformations, an Integrated Information Catalog, QMF for Windows, and Query Patroller.

Information Catalog

The Information Catalog is a tool for end-users to help easily find, understand, and

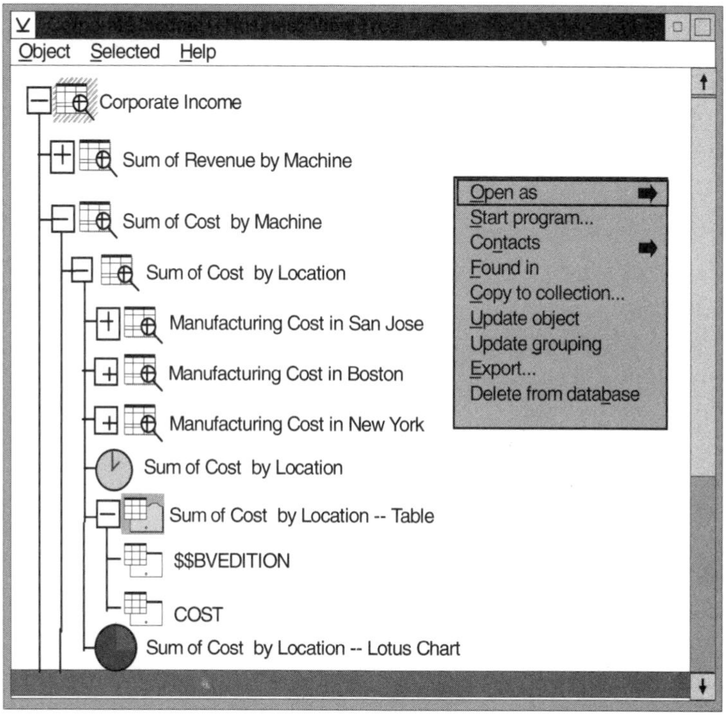

Fig. 1–21 *Information Catalog*

access available information in the corporation. This graphical tool uses a Business View Model, built by the Data Warehouse Administrator, that can be used by the business user to navigate through the data in an enterprise. It allows users to:

- Populate the catalog through metadata interchange with the Data Warehouse Center and other analytical and reporting tools

- Directly register shared information objects
- Navigate or search across the objects to find relevant information
- Display the metadata about the object
- Launch the tools used to render the information for the end-user

 The Information Catalog keeps metadata on data that end-users need to access. This tool automates the exchange of metadata with the Data Warehouse Center.

Query Management Facility

Query Management Facility (QMF) for Windows is an easy-to-use query and reporting tool for publishing reports either locally or onto the Internet. It also easily integrates with other Windows desktop tools. End-users can easily do the following:

- Build queries and reports easily using its graphical interface
- Integrate query results with desktop tools such as spreadsheets and personal databases
- Rapidly build data access and update applications
- Exploit DB2 performance and all of its SQL capabilities

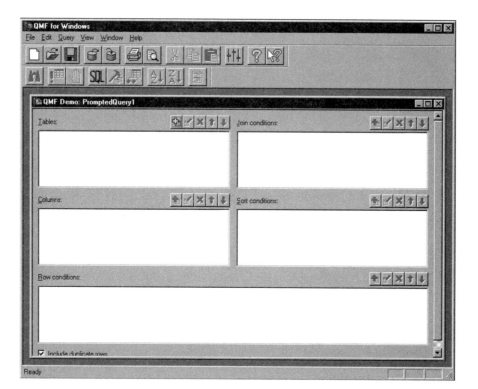

Fig. 1–22 *QMF for Windows*

QMF for Windows can also be used to access DB2 on OS/390 directly if DB2 Connect is installed.

DB2 Query Patroller

DB2 Query Patroller controls and monitors query execution while exploiting the capabilities of uniprocessors, SMP systems, and MPP systems. DB2 Query Patroller works with queries to prioritize and schedule user queries based on user profiles and cost analysis performed on each query. Large queries are put on hold and scheduled for a later time during off-peak hours. Queries with high priority (based on user profiles) are promoted to the top of the schedule. In addition, DB2 Query Patroller monitors resource utilization statistics to determine which CPUs are the least used. Then it provides load distribution functionality that increases the number of users allowed to submit queries at any given time as well as decreases the response time for a query.

DB2 Query Patroller greatly improves the scalability of a data warehouse by allowing hundreds of users to safely submit queries on multi-terabyte class systems. Its components span the distributed environment to better manage and control all aspects of query submission.

DB2 Query Patroller acts as an agent on behalf of the end-user. It prioritizes and schedules queries so that query completion is more predictable and computer resources are efficiently utilized. After an end-user submits a query, DB2 Query Patroller frees up the user's desktop so that he or she can perform other work, or even submit other queries, while waiting for the original query results. DB2 Query Patroller obtains the query cost from the DB2 Optimizer and then schedules and dispatches those queries so that the load is balanced across the installation-specified nodes.

DB2 Query Patroller sets individual user and user class priorities as well as user query limits. This enables the data warehouse to deliver the needed results to its most important users as quickly as possible. If desired, an end-user can choose to receive notice of scheduled query completion through electronic mail.

DB2 Query Patroller consists of components running on the database server and end-users' desktops. DB2 Query Patroller is made up of several components, each having a specific task in providing query and resource management.

 DB2 Query Patroller traps all dynamic queries running against DB2 and is now an integrated component of DB2 UDB V7.1 Warehouse Manager.

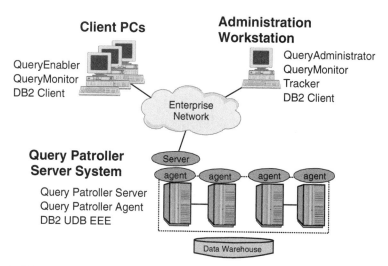

Fig. 1–23 *DB2 Query Patroller components*

The Server is the core component of DB2 Query Patroller. It provides an environment for storing user profiles, setting up system parameters, maintaining job lists, and storing node information. The DB2 Query Patroller system administrator has an interface to the Server to perform these tasks. The Server component executes on a node within the Database Management System (DBMS) called the Management Node.

The Administrator component gives a DBA or system administrator the tools needed to manage the DB2 Query Patroller environment. This tool allows for the management and viewing of queries. The administrator provides menus to display job lists and history, user profiles, node information, and system parameters. It also provides for the display of utilization graphs.

DB2 Data Links Manager

DB2 Data Links Manager can be used to build applications that need to combine the search capabilities of SQL with the advantages of working directly with files to manipulate raw data. A reference is stored for each external file, along with meta-data that describes the contents of each file.

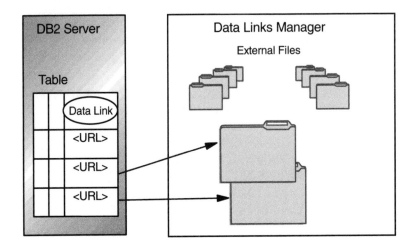

Fig. 1–24 *DB2 Data Links Manager*

DB2 Data Links Manager uses the DATALINK data type, which points to an external file, and the DB2 Data Links Manager components.

You use the DATALINK data type, just like any other data type, to define columns in tables. The DATALINK values encode the name of the Data Links Server containing the file and the file name in terms of a Uniform Resource Locator (URL).

Using DB2 Data Links Manager means that external files can be backed up with the database and SQL Data Control Language statements (GRANT and REVOKE) can be used to control permissions to those files.

Examples of applications that can use the DATALINK data type are:

- Medical applications, in which X-rays are stored on the file server and the attributes are stored in the database.
- Entertainment industry applications that perform asset management of video clips. The video clips are stored on a file server, but attributes about the clips are stored in a database. Access control is required for accessing the video clips based on database privileges of accessing the metainformation.
- World Wide Web applications to manage millions of files and allow access control based on database privileges.
- Financial applications, which require distributed capture of check images, and a central location for those images.

- CAD and CAM applications, where the engineering drawings are kept as files, and the attributes are stored in the database. Queries are run against the file attributes.

Even though the DATALINK column represents an object that is stored outside the database system, you can use SQL queries to search metadata to obtain the file name that corresponds to the query result. You can create indexes on videos, images, text (and so on), and store those attributes in tables along with the DATALINK column. With a central repository of files on the file server and DATALINK data types in a database, you can obtain answers to questions like "what do I have?" and "find what I am looking for."

The DB2 Data Links Manager supports DCE Distributed File System (DFS), supports archiving of linked files to third-party backup solutions, and supports replication using DB2 DataPropagator.

DATALINK Compared to Relational Extenders and LOBs

The DB2 Relational Extenders provide a similar functionality. They keep the metadata that describes the raw data for objects so that you can search on the important aspects of those objects. The extenders allow you to specify whether the object itself is to be maintained either in or outside the database. The extenders, however, do not provide referential integrity between the files on a file server and their references in the database. Thus, it is possible to independently delete either the reference or the file. Moreover, the extenders provide neither access control to the related files nor coordinated backup and recovery of the database and the files.

In contrast to the LOB data type, applications cannot use SQL to access the data in the referenced files. The application gets the file names and uses the file APIs (read/write) to get or manipulate the content.

DB2 Administration

Database administrators have a number of graphical-based tools they can use to manage and administer DB2 databases. Alternatively, a DBA can also use script-based tools to administer the database environment. The main tools available with DB2 will now be examined.

Control Center

The Control Center is the central point of administration for DB2. The Control Center provides the user with the tools necessary to perform typical database administration tasks. It allows easy access to other server administration tools, gives a clear overview of the entire system, enables remote database management, and provides step-by-step assistance for complex tasks.

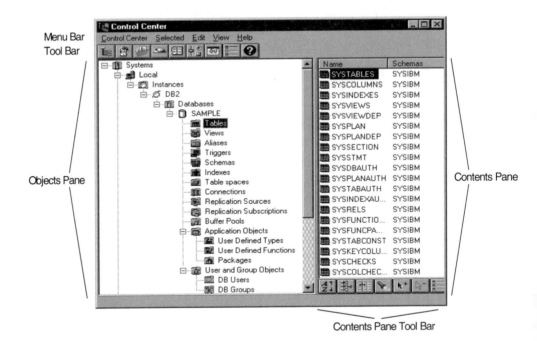

Fig. 1–25 *DB2 Control Center*

The Systems object represents both local and remote machines. To display all the DB2 systems that your system has cataloged, expand the object tree by clicking on the plus sign (+) next to Systems. The left portion of the screen lists available DB2 systems (local and remote). From this example, the system LOCAL contains a DB2 instance, DB2, in which the database SAMPLE is located. When Tables is highlighted, details about each system is shown in the Contents Pane. A number of the existing tables in the SAMPLE database are displayed.

The main components of the Control Center are:

- Menu Bar - Used to access Control Center functions and online help.
- Tool Bar - Used to access the other administration tools.
- Objects Pane - This is shown on the left-hand side of the Control Center window. It contains all the objects that can be managed from the Control Center as well as their relationship to each other.
- Contents Pane - This is found on the right side of the Control Center window and contains the objects that belong or correspond to the object selected on the Objects Pane.
- Contents Pane Toolbar - These icons are used to tailor the view of the objects and information in the Contents pane. These functions can also be selected in the View menu.

Hover Help is also available in the Control Center, providing a short description for each icon on the tool bar as you move the mouse pointer over the icon.

Other Tools Available from the Control Center

By using the Control Center Tool Bar, you can access other administration tools to help you manage and administer databases in your environment:

- Satellite Center - Used to manage the satellite environment.
- Data Warehouse Center - Used to build the data mart/warehouse.
- Command Center - This provides an interactive window that allows input of SQL statements or DB2 commands, the viewing of execution results, and explain information. The graphical command utility is the preferred method for text commands as it provides enormous flexibility and function; interacts with the Script Center.
- Script Center - Used to create, schedule, and manage scripts that can contain SQL statements, DB2 commands, or operating systems commands.
- Alert Center - used to view performance variables that have reached a threshold. For example, use the Alert Center to work with alerts generated by DB2.
- Journal - This keeps a record of all script invocations, all DB2 messages, and the DB2 recovery history file for a database. It is used to show the results of a job and, contents of a script and also to enable or disable a job.
- License Center - Used to manage licenses and check how many connections are used.

- Stored Procedure Builder - This tool enables the creation and testing of DB2 stored procedures.
- Tools Settings - Allows you to configure the DB2 graphical tools and some of their options.
- Information Center - Provides the user with quick access to the DB2 product documentation. Information is available about common tasks, problem determination, DB2 online manuals and the sample programs provided with DB2.

The graphical tool set provided with DB2 is full functioned and very powerful, allowing you to administer and access your DB2 system from graphical interfaces.

Wizards

Wizards (formerly known as SmartGuides) are tutors that help you create objects and perform other database operations. Each Wizard has detailed information available to help the user. The DB2 Wizards are integrated into the administration tools and assist in completing administration tasks. For example, the Add Database Wizard is used to set up communications on a DB2 client with a database on a DB2 server and is invoked from the Client Configuration Assistant (CCA).

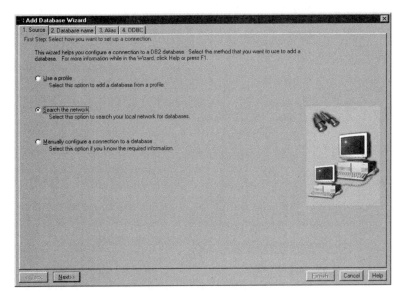

Fig. 1–26 *Client Configuration Assistant - Add Database Wizard*

Fig. 1–26 shows that there are a number of ways to add a remote database. You do not have to know the syntax of commands or even the location of the remote database server. One option searches the network, looking for valid DB2 servers.

The Configure Performance Wizard (Fig. 1–27) can be used to get a database system up and running quickly.

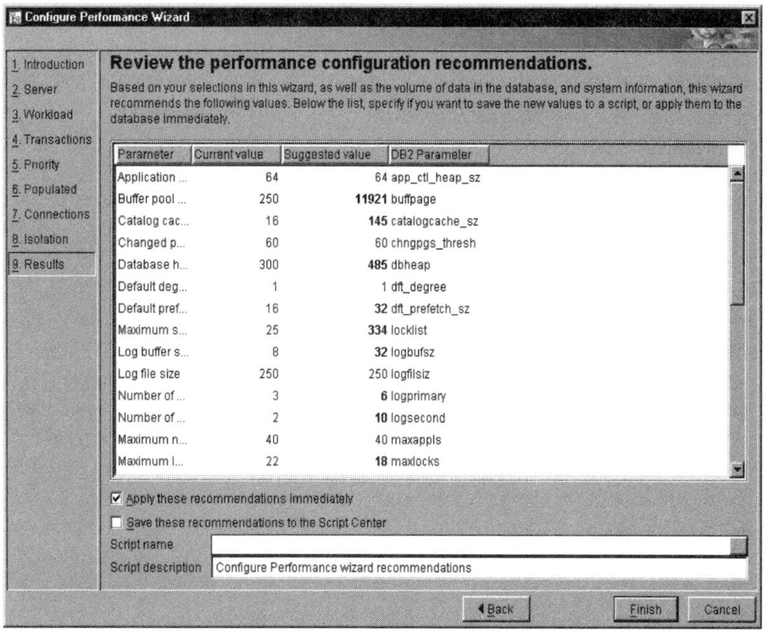

Configure Performance Wizard

Review the performance configuration recommendations.

Based on your selections in this wizard, as well as the volume of data in the database, and system information, this wizard recommends the following values. Below the list, specify if you want to save the new values to a script, or apply them to the database immediately.

1. Introduction
2. Server
3. Workload
4. Transactions
5. Priority
6. Populated
7. Connections
8. Isolation
9. Results

Parameter	Current value	Suggested value	DB2 Parameter
Application ...	64	64	app_ctl_heap_sz
Buffer pool ...	250	11921	buffpage
Catalog cac...	16	145	catalogcache_sz
Changed p...	60	60	chngpgs_thresh
Database h...	300	485	dbheap
Default deg...	1	1	dft_degree
Default pref...	16	32	dft_prefetch_sz
Maximum s...	25	334	locklist
Log buffer s...	8	32	logbufsz
Log file size	250	250	logfilsiz
Number of ...	3	6	logprimary
Number of ...	2	10	logsecond
Maximum n...	40	40	maxappls
Maximum l...	22	18	maxlocks

☑ Apply these recommendations immediately
☐ Save these recommendations to the Script Center
Script name
Script description Configure Performance wizard recommendations

◀ Back   Finish   Cancel

Fig. 1–27 *Configure Performance Wizard*

Invoked from the DB2 Control Center, the wizard extracts information from the system and asks questions about the database workload. It then runs a series of calculations designed to determine an appropriate set of values for the database and database manager configuration variables. You can choose whether to apply the changes immediately or to save them in a file that can be executed at a later time.

DB2 Wizards include:

- Create, Add, Backup, Restore Database
- Configure multisite update
- Create Table
- Create Table Space
- Create Index
- Configure Performance

The Command Line Processor (CLP)

The Command Line Processor (CLP) is a component common to all DB2 products. It is a text-based application that is used to execute SQL statements and DB2 commands. For example, you can create a database, catalog a database, and issue dynamic SQL statements from the CLP.

 Note: The commands and statements issued through the DB2 CLP can also be issued through the DB2 Command Center, which is a preferred graphical interface.

```
C:\>db2 list db directory

 System Database Directory

 Number of entries in the directory = 1

Database 1 entry:

  Database alias                = DB2CERT
  Database name                 = DB2CERT
  Local database directory      = G:\DB2
  Database release level        = 9.00
  Comment                       =
  Directory entry type          = Indirect
  Catalog node number           = 0
```

Fig. 1–28 *Command Line Processor*

Fig. 1–28 shows a command and its output as executed from the Command Line Processor. The Command Line Processor can be used to issue interactive SQL statements or DB2 commands. The statements and commands can be placed in a file and executed in a batch environment or they can be entered in interactive mode.

The DB2 Command Line Processor (CLP) is provided with all DB2 Universal Database, DB2 Connect, and DB2 Developer's products and Clients.

All SQL statements issued from the Command Line Processor are dynamically prepared and executed on the database server. The output, or result, of the SQL query is displayed on the screen by default.

All of the DB2 commands are documented in the *DB2 UDB V7.1 Command Reference*.

Visual Explain

Other graphical tools can be used for tuning or monitoring performance. Visual Explain is a graphical utility that provides a visual representation of the access plan that DB2 uses to execute an SQL statement.

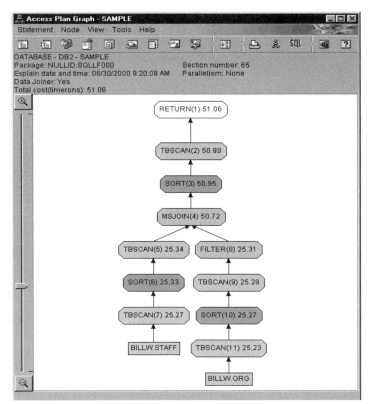

Fig. 1–29 *Access Plan Graph in Visual Explain*

Visual Explain can be invoked from the Control Center or from the Command Center. Fig. 1–29 shows the type of information that is displayed. This example shows that two tables are being accessed and an approximation of the cost of the query is also provided in the Visual Explain output. The estimated query costs represent the complexity and resource usage expected for a given SQL query. More details on the usage of Visual Explain are provided in "Monitoring and Tuning" on page 583.

Performance Monitor

The Performance Monitor is a graphical tool that displays information from the two basic monitoring facilities: Snapshot Monitor and Event Monitor.

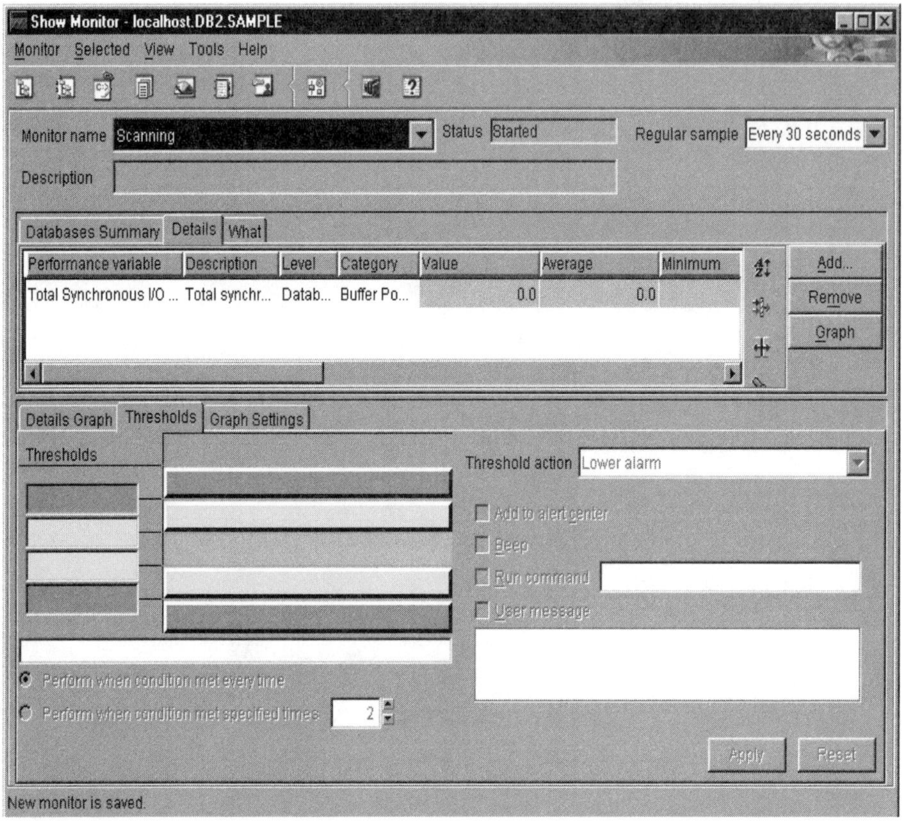

Fig. 1–30 *Performance Monitor*

The *Snapshot Monitor* captures database information at specific intervals. The interval time and data represented in the performance graph can be configured. Fig. 1–30 is an example of Snapshot Monitor output that displays various pieces of information and threshold actions. The Snapshot Monitor can help analyze performance problems, tune SQL statements, and identify exception conditions based on limits or thresholds.

The *Event Monitor* captures database activity events as defined by the event monitor definition. Event Monitor records are usually stored on disk and then analyzed after the data has been captured. The *Event Analyzer* graphical tool provided with DB2 can be used to analyze the captured data. More details on the usage of the DB2 monitors are provided in "Monitoring and Tuning" on page 583.

The DB2 folder is created on the desktop for environments such as Windows or OS/2. This DB2 folder is typically used to invoke the graphical tools provided with DB2. Fig. 1–31 shows some of the components of the DB2 product as they appear in the DB2 folder. A component usually relates to an executable application or utility.

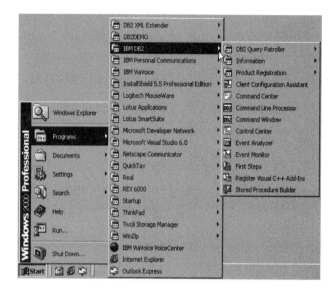

Fig. 1–31 *DB2 desktop folder (Windows)*

The graphical tools integrated with DB2 support these functions:

- Create, alter, and drop databases, table spaces, tables, views, indexes, triggers, schemas, users, user groups, and aliases
- Load, import, export, and reorganize data and gather statistics
- Schedule jobs to run unattended
- Back up and restore databases
- Monitor and tune performance
- Tune queries using access path analysis
- Manage data replication

The following are also available in the DB2 desktop folder:

- Query Patroller - These are the client interfaces to Query Patroller: QueryAdmin, QueryMonitor, and Tracker.
- Information - This folder contains the DB2 online books in HTML format and the release notes that are provided with the product.

- Client Configuration Assistant (CCA) - This is a graphical tool that is used to configure access to remote databases. It can be invoked from the DB2 Desktop folder or from the command line with the `db2cca` command.
- Command Line Processor (CLP) - The CLP is a text-based program that allows you to enter DB2 commands or SQL statements.
- Command Window (Windows platform).
- Command Center - a graphical tool that allows you to enter one or more DB2 commands and statements, store the commands as scripts, view the explain information for a statement, and schedule scripts via the Script Center.
- Control Center - The central point of administration for DB2 Universal Database. This tool allows you to access other tools such as the Command Center and the Journal.
- Event Analyzer - This allows you to access information on database activities collected by event monitors.
- Event Monitor - This allows you to work with DB2 event monitors including creating, starting, stopping, and removing event monitors.
- First Steps - This allows you create the `SAMPLE` database, view sample contents, and access the on-line DB2 library.
- Start/Stop HTML Search Server - This enables (or disables) the searching of a topic in the online books.
- Stored Procedure Builder - assists with the creation of stored procedures that run on DB2 servers
- SQL Assist - a graphical online tool that can be used to build Select, Insert, Update, and Delete statements

Summary

This chapter discussed the DB2 Version 7.1 products for UNIX, Linux, Windows, and OS/2. There are a number of offerings available:

- DB2 Universal Database
- DB2 Connect
- DB2 Universal Developer's Edition
- DB2 OLAP Server Starter Kit
- DB2 Data Warehouse Center

These products provide specific function that allow you to build a complete database environment. In this chapter, the various DB2 packaging options were reviewed and the applications they might support:

- DB2 UDB Everyplace Edition
- DB2 UDB Satellite Edition
- DB2 UDB Personal Edition
- DB2 UDB Workgroup Edition
- DB2 UDB Enterprise Edition
- DB2 UDB Enterprise-Extended Edition

DB2 Connect provides access to DRDA host databases. It is available as DB2 Connect Personal Edition and DB2 Connect Enterprise Edition. The ability to connect to a host database is also included in the DB2 Enterprise and Enterprise-Extended Edition products.

DB2 Satellite Edition and DB2 Everyplace supports occasionally connected systems. DB2 Data Links Manager extends the functions of an RDBMS to files stored outside the database. DB2 Query Patroller provides query and resource management for decision support systems.

This chapter also introduced some of the graphical and command line tools available in DB2. The Command Line Processor (CLP) is a text-based application that allows you to enter DB2 commands and SQL statements and is found in all DB2 products. From the desktop, an administrator can configure remote and local systems, administer instances and databases, and create database objects. In the remaining chapters, additional DB2 functions and tools will be examined in how they assist the end-user, application developer, and administrator.

Product Overview

2

Getting Started

- ◆ INSTALLING DB2 SERVERS
- ◆ INSTALLING DB2 CLIENTS
- ◆ CREATING INSTANCES
- ◆ SETTING UP THE ENVIRONMENT

*T*his chapter provides an overview of the first steps in getting started with setting up a DB2 database server. A few steps are required before the creation of a DB2 database and accessing the database using SQL. First, the installation process for DB2 in various operating environments will be examined.

A distributed installation will also be reviewed. If you are planning to install DB2 products across your network, a network-based distributed installation can be significant. Rolling out multiple identical copies of DB2 products is possible with this method.

Once the DB2 products have been installed, the environment that is created by the installation process will be examined. This requires understanding the different levels of managing the DB2 environment from a global, instance, and user perspective. DB2 databases are created within an instance on a DB2 database server. The management of multiple instances including administration commands will also be reviewed.

Product Installation

This section discusses installation of DB2 Universal Database Windows, OS/2, and UNIX. There are some differences between the platforms, but once the DB2 product is installed, the administration is very similar within the DB2 family of database servers.

The installation process detects the active communication protocols on your system and configures them to work with DB2. Two instances are created when DB2 is installed. A global instance called the DB2 Administration Server (DAS) instance is created. The DAS instance is used by the DB2 administration tools, including the Control Center and the Client Configuration Assistant, to satisfy the requests. The second instance, called DB2, is used to create and manage databases.

Windows and OS/2 Installation

This section discusses installing DB2 distributed on Windows and OS/2; our example is Windows NT.

Before beginning the installation on a Windows NT machine, make sure that the user account that will be used to perform the installation is:

- Defined on the local machine
- A member of the Local Administrator's group
- Given the *Act as part of the operating system* advanced user right

To install, insert the CD-ROM into the drive. The auto-run feature automatically starts the setup program. The setup program will determine the system language and launch the setup program for that language. If the setup program fails to auto-start, execute the following command from an operating system window:

```
x:\setup.exe
```

x represents the CD-ROM drive.

Fig. 2–1 *DB2 Welcome screen for Windows NT installation*

Fig. 2–1 shows the Welcome window. Click on **Next** to continue.

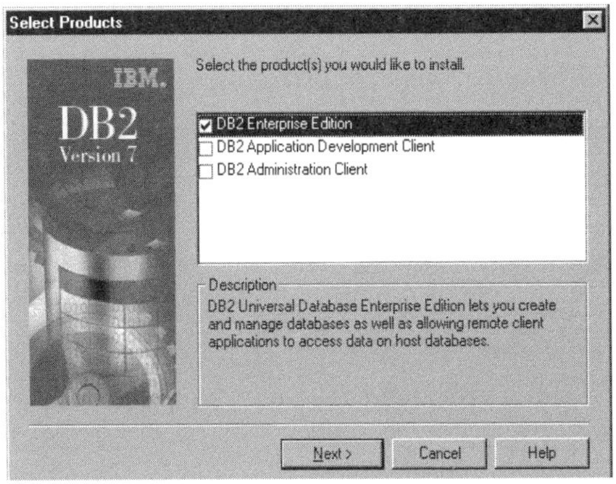

Fig. 2–2 *DB2 product selection screen for Windows NT*

Fig. 2–2 shows you the products you can install. For this example, Enterprise Edition is selected.

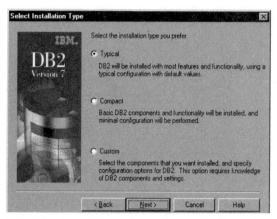

Fig. 2–3 *Windows NT selection screen for installation type*

There are three types of installation:

- **Typical** installs those DB2 components that are used most often, including all required components, ODBC support, documentation, and commonly used DB2 tools such as the Control Center, Client Configuration Assistant, and the Information Center. The DAS instance and the DB2 instance are created during this install.

- **Compact** installs only the required DB2 components and ODBC support. The DAS instance and DB2 instance are also created.

- **Custom** installs only the components that you select. You are given the option of when to start the DAS and DB2 instances as part of the Custom installation process.

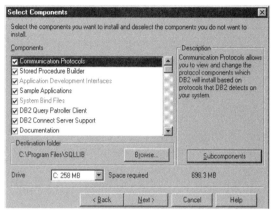

Fig. 2–4 *DB2 component screen*

Fig. 2–4 illustrates some of the choices available with a custom install. Notice the amount of disk that is available on the drive. The products will be installed in the `C:\Program Files\SQLLIB` directory. You can change the drive and the install directory from this window. Highlight a component and click **Details** to select sub-components. The following example is for the Control Center.

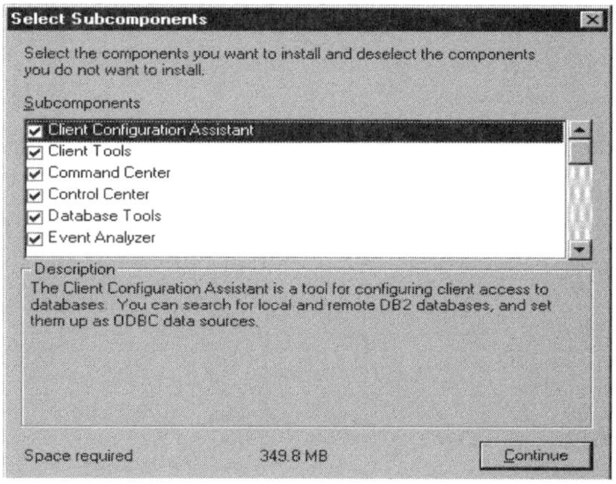

Fig. 2–5 *DB2 subcomponents*

Fig. 2–5 shows the available subcomponents and disk requirements for the selected installation. Notice that once an item is selected, a description of that item is provided. Click **Continue** to go back to the previous window (Fig. 2–4) and then, clicking on **Next**, the following window appears:

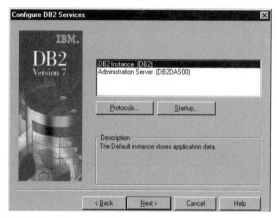

Fig. 2–6 *Configure DB2 services*

Fig. 2–6 shows instances that are being created, a DB2 instance for managing databases, and the DB2 Administration Server instance (DAS). The setup program customizes DB2 to use the communication protocols detected on your system. Highlight the DB2 Instance and Click **Protocols**; the following window appears:

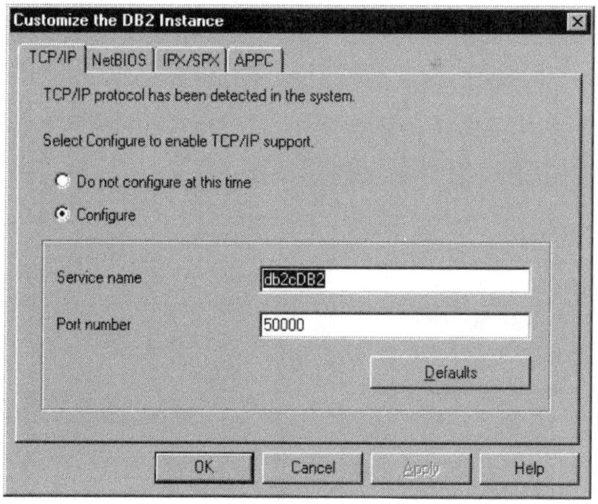

Fig. 2–7 *DB2 instance protocols configuration (TCP/IP)*

The DB2 installation utility examines your system to see what communication protocols are installed and configured to use with the DB2 instance and the DAS. If you select Typical or Compact install (Fig. 2–3 on page 54), communication protocol configuration is done automatically. The Custom install option allows you to explicitly configure communication protocols. Fig. 2–7 shows that TCP/IP has been detected. The values shown in Fig. 2–7 will be used for TCP/IP settings with the DB2 instance unless changed at this time.

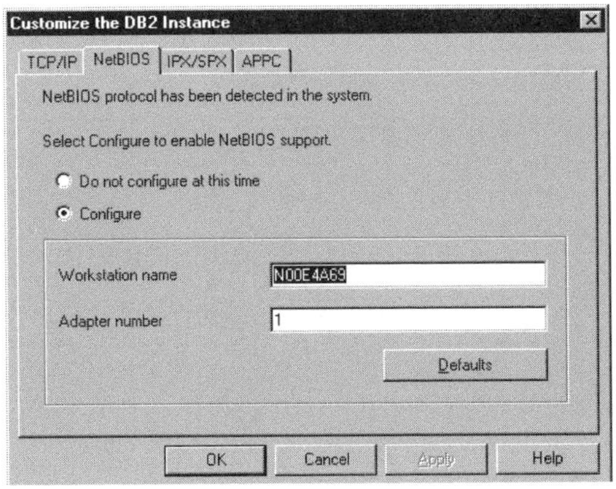

Fig. 2–8 *DB2 instance protocols configuration (NetBIOS)*

Fig. 2–8 shows that NetBIOS has been detected as well. The values shown in Fig. 2–8 will be used for NetBIOS settings with the DB2 instance unless changed at this time. Click **OK** to go back to the previous window (Fig. 2–6). Now, let us customize communication protocols for the DAS instance.

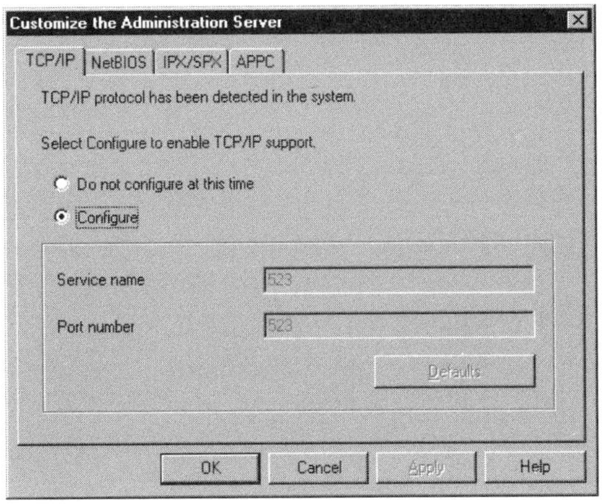

Fig. 2–9 *DB2 Administration Server protocols configuration (TCP/IP)*

The protocol configuration for the DAS instance is similar to that of the DB2 instance. Notice the same protocols were detected on your system. Changes can be made at this time. However, notice TCP/IP settings for the DAS instance cannot be altered. These are indicated by the gray-shaded areas in the communication-specific windows. You are not allowed to change the port number for TCP/IP or the socket number for IPX/SPX for the DAS instance since these values are reserved within DB2.

Getting Started

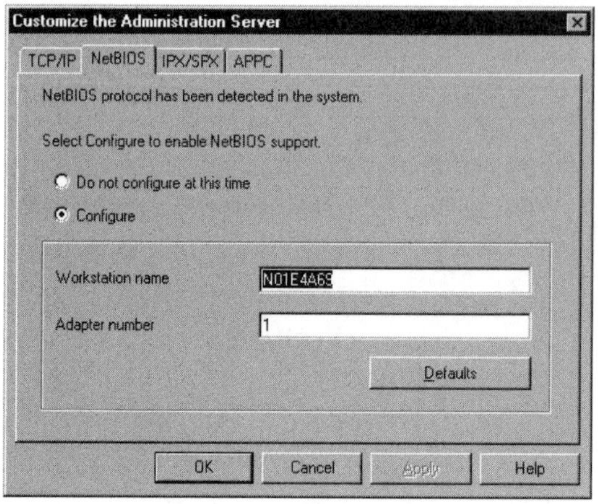

Fig. 2–10 *Administration Server protocols configuration (NetBIOS)*

Notice that you can change the communication settings for NetBIOS.

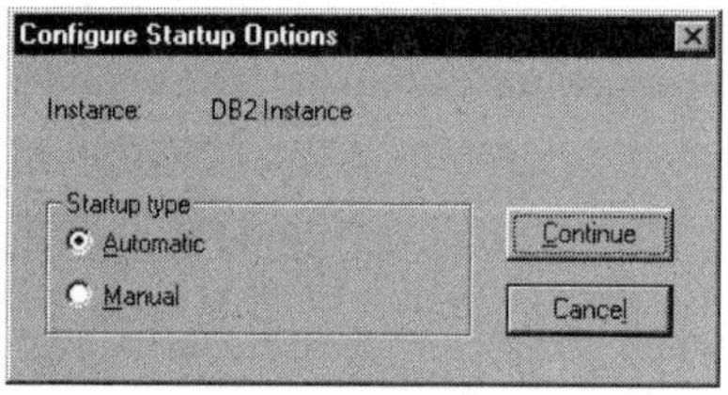

Fig. 2–11 *Select start options (DB2 instance)*

Clicking **Startup** on the Configure DB2 Services window (Fig. 2–6 on page 56) brings up the window shown in Fig. 2–11. By default, the DB2 instance will be automatically started when your server boots. You can choose whether to have the DB2 instance started automatically. You may also change these start options after DB2 has been installed.

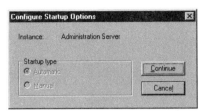

Fig. 2–12 *Select start options (Administration Server instance)*

Fig. 2–12 shows the start option for the DAS instance. Notice that you are not allowed to change the start option for the DAS instance. You may change these start options after DB2 has been installed.

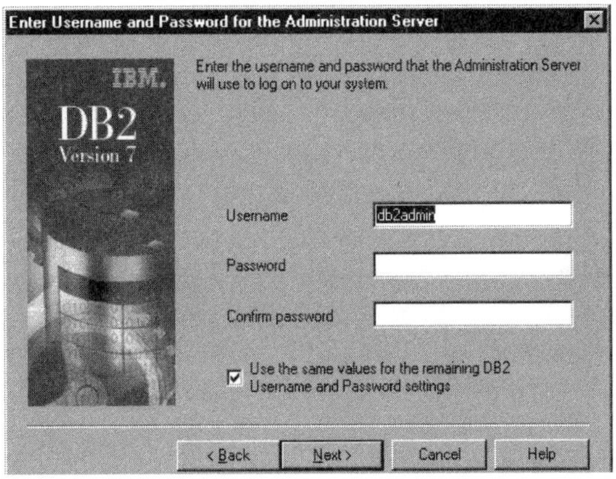

Fig. 2–13 *Username and password for the Administration Server*

After setting up communication for the DAS and DB2 instances, the Administration Server logon screen appears. From here, you can change the default username and password used by the DAS instance. The username you specify here must conform to DB2's naming rules. See the manual *DB2 UDB V7.1 Quick Beginnings* for each platform for more information about the naming rules.

 DB2 V7.1 supports up to 30-byte DB2 userids, authids, and schema names.

If you want to specify an existing user account, it must:

- Be defined on the local machine
- Belong to the Local Administrator's group
- Have the *Act as part of the operating system* advanced user right

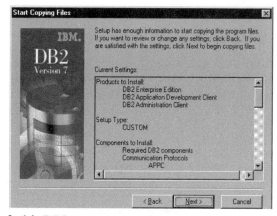

Fig. 2–14 *DB2 component summary*

Once you have entered values for username and password, the installation utility displays a summary report. The summary report shows the selections that you have made. After viewing your choices, you can continue with the installation or make changes. The DB2 products are then installed on your system. After the installation of the DB2 product is completed, you must reboot your system. Upon completion, the First Steps screen appears. How to use the First Steps will be discussed in the section "Using First Steps" on page 82.

Windows and OS/2 Install Directory Structure

It is useful to understand where the DB2 products are installed. Some of the structure is displayed below:

```
\sqllib          - Readme file, etc.

\sqllib\adsm     - ADSTAR Distributed Storage Manager files
       \bin      - Binary executable files
       \bnd      - Bind files for utilities
       \cc       - Control Center files
       \cfg      - Default system configuration files
       \conv     - Code page conversion table files
       \DB2      - Default instance directory
       \DB2DAS00 - Default DAS instance Directory
       \doc      - On-line Books
       \function - Default location for UDFs
       \function\unfenced - Default location for unfenced UDFs
       \help     - On-line help files
       \java     - Java programs
       \java12   - JDK 1.2 support files
       \misc     - DB2 tools and utilities
       \msg\prime- Message files
       \qp       - Query Patroller Client files
       \samples  - Sample programs, sample scripts
       \spmlog   - DB2 Syncpoint Manager log file
       \thnsetup- Installation files for thin clients
```

Fig. 2–15 *Windows and OS/2 install directory structure*

The files and directories in Fig. 2–15 are created under the `sqllib` directory on the drive where DB2 is installed (`c:\SQLLIB`, for example). Do not attempt to delete or modify any of these files. The actual directory structure may be different than the one displayed depending on the DB2 products installed. You can choose a directory different than `SQLLIB`.

UNIX and Linux Installation

In the UNIX and Linux environments, it is recommended to used the db2setup utility to install DB2 and its various components. This utility uses a text-based interface and offers similar options as the graphical interface available on Intel environments. The administrator can select from the following installation methods:

- The db2setup utility. This program is supplied with the DB2 product and is the recommended installation method. It is similar to the setup program for Windows or OS/2 in that it detects and configures communication protocols to use

Getting Started

with the DAS and DB2 instances. The other methods require you to manually configure your system.

- The install command found in your operating system environment. For example, in AIX, the installp command will install the DB2 products. Using this command requires you to know the complete syntax.

- There may be an installation utility available in your operating system environment. For example, in AIX, the System Management Interface Tool (SMIT) is available to install software. This is a better choice than using the install command. However, there is no communication detection and configuration performed. Also, the DAS and DB2 instance are not created.

> **Note:** The following Linux environments have been tested with DB2: Red Hat Linux, Caldera Open Linux, Turbo Linux, SuSE Linux.

The db2setup utility is the recommended choice to install DB2. This utility is consistent across all UNIX and Linux environments. To run the db2setup utility, perform the following steps:

1. Log in as a user with root authority.

2. Mount the CD-ROM file system.

3. Change to the directory where the CD-ROM is mounted by entering the **cd / cdrom** command where **cdrom** is the mount point of your product CD-ROM.

4. Enter the **./db2setup** command

5. Select **Install** and press Enter. The Install DB2 V7 window appears (this text-based screen is similar to the graphical screens produced when installing on an Intel-based environment).

6. Select the products desired and that are licensed for the installation. Press **Tab** to move between available options and fields. Press **Enter** to select or deselect an option. Selected options are denoted by an asterisk. When a DB2 product is selected to install, you can choose the product's **Customize** option to view and change the optional components that will be installed.

> **Note:** For some operating environments, you may have to modify the Kernel configuration parameters to install and run DB2; see the *Quick Beginnings for UNIX* manual for details. Also, the following shells are supported: bash, Bourne, Korn.

UNIX Install Directory Structure

The directory for installation of the DB2 products will vary depending on your UNIX environment. For example, in AIX, DB2 products are installed in the `/usr/lpp/db2_vv_rr` directory where `vv` represents the version of DB2 and `rr` represents the release. The directory structure created under `/usr/lpp/db2_07_01` will be similar to the following:

```
Readme          - Readme file, etc.
adm             - System administrator and executable files
adsm            - ADSTAR Distributed Storage Manager files
bin             - Binary executable files
bnd             - Bind files for utilities
cc              - Control Center files
cfg             - Default system configuration files
conv            - Code page conversion table files
doc             - On-line Books
function        - Default location for UDFs
function/unfenced Default location for unfenced UDFs
install         - Installation program
instance        - Instance scripts
java            - Java programs
lib             - Libraries
map             - Map files for DB2 Connect
misc            - DB2 tools and utilities
msg/$L          - Message catalogs
samples         - Sample programs, sample scripts
```

Fig. 2–16 *UNIX install directory structure*

Depending on the products you are installing, some of these directories may not exist. When an instance is created, symbolic links are created under the home directory of the DB2 instance owner. These links point to the directory where DB2 was installed.

DB2 software registration is handled automatically if you installed your DB2 product from a CD-ROM using the DB2 Installer program. If you installed DB2 using the operating system's native installation tools, you must use the `db2licm` command to register DB2.

```
db2licm -a /cdrom/db2/license/filename.lic
```

`/cdrom` represents the CD-ROM mount directory and `filename.lic` represents the file containing valid license information.

Getting Started

It is possible to install different versions of DB2 products on the same UNIX server because the product files will be installed in a different path.

DB2 Client Installation

At this time, the installation of a DB2 Server on Windows, OS/2, and UNIX has been demonstrated. The installation considerations of the DB2 clients will now be examined.

The DB2 client provides a runtime environment that is required for DB2 applications to access database resources. The DB2 client contains the communications infrastructure to communicate with remote database servers. You can also execute SQL, bind packages, use data manipulation utilities (Import/Load/ Export), and catalog remote nodes and databases. Most of the database administrator tasks can be performed from a DB2 client.

There are three types of DB2 clients you can install:

- **DB2 Run-Time Client** provides the ability to access DB2 databases and a basic application execution environment.
- **DB2 Administration Client** provides all the features of the DB2 Run-Time Client and includes all the DB2 Administration GUI tools, documentation, and support for Thin Clients.
- **DB2 Software Developer's Kit (SDK)** client provides all the features of the DB2 Administration Client and also includes libraries, header files, documented APIs, and sample programs to build character-based, multimedia, and object-oriented applications.

A Thin Client is not an installable component; however, it is a type of DB2 client. You can install a DB2 Administration Client on a code server and have Thin Client workstations access the code across a LAN connection. The benefits of a thin client are reduced disk space on each DB2 client and easier software changes and updates. See the manual *Installation and Configuration Supplement* for more information.

Remember that licensing is controlled on the DB2 Server or the DB2 Connect Server and not on each of the client workstations. Each operating system is slightly different, but the installation process is similar on all platforms.

Installing the DB2 Client on Windows and OS/2

The DB2 client installation for Windows and OS/2 is similar to the server installation; our example is the DB2 Administration Client. The DB2 Administration Client will install the following components by default:

- DB2 Run-Time Client
- Communication protocol
- ODBC Support
- Java Enablement
- System Bind Files
- GUI tools
- DB2 Query Patroller Client
- Documentation

You may select the optional products to install. After completing the installation, you must reboot your system to make the products available.

> **Note:** The installation program creates DB2 program groups and items, updates the Windows registry, and creates a client instance called DB2.

> **Note:** In Windows you must make sure the user account used to install the product is defined on the local machine, belongs to the Local Administrator's group and has the *Act as part of the operating system* advanced user right.

Installing the DB2 Client on UNIX

The DB2 client installation for UNIX platforms is similar to the server installation for UNIX. The components installed will depend on whether you elect to use defaults that include:

- DB2 Run-Time Client
- Java Enablement
- Codepage Conversion Support

The preferred method for installation is to use the DB2 Installer program. During the installation process, you will be prompted to create a DB2 instance, or a default one will be used. A DB2 client instance cannot contain local databases. A DB2 client requires that the proper links to the DB2 product files have been created.

Distributed Installation

Distributed installation is an installation method to make rolling out multiple identical copies of DB2 products possible. If you are planning to install DB2 products across your network, a network-based distributed installation can be significant.

Before starting an installation of DB2 products, you need to prepare an ASCII file called a response file that can be customized with the setup and configuration data that will automate an installation. The setup and configuration data would have to be entered during a normal install; however, with a response file, the installation can proceed without any intervention.

A response file specifies such configuration and setup parameters as the destination directory and the products and components to install. It can also be used to set up the following settings:

- Global DB2 registry variables
- Local DB2 registry variables
- Database manager configuration settings

You can use a response file to install an identical configuration across every system on your network or to install multiple configurations of a DB2 product. For example, you can customize a response file that will install a DB2 Administration Client. You can then distribute this file to every system where you want this product to be installed.

There are two ways to prepare a response file:

- Modify a provided sample response file.
- Use the *Response file generator.*

Sample Response Files

The DB2 CD-ROM includes a ready-to-use sample response file with default entries. The sample response files are located in:

- `x:\db2\common` (Windows)
- `x:\db2\os2\language` (OS/2)
- `/cdrom/db2/install/sample` (UNIX)

x represents your CD-ROM drive, `language` represents the two-character code that represents your language (for example, `EN` for English), and `/cdrom` represents the path on which the CD-ROM file system is mounted.

For example, the `db2admcl.rsp` file is provided for the installation of the DB2 Administration Client. A part of `db2admcl.rsp` file is shown in Fig. 2–17.

```
* General Options
* ----------------
PROD                = ADMIN_CLIENT
*FILE               = C:\SQLLIB
*TYPE               = 0,1,2 (0=compact,1=typical,2=custom)
*COMP               = APPC
*COMP               = IPXSPX
*COMP               = NAMED_PIPES
*COMP               = NETBIOS
*COMP               = TCPIP
*COMP               = ODBC_SUPPORT
*COMP               = JDBC_SUPPORT
*COMP               = SQLJ_SUPPORT
*COMP               = IBMJRE
```

Fig. 2–17 *Sample response file*

You can copy a sample response file into a hard disk drive and modify each parameter. See the manual *Installation and Configuration Supplement* for more information about available parameters for a response file.

Response File Generator

The response file generator utility creates a response file from an existing installed and configured DB2 product. You can use the generated response file to recreate the exact setup on other machines.

For example, you could install and configure a DB2 Run-Time client to connect to various databases across your network. Once this client is installed and configured to access all the database that your users must have access to, you can run the response file generator to create a response file and a profile for each instance.

To generate a response file, execute the following command:

```
db2rspgn -d x:\path
```

A response file is generated in the path you specify with the -d option. The file name is fixed depending on which product has been installed. For example, the db2admcl.rsp file is generated for the Administration Client. In addition to the response files, instance profiles are generated in the same path for all instances in this machine. Each instance profile has the settings of DB2 registry variables, database manager configuration parameters, node directory, database directory, and so on. If you are planning to set up and configure identical DB2 products, you only need to specify the installation response file when you perform the installation. The installation response file that was created by the response file generator will automatically call each instance profile. You only need to ensure that the instance profiles are located in the same drive and directory as the installation response file.

 Note: The response file generator is only available on OS/2 and Windows.

Distributed Installation with a Response File

With a response file, the installation can proceed without any intervention. You can configure a CD-ROM drive or a hard disk drive to be shared and make the DB2 install files and response files accessible to the machines where the DB2 product will be installed. To use a response file, you use the same installation program as the normal installation with the option to specify a response file. For Windows NT/9x, execute the following command:

```
setup /U x:\path\response_file /L y:\path\logfile
```

You specify a response file with the /U option. The /L option is used to specify the log file for this installation. The default log file is x:\db2log\db2.log (x: is the boot drive).

For UNIX, execute the following command:

```
db2setup -r /path/response_file
```

You specify a response file with the -r option. The log of this installation is written into /tmp/db2setup.log.

For OS/2, modify the sample cmd file provided in the directory x:\db2\os2\language and use it.

After the installation and configuration is completed, you should check the log file for any errors or problems.

The DB2 Environment

Before creating and working with databases, you need to understand the DB2 environment. The DB2 environment controls many database-related factors, such as what protocols may be used for accessing remote databases, what paths should be used by applications when searching for database-related files, how much memory will be allocated for various buffers that databases and applications use, and how the system will behave in certain situations. This complex environment is controlled by several different mechanisms including:

- DB2 Profile Registry
- Environment variables
- Configuration parameters

This section discusses the DB2 Profile Registry and environment variables. Configuration parameters are discussed throughout the remainder of this book.

DB2 Profile Registry

Much of the DB2 environment is controlled by entries stored in the DB2 Profile Registry. The objective of the Profile Registry is to consolidate the DB2 environment, so that key controlling factors are centrally located and easily managed. Many of the Registry values control DB2 interfaces or communication parameters, so the variables that are set in the registry may vary by platform. The following are some of the parameters that may be set in the DB2 Registry:

- `DB2CODEPAGE` - This applies to all platforms. If not set, DB2 will use the code page set for the operating system.
- `DB2DBDFT` - The default database for implicit connections.
- `DB2COMM` - This applies to all DB2 servers that participate in a distributed DB2 environment. It specifies which DB2 communication listeners are started with DB2.
- `DB2NBADAPTERS` - This applies only to DB2 for Windows and DB2 for OS/2 servers, specifying which local adapters to use for NetBIOS communication.

 Note: You don't have to reboot your system after making changes to the DB2 Registry.

For a complete list of parameters and values, refer to the *DB2 UDB V7.1 Administration Guide*.

Getting Started

Managing the DB2 Profile Registry

There are some values in the DB2 Profile Registry that are applied globally for the system, some that are applied across database partitions if the database is partitioned, and some that are applied only for a particular instance. The DB2 Profile Registry is divided into four registries. They are:

- DB2 Instance-Level Profile Registry - The majority of DB2 registry variables are placed within this registry. The variable settings for a particular instance are kept here.
- DB2 Global-Level Profile Registry - If a variable is not set for a particular instance, this registry is used. This registry contains the machinewide variable settings.
- DB2 Instance Node-Level Profile Registry - In a system where the database is divided across different database partitions, this registry resides on every particular database partition.
- DB2 Instance Profile Registry - This registry contains a list of all instance names recognized by this system.

The db2set Command

The registry information is stored in files containing variable names and values. However, these files should not be edited or manipulated directly. To update registry values, use the db2set command. Any changes made to the values in the registry are applied dynamically, and you do not need to reboot your system for the changes to take effect. The DB2 registry applies the updated information to the DB2 applications started after the changes are made. For example, if changes are made at the instance level, you must issue a db2stop to stop the instance followed by a db2start.

Using the db2set command with the -all option, you can see the list of all of the profiles variables set for your environment.

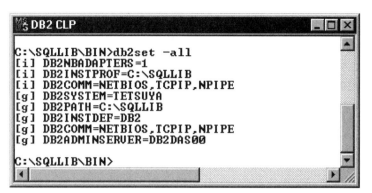

Fig. 2–18 *The db2set -all command*

The output of the db2set command with the -all option is shown in Fig. 2–18. Notice that the instance-level settings are preceded with an [i] and the global settings are preceded with a [g].

The following are some examples of usage of the db2set command:

To set a parameter for the current instance:

```
db2set parameter=value
```

To set a parameter's value for a specific instance:

```
db2set parameter=value -i instance_name
```

To set a parameter at the global level:

```
db2set parameter=value -g
```

To view a list of all variables that can be set in the profile registry:

```
db2set -lr
```

Environment Variables

There are some environment variables that may or may not be stored in the DB2 Profile Registry (depending on the operating system). They are system environment variables used by DB2 that must be stored in a location where the platform stores its system variables. The following are examples of DB2 system environment variables:

- DB2INSTANCE - Specifies the active DB2 instance
- DB2PATH - Specifies the path for the DB2 executables
- DB2INSTPROF - The environment variable used to specify the location of the instance directory if different than DB2PATH (OS/2 only)

A summary of the locations of these DB2 environment variables is shown below. For further details on environment variables and on which operating system platforms you may see them or need them, please refer to the *DB2 Administration Guide*.

Table 2–1 *DB2 Environment Variables*

Operating System	Location of DB2 Environment Variables
Windows NT/2000	System Environment Variables, specifies the system within the System icon from the Control Panel
OS/2	CONFIG.SYS used by OS/2, located on the OS/2 installation drive
UNIX	Within a script file called db2profile (Bourne or Korn shell) or db2cshrc (C shell) depending on the UNIX platform. Incorporated with the user's initialization file (.profile or .login)

Hierarchy of the DB2 Environment

Since there are multiple places where a variable can be set, DB2 uses a hierarchy to determine where it will look to determine a variable's value. It uses the following search order:

1. The session's environment variables
2. DB2 Profile Registry variables set in the instance node level profile
3. DB2 Profile Registry variables set using db2set for the session
4. DB2 Profile Registry variables set at the instance level using the -i option of db2set
5. DB2 Profile Registry variables set at the global level

Although most DB2 environment settings can be set either in the DB2 Profile Registry or in the operating system environment, it is strongly recommended that the DB2 Profile Registry be used whenever possible. If DB2 variables are set outside of the DB2 Registry, remote administration of those variables is not possible and any changes made mean that the system (except UNIX) must be rebooted for any changes in the value of the variables to take effect.

Using the Command Line Processor

The Command Line Processor (CLP) was introduced in Chapter 1. This section discusses how the CLP is used in the DB2 environment, especially, to make changes at the session level. It is important to note that all commands can also be issued from the DB2 Command Center and, if available on your platform, the DB2 Command Window.

When using the Command Line Processor, be careful that the operating system does not parse your SQL statements. If you enclose any SQL statements or DB2 commands within quotation marks, it will ensure that they are not parsed by the operating system. Within the Command Line Processor (CLP) you can issue operating system commands by prefacing them with an exclamation mark (!). For example:

```
db2 => !dir c:\
```

If the command exceeds the limit allowed by the operating system, use a backslash (\) as the line continuation character.

The complete syntax and explanation of all commands is documented in the *DB2 UDB V7.1 Command Reference*. You can obtain syntax and information for all of the DB2 commands from the Command Line Processor:

DB2 ?   displays a list of all DB2 commands
DB2 ? command   displays information about a specific command
DB2 ? SQLnnnn   displays information about a specific SQLCODE
DB2 ? DB2nnnn   displays information about DB2 error

To examine the current CLP settings, issue the following command:

```
db2 => LIST COMMAND OPTIONS
```

```
Command Line Processor Option Settings

 Backend process wait time (seconds)        (DB2BQTIME) = 1
 No. of retries to connect to backend       (DB2BQTRY)  = 60
 Request queue wait time (seconds)          (DB2RQTIME) = 5
 Input queue wait time (seconds)            (DB2IQTIME) = 5
 Command options                            (DB2OPTIONS) =

Option Description                                    Current Setting
------ --------------------------------------------- ---------------

  -a  Display SQLCA                                  OFF
  -c  Auto-Commit                                    ON
  -e  Display SQLCODE/SQLSTATE                       OFF
  -f  Read from input file                           OFF
  -l  Log commands in history file                   OFF
  -o  Display output                                 ON
  -p  Display interactive input prompt               ON
  -r  Save output to report file                     OFF
  -s  Stop execution on command error                OFF
  -t  Set statement termination character            OFF
  -v  Echo current command                           OFF
  -w  Display FETCH/SELECT warning messages          ON
  -z  Save all output to output file                 OFF
```

Fig. 2–19 *Command Line Processor option settings*

Fig. 2–19 shows the default settings. These settings can be updated globally or for each CLP session using the DB2OPTIONS profile variable.

```
db2 ? UPDATE COMMAND OPTIONS
```

This command displays all the available options, the possible values for each option, and the usage of the UPDATE COMMAND OPTIONS command.

```
db2 UPDATE COMMAND OPTIONS USING *OPTIONS...*
```

This command changes the value of one or more options for a CLP session.

The Command Line Processor has two parts: a front-end process and a back-end process. The front-end process is called `db2` and the back-end is `db2bp`. The back-end process will maintain a connection to the database. To release this connection, use the `TERMINATE` command. To end an interactive DB2 session, issue the `QUIT` command. (This does not release the database connection.)

DB2 for Windows CLP Considerations

DB2 for Windows does not allow the DB2 Command Line Processor to be used in every operating system window. A DB2 command window or the DB2 Command Line Processor program itself must be used to issue any CLP statements. A command window can be started by clicking on **Start** and selecting **Programs → DB2 for Windows NT → Command Window** or by executing the command `db2cmd`. As indicated earlier, the DB2 Command Center can also be used and is the suggested method as it allows entry of multiple commands/statements, saving these to a script, and viewing the explain output of a statement.

Getting Started

DAS and DB2 Instances

There are two types of instances: a DB2 Administration Server (DAS) instance and a DB2 instance. Both of these instances may be created during the installation process. The similarities and differences between these instances are reviewed in the following sections.

DB2 Administration Server (DAS) Instance

The DB2 Administration Server (DAS) instance is a special DB2 instance for managing local and remote DB2 servers. The DAS instance is used by the DB2 administration tools, including the Control Center and the Client Configuration Assistant, to satisfy requests. The db2admin commands allow you to start, stop, and configure the DAS instance and catalog nodes.

The DAS instance must be running on every DB2 server that you want to administer remotely or detect using the client configuration search method. The DAS instance provides remote clients with the information required to set up communications to access the DB2 server instances. You can create only one DAS instance for each machine. When the DAS instance is created, the DB2 global-level profile registry variable DB2ADMINSERVER is set to the name of the DAS instance.

The DB2 Administration Server instance will:

- Obtain the configuration of the operating system
- Obtain user and group information
- Start/Stop DB2 instances
- Set up communications for a DB2 server instance
- Attach to an instance to perform administration tasks for a database
- Provide a mechanism to return information about the DB2 servers to remote clients
- Collect information results from DB2 Discovery

In order to start administration from a remote client, the user must have SYSADM authority in the DB2 Administration Server instance. Once the instance and the databases are registered, the user must also hold the appropriate authorities and privileges for each administration task.

The Administration Server instance is automatically created in DB2 installations (Windows and OS/2 only) of the DB2 products. You can also manually create the DAS instance after product installation.

The automatic installation process performs the following tasks related to configuring communications:

- Detects the communication protocols installed on the machine.
- Determines protocol information required by DB2, such as workstation name if NetBIOS is detected.
- Sets the properties for each communication protocol with the previously determined information.
- Allows the user to optionally customize the communication protocols properties.
- Updates the files required for each protocol. For example, it modifies the services file if the TCP/IP protocol is detected.
- Sets the communication variables for the DAS instance and the DB2 instance using the customized properties for the protocols.
- Creates the DB2 Administration Server instance (optional on UNIX).
- Creates the DB2 server instance (optional).
- Updates the database manager configuration file with the appropriate communications settings.

Managing the DAS Instance

The DB2 Administration Server instance is created during the install process. If you do not specify the name of the DAS instance, the default instance name is used. The UNIX default is `db2as`, and on Windows NT/9x and OS/2 it is `DB2DAS00`.

Note: The Administration Server instance is created in a manner similar to any other DB2 instance; however, there are no databases associated with it.

The following are some of the commands used to administer the DAS instance:

- `db2admin start` - Starts the DB2 Administration Server instance.
- `db2admin stop` - Stops the DB2 Administration Server instance.
- `dasicrt` - Creates the DAS instance in UNIX.
- `dasidrop` - Drops the DAS instance in UNIX.
- `db2admin create` - Creates the DAS instance in Windows NT/9x and OS/2.
- `db2admin drop` - Drops the DAS instance in Windows NT/9x and OS/2.
- `db2 get admin cfg` - Displays the database manager configuration file of the DAS.

- `db2 update admin cfg` - This command allows you to update individual entries in the database manager configuration file for the DAS instance.
- `db2 reset admin cfg` - Resets the configuration parameters to the recommended defaults. The changes become effective only after the `db2admin start` is executed.

DB2 Instances

A DB2 instance is defined as a logical database server environment. DB2 databases are created within DB2 instances on the database server. The creation of multiple instances on the same physical server provides a unique database server environment for each instance. For example, you can maintain a test environment and a production environment on the same machine.

Each instance has an administrative group associated with it. This administrative group must be defined in the instance configuration file known as the *database manager configuration file*. Creating user IDs and user groups is different for each operating environment.

The installation process creates a default DB2 instance. This is the recommended method for creating instances. However, instances may be created (or dropped) after installation.

DB2 Instances on Windows and OS/2

The default instance created during the installation of DB2 for Windows NT/9x and OS/2 is called DB2. The DB2 environment variables are set during install. If you want another instance, you can create the additional instance using the command `db2icrt`. The instance name is specified at creation time and does not have to directly correspond to a user ID as it does in UNIX environments.

DB2 Instance Considerations on Windows NT

Installing DB2 for Windows NT/2000 is similar to installing DB2 for OS/2. As in OS/2, a default instance is created called DB2. However, the DB2 instance is defined as a Windows NT service. Therefore, the DB2 instance name must adhere to any naming rules for Windows services. The DAS instance is defined as a Windows service as well. Another service created during installation is called the *DB2 Security Server.* When the authentication type is set to CLIENT, and TRUST_CLNTAUTH is set to CLIENT, and you specify a user ID/password on the connect, the DB2 security server needs to be started on the client machine. You can configure these services to start automatically. Click the **Services** icon located in the Windows Control Panel to verify the existence and status of these services.

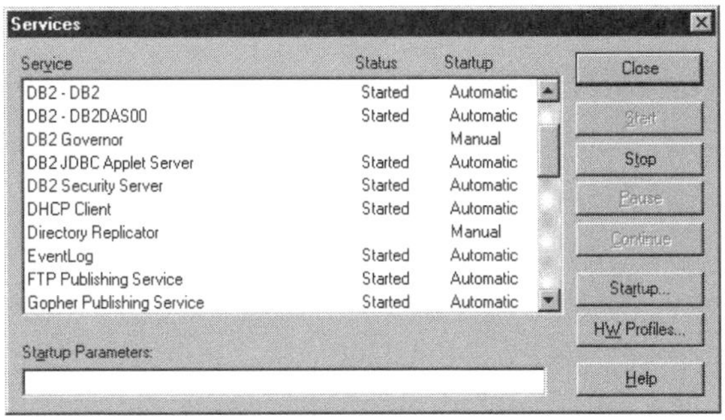

Fig. 2–20 *Windows Services*

Fig. 2–20 shows the Control Panel for Windows NT/2000 Services. The instance can be started from this control panel or from an operating system window using the command NET START DB2. The DB2 for Windows NT/2000 Security service can be started with the command NET START DB2NTSECSERVER. The Administration Server can be started by using NET START DB2DAS00 where DB2DAS00 is the name of the DAS instance.

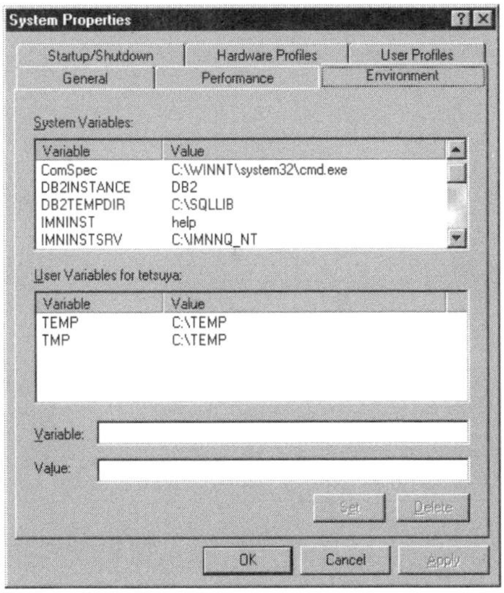

Fig. 2–21 *Environment variable screen (Windows only)*

The environment variables are set during installation. To verify these environment variables, examine the System folder of the Program Manager Control Panel.

Note: DB2 for OS/2 sets the environment variable DB2INSTANCE=DB2 in the *CONFIG.SYS* file during installation.

DB2 Instances on UNIX

Before executing the command to create an instance on the UNIX platform (db2icrt), an instance group and an instance owner must be created within UNIX.

To create the user, group, and instance in UNIX, you must be the UNIX system administrator (root authority). The group, user, and instance are created for you at install. The default instance name used in the installation process is db2inst1. To create another instance, follow the steps below.

Create a group if one is not already defined:

```
mkgroup db2grp2
```

Create a user who will be the instance owner and is a member of the group created in the previous step:

```
mkuser pgrp=db2grp2 db2inst2 passwd db2test
```

Execute the DB2 command to create an instance:

```
db2icrt -u db2fenc2 db2inst2
```

 Note: Remember that all commands are case sensitive in UNIX environments.

You have to specify the user name, which can run fenced user-defined functions with the -u option. User defined functions are described in detail in "Advanced SQL" on page 325. For security purposes, it is recommended that you use a user in which fenced UDFs will execute different than that of the DB2 instance owner.

One of the files placed in the instance owner's home directory under the *sqllib* subdirectory is a DB2 setup (profile) file. Depending on the UNIX shell you are using, the file will be called `db2profile` (Bourne or Korn shell) or `db2cshrc` (C shell). This profile must be executed before using the DB2 instance. It is usually added to the user's login profile to ensure that it is executed when the user enters the system.

Starting the DB2 Instance

Now that a DB2 instance has been created, it must be initialized or the instance be started. The process of starting an instance is similar to starting a network file server; until the instance is started, the clients will not be able to access the databases on the server.

The command to start a DB2 instance is called `db2start`. This command will allocate all of the required DB2 resources on the server. These resources include memory and communications support.

```
db2start
SQL1064N DB2START processing was successful.
```

On Windows NT, you may also start an instance with the command:

```
net start instance_name
```

Stopping the DB2 Instance

The command to stop the current database manager instance is `db2stop`. Messages are sent to standard output indicating the success or failure of the `db2stop` command.

```
DB2STOP
SQL1064N DB2STOP processing was successful.
```

On Windows NT, you may also stop an instance with the command:

```
net stop instance_name
```

Using First Steps

First Steps is a graphical tool that helps you get started using DB2 UDB. On Windows NT, for instance, one of the options is to create the sample database. Click on **Start** and select **Programs → DB2 for Windows NT → First Steps**. This will bring up the First Steps main screen.

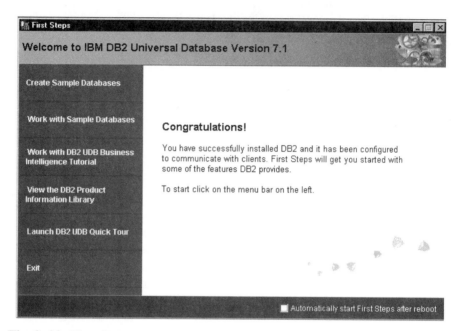

Fig. 2–22 *First Steps main menu*

First Steps has a number of options; all are available by clicking on the icon next to the action. You can:

- Create the sample databases. DB2 now includes the SAMPLE database, along with OLAP and Data Warehousing databases that you can use to try out the new features in the product.
- Work with the sample databases. You can, for example, list the tables and view their contents.
- Work with the DB2 UDB Business Intelligence tutorial. This tutorial provides an end-to-end guide for typical business intelligence tasks.
- View the product information library. This is helpful in finding out what DB2 UDB information is available online and how it is organized.

Once you have create the various databases or explored the features of DB2, you can click on EXIT to close this panel.

Summary

In this chapter, the process of installing DB2 on various platforms was demonstrated. The creation of a DB2 instance and the DB2 Administration Server (DAS) were also demonstrated and their roles in a DB2 system were discussed.

A DB2 instance can be defined as a logical database server environment. For each environment, the instance creation process including any special user ID and group setup required was reviewed.

The DB2 environment variables were discussed, specifically that they are defined on every DB2 system including DB2INSTANCE and DB2PATH. The location of the definition of the DB2 environment variables differs by platform. Also discussed were the DB2 profile variables and the DB2 Profile Registry and how the various levels of the registry can contain different levels of information and how searching through these levels can affect your system.

Throughout this chapter, two common interfaces were used: the Command Line Processor and the Control Center. Processing DB2 commands was also demonstrated by using the Command Center. The Command Line Processor has default settings that can be modified for each session or changed globally using the DB2OPTIONS profile variable. Finally, examples of how to execute DB2 commands and SQL statements from a file were demonstrated using the Command Line Processor.

Instance management including starting and stopping a DB2 instance was reviewed. DB2 for Windows NT/2000 is integrated with the Windows NT/2000 services environment, and each DB2 instance is a Windows NT/2000 service. The commands used to start and stop the instance are db2start and db2stop.

Getting Started

C H A P T E R 3

Getting Connected

- ◆ CONNECTING TO A REMOTE DATABASE
- ◆ AUTOMATING CONFIGURATIONS
- ◆ USING DISCOVERY
- ◆ USING ACCESS PROFILES
- ◆ BINDING DATABASE UTILITIES
- ◆ ATTACHING TO A LOCAL INSTANCE

DB2 databases can be accessed by applications that run on the same machine as the database or from a remote machine by using a distributed connection. In addition to providing client access to a centralized database running on a server, distributed connections can also be used to perform administrative tasks on the database server by a Database Administrator using a client workstation. The following diagram illustrates in more detail a remote client connecting to a DB2 server:

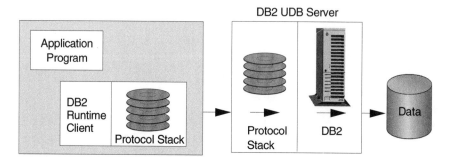

Fig. 3–1 *Remote client flow to DB2 server*

All remote clients use a communications product to support the protocol the client uses when accessing a remote database server. This protocol support is either part of the client's operating system or available as a separate product.

The protocol stack must be installed and configured before a remote client can communicate with a remote DB2 server.

DB2 provides many different methods for configuring a remote client that wants to access a DB2 database server. Though the methods may differ, the steps are basically the same:

- Make sure that the communication product is installed and configured on the client workstation. The following protocols are supported: TCP/IP, NetBIOS, Named Pipes, IPX/SPX, and APPC.

- Perform the communication-specific steps. For example, if using TCP/IP, update the services file on the server with the port number(s) that the database server is listening on.

- Catalog the remote node. This is the database server to which you want to establish the connection.

- Catalog the remote database. A DB2 database server can support both local and remote clients concurrently.

These configuration steps may be done in a number of ways. This section discusses some of the methods.

The easiest way to configure a remote client for communication with a DB2 server is by using one of the graphical tools. Which method you use depends on your particular environment and requirements.

Note: Normally, the communication settings for the DB2 server are configured during installation.

Roadmap to Distributed Communications

There are several methods you can use to set up communications between a DB2 client and a DB2 server. The methods will first be introduced to help you decide which is the most suitable for your requirements. Later in this chapter, examples of each method will be presented.

DB2 Discovery

DB2 Discovery is a helpful concept to understand before attempting to set up distributed connections.

DB2 Discovery allows you to automate the configuration of remote clients connecting to DB2 databases. You can easily catalog a remote database from a client workstation without having to know any detailed communication-specific information. From the client, DB2 Discovery requests information from DB2 servers to return to the client issuing the discovery request. A discovery message is sent to the DB2 servers, and if the servers are configured to support the discovery process, data is returned to the client.

The returned data includes:

- A list of instances on the DB2 server that have discovery enabled and information about the protocols that each instance supports for client connection
- The databases that are defined within the instances and have discovery enabled, including name and description for each available database

Both the database server and the client have control over DB2 Discovery. Using the configuration parameters, the user can control:

- Whether discovery is disabled or enabled as well as the discovery method that will be used, if it is enabled
- The protocols that DB2 Discovery uses
- If an instance can be discovered
- If a database can be discovered

See "Configuring DB2 Discovery" on page 130 for more details.

Getting Connected

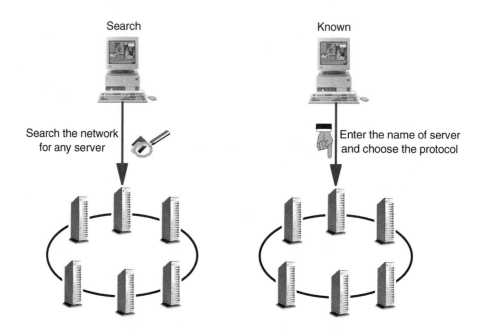

Fig. 3–2 *Discovery methods*

There are two methods of DB2 discovery, search and known.

The search method searches the network for valid DB2 database servers that a client workstation can access. You do not need to provide specific communication information. The remote client, using the Client Configuration Assistant, searches the network to obtain a list of valid servers.

In the known discovery method, you must provide some communication-specific information about the server that you want to access. You need to supply:

- A protocol that is configured and running on the Administration Server instance on the server
- The protocol to be used to connect to the DB2 Administration Server
- A server name

The use of the Client Configuration Assistant is discussed later in this chapter.

Automated Configuration Using Discovery

If you use this type of *automated configuration*, you do not need to provide any detailed communications information to enable the DB2 client to contact the DB2 server.

As mentioned earlier, discovery works in one of two ways:

- *Search discovery* - the DB2 client searches for DB2 servers on the network.
- *Known discovery* - one particular server is queried for information about the instances and databases defined there.

You can use either the Client Configuration Assistant or the Control Center to exploit discovery-based configuration, and this method is normally used to configure small numbers of clients.

Step-by-step examples of using discovery are given in "Configuring DB2 Clients" on page 94.

 Note: The DAS instance must be configured and running on each DB2 server you wish to locate in this manner.

Automated Configuration Using Access Profiles

Access profiles are another automated method to configure a DB2 client to access remote DB2 servers and their databases. An access profile contains the information that a client needs to catalog databases to a DB2 server.

As with discovery, when using access profiles, you do not need to provide any detailed communications information to enable the DB2 client to contact the DB2 server.

Two types of access profiles exist:

- *Server access profiles* are created from DB2 servers and contain information about all the instances and databases the DB2 server has cataloged.
- *Client access profiles* are used for duplicating the cataloged databases and/or the client settings (dbm cfg, CLI/ODBC) from one client to another.

Both types of profiles can be exported and then imported to another DB2 system. Use of access profiles is typical for configuring a large number of clients.

The DB2 Control Center can be used to export and then import a server access profile for a system. A client access profile is exported, then imported using the DB2 Client Configuration Assistant (CCA).

Step-by-step examples of using access profiles are given in "Using Access Profiles" on page 106.

If you have a large number of clients to configure, you should also consider making use of DCE Directory Services or LDAP (Lightweight Directory Access Protocol). These features allow you to store catalog information in one centralized location. Each client just needs to know the centralized location to be able to connect to any database that has been made available in the network. See the *DB2 UDB V7.1 Administration Guide* for more details about LDAP.

 In the Windows environment, DB2 V7.1 supports Windows 2000 Active Directory as the LDAP Server and single sign-on using Kerberos security.

DB2 for OS/390 and DB2 for OS/400 do not support a searched discovery-based configuration. However, if you have a DB2 Connect server already configured with connections to either of these host servers, DB2 Discovery will search for your DB2 Connect server. You can then choose to connect through the DB2 Connect server or use its information to configure a direct connection to the host (if you have the appropriate DB2 Connect software installed on your local client machine).

Manual Configuration

It is also possible to manually configure a database connection. To do this, you need to know the details of the communications setup between the client and the server.

You can use a manual configuration to your host databases or use discovery to connect through a DB2 Connect server or use that information for a direct connection from your client as described in the previous section.

There are two ways to manually configure connections:

- Using the Manual option in the CCA - in this case, you are prompted via a GUI interface for all the values to enter.
- Using the CATALOG NODE/DB commands - in this case, you must know the syntax of the commands and enter the commands from a command line interface.

In either case, manual configuration must be used to exploit some advanced options that are not available using automated methods; for example, choosing the location where authentication should take place.

The advantage of using the CATALOG NODE/DB commands is that the configuration steps can be put into scripts so that the configuration can be redone if necessary.

Step-by-step examples of performing manual configurations are given in "Manual Configuration" on page 112.

DB2 Directories

Access to both local and remote databases uses entries in the DB2 directories. The directories hide the requirement for the user to know where a database actually resides. Users are able to connect to local databases and remote databases (including DRDA databases) by specifying a database name. The directories that make this possible are:

- System database directory
- Local database directory
- Node directory
- DCS directory
- Administration node directory

System Database Directory

The *system database directory* resides in the SQLDBDIR subdirectory in the instance directory. This directory is used to catalog both local and remote databases. The directory contains the database name, alias, type, and node where the database resides. If the database is local, a pointer to the local database directory is located in the system database directory. If the database is remote, there is a pointer to the node directory.

Local Database Directory

The *local database directory* resides in every drive/path that contains a database. It is used to access local databases in that subdirectory. Each entry in the directory contains the database name, alias, type, and location information about the database.

Node Directory

Each database client maintains a *node directory*. The node directory contains entries for all instances that the client will access. The node directory contains communication information about the network connection to the instance. If multiple instances exist on a remote machine, then each instance must be cataloged as a separate node before you are able to access any information contained within the instance.

Getting Connected

DCS Directory

The connection information for DRDA host databases is different from the information for LAN-connected databases. A separate directory maintains this host information. This directory is the *DCS directory*. It only exists if the DB2 Connect product is installed on your system. The DCS directory stores information used by the database manager to access databases on a DRDA Application Server.

Administration Node Directory

The *administration node directory* contains one definition for each remote system that is known to a DB2 client. Most of the entries for this directory are made during product installation, by the Control Center, or by the CCA.

Examining DB2 Directories

Consider a scenario with two systems, a database server and a remote client. From the database server, issue the LIST DB DIRECTORY command to list the contents of the system database directory. The output is as follows:

```
System Database Directory

Number of entries in the directory = 4

Database 1 entry:

  Database alias                    = DB2CERT
  Database name                     = DB2CERT
  Local database directory          = /home/db2
  Database release level            = 9.00
  Comment                           = DB2 Certification DB
  Directory entry type              = Indirect
  Catalog node number               = 0

Database 2 entry:

  Database alias                    = MYDB
  ...
```

The results display that there are four databases cataloged on the server. The first database is the DB2CERT database.

The local database directory is set to /home/db2. If more detail is desired, the local database directory can be examined by using the command: `list db directory on /home/db2`. This provides more detailed information regarding the location of some of the database files.

Next, examine the contents of two directories on the client workstation: the system database directory and the node directory. A client does not have a local database directory since it does not usually contain local databases. The command to examine the system database directory is `LIST DB DIRECTORY`. Here is the output:

```
System Database Directory

Number of entries in the directory = 2

Database 1 entry:

   Database alias                = MYCERT
   Database name                 = DB2CERT
   Node name                     = DB2AIX
   Database release level        = 9.00
   Comment                       = DB2 Certification DB
   Directory entry type          = Remote
   Catalog node number           = 0

Database 2 entry:

   Database alias                = OTHERDB
   ...
```

The database alias name of the database on the client is called MYCERT. This name corresponds to the actual database name on the server (DB2CERT). Note that the directory entry type is *indirect* on the server for the DB2CERT database and the type is *remote* on the client.

Note: When a database is created, an entry is automatically placed in the system database directory and the local database directory on the server.

When cataloging the remote database on the client, the database name on the client must match the database alias on the server. The database alias specified on the client workstation is used in the CONNECT statement. Therefore, the name used to CONNECT to the DB2CERT database is MYCERT.

Getting Connected

There is always an associated *node name* with a client system database directory entry. The node name (in this example DB2AIX) defines the location of the DB2 server on the network.

To discover more information about the location of the database server, examine the DB2AIX node entry in the node directory using the LIST NODE DIRECTORY command. The output is as follows:

```
Node Directory

Number of entries in the directory = 1

Node 1 entry:

    Node name                           = DB2AIX
    Comment                             =
    Protocol                            = TCPIP
    Hostname                            = db2aix
    Service name                        = db2tcp1
```

The DB2AIX node name corresponds to a TCP/IP connection. The TCP/IP host name for the DB2 server is db2aix and the service name is db2tcp1. The TCP/IP information in the client's node directory must match the information in the server's DBM configuration file.

There are other options available when cataloging a database and node, such as where authentication takes place. These options are explained in detail in "Controlling Data Access" on page 145.

Configuring DB2 Clients

DB2 provides several different methods for configuring a remote client that needs to access a DB2 database server, as detailed in "Roadmap to Distributed Communications" on page 87. In this section, more details and examples of using these methods will be reviewed.

Automated Configuration Using Discovery

You can use the discovery function of DB2 to automate the addition of remote databases. This can be done in one of two ways:

- Enter the name of the machine on the network (e.g., the hostname if using TCP/IP and then use discovery to automatically return the instances and databases on that machine (*known discovery*).

- Search the network for machines, and then use discovery to automatically return the instances and databases on each machine (*search discovery*).

You can use either the Client Configuration Assistant or the Control Center to perform automated configuration. This is an example of using the CCA to perform known discovery.

Known Discovery Using the CCA

You can access the CCA from the desktop or from the command line using the db2cca command.

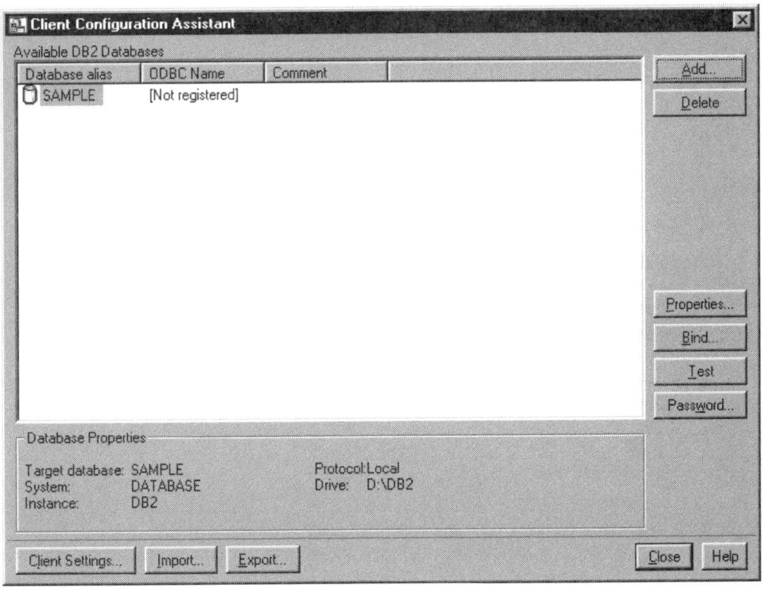

Fig. 3–3 *Client Configuration Assistant (CCA)*

If no databases are yet cataloged on the client, the Welcome panel is displayed (Fig. 3–3). Otherwise, the databases that are cataloged on your client workstation are displayed under Available DB2 Databases in the main CCA panel. To add another database, click on the **Add** button (or the **Add Database** button from the Welcome panel). The Add Database Wizard panel will appear to guide you through the adding of the new database.

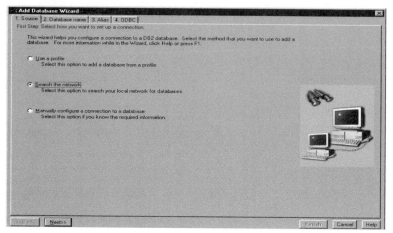

Fig. 3–4 *CCA - Add Database Wizard*

Select the **Search the network** radio button. Click on the **Next** push button.

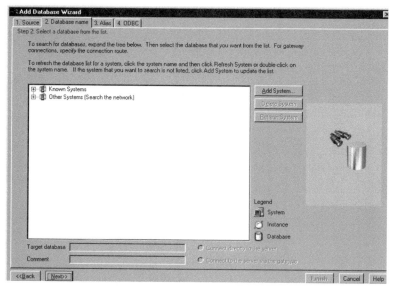

Fig. 3–5 *CCA - Target database (1)*

You can check if the database server is already known to the client by clicking on the [+] next to Known Systems in Fig. 3–5. If it is not, then click on the **Add System** push button. If it is already known, then expand the system until you see the desired database, as in Fig. 3–7.

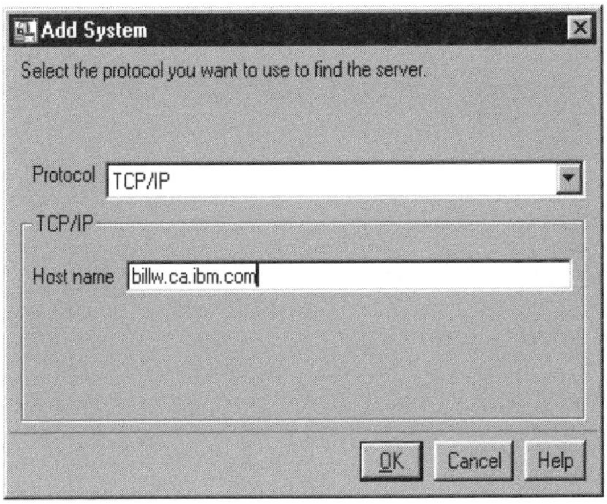

Add System   ☒

Select the protocol you want to use to find the server.

Protocol   TCP/IP   ▼

┌ TCP/IP ─────────────────────────

Host name   billw.ca.ibm.com

    OK   Cancel   Help

Fig. 3–6 *CCA - Add System*

Choose the protocol in the Add System panel. The contents of the rest of the panel changes according to the protocol you select. Fig. 3–6 shows the panel for TCP/IP. Here are all the supported protocols together with the parameters for each protocol:

- TCP/IP - Server hostname/IP address, port number
- NetBIOS - Server workstation name, adapter number
- Named Pipe - Server computer name, instance
- IPX/SPX - Server internetwork address, socket number. If using file server addressing, file server name and object name.

You should check that the machine is properly configured on the network before clicking OK. For example, if using TCP/IP, ping the hostname to check it is available.

 Note: You cannot use known discovery with the APPC protocol.

If the system is located, then it is displayed under Known Systems, together with all its instances and databases:

Getting Connected

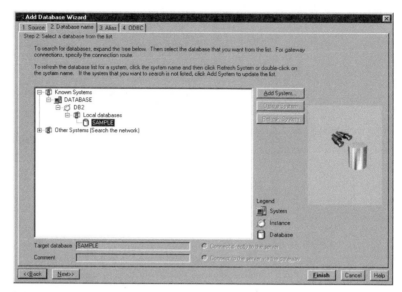

Fig. 3–7 *CCA - Target database (2)*

Select the database that you wish to connect to. You can select the **Alias** and **ODBC** tabs at the top of the panel (or use the **Next** push button) to specify a database alias name for the database and/or to select CLI/ODBC options for the database.

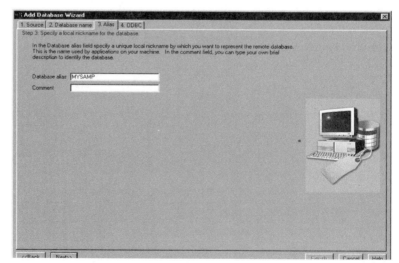

Fig. 3–8 *CCA - Alias for remote database*

Choose an alias for the database and optionally add a description. Click **Next**.

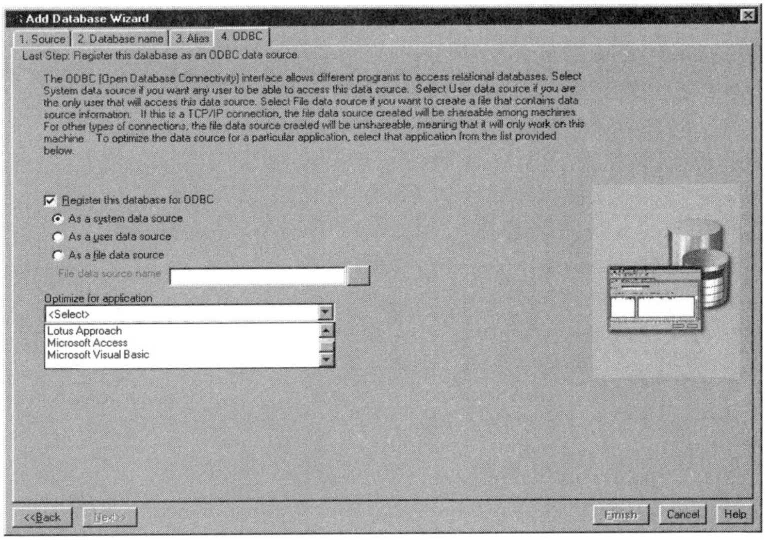

Fig. 3–9 *CCA - ODBC settings*

You can register the database as an ODBC data source. By default the "Register this database for ODBC" check box is ticked. You can choose an application from the "Optimize for Application" selection box to optimize the ODBC settings for that application. Click **Done** when finished.

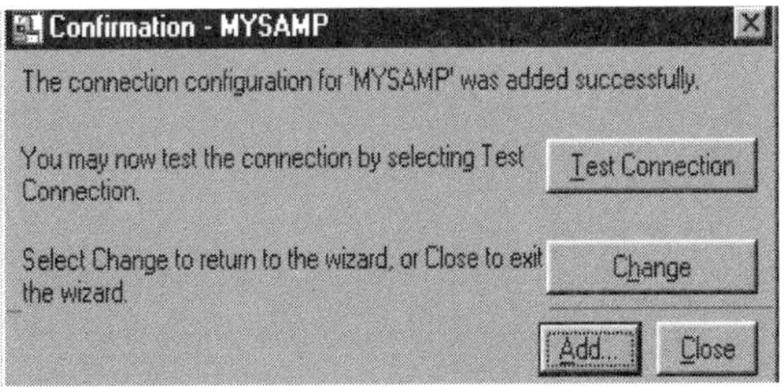

Fig. 3–10 *CCA - Connection added successfully*

You can test the connection that has been added by clicking on **Test Connection**.

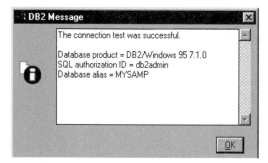

Fig. 3–11 *CCA - Test connection*

Enter the user ID and password to be used when connecting to the remote database. On this panel you can also change the password for the user ID defined at the database server machine. If the connection is successful, you will see a pop-up message similar to this:

Fig. 3–12 *CCA - Test connection successful*

Note that this example assumes that the installation defaults for discovery on the client and the server have not been changed. For details on how to alter the default behavior, see "Configuring DB2 Discovery" on page 130.

Search Discovery Using the CCA

Instead of entering the machine identifier (known discovery), you can use the CCA to find databases on your local network (search discovery).

Start the Client Configuration Assistant (CCA) and click on the **Add** push button on the CCA's main panel to start the Add Database Wizard.

Select the **Search the network** radio button. Click on the **Next** push button.

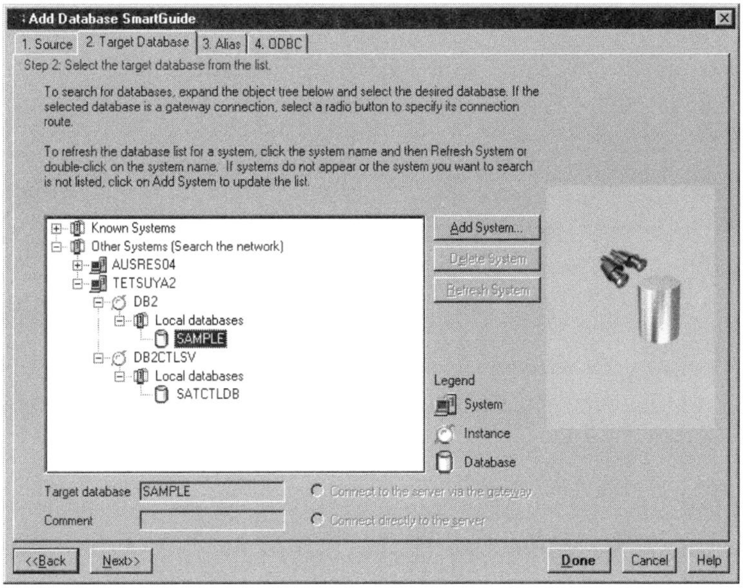

Fig. 3–13 *CCA - Target database after search*

As in the previous example using known discovery, you should first check in the Known Systems to make sure that the database server is not already known to the client.

If the system that contains the database you require is not listed, click on the **[+]** sign beside the "Other Systems (Search the network)" icon to search the network for additional systems. When the search is over, the list of discovered systems is displayed. Click on the **[+]** sign beside the system you require to get a list of the instances and databases defined there (Fig. 3–13). Select the database that you want to add and proceed as shown in the known discovery example.

If the system you want is not listed, it can be added to the list of systems by clicking on the **Add Systems** push button.

> **Note:** Only the TCP/IP and NetBIOS protocols are supported for search discovery.

Using search discovery may appear to be simpler than known discovery. However, in larger networks, routers and bridges can filter the messages search discovery uses to find DB2 servers on the network. This may result in an incomplete or even empty list. In these cases, use known discovery.

Known Discovery Using the Control Center

You can also use the Control Center to configure remote database connections using discovery. The Control Center is accessed from the desktop or by entering db2cc at a command line.

To add a database using known discovery, right-click on **Systems** and choose **Add** from the menu:

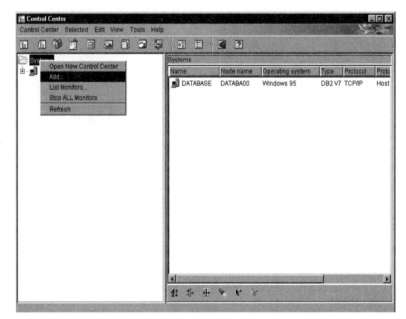

Fig. 3–14 *Control Center - Add System (1)*

The Add System panel is displayed:

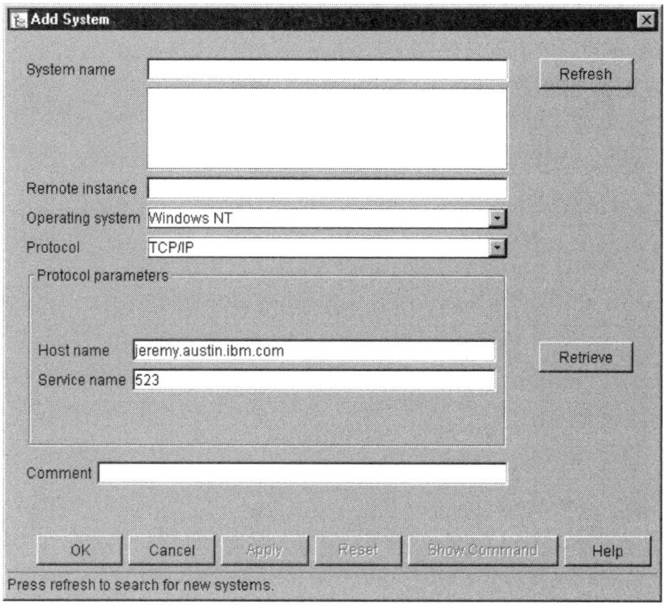

Fig. 3–15 *Control Center - Add System (2)*

In this panel, choose the protocol you wish to use. As with the CCA, the contents of the Protocol parameters box changes according to the protocol. Here are the protocols you can choose along with their parameters:

- TCP/IP - Server hostname/IP address, port number
- NetBIOS - Server workstation name, adapter number
- Named Pipe - Server computer name, instance
- IPX/SPX - Server internetwork address, socket number; if using file server addressing, file server name and object name

You should check that the system is available on the network before clicking on **Retrieve**.

If the system is found, then the System name, Remote instance, and Operating system fields are filled in on this panel. Click **OK** to return to the Control Center.

In this panel (and other Add panels), you can click on **Show Command** to see the DB2 CATALOG command that is actually being executed.

Note: APPC is not supported for known discovery.

You should now see the system displayed in the Control Center under Systems.

Next, click on the **[+]** next to the system to display the instances. Right-click on instances and select **Add** from the menu to display the Add Instance panel:

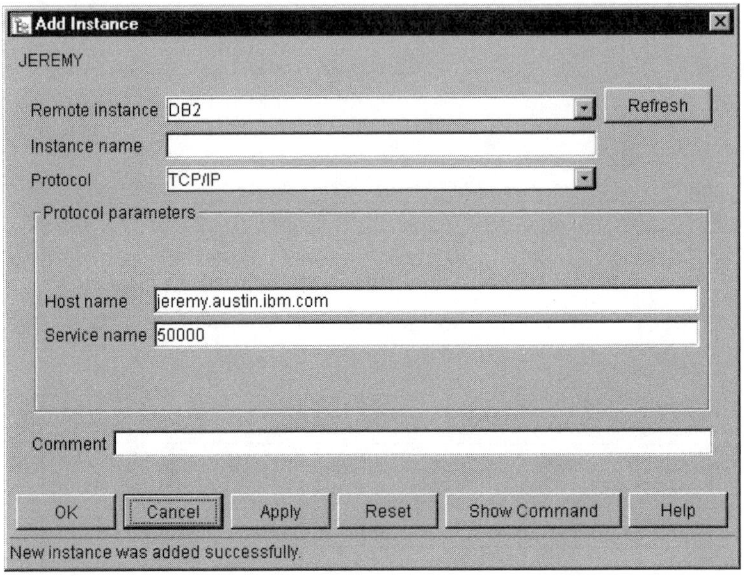

Fig. 3–16 *Control Center - Add Instance*

Click on **Refresh** to display a list of instances at the remote system. Choose the instance you require and you should see the protocol parameters filled in for you.

Click **OK** to return to the Control Center.

Expand the instance by clicking on the **[+]** next to it. Right-click on Databases and select **Add** from the menu to display the Add Database panel:

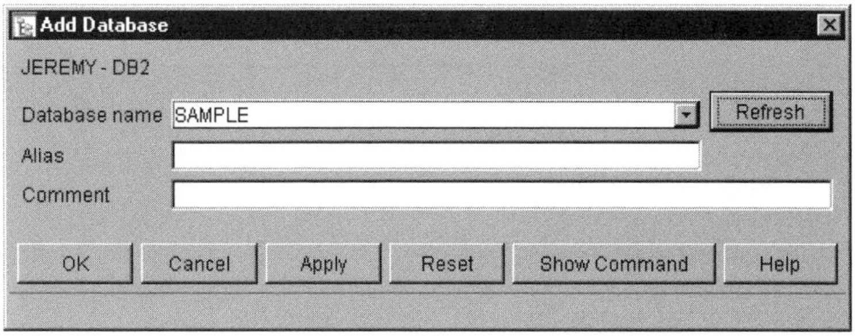

Fig. 3–17 *Control Center - Add Database*

Click on **Refresh** to display a list of databases at the remote system. Choose the database you require and optionally enter an Alias for the remote database. Click **OK** to return to the Control Center.

Click on the [+] next the database to display the database objects. To verify the configuration, you can click on **Tables**, and a connection will be made to the remote database.

Search Discovery Using the Control Center

You can also use search discovery to add a remote database using the Control Center. In the Control Center, right-click on **Systems**, and choose **Add** from the menu to display the Add System panel:

Getting Connected

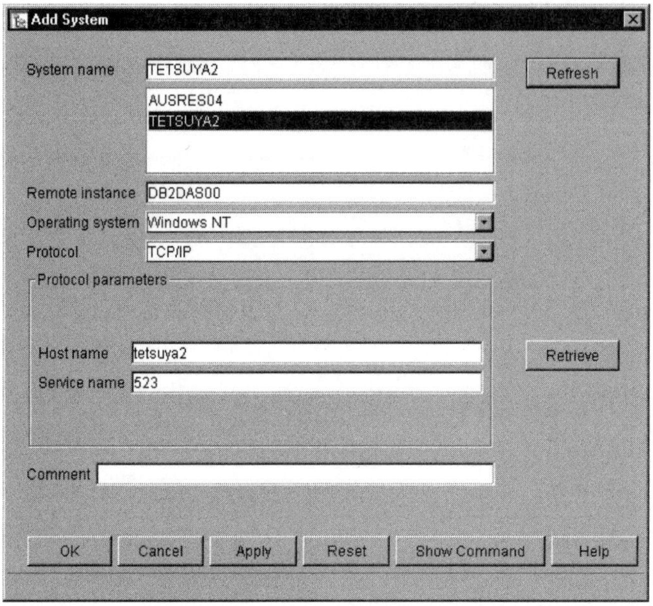

Fig. 3–18 *Control Center - Add System using search*

To initiate search discovery, click on **Refresh**.

When the search is over, the list of systems is displayed. Select the system you require and click OK to return to the Control Center.

Note: Only the TCP/IP and NetBIOS protocols are supported for search discovery.

If the system you want is not listed, you can choose a protocol, enter the protocol-specific parameters, and click **Retrieve**. This is using known discovery.

The rest of the procedure is the same as performing known discovery from the Control Center. To follow the steps, go to "Known Discovery Using the Control Center" on page 102.

Using Access Profiles

Access profiles are another automated method to configure a DB2 client to access remote DB2 servers and their databases. An access profile contains the information that a client needs to catalog databases on a DB2 server. Two types of access profiles exist, client and server.

Using a Server Access Profile

A server access profile is a file that contains information about all instances on the DB2 server and all the databases within each instance. This file can be generated from the Control Center.

The first part of the process is to generate the access profile from the server.

Fig. 3–19 shows the option to generate a server access profile in the Control Center for the system called DATABASE. When **Export Server Profile** is selected, a window appears where you specify the path and file name to store the profile. Once this information is entered, the generation process starts and a message appears when the process completes.

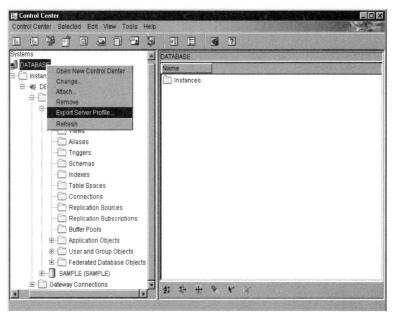

Fig. 3–19 *Control Center - Export Server Profile*

The generated file is a text file and can be viewed but should not be changed.

The generation of an access profile requires that the DISCOVER configuration parameter of the DAS instance be set to either SEARCH or KNOWN. When the profile is generated, it includes all the instances that have ENABLE in the DISCOVER_INST database manager configuration parameter and all the databases that have the DISCOVER_DB database configuration parameter set to ENABLE. See "Configuring DB2 Discovery" on page 130 for more details about these settings.

The second part of the process is to import the server access profile to one or many client machines. To do this, the profile file must be made available to the DB2 client machine (e.g., via the LAN or by diskette) and then be imported using the CCA or the Control Center.

If you wish to import all the information in the access profile, select **Import** from the CCA main panel and then locate the profile file. In this case, when you select the profile file, the Import Profiles panel is displayed:

Fig. 3–20 *Import Server Access Profile - Options*

You can select all the information or choose Customize and select only information related to the Client Settings (the local DBM CFG settings), the CLI/ODBC common settings (from the db2cli.ini file), the APPC stack settings, the configured databases, and/or the NetBIOS name.

When you import client settings, CLI/ODBC common parameters, or local APPC configuration information, the imported values will overlay current values on your system.

If you wish to import only the database settings, start the CCA, select **Add**, and then select **Use an Access Profile**. In the panel shown in Figure 3–21, use the File entry to locate the profile file.

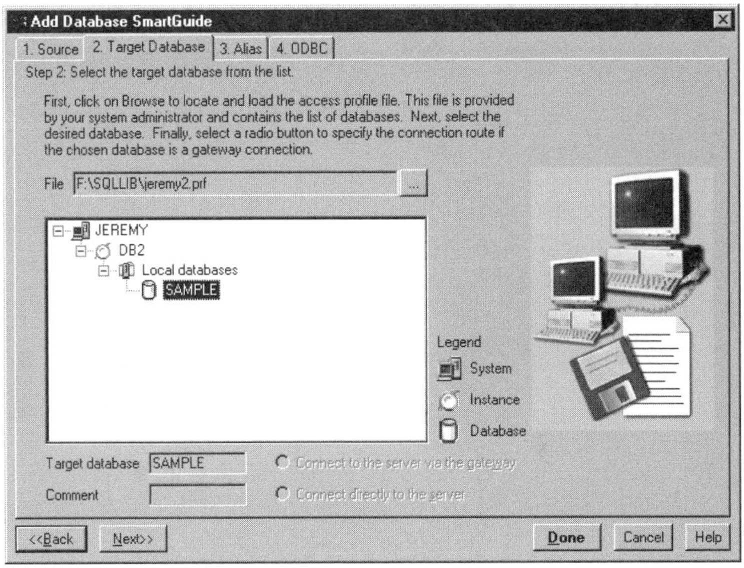

Fig. 3–21 *Import Server Access Profile*

A list of databases (and the systems and instances they belong to) is then displayed in the list of target databases. You can then choose one to catalog. The rest of the configuration then proceeds as for a database located by discovery. (See "Known Discovery Using the CCA" on page 95 for details.)

Alternatively, you can import a server access profile using the Control Center. Expand the required system and then right-click on an instance. Select **Import Server Profile** from the pop-up menu (see Fig. 3–22). Select the file containing the access profile. After the operation completes, refresh the list of systems to see the newly added system.

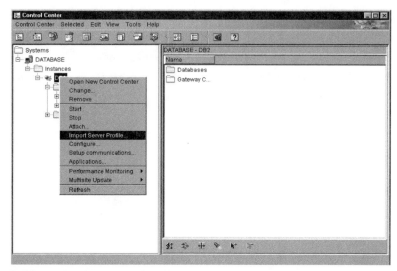

Fig. 3–22 *Control Center - Import Server Access Profile*

Using a Client Access Profile

A client access profile is a file that contains information about all remote databases cataloged at a client and can also contain information about the local DBM CFG settings, the CLI/ODBC setttings, the APPC stack settings, and the NetBIOS name. This file can be generated using the CCA.

The first part of the process is to generate the access profile from the client.

Start the CCA and click on **Export** from the main panel. The Select Export Options panel is displayed:

Fig. 3–23 *Export Client Access Profile - Options*

In this panel, you can choose to export all information, only database-related information, or select exactly which information to export (Customize). If you choose the last option, the Customize Export panel is displayed:

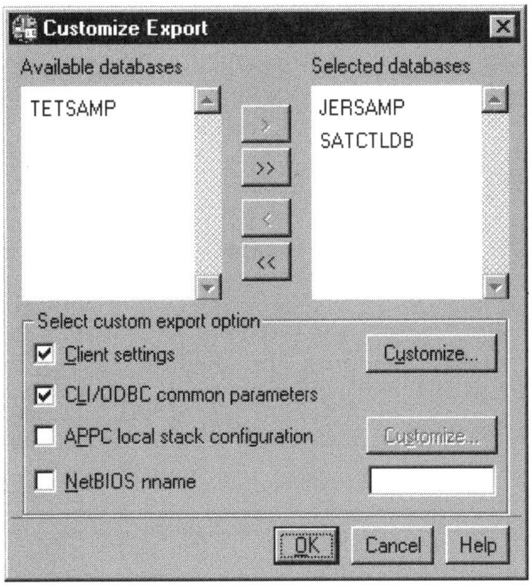

Fig. 3–24 *Customize Export of Client Access Profile*

In this panel, you can select which cataloged databases to export by double-clicking on the entries under Available databases to move them to the Selected databases list. The local client settings (DBM DFG) and/or the APPC stack settings can be customized before export, and the NetBIOS name can be specified.

When you click OK, you are prompted to choose a file name for the client access profile.

The second part of the process is to import the client access profile to other client machines. To do this, the profile file must be made available to the DB2 client machine (for example via the LAN or by diskette), and then be imported using the CCA.

If you wish to import all the information in the access profile, you should select **Import** from the CCA main panel, and then locate the profile file. In this case, when you select the profile file, you can then choose what information to use from the file. You can select all the information that was exported, or choose Customize and select only information related to the Client Settings (the local DBM cfg settings), the CLI/ODBC common settings (from the db2cli.ini file), the APPC stack settings, the configured databases, and/or the NetBIOS name.

If you wish to import only the database settings, start the CCA, select **Add,** and then select **Use an Access Profile**. As in the panel shown in Figure 3–21, use the File entry panel to locate the profile file.

A list of databases (and the systems and instances they belong to) is then displayed in the list of target databases. You can then choose one to catalog. The rest of the configuration then proceeds as for a database located by discovery. (See "Known Discovery Using the CCA" on page 95 for details.)

Manual Configuration

You can configure a database connection manually using the CCA, the DB2 Control Center, the DB2 Command Center, or the DB2 Command Line Processor (CLP). In this section, both the CCA and the DB2 Command Line Processor will be demonstrated. Commands entered from the DB2 CLP can also be entered from the DB2 Command Center to take advantage of the features of the DB2 Command Center. To configure a connection using one of the above methods, you must know the following:

- One of the protocols supported by the server instance containing the database
- The protocol connection information required to configure the connection to the server instance
- The server name
- The name of the database on the remote server

Manual configuration using the CCA will now be reviewed. With the information listed above, the Add Database Wizard can be used to guide you through the steps necessary to add the database connection.

Manual Configuration Using the CCA

Start the Client Configuration Assistant (CCA) and click on **Add** in the CCA's main panel to start the Add Database Wizard. Select **Manually configure a connection to a DB2 database** and click on **Next**.

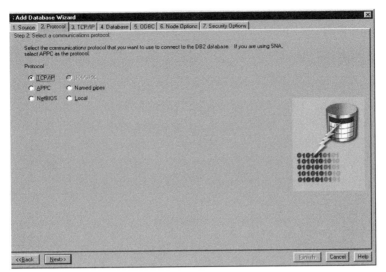

Fig. 3–25 *CCA manual configuration - Select protocol*

Select the protocol that you will use to connect to the database.

All of the protocols that DB2 supports are listed here, including APPC. If you have chosen APPC, your operating system choices are LAN-based, OS/390 or MVS, OS/400, VM, or VSE. If you choose TCP/IP, your choices are LAN-based, OS/390, OS/400, or VM.

Click on **Next**.

Getting Connected

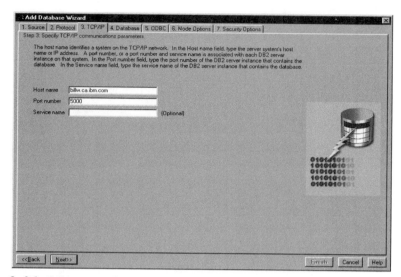

Fig. 3–26 *CCA manual configuration - Enter protocol-specific details*

Enter the required protocol parameters. These parameters differ according to the protocol selected. These are the supported protocols together with their associated parameters:

- TCP/IP - Server hostname/IP address, port number
- NetBIOS - Server workstation name, adapter number
- Named Pipe - Server computer name, instance
- IPX/SPX - Server internetwork address, socket number; if using file server addressing, file server name and object name
- APPC - Server symbolic destination name

You should check that the machine is properly configured on the network before clicking on OK. For example, if using TCP/IP, ping the hostname to check it is available.

Click on the **Next** push button.

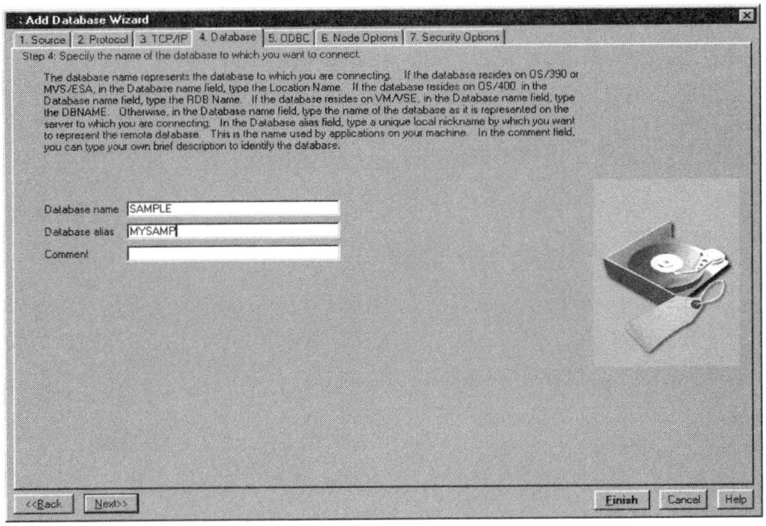

Fig. 3–27 *CCA manual configuration - Enter database details*

Enter the name of the database (as known at the server) in the Database name field.

You can accept the same name as the local alias for the database or change the alias to a name of your choice. You can also enter a description.

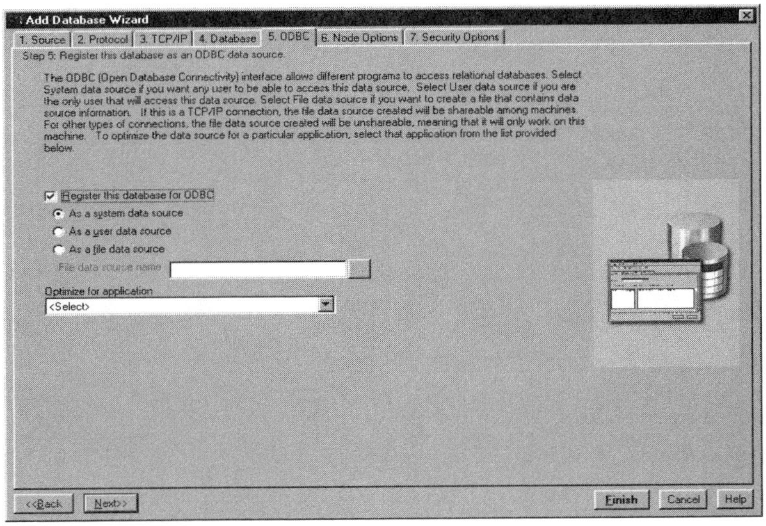

Fig. 3–28 *CCA manual configuration - Enter ODBC settings*

On the next panel (Figure 3–28) you can enter the ODBC settings.

Getting Connected

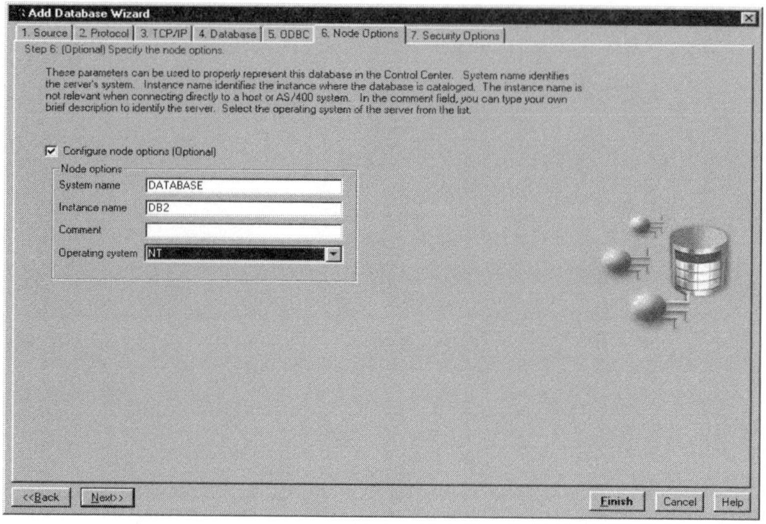

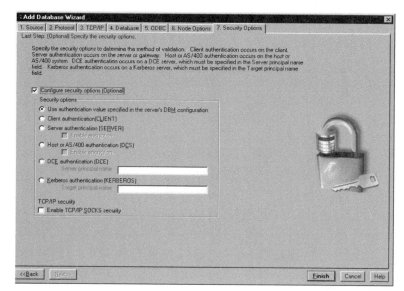

Fig. 3–29 *CCA manual configuration - Enter node options*

The next panel allows you to enter options relating to the remote node. You should fill in these values as they affect the behavior of the Control Center. The System and Instance names are given by the values of DB2SYSTEM and DB2INSTANCE at the server. You should also select the operating system of the remote system.

Fig. 3–30 *CCA manual configuration - Enter security options*

In the final panel, there are many options relating to security that may be specified.

You can specify where authentication of the user takes place at the server (the default), at the client, on a host or OS/400, or on a DCE server). These options are explained in more detail in "Controlling Data Access" on page 145. You can also choose to use SOCKS security for TCP/IP connections, which allows you to access a remote database outside your firewall.

Using the CATALOG Commands

You can also use the CATALOG NODE and CATALOG DB commands from the DB2 Command Center or the DB2 Command Line Processor (CLP) to add a remote database.

Before cataloging a remote database, you should check that the client machine can communicate with the remote DB2 server. The client must then catalog the remote node and the remote database.

The format of the CATALOG NODE command depends on the protocol that you use. The TCP/IP, NetBIOS, Named Pipe, IPX/SPX, and APPC protocols are supported.

Other cataloguing for APPN, LDAP, and APPCLU nodes are not described in this book. For details on these cataloguing options, please refer to the DB2 Command Reference.

Cataloging a TCP/IP Node

When cataloging a TCP/IP node to communicate with a DB2 database server, you must specify a node name after CATALOG TCPIP NODE. This node name will be used in the CATALOG DB command and must be unique in the client node directory.

```
catalog tcpip node mynode
remote billw.ca.ibm.com
server 50000
```

To specify the remote machine, you can use the host name or IP address as the value for the REMOTE parameter.

The SERVER parameter specifies either the service name or the port number used by the database server. These values are located in the /etc/services file (e.g., on AIX) at the server. This identifies which instance to use at the DB2 server instance.

Once the node has been cataloged, the remote database can be cataloged.

Getting Connected

```
catalog db sample
as mysamp
at node mynode
```

 Note: In this chapter, the basic CATALOG command options are presented. There are many more options you can use - for details on these options, please refer to the *DB2 UDB V7.1 Command Reference*.

The database name you use after CATALOG DB must match the name of the database alias at the server. You can specify an alias for the remote database by specifying a different name for the value of the AS parameter. You will then use this alias to connect to the remote database. The node name you use for the AT NODE parameter must match the node name you used in the CATALOG TCPIP NODE command (in this example, mynode).

Once the remote database has been configured, you can test the connection using the CONNECT statement. For example:

```
connect to mysamp user db2admin using db2admin
```

Cataloging a NetBIOS Node

When cataloging a NetBIOS node to communicate with a DB2 database server, you must specify a node name after CATALOG NETBIOS NODE. This node name will be used in the CATALOG DB command and must be unique in the client node directory.

```
catalog netbios node billw
remote N01FCBE3
adapter 0
```

To specify the remote machine, you can use the server workstation name as the value for the REMOTE parameter. You should check that the machine is available on the network.The ADAPTER parameter specifies the outgoing local logical LAN adapter number.

The workstation name of the client (NNAME) must be defined in the client's DBM configuration file. This is usually done during the installation.

Once the node has been cataloged, the remote database can be cataloged (as shown for the TCP/IP node example).

Cataloging a Named Pipe Node

When cataloging a Named Pipe node to communicate with a DB2 database server, you must specify a node name after CATALOG NPIPE NODE. This node name will be used in the CATALOG DB command and must be unique in the client node directory.

```
catalog npipe node mynode
remote billw
instance db2
```

To specify the remote machine, you use the Computer Name of the database server as the value for the REMOTE parameter. This is specified in the Identification Tab of the Network folder in Windows. You should check that the machine is available on the network.

The INSTANCE parameter specifies the instance on the server where the database resides.

Once the node has been cataloged, the remote database can be cataloged (as shown for the TCP/IP node example).

Cataloging an IPX/SPX Node

When cataloging an IPX/SPX node to communicate with a DB2 database server, you must specify a node name after CATALOG IPXPSX NODE. This node name will be used in the CATALOG DB command and must be unique in the client node directory.

```
catalog ipxspx node mynode
remote *
server 00000001.08005AB80EE4.879E
```

If direct addressing is being used, then you use the internetwork address of the server as the value for the SERVER parameter. A value of * can be used for the REMOTE parameter.

The DB2 server's internetwork address can be found by executing the db2ipxad utility at the DB2 server.

Getting Connected

If fileserver addressing is being used, then you use the server's IPX/SPX fileserver name as the value for the REMOTE parameter. The IPX/SPX object name, which represents the DB2 server instance, is used for the SERVER parameter.

This information can be found in the server's database manager configuration file.

Once the node has been cataloged, the remote database can be cataloged (as shown for the TCP/IP node example).

Cataloging an APPC Node

When cataloging an APPC node to communicate with a DB2 database server, you must specify a node name after CATALOG APPC NODE. This node name will be used in the CATALOG DB command and must be unique in the client node directory.

```
catalog appc node mynode
remote db2cpic00
security same
```

To specify the remote machine, you use the symbolic destination name used in the CPI-C Side Information profile as the value for the REMOTE parameter. You should check that the machine is available on the network.

The level of security can be specified as SAME, SECURITY, or PROGRAM. For details of these security types, please refer to the *DB2 UDB V7.1 Command Reference*.

Once the node has been cataloged, the remote database can be cataloged (as shown for the TCP/IP node example).

Summary of Configuring Connections

Choosing a client configuration method will depend on the number of database clients, the number of different configurations needed and the network complexity. The following table gives general recommendations on when to use each configuration method.

Table 3–1 *Choosing a Configuration Method*

Environment Considerations	Configuration Method
Large number of clients to configure Clients may have access to different databases	Server Access Profile
Large number of clients to configure Clients will have access to the same databases	Client Access Profile

Table 3–1 *Choosing a Configuration Method (Continued)*

Environment Considerations	Configuration Method
Large network with many routers and bridges	Known discovery
Simple network Many clients Dynamic environment, new servers added frequently	Search discovery
Using APPC protocol Need advanced options	Manually from CCA
Need to be able to redo the setup using scripts	CATALOG NODE/DB

Configuring Communications

During the installation of a DB2 server, the setup program will try to detect any protocols that are installed and configured on the server machine. It will then configure DB2 to use those protocols. Default values are available that can be overridden by the user. However, if you install a new protocol stack, or reconfigure an existing protocol stack after installing DB2, you will have to manually configure DB2 to use the new protocol information.

DB2 keeps information about communications in:

- The DB2 instance (DBM CFG) on the server
- The DAS instance (ADMIN CFG) on the server
- The DB2 instance (DBM CFG) on the client
- The DB2 Profile Registry (server and client)
- Protocol-specific locations - for example, the services file for TCP/IP

The ways to view and change DB2 Discovery settings will now be examined and the parameters that can affect its behavior.

Configuring the DB2 Instance for Communications

This section discusses the steps necessary to configure a DB2 server to receive incoming database requests. There are a number of communication protocols supported by DB2: APPC, NetBIOS, TCP/IP, Named Pipe, and IPX/SPX. Not all these protocols are supported on all DB2 server platforms.

Note: The underlying communication support (software) needs to be installed prior to enabling communication with DB2.

Two methods exist to assist with the communications configuration: using the DB2 Control Center and using a command line interface to update configuration files and other configuration information.

Using the Control Center

You can set up communications for local instances using the Control Center. The following steps are needed:

Open the Control Center and click on the [+] sign next to a local system that you want to configure. Open the **Instances** icon. Right-click on the instance you require and select **Setup communications** from the menu.

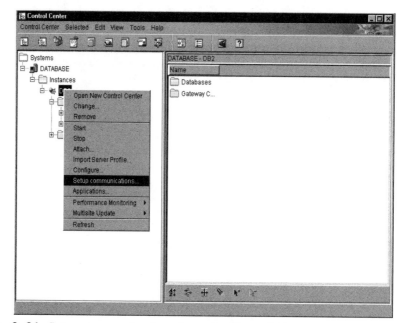

Fig. 3–31 *Setup communications from the Control Center*

Once it is clicked, all possible communication protocols are shown:

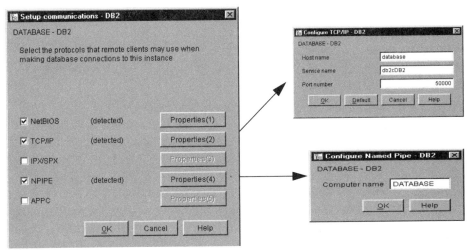

Fig. 3–32 *Setup communications - TCP/IP and Named Pipe*

The protocols that were detected at the server during installation are marked as detected.

Figure 3–32 shows that TCP/IP and Named Pipes were detected. This means, for example, that remote clients can access the DB2 instance using TCP/IP. To change the settings for TCP/IP, click on **Properties(2)**. Here, the defaults for the service name (db2cDB2) and port number (50000) have been specified.

If you need to configure protocols that were not detected (e.g., APPC), you can click in the check box next to the protocol, then in the Properties box for the protocol to change the communications settings.

Once you have set the properties for the protocol, a message is displayed, reminding you that you must restart the instance because the database manager configuration file was updated.

Click on the **OK** button. From the Setup communications panel, either configure the next protocol or click on the **OK** button. The message to restart the instance appears once again. Click on the **OK** button. Now the instance has been configured with the specified protocols. You must stop and then restart the instance for the changes to take effect. You can restart the instance from the Control Center.

The following sections explain how to set up the server communications manually. These steps need to be done for instances created with the db2icrt command, where a local Control Center is not available.

Getting Connected

Using the Command Line Processor

If you configure DB2 to use new protocols using the CLP, then you must modify the value for DB2COMM for the DB2 instance accordingly. The setting of this registry variable is done using the db2set command, and the value is stored in the profile registry. If more than one protocol is used, the protocol values are separated by a comma. For example, to enable TCP/IP and NetBIOS communications on a DB2 server, set the DB2COMM registry variable as follows:

```
db2set -i db2comm=tcpip,netbios
```

The DB2COMM variable should be updated in your environment so that no errors are detected when the instance is started and protocol support start-up is attempted.

There are several other communication variables that can be changed depending on the remote clients you are supporting and the communication protocol. For example, DB2SERVICETPINSTANCE is a communication variable used with APPC to support down-level remote clients. NetBIOS has a number of parameters that can be set for performance reasons.

Not only must the registry variables be updated, but the associated DBM configuration parameters must also be updated to complete the configuration support for a protocol.

When updating the database manager configuration, you need to be a member of the instance administration group (SYSADM). The required information will be examined by using five scenarios.

The UPDATE DBM CONFIG USING <option> <value> command should be used to modify any of the DBM configuration parameters from a command window environment. You can also do this through the DB2 Control Center by right-clicking your mouse on the instance you wish to update, choose the **Configure** option, and then choose the **Communications** tab (Fig. 3–33). You then modify the entries you wish to update.

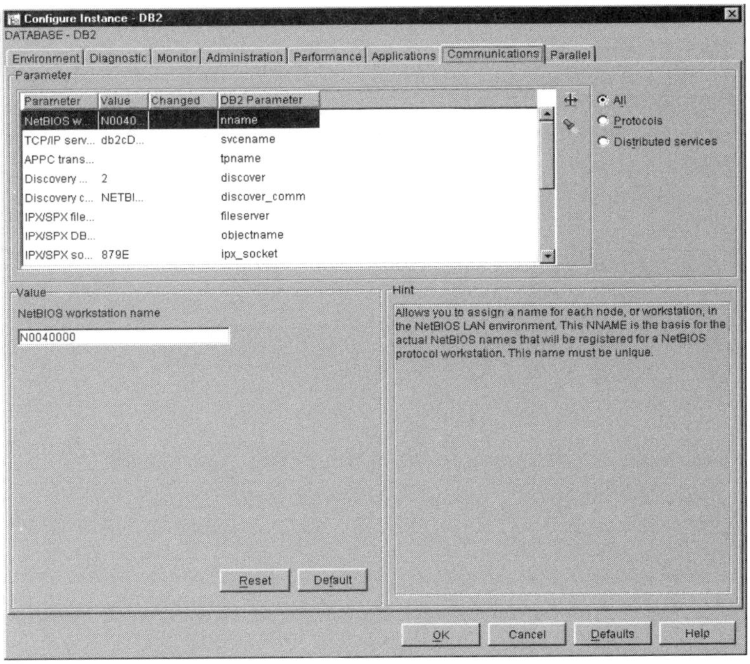

Fig. 3–33 *Configure Instance - Communications*

TCP/IP

To enable the TCP/IP protocol, the DB2 server must have the DB2COMM registry variable include TCPIP. You also need to update the service name defined in the services file and the DBM configuration file on the database server.

> **Note:** The updating of the services file must be performed on the DB2 server. The services file is updated using an editor and cannot be updated from DB2.

The parameter in the database manager configuration file is called SVCENAME. The service name is assigned as the main connection port name for the instance and defined in the services file. For example, if the name defined in the services file is db2tcp, the command is the following:

```
update dbm cfg using svcename db2tcp
```

Getting Connected

After this command, the DB2 instance must be restarted.

NetBIOS

To enable the NetBIOS protocol, the DB2 server must have the DB2COMM registry variable include NETBIOS. The workstation name (NNAME) on both the client and server must be set. This name must be unique within the network. A NetBIOS error will occur if the workstation name is not unique.

For example, if the NNAME is db200, the command is:

```
update dbm cfg using NNAME db200
```

After this command, the DB2 instance must be restarted.

Named Pipes

To enable the Named Pipes protocol, the DB2 server must have the DB2COMM registry variable include NPIPE. This protocol only applies for Windows systems. No configuration in the DBM configuration file is required.

IPX/SPX

To enable IPX/SPX connections, you must ensure that the DB2 IPX/SPX communications manager has been enabled on the DB2 server. Set the DB2COMM registry variable to include IPXSPX. There are two methods of enabling the DB2 server to accept IPX/SPX connections on a network: fileserver addressing or direct addressing.

A DB2 client locates the DB2 server via the NetWare fileserver when fileserver addressing is used. Direct addressing avoids this step because the DB2 client has the address of the DB2 server and can therefore communicate directly with the DB2 server.

If only direct addressing will be used to communicate from a client to the server, set the FILESERVER and OBJECTNAME database manager configuration parameters to * (asterisk). For the IPX_SOCKET parameter, you can select a hex number representing the connection endpoint identifier that specifies a well-known socket number and represents the connection endpoint in a DB2 server's Netware Internetwork Address. It must be unique for each DB2 server instance and unique among all IPX/SPX applications running on one workstation. DB2 has registered well-known sockets with Novell in the range 0x879E to 0x87A1, with the default value of 0x879E.

If you run more than four instances on the server machine, you must prevent socket collisions for instances five and up by choosing a socket number that is not 0x0000, in the dynamic socket range 0x4000 to 0x7FFF, or in the range 0x8000 to 0x9100. (These are well known sockets that are registered to various applications.) The maximum value for this parameter is 0xFFFF.

Here is an example of configuring a DB2 server using direct addressing:

```
update dbm cfg using fileserver *
objectname *
ipx_socket 879F
```

If both fileserver and direct addressing will be used to communicate from a client to a server, then set the the FILESERVER parameter in the DBM configuration to the name of your Netware fileserver. This is the name of the fileserver where the DB2 server instance is registered. The OBJECTNAME represents the DB2 server instance on the network. It must be unique for all DB2 server instances registered at the same NetWare fileserver. IPX_SOCKET should be specified as for direct addressing.

An example of configuring the DB2 server using fileserver addressing follows:

```
update dbm cfg using fileserver ipxfs
objectname DB2
ipx_socket 897F
```

When fileserver addressing is used, the DB2 server instance must be registered at the NetWare fileserver. During the registration process, you must specify a user ID that has Supervisor or Workgroup Manager security equivalence. It is the user ID used to login to the NetWare server.

The DB2 server can be registered using the following command:

```
register db2 server in nwbindery
user user1 password pass1
```

The DB2 instance must be restarted for the changes to take effect.

Getting Connected

APPC

For APPC, you need to know the transaction program name (TPNAME) that DB2 is using. For example, if the TPNAME on the server is db2tp00, the command is:

```
update dbm cfg using tpname db2tp00
```

The instance must be stopped and restarted when any changes are made in the database manager configuration file for the changes to take effect.

Configuring the DAS Instance

This section discusses the steps necessary to configure the DAS server on a DB2 server to enable distributed connections to be established.

Usually, communications protocols are detected and configured for the DAS instance during the installation process. This section describes how the DAS instance communications settings can be configured after installation.

If you install and configure a new communications protocol after the DAS instance has been created, you should update the DAS instance configuration on your machine as necessary to accommodate the new protocol. This is the only time you should need to modify these settings. You can use the UPDATE ADMIN CFG command from the CLP to do this.

NetBIOS

The parameter that controls the NetBIOS Workstation name in the DAS instance configuration is NNAME. To change this, use the following command:

```
update admin cfg using nname <wsname>
```

where <wsname> is the value you wish to use for NNAME.

TCP/IP

The parameter that controls the TCP/IP service to be used by the DAS instance is SVCENAME. This is set to the port number 523, which is reserved for the DAS instance and cannot be changed.

IPX/SPX

The parameter in the DAS instance configuration that controls the IPX/SPX settings is IPX_SOCKET, which represents a connection point in the computers internetwork address. The socket number needs to be unique for each DB2 instance and unique within the computer to ensure that the DAS instance can listen for incoming remote client requests. To alter this, use the following command:

```
update admin cfg using IPX_SOCKET <socname>
```

where <socname> is the value you wish to use for IPX_SOCKET. The default value is 87A2. You should not change this value.

Named Pipes

You cannot alter the Computer Name from a Command Window, as it is not held in the DAS instance configuration. To change this parameter you must use the Network settings from the Windows NT Control Panel.

APPC

The parameter that controls the transaction program name for the DAS instance is TPNAME. To change this parameter, use the following command:

```
update admin cfg using TPNAME <tpname>
```

where <tpname> is the value you wish to use for TPNAME.

> **Note:** If you configure a new protocol, you must set the registry variable DB2COMM for the DAS instance to include the new protocol. For example:
> db2set -i DB2DAS00 DB2COMM=TCPIP,NPIPE

Getting Connected

Configuring DB2 Discovery

As well as needing to have the communication protocols installed and configured, there are various parameters that need to be correctly configured for Discovery to work. As mentioned previously, as long as DB2 is installed after the communications protocols have been installed and configured, these Discovery-related parameters should be set automatically. However, if you add a new communications protocol after DB2 is installed, or if Discovery is not working, you may need to check the parameter settings. Table 3–2 shows the configuration parameters that affect Discovery on both the client and the server.

Table 3–2 *Parameters that Affect Discovery*

Client DB2 Instance	Server DAS Instance	Server DB2 Instance	Server Database
DISCOVER	DISCOVER	DISCOVER_INST	DISCOVER_DB
DISCOVER_COMM	DISCOVER_COMM		

Each parameter and its function is briefly discussed:

DISCOVER in Client DBM CFG

This is a parameter in the database manager configuration file (dbm cfg). The default setting for this parameter is SEARCH. If this parameter is set to SEARCH, either search or known discovery can be used from the client. If this parameter is set to KNOWN only known discovery can be used. If this parameter is set to DISABLE, both known and search discovery are disabled.

DISCOVER_COMM in Client DBM CFG

This is a parameter in the database manager configuration file (dbm cfg). When configured on the client, this parameter specifies which communications protocol(s) will be used for issuing search discovery messages. This parameter can be configured with a single setting or multiple settings separated by commas. When using search discovery, it should be set to TCP/IP, NETBIOS, IPX/SPX, or a combination thereof depending on the communications protocol you wish to use. Note that this parameter has no effect on known discovery.

DISCOVER in Server ADMIN CFG

This is a parameter in the DAS instance configuration file (admin cfg). The default setting for this parameter is SEARCH. If this parameter is set to SEARCH, the server can respond to either search or known discovery requests. If this parameter is set to KNOWN only known discovery requests can be responded to. If this parameter is set to DISABLE, both known and search discovery requests are rejected.

DISCOVER_COMM in Server ADMIN CFG

This is a parameter in the DAS instance configuration file (admin cfg). It specifies the communication protocols that a DAS instance will listen on for search discovery requests. This parameter can be configured with a single setting or multiple settings separated by commas. When using search discovery, it should be set to TCP/IP, NETBIOS, or IPX/SPX (as above) depending on the communications protocol you wish to use. Note that this parameter has no effect on known discovery.

Getting Connected

DISCOVER_INST in Server DBM CFG

This is a parameter in the database manager configuration file (dbm cfg). This parameter can be set to ENABLE or DISABLE. If set to ENABLE the DB2 instance can be discovered. If, however, this parameter is set to DISABLE the DB2 instance cannot be discovered. This gives you the ability to hide a DB2 instance from discovery. If the discovery of an instance is disabled, all databases associated with that instance will be hidden also (see "Restricting Discovery" on page 133). The default setting for this parameter is ENABLE.

DISCOVER_DB in Server DB CFG

This is a parameter in the database configuration file (db cfg) for a particular database. This parameter acts in a similar fashion to the DISCOVER_INST DB2 instance parameter. The difference is that this parameter enables you to hide a database from discovery. For each database in a DB2 instance you can set this parameter to either ENABLE or DISABLE. This enables you to control which databases in an instance are shown on a Discovery request (see "Restricting Discovery" on page 133). The default setting for this is ENABLE.

Note: The DB2COMM registry variable at the server DAS instance and the server DB2 instance must be set to the communications protocols that listen for discovery requests.

Note: The DISCOVER and DISCOVER_COMM parameters in the database manager configuration file (dbm cfg) on a DB2 server affect discovery only if a discovery request is initiated from the DB2 server, in other words, when the DB2 server behaves as a client to another DB2 server.

Note: When using the search mode of discovery, at least one protocol set in DISCOVER_COMM on the client must match the values set in the DISCOVER_COMM on the server. If there is no match, the server will not respond to the client's requests.

Restricting Discovery

As well as enabling discovery for either the search and known methods, it is also possible to disable discovery so your DB2 server cannot be located on the network. This is achieved by setting the DAS instance parameter DISCOVER to DISABLE. It is also possible to configure discovery on a DB2 server in a hierarchical manner. You can disable or enable at the DB2 server level, instance level, and database level. This provides you with the ability to enable discovery of your DB2 server while hiding certain instances and/or databases (Fig. 3–34).

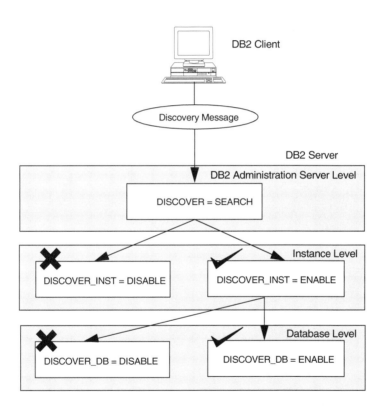

Fig. 3–34 *Discovery hierarchy*

To set the discovery parameters for the DAS instance on the server, you can use the Command Center or CLP. For example, to set the DISCOVER parameter to SEARCH and the DISCOVER_COMM parameter to TCP/IP, enter the following commands:

```
update admin cfg using discover search
update admin cfg using discover_comm tcpip
```

Getting Connected

To view the parameter values currently set for the DAS instance, enter the following command:

```
get admin cfg
```

To set the discovery parameters for the DB2 instance or a database on the server, you can use the Control Center. Select the object, right-click on the mouse and select **Configure**.

To set the discovery parameters for the DB2 client, you can use the Client Configuration Assistant. Click on the **Client Settings** button and go to the Communications tag. Alternatively, you can use the `update dbm cfg` command from the CLP or Command Center, or if you choose, you can use the graphical interface of the DB2 Control Center to update configuration parameters.

Binding Utilities

When a remote client wants access to a database server, the database utilities must be bound on the server for the client to use. The database utilities that a remote client must bind to the DB2 server include:

- CLI/ODBC support
- DB2 Command Line Processor
- Data import/export utilities
- REXX support

If you create a new database on the server, packages for the database utilities must also be created in the system catalog tables. All of the client utility packages are contained in a file called `db2ubind.lst`. Call Level Interface and ODBC packages are grouped together in the `db2cli.lst` file. These packages can be created by executing the `BIND` command from the client workstation after a connection has been made to the server database.

The `BIND` command must be run separately for each database that you wish to access. Once a package has been successfully bound to the database, all DB2 clients can access it. If you have different types or versions of clients on your network, you must bind the utilities from each type and version of client.

Note: Bind files can be different for each client platform and each version of DB2. You have to bind them for each platform you want to use. Every time you install an update to the DB2 product that comes with new bind files, you also have to bind the new files.

Here is an example binding from an OS/2 client to the DB2CERT database that is on an AIX server. Issue the following commands:

```
connect to db2cert
bind @db2ubind.lst blocking all grant public
```

The output from the BIND command can be sent to a file using the MESSAGES parameter. By default, the information is displayed to the screen.

Note: The symbol @ is used to specify that db2ubind.lst is a list of bind files and is not a bind file itself.

When a bind is performed, you should ensure that there are no errors encountered. If errors are encountered, the package will not be created in the database. Common errors include nonexistent database objects used in static SQL.

The GRANT PUBLIC option in the BIND command were used. This option is used to provide EXECUTE and BIND privileges to all users that can access the database. Also note that there are different BIND command options for DRDA (host) databases, such as DB2 for OS/390. (See the *DB2 UDB V7.1 Command Reference* for details.) The output of a successful BIND command should be similar to this excerpt:

Getting Connected

```
LINE    MESSAGES FOR db2ubind.lst
------  ------------------------------------------------------------
        SQL0061W The binder is in progress.

LINE    MESSAGES FOR db2clpnc.bnd
------  ------------------------------------------------------------
        SQL0595W Isolation level "NC" has been escalated to "UR".
             SQLSTATE=01526

LINE    MESSAGES FOR db2arxnc.bnd
------  ------------------------------------------------------------
        SQL0595W Isolation level "NC" has been escalated to "UR".
             SQLSTATE=01526

LINE    MESSAGES FOR db2ubind.lst
------  ------------------------------------------------------------
        SQL0091N Binding was ended with "0" errors and "2" warnings.
```

The utilities that are bound include IMPORT, EXPORT, LOAD, CLP, BACKUP, RESTORE, and REORG. The db2ubind.lst file contains the list of bind (.bnd) files that are required to create the packages for these utilities.

Note: Remember you must have BINDADD authority to create a new package in a database. If the package exists, then BIND privilege for the package is the only requirement needed to update the package.

Binding Utilities Using the CCA

Binding utilities can also be done with the Client Configuration Assistant. In this example, binding the utilities to a DB2 for OS/390 database will be demonstrated.

To do this, the user performing the bind operations must have SYSCTRL or SYSADM authority or be granted the BINDADD or CREATE IN COLLECTION NULLID privileges.

Note: While the CCA is convenient to use, it gives you only a subset of the BIND options available from the command line interface.

Start the CCA. Select the DB2 for OS/390 database that has been catalogued. Click on the **Bind** button and the Bind Database dialog will pop up.

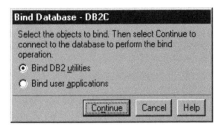

Fig. 3–35 *Bind Database Utilities*

Select **Bind DB2 utilities** and click on **Continue**.

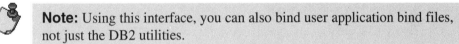

Note: Using this interface, you can also bind user application bind files, not just the DB2 utilities.

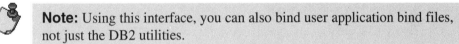

Fig. 3–36 *Bind Utilities - Connect to DB2 Database*

Complete the **Connect To DB2 Database** panel by filling in a valid user ID and password, then click on **OK**. The Bind Utilities dialog pops up.

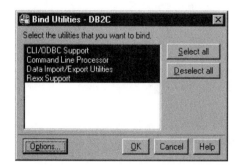

Fig. 3–37 *Bind Utilities - Select utilities*

Select one or more utilities from the list:

- CLI/ODBC Support - If you want to use ODBC or CLI applications
- Command Line Processor - If you want to use interactive SQL from the DB2 command line interface
- Data Import/Export Utilities - If you want to import or export data on the DB2 for OS/390 database to or from the client
- REXX Support - If you want to use the REXX SQL interface

To change or review the bind options, click on the **Options** push button.

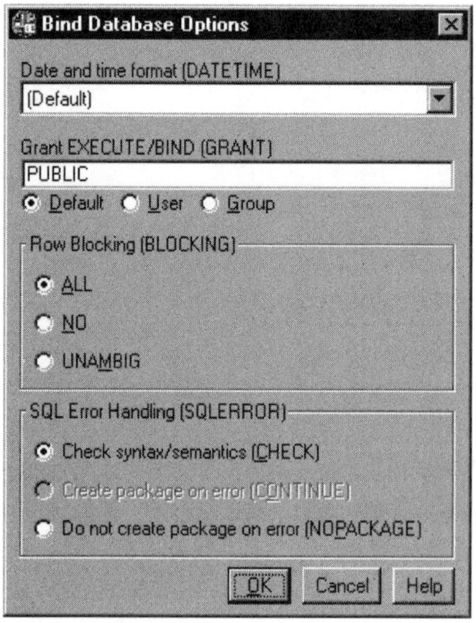

Fig. 3–38 *Bind Utilities - Options*

For "Date and time format," it is suggested you select the default value.

This selection sets a date and time format based on the country setting of the database. Please refer to the *DB2 UDB V7.1 SQL Reference* for the other options. For "Grant EXECUTE/BIND," enter a specific user, group, or PUBLIC. A value of PUBLIC means that all users will be granted EXECUTE and BIND privilege for this package. If a user has the same name as a group, select the User or Group radio-button to tell DB2 whether the name refers to a user or a group. For "Row Blocking," select **All**. This is the same as the BLOCKING ALL option of the BIND command.

If you are binding to a DRDA database, for "SQL Error Handling," select **Create package on error**. This is the same as the SQLERROR CONTINUE option of the BIND command.

Click on **OK** to return to the Bind Utilities dialog. Click on **OK** on the Bind Utilities dialog to start the bind process. Details about the bind progress as well as warnings and errors will be displayed in the Bind Results dialog.

Instance Administration

This section discusses how to administer DB2 instances, both locally and remotely. Certain tasks in DB2 can only be performed at the instance level, such as creating a database, forcing users off databases, monitoring a database, or updating the database manager configuration. Other tasks require a database connection, such as issuing SQL Data Manipulation Language (DML) statements, using the LOAD utility, or using the BIND command.

Both remote and local administration of instances can be done using the Control Center. The ATTACH command can be used from the command line for both local and remote administration tasks.

To attach to an instance, you can use the ATTACH command. The syntax of the ATTACH command is as follows:

```
ATTACH [TO nodename] [USER username [USING password]]
```

If the ATTACH command is executed without arguments, the node name you are currently attached to is returned. If you attempt to attach to an instance while attached to another instance, the current instance will be detached and the new attachment is attempted. In other words, you can only be attached to one instance at a time.

> **Note:** The currently active instance can be identified using the GET INSTANCE command, which returns the value of the DB2INSTANCE environment variable.

Database connections are independent of instance attachments. A single application can maintain several database connections at the same time it has an instance attachment, but it can only maintain a single instance attachment at any one time. The database connection can be implicit or explicit. An implicit database connection will connect to the database specified by the DB2DBDFT registry variable. An explicit database connection can be made using the CONNECT TO DATABASE statement.

The local instance is determined by the value contained in the DB2INSTANCE variable. When attached to a second instance, you are using the directory services of the local instance. You cannot make catalog changes or list, update, or reset catalogs for database, node, or DCS directories in the second instance.

Local Instance Administration

After DB2 has been installed on a server and an instance created, a user can access this instance in one of two ways:

- By setting the DB2INSTANCE environment variable to the name of the instance. The DB2PATH environment variable must be set to the location of the DB2 executables. This is known as an *implicit attachment*.

- By cataloging a local instance and issuing the ATTACH command. This is known as an *explicit attachment*.

Instance Attach Scenario

This scenario examines a situation in which a local user wants to access two instances on the same database server without changing the environment when the user logs into the system.

The two local instances are called db2test and db2. They are located on an AIX database server. The user, Dana, is a local user on the database server. Dana has set the DB2INSTANCE and DB2PATH variables to allow access to the db2test instance. In AIX, Dana would edit her profile to include the following entry:

```
. /home/db2test/sqllib/db2profile
```

Dana also wants to access the db2 instance on the same server. To do this, she catalogs the db2 instance as a local node by using the following command:

```
catalog local node mydb2 instance db2
```

In this example:

- local identifies that this is a local instance.
- mydb2 is the local alias for the node to be catalogued.
- db2 is the name of the local instance to be accessed.

The contents of the node directory can be examined using the LIST NODE DIRECTORY command:

```
Node Directory

Number of entries in the directory = 2

Node 1 entry:

Node name                   = MYDB2
Comment                     =
Protocol                    = LOCAL
Instance name               = db2
```

To access a database in the instance named db2, Dana must catalog the local database using the following command:

```
catalog db db2cert as mycert at node mydb2
```

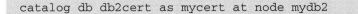

In this example:

- db2cert is the name of the database as it exists in the instance on the database server.
- mycert is the alias that user Dana will use when connecting.
- mydb2 is the local alias given to the local instance by Dana in the CATALOG NODE command.

If Dana issues the LIST DB DIRECTORY command, the output is similar to the following:

```
System Database Directory

Number of entries in the directory = 1

Database 1 entry:

    Database alias                    = MYCERT
    Database name                     = DB2CERT
    Local database directory          = /home/db2test
    Database release level            = 9.00
    Comment                           =
    Directory entry type              = Remote
    Catalog node number               = 0
```

Notice that the entry is a REMOTE type. The database has been cataloged via the mydb2 node. This is, in fact, a local node on the same workstation. A local node is essentially another DB2 instance. In this case, the instance is called db2 as shown above.

Attaching to an Instance Using the Control Center

So far, DB2 commands have been used to attach to an instance. This can also be done using the Control Center. To do this, right-click on the required instance and select Attach from the menu as shown here:

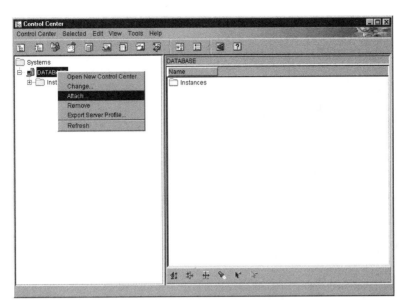

Fig. 3–39 *Attaching to an instance*

An attachment being made to the JEREMY instance is displayed. To be able to perform administrative tasks at a remote instance, you should log on to the instance as the DAS instance owner.

Summary

This chapter presented an overview of configuration methods that can be used to set up a remote database connection. The concept of directories within DB2 was discussed as well as how the information contained in the directories is used to access databases, both locally and remotely.

Step-by-step examples of configuring connections on DB2 clients using each of the possible methods. You can use automated methods to set up communications or use manual methods.

The steps that a database server must perform to communicate with a remote client using one of the supported protocols if the protocol was not detected during installation or changed after installation was demonstrated.

How to bind the utilities to the server database when the client and server are on different systems was reviewed.

Finally, the ATTACH command is explained, which allows both local and remote users to access an instance to perform tasks such as creating or monitoring a database. Attaching to a remote instance can be done using the ATTACH command or the Control Center.

CHAPTER 4

Controlling Data Access

- ◆ AUTHENTICATING USERS
- ◆ ASSIGNING AUTHORITIES
- ◆ ASSIGNING PRIVILEGES
- ◆ USERS AND GROUPS
- ◆ WINDOWS NT/2000 CONSIDERATIONS
- ◆ AUDIT FACILITY

*S*ecurity is an important consideration whenever data is stored in a relational database management system. In this chapter, we discuss controlling data access using many different methods. Access to data within DB2 is controlled at many levels including instance, database, database object, and application packages. The topics of authentication of user IDs and passwords are discussed. We configure groups of typical database users such as database administrators, system administrators, transactional processing personnel, and decision support users. Each of these database user types may require different access privileges. We will also discuss the Audit facility. It allows you to monitor security-related events.

 DB2 UDB Version 7.1 introduces support for the Windows 2000 platform. Throughout this chapter, references to Windows NT also refers to Windows 2000 unless specifically stated.

Security

When working with or using a Relational Database Management System (RDBMS), access to it needs to be controlled. There are three factors to consider when controlling access to an RDBMS:

- Who will access it? Users of the RDBMS may need to be known at the database server.
- What will be accessed? DB2 has various objects that can be accessed by users and administrators, such as instances, databases, tables, and views.
- What type of access is allowed? This refers to which actions a user is permitted to perform on DB2 objects, such as creating, updating, or deleting records or objects.

Overview of Security

There are three levels of security that control access to a DB2 system. The first level controls the access to the instance. The second level controls the access to the database. The last level relates to the access of data or data-associated objects within the database.

All access to the instance is managed by a security facility external to DB2. The security facility can be part of the operating system or a separate product. It allows the system to make sure that the user really is who he or she claims to be and may also control access to other objects such as files and programs. Users and groups to which they may belong are normally used by these security facilities.

Access to a database and its data objects is controlled at the database level by the DB2 database manager. Here, administrative authorities and user privileges defined in the database are used to control access.

The database administrator must ensure that sensitive information is not accessed by those without a *need to know*. A security plan for DB2 should be developed by defining your objectives and implementing them using the correct privileges and authorities.

Authentication

The first step in managing security is to verify the user's identity. This is called *authentication*. Authentication is the operation of verifying whether a user is who he or she claims to be. This is typically accomplished by forcing the user to provide a valid user ID and password. Every time a user tries to connect to a local or remote database, he or she is authenticated. DB2 will pass all user IDs and passwords to the operating system or external security facility to be verified.

When configuring the connection between DB2 clients and DB2 servers, you can specify where authentication should take place, for example, at the client or at the server. One can also specify which clients should be allowed to authenticate users at the client and which ones at the server. DB2 groups the different clients into three groups:

Untrusted Clients

These are clients running operating systems that do not have integrated security facilities. They include Windows 95/98,Windows 3.x, and Macintosh.

Trusted Clients

These clients run on operating systems that have integrated security facilities as part of the operating system. Trusted clients include Windows NT, Windows 2000, OS/2, all the supported UNIX operating systems, MVS, OS/390, VM, VSE, and AS/400.

Host Clients

This group is a subset of the trusted client group. They run on one of the following operating systems: MVS, OS/390, VM, VSE, or AS/400.

Supplying a User ID and a Password for Authentication

A user is able to establish a connection between the client and an instance on the server or between a client and a database on the server. DB2 has two commands that can be used to establish these connections. For an instance connection, the ATTACH command is used. For a database connection, the CONNECT statement is used. With both, the user may or may not supply a user ID and password. If it is not supplied and the authentication type is CLIENT (the authentication type is discussed later), DB2 may use the user ID and password with which the user is logged on at the client for authentication. It may also prompt the user to supply a user ID and password. If the user ID and password is supplied with either ATTACH or CONNECT, DB2 will use them to authenticate the user. The user ID and password specified may differ from those used to log on to the client.

In addition, the user can also request a password change by supplying the user ID, password, new password, and confirmation of the new password. DB2 will authenticate the user first before requesting the password change from the security facility. Connecting to a database in an embedded SQL program does not require a user to supply the confirmation of the new password.

Controlling Data Access

Example 1

A user wants to connect to the database named SAMPLE using his user ID PETE and his password MYPASS. The statement he would use would look like this:

```
CONNECT TO SAMPLE USER PETE USING MYPASS
```

Example 2

The same user as in Example 1 wants to connect to a database named SAMPLE, but he wants to change his password from MYPASS to NEWPWD. The statement he would use is:

```
CONNECT TO SAMPLE USER PETE USING MYPASS
    NEW NEWPWD CONFIRM NEWPWD
```

Example 3

The user specified by the host variable USERID wants to connect to the database named SAMPLE in an embedded SQL program, and he wants to change his password from the one specified by the host variable OLDPWD to NEWPWD. The SQL statement he would use is:

```
EXEC SQL CONNECT TO SAMPLE USER:USERID USING:OLDPWD
    NEW:NEWPWD
```

Controlling Where Authentication Takes Place

The *authentication type* defines where and how authentication will take place, for example, at the client or at the server. It can be specified at each machine taking part in establishing the connection. Authentication types are available depending on the environment. We will be looking at two environments commonly used to describe the authentication types available and what they will achieve.

Environment 1: Client Connected Directly to DB2 UDB Server

This environment consists of only two types of machines: servers and clients. The location where the authentication takes place is determined by the value of authentication parameter in the database manager configuration file at the DB2 server. You can, optionally, specify the authentication type at the DB2 client when cataloging a database; however, it must match the value of authentication parameter at the DB2 server. The exception is when DCE_SERVER_ENCRYPT is specified at the DB2 server. This is explained later.

Authentication types at the DB2 UDB server

At the server, the authentication type is defined in the database manager configuration file. This file is used to configure the instance with which it is associated. Its definition is shared among all the databases in the instance; therefore, if an authentication type is chosen for the instance, all the databases in that instance will use that authentication type, and all users connecting to a database in this instance are authenticated based on this authentication type. The authentication types available at the server are:

- **SERVER**

  This forces all authentication to take place at the server; therefore, a user ID and a password must be supplied when attaching to an instance or connecting to a database. The DB2 software at the client will not encrypt the password before it is sent to the server.

- **SERVER_ENCRYPT**

  This is the same as authentication SERVER in the sense that all authentication will take place at the server. However, all passwords are encrypted by DB2 at the client before they are sent to the server. At the server, it is decrypted and authenticated. It is important to note that if a password change is requested, the new password will not be encrypted before it is sent to the server.

- **CLIENT**

  Using this authentication type gives permission to the client to authenticate users on behalf of the server. It does not guarantee that authentication will take place at the client exclusively. We will discuss this setting in detail in a later section.

- **DCE**

  Specify this authentication type if the operating system will not be used to authenticate a user either on the server or on the client. Before using this type of authentication, you will have to install and configure DCE security software.

- **DCE_SERVER_ENCRYPT**

  If the authentication type DCE is specified, no connection with authentication types other than DCE is accepted. DCE_SERVER_ENCRYPT allows various clients with different authentication types to connect to the DB2 server. The client authentication types allowed to connect to a server with `DCE_SERVER_ENCRYPT` authentication type are `DCE`, `SERVER`, and `SERVER_ENCRYPT`.

Table 4–1 shows which authentication type will be used when `DCE_SERVER_ENCRYPT` is chosen at the server depending on the authentication type specified at the client.

Table 4–1 *DCE_SERVER_ENCRYPT*

Client Authentication Type	Server Authentication Type	Authentication Type Used
DCE	DCE_SERVER_ENCRYPT	DCE
SERVER	DCE_SERVER_ENCRIPT	SERVER
SERVER_ENCRYPT	DCE_SERVER_ENCRYPT	SERVER_ENCRYPT

- **KERBEROS**

  This authentication type is used when both the DB2 client and server are on operating systems that support the Kerberos security protocol. The Kerberos security protocol performs authentication as a third-party authentication service by using conventional cryptography to create a shared secret key. This key becomes a user's credential and is used to verify the identity of users during all occasions when local or network services are requested. The key eliminates the need to pass the user name and password across the network as clear text. Using the Kerberos security protocol enables the use of a single sign-on to a remote DB2 server.

- **KRB_SERVER_ENCRYPT**

  It specifies that the server accepts KERBEROS authentication or encrypted SERVER authentication schemes. If the client authentication is KERBEROS, the client is authenticated using the Kerberos security system. If the client authentication is not KERBEROS, then the system authentication type is equivalent to SERVER_ENCRYPT.

KERBEROS and KRB_SERVER_ENCRYPT are new to DB2 UDB Version 7.1. The Kerberos authentication types are only supported on clients and servers running Windows 2000.

Authentication types at the client

The authentication at the client is specified in the system database directory using the catalog database command; however, you can omit specifying an authentication type at the client. If you specify an authentication type at the client, you must keep it the same as the server except if DCE_SERVER_ENCRYPT is used at the server. Not doing so may cause the connection to fail. The meanings of these authentication types are the same as the ones used at the server.

At the client the following authentication types are available:

- **SERVER**
- **SERVER_ENCRYPT**
- **CLIENT**
- **KERBEROS**
- **DCE**

If CLIENT is used, two other parameters in the database manager configuration file are evaluated to determine where the authentication will take place: at the client or at the server. These parameters are TRUST_ALLCLNTS and TRUST_CLNTAUTH. For more information on these parameters, please read the sections covering these parameters in more detail later in this chapter.

Example 1

In this example, we will show where the authentication type is specified at the client and the server. We decided that all authentication should take place at the server, so we chose authentication type SERVER at the server and the client. This will allow all user IDs and passwords to be sent to the database server for authentication. All passwords will be sent to the server unencrypted. Fig. 4–1 shows the authentication type setting in the database manager configuration file of the server and the authentication type in the system database directory of the client.

Controlling Data Access

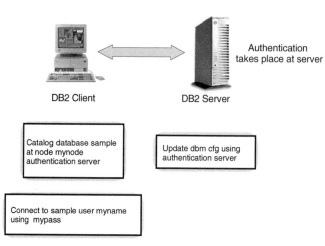

Fig. 4–1 *Example 1 - Authentication server*

Environment 2: Client Connecting to a Host Database via DB2 Connect

In this environment, there are three types of machines taking part in establishing the connection: clients, a DB2 Connect server, and a host database server. DB2 Connect Enterprise Edition will have to be installed on the DB2 Connect server machine. The client connects to the DB2 Connect server using a standard DB2 supported protocol, and then a connection is made from the DB2 Connect server to the host server using a DRDA protocol. In this environment, the location where the authentication takes place is determined by the AUTHENTICATION parameter specified in the CATALOG DATABASE command executed at the DB2 Connect server.

Authentication types at the DB2 Connect server

We can configure the client and DB2 Connect server so authentication can take place at the client, the DB2 Connect server, or the host server. Valid authentication types on the DB2 Connect server include:

- **SERVER**

  In this case, authentication takes place on the DB2 Connect server, and the password is not encrypted before it is sent to the DB2 Connect server.

- **SERVER_ENCRYPT**

  This is the same as SERVER, but the password is encrypted by the client before it is sent.

- **DCS**

  Authentication takes place at the host database server.

- **DCS_ENCRYPT**

  Authentication takes place at the host database server and the password is encrypted.

- **DCE**

  This allows an external security facility to do the authentication on behalf of the host database server. It is currently supported only on hosts running DB2 for MVS version 5.1 and higher.

- **CLIENT**

  This allows a client to authenticate the user on behalf of the host database server.

Authentication types at the client

On the client, valid authentication types include:

- **SERVER**
- **SERVER_ENCRYPT**
- **DCS**
- **DCS_ENCRYPT**
- **CLIENT**
- **DCE**

Table 4–2 shows where authentication will take place given combinations of the client's and server's authentication type, and also it shows whether the flowing password is encrypted. In this table, N/A means that the password does not flow.

Table 4–2 *Authentication Options Between Client, DB2 Connect, and Host*

Client Authentication Type	DB2 Connect Server Authentication Type	Authenticated at	Client to DB2 Connect Server Encryption	DB2 Connect Server to Host Encryption
SERVER	SERVER_ENCRYPT	DB2 Connect Server	No	N/A
SERVER_ENCRYPT	SERVER_ENCRYPT	DB2 Connect Server	Yes	N/A
DCS	SERVER_ENCRYPT	DB2 Connect Server	No	N/A

Table 4–2 *Authentication Options Between Client, DB2 Connect, and Host (Continued)*

Client Authentication Type	DB2 Connect Server Authentication Type	Authenticated at	Client to DB2 Connect Server Encryption	DB2 Connect Server to Host Encryption
DCS_ENCRYPT	SERVER_ENCRYPT	DB2 Connect Server	Yes	N/A
SERVER_ENCRYPT	SERVER	DB2 Connect Server	Yes	N/A
DCS_ENCRYPT	SERVER	DB2 Connect Server	Yes	N/A
DCS	SERVER	DB2 Connect Server	No	N/A
SERVER	SERVER	DB2 Connect Server	No	N/A
SERVER_ENCRYPT	DCS	Server	Yes	No
DCS_ENCRYPT	DCS	Server	Yes	No
SERVER	DCS	Server	No	No
DCS	DCS	Server	No	No
SERVER	DCS_ENCRYPT	Server	No	Yes
DCS	DCS_ENCRYPT	Server	No	Yes
SERVER_ENCRYPT	DCS_ENCRYPT	Server	Yes	Yes
DCS_ENCRYPT	DCS_ENCRYPT	Server	Yes	Yes
DCE	DCE	DCE Server	Yes	Yes
CLIENT	CLIENT	Client	N/A	N/A

Example 2

In this example, we configured a client to a DB2 Connect server to DB2 OS/390 connection using TCP/IP as the communication protocol between the client and the DB2 Connect server and APPC between the DB2 Connect server and DB2 OS/390. Since APPC encrypts the passwords for us, there is no need to use the DCS_ENCRYPT option on the DB2 Connect server. We will, however, use the DCS_ENCRYPT authentication type on the client. This will allow the password to be encrypted at the client before it is passed to the DB2 Connect server. It will be decrypted at the DB2 Connect server and passed securely to the host using APPC as the communications protocol.

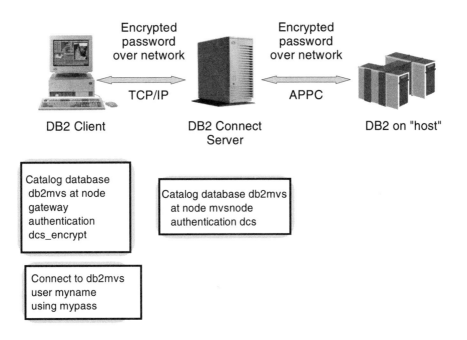

Fig. 4–2 *Example 2 - Authentication DCS/DCS_ENCRYPT*

Note: The encrypted authentication types may not be supported on all DB2 platforms. Please refer to your particular platform to find out if it will support encryption authentication as a client or server.

Table 4–3 shows the valid options for each of the four locations where authentication can be explicitly defined.

Table 4–3 *Authentication Setup and Options*

Specified at	Available Options	How to Specify
Client	CLIENT	CATALOG DATABASE *dbname*
	SERVER	AT NODE *nodename*
	SERVER_ENCRYPT	AUTHENTICATION xxx
	DCE	

Table 4–3 *Authentication Setup and Options*

Specified at	Available Options	How to Specify
Server	CLIENT SERVER SERVER_ENCRYPT DCE DCE_SERVER_ENCRYPT	UPDATE DBM CFG USING AUTHENTICATION xxx
Client (connection to host)	SERVER SERVER_ENCRYPT DCS DCS_ENCRYPT DCE *(DB2 for OS/390 V5.1 +)*	CATALOG DATABASE *dbname* AT NODE *nodename* AUTHENTICATION xxx
DB2 Connect server	SERVER SERVER_ENCRYPT DCS DCS_ENCRYPT DCE *(DB2 for OS/390 V5.1+)*	CATALOG DATABASE *dbname* AT NODE *nodename* AUTHENTICATION xxx

The TRUST_ALLCLNTS and TRUST_CLNTAUTH Parameters

If an instance is set to authentication type CLIENT, two other database manager configuration parameters determine where the final authentication will actually take place: TRUST_ALLCLNTS and TRUST_CLNTAUTH.

TRUST_ALLCLNTS

DB2 allows the administrator to decide whether to trust all clients. In other words, the administrator can specify whether all clients can authenticate users. If there are clients that do not have a reliable security facility, you probably do not want them to authenticate users. You can configure this by changing the TRUST_ALLCLNTS parameter in the database manager configuration file of the database server. This is an instance level configuration file; so, all databases in the instance will use the same setting.

The TRUST_ALLCLNTS parameter can be set to one of three values:

- **YES**

  Setting the parameter to YES forces all clients, whether or not they are trusted, to authenticate at the client. As Fig. 4–3 shows, all clients will be allowed to authenticate on behalf of the database server if the authentication type is set to CLIENT.

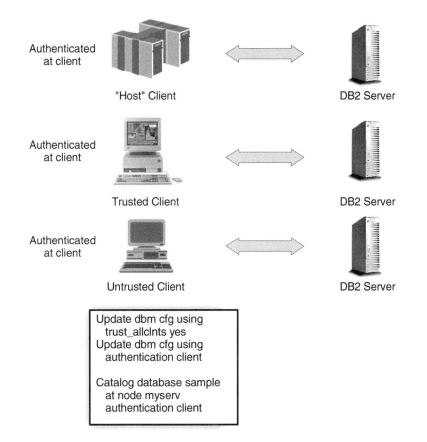

Fig. 4–3 *TRUST_ALLCLNTS set to YES*

- **NO**

  If NO is set, all untrusted clients will be authenticated at the server, meaning that a user ID and a password must be provided, and all trusted clients will be authenticated at the client machine. See Fig. 4–4.

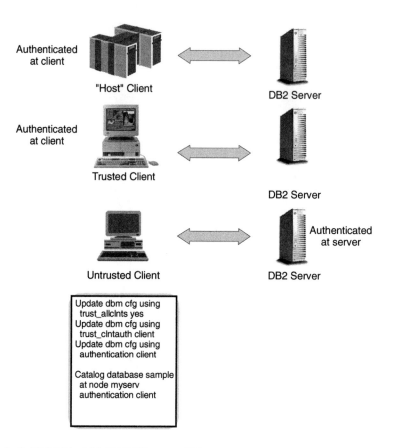

Authenticated
at client

"Host" Client

DB2 Server

Authenticated
at client

Trusted Client

DB2 Server

Authenticated
at server

Untrusted Client

DB2 Server

Update dbm cfg using
 trust_allclnts yes
Update dbm cfg using
 trust_clntauth client
Update dbm cfg using
 authentication client

Catalog database sample
 at node myserv
 authentication client

Fig. 4–4 *TRUST_ALLCLNTS set to NO*

- **DRDAONLY**

  If DRDAONLY is used, only MVS, OS/390, VM, VSE, and OS/400 clients are
  allowed to authenticate users on behalf of the database server. Remember, using
  DRDAONLY does not imply a Windows NT client or an AIX client even if DRDA
  is used. See Fig. 4–5.

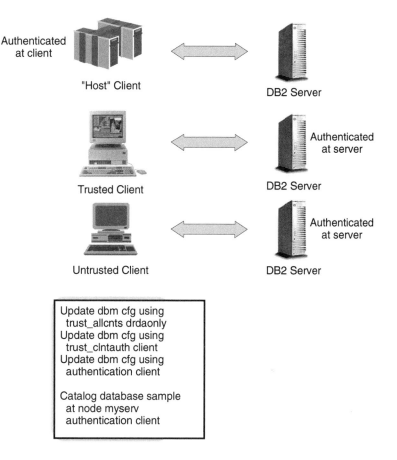

Fig. 4–5 *TRUST_ALLCLNTS set to DRDAONLY*

TRUST_CLNTAUTH

This is a parameter of the database manager configuration file on a DB2 server. This parameter allows you to specify where the authentication will take place when a user ID and a password are supplied with a CONNECT statement or an ATTACH command. This parameter is only used if the authentication type is CLIENT and affects clients that can authenticate users on behalf of a server; in other words, it affects all clients if TRUST_ALLCLNTS is set to YES, trusted clients and host clients if TRUST_ALLCLNTS is set to NO, and only host clients if TRUST_ALLCLNTS is set to DRDAONLY. Valid values for this parameter are:

- **CLIENT** (default)

The authentication is done at the client; a user ID and a password are not required. If user ID and password are not supplied, the authentication will take place on the client with the user ID and password that the user used to log on to the client.

- **SERVER**

If SERVER is specified, the authentication is done at the server if a user ID and a password are provided with a CONNECT statement or an ATTACH command.

Fig. 4–6 shows portions of a trusted client connection configuration with a DB2 server. In this example, the authentication type is CLIENT. The TRUST_ALLCLNTS is set to NO. This will allow only trusted clients to authenticate users on behalf of the DB2 server. The TRUST_CLNTAUTH is set to SERVER. Therefore, if a user ID and a password are supplied with a CONNECT statement, they will be sent to the server for authentication. If user ID and password are not supplied, the authentication will take place on the client based on the user ID and password that the user used to log on to the client.

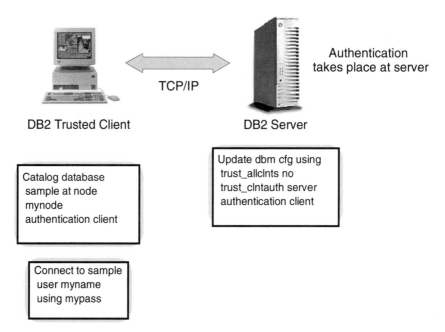

Authentication takes place at server

TCP/IP

DB2 Trusted Client   DB2 Server

Update dbm cfg using
trust_allclnts no
trust_clntauth server
authentication client

Catalog database
sample at node
mynode
authentication client

Connect to sample
user myname
using mypass

Fig. 4–6 *Trust_clntauth set to SERVER*

Cataloging Databases

DB2 has multiple directories that are used to access databases. These directories allow DB2 to find databases known to it whether they are on the local system or a remote system. The system database directory contains a list and pointer to where all the known databases can be found. The node directory contains information relating to how and where remote systems or instances can be found. To put an entry into any of these directories, a CATALOG command is used. To remove an entry, the UNCATALOG command is used.

When setting up the database server, you can choose who should be able to catalog and uncatalog databases. This can be done in the database manager configuration file by setting the CATALOG_NOAUTH parameter. The two available values this can be set to are YES and NO. NO is the default value for a DB2 server with local and remote clients and prevents users without SYSADM or SYSCTRL authority from using the CATALOG or UNCATALOG commands. Setting it to YES allows other users to use these commands. YES is the default value for a DB2 client, a Satellite database server with local clients, and a DB2 server with local clients.

Setting the Authentication Type

The authentication type is specified in the database manager configuration file that is shared among all the databases contained in the instance. Therefore, all the databases in an instance will have the same authentication type. You can check the authentication type associated with the current instance with the following command:

```
GET DATABASE MANAGER CONFIGURATION
```

The current authentication type will be seen next to the AUTHENTICATION parameter in the database manager configuration file. The default setting for AUTHENTICATION is SERVER. To change it, issue the following command:

```
UPDATE DBM CFG USING AUTHENTICATION CLIENT
db2stop
db2start
```

Notice that we have used a shorthand method of the command within the CLP. Database Manager can be abbreviated to DBM, and CONFIGURATION can be abbreviated to CFG.

Note: The changes to the instance will take effect when the instance is stopped and restarted.

You must be a member of the SYSADM group for the instance (discussed later) to make changes to the parameters in the database manager configuration file.

The client authentication type of a connection is stored in the system database directory. This is a listing of all the databases known to the system. To look at it, use the following command:

```
LIST DATABASE DIRECTORY
```

All the remotely cataloged databases will show the authentication type with which the client will attempt to connect to the server. To change the authentication type for a connection, the database needs to be uncataloged from the database directory and recataloged with the new authentication type. Here is a sample of the catalog command; it catalogs a remote database named sample at a node named mynode using authentication SERVER.

```
CATALOG DATABASE sample AT NODE mynode AUTHENTICATION
SERVER
```

Authorities and Privileges

After successful authentication, access to the database objects is controlled by DB2 itself. Access to these objects is controlled by associating *privileges* or *authorities* to users. Authorities are normally required for maintaining databases and instances. They are a high level set of user's rights that allow users to do actions such as backup or create databases. Privileges are normally granted to users to work with objects in the database, such as tables. For example, a user may have SELECT and UPDATE privileges on a table.

Authorities

As mentioned above, authorities are used to control access to objects within an instance or for administrative tasks.

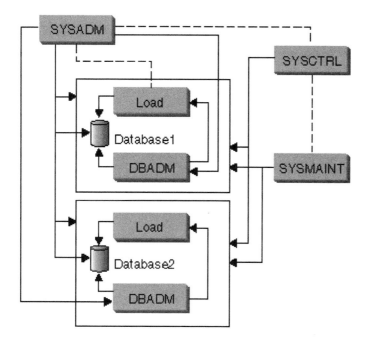

Fig. 4–7 *Authorities*

There are five authorities in DB2:

- **SYSADM** - System Administration Authority
- **SYSCTRL** - System Control Authority
- **SYSMAINT** - System Maintenance Authority
- **LOAD** - Load Table Authority
- **DBADM** - Database Administration Authority

Authorities in DB2 provide a hierarchy for administration capabilities as shown in Fig. 4–7. Authorities are assigned to a group of users. Exceptions to this rule include the DBADM and LOAD authority since they can be granted to a user or a group. If a certain authority is given to a group, each member of that group has the same DB2 authority unless they have had that authority explicitly revoked.

Controlling Data Access

The LOAD authority was introduced in DB2 UDB Version 7.1. This allows database administrators to grant authority to users or developers for bulk loading of data into DB2 without requiring them to have DBA capabilities.

SYSADM Authority

At the top of this hierarchy is the DB2 System Administrator or SYSADM authority. Any member of the SYSADM group is able to perform any of the DB2 administration operations as well as to access all database objects. SYSADM group members are the only users that are allowed to configure the DB2 instance.

On UNIX systems, the SYSADM group is set to the primary group of the instance owner by default.

On a Windows NT system, a member of the local administrator group has to install DB2 at which time the default instance named DB2 will be created. The default SYSADM authority will be granted to all the local administrators on the machine where DB2 is installed.

To give a group SYSADM authority, change the SYSADM_GROUP parameter in the database manager configuration file to the name of the group.

SYSCTRL Authority

System control (SYSCTRL) authority provides the ability to perform almost any administration task. A member of the SYSCTRL user group does not have authority to access database objects or modify the instance configuration file (DBM configuration). SYSCTRL offers almost complete control of database objects defined in the DB2 instance but cannot access user data directly unless explicitly granted the privilege to do so. A user with this authority or higher can perform the following functions and all the functions of SYSMAINT authority:

- Create or drop a database
- Force applications
- Restore to a new database
- Create, drop, or alter a table space

SYSMAINT Authority

SYSMAINT, or System Maintenance authority, allows the execution of maintenance activities but does not allow access to user data. Only users with this level of authority or higher (SYSADM or SYSCTRL) can perform the following tasks:

- Update database configuration files
- Back up databases and table spaces
- Restore to an existing database
- Perform roll forward recovery
- Restore table spaces
- Start and stop the DB2 instance
- Run the database monitor
- Start and stop traces
- Query the state of a table space
- Update log history files
- Quiesce a table space
- Reorganize a table
- Execute the runstats utility

LOAD Authority

Users granted LOAD authority can run the LOAD utility without the need for SYSADM or DBADM authority. This allows users to perform more DB2 functions and gives database administrators more granular control over the administration of their database. Users with LOAD authority can perform the following tasks:

- If they have INSERT privilege on a table, they can use the LOAD command or the AutoLoader utility to load data into a table.
- If they have INSERT privilege on a table, they can LOAD RESTART or LOAD TERMINATE if the previous load operation is a load to insert data.
- If the previous load operation was a LOAD REPLACE, the DELETE privilege must also have been granted to that user before the user can LOAD RESTART or LOAD TERMINATE.
- If the exception tables are used as part of a LOAD, the user must have INSERT privilege on the exception tables.
- The user with LOAD authority can perform QUIESCE TABLESPACES FOR TABLE, RUNSTATS, and LIST TABLESPACES commands.

DBADM Authority

At the database level, there is the DBADM authority. A DBADM can do any administrative task on the database, such as loading data, creating objects within the database, and monitoring database activity. DBADM has complete authority over the database and may query, drop, or create any table and set privileges for users within the database. The creator of a database will automatically have DBADM authority for the new database. Other users may be granted the DBADM authority by a SYSADM user

Controlling Data Access

using the GRANT statement. It is possible to hold DBADM authority for multiple databases.

Table 4–4 shows some of the valid tasks for the various DB2 privilege levels. The DBADM column has * beside entries that are related to LOAD authority only.

Table 4–4 *Database Authorities and Valid Tasks*

Function	SYSADM	SYSCTRL	SYSMAINT	DBADM
UPDATE DBM CFG	YES			
GRANT/REVOKE DBADM	YES			
ESTABLISH/CHANGE SYSCTRL	YES			
ESTABLISH/CHANGE SYSMAINT	YES			
FORCE USERS	YES	YES		
CREATE/DROP DATABASE	YES	YES		
RESTORE TO NEW DATABASE	YES	YES		
UPDATE DB CFG	YES	YES	YES	
BACKUP DATABASE/TABLE SPACE	YES	YES	YES	
RESTORE TO EXISTING DATABASE	YES	YES	YES	
PERFORM ROLL FORWARD RECOVERY	YES	YES	YES	
START/STOP INSTANCE	YES	YES	YES	
RESTORE TABLE SPACE	YES	YES	YES	
RUN TRACE	YES	YES	YES	
OBTAIN MONITOR SNAPSHOTS	YES	YES	YES	
QUERY TABLE SPACE STATE	YES	YES	YES	YES*
PRUNE LOG HISTORY FILES	YES	YES	YES	YES
QUIESCE TABLE SPACE	YES	YES	YES	YES*
LOAD TABLES	YES			YES*
SET/UNSET CHECK PENDING STATUS	YES			YES
CREATE/DROP EVENT MONITORS	YES			YES

Security Considerations

The authorities SYSADM, SYSCTRL, and SYSMAINT are not established using the GRANT statement. These three authorities are associated with groups and are specified at the instance level. As such, they must be set or changed in the database manager configuration file. The parameters are SYSADM_GROUP, SYSCTRL_GROUP, and SYSMAINT_GROUP. There are no default values for them.

A member of the system administration group (SYSADM) can either set or modify these authorities for the instance. For example, to change the SYSCTRL group to db2cntrl, the following commands would be issued.

```
UPDATE DATABASE MANAGER CONFIGURATION USING SYSCTRL_GROUP
db2cntrl
db2stop
db2start
```

The UPDATE DATABASE MANAGER CONFIGURATION command (or UPDATE DBM CFG) requires the USING option with the parameter to be updated followed by the new value. For any changes to take effect, the instance must be stopped and restarted. For the instance to be successfully stopped, all database connections must be released and attachments terminated. The new values in the DBM configuration file are as follows:

```
SYSADM   group name    (SYSADM_GROUP)    =
SYSCTRL  group name    (SYSCTRL_GROUP)   = db2cntrl
SYSMAINT group name    (SYSMAINT_GROUP)  =
```

The user group db2cntrl should match an existing operating system group. DB2 does not verify that the operating system group exists during the modification of the DBM configuration file. Therefore, the database administrator must ensure that the operating system user IDs and groups are set properly.

The group authorities are also related to the security mechanisms of the operating system. For example, a UNIX user who is placed in the db2cntrl group has access controlled within DB2 according to the SYSCTRL authority. But, the same user can have special access to their UNIX file system also.

Note: The creation of users and group assignments should be strictly controlled on any DB2 server.

Privileges

A privilege is the right to create or access a database object. DB2 authorities and privileges on database objects are hierarchical in nature. Fig. 4–8 shows the hierarchy of authorities and privileges within DB2.

Privileges are stored in the system catalog tables within the database. There are three types of privileges: *Ownership*, *Individual*, and *Implicit*.

1. Ownership or CONTROL privileges - For most objects, the user who creates an object has full access to that object. CONTROL privilege is automatically granted to the creator of an object. There are some database objects, such as views, that are exceptions to this rule.

    Having CONTROL privilege is like having ownership of the object. You have the right to access an object, give access to others, and give others permission to grant privileges on the object. Privileges are controlled by users with ownership or administrative authority. These users can grant or revoke privileges using GRANT or REVOKE SQL statements.

2. Individual privileges - These are privileges that allow you to perform a specific function, sometimes on a specific object. These privileges include SELECT, DELETE, INSERT, and UPDATE.

3. Implicit privileges - An implicit privilege is one that is granted to a user automatically when that user is explicitly granted certain higher level privileges. These privileges are not revoked when the higher level privileges are explicitly revoked.

    In addition, an implicit privilege can also be associated with a package. As an example, when a user executes a package that involves other privileges, they obtain those privileges while executing the package. They do not necessarily require explicit privilege on the data objects accessed within the package. These privileges can also be called *indirect* privileges.

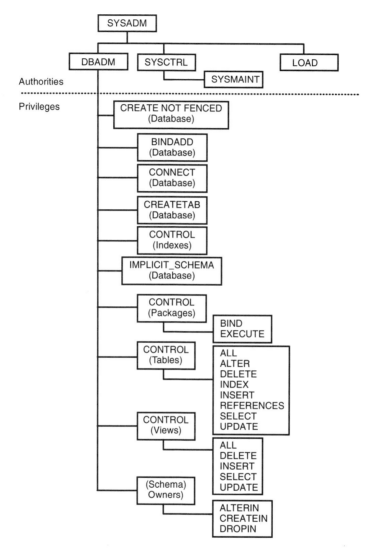

Fig. 4–8 *Hierarchy of authorizations and privileges on database objects*

Database Object Privileges

For each DB2 object, a specific authority or privilege is required to create it, and a specific authority or privilege is needed to have control over it. The following list describes the privileges on various objects within the database.

- **Database authorities** - These include the ability to create and access a database. Any creator of a database automatically receives DBADM authority. The DBADM can issue any SQL statement against the database. The DBADM can grant connect privilege, the ability to create tables or new packages in the database, the ability to create a schema implicitly, and the ability to create unfenced stored procedures or user-defined functions.

The IMPLICIT_SCHEMA privilege allows the user to create an object without specifying the schema name. The object will be assigned a schema that is the authorization ID of the user. This *implicitly created* schema is owned by SYSIBM. The group PUBLIC (anyone who can connect to the database) is given the privilege to create objects in the schema.

 Note: When a database is created, certain privileges are automaticlaly granted to the group PUBLIC. If you want to control who can do what on the database, a DBADM or SYSADM user must revoke these privileges from PUBLIC (these include CREATETAB and BINDADD).

- **Schema privileges** - These include the permissions to create, alter, or drop objects within schemas in a database. The owner of the schema has all these permissions and the ability to grant them to others. The objects that are manipulated within schemas include tables, views, indexes, packages, user-defined data types, user-defined functions, triggers, stored procedures, and aliases.

- **Table privileges** - CONTROL privilege on a table or view can only be granted by a user who has SYSADM or DBADM authority. (However, the creator of the table implicitly gets CONTROL privilege on that table.) Having CONTROL privileges on a table allows you to add columns to it, create a primary key, delete, retrieve, update, or insert rows in the table, create an index, create referential constraints on the table, grant these privileges to others, use the EXPORT utility, and perform maintenance such as reorganizing or updating statistics on the table.

  The UPDATE *on column* privilege allows users to modify only the specified columns of the table or view. In a similar way, the REFERENCE *on column* privilege allows the creation of foreign keys only on the stated columns.

- **View privileges** - To create a view, you must be able to issue the SQL SELECT statement or have CONTROL privilege on every table or view that is referenced. You need to have CONTROL privilege on the view to grant delete, insert, select, and update privileges on the view unless the view is defined as a read-only view. The privileges required must be explicitly held by the user or be granted to PUBLIC. (Alternately holding the WITH GRANT OPTION for each additional privilege will also suffice.)

- **Index privileges** - The user that creates the index receives CONTROL privileges on the index. This means that the user can drop the index. The table-level index privilege allows a user to create a new index on the table.

- **Package privileges** - The creator of a package automatically receives CONTROL privilege on the package. That user can grant other users the ability to rebind or execute the package. However, the person that rebinds a package must have the necessary privileges to access the objects referenced in the embedded static SQL statements. The required privileges must be obtained before doing the rebind, either explicitly through grants or through the privileges that were granted to the PUBLIC group or by being a SYSADM or DBADM user.

CONTROL privilege on a package also allows you to drop the package. Any user who has EXECUTE privilege on the package can execute the statements within the scope of that package without the explicit privileges on the static SQL statement objects required.

Note: To bind a new package to the database, you must have BINDADD database authority or you must be in the SYSADM group or be a DBADM.

There are two SQL statements used to administer privileges:

- The GRANT statement gives privileges to a user.
- The REVOKE statement takes privileges away from a user.

For example, suppose you want user Andrew to be able to drop the candidate table in the db2cert database. The statement would be as follows:

```
GRANT CONTROL ON TABLE candidate TO Andrew
```

The CONTROL option of the GRANT statement gives Andrew the ability to drop the candidate table or view. Unless Andrew is a SYSADM or DBADM, he cannot give another user the CONTROL privilege on the candidate table. The privileges and authorities combine to control the access to the database objects.

To grant privileges on database objects, a user must have SYSADM authority, DBADM authority, CONTROL privilege, or have a privilege WITH GRANT OPTION on that object. A user can grant privileges only on existing database objects. A user must have SYSADM or DBADM authority to grant CONTROL privilege to another user. To grant DBADM authority, a user must have SYSADM authority. Table 4–5 summarizes some of the privileges required for database objects within DB2 to perform the following:

- Create a resource (database, schema, table, view, index, or package)
- Control a resource

Table 4–5 *Privileges and Authorities Related to Database Objects*

Object	Authority/Privilege Needed to Create	Authority/Privilege Needed to Control	Other Possible Privileges on Object
DATABASE	SYSADM	DBADM	CONNECT BINDADD CREATETAB CREATE_NOT_FENCED IMPLICIT_SCHEMA CONNECT
SCHEMA	DBADM or IMPLICIT_SCHEMA	Ownership or IMPLICIT_SCHEMA	CREATEIN ALTERIN DROPIN
PACKAGE	BINDADD	CONTROL	BIND EXECUTE
TABLE or VIEW	CREATETAB (Table) CONTROL or SELECT (View)	CONTROL	SELECT (Table/View) INSERT (Table/View) DELETE (Table/View) UPDATE (Table/View) ALTER (Table) INDEX (Table) REFERENCES (Table)
INDEX	INDEX	CONTROL	NONE

Table 4–5 *Privileges and Authorities Related to Database Objects (Continued)*

Object	Authority/Privilege Needed to Create	Authority/Privilege Needed to Control	Other Possible Privileges on Object
ALIAS	If the schema differs from current authid, requires DBADM or IMPLICIT_SCHEMA. If schema is the same as an existing schema, may need CREATEIN privilege.	CONTROL	NONE
DISTINCT TYPE (UDT)	If the schema differs from current authid, requires DBADM or IMPLICIT_SCHEMA. If the schema is the same as an existing schema, may need CREATEIN privilege.	CONTROL	NONE
USER DEFINED FUNCTION (UDF)	If the schema differs from current authid, requires DBADM or IMPLICIT_SCHEMA. If the schema is the same as an existing schema, may require CREATIN privilege.	CONTROL	NONE

Objects manipulated within a schema must be able to use the schema before their creation. The privilege to create in the schema can be given either with the IMPLICIT_SCHEMA authority or by the CREATEIN privilege.

There are other situations that require special privileges. When creating DB2 applications or using DB2 applications, there are additional security considerations.

Application Development Privileges

There are certain privileges that apply only to application developers. Each step of the development process requires certain privileges on database objects. Let us examine the application development steps and the required privileges.

Table 4–6 summarizes the authorities and privileges needed for various tasks.

Controlling Data Access

Table 4–6 *Privileges Required for Application Development*

Action	Privileges Required
Precompile to bindfile	CONNECT on database
Create a new package	CONNECT on database BINDADD on database Privileges needed to execute each static SQL statement explicitly or to PUBLIC
Modify an existing package	CONNECT on database BIND on package Privileges needed to execute each static SQL statement explicitly or to PUBLIC
Re-create an existing package	CONNECT on database BIND on package
Execute a package	CONNECT on database EXECUTE on package
Drop a package	CONNECT on database CONTROL on package or creator of package

An embedded SQL program must have the SQL statements prepared and bound as a package in the DB2 database. The preparation step for a program with static embedded SQL does not require any privileges for the database objects. When the proper privileges on the object are not held or the objects do not exist, warning messages will be generated. The objects must exist during the bind phase as the existence and privileges of the objects are verified.

If the program contains dynamic embedded SQL statements, the statements are prepared and executed at runtime. There are no special requirements to verify a package for dynamic embedded SQL statements because there are no database objects referenced.

To create a new package for any embedded SQL application, you need CONNECT privilege and BINDADD authority on the database. Since the access plans for static embedded SQL statements are created during the prep or bind phase, you may wish to update the plan using the REBIND command or BIND the package using the bind files as input. You need BIND privilege on the package to update its contents. To execute a package, you need EXECUTE privilege on the package.

Let us look at a sample scenario where all the privileges granted to PUBLIC, except CONNECT, were removed and determine the necessary authorities and privileges on the database objects, according to the function that a user will be performing. In our scenario, we have a database where one of the applications, `app1`, is used to manipulate names and addresses.

User George wants to execute a program called app1. He also wants to be able to have his own table called George.personal to store other data. Therefore, we grant George EXECUTE privilege for the app1 package. We also grant George the CONTROL privilege for the George.personal table. We could have given him CREATETAB authority for the database and let him create the table, but this would allow him the ability to create many tables. Remember, the app1 package must exist in the database before we can grant George EXECUTE privilege.

Katrina is the application developer who is writing the app1 program. She needs to have SELECT, INSERT, UPDATE, and DELETE access to the various tables in the database. We need to GRANT the required privileges to Katrina. She needs to be able to add the new package in the database and execute the application to test it; therefore, we will give her BINDADD authority.

Bill needs to be able to load data using the LOAD command into various tables, but he will never execute the application. He needs DBADM authority. He could also be given SYSADM authority, but, for security reasons, we have only one user with SYSADM authority.

Another option for Bill is to grant him LOAD authority on the database, rather than DBADM authority. In DB2, we can use the LOAD authority to allow him to run the LOAD utility against this table.

The new LOAD authority is granted similar to other database privileges:

```
GRANT LOAD ON DATABASE TO USER BILL
```

This LOAD authority grants Bill the authority to use the LOAD utility in this database. SYSADM and DBADM also have this authority by default. However, if a user only has LOAD authority (not SYSADM or DBADM), the user is also required to have table-level privileges.

Shirley needs to be able to create a database to store personal information. Shirley is given SYSADM authority for the DB2 instance. Therefore, only Shirley can create the database and modify the DBM configuration file for the instance.

Note: SYSADM, SYSCTRL, and SYSMAINT cannot be granted in the same way as DBADM. They must be defined in the database manager configuration file.

Controlling Data Access

Let us examine Fig. 4–9 to understand the required authorities and privileges for the scenario we have just discussed.

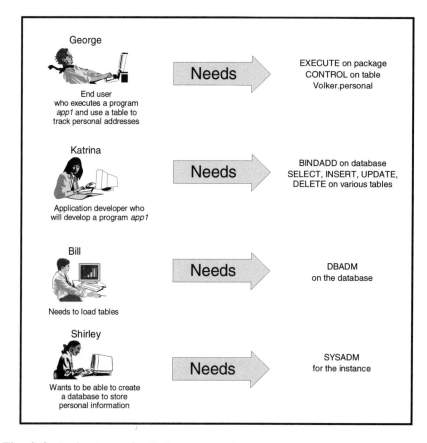

Fig. 4–9 *Authority and privilege scenario*

Privileges of Groups

In addition to granting privileges to users of the database, one could grant privileges to groups. These group definitions are not done in DB2 but in the operating system or external security facility (using DCE). A group consists of one or more users as defined in the security system. Every member of the group will have the same access privileges and authorities as were granted to the group they belong to unless they have been granted higher privileges individually or have had privileges individually revoked.

In addition to those groups, DB2 also has one special group definition: the PUBLIC group. This group consists of all users, and CONNECT privilege is granted automatically to the PUBLIC group. Granting a privilege to PUBLIC provides all users with the privilege. There are certain privileges granted to PUBLIC by default. For example, all database users have SELECT privilege on the system catalog tables. You may decide to remove the privilege using the REVOKE statement after creating the database.

Explicit and Implicit Privileges and Authorities

Privileges and authorities within DB2 can be obtained either implicitly or explicitly. As a database administrator, you should be aware of the ways that users can obtain access to objects in your databases. This section examines the various ways that privileges and authorities can be obtained or revoked.

If a user who has SYSADM or SYSCTRL authority creates a database, the user is implicitly granted DBADM authority on that database. If that user has SYSADM or SYSCTRL authority removed, they maintain their DBADM authority on each database they created. Removing DBADM authority must be done explicitly for each database using the REVOKE statement.

When a user is granted DBADM authority on a database, the user is also implicitly granted CONNECT, CREATETAB, BINDADD, IMPLICIT_SCHEMA, and CREATE_NOT_FENCED privileges. If DBADM authority is later revoked, the implicitly granted privileges remain unless they are explicitly revoked.

When a user is granted CONTROL privilege on a table, the user is implicitly granted all of the other table privileges with the capability to allow others access to it. If the CONTROL privilege is removed, the implicitly granted privileges remain unless they are explicitly revoked. All remaining privileges for the table can be explicitly removed using the REVOKE ALL statement.

```
REVOKE ALL ON tablename FROM username/groupname
```

SYSADM or DBADM authority or a user with CONTROL privilege on the table or view is required to revoke a privilege that was granted through the use of the WITH GRANT option. Note that, if Bill is granted privileges and the WITH GRANT option is specified, Bill can, subsequently, grant privileges to other users. If Bill has privileges revoked, the privileges granted by Bill are unaffected. In other words, there is no cascade effect when using the WITH GRANT option.

Determining Privileges and Authorities on a Database

Information about authorities and privileges is maintained in the following system catalog views:

- SYSCAT.DBAUTH - Contains database authorities
- SYSCAT.TABAUTH - Contains table and view privileges
- SYSCAT.PACKAGEAUTH - Contains package privileges
- SYSCAT.INDEXAUTH - Contains index privileges
- SYSCAT.SCHEMAAUTH - Contains schema privileges

To examine the groups specified for SYSADM, SYSCTRL, and SYSMAINT, view the database manager (DBM) configuration file. For all other authorities and privileges, examine the system catalog views listed in this section to determine the users and groups that have access rights. You may also use the DB2 Control Center to easily view and change the privileges and authorities granted to individual users and groups.

Group and User Support (UNIX)

Some operating systems will allow the same name for a user and a group. This can cause confusion for authorization and privilege checking within DB2.

Note: OS/2 and Windows NT/2000 do not permit a group and a user to have the same name.

Let us look at how DB2 handles the different scenarios regarding groups and users. Suppose we have a user named austin. We want to give this user the ability to perform a SELECT on the candidate table:

```
GRANT SELECT ON candidate TO austin
GRANT SELECT ON candidate TO USER austin
```

Both of these statements give SELECT privilege on the candidate table to the user named austin. Suppose we have a group named austin:

```
GRANT SELECT ON candidate TO austin
GRANT SELECT ON candidate TO GROUP austin
```

If there is no user named austin defined in the operating system, the members of the group named austin will be given the SELECT privilege. It is best to specify if the name is an individual user or a group. Therefore, the following statements specify that both the group and the user should be given SELECT privilege:

```
GRANT SELECT ON candidate TO USER austin
GRANT SELECT ON candidate TO GROUP austin
```

This will give both user `austin` and group `austin` the privilege on the `candidate` table. The GRANT and REVOKE statements can include either the USER or GROUP keyword to indicate the level of privilege that should be provided or removed.

Windows NT/2000 Considerations

Windows NT implements the user and group management in a slightly different manner than other operating systems. For example, a Windows NT user can belong to a group, which, in turn, belongs to another group. DB2 for Windows NT/2000 has added functionality to exploit and use this unique implementation of user and group management in Windows NT. In this section, we will briefly discuss the basic concepts of user management as implemented by Windows NT. We will then explain how DB2 for Windows NT exploits it.

When using Windows NT, one can group users and resources in two ways: workgroup and domains.

Workgroups

A *workgroup* is a collection of Windows workstations. It can contain computers running various operating systems. A workgroup is identified by a unique name shared among all the workstations in the workgroup. Each workstation manages and maintains its own set of users and/or resources. Resources, such as shared disks and printers, can be made available to all workstations in the workgroup. A user remotely accessing such a resource will be authenticated on the resource server; that is, the user will have to have a user ID on the resource server and the right to work with the resource being accessed. The definition of the user and the rights is local to the resource server and is not shared among the workstations in the workgroup.

Domains

A Windows NT *domain* (hereafter referred to as a domain) is a collection of client workstations and server computers identified by a unique name that share a single security permissions (domain) database.

In every Windows NT domain, there must be one Primary Domain Controller (PDC). The PDC is a server running Windows NT Server. It holds the Security Access Manager (SAM) database (not a DB2 database) used to store information about all the users in the domain, their passwords, groups, and logon scripts.

Controlling Data Access

Each Windows NT domain may also have one or more Backup Domain Controllers (BDCs). These BDCs store an copy of the SAM database located on the PDC. All changes to the PDCs SAM database are broadcast to the BDCs at configurable time intervals, thus keeping all the domain controllers synchronized.

Finally, the domain may also consist of multiple workstations running an assortment of operating systems, such as Windows 95/98, Windows NT Server, Windows NT Workstation, Windows 2000 Professional, and Windows 2000 Server.

Users

Users can be defined as part of the domain (domain users) or as a local user on a workstation or server in the domain. If a domain user logs on to the domain, the user ID and password will be verified by any one of the domain controllers, PDC, or BDCs.

Local users on workstations in the domain do not have access to resources within the domain.

Local users on the domain controller have access to all the resources in the domain. Their user IDs are not valid outside the bounds of the domain. These should not be confused with users defined locally to workstations within the domain.

Domain users are defined on the domain controller. These users have access to all the resources in the domain as do local users defined on domain controllers. The difference lies in that domain users might have access to resources outside the bounds of the domain. This is true when a trust relationship is defined between two domains.

Groups

A group is a collection of users and can give access to resources. If a user belongs to a group and the group has been given access to a resource, the user will also have access to that resource. There are two types of groups to which users can belong: *local groups* and *global groups*.

Global groups are defined on the domain controller. These groups can be granted access to resources in their domain as well as resources at trusting domains. Only domain users may belong to a global group.

Local groups are defined on domain controllers or on workstations, and like local users defined on domain controllers, have access to the resources within the domain. They cannot be granted access to resources outside their domain. The following can be made part of a local group:

1. Local users
2. Domain users
3. Global groups from the domain
4. Any domain users belonging to a trusted domain
5. Any global groups belonging to a trusted domain

Local groups not defined on domain controllers can only be granted access to resources on the machine they are defined on. They may include any of the following:

1. Local users
2. Domain users
3. Global groups
4. Any domain user belonging to a trusted domain
5. Any global group belonging to a trusted domain

Trusted and Trusting Domains

In a large environment, users from multiple domains may need access to common data. *Trust relationships* are defined to allow users to log on to one domain yet be able to access resources in various trusting domains.

To be able to access these resources, a trust relationship needs to be set up between the two domains. If a user defined in domain A needs to have access to a resource in domain B, domain B needs to trust domain A to authenticate the user. Once this relationship is set up, domain A is referred to as the trusted domain, and domain B is referred to as the trusting domain. See Fig. 4–10.

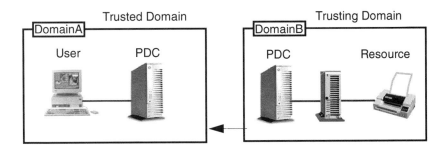

Fig. 4–10 *Windows NT trusted domain*

If there is a user in domain B that wants to access a resource in domain A, a second relationship needs to be set up in which domain A trusts domain B.

Trusts relationships are not transitive. For example, if domain C trusts domain B and domain B trusts domain A, domain C does *NOT* implicitly trust domain A. If there is a requirement for domain C to trust domain A, an explicit trust relationship needs to be defined.

Models of Domain Trust

Trust relationships between domains lend themselves to very complex domain architectures. The following are some commonly used domain architectures:

The single domain model

In the *single domain model*, there is only one domain; all servers and workstations belong to this domain as shown in Fig. 4–11.

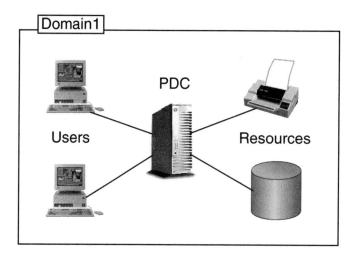

Fig. 4–11 *Single domain model*

The master domain model

The *master domain model* centralizes all the users in one domain, whereas most of the resources belong to various other domains. This model lends itself to centralized user management, where the resources are managed within their particular domains. See Fig. 4–12.

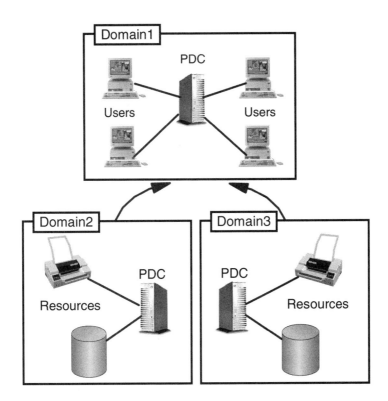

Fig. 4–12 *Master domain model*

The multiple master domain model

In the *multiple master domain model*, users are spread across multiple domains and resources are spread across multiple domains. Trust relationships are established between all user domains in both directions and between each resource domain and each master domain (one way). See Fig. 4–13.

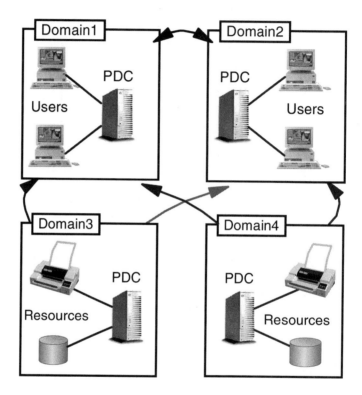

Fig. 4–13 *Multiple master domain model*

The complete trust model

If all the domains in the environment have both users and resources, a two-way trust relationship is set up between each and every domain. This model is called the *complete trust model*. See Fig. 4–14.

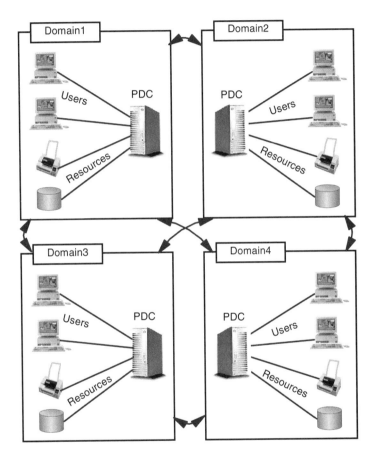

Fig. 4–14 *Complete trust domain model*

DB2 UDB for Windows NT/2000 Authentication and Security

As mentioned before, DB2 for Windows NT exploits the native Windows NT security system to assist in the management of the RDBMS security. In this section, we will be discussing how this is done.

When a user attempts to connect to a DB2 database on Windows NT (assume authentication type is server), DB2 passes the user ID and password to Windows NT for authentication. DB2 uses Windows NT to attempt to authenticate the user in the following order of user information:

1. Local SAM

2. Domain controller

3. Trusted domain controllers

Local SAM, in this case, refers the SAM of a client, a server, or a gateway depending on which authentication type is specified.

If the authentication type is SERVER, the DB2 server attempts to authenticate the user at the server machine. If the user is not defined in the server machine's SAM, the authentication will be attempted on the domain controller of the domain that the DB2 server belongs to. If the user is not defined there either, the authentication will be attempted at the domain controllers of the trusted domains. If the user is not defined there, the authentication will fail.

If a userA is defined on the local server and a userA is also defined on the domain controller, authentication will take place at the local server. Notice that these two user accounts are independent and may have different passwords. Therefore, using the user ID userA and the password defined at the domain controller results in an error.

The order in which the trusted domains are checked is random; therefore, make sure the user ID of a trusted domain is unique among all the trusted domains.

Once authentication is done, the group list is enumerated at the machine where the user is defined.

Granting Privileges and Authorities

In the DB2 for Windows NT environment, administrators are allowed to grant privileges and authorities to the following:

- Locally defined user
- Local user defined on the domain controller
- Domain user
- Trusted domain user
- Local group to which the user directly belongs
- Global group to which the user directly belongs
- Local group that contains a global group to which the user belongs

DB2_GRP_LOOKUP

In a Windows NT domain environment, a group list for the authenticated user is enumerated at the machine where the authentication is done; so, if the user is defined at a domain controller of the trusted domain and the database administrator does not have the administrative authority for the domain, managing membership of the group the user belongs to is not possible. The DB2_GRP_LOOKUP registry variable allows DB2 administrators to specify where the list of groups a user belongs to should be enumerated.

If it is set to LOCAL at the DB2 server, the list of groups is enumerated using the local SAM at the DB2 server. By setting this value, the database administrator does not need to have the administrative authority for Windows NT domains. What he or she needs to be is the local administrator.

If this registry variable is set to DOMAIN, you are telling DB2 to always enumerate groups and validate user accounts on the user account's Windows NT domain.

If you do not set this registry variable, the list of groups a user belongs to will be enumerated as follows: The local SAM will be queried first, followed by the domain controller of the domain the DB2 server belongs to. Then, all the PDCs of the trusted domains will be queried. DB2 is told where the user account was validated and will use that location to enumerate groups.

Controlling Data Access

Auditing

Even though DB2 allows an administrator the ability to limit access to databases and database objects to those users requiring it, it is necessary to monitor system use and possible system abuse. The DB2 *audit facility* provides this function.

The audit facility is associated with an instance. It records auditable events associated with the instance and databases within it. It can be active even though the instance it is monitoring is not active. Only users with SYSADM authority can use the audit facility. The audit facility uses a binary configuration file located in the security directory within the instance directory.

For each operation a user executes on a DB2 system, such as a select statement, one or more audit records may be generated. These audit records are categorized into the following groups:

- AUDIT All records logged associated with the audit facility.
- CHECKING Events logged due to authorization checking when accessing DB2 objects.
- OBJMAINT Records logged caused by dropping or creating objects.
- SECMAINT Records logged due to changing SYSADM_GROUP, SYSCTRL_GROUP, SYSMAINT_GROUP, grant/revoke DBADM, or any privileges on any database objects.
- SYSADMIN Records logged for operations that required SYSADM, SYSCTRL, and SYSMAINT authority.
- VALIDATE Records are generated when authenticating users or retrieving system security information.
- CONTEXT This type of audit record shows detailed information about an operation. This operation may have caused multiple records to be logged in the audit log. Such records can be associated with the CONTEXT record using the event correlator field.

The audit facility may generate multiple audit records for a single operation, each of which may belong to a different record category.

Buffering Audit Log Writes

When configuring the audit facility, a SYSADM user can specify whether the audit facility should write audit records directly to disk in a synchronous mode or buffer the records in an audit buffer for asynchronous writing. This buffer size can be specified using the AUDIT_BUFF_SZ parameter of the database manager configuration file. If the AUDIT_BUFF_SZ is set to 0, all audit record writing will be done synchronously; any number larger than zero indicates the buffer size as a multiple of 4KB.

If a buffer size is specified, the buffer will be written out to disk if the buffer is full or at regular intervals. The SYSADM can also force the buffer to be flushed to disk.

Handling Audit Facility Errors

A SYSADM user can also specify how an error occurring in the audit facility should be handled by setting the ERRORTYPE when the audit facility is configured. By setting it to AUDIT, any error occurring in the audit facility will return the SQLCODE of the error to the application for which the audit record was logged during the failure. It will also cause the operation attempted by the application to fail. If the ERRORTYPE is set to NORMAL, none of the applications executing will be affected if an attempt to generate an audit record fails.

Configuring the Audit Facility

Before starting the audit facility, you need to configure it. Use the db2audit configure command to configure it. The syntax for the command is as follows:

```
db2audit CONFIGURE SCOPE scope STATUS status
    ERRORTYPE errortype
```

The SCOPE refers to which set of audit record categories should be logged. If ALL is specified as the category, it includes all the categories except the CONTEXT category.

The STATUS refers to whether an event should be logged if it returned successfully, failed, or both. The available values are success, failure, or both.

The ERRORTYPE is as discussed above.

Looking at the Current Configuration

To see how the audit facility configuration looks, use the following command:

```
db2audit DESCRIBE
```

Starting the Audit Facility

Once the audit facility is configured, it can be started independently of whether the instance is started. Use the following command:

Controlling Data Access

```
db2audit START
```

Flushing the Audit Buffer

Before extracting an audit log, the SYSADM user may want to make sure the audit buffer is flushed to disk. Use the following command:

```
db2audit FLUSH
```

Extracting the Audit Log

When the audit facility is started, it starts generating a binary audit log. This binary audit log can be extracted by a SYSADM user to one of two formats. One of the formats is a text file containing the audit records. The other format (delasc) generates an ASCII-delimited file for each audit record category monitored. The file names correspond to the category names (listed on page 188). When choosing this output type, the users can also override the default delimiter *0xFF* by specifying the delimiter to use. These files can then be used to populate tables in a database by using the load or import commands.

For example, the SYSADM user of an instance wants to extract all the records in the validate and checking categories for the database sample to delimited ASCII files using the "!" character as the delimiter. The command the user would use is:

```
db2audit EXTRACT delasc DELIMITER ! CATEGORY validate,
     checking DATABASE sample
```

The output of this command will be two files named VALIDATE.DEL and CHECK-ING.DEL. The default delimiter *0xFF* was overridden by the DELIMITER option.

If the SYSADM user wants to extract all the context records to a text file, the command the user would use looks like this:

```
db2admin EXTRACT file myfile.txt CATEGORY context
     DATABASE sample
```

In this case, the output will be in a file named `myfile.txt`. If the file existed prior to executing the command, the command will fail. Fig. 4–15 shows a sample of the output. It seems that a user named `AUSRES30` created a table named `TEST` from the command line on the server.

```
timestamp=1999-03-15-11.55.35.464000;category=CONTEXT;
  audit event=EXECUTE_IMMEDIATE;
  event correlator=22;
  database=SAMPLE;userid=AUSRES30;authid=AUSRES30;
  application id=*LOCAL.DB2.990315172709;
  application name=db2bp.exe;
  package schema=NULLID;package name=SQLC28N5;
  package section=203;text=create table test (col1 char(10)
not null primary key, col2 char(10)) in userspace1;

timestamp=1999-03-15-11.55.35.564000;category=CONTEXT;
  audit event=COMMIT;
  event correlator=22;
  database=SAMPLE;userid=AUSRES30;authid=AUSRES30;
  application id=*LOCAL.DB2.990315172709;
  application name=db2bp.exe;
  package schema=NULLID;package name=SQLC28N5;
```

Fig. 4–15 *The audit log*

Pruning the Audit Log

To delete all the audit records from the audit log, use the following command:

```
db2audit PRUNE all
```

If the audit facility is set up to record events categorized as `AUDIT` events, an entry will be made in the audit log after the log has been cleared.

Another way to prune is to specify the date/time before which all entries should be cleared out of the audit log.

```
db2audit PRUNE DATE yyyymmddhh PATHNAME pathname
```

Adding the optional `pathname` allows the `SYSADM` user to prune the audit log if the drive or file system on which it is logged becomes full.

Controlling Data Access

Stopping the Audit Facility

To stop the audit facility, use the following command:

```
db2audit STOP
```

One possible flow of the audit facility is shown in Fig. 4–16. First, the audit facility is configured and checked, then it is started. If the SYSADM user wants to look at the audit log, the audit buffer must be flushed and the audit log extracted either as a flat file or as delimited files that the user can use to populate audit tables. At some point, the user can stop the audit facility and, if desired, clear the audit log of all or some of the records. It is important to note that the SYSADM user could have stopped the audit facility and extracted the audit log.

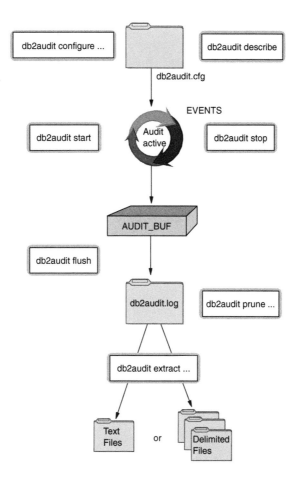

Fig. 4–16 *The audit facility*

Summary

This chapter discussed a number of topics relating to accessing data. We discussed security, first to the database and then within DB2. We talked about authentication. There are four different methods of authentication: SERVER, CLIENT, DCE, and DCS. To encrypt passwords flowing to a server, you can specify two authentication types: SERVER_ENCRYPT and DCS_ENCRYPT. The other value that can be specified at the DB2 server is DCE_SERVER_ENCRYPT. By setting this value, you can have the SERVER authentication, SERVER_ENCRYPT authentication, and DCE authentication dependent on the value specified at the DB2 client. Depending on the DB2 products installed, authentication tells where the user is to be validated. The authentication type can be set in the database manager configuration. All databases within the instance will have the same authentication type.

We talked about several of the authorization levels within DB2: SYSADM, SYSCTRL, SYSMAINT, and DBADM. SYSADM has system administrative authority over the instance and is able to perform any administration operations as well as access any information from any database that exists within that instance. SYSCTRL does not have the authority to access the database (unless explicitly granted), nor can SYSCTRL modify the database manager configuration. SYSMAINT also cannot access user data. SYSMAINT allows you to perform functions, such as backup or restore databases and table spaces, start and stop the instance, and use the database monitor. At the database level, DBADM has complete authority over the database objects. This authority includes creating or dropping tables, performing a query, and setting privileges for other users of the database. We also examined the granting and revoking of database object privileges using the GRANT and REVOKE SQL statements.

We also talked about the considerations when the DB2 server belongs to a Windows NT domain. DB2 attempts to authenticate users using the SAM of the local machine, the domain controller of the current domain, and the domain controllers of the trusted domains. The group list of the authenticated user is enumerated at the machine at which the user is defined.

Finally, we talked about the DB2 audit facility. It allows you to monitor security-related events and possible system abuse.

Using SQL

Database Objects

- ◆ CREATING DATABASE OBJECTS
- ◆ DATA TYPES
- ◆ TABLES
- ◆ CONSTRAINTS
- ◆ VIEWS
- ◆ INDEXES

*T*he standard language of relational database access is Structured Query Language (SQL). SQL is not a programming language. It was designed for the single purpose of accessing structured data. Every Relational Database Management System (RDBMS) implements a slightly different level of SQL.

In this chapter we examine the DB2 implementation of the SQL language. If you are familiar with other RDBMS products, you will already understand many aspects of the DB2 implementation of SQL thanks to the industry acceptance of SQL standards.

We first examine the DB2 database objects that can be referenced from an SQL statement; then, we examine the SQL language elements. A database object, for the purpose of this book, is any component of a DB2 database, such as table spaces, tables, columns, views, indexes, packages, logs, and locks. It is important to note that some of these database objects cannot be directly referenced using the SQL language.

Many of these objects can be directly referenced from an SQL statement; thus, it is important to understand their purpose.

SQL is divided into three major categories:

- DDL (Data Definition Language) - Used to create, modify, or drop database objects
- DML (Data Manipulation Language) - Used to select, insert, update, or delete database data (records)
- DCL (Data Control Language) - Used to provide data object access control

As SQL has evolved, many new statements have been added to provide a more complete set of data access methods. We explore some of these features, including constraints, triggers, outer joins, large object data access, and common table expressions.

Later in this chapter, the use of DDL (Data Definition Language) to create database objects is discussed.

DCL is discussed in "Controlling Data Access" on page 145.

Understanding Database Objects

A database is an organized collection of related objects. Each database has its own system catalog, log files, security, and tuning parameters.

Structured Query Language (SQL) is used throughout the database industry as a common method of issuing database queries. SQL is considered a language, composed of statements, functions, and data types. An SQL statement is used to access database objects using relational operations. Before we examine the SQL language, we need to understand some DB2 terminology. We will be referring to the basic components or objects that are defined for each DB2 database. These objects include:

- Data types
- Tables
- Schemas
- Table spaces
- Views
- Indexes
- Packages
- Buffer pools
- Transactions
- Locks
- Triggers
- Stored procedures
- Log files

Data Types

Data types are used to define a column attribute when creating a table. The data type of a column indicates the length of the values in it and the kind of data that is valid for it. There are two major categories of data types in DB2.

- Built-in data types
- User-defined data types

Built-in data types are defined by DB2. DB2 supports a number of built-in data types that are described later in this chapter. DB2 also provides support for *user-defined data types*. User-defined types are classified into the following three types:

- User-defined distinct type
- User-defined structured type
- User-defined reference type

User-defined distinct types (UDT) enable you to create a new data type that has its own semantics based on existing built-in data types. *User-defined structured types* enable you to create a structure that contains a sequence of named attributes each of which has a data type. This is one of the extensions of DB2 Object Relational functions. A *user-defined reference type* is a companion type to a user-defined structured type. Similar to a user-defined distinct type, a user-defined reference type is a scalar type that shares a common representation with one of the built-in data types. A user-defined reference type may be used to reference rows in another table that uses a user-defined structured type. User-defined distinct types (UDTs) will be discussed in this chapter, and user-defined structured types and user-defined reference types will be discussed in "Advanced SQL" on page 325.

> User-defined structured types allow a user to create structures in DB2 and use them as columns within a table. In addition, structures can contain other structures. This is one way that DB2 extends the relational model to be more object-oriented.

Tables

A *table* is an unordered set of data records. It consists of columns and rows (generally known as records). Each column is based on a data type. Tables, once created and populated with data, are referenced in the FROM clause of the SQL statements. There are three types of tables:

- Permanent (base) tables
- Temporary (declared) tables
- Temporary (derived) tables

We only discuss permanent tables in this chapter. These tables are created using the CREATE TABLE statement and each is a logical representation of the way the data is physically stored on disk. We discuss the temporary tables in "Advanced SQL" on page 325.

> Temporary declared tables are new to this release. This feature lets the application developer or user create temporary tables that are used only during the duration of the program. This feature is particularly important for stored procedures that require temporary storage during the execution of the program.

Schemas

Schemas are database objects used in DB2 to logically group a set of database objects. Most of the database objects are named using a two-part naming convention (`schema_name.object_name`). The first part of the name is referred to as the schema (otherwise known as a qualifier for the database object). The second part is the *object name*.

When you create an object and do not specify a schema, the object will be associated with an *implicit schema* using your *authorization ID*. When an object is referenced in an SQL statement, it is also implicitly qualified with the authorization ID of the issuer (dynamic SQL) if no schema name is specified in the SQL statement.

The `CURRENT SCHEMA` special register contains the default qualifier to be used for unqualified objects referenced for dynamic SQL statements issued from within a specific DB2 connection. This value can be modified by the user with the `SET CURRENT SCHEMA` statement. Static SQL statements are qualified with the authorization ID of the person binding the application (by default). For example, if user `katrina` connected to the database and created a table called `tasks`, the complete name of the table as stored in the database would be: `KATRINA.TASKS`. You can use the `QUALIFIER` option of the `BIND` command to define the default qualifier at bind time.

One additional schema qualifier introduced in DB2 UDB Version 7.1 is the `SESSION` qualifier. This keyword is used for temporary tables that are created and used during a connection. The `SESSION` qualifier is discussed later in the section on "The DECLARE Statement" on page 208

> The `SESSION` qualifier is a form of schema that is used by DB2 Version 7. When a program or user declares a temporary table, the only way to reference it in the SQL is through the use of the `SESSION` qualifier. If the `SESSION` qualifier is not used, DB2 will attempt to find the table using the current schema.

Table Spaces

Table spaces are the logical layers between the database and the tables stored in that database. Table spaces are created within a database, and tables are created within table spaces. DB2 supports two kinds of table spaces:

- System Managed Space (SMS) - The operating system's file system manager allocates and manages the space where the table is to be stored. An SMS table space is the default table space type.
- Database Managed Space (DMS) - The database manager controls the storage space. This table space is, essentially, an implementation of a special purpose file system designed to best meet the needs of the database manager.

When a table is being defined using the CREATE TABLE statement, you can explicitly state in which table space the table data will reside. Table spaces provide the database administrator with the ability to control the location of the database objects. You can define any number of table spaces within a single database.

Views

Views are logical tables that are derived from one or more base tables or views and can be used interchangeably with base tables when retrieving data. When changes are made to the data shown in a view, the data is changed in the table itself. Views do not contain real data. Only the definition exists in the database. A view can be created to limit access to sensitive data while allowing more general access to other data. Views can be deletable, updatable, insertable, and read-only. The classification indicates the kind of SQL operation that is allowed while using the view.

Indexes

Indexes are physical objects that are associated with a single table. Any permanent table (user table or system table) can have indexes defined on it. You cannot define an index on a view. You can define multiple indexes for a single table. Indexes are used for two primary reasons:

- Ensure uniqueness of data values
- Improve SQL query performance

Indexes can be used to access data in a sorted order more quickly and avoid the time-consuming task of sorting the data using temporary storage. In Version 7, indexes can also be created on computed columns so that the optimizer can save computation time by using the index instead of doing the calculations. The index will be maintained automatically by DB2 as data is inserted, updated, and deleted.

Computed columns in Version 7 can also have indexes created on them. These indexes can then be used by DB2 to improve the performance of queries that include calculations that can be resolved by the use of the index. Another important feature in index creation is the ability to add additional values to the index, which can be used by the optimizer to get nonkey data. This can also result in much faster performance for queries, which can get their answer sets from the index rather than from the data pages.

Database Objects

> **Note:** The maintenance overhead of indexes will negatively impact the performance of INSERT, UPDATE, and DELETE statements.

Indexes can be defined in ascending or descending order. (Ordering is dependent on the code page.) They can be defined as unique or nonunique, and they can involve a single column's data values or multiple columns' data values. They can also be defined to support both forward and reverse scans. An index can also contain additional fields that are not part of the key itself to allow for faster access to commonly requested data. Instead of having to read data pages, the optimizer can use the index directly to retrieve values. The Visual Explain utility will provide index usage information for every explainable SQL statement (if the explain data is gathered).

Packages

Packages are database objects that contain executable forms of SQL statements. These packages contain statements that are referenced from a DB2 application. A package corresponds to a program source module.

> **Note:** Only the corresponding program source module can invoke the contents of the package.

Packages are stored in the database system catalog tables. The packages contain the DB2 access plan that was selected by DB2 during the BIND or PREP process. This type of BIND is known as static binding since it is performed prior to the execution of the SQL statement. Packages cannot be directly referenced in an SQL data manipulation (DML) statement.

Most applications that access a DB2 database will have a package or group of packages stored (bound) in the system catalog tables.

Buffer Pools

Buffer pools are database objects used to cache database data pages in memory. If an object's data page is placed in a buffer pool, physical I/O access to disks will be avoided. Buffer pools can be assigned to cache only a particular table space's data. This is assigned within the table space definition.

Every DB2 database must have a buffer pool. For each new database created, DB2 will define the IBMDEFAULTBP buffer pool. This is the default buffer pool for the database.

The CREATE BUFFERPOOL SQL statement is used to define buffer pools other than the default IBMDEFAULTBP buffer pool. Once a buffer pool is created, it can be assigned to a certain table space using the CREATE TABLESPACE statement or the ALTER TABLESPACE statement.

The SYSCAT.BUFFERPOOLS system catalog view contains the information for the buffer pools defined in the database.

Transactions

A *transaction* is a set of one or more SQL statements that execute as a single operation. The term *unit of work* is synonymous with the term *transaction*. There is no physical representation of a transaction because it is a series of instructions (SQL statements). You can think of transactions as activity in the database that is tracked using the database log files.

A transaction is treated as a single operation; it either succeeds or fails. A transaction is started implicitly with the first executable SQL statement in a program. The transaction is completed when either an explicit COMMIT or a ROLLBACK statement is encountered. An implicit COMMIT or ROLLBACK can occur when a DB2 application terminates.

Version 7 introduces the notion of SAVEPOINTS to a transaction commit scope. This allows a developer to "save" intermediate steps in their SQL and allows them to selectively rollback to this savepoint without losing earlier work. More details on COMMIT, ROLLBACK, and SAVEPOINTS can be found in "Development SQL" on page 719

SAVEPOINTS are a technique for saving work between COMMIT and ROLLBACK points. This makes application development more flexible, especially with the use of stored procedures.

Note: It is best to COMMIT or ROLLBACK any outstanding SQL transactions explicitly prior to terminating a DB2 application. Otherwise, the result of any outstanding transactions during application termination will vary in different operating environments.

Database Objects

Locks

DB2 is a multiuser database product. As users request data, the DB2 locking mechanism attempts to avoid resource conflicts yet still provide full data integrity. As SQL statements are processed, the transactions may obtain locks. The locks are released when the resource is no longer required at the end of the transaction. The locks are stored in memory on the database server (in a structure known as the *locklist*). DB2 supports two types of locks, table locks and row locks.

The locking strategy used by DB2 during transaction processing is specified using an *isolation level* as defined when binding the application. CLI applications set the isolation level in the db2cli.ini file.

Log Files

A number of *log files* are associated with each DB2 database. As transactions are processed, they are tracked within the log files. DB2 will track all of the SQL statements that are issued for a database within its database log files.

DB2 uses a *write-ahead logging method* that ensures that the changes to the database will be applied (even during a crash recovery scenario). The changes are first written to the log files and, at a later time, these changes are applied to the physical database tables.

Log files can now be 32GB in size in Version 7.1! This should allow long-running transactions to finish without filling up the log file.

Creating a DB2 Database

A DB2 database must exist before any of the database objects can be created in it. The database must be given a name. (There is no schema associated with the database.) Once the database has been created, the next logical step is to create the table spaces that will be used to store the user tables.

Note: The CREATE DATABASE command is not an SQL statement but is a DB2 command. The database name can be 1 - 8 characters long.

When you create a database without any table space options, three SMS table spaces are created by default:

- SYSCATSPACE - Contains the system catalog tables
- TEMPSPACE1 - Holds temporary tables used by DB2
- USERSPACE1 - Contains the user tables unless other user table spaces are created

These table spaces can be specified as DMS table spaces in the CREATE DATABASE command. In addition, a fourth tablespace type, USER Temporary tablespace, needs to be defined for this system for any temporary tablespaces that might be used by an application or user.

Please refer to "Data Storage Management" on page 409 for more information about a database and table spaces.

Temporary tables that are DECLARED in a transaction require the use of a USER Temporary Tablespace. This needs to be created and authority be granted to users before temporary tables are used.

Managing Database Objects

To create, modify, or delete objects in a database, SQL Data Definition Language (DDL) is used.

Using SQL Data Definition Language (DDL)

The DDL contains four main SQL statements:

* `CREATE`
* `ALTER`
* `DROP`
* `DECLARE`

 The `DECLARE` statement is new in Version 7 and is used for temporary tables used in an application. This can only be used for temporary objects and requires the use of USER temporary tablespaces.

The CREATE Statement

```
CREATE <database object>....
```

The `CREATE` statement is used to create database objects. Some examples of the `<database object>` that can be created are:

* Table
* Index
* Schema
* View
* User-defined function
* User-defined data type
* Buffer pool
* Table space
* Stored procedures
* Trigger

The creation of any database object using DDL will result in an update to the system catalog tables. Special database authorities or privileges are required to create database objects.

Database objects are used for different purposes. Some are used to define a condition or relationship (index, trigger), and others are a logical representation of the data as it is physically stored on disk (table, table space).

The DECLARE Statement

```
DECLARE <database object>....
```

The DECLARE statement is very similar to the CREATE statement, except that it is used to create temporary tables that are used only during a connection. The only object that can be DECLARED is a table, and it must be placed into an existing USER TEMPORARY tablespace.

The creation of a temporary table will not result in any update to the system catalog tables, so locking, logging, and other forms of contention are avoided with this object.

DECLARED tables can be DROPPED and ALTERED, but no other database objects (such as views or triggers) can be created to act against them. Temporary tables do allow for the specification of a partitioning key, which can be beneficial in a clustered (DB2 EEE) environment.

Once a table is declared, it can be referenced like any other SQL table. The SQL in the following example shows a table being declared and then used in a subsequent SQL statement.

```
DECLARE GLOBAL TEMPORARY TABLE T1
   LIKE TRANSACTIONS
   ON COMMIT PRESERVE ROWS NOT LOGGED IN SESSIONTEMP;

INSERT INTO SESSION.T1
   SELECT * FROM TRANSACTIONS WHERE SALES < 3000;

SELECT * FROM SESSION.T1;
```

The DECLARE statement is used to create temporary tables that are used only during the duration of an application or stored procedure. The table does not cause any logging or contention against the SYSTEM catalog tables and is very useful for working with intermediate results.

The DROP Statement

```
DROP <database object>....
```

The DROP statement is used to remove constraints or definitions from the system catalog tables (and hence the database itself). Since the system catalog tables cannot be directly deleted from, the DROP statement is used to remove data records from these tables. Since database objects can be dependent on other database objects, the act of dropping an object can result in a related object being rendered invalid. You can drop any object created with the CREATE <database object> and the DECLARE <table> statements.

The ALTER Statement

```
ALTER <database object>....
```

The ALTER statement allows you to change some characteristics of the database object. (The database object must already exist in the database.) Some examples of the <database object> that can be altered are:

- Table
- Table space
- View
- Buffer pool

Note: You cannot alter an index. You must drop and create a new index.

Every time you issue a DDL statement (except for the DECLARE statement), the system catalog tables will be updated. The update will include a creation or modification timestamp and the authorization ID of the creator (modifier).

Note: It is useful to store all of the DDL statements for the database in a script file to allow for easier creation of the database objects. This script can either be used from the DB2 CLP or the DB2 Command Center.

Note: It is possible to extract the DDL of database objects from an existing DB2 database using the DB2LOOK utility program.

Let's look in detail at some of the objects that can be created in a database. We will cover data types, tables, views, and indexes.

Data Types

Data types are used to specify the attribute of the columns when creating a table. Before discussing a table or other objects, we have to understand the various data types supplied by DB2 or created by the users. There are three types of user-defined data types: user-defined distinct types (UDT), user-defined structured types and user-defined reference types. In this chapter, we will talk about UDTs. User defined structured types and user defined reference types will be discussed in "Advanced SQL" on page 325.

First let us look at the built-in data types supplied by DB2.

DB2-Supplied Data Types

When the database design is being implemented, any of these data types can be used. Data is stored in DB2 tables that are composed of columns and rows. Every DB2 table is defined by using columns. These columns must be one of the built-in DB2 data types or user-defined data types. Every DB2-supplied data type belongs to one of these three major categories (Datalink is not included in this categorization list but is represented in the figure below):

- Numeric
- String (Binary, Single Byte, Double Byte)
- Datetime

The valid built-in DB2 data types are shown in Fig. 5–1.

Database Objects

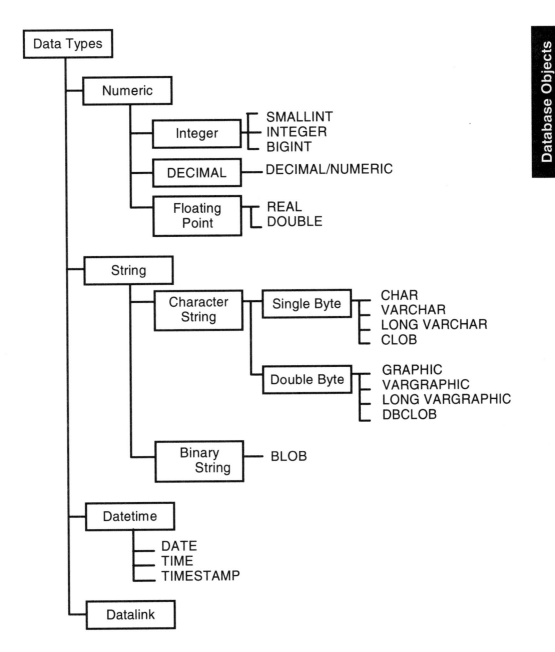

Fig. 5–1 *DB2-supplied data types*

Numeric Data Types

The six DB2 data types that can be used to store numeric data are:

- SMALLINT
- INTEGER
- BIGINT
- DECIMAL/NUMERIC
- REAL
- DOUBLE

These data types are used to store different numeric types and precisions. The precision of a number is the number of digits used to represent its value. The data is stored in the DB2 database using a fixed amount of storage for all numeric data types. The amount of storage required increases as the precision of the number goes up.

You must also be aware of the range limits of the data types and the corresponding application programming language when you are manipulating these numeric fields.

Some data values are of the integer type by nature, such as the number of test candidates. It would be impossible to have a number representing a number of people that contains fractional data (numbers to the right of the decimal). On the other hand, some values require decimal places to accurately reflect their value, such as test scores. These two examples should use different DB2 data types to store their values (SMALLINT and DECIMAL, respectively).

Numeric values should not be enclosed in quotation marks. If they are, the value is treated as a character string. Even if a field contains numbers in its representation, a DB2 numeric data type should be used to represent the data only if arithmetic operations should be allowed.

Small integer (SMALLINT)

A small integer uses the least amount of storage in the database for each value. An integer does not allow any digits to the right of the decimal.

The data value range for a SMALLINT is -32768 to 32767. The precision for a SMALLINT is 5 digits (to the left of the decimal). Two bytes of database storage are used for each SMALLINT column value.

Integer (INTEGER)

An INTEGER takes twice as much storage as a SMALLINT but has a greater range of possible values.

The range value for an INTEGER data type is -2,147,483,648 to 2,147,483,647. The precision for an INTEGER is 10 digits to the left of the decimal. Four bytes of database storage are used for each INTEGER column value.

Big integer (BIGINT)

The BIGINT data type is available for supporting 64-bit integers. The range for BIGINT is -9,223,372,036,854,775,808 to +9,223,372,036,854,775,807. As platforms include native support for 64 bit integers, the processing of large numbers with BIGINT is more efficient than processing with DECIMAL and more precise than DOUBLE or REAL. Eight bytes of database storage are used for each BIGINT column value.

Decimal (DECIMAL/NUMERIC)

A DECIMAL or NUMERIC data type is used for numbers with fractional and whole parts. The DECIMAL data is stored in a packed format.

The precision and scale must be provided when a decimal data type is used. The precision is the total number of digits (range from 1 to 31), and the scale is the number of digits in the fractional part of the number. For example, a decimal data type to store currency values of up to $1 million would require a definition of DECIMAL(9,2). The terms NUMERIC, NUM, DECIMAL, and DEC can all be used to declare a decimal/numeric column. If a decimal data type is to be used in a C program, the host variable must be declared as a double. A DECIMAL number takes up p/2 + 1 bytes of storage, where p is the precision used. For example, DEC(8,2) would take up 5 bytes of storage (8/2 + 1), whereas DEC(7,2) would take up only 4 bytes (truncate the division of p/2).

> **Note:** If the precision and scale values are not supplied for a DECIMAL column definition, a default value (5,0) is used. This column would take up 3 bytes of space in the row.

Single-precision floating-point (REAL/FLOAT)

A REAL data type is an approximation of a number. The approximation requires 32 bits or 4 bytes of storage. To specify a single-precision number using the REAL data type, its length must be defined between 1 and 24 (especially if the FLOAT data type is used, as it can represent both single- and double-precision and is determined by the integer value specified).

Double-precision floating-point (DOUBLE/FLOAT)

A DOUBLE or FLOAT data type is an approximation of a number. The approximation requires 64 bits or 8 bytes of storage. To specify a double-precision number using the FLOAT data type, its length must be defined between 25 and 53.

Note: Exponential notation is used to represent REAL, DOUBLE, and FLOAT data values.

String Data Types

This section discusses the string data types that include CHAR, VARCHAR, and LONG VARCHAR.

Fixed-length character string (CHAR)

Fixed-length character strings are stored in the database using the entire defined amount of storage. If the data being stored always has the same length, a CHAR data type should be used. In Fig. 5–2, the Candidate ID field is defined as a fixed-length character string of 8 characters.

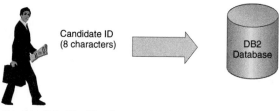

Character Data (Fixed length - up to 254 bytes/column)

Fig. 5–2 *Fixed-length character strings (CHARs)*

Using fixed-length character fields can potentially waste disk space within the database if the data is not using the defined amount of storage. However, there is overhead involved in storing varying-length character strings. The term CHARAC-TER can be used as a synonym for CHAR.

The length of a fixed-length string must be between 1 and 254 characters. If you do not supply a value for the length, a value of 1 is assumed.

Database Objects

Note: Character strings are stored in the database without a termination character. Depending on the development environment, a null-terminator may or may not be appended to the end of a character string when the data is stored or retrieved.

Varying-length character string (VARCHAR)

Varying-length character strings are stored in the database using only the amount of space required to store the data. The individual names, in our example, are stored as varying-length strings (VARCHAR) because each persons name has a different length (up to a maximum length of 30 characters). The term CHAR VARYING or CHARACTER VARYING can be used as a synonym for VARCHAR.

If a varying-length character string is updated and the resulting value is larger than the original, the record will be moved to another page in the table. These data records are known as *tombstone* records or pointer records. Too many of these records can cause significant performance degradation since multiple pages are required to return a single data record. The maximum length of a VARCHAR column is 32,672 bytes.

Varying-length long character strings (LONG VARCHAR)

This data type is used to store character data with a varying length. In the past it was used when the VARCHAR was not large enough; however, with the increase of the VARCHAR column to 32,672, the LONG VARCHAR data type may not be used as often.

A VARCHAR column has the restriction that it must fit on one database page. This means that a 4K page would allow a VARCHAR of approximately 4000 characters long, an 8K page would be 8000 and so on up to a 32K page. This means that you must create a tablespace for this table that can accommodate the larger page size, and you must have sufficient space in the row to accommodate this string. A LONG VARCHAR only takes up 24 bytes of space in the row, no matter what the length is. The LONG VARCHAR format will result in the strings being stored in a separate database page, and this will result in longer processing time for these strings since the database will always need to make an extra hop to get to this data.

The maximum length of a LONG VARCHAR column is 32,700.

Note: LONG VARCHAR data types are similar to CLOB data types. (Both types have usage restrictions.)

 Note: The FOR BIT DATA clause can be used following a character string column definition. During data exchange, code page conversions are not performed. Rather data is treated and compared as binary (bit) data.

Character large object (CLOB)

Character large objects are varying-length SBCS (single-byte character set) or MBCS (multibyte character set) character strings that are stored in the database. There is a code page associated with each CLOB. For more details regarding a DB2 code page, please see "Code Page Considerations" on page 230 CLOB columns are used to store greater than 32KB of text. The maximum size for each CLOB column is 2GB (gigabytes). Since this data type is of varying length, the amount of disk space allocated is determined by the amount of data in each record. Therefore, you should create the column specifying the length of the longest string.

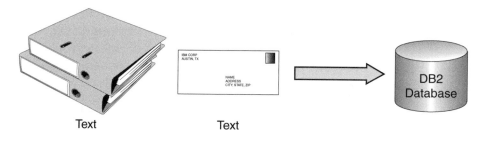

Text   Text

Fig. 5–3 *CLOB character strings*

Double-byte character strings (GRAPHIC)

The GRAPHIC data types represent a single character using 2 bytes of storage. The GRAPHIC data types include:

GRAPHIC (fixed length - maximum 127 characters)

VARGRAPHIC (varying length - maximum 16336 characters)

LONG VARGRAPHIC (varying length - maximum 16350 characters).

Double-byte character large objects (DBCLOB)

Double-byte character large objects are varying-length character strings that are stored in the database using 2 bytes to represent each character. There is a code page associated with each column. DBCLOB columns are used for large amounts (>32KB) of double-byte text data such as Japanese text.

The maximum length should be specified during the column definition because each data record will be variable in length.

Binary large object (BLOB)

Binary large objects are variable-length binary strings. The data is stored in a binary format in the database. There are restrictions when using this data type including the inability to sort using this type of column. The BLOB data type is useful for storing nontraditional relational database information as shown in Fig. 5–4.

The maximum size of each BLOB column is 2GB (gigabytes). Since this data type is of varying length, the amount of disk space allocated is determined by the amount of data in each record, not by the defined maximum size of the column in the table definition.

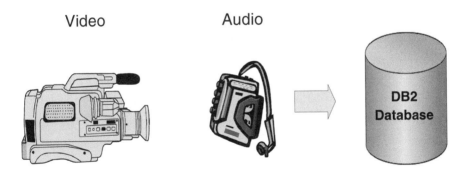

Fig. 5–4 *Binary large objects (BLOBs)*

Large Object Considerations

Traditionally, large unstructured data was stored somewhere outside the database. Therefore, the data could not be accessed using SQL. Besides the traditional database data types, DB2 implements data types that will store large amounts of unstructured data. These data types are known as Large Objects (LOBs). Multiple LOB columns can be defined for a single table.

DB2 provides special considerations for handling these large objects. You can choose not to log the LOB values to avoid exhausting the transaction log files.

There is a NOT LOGGED option that can be specified during the CREATE TABLE statement for each LOB column that you want to avoid logging any modifications. If you would like to define a LOB column greater than 1GB, you must specify the NOT LOGGED option.

There is also a COMPACT option that can be specified during the CREATE TABLE statement. This option is used to avoid allocating extra disk space when storing these large data objects, not for the compression of these objects!

In a database, you may choose to use BLOBs for the storage of pictures, images, or audio or video objects, along with large documents. BLOB columns will accept any binary string without regard to the contents.

If you would like to manipulate textual data that is greater than 32 KB in length, you would use CLOB or a character large object data type. For example, if each test candidate were required to submit their resume, the resume could be stored in a CLOB column along with the rest of the candidate's information. There are many SQL functions that can be used to manipulate large character data columns.

Date and Time Data Types

There are three DB2 data types specifically used to represent dates and times:

*   DATE - This data type is stored internally as a (packed) string of 4 bytes. Externally, the string has a length of 10 bytes (MM-DD-YYYY - this representation can vary and is dependent on the country code).

*   TIME - This data type is stored internally as a (packed) string of 3 bytes. Externally, the string has a length of 8 bytes (HH-MM-SS - this representation may vary).

*   TIMESTAMP - This data type is stored internally as a (packed) string of 10 bytes. Externally, the string has a length of 26 bytes (YYYY-MM-DD-HH-MM-SS-NNNNNN).

From the user perspective, these data types can be treated as character or string data types. Every time you need to use a datetime attribute, you will need to enclose it in quotation marks. However, datetime data types are not stored in the database as fixed-length character strings.

DB2 provides special functions that allow you to manipulate these data types. These functions allow you to extract the month, hour, or year of a datetime column.

The date and time formats correspond to the country code of the database or a specified format (since the representation of dates and times varies in different countries). Therefore, the string that represents a date value will change depending on the country code (or format specified). In some countries, the date format is DD/MM/YYYY, whereas in other countries, it is YYYY-MM-DD. You should be aware of the country code/format used by your application to use the correct date string format. If an incorrect date format is used, an SQL error will be reported.

As a general recommendation, if you are interested in a single element of a date string, say month or year, always use the SQL functions provided by DB2 to interpret the column value. By using the SQL functions, your application will be more portable.

Note: TIMESTAMP fields use the most storage, but they contain the most accurate time since they include microseconds.

We stated that all datetime data types have an internal and external format. The external format is always a character string. Let us examine the various datetime data type formats available in DB2.

Date string (DATE)

There are a number of valid methods of representing a DATE as a string.

Table 5–1 *Valid Date Formats*

Format Name	Abbreviation	Date Format
International Standards Organization	ISO	YYYY-MM-DD
IBM USA Standard	USA	MM/DD/YYYY
IBM European Standard	EUR	DD.MM.YYYY
Japanese Industrial Standard	JIS	YYYY-MM-DD
Site Defined	LOC	Depends on database country code

Any of the string formats shown in Table 5–1 can be used to store dates in a DB2 database. When the data is retrieved (using a SELECT statement), the output string will be in one of these formats. There is an option of the BIND command called DATETIME, which allows you to define the external format of the date and time values. The abbreviation column in Table 5–1 contains some possible values for the DATETIME option of the BIND command.

Time string (TIME)

There are a number of valid methods for representing a TIME as a string. Any of the string formats in Table 5–2 can be used to store times in a DB2 database. When data is retrieved, the external format of the time will be one of the formats shown in Table 5–2.

Table 5–2 *Valid Time Formats*

Format Name	Abbreviation	Date Format
International Standards Organization	ISO	HH.MM.SS
IBM USA Standard	USA	HH:MM AM or PM
IBM European Standard	EUR	HH.MM.SS
Japanese Industrial Standard	JIS	HH:MM:SS
Site Defined	LOC	Depends on the database country code

There is a BIND option, called DATETIME, which allows you to define the external format of the date and time values. The abbreviation column in Table 5–2 contains some possible values for the DATETIME BIND option.

Note: Regardless of the date and time format of the applications, TIME data types have the same internal representation. Their external representation can be changed with the BIND option.

Timestamp string (TIMESTAMP)

The timestamp data type has a single external format. Therefore, the DATETIME BIND option does not affect the external format of timestamps. Timestamps have an external representation as YYYY-MM-DD-HH.MM.SS.NNNNNN (Year-Month-Day-Hour-Minute-Seconds-Microseconds).

External File Data Types (DATALINK)

A DATALINK value is an encapsulated value that contains a logical reference from the database to a file stored in a Data Links Manager Server, which is outside the database (See "DB2 Data Links Manager" on page 37). The attributes of this encapsulated value are as follows:

• Link type - The currently supported type of link is a URL (Uniform Resource Locator).

- Scheme - For URLs, this is a value like HTTP or FILE. The value, no matter what case it is entered in, is stored in the database in uppercase characters. If a value is not specified, FILE is included in the DATALINK value.
- File server name - The complete address of the file server. The value, no matter what case it is entered in, is stored in the database in uppercase characters. If a value is not specified, the file server name of the database server is selected and included in the DATALINK value.
- File path - The identity of the file within the server. The value is case-sensitive and, therefore, it is not converted to uppercase characters when stored in the database.
- Access control token - When appropriate, the access token is embedded within the file path. It is generated dynamically when a DATALINK value is extracted, and it is not necessary to provide it when a DATALINK value is inserted. In other words, it is not a permanent part of the DATALINK value that is stored in the database.
- Comment - Up to 254 bytes of descriptive information. This is intended for application specific uses such as further or alternative identification of the location of the data.

Insert and extract DATALINK values

When you are inserting rows into a table that has DATALINK columns, you should use a built-in scalar function, DLVALUE, to provide each attribute of the DATALINK value.

To extract encapsulated attributes of the DATALINK value, DB2 provides several built-in scalar functions, such as DLLINKTYPE, DLURLSCHEME, DLURLSERVER, DLURLCOMPLETE, DLURLPATH, DLURLPATHONLY, and DLCOMMENT.

Refer to the *DB2 UDB V7.1 SQL Reference* for more detailed information about these built-in scalar functions.

User-Defined Data Types

User-defined types (UDTs) allow a user to extend the data-types that DB2 understands in a database. UDTs can be classified into three types:

- User-defined distinct type - User-defined data types (UDTs) can be created on an existing data type or on other user-defined data types. UDTs are used to define further types of data being represented in the database. If columns are defined using different UDTs based on the same base data type, these UDTs cannot be directly compared. This is known as *strong typing*. DB2 provides this strong data typing to avoid end-user mistakes during the assignment or comparison of different types of real-world data.

- User-defined reference type - A UDT can also be a user-defined reference type used to reference rows in another table that uses a user-defined structured type. A structured type can be a subtype of another structured type (called supertype) defining a type hierarchy. User-defined structured types (for type hierarchy) will be discussed in "Advanced SQL" on page 325.
- User-defined structured (or abstract) data type - Structured type support has been extended to provide the ability to create tables with structured type columns. Additionally, structured types can be nested within a structured type. This means that the attributes of structured type are no longer restricted to the base SQL types, they can now be of another structured type. User-defined structured type as discussed in "Advanced SQL" on page 325.

The user-defined structured (abstract) data type allows the DBA or developer to create columns that are actually made up of a structure. This is part of the object-relational support found within DB2.

The SYSCAT.DATATYPES catalog view allows you to see the UDTs that have been defined in your database.

Creating User-Defined Distinct Types (UDTs)

Let us say we have a table that will be used to store different measures of weight such as pounds and kilograms. We should use a numeric data type for these columns since arithmetic operations are appropriate. We will use the INTEGER data type as the base DB2 data type for the UDTs, KILOGRAM and POUND. The values represent different units and, therefore, should not be directly compared.

Note: User-defined data types (UDTs) can be based on other UDTs or existing DB2 data types.

Here we define two new data types: KILOGRAM and POUND. These data types will be based on the integer (INTEGER) data type. Once the KILOGRAM and POUND UDTs have been defined, they can be referenced in the CREATE TABLE statement.

When the UDTs are defined, system-generated SQL functions are created. These functions are known as *casting functions*. The casting functions allow comparison between the UDT and its base type. In the real world, you cannot directly compare pounds and kilograms without converting one of the values. In DB2, a user-defined function is required.

Let us create the user-defined data types for pound and kilogram.

```
CREATE DISTINCT TYPE pound
       AS INTEGER WITH COMPARISONS
CREATE DISTINCT TYPE kilogram
       AS INTEGER WITH COMPARISONS
```

In the example above, we are creating the new data types known as POUND and KILOGRAM.

The keyword DISTINCT is mandatory for all user-defined data types. The WITH COMPARISONS clause is also a mandatory clause (except for LOB, LONG, and DATALINK data types). Let us create a table using the pound and kilogram data types.

```
CREATE TABLE health
   (f_name VARCHAR(30),
    weight_p POUND,
    weight_k KILOGRAM)
```

The new data types are used in the table definition just like the DB2 built-in data types. DB2 will not allow you to compare or perform arithmetic operations on the POUND and KILOGRAM typed columns directly. A casting function would need to be used to perform arithmetic operations using the columns defined with these types. In other words, you could not use built-in functions, such as the average function (AVG), for a column defined as POUND or KILOGRAM, unless you use the appropriate casting functions or create a new user-defined function that can use those UDTs as an input parameter.

The following SQL statement would result in an error. The data type for the constant value of 30 is of type INTEGER. An INTEGER data type cannot be directly compared with the POUND data type.

```
SELECT f_name, weight_p
FROM health
WHERE weight_p > 30
```

To resolve the error, a cast of the constant value of 30 is required. By casting, the value of 30 is treated as an POUND data type. In the following example, the

`POUND(INTEGER)` casting function is being used to convert the value of 30 to the `POUND` data type.

```
SELECT f_name, weight_p
FROM health
WHERE weight_p > POUND(30)
```

Let us look at a simple example of a UDT involving telephone numbers. This example is here for the purpose of describing the use of user-defined types. Be aware that this example would not restrict the phone number to be numeric. You always compare phone numbers with other phone numbers; you do not compare them with street numbers or department numbers. This means that a column representing telephone numbers would be an ideal candidate to be defined using a distinct type or UDT.

Should telephone numbers be stored as numeric or string data? Does it make sense to perform arithmetic operations on a telephone number? No, a telephone number has no significant mathematical properties (e.g., adding one to your telephone number is not a useful operation). Therefore, we should base the new data type on a `CHARACTER` or `CHAR` type. A varying-length character string or `VARCHAR` is not required because the length of a telephone number is consistent.

Let us create a user-defined data type for the telephone numbers. This will ensure that all the columns containing telephone numbers share the same data type.

 Note: The valid data values for a user-defined data type cannot be specified. Therefore, any valid value for the base data type is allowed. Additional constraints should be placed on the data value within the table.

The SQL statement to create the distinct type `phoneno` is shown.

```
CREATE DISTINCT TYPE phoneno
          AS CHAR(10) WITH COMPARISONS
```

The creation of this user-defined data type will result in the creation of the following casting functions:

- CHAR(PHONENO), which translates data values from the PHONENO data type to the base data type CHAR
- PHONENO(CHAR), which translates data values from the base data type CHAR to the PHONENO data type

In fact, DB2 will create two PHONENO casting functions: one that converts fixed CHAR strings and another that works with VARCHAR columns. The number of casting functions created will vary according to the base data type being used. In addition, a casting function VARCHAR(PHONENO) is also created.

Let us say that we have two columns that represent phone numbers: HPHONE (home phone number) and WPHONE (work phone number). Both of these columns should be defined using the same data type PHONENO.

Here are some examples of using these columns in expressions:

- An expression involving the same data type (phoneno) -
  phoneno = HPHONE or HPHONE <> WPHONE
- An expression using the casting function PHONENO(CHAR) -
  HPHONE = PHONENO('5555551234')
- A similar expression using the casting function CHAR(PHONENO) -
  CHAR(hphone) = '5555551234'

Removing a User-Defined Distinct Type

User-defined distinct types (UDTs) are defined at the database level. They can be created and dropped from a database by the database administrator. If tables have been defined using a UDT, you will not be allowed to drop the UDT. The table would need to be dropped before the UDT could be dropped.

Assuming there is no table defined using the pound data type, you could remove the definition of the pound data type using the following statement.

```
DROP DISTINCT TYPE pound
```

The DROP DISTINCT TYPE statement will drop the pound data type and all of its related casting functions.

> **Note:** Remember that if you do not qualify a DB2 object, the current
> authorization ID will be used as the schema name. For example, if you are
> connected to the database as user geoffrey, the drop statement in the previ-
> ous example would attempt to drop the data type geoffrey.pound

Null Value Considerations

A null value represents an unknown state. Therefore, when columns containing
null values are used in calculations, the result is unknown. All of the data types discussed in the previous section support the presence of null values. During the table
definition, you can specify that a valid value must be provided. This is accomplished by adding a phrase to the column definition. The CREATE TABLE statement
can contain the phrase NOT NULL following the definition of each column. This will
ensure that the column contains a known data value.

Special considerations are required to properly handle null values when coding a
DB2 application. DB2 treats a null value differently than it treats other data values.

> **Note:** Relational databases allow null values. It is important to remem-
> ber that they can be appropriate for your database design.

To define a column not to accept null values, add the phrase NOT NULL to the end of
the column definition, for example:

```
CREATE TABLE t1 (c1 CHAR(3) NOT NULL)
```

From the example above, DB2 will not allow any null values to be stored in the c1
column. In general, avoid using nullable columns unless they are required to implement the database design. There is also overhead storage you must consider. An
extra byte per nullable column is necessary if null values are allowed.

Null with Default

When you insert a row into a table and omit the value of one or more columns, those columns may either be populated using a null value (if the column is defined as nullable) or a defined default value (if you have specified this to be used). If the column is defined as not nullable, the insert will fail unless the data has been provided for the column. DB2 has a defined default value for each of the DB2 data types, but you can provide a default value for each of the columns. The default value is specified in the CREATE TABLE statement. By defining your own default value, you can ensure that the data value has been populated with a known value.

In Fig. 5–5, we can see how the default values can be specified in a CREATE TABLE statement.

```
CREATE TABLE Staff
(ID SMALLINT NOT NULL,
 NAME VARCHAR(9),
 DEPT SMALLINT not null with default 10,
 JOB CHAR(5),
 YEARS SMALLINT,
 SALARY DECIMAL(7,2),
 COMM DECIMAL(7,2) with default 15);
```

Fig. 5–5 *Defining user default values for columns*

Now, all the INSERT statements that omit the DEPT column will populate the column with the default value of 10. The COMM column is defined as with default. In this case, you can choose at insert time between null or the default value of 15.

To ensure that the default value is being used during an INSERT operation, the keyword DEFAULT should be specified in the VALUES portion of the INSERT statement. Fig. 5–6 shows two examples of inserting a record with user-defined default values. In this case, both cause the same result.

```
INSERT INTO STAFF
 values(360,'Chihoko',DEFAULT,'SE',8,20000,DEFAULT);

INSERT INTO STAFF (ID,NAME,JOB,YEARS,SALARY)
 values(360,'Chihoko','SE',8,20000,);

The result is

ID       NAME       DEPT   JOB   YEARS  SALARY      COMM
------   --------   ----   ----- ------ --------    --------
   360 Chihoko        10 SE          8  20000.00      15.00

1 record(s) selected.
```

Fig. 5–6 *Inserting a record with default value*

 Columns can also contain generated values, including a new sequence
number value.

Identity Column

The previous section discussed how columns can be populated with values if no
value was supplied by the user. It is also possible to have DB2 generate sequence
numbers or other values as part of a column during record insertion.

In the majority of applications, a single column within a table represents a unique
identifier for that row. Often this identifier is a number that gets sequentially
updated as new records are added.

In DB2, a feature exists that will automatically generate this value on behalf of the
user. Fig. 5–7 shows a table definition with the EMP_NO field being automatically
being generated as a sequence.

```
CREATE TABLE EMPLOYEE (
  EMPNO  INT GENERATED ALWAYS AS IDENTITY,
  NAME CHAR(10));

INSERT INTO EMPLOYEE(NAME) VALUES 'George','Bill';

SELECT * FROM EMPLOYEE;

EMPNO          NAME
-----------    -----------
          1    George
          2    Bill
```

Fig. 5–7 *Inserting records with generated values*

If the column is defined with GENERATED ALWAYS, then the INSERT statement cannot specify a value for the EMPNO field. By default, the numbering will start at 1 and increment by 1. The starting and increment values can be modified as part of the column definition:

```
CREATE TABLE EMPLOYEE (
  EMPNO  INT GENERATED ALWAYS AS
     IDENTITY(START WITH 100, INCREMENT BY 10)),
  NAME CHAR(10));

INSERT INTO EMPLOYEE(NAME) VALUES 'George','Bill';

SELECT * FROM EMPLOYEE;

EMPNO          NAME
-----------    -----------
        100    George
        110    Bill
```

Fig. 5–8 *Inserting records with generated values*

In addition, the default value can be GENERATED BY DEFAULT, which means that the user has the option of supplying a value for the field. If no value is supplied (using the DEFAULT keyword), DB2 will generate the next number in sequence.

One additional keyword is available as part of IDENTITY columns. As a DBA, you can decide how many numbers should be "pregenerated" by DB2. This can help reduce catalog contention since DB2 will store the next n numbers in memory rather than go back to the catalog tables to determine which number to generate next.

Identity columns are restricted to numeric values (integer or decimal) and can only be used in one column in the table definition. The GENERATE keyword can be used for other columns, but they cannot be IDENTITY columns.

The GENERATE keyword can be applied to other columns to generate values automatically in the table without the programmer or user having to include it. For instance, the EMPLOYEE table could include two columns that are components of the individuals pay.

```
CREATE TABLE EMPLOYEE (
    EMPNO   INT GENERATED ALWAYS AS IDENTITY,
    NAME    CHAR(10),
    SALARY  INT,
    BONUS   INT,
    PAY     INT GENERATED ALWAYS AS (SALARY+BONUS)
    );

INSERT INTO EMPLOYEE(NAME, SALARY, BONUS) VALUES
    ('George',20000,2000),
    ('Bill',30000,5000);

SELECT * FROM EMPLOYEE;

EMPNO        NAME        SALARY      BONUS       PAY
-----------  ----------  ----------- ----------- -----------
          1  George           20000        2000       22000
          2  Bill             30000        5000       35000
```

Fig. 5–9 *Inserting records with a generated column*

The EMPNO is generated as an IDENTITY column, and the PAY value is calculated automatically by DB2. If the SALARY or BONUS fields are modified at a later time, DB2 will recalculate the PAY column. A GENERATED column has the same options as the IDENTITY field has. The value can be either calculated ALWAYS or generated by DEFAULT.

For more information on this powerful feature, please refer to the *DB2 UDB V7.1 SQL Reference* manual.

Code Page Considerations

A character *code page* is associated with all DB2 character data types (CHAR, VARCHAR, CLOB, DBCLOB). This code page is set at the database level during the CREATE DATABASE command.

Database Objects

A code page can be considered a reference table that is used to convert alphanumeric data to binary data stored in the database. A DB2 database can only use a single code page. The code page is established during the CREATE DATABASE command using the options CODESET and TERRITORY. The code page can use a single byte to represent an alphanumeric (a single byte can represent 256 unique elements) or multiple bytes.

Languages such as English contain relatively few unique characters; therefore, a single byte code page is sufficient to store data. Languages like Japanese require more than 256 elements to represent all of the unique characters; therefore, a multi-byte code page (usually a double-byte code page) is required.

A code point is the unique value used to locate the character within the code page. DB2 will attempt to perform code page conversion if the application and the database have not been defined using the same code page.

	0	1	2	3	4	5	6	7	8	9	A	B	C	D	E	F
0				0	@	P	`	p								
1			!	1	A	Q	a	q								
2			"	2	B	R	b	r								
3			#	3	C	S	c	s								
4			$	4	D	T	d	t								
5			%	5	E	U	e	u								
6			&	6	F	V	f	v								
7			"	7	G	W	g	w								
8			(	8	H	X	h	x								
9			)	9	I	Y	i	y								
A			*	:	J	Z	j	z								
B			+	;	K	[	k	{								
C			,	<	L	\	l	|								
D			-	=	M	]	m	}								
E			.	>	N	^	n	~								
F			/	?	O	_	o									

Fig. 5–10 *Code page*

In Fig. 5–10, an example code page is shown. This example represents a portion of the ASCII character set (e.g., hexadecimal code point 41 represents the character A).

Note: Binary strings, such as FOR BIT DATA column specifications and BLOB columns, are not associated with the database code page.

When a DB2 application is bound to a DB2 database, the application and database code page are compared. If the code pages are not equal, code page conversion will be attempted for each SQL statement. If you are using a code page other than that of the database you are accessing, it is important to ensure that the code pages are compatible and conversion can be accomplished.

By default, the collating sequence of a database is defined according to the codeset used in the CREATE DATABASE command. If you specify the option COLLATE USING SYSTEM, the data values are compared based on the TERRITORY specified for the database. If the option COLLATE USING IDENTITY is used, all values are compared using their binary representation in a byte-to-byte manner.

When you need to store data in its native (binary) format, avoid using data types with code pages. It is generally advantageous to have the application and the database code page the same to avoid the code page conversion process.

Unicode Support in DB2

The *Unicode* character encoding standard is a fixed-length, character-encoding scheme that includes characters from almost all the living languages of the world. Unicode characters are usually shown as U+xxxx, where xxxx is the hexadecimal code of the character. Each character is 16 bits (2 bytes) wide regardless of the language. While the resulting 65,536 code elements are sufficient for encoding most of the characters of the major languages of the world, the Unicode standard also provides an extension mechanism that allows for encoding as many as a million more characters. This extension reserves a range of code values (U+D800 to U+D8FF, known as *surrogates*) for encoding some 32-bit characters as two successive code elements.

DB2 supports ISO/IEC 10646 standard UCS-2, that is, Unicode without surrogates. UCS-2 is implemented with UTF-8 (UCS Transformation Format 8) algorithmic transformation. DB2 supported codepage/CCSIDs are shown in Table 5–3.

Table 5–3 *Supported Code Pages/CCSIDs*

CP/CCSID	Single-Byte (SBCS) Space	Double-Byte (DBCS) Space
1200	N/A	U+0020
13488	N/A	U+0030

These are handled the same way except for the value of their DBCS space. Regarding the conversion table, since code page 1200 is a super set of CCSID 13488, the exact same tables are used for both.

UTF-8 has been registered as CCSID 1208, which is used as the multibyte (MBCS) code page number for the UCS-2/UTF-8 support of DB2. This is the database code page number and the code page of character string data within the database. The double-byte code page number (for UCS-2) is 1200, which is the code page of graphic string data within the database.

When a database is created in UCS-2/UTF-8, CHAR, VARCHAR, LONG VARCHAR, and CLOB data are stored in UTF-8, and GRAPHIC, VARGRAPHIC, LONG VAR-GRAPHIC, and DBCLOB data are stored in UCS-2. We will simply refer to this as a UCS-2 database.

If you are working with character string data in UTF-8, you should be aware that ASCII characters are encoded into 1-byte lengths; however, non-ASCII characters are encoded into 2- or 3-byte lengths in a multiple-byte character code set (MBCS). Therefore, if you define an n-byte length character column, you can store strings anywhere from n/3 to n characters depending on the ratio of ASCII to non-ASCII characters.

Following is the example to create a UCS-2 database named UCS2DB with the territory code for United States.

```
CREATE DATABASE UCS2DB USING CODESET UTF-8 TERRITORY US
```

 Note: Code set should be specified in uppercase characters.

For further DB2-supported code set or territory information, please refer to the *National Language Support (NLS) section in the DB2 UDB V7.1 Administration Guide.*

Selecting the Correct Data Type

Knowledge of the possible data values and their usage is required to be able to select the correct data type. Specifying an inappropriate data type when defining the tables can result in:

- Wasted disk space
- Improper expression evaluation
- Performance considerations

A small checklist for data type selection is shown in Table 5–4.

Table 5–4 *Data Type Checklist*

Question	Data Type
Is the data variable in length?	VARCHAR
If the data is variable in length, what is the maximum length?	VARCHAR
Do you need to sort (order) the data?	CHAR, VARCHAR, NUMERIC
Is the data going to be used in arithmetic operations?	DECIMAL, NUMERIC, REAL, DOUBLE, BIGINT, INTEGER, SMALLINT
Does the data element contain decimals?	DECIMAL, NUMERIC, REAL, DOUBLE
Is the data fixed in length?	CHAR
Does the data have a specific meaning (beyond DB2 base data types)?	USER DEFINED TYPE
Is the data larger than what a character string can store, or do you need to store non-traditional data?	CLOB, BLOB, DBCLOB

When using character data types, the choice between CHAR and VARCHAR is determined by the range of lengths of the columns. For example, if the range of column length is relatively small, use a fixed char with the maximum length. This will reduce the storage requirements and could improve performance.

Remember that you need to create page sizes that are large enough to contain the length of a row in a table. This is particularly important for tables with large character columns.

Tables

Tables consist of columns and rows that store an unordered set of data records. Tables can have constraints to guarantee the uniqueness of data records, maintaining the relationship between and within tables, and so on. A constraint is a rule that the database manager enforces. There are three types of constraints:

- Unique constraint - Ensures the unique values of a key in a table. Any changes to the columns that comprise the unique key are checked for uniqueness.
- Referential integrity - Enforces referential constraints on insert, update, and delete operations. It is the state of a database in which all values of all foreign keys are valid.
- Table check constraint - Verifies that changed data does not violate conditions specified when a table was created or altered.

Unique Constraints

A *unique constraint* is the rule that the values of a key are valid only if they are unique within the table. Each column making up the key in a unique constraint must be defined as NOT NULL. Unique constraints are defined in the CREATE TABLE statement or the ALTER TABLE statement using the PRIMARY KEY clause or the UNIQUE clause.

A table can have any number of unique constraints; however, a table cannot have more than one unique constraint on the same set of columns.

> **Note:** The UNIQUERULE column of the SYSCAT.INDEXES view indicates the characteristic of the index. If the value of this column is P, the index is a primary key, and if it is U, the index is an unique index (but not a primary key).

When a unique constraint is defined, the database manager creates (if needed) a unique index and designates it as either a primary or unique system-required index. The enforcement of the constraint is through the unique index. Once a unique constraint has been established on a column, the check for uniqueness during multiple row updates is deferred until the end of the update (deferred unique constraint).

A unique constraint can also be used as the parent key in a referential constraint.

Referential Integrity

Referential integrity allows you to define required relationships between and within tables. The database manager maintains these relationships, which are expressed as referential constraints and requires that all values of a given attribute or table column also exist in some other table column. Fig. 5–11 shows an example of the referential integrity between two tables. This constraint requires that every employee in the EMPLOYEE table must be in a department that exists in the DEPARTMENT table. No employee can be in a department that does not exist.

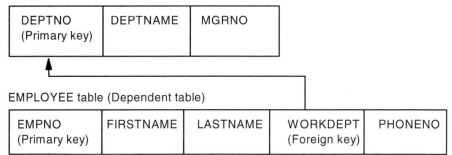

Fig. 5–11 *Referential integrity between two tables*

A *unique key* is a set of columns in which no two values are duplicated in any other row. Only one unique key can be defined as a primary key for each table. The unique key may also be known as the *parent key* when referenced by a foreign key.

A *primary key* is a special case of a unique key. Each table can only have one primary key. In this example, DEPTNO and EMPNO are the primary keys of the DEPARTMENT and EMPLOYEE tables.

A *foreign key* is a column or set of columns in a table that refer to a unique key or primary key of the same or another table. A foreign key is used to establish a relationship with a unique key or primary key and enforces referential integrity among tables. The column WORKDEPT in the EMPLOYEE table is a foreign key because it refers to the primary key, column DEPTNO, in the DEPARTMENT table.

A parent key is a primary key or unique key of a referential constraint.

A *parent table* is a table containing a parent key that is related to at least one foreign key in the same or another table. A table can be a parent in an arbitrary number of relationships. In this example, the DEPARTMENT table, which has a primary key of DEPTNO, is a parent of the EMPLOYEE table, which contains the foreign key WORKDEPT.

A dependent table is a table containing one or more foreign keys. A dependent table can also be a parent table. A table can be a dependent in an arbitrary number of relationships. For example, the EMPLOYEE table contains the foreign key WORKDEPT, which is dependent on the DEPARTMENT table that has a primary key.

A referential constraint is an assertion that non-null values of a designated foreign key are valid only if they also appear as values of a unique key of a designated parent table. The purpose of referential constraints is to guarantee that database relationships are maintained and data entry rules are followed.

Enforcement of referential constraints has special implications for some SQL operations that depend on whether the table is a parent or a dependent. The database manager enforces referential constraints across systems based on the referential integrity rules. The rules are

* INSERT rule
* DELETE rule
* UPDATE rule

INSERT Rules

The INSERT rule is implicit when a foreign key is specified.

You can insert a row at any time into a parent table without any action being taken in the dependent table.

You cannot insert a row into a dependent table unless there is a row in the parent table with a parent key value equal to the foreign key value of the row that is being inserted unless the foreign key value is null.

If an INSERT operation fails for one row during an attempt to insert more than one row, all rows inserted by the statement are removed from the database.

DELETE Rules

When you delete a row from a parent table, the database manager checks if there are any dependent rows in the dependent table with matching foreign key values. If any dependent rows are found, several actions can be taken. You determine which action will be taken by specifying a delete rule when you create the dependent table.

* RESTRICT - This rule prevents any row in the parent table from being deleted if any dependent rows are found. If you need to remove both parent and dependent rows, delete dependent rows first.
* NO ACTION - This rule enforces the presence of a parent row for every child after all the referential constraints are applied. This is the default. The difference between NO ACTION and RESTRICT is based on when the constraint is enforced. See the *DB2 UDB V7.1 SQL Reference* for further details.

- CASCADE - This rule implies that deleting a row in the parent table automatically deletes any related rows in the dependent table.
- SET NULL - This rule ensures that deletion of a row in the parent table sets the values of the foreign key in any dependent row to null (if nullable). Other parts of the row are unchanged.

UPDATE Rules

The database manager prevents the update of a unique key of a parent row. When you update a foreign key in a dependent table and the foreign key is defined with NOT NULL option, it must match some value of the parent key of the parent table. Two options exist:

- RESTRICT - The update for the parent key will be rejected if a row in the dependent table matches the original values of the key.
- NO ACTION - The update operation for the parent key will be rejected if any row in the dependent table does not have a corresponding parent key when the update statement is completed (excluding after triggers). This is the default.

Check Constraints

Table-check constraints will enforce data integrity at the table level. Once a table-check constraint has been defined for a table, every UPDATE and INSERT statement will involve checking the restriction or constraint. If the constraint is violated, the data record will not be inserted or updated, and an SQL error will be returned.

A table-check constraint can be defined at table creation time or later using the ALTER TABLE statement.

The table-check constraints can help implement specific rules for the data values contained in the table by specifying the values allowed in one or more columns in every row of a table. This can save time for the application developer since the validation of each data value can be performed by the database and not by each of the applications accessing the database.

The check constraint's definition is stored in the system catalog tables, specifically the SYSIBM.SYSCHECKS table. In addition you can use the SYSCAT.CHECKS system catalog view to view the check constraint definitions.

Adding Check Constraints

When you add a check constraint to a table that contains data, one of two things can happen:

- All the rows meet the check constraint.
- Some or all the rows do not meet the check constraint.

In the first case, when all the rows meet the check constraint, the check constraint will be created successfully. Future attempts to insert or update data that does not meet the constraint business rule will be rejected.

When there are some rows that do not meet the check constraint, the check constraint will not be created (i.e., the ALTER TABLE statement will fail). The ALTER TABLE statement, which adds a new constraint to the EMPLOYEE table, is shown below. The check constraint is named check_job. DB2 will use this name to inform us which constraint was violated if an INSERT or UPDATE statement fails. The CHECK clause is used to define a table-check constraint.

```
ALTER TABLE EMPLOYEE
  ADD CONSTRAINT check_job
  CHECK (JOB IN ('Engineer','Sales','Manager'));
```

An ALTER TABLE statement was used because the table had already been defined. If there are values in the EMPLOYEE table that conflict with the constraint being defined, the ALTER TABLE statement will not be completed successfully.

It is possible to turn off constraint checking to let you add a new constraint. The SET INTEGRITY statement enables you to turn off check constraint and referential constraint checking for one or more tables. When you turn off the constraint checking for a table, it will be put in a CHECK PENDING state, and only limited access to the table will be allowed. For example, once a table is in a check-pending state, use of SELECT, INSERT, UPDATE, and DELETE is disallowed on a table. See the *DB2 UDB V7.1 SQL Reference* for the complete syntax of the SET INTEGRITY statement.

Note: The SET CONSTRAINTS statement is replaced by the SET INTEGRITY statement in DB2 Universal Database V6.1. The SET CONSTRAINTS statement is still supported for backward compatibility.

Note: It is a good idea to label every constraint (triggers, table-check, or referential integrity). This is particularly important for diagnosing errors that might occur.

Modifying Check Constraints

As check constraints are used to implement business rules, you may need to change them from time to time. This could happen when the business rules change in your organization.

There is no special command used to change a check constraint. Whenever a check constraint needs to be changed, you must drop it and create a new one. Check constraints can be dropped at any time, and this action will not affect your table or the data within it.

When you drop a check constraint, you must be aware that data validation performed by the constraint will no longer be in effect. The statement used to drop a constraint is the ALTER TABLE statement.

The following example shows how to modify the existing constraint. After dropping the constraint, you have to create it with the new definition.

```
ALTER TABLE EMPLOYEE DROP CONSTRAINT check_job;
```

```
ALTER TABLE EMPLOYEE
  ADD CONSTRAINT check_job
  CHECK (JOB IN ('OPERATOR','CLERK'));
```

Physical DB2 Tables

In DB2, there are two types of permanent tables. One type is the system catalog tables and the other is the user tables.

System Catalog Tables

There are special tables used by DB2 that contain information about all objects within the database and are created for you when the database is created (for instance using the CREATE DATABASE command). These tables are called system catalog tables and they are examined by DB2 during query processing. Some of the information contained in the system catalog tables includes:

- Table/Index definitions
- Column data types
- Defined constraints
- Object dependencies
- Object privileges

When SQL Data Definition Language (DDL) statements are issued, the system catalog tables may in fact be updated for you. There are a number of base system tables and views in a DB2 database, and they always reside in a special table space called SYSCATSPACE.

> **Note:** To display the names of the system catalog tables and views along with their creation time enter the command LIST TABLES FOR SYSTEM or LIST TABLES FOR SCHEMA schemaname (SYSIBM, SYSCAT, or SYSSTAT).

The system catalog table data cannot be modified using an INSERT or DELETE SQL statement. However, some of the table data can be modified. For example, the COMMENT ON statement and ALTER statement will update information stored in the system catalog tables. For more details on the use of the ALTER statement, please refer to "The ALTER Statement" on page 209 and to the *DB2 UDB V7.1 SQL Reference.*

The system tables also contain statistical information about the tables in the database. For example, the number of physical pages allocated for each table is stored in the system catalog tables. The statistical information is calculated and updated by the RUNSTATS command.

Database object privileges, such as INSERT, SELECT, and CONTROL, are also maintained within the system catalog tables. The privileges are established using special SQL statements known as Data Control Language (DCL) statements. The primary DCL statements are GRANT and REVOKE. These statements were discussed in "Controlling Data Access" on page 145.

The system catalog tables are primarily for read-only purposes since they are maintained by DB2. However, there is a special set of system catalog views that are updatable. This is a special set of views defined on the system catalog tables that are used to update database statistics. These views are defined in the SYSSTAT schema. For example, these views can be used to force the DB2 optimizer to change the access path when executing a query relating to a certain table.

Note: Use the RUNSTATS command to update the database statistics. Update the SYSSTAT schema views to perform *what if* analysis of performance statistics.

There is also a set of read-only views defined for the system catalog base tables. To determine information about a DB2 database, the most common method is to issue SELECT statements against the system catalog tables. There are views defined for this purpose and they have the schema name SYSCAT.

The system catalog base tables are defined under the SYSIBM schema. However, you should query the SYSCAT views instead.

In general, there is at least one system catalog table for each of the database object types. Table 5–5 lists some of the system catalog views.

Table 5–5 *System Catalog Tables and Views*

Database Object	SYSCAT System Catalog Views	SYSSTAT Updatable Views
Table space	TABLESPACES	-
Table	TABLES	TABLES
Schema	SCHEMATA	
View	VIEWS	-
Column	COLUMNS	COLUMNS
Index	INDEXES	INDEXES
Package	PACKAGES	-
Trigger	TRIGGERS	-
Data Type	DATA TYPES	-
Stored Procedures	PROCEDURES	-
Constraint	CHECKS	-
Referential Integrity	REFERENCES	-
Function	FUNCTIONS	FUNCTIONS
Buffer Pool	BUFFERPOOLS	

The number of views defined within the SYSCAT schema or defined within the SYSSTAT schema can differ based on the version of DB2. Remember, the SYSSTAT schema views are used for updating statistical information for the database. An attempt to update any nonstatistical value is rejected by DB2.

User Tables

The CREATE TABLE statement allows you to define a new table. The definition must include its name and the attributes of its columns. The definition may include other attributes of the table such as its primary key or check constraints.

Once the table is defined, column names and data types cannot be modified. Exceptions to this include increasing the length of a varchar column or modifying a reference type column to add a scope. However, new columns can be added to the table (be careful when adding new columns since default data values will be used for existing records). In addition, after a table is created you can change table options such as PCTFREE, the DATA CAPTURE option, LOCK SIZE, LOGGING, or APPEND MODE.

The RENAME TABLE statement can change the name of an existing table.

> **Note:** The longest unqualified table name is 128 bytes and the longest unqualified column name is 30 bytes.

The maximum number of columns that a table can consists of is 1012. This maximum will vary depending on the data page size. DB2 supports 4K, 8K, 16K, and 32K data page sizes. Table 5–6 shows the maximum number of columns in a table and maximum length of a row by page size.

Table 5–6 *Table Limits*

	4k Page Size	8k Page Size	16k Page Size	32k Page Size
Most columns in a table	500	1012	1012	1012
Maximum row length (Bytes)	4005	8101	16293	32677
Maximum table size (per partition) (GB)	64	128	256	512

User tables are always created within a table space. Users can specify the table space name in which the table will be created. Tables and indexes can be placed separately into different table spaces (using DMS table spaces). LOB columns can also be placed into another table space in which the table is created (using DMS table spaces). If the table space name is not specified explicitly when creating a table, a table space for the table is determined as follows:

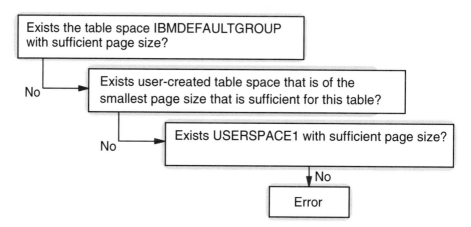

Fig. 5–12 *How DB2 chooses a table space for a table*

For detailed information about table spaces, please refer to "Data Storage Management" on page 409.

After creating a table, user data can be placed into the table using one of these methods:

- INSERT statement
- IMPORT command
- LOAD command

Note: The terms *utility* and *command* are used interchangeably throughout the book. All of the DB2 utilities are documented in the *DB2 UDB V7.1 Command Reference*, but they can also be issued from an application using an API defined in the *DB2 UDB V7.1 API Reference*.

Not logged table

The NOT LOGGED INITIALLY option of the CREATE TABLE statement saves the overhead of logging the data. Any changes made to the table by an INSERT,

DELETE, UPDATE, CREATE INDEX, DROP INDEX, or ALTER TABLE operation in the same unit of work in which the table is created are not logged.

For the table created with the NOT LOGGED INITIALLY option, you can activate the not logged mode using the ALTER TABLE statement with the ACTIVATE NOT LOGGED INITIALLY option. Any changes made to the table by an INSERT, DELETE, UPDATE, CREATE INDEX, DROP INDEX, or ALTER TABLE operation in the same unit of work in which the table is initially altered are not logged either. This option is useful for situations where a large result set needs to be created with data from an alternate source (another table or file) and recovery of the table is not necessary.

If you really need a temporary table that is only used during the duration of a program, use the DECLARE statement instead. This will result in no catalog contention, no logging, and no lock contention.

Note: When the unit of work is committed, all changes that were made to the table during the unit of work are flushed to disk.

Note: When you run the ROLLFORWARD utility and it encounters a log record that indicates that a table in the database was created with the NOT LOGGED INITIALLY option, the table will be marked as unavailable. After the database is recovered, an error will be issued if any attempt is made to access the table (SQL1477N Table " " cannot be accessed. SQL-STATE=55019). The only operation permitted is to drop the table.

Fig. 5–13 shows sample CREATE TABLE statements. This sample creates two tables. This definition includes unique constraints, check constraints, referential integrity, and not-logged-initially attributes. In this example,

- The DEPARTMENT table has a primary key that consists of column DEPTNUMB.
- The EMPLOYEE table has a check constraint that says JOB should be Sales, Mgr, or Clerk.
- The default value is defined for the column HIREDATE in the EMPLOYEE table.
- EMPLOYEE table has a primary key that consists of column ID
- A Referential constraint is defined between the DEPARTMENT table and the EMPLOYEE table.
- The EMPLOYEE table is created in the table space HUMRES, and its index is created in the table space HUMRES_IDX.

- Any changes made to the table by an INSERT, DELETE, UPDATE, CREATE INDEX, DROP INDEX, or ALTER TABLE operation in the same unit of work in which the EMPLOYEE table is created are not logged for the EMPLOYEE table.

```
CREATE TABLE Department
(Deptnumb SMALLINT NOT NULL,
 Deptname VARCHAR(20),
 Mgrno SMALLINT,
 PRIMARY KEY(Deptnumb)
);

CREATE TABLE Employee
(Id          SMALLINT     NOT NULL,
 Name        VARCHAR(9)   NOT NULL,
 Dept        SMALLINT,
 Job         CHAR(5) CHECK (Job IN
('Sales','Mgr','Clerk')),
 Hiredate    DATE WITH DEFAULT CURRENT DATE,
 Salary      DECIMAL(7,2),
 Comm        DECIMAL(7,2),
CONSTRAINT UNIQUEID PRIMARY KEY(Id),
FOREIGN KEY(Dept) references DEPARTMENT(Deptnumb)
                              ON DELETE RESTRICT)
IN HUMRES
INDEX IN HUMRES_IDX
NOT LOGGED INITIALLY;
```

Fig. 5–13 *Create Table statement examples*

Modifying a Table

After creating a table, the ALTER TABLE statement enables you to modify existing tables. The ALTER TABLE statement modifies existing tables by:

- Adding one or more columns to a table
- Adding or dropping a primary key
- Adding or dropping one or more unique or referential constraints
- Adding or dropping one or more check constraint definitions
- Altering the length of a VARCHAR column
- Altering a reference type column to add a scope
- Altering or dropping a partitioning key
- Changing table attributes such as the DATA CAPTURE, PCTFREE, LOCKSIZE, or APPEND mode option
- Activating the not logged initially attribute of the table

In this chapter, not all of these operations are discussed. Refer to the *DB2 UDB V7.1 SQL Reference* for each option of the ALTER TABLE statement.

Some of the attributes of a table can be changed only after the table is created. For example, if users want to change the default lock level or enable insert by append mode for a table, the `ALTER TABLE` statement should be issued for a table. Fig. 5–14 shows us the `ALTER TABLE` statement with these options used.

```
ALTER TABLE Employee
  ACTIVATE NOT LOGGED INITIALLY
  LOCKSIZE TABLE
  APPEND ON
  VOLATILE;
```

Fig. 5–14 *Alter Table statement*

The `LOCKSIZE` option indicates the granularity of locks used when the table is accessed; in this case, the use of a table lock. By default, row-level locks are used when tables are accessed. This option of the `ALTER TABLE` statement allows locking to be pushed up to the table level. Using table-level locks may improve the performance of queries by reducing the number of locks that need to be obtained and released. However, concurrency may be reduced since all locks are held over the complete table.

The `APPEND ON` option indicates whether data is appended to the end of a table or inserted where free space is available. Specifying `APPEND ON` can improve performance by allowing for faster inserts and eliminating the maintenance of free space information. Note that the table must not have a clustered index when specifying this option.

If you want to activate the `NOT LOGGED` attribute of the table for the current unit of work, the `ACTIVATE NOT LOGGED INITIALLY` option enables you to do this. However, notice that if you want to specify this option, the table must have been originally created with the `NOT LOGGED INITIALLY` attribute, and the create table transaction committed.

The `VOLATILE` parameter indicates to the optimizer that the cardinality of the table can vary significantly at run time, from empty to quite large. To access the table, the optimizer will use an index scan rather than a table scan, regardless of the statistics, if that access is index only (all columns referenced are in the index) or that access is able to apply a predicate in the index scan. An optional key word, `CARDINALITY`, is used to indicate that it is the number of rows in the table that is volatile and not the table itself.

Removing a Table

When you want to remove a table, issue this statement:

```
DROP TABLE EMPLOYEE;
```

Note that any objects that are directly or indirectly dependent on this table are deleted or made inoperative, for example, indexes, triggers, and views. Whenever a table is deleted, its description is deleted from the catalog and any packages that reference the object are invalidated.

To delete all of the rows from a table, without actually dropping it, you can use the ALTER TABLE statement:

```
ALTER TABLE name NOT LOGGED INITIALLY WITH EMPTY TABLE
```

The advantage of using this format over a DROP table is that all of the security definitions, indexes, and other database objects are preserved.

Views

Views are logical tables that are created using the CREATE VIEW statement. Once a view is defined, it may be accessed using DML statements, such as SELECT, INSERT, UPDATE, and DELETE, as if it were a base table. A view is a temporary table and the data in the view is only available during query processing. We will talk about the typed view in "Advanced SQL" on page 325.

With a view, you can make a subset of table data available to an application program and validate data that is to be inserted or updated. A view can have column names that are different from the names of corresponding columns in the original tables. The use of views provides flexibility in the way the application programs and end-user queries look at the table data.

A sample CREATE VIEW statement is shown below. The original table, EMPLOYEE, has columns named SALARY and COMM. For security reasons, this view is created from the ID, NAME, DEPT, JOB, and HIREDATE columns. In addition, we are restricting access on the column DEPT. This definition will only show the information of employees who belong to the department whose DEPTNO is 10.

```
CREATE VIEW EMP_VIEW1
(EMPID,EMPNAME,DEPTNO,JOBTITLE,HIREDATE)
AS SELECT ID,NAME,DEPT,JOB,HIREDATE FROM EMPLOYEE
   WHERE DEPT=10;
```

After the view has been created, the access privileges can be specified. This provides data security since a restricted view of the base table is accessible. As we have seen above, a view can contain a WHERE clause to restrict access to certain rows or can contain a subset of the columns to restrict access to certain columns of data.

 Note: A view is always defined using a SELECT statement.

The column names in the view do not have to match the column names of the base table. The table name has an associated schema as does the view name.

Once the view has been defined, it can be used in DML statements such as SELECT, INSERT, UPDATE, and DELETE (with restrictions). The database administrator can decide to provide a group of users with a higher level privilege on the view than the base table.

Views with Check Option

If the view definition includes conditions (such as a WHERE clause) and the intent is to ensure that any INSERT or UPDATE statement referencing the view will have the WHERE clause applied, the view must be defined using WITH CHECK OPTION. This option can ensure the integrity of the data being modified in the database. An SQL error will be returned if the condition is violated during an INSERT or UPDATE operation.

Fig. 5–15 is an example of a view definition using the WITH CHECK OPTION. The WITH CHECK OPTION is required to ensure that the condition is always checked. You want to ensure that the DEPT is always 10. This will restrict the input values for the DEPT column. When a view is used to insert a new value, the WITH CHECK OPTION is always enforced.

```
CREATE VIEW EMP_VIEW2
(EMPNO,EMPNAME,DEPTNO,JOBTITLE,HIREDATE)
AS SELECT ID,NAME,DEPT,JOB,HIREDATE FROM EMPLOYEE
    WHERE DEPT=10
WITH CHECK OPTION;
```

Fig. 5–15 *View definition using* WITH CHECK OPTION

If the view in Fig. 5–15 is used in an INSERT statement, the row will be rejected if the DEPTNO column is not the value 10. It is important to remember that there is no data validation during modification if the WITH CHECK OPTION is not specified.

If the view in Fig. 5–15 is used in a SELECT statement, the conditional (WHERE clause) would be invoked and the resulting table would only contain the matching rows of data. In other words, the WITH CHECK OPTION does not affect the result of a SELECT statement.

The WITH CHECK OPTION must not be specified for the following views:

- Views defined with the READ ONLY option (a read only view)
- Views that reference the NODENUMBER or PARTITION function, a nondeterministic function (e.g., RAND), or a function with external action
- Typed views (refer to "Advanced SQL" on page 325 for detailed information about typed views)

Nested View Definitions

If a view is based on another view, the number of predicates that must be evaluated is based on the WITH CHECK OPTION specification.

If a view is defined without WITH CHECK OPTION, the definition of the view is not used in the data validity checking of any insert or update operations. However, if the view directly or indirectly depends on another view defined with the WITH CHECK OPTION, the definition of that super view is used in the checking of any insert or update operation.

If a view is defined with the WITH CASCADED CHECK OPTION or just the WITH CHECK OPTION (CASCADED is the default value of the WITH CHECK OPTION), the definition of the view is used in the checking of any insert or update operations. In addition, the view inherits the search conditions from any updatable views on which the view depends. These conditions are inherited even if those views do not include the WITH CHECK OPTION. Then, the inherited conditions are multiplied together to conform to a constraint that is applied for any insert or update operations for the view or any views depending on the view.

As an example, if a view V2 is based on a view V1, and the check option for V2 is defined with the WITH CASCADED CHECK OPTION, the predicates for both views are evaluated when INSERT and UPDATE statements are performed against the view V2. Fig. 5–16 shows a CREATE VIEW statement using the WITH CASCADED CHECK OPTION. The view EMP_VIEW3 is created based on a view EMP_VIEW2, which has been created with the WITH CHECK OPTION (Fig. 5–15). If you want to insert or update a record to EMP_VIEW3, the record should have the values DEPTNO=10 and EMPNO>20.

> **Note:** Notice that the condition DEPTNO=10 is enforced for inserting or updating operations to EMP_VIEW3 even if EMP_VIEW2 does not include the WITH CHECK OPTION.

```
CREATE VIEW EMP_VIEW3 AS
  SELECT EMPNO,EMPNAME,DEPTNO FROM EMP_VIEW2
     WHERE EMPNO >20
WITH CASCADED CHECK OPTION;
```

Fig. 5–16 *View definition using the* WITH CASCADED CHECK OPTION

We can also specify the WITH LOCAL CHECK OPTION when creating a view. If a view is defined with the WITH LOCAL CHECK OPTION, the definition of the view is used in the checking of any insert or update operations. However, the view does not inherit the search conditions from any updatable views on which it depends.

As an example, refer to the nested view example shown in Fig. 5–17.

```
CREATE TABLE T1
    (C1 INT, C2 INT, C3 INT, C4 INT, C5 INT);
CREATE VIEW V1 AS
     SELECT * FROM T1 WHERE C1=1;
CREATE VIEW V2 AS
     SELECT * FROM V1 WHERE C2=1 WITH LOCAL CHECK OPTION;
CREATE VIEW V3 AS
     SELECT * FROM V2 WHERE C3=1;
CREATE VIEW V4 AS
     SELECT * FROM V3 WHERE C4=1 WITH CASCADED CHECK OPTION;
CREATE VIEW V5 AS
     SELECT * FROM V4 WHERE C5=1;
```

Fig. 5–17 *Nested view table and view creation statements*

We created one table and five views. V2 depends on V1, V3 on V2, V4 on V3, and V5 on V4. V2 includes WITH LOCAL CHECK OPTION and V4 includes WITH CASCADED CHECK OPTION.

Let us test some insert statements against these views.

1. This insert statement succeeds because the view V1 does not include the WITH CHECK OPTION.

```
INSERT INTO V1 VALUES (2,1,1,1,1);
```

2. The next insert statement will cause an error because V2 includes the WITH LOCAL CHECK OPTION, and the value does not conform to the definition of V2.

```
INSERT INTO V2 VALUES (1,2,1,1,1);
```

3. The following insert statement succeeds because V2 includes the WITH LOCAL CHECK OPTION, which means the definition of V2 is used for the checking but the one of V1 is not. Therefore, it succeeds regardless of the value of the column C1.

```
INSERT INTO V2 VALUES (2,1,1,1,1);
```

4. The next insert returns an error even though V3 does not include the WITH CHECK OPTION, because V3 inherits search conditions from the views on which V3 depends directly or indirectly if those views have the WITH CHECK OPTION. Therefore, the search condition of V2, which is C2=1, is inherited and used for the checking of this insert.

```
INSERT INTO V3 VALUES (1,2,1,1,1);
```

5. The next insert succeeds because V3 does not inherit the definition of V1.

```
INSERT INTO V3 VALUES (2,1,1,1,1);
```

6. The next insert should return an error because V4 includes the WITH CASCADED CHECK OPTION, but the value does not conform to the definition of V4.

```
INSERT INTO V4 VALUES (1,1,1,2,1);
```

7. These insert statements return errors because V4 inherits all search conditions of V4, V3, V2, and V1. Each of these statements does not conform to the definition of V3 or V1.

```
INSERT INTO V4 VALUES (1,1,2,1,1);
INSERT INTO V4 VALUES (2,1,1,1,1);
```

8. This one succeeds because V5 does not include WITH CHECK OPTION, which means the condition C5=1 is not used.

```
INSERT INTO V5 VALUES (1,1,1,1,2);
```

9. This insert statement returns an error for the same reason as does the fourth example: V5 inherits the definition of V4, that is C4=4. This insert does not conform to this condition.

```
INSERT INTO V5 VALUES (1,1,1,2,1);
```

10. This last example returns an error because the inserting row is checked using V4 and V4 inherits the definition of V3.

```
INSERT INTO V5 VALUES (1,1,2,1,1);
```

The inserting of rows into V5 must conform to the search conditions of V1, V2, V3, and V4. If the WITH LOCAL CHECK OPTION is specified for V4, the search conditions of V2 and V4 must be met. If the WITH CHECK OPTION is not specified for V4, the search condition of V2 must be met.

Modifying a View

Views are temporary table definitions. The view definition is stored in the system catalog tables. Therefore, if a backup of the database is performed, the view definition is contained in the backup image. The data contained in the view is only available when the view is being referenced in an SQL statement.

Unlike some other DB2 objects, a view definition cannot be altered using the ALTER statement. If a view definition needs to be changed in any way, the original view must be dropped and re-created with the desired configuration. (Note that in V7.1 there is the option to use the ALTER VIEW statement to alter a reference type column to alter the scope; however, this is the only action on a view definition that can be done.)

A view can become inoperative if any of the referenced database objects are dropped from the database. These view dependencies are stored in the system catalog view called SYSCAT.VIEWDEP.

The system catalog view SYSCAT.VIEWS and the system catalog table SYSIBM.SYSVIEWS contain a column called VALID that contains the character X if the view has become inoperative. If the base table EMPLOYEE is dropped, the views EMP_VIEW1 and EMP_VIEW2 would become inoperative as shown in Fig. 5–18.

```
SELECT VIEWNAME,VIEWCHECK,READONLY,VALID
FROM SYSCAT.VIEWS
WHERE VIEWSCHEMA ='DB2ADMIN'


VIEWNAME              VIEWCHECK READONLY VALID
-----------------     --------- -------- -----
EMP_VIEW1             N         N        X
EMP_VIEW2             C         N        X

 2 record(s) selected.
```

Fig. 5–18 *Inoperative views*

Two inoperative views are shown in Fig. 5–18 since the valid column contains the value X (a value of Y means that the view is valid). The query in Fig. 5–18 does not show the contents of the TEXT column. This column contains the original CREATE VIEW statement text. The column VIEWCHECK corresponds to the WITH CHECK OPTION in the CREATE VIEW statement. A value of N means that no check option was specified, L means that the WITH LOCAL CHECK OPTION was specified, and C means that the WITH CASCADED CHECK OPTION was specified.

Note: A view will always enforce the base table constraints. These constraints could include a primary key, foreign key, table-check, or not-null constraint.

Removing a View

When you want to remove a view, issue the statement:

```
DROP VIEW EMP_VIEW1;
```

Note that when the specified view is deleted, the definition of any view or trigger that is directly or indirectly dependent on that view is marked inoperative, and any packages dependent on a view that is dropped or marked inoperative will be invalidated.

View Classifications

Views can be classified by the operations they allow. Views can be deletable, updatable, insertable, and read only. Essentially a view type is established according to its update capabilities, and the classification of the view indicates the kind of SQL operation that can be performed using the view.

Referential and check constraints are not taken into account when determining the classification of the view.

The rules determining the classification of a view are numerous and are not listed here. For details on DB2 V7.1 on the classification of views, please refer to the CREATE VIEW statement description in the *DB2 UDB V7.1 SQL Reference*.

Indexes

An *index* is a list of the locations of rows sorted by the contents of one or more specified columns. Indexes are typically used to improve the query performance. However, they can also serve a logical data design purpose. For example, a unique index does not allow the entry of duplicate values in columns, thereby guaranteeing that no rows of a table are the same. Indexes can be created to specify ascending or descending order by the values in a column. The indexes contain a pointer, known as a *record id (RID)*, to the physical location of the rows in the table.

These are two main purposes for creating indexes:

- To ensure uniqueness of values
- To improve query performance

More than one index can be defined on a particular base table, which can have a beneficial effect on the performance of queries. However, the more indexes there are, the more the database manager must work to keep the indexes up-to-date during update, delete, and insert operations. Creating a large number of indexes for a table that receives many updates can slow down processing.

Unique Index and Non-unique Index

A *unique index* guarantees the uniqueness of the data values in a table's columns. The unique index can be used during query processing to perform faster retrieval of data. The uniqueness is enforced at the end of the SQL statement that updates rows or inserts new rows. The uniqueness is also checked during the execution of the CREATE INDEX statement. If the table already contains rows with duplicate key values, the index is not created.

A *nonunique index* can also improve query performance by maintaining a sorted order for the data.

Depending on how many columns are used to define a key, you can have one of the following types:

- An *atomic key* is a single column key.
- A *composite key* is composed of two or more columns.

The following are types of keys used to implement constraints:

- A *unique key* is used to implement unique constraints. A unique constraint does not allow two different rows to have the same values on the key columns.
- A *primary key* is used to implement entity integrity constraints. A primary key is a special type of unique key. There can be only one primary key per table. The primary key column must be defined with the not null option.
- A *foreign key* is used to implement referential integrity constraints. Referential constraints can only reference a primary key or unique constraint. The values of a foreign key can only have values defined in the primary key or unique constraint they are referencing or NULL values. (A foreign key is not an index.)

Referential Integrity and Indexes

We have discussed how defining a primary key will ensure the uniqueness of column values and that the primary key is maintained using an index. The index supporting a primary key is known as the primary index of the table. If a constraint name is not provided, DB2-generated indexes are given the name SYSIBM.SQL<timestamp>.

Indexes supporting primary or unique key constraints cannot be dropped explicitly. To remove primary or unique key constraints indexes, you need to use the ALTER TABLE statement. Primary key indexes are dropped with the DROP PRIMARY KEY option. Unique key indexes are dropped using the DROP UNIQUE (CONSTRAINT NAME) option.

> **Note:** DB2 uses unique indexes and the NOT NULL option to maintain primary and unique key constraints.

Null Values and Indexes

It is important to understand the difference between a primary or unique key constraint and a unique index. DB2 uses two elements to implement the relational database concept of primary and unique keys: unique indexes and the NOT NULL constraint. Therefore, unique indexes do not enforce the primary key constraint by themselves since they can allow a null value. Null values are unknown, but, when it comes to indexing, a null value is treated as equal to all other null values. You cannot insert a `NULL` value twice if the column is a key of a unique-index because it violates the uniqueness rule for the index.

General Indexing Guidelines

Indexes consume disk space. The amount of disk space will vary depending on the length of the key columns. The size of the index will increase as more data is inserted into the base table. Therefore, consider the disk space required for indexes when planning the size of the database. Some of the indexing considerations include:

- Primary and unique key constraints will always create a system-generated unique index.
- It is usually beneficial to create indexes on foreign key constraint columns.

You can estimate the disk space consumed by an index using the Control Center. If you are creating an index using the Control Center, you can see the **Estimate Size** button. Clicking this button brings up the Estimate Size panel. You can supply the total number of rows and so forth from this panel and get the estimated size.

Note: The most columns possible in an index key is 16 and the most indexes allowed on a table is 32767 (or storage). The longest index key that includes all overhead is 1024 bytes.

Index Only Access (Unique Index Include)

The `INCLUDE` clause specifies additional columns to be appended to the set of index key columns. Any columns included with this clause are not used to enforce uniqueness. These included columns may improve the performance of some queries through index only access. This option may:

- Eliminate the need to access data pages for more queries
- Eliminate redundant indexes
- Maintain the uniqueness of an index

See the following example. If `select empno,firstnme,job from empno` is issued to the table on which this index resides, all of the required data can be retrieved from the index without reading data pages. It may improve performance.

```
CREATE UNIQUE INDEX EMP_IX
  ON EMPLOYEE(EMPNO)
  INCLUDE(FIRSTNME,JOB)
```

Bi-Directional Index

The ALLOW REVERSE SCANS index creation clause enables both forward and reverse scans, that is, in the order defined at index creation time and in the opposite (or reverse) order. This option allows you to:

- Facilitate MIN and MAX functions
- Fetch previous key
- Eliminate the need for the optimizer to create a temporary table for the reverse scan
- Eliminate redundant reverse order index

If the index is ordered in ascending order from left to right across its leaf pages, a bidirectional index contains leaf pointers pointing in both directions, that is, to left and right neighboring leaf pages. Therefore, a bidirectional index can be scanned or leaf-traversed from left to right (ascending) or right to left (descending). For example:

```
CREATE UNIQUE INDEX EMP_IX
  ON EMPLOYEE(EMPNO)
  INCLUDE(FIRSTNME,JOB)
  ALLOW REVERSE SCANS;
```

In this example, if you issue select * from EMPLOYEE order by EMPNO desc to the EMPLOYEE table, a sort operation will not take place.

Modifying an Index

Index attributes cannot be changed without re-creating the index definition. For example, you cannot add a column to the list of key columns without dropping the previous definition and creating a new index. You can add a comment to describe the purpose of the index using the COMMENT ON statement.

If you want to modify your index, you have to drop the index first and then create the index again. There is no ALTER INDEX statement.

Removing an Index

When you want to remove an index, issue the following statement:

```
DROP INDEX EMP_IX;
```

Note that packages having a dependency on a dropped index or index specification are invalidated.

Index Advisor

The DB2 V7.1 Index Advisor is a utility for automatically recommending indexes for the user to create. The Index Advisor helps you to:

- Find the best indexes for a problem query
- Find the best indexes for a set of queries (a workload), subject to resource limits that are optionally applied
- Test an index on a workload without having to create the index

The Index Advisor can be invoked using either:

- A SmartGuide, called the Index SmartGuide, available from the Control Center.
- The command `db2advis`

For more information on the Index Advisor, refer to the *DB2 UDB V7.1 Administration Guide: Performance.*

Database Design and Implementation

The best way to understand data type selection is to design a database and implement the design using DB2. We will create a database that can be used to schedule and track the results of a certification program. This database will be used to illustrate many aspects of the SQL language and features of DB2.

This database will be used to schedule test candidates' exams and, following the completion of the test, it will contain the candidates' test scores.

The database and its application will need to perform the following tasks:

1. Insert/update/delete testing center information

2. Insert/update/delete test information

3. Insert/update/delete test candidate information

4. Guarantee a uniquely identified test name, regardless of the test number

5. Schedule a candidate to take a test

6. Update candidate test scores once exams have been completed

7. Determine which candidates qualify for certification

8. Generate various reports on the candidates and tests

The database will be named DB2CERT. The data to be stored in the DB2CERT database can easily be grouped into three reference tables and a fourth table used to relate the other tables. The primary relationship can be defined as *a test candidate takes a specific test at a test center.*

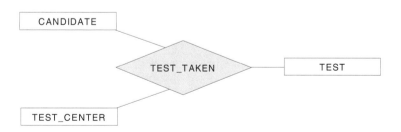

Fig. 5–19 *Tables for the DB2CERT database*

Fig. 5–19 shows the relationships within the problem domain. The rectangles represent the base tables: CANDIDATE, TEST_CENTER, and TEST. The fourth table is a relationship table called TEST_TAKEN.

DB2CERT Database Table Descriptions

The following is a list of tables that will be used in the DB2CERT database:

- The CANDIDATE table stores information about each test candidate for the DB2 Certification Program. Data such as candidate name, address, candidate ID, and phone number will be stored in this table. A data record represents a single test candidate (person).

- The TEST_CENTER table stores information about the test centers where a candidate can take a DB2 Certification exam. Data such as the test-center name, address, number of seats at the test center, test center ID, and its phone number will be stored in this table. A data record represents a single test-center location.

- The TEST table stores information about each of the DB2 Certification exams. Data such as the test name, type, test ID, cut score (passing percentage) and the length of each test will be stored in this table. A data record represents a single test. For our example, there are three tests in the DB2 Certification Program; therefore, there are only three data records in this table. A test name must be uniquely identified.

- The TEST_TAKEN table associates the records from the other three tables. It serves the dual purpose of scheduling tests and tracking each test result. Data such as the candidates' test scores, date_taken, start time, and seat number will be stored in this table. This will be the most active of the four tables since multiple exams must be taken by each candidate to become certified, and each test taken will have a corresponding data record in this table.

Once you have defined the tables and their relationships, the following should be defined:

1. User-defined data types

2. Columns or attributes for the tables

3. (Optional) primary keys (PK) for the tables

4. (Optional) unique keys for the tables

5. (Optional) foreign keys (referential constraints) for the tables

6. (Optional) table check constraints for the tables

7. (Optional) triggers for the database

In Fig. 5–20, the database design is shown. The rectangles represent the entities or tables. The columns or attributes are shown as ellipses. Note that some of the columns are derived columns. A derived column is a column that represents a concept and not a physical attribute of an object. The derived columns are included in the model since their values will be populated by the database using a constraint mechanism.

We must map the attributes shown in Fig. 5–20 to DB2 as supported data types or user-defined data types. To demonstrate some of the powerful features of DB2, we have decided to create distinct types for many of the attributes.

It is beneficial to have a primary key defined for each of the tables since this will ensure uniqueness of the data records. The attributes that are <u>underlined</u> will be used as primary keys. We will also create unique keys to illustrate their use. Unique key attributes are <u>double underlined</u>.

In the previous section, we mentioned that there will be four tables in the DB2CERT database. However, the design shown in Fig. 5–20 has only three tables defined: They are shown as rectangles. There is an implied table defined in the relationship *candidate takes a test*. A table is required to store each occurrence of a candidate taking a certification test.

We will impose a restriction on the candidates: They can only take the test once on any given day. A candidate can take different tests on the same day, but not the same test. With this restriction in place, we will define a primary key for the *test_taken* table as a composite key including NUMBER (test ID), CID (candidate ID) and DATE_TAKEN (the date of the test). By defining the primary key as a combination of these three values, we can enforce this constraint.

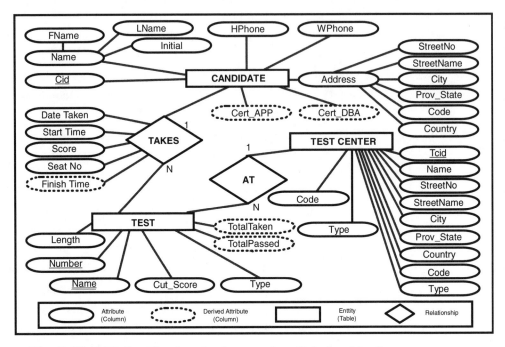

Fig. 5–20 *DB2 Certification database entity - Relationship diagram*

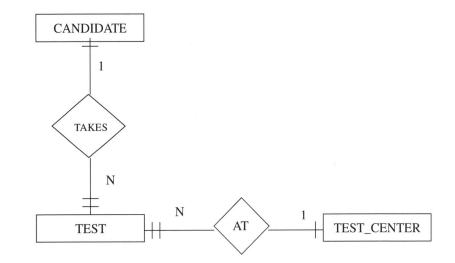

Fig. 5–21 *DB2 Certification database entity - Basic relationship diagram*

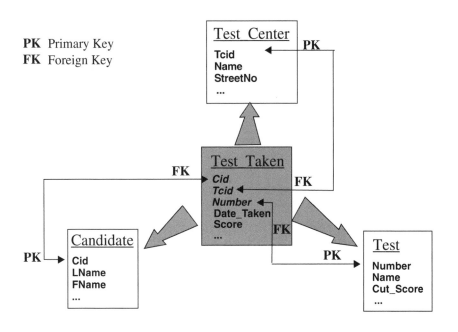

Fig. 5–22 *DB2 Certification database - Referential integrity*

The diamond shapes are used to describe the relationships between the tables, including the parent-child relationship. For example, there is a one-to-many relationship between the CANDIDATE and the TEST_TAKEN table because a single candidate can take many tests. This relationship is shown by denoting the values of 1 and N (many) on the appropriate side of the diamond.

The database design shown in Fig. 5–20 is just one type of diagramming technique. A logical database design can be represented in a number of ways, but it should not dictate the physical implementation of the database. We have included it here because it will be used in many of the SQL statements throughout the rest of the book.

Define User-Defined Data Types

If you wish to utilize user-defined data types, they must exist in your database before they can be referenced in a CREATE TABLE statement.

We have decided to create a number of user-defined data types as shown in Fig. 5–23. The candidate_id, test_id, center_id, and phone data types are all based on the fixed-length character (CHAR) data type. These attributes were chosen to be user defined because they have meaning in their structure, and they should not be used in expressions with other character data types. For example, a telephone number data type could be defined and then a user-defined function could be created to extract the area code. The function would only be used for phone data types.

```
CREATE DISTINCT TYPE candidate_id AS CHAR(8)
    WITH COMPARISONS
CREATE DISTINCT TYPE test_id AS CHAR(6)
    WITH COMPARISONS
CREATE DISTINCT TYPE center_id AS CHAR(4)
    WITH COMPARISONS
CREATE DISTINCT TYPE phone AS CHAR(10)
    WITH COMPARISONS
CREATE DISTINCT TYPE score AS DECIMAL(6,2)
    WITH COMPARISONS
CREATE DISTINCT TYPE minutes AS SMALLINT
    WITH COMPARISONS
```

Fig. 5–23 *Defining the user-defined data types*

We also decided to create some numeric user-defined data types, including the data types `score` and `minutes`.

Defining Columns

Designing a database involves many considerations. We will only examine some of these considerations in this book. If we use the database design in Fig. 5–20 as a starting point, we can start creating database objects.

The first step in creating a database is to issue the CREATE DATABASE command. This command is not part of the SQL since each database product has a different syntax for the creation of a database. An important consideration during the creation of the database (from a design point of view) is the specification of the CODESET and TERRITORY. For more information code pages, see See "Code Page Considerations" on page 230.

Once the database has been created, we can start creating objects. We can create distinct (user-defined) data types as shown in Fig. 5–23. Let us start creating tables. The database design had a number of attributes shown. Each of these attributes will be a column in the table definitions.

Every DB2 table contains one or more columns. The tables and their corresponding columns are given names. In the previous sections, we discussed all of the data types that can be used for column definitions.

Database Objects

Data is placed in a DB2 table using the SQL statement INSERT or UPDATE. (The LOAD and IMPORT utilities are other options.) Usually, it is desirable for each column, or data value, to have a value. Sometimes, there is no value provided for a column during the INSERT statement. If the column is defined as NOT NULL, the INSERT statement will fail. If a default value is defined, it will be stored.

The table in Fig. 5–24 is called DB2CERT.CANDIDATE and contains 15 columns.

Each column is given a name and a data type. There are three user-defined data types being used in the DB2CERT.CANDIDATE table. These data types are CANDIDATE_ID, PHONE, and BITMAP. There are also constraints defined for the valid values for some of the columns. For example, the null constraint is specified for all of the columns except HPHONE, WPHONE, INITIAL, and PHOTO.

```
CREATE TABLE db2cert.candidate (
    Cid candidate_id NOT NULL,
    LName VARCHAR(30) NOT NULL,
    FName VARCHAR(30) NOT NULL,
    Initial CHAR(1),
    HPhone phone,
    WPhone phone,
    StreetNo VARCHAR(8) NOT NULL,
    StreetName VARCHAR(20) NOT NULL,
    City VARCHAR(30) NOT NULL,
    Prov_State VARCHAR(30) NOT NULL,
    Code CHAR(6) NOT NULL,
    Country VARCHAR(20)) NOT NULL,
    Cert_DBA CHAR(1) NOT NULL WITH DEFAULT 'N',
    Cert_APP CHAR(1) NOT NULL WITH DEFAULT 'N',
CONSTRAINT Unique_Candidate
PRIMARY KEY (Cid));
```

Fig. 5–24 *Creating the* CANDIDATE *table*

Keys

Keys are a special set of columns defined on a table. They can be used to uniquely identify a row or to reference a uniquely identified row from another table. Keys can be classified either by the columns they are composed of or by the database constraint they support.

Depending on how many columns are used to define a key, you can have one of the following types:

- An *atomic key* is a single column key.
- A *composite key* is composed of two or more columns.

The following are types of keys used to implement constraints:

- A *unique key* is used to implement unique constraints. A unique constraint does not allow two different rows to have the same values in the key columns.
- A *primary key* is used to implement entity integrity constraints. A primary key is a special type of unique key. There can only be one primary key per table. The primary key column must be defined with the NOT NULL option.
- A *foreign key* is used to implement referential integrity constraints. Referential constraints can only reference a primary key or unique key. The values of a foreign key can only have values defined in the primary key or unique key they are referencing or the NULL value.

Defining Primary Keys

It is sometimes beneficial to define a primary key for each of your DB2 tables since this will guarantee the uniqueness of a column value or group of column values (composite key). In Fig. 5–24, the primary key for the table candidate is defined as the column Cid (candidate ID). By specifying this column as a primary key, DB2 will create a system-unique index if one does not already exist.

Let us look at the other tables representing the tests and the test centers. In Fig. 5–25, the test and test_center tables are shown. These tables each have a primary key defined.

In our example, the primary key constraint was given a name (unique_test and unique_center) for referencing purposes. If a name is not provided, DB2 will assign a system-generated name to the constraint.

```
CREATE TABLE db2cert.test (
Number test_id NOT NULL,
Name    VARCHAR(50) NOT NULL,
Type    CHAR(1)     NOT NULL,
Cut_Score score     NOT NULL,
Length minutes      NOT NULL,
TotalTaken SMALLINT NOT NULL,
TotalPassed SMALLINT NOT NULL,
CONSTRAINT Unique_Test
PRIMARY KEY(Number),
CONSTRAINT Unique_Test_Name UNIQUE (Name),
CONSTRAINT Test_Type CHECK (Type IN ('P','B')))

CREATE TABLE db2cert.test_center (
Tcid center_id      NOT NULL,
Name VARCHAR(40)    NOT NULL,
StreetNo VARCHAR(8) NOT NULL,
StreetName VARCHAR(20) NOT NULL,
City VARCHAR(30)    NOT NULL,
Prov_State VARCHAR(30) NOT NULL,
Country VARCHAR(20) NOT NULL,
Code CHAR(6)        NOT NULL,
Type CHAR(1)        NOT NULL,
Phone phone         NOT NULL,
No_Seats SMALLINT NOT NULL,
CONSTRAINT Unique_Center
PRIMARY KEY (Tcid))
```

Fig. 5–25 *Defining the test and test_center tables*

Defining Unique Keys

Unique keys can be used to enforce uniqueness on a set of columns. A table can have more than one unique key defined. The test table definition in Fig. 5–25 uses a unique constraint (Unique_Test_Name) on column Name to ensure that a test name is not used twice. There is also a primary key constraint on the column Number to avoid duplicate test numbers.

Having unique constraints on more than one set of columns of a table is different than defining a composite unique key that includes the whole set of columns. For example, if we define a composite primary key on the columns Number and Name, there is still a chance that a test name will be duplicated using a different test number.

Note: A unique index is always created for primary (if one does not already exist) or unique key constraints. If you define a constraint name, it will be used to name the index; otherwise, a system-generated name will be used for the index.

Defining Foreign Keys

A foreign key is a reference to the data values in another table. There are different types of foreign key constraints. Let us look at the remaining table in the DB2 Certification database and, in particular, its foreign key constraints. In Fig. 5–26, there is one composite primary key defined and three foreign key constraints.

The primary key is defined as the columns cid, tcid, and number. The foreign key constraints will perform the following:

- If a record in the candidate table is deleted, all matching records in the test_taken table will be deleted (DELETE CASCADE).
- If a test center in the test_center table is deleted, all of the matching records in the test_taken table will be deleted (DELETE CASCADE).
- If a test in the test table is deleted and there are matching records in the test_taken table, the DELETE statement will result in an error (DELETE RESTRICT).
- If a test in the test table is updated and there are matching records in the test_taken table, the UPDATE statement will result in an error (UPDATE RESTRICT).

Note: A foreign key constraint always relates to the primary or unique constraint of the table in the references clause.

```
CREATE TABLE db2cert.test_taken (
   Cid candidate_id NOT NULL,
   Tcid center_id NOT NULL,
   Number test_id NOT NULL,
   Date_Taken date NOT NULL WITH DEFAULT,
   Start_Time TIME NOT NULL,
   Finish_Time TIME NOT NULL,
   Score score,
   Seat_No CHAR(2) NOT NULL,
   CONSTRAINT number_const
PRIMARY KEY (Cid,Tcid,Number),
FOREIGN KEY (Cid)
   REFERENCES db2cert.candidate ON DELETE CASCADE,
FOREIGN KEY (Tcid)
   REFERENCES db2cert.test_center ON DELETE CASCADE,
FOREIGN KEY (Number)
   REFERENCES db2cert.test ON DELETE RESTRICT
                            ON UPDATE RESTRICT)
```

Fig. 5–26 *Defining the test_taken table*

Defining parent-child relationships between tables is known as declarative referential integrity because the child table refers to the parent table. These constraints are defined during table creation or by using the ALTER TABLE SQL statement. DB2 will enforce referential constraints for all INSERT, UPDATE, and DELETE activity.

Summary

In this chapter, we concentrated on the SQL Data Definition Language (DDL). DDL is used to create, modify, and remove database objects. There are three main statements in DDL: CREATE, ALTER, and DROP. If you want to use a DB2 database, you may learn DDL first to create some database objects. There are many kinds of objects in a DB2 database. Some of them are created by a DB2 command, and some of them are created by DDL statements.

Here we focused on data types, tables, views, and indexes among the database objects created by DDL. A data type is used to specify the attribute of columns in a table. DB2 has two kinds of data types: built-in data types and user-defined data types. The built-in type is a DB2-supplied data type and falls into four main categories: Numeric, String (including large object [LOB]), Datetime, and Datalink. Character data types (part of the String category) are associated with a character codepage. We also discussed that DB2 supports Unicode. The user-defined data type enables you to create your application-oriented data type based on the built-in data type.

A table consists of columns and rows and stores an unordered set of records. Each column has a data type as one of the attributes. A table itself can have some rules called CONSTRAINTS to guarantee the uniqueness of records or maintain the relationship between and within tables. It helps application programmers to evaluate the records or maintain the consistency between the tables. A view may also reduce some application development workload. A logical table is created and is based on the physical table or other views. A view can be created to limit access to sensitive data while allowing more general access to other data. An index is one of the most important objects for performance. It can also be used to guarantee the uniqueness of each record. We also introduced some new options in the CREATE and ALTER statements.

Manipulating Database Objects

- ◆ DATA MANIPULATION LANGUAGE

- ◆ RETRIEVING DATA

- ◆ INSERTING DATA

- ◆ UPDATING DATA

- ◆ DELETING DATA

- ◆ VIEW CLASSIFICATION

*I*n the previous chapter, we discussed the definition of various database objects using the Data Definition Language (DDL). In this chapter, we start manipulating the database objects using the portion of SQL known as Data Manipulation Language (DML). We will be populating (inserting) data into the database and retrieving the data using many powerful methods. Depending on the sophistication of the database users, they can use SQL to query the database. The majority of the SQL statements within a DB2 application involve DML statements. Therefore, application developers must understand the various methods of inserting, updating, and retrieving data from the database. We will start with simple retrieval statements and gradually introduce more complex methods of data manipulation. The DB2 Certification database will be used for most of the examples. There are four main DML SQL statements we consider: SELECT, INSERT, UPDATE, and DELETE.

Data Retrieval

SQL is based on mathematical principles, specifically set theory and relational algebra. The data is stored in the database as unordered sets of data records.

SQL is a set-oriented language and many of its language elements are directly related to relational algebraic terms, such as *PERMUTATION*, *PROJECTION*, *RESTRICTION*, and *JOIN*.

A set of data is represented in a DB2 database as a table or a view and is stored in a DB2 table without regard to order. To retrieve data in a particular order, an ORDER BY phrase must be added to a SELECT statement. Similarly, if the data is to be grouped, then a GROUP BY phrase must be added to the statement.

Now, let's review the DB2CERT database design defined in the previous chapter and manipulate data using various SQL statements. There are three main tables: CANDIDATE, TEST, and TEST_CENTER. Each of these tables represents a set of records that correspond to a test candidate (person), a test, and a test center (location). There is an associative table, known as the test_taken table, that is used to reflect the relationships among the three main tables. The test_taken table is used to schedule the test candidates and also to maintain their test scores.

 Note: The longest SQL statement is 65,535 bytes.

 Note: Remember that to execute any operation, one must have the necessary privileges.

Retrieving the Entire Table

The most basic of all retrieval command involves the SELECT statement with no other operators other than the name of the table. This SQL statement retrieves all of the candidates who have taken a DB2 Certification exam. The information requested is contained in the table TEST_TAKEN.

```
SELECT * FROM db2cert.test_taken
```

SQL is a data access language that consists of language statements and clauses. There are many optional clauses that can be used to modify the output. The output of a SELECT statement is known as a result set or result table. The results from the SELECT statement are shown next.

```
CID TCID NUMBER DATE_TAKEN START_TIME FINISH_TIME SCORE PASS_FAIL SEAT_NO
--- ---- ------ ---------- ---------- ----------- ----- --------- -------
111 TX01 500    01/01/2000 11:30:00   12:30:00       65 Y         1
111 TX01 501    02/02/2000 10:30:00   11:45:00       73 Y         1
111 TX01 502    03/03/2000 12:30:00   13:30:00       67 Y         1
222 TR01 500    01/01/2000 14:00:00   15:30:00       55 N         2
222 TR01 502    01/02/2000 09:00:00   10:15:00       53 N         2
222 TR01 502    02/18/2000 10:00:00   11:30:00       75 Y         2
333 TX01 500    03/01/2000 11:30:00   13:00:00       82 Y         2
333 TX01 501    12/29/2000 14:00:00   -               - -        1
333 TX01 502    03/02/2000 14:00:00   14:30:00       92 Y         1

    9 record(s) selected.
```

Fig. 6–1 *Query result from simple SELECT statement*

In SQL, the asterisk or star character (*) is used to indicate that all columns of a table are being referenced. In this example, the SQL statement refers to all of the columns defined for the DB2CERT.TEST_TAKEN table.

If the table is altered and a new column is added to the table definition, the result set would contain the new column.

Note: Adding a new column to an existing table will result in default values being populated for the existing rows.

Since the output of the SQL statement using the asterisk(*) character varies according to the table definition, it is recommended that you specify all of the column names you want to see in the SELECT statement.

We could have obtained the same result as in Fig. 6–1 with the following SQL statement.

```
SELECT cid, tcid, number,date_taken,start_time,
       finish_time,score,seat_no
FROM db2cert.test_taken;
```

This SQL statement will provide the same result table even if new columns are added to the table definition.

Note: The asterisk (*) character is used to refer to all of the columns defined for a table. The order of the columns in the result table is the same order as specified in the CREATE TABLE or CREATE VIEW statement.

The FROM clause is required for the DML SQL statement since it describes the location (table or view) of the data. Our example references a single table called db2cert.test_taken. The SELECT and FROM clauses are required in all data retrieval statements. The list of columns following the SELECT keyword is referred to as the *select list*.

Projecting Columns from a Table

Projection is a relational operation that allows you to retrieve a subset of the defined columns from a table. The next example restricts the output from the select command so that only the candidate ID, test center, and test number attributes from the test_taken table are shown (Fig. 6–1).

```
SELECT cid,tcid,number FROM db2cert.test_taken
```

The output of this SELECT statement is shown in Fig. 6–2. The order of the columns in the result table will always match the order in the select list. The order of the columns as they were defined in the CREATE TABLE or CREATE VIEW statement is ignored when a select list is provided in the SQL statement. In this example, the order of the columns is similar to the order in the CREATE TABLE statement, since the CID column was defined prior to TCID and NUMBER columns.

```
CID TCID NUMBER
--- ---- ------
111 TX01 500
111 TX01 501
111 TX01 502
222 TR01 500
222 TR01 502
222 TR01 502
333 TX01 500
333 TX01 501
333 TX01 502

  9 record(s) selected.
```

Fig. 6–2 *Result table of a projection*

Changing the Order of the Columns

Permutation is the relational operation that allows you to change the order of the columns in your result table. Permutation is used every time you select columns in an order different than the order defined in the CREATE TABLE statement. For example, to display the test center ID prior to the candidate IDs and the test number you could execute the following:

```
SELECT tcid,cid,number FROM db2cert.test_taken
```

The result of this SELECT statement specifies a select list in a different order than was defined in the table shown in Fig. 6–3.

```
TCID CID NUMBER
---- --- ------
TX01 111 500
TX01 111 501
TX01 111 502
TR01 222 500
TR01 222 502
TR01 222 502
TX01 333 500
TX01 333 501
TX01 333 502

  9 record(s) selected.
```

Fig. 6–3 *Result table of a permutation*

Note: We refer to the output of a SELECT statement as the *result table* because the output of all SELECT statements can be considered a relational table.

Restricting Rows from a Table

Restriction is a relational operation that will filter the resulting rows of a table. Restriction can be accomplished through the use of *predicates* defined in an SQL WHERE clause.

Note: A predicate is a condition placed on the data. The result of the condition is TRUE, FALSE, or UNKNOWN.

To restrict the result set, we need to add a WHERE clause to the SQL statement. The WHERE clause specifies conditions or predicates that must be evaluated by DB2 before the result table is returned to the end-user. There are many valid types of predicates that can be used. In the following example, the equality (=) predicate is being used to restrict the records to only those candidates who have taken a DB2 Certification test at the test center TR01.

```
SELECT tcid,cid FROM db2cert.test_taken
                              WHERE tcid ='TR01'
```

The WHERE clause also accepts other comparison operators, such as greater than (>), less than (<), greater than or equal to (>=), less than or equal to (<=), and not equal to (<>). This statement is an example of a *basic predicate*. A basic predicate compares two values.

Note: Trying to execute this example SQL statement will result in a data type compatibility error, because the column tcid is defined with a user-defined distinct data type (UDT).

Predicate Evaluation for UDTs

The column tcid was defined as a *user-defined distinct data type* (UDT). To make the comparison in the WHERE clause valid, a casting function needs to be used. This technique is shown below:

```
SELECT tcid, cid FROM db2cert.test_taken
    WHERE tcid=CAST('TR01' AS db2cert.center_id)
```

Predicate evaluation requires that the data types be compatible (same data type or a compatible data type).

We can accomplish the data type conversion (cast) using one of two methods:

- Use the CAST expression
- Use a casting function

In the example above, we used the CAST expression to perform a comparison using compatible data types.

The CAST expression requires that you specify the input data value and the output data type. In our example, the input data value is TR01 and the output data type is db2cert.center_id (the full two-part name of the UDT).

The other method of converting UDTs involves the use of a system-generated SQL function known as a *casting function*. When we created the user-defined data type called db2cert.center_id, functions to cast between the distinct type (db2cert.center_id) and its source type (CHAR) and six comparison operators (=, <>, <, <=, >, and >=) are also generated.

The following example uses the casting function:

```
SELECT tcid,cid FROM db2cert.test_taken
        WHERE tcid=db2cert.center_id('TR01')
```

The casting function used in this example is called db2cert.center_id. It is easy to remember the name of the casting function, since it is the same as the UDT itself. It is also possible to cast the left-side argument using the CHAR() casting function as follows:

```
SELECT tcid,cid FROM db2cert.test_taken
            WHERE CHAR(tcid)='TR01'
```

Restricting Rows Using Multiple Conditions

It is possible to combine multiple conditions (predicates) in a single SQL statement. The predicates can be combined using boolean operators, such as the AND operator. These operators allow you to combine multiple conditions in a single SQL statement. The order of the predicate evaluation will not affect the result set (known as set closure). The DB2 optimizer will decide the order in which the conditions are applied to maximize query performance based on statistical information and other factors.

The next example retrieves the records for the test candidates who took a test at test center TR01 and achieved a score greater than 65. The rows that satisfy the predicates are known as the *qualifying rows*. The following example is an SQL statement using multiple predicates:

```
SELECT tcid,cid,score
FROM db2cert.test_taken
        WHERE tcid=db2cert.center_id('TR01')
        AND score > db2cert.score(65)
```

Manipulating Database Objects

In addition to user-defined datatypes, DB2 UDB Version 7.1 introduces structured types that can be used within table definitions. User-defined types and structured types allow for greater control of data comparisons within a database as well as giving the relational model a more object-oriented feel. However, UDTs require the use of casting functions and may require more knowledge by end-users and developers.

Selecting Columns from Multiple Tables

There are basically two operations that combine columns from multiple tables in a single SQL statement. These operations are:

- Cartesian product
- Join

Cartesian Product

A *cartesian product* is a relational operation that will merge all the values from one table with all the values from another table. This operation is not used frequently because the result table can be very large.

The number of rows in the result table is always equal to the product of the number of rows in the qualifying rows for each of the tables being accessed.

The following example is a cartesian product of all test numbers and test names from the test table.

```
SELECT number,name FROM db2cert.test

NUMBER NAME
------ --------------------------------------------------------
500    DB2 Fundamentals
501    DB2 Administration
502    DB2 Application Development

 3 record(s) selected.
```

Fig. 6–4 *Simple query (1)*

The following example is a simple select of all candidates from the test_taken table.

```
SELECT cid,tcid FROM db2cert.test_taken

CID TCID
--- ----
222 TR01
222 TR01
222 TR01
111 TX01
111 TX01
111 TX01
333 TX01
333 TX01
333 TX01

  9 record(s) selected.
```

Fig. 6–5 *Simple query (2)*

An example of a cartesian product result table is shown in Fig. 6–6.

```
SELECT db2cert.test_taken.number,cid,tcid
    FROM db2cert.test_taken,db2cert.test

NUMBER CID TCID
------ --- ----
500    111 TX01
501    111 TX01
502    111 TX01
500    222 TR01
502    222 TR01
502    222 TR01
500    333 TX01
501    333 TX01
502    333 TX01
500    111 TX01
501    111 TX01
502    111 TX01
500    222 TR01
502    222 TR01
502    222 TR01
500    333 TX01
501    333 TX01
502    333 TX01
500    111 TX01
501    111 TX01
502    111 TX01
500    222 TR01
502    222 TR01
502    222 TR01
500    333 TX01
501    333 TX01
502    333 TX01

  27 record(s) selected.
```

Fig. 6–6 *Cartesian product query*

There are two tables referenced in the FROM clause of this query. The tables are separated by commas. There is no relationship expression in the FROM clause. This type of query results in a cartesian product.

The result table is a representation of all possible combinations of the input tables. The `test` table has three rows and the `test_taken` table has nine rows. Therefore, the `select` statement shown in Fig. 6–6 returns 27 rows. Note the first column name in Fig. 6–6. It is necessary to fully qualify the column name by providing the schema name and table name with the column name because this column exists in both the `test` table and `test_taken` table. In this case, we needed to specify that the number column is to be retrieved from the `db2cert.test_taken` table and not the `db2cert.test` table.

By adding a predicate to a cartesian product SQL query, the result table can represent a more useful representation of the data. In Fig. 6–7, the query represents all of the tests that were taken by the candidate whose ID is `111`.

```
SELECT db2cert.test_taken.number,cid,tcid
   FROM db2cert.test_taken,db2cert.test
      WHERE cid=db2cert.candidate_id('111')

NUMBER CID TCID
------ --- ----
500    111 TX01
500    111 TX01
500    111 TX01
501    111 TX01
501    111 TX01
501    111 TX01
502    111 TX01
502    111 TX01
502    111 TX01

  9 record(s) selected.
```

Fig. 6–7 *Cartesian product with a predicate*

Adding a WHERE clause to your query does not always provide the desired result. In the example shown in Fig. 6–7, you want to know all of the tests that were taken by the candidate whose ID is `111` and the query returns nine rows. However, as the result in Fig. 6–1 shows, the candidate took only three tests. The query in Fig. 6–7 uses a WHERE clause to filter out the candidates whose ID is `111` from the `test_taken` table, but there was no filter on the `test_center` table. Therefore, the result of the query would always be a multiple of the number of testing centers. Usually, when multiple tables are referenced, you should include a cross-table relationship using a table merge or join method as shown in Fig. 6–8. We will examine table join methods in the next section.

```
SELECT db2cert.test_taken.number,cid,tcid
   FROM db2cert.test_taken,db2cert.test
      WHERE cid=db2cert.candidate_id('111')
            AND db2cert.test_taken.number=db2cert.test.number

NUMBER CID TCID
------ --- ----
500    111 TX01
501    111 TX01
502    111 TX01

  3 record(s) selected.
```

Fig. 6–8 *Join tables example*

Join

To avoid data redundancy it is recommended that the database tables be *normalized*. Following a normalization process, a number of related tables will exist. To satisfy some of the required queries, the tables must be reconstructed. The tables are reconstructed temporarily using a table join strategy to produce a single-result table.

The result tables in the previous examples usually provided candidate ID numbers and not the complete name of the test candidates. The candidate IDs are stored in the test_taken table, and the full names are stored in the candidate table. To obtain the name of a candidate, the data must be retrieved from the candidate table using a relationship or join strategy.

Consider an example that will list the name and phone numbers of candidates who were registered to take a DB2 Certification test in 2000. To accomplish this, we need to select data from two different tables:

- db2cert.candidate
- db2cert.test_taken

Let's retrieve a list of candidate names, phone numbers, and IDs from the candidate table. The candidate names were stored in multiple columns to allow for easy retrieval by last name.

```
SELECT fname,initial,lname,hphone,cid
   FROM db2cert.candidate
```

The output of this example follows. Pay special attention to the values in the CID column. It will be used as the *join column* in the next example.

```
FNAME      INITIAL LNAME       HPHONE     CID
---------  ------- ----------  ---------- ---
Bill       W       Wong        1115551234 111
George             Baklarz     2226543455 222
Susan      M       Visser      4442314244 333
Glen       R       Sheffield   5552143244 444
Jim        G       Stittle     6662341234 555
Kevin      W       Street      7773142134 666
Bert       F       Nicol       8886534534 777
Paul       C       Zikopoulos  9992112212 888

 8 record(s) selected..
```

Fig. 6–9 *A sample query result*

Now, let's retrieve the ID numbers of those candidates who were registered to take the test in 2000.

```
SELECT distinct cid FROM db2cert.test_taken
                WHERE YEAR(date_taken) = 2000
```

```
CID
---
222
111
333

 3 record(s) selected.
```

Fig. 6–10 *Retrieving the candidate IDs*

The candidate IDs in the test_taken table must correspond to a candidate ID in the candidate table because of the declarative referential integrity constraints. The parent table in the relationship is the candidate table and the child table (dependent table) is the test_taken table.

The result table from the second query in Fig. 6–10 does not include the test candidate 444 since that candidate did not have a test scheduled for 2000. We need to join the two result tables based on the candidate ID values. This column is known as the *join column*.

> **Note:** Query performance can significantly improve if the join columns are appropriately indexed.

The following single query will satisfy the end-user requirement.

```
SELECT distinct fname,initial,lname,hphone
    FROM db2cert.test_taken,db2cert.candidate
    WHERE YEAR(date_taken) = 2000
        AND db2cert.test_taken.cid=db2cert.candidate.cid
```

A table join requires a predicate that includes an expression based on columns from the tables referenced in the FROM clause. This is known as a *join predicate*. The FROM clause has not changed from the cartesian product examples. The only difference is in the join predicate (test_taken.cid = candidate.cid).

> **Note:** This kind of join operation is also known as INNER JOIN. An inner join displays only the rows that are present in both of the joined tables.

The table names needed to be explicitly stated because there is a column named cid in both of the referenced tables. When multiple tables are being accessed in a single query, you have to qualify the column names with the table name.

> **Note:** An error will occur if the columns being referenced are ambiguous (not properly qualified).

There is no defined limit, except in storage, to the number of tables that can be referenced in a single SQL statement. However, there is a 1012 column limit in the SELECT list of a query. (If the page size is 4K, the maximum number of columns in a select list is 500.)

Using Correlation Names

If each of the columns needed to be fully qualified with the table name, such as tableschema.tablename.columnname, the queries would become very large and cumbersome to work with. Fortunately, there is an easier way to qualify the ambiguous columns resulting from a multitable SELECT statement.

**Manipulating
Database Objects**

The columns can be qualified using a *correlation name*. A correlation name is a temporary alias for the tables referenced in an SQL statement. We rewrite the previous query using correlated names as follows:

```
SELECT distinct fname,initial,lname,hphone
    FROM db2cert.test_taken tt, db2cert.candidate c
    WHERE YEAR(date_taken) = 2000
                AND tt.cid = c.cid
```

The correlation name immediately follows the name of the table as stated in the FROM clause. In this example, the correlated name for the test_taken table is tt and the correlated name for the candidate table is c.

The correlated names are accessible within the SQL statement only. Following the execution of the SQL statement, the correlation name is no longer defined. Once a correlation name has been defined, it can be referenced in the rest of the query instead of the table name.

Note: Use simple, easy-to-remember correlation names. Table initials are good candidates for correlation names.

Sorting Your Output

We have been retrieving data from one or more tables. The order of the result table has not been specified in any of the SQL statements. The data is retrieved in an undetermined order if there is no ORDER BY clause in the SQL statement.

The following example produces a list of the test candidates in alphabetical order by last name for the candidates who have taken a DB2 Certification test at the TR01 test center.

```
SELECT lname,initial,fname
    FROM db2cert.candidate c,db2cert.test_taken tt
        WHERE c.cid=tt.cid
          AND tcid=db2cert.center_id('TR01')
        ORDER BY lname
```

This example contains a new clause, ORDER BY. After the ORDER BY clause, you can list the columns that will specify the sort order and the type of sort.

The SQL can be modified so that the output is changed to descending order by last name and a secondary order column on the first name in ascending order.

```
SELECT lname,fname,hphone
    FROM db2cert.candidate c,db2cert.test_taken tt
        WHERE c.cid=tt.cid
            AND tcid=db2cert.center_id('TR01')
            ORDER BY lname DESC, fname
```

In this example, the DESC keyword that follows the lname column indicates that the result table should be in descending order based on the last name. More than one record can have the same last name. This situation is quite common. There is a second column specified in the ORDER BY clause, fname. There is no keyword specifying the sort sequence based on the fname column. Therefore, the default ordering sequence (ascending) is used.

The next example contains three columns: lname, fname, and hphone. You can reference the column that should be used to sort the data using the column name or by specifying its position in the SELECT list. Using the column position is very useful when the column in the select list is made up of derived columns (calculated columns) that have no explicit name.

```
SELECT lname,fname,hphone
    FROM db2cert.candidate c,db2cert.test_taken tt
        WHERE c.cid=tt.cid
            AND tcid=db2cert.center_id('TR01')
            ORDER BY 1 DESC, 2
```

In this example, the sort order is specified using the column position. Therefore, the query result is exactly the same as the previous example.

You can also rename a column using an *alias*. The alias can then be referenced in the ORDER BY clause.

Note: The ORDER BY clause must be the last clause in your SQL statement.

Manipulating Database Objects

Derived Columns

There are some cases when you will need to perform calculations on the data. The SQL language has some basic mathematical and string functions built in. Mathematical operations include standard addition, subtraction, multiplication, and division.

The calculation can be defined in the WHERE clause of the SQL statement or the SELECT list. Suppose that you need to calculate a passing rate for a DB2 test. The passing rate is defined as the percentage of candidates that pass the test (totalpassed*100/totaltaken). The following SQL statement will accomplish this for us for test number 500:

```
SELECT number, totalpassed*100/totaltaken
      FROM test
      WHERE number=test_id('500')
```

In this example, the second column of the output list is a calculated column. Remember that you must use the column position if you want to use this calculated column for the ORDER BY clause unless you name it (as we now discuss).

 Note: Occasionally, the results of a derived column may not display as expected. The example using totalpassed*100/totaltaken will result in a value of 66 being retrieved. Since both the totalpassed and totaltaken columns are integers, the final result is also an integer and the fractional part is discarded. If this is not your desired result, you should use other functions (like decimal) to change the way the calculation is done or displayed.

Naming Derived/Calculated Columns

You can specify a column name for any expression. By providing the derived (calculated) column with a name, the ORDER BY clause can reference the derived name to allow for a more readable SQL statement.

The following SQL calculates the percentage of people that have passed the DB2 Certification exams and orders the output in descending order of the passing rate.

```
SELECT number,totalpassed*100/totaltaken AS PassedRate
    FROM test
    ORDER BY PassedRate DESC
```

The AS clause is used to rename the default name of an element in the select list. In this example, we are giving the name of PassedRate to the result of the division of columns totalpassed by totaltaken. The named column is used in the query to specify the column that should be used for the sorting of the output.

DB2 Functions

In DB2, there are different types of functions provided. For example, two types of functions provided by DB2 are scalar and column functions (a third type of function called a *table function* is not discussed here - for details on this function please refer to the *DB2 UDB V7.1 SQL Reference*):

- *Scalar functions* (also known as row functions) provide a result for each row of the result table. A scalar function can be used any place an expression is allowed.
- *Column functions* (also known as vector functions). They work with a group of rows to provide a result. The group is specified using a FULLSELECT and optionally grouped using the GROUP BY clause.

In this section, we introduce you to some of the SQL functions provided with DB2. SQL functions are categorized by their implementation type. Either the functions are built-in or they are extensions of DB2 and are known as user-defined functions (UDFs).

- *Built-in functions* are defined within the SQL standards, and they are provided by DB2. These can be either scalar, column or table functions.
- *User-defined functions (UDFs)* are not defined within the SQL standards because they are extensions of the current SQL language. These functions can be developed by a DB2 administrator or application developer. Once the UDFs have been created, they can be invoked by any end-user with the proper privileges. Some of the new functions provided in DB2 are scalar UDFs. The functions with the schema name of SYSFUN are provided by DB2.

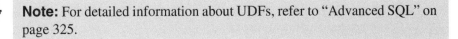

Note: For detailed information about UDFs, refer to "Advanced SQL" on page 325.

Scalar Functions

Scalar functions are applied to each row of data, and there is a per-row result provided. If we wanted to retrieve only the first three digits of telephone numbers for each candidate, we could use a scalar function. The function that will be used is called SUBSTR. The arguments for this function include a string data type column, a beginning offset, and length. The output data type and attribute of the function depend on the input data type and attribute.

The following example retrieves the telephone area code for the column wphone.

```
SELECT lname, SUBSTR(CHAR(wphone),1,3)
                    FROM db2cert.candidate
```

The SUBSTR function is a scalar function. In this example, SUBSTR returns a character string of three characters.

The result string corresponds to the first three characters of the wphone column. This function is known as a string function because it works with any string data type. If we wanted to provide the output column with a meaningful name, we could provide an alias, as was done for calculated columns.

In the example above, the substring starts from the beginning of the string because we indicate one (1) as the second parameter of the function. The length of the resulting string is indicated in the third argument. In our example, the length is three. Note that the data type of the wphone column is phone, so a casting function is used to convert the phone data type to the char data type.

The following query will provide the month when the exam was taken. The input for this function is a DATE string and the output is a character string.

```
SELECT fname, MONTHNAME(date_taken)
            FROM candidate c, test_taken tt
            WHERE c.cid=tt.cid
```

Column Functions

Column functions provide a single result for a group of qualifying rows for a specified table or view. Many common queries can be satisfied using column functions where they include common tasks, such as finding the smallest value, the largest value, or the average value for a group of data records.

Let's obtain the maximum length of time of any of the DB2 Certification exams:

```
SELECT MAX(smallint(length)) FROM test
```

Because the column `length` is specified as the `minutes` data type, a casting function is required to convert the `minutes` data type to the `smallint` data type in this example.

If we added a WHERE clause to this example, the maximum would represent the maximum length for the qualifying rows, since the predicate is used to filter the data prior to the application of the MAX function.

This next example calculates the average of the number of seats for all of the test centers. Notice the column function AVG is used in this example:

```
SELECT AVG(noseats) FROM test_center
```

DB2 does provide many more built-in functions. If you are interested in calculating statistical information, you can use Business Intelligence-related functions, such as CORRELATION, COVARIANCE, and some regression functions. See the *DB2 UDB V7.1 SQL Reference* for more detailed information.

Grouping Values

Many queries require some level of aggregated data. This is accomplished in SQL through the use of the GROUP BY clause.

The following SQL obtains the average number of seats for each country:

```
SELECT country, AVG(noseats) FROM test_center
                                        GROUP BY country
```

This SQL statement obtains the average number of seats per country and the GROUP BY clause tells DB2 to group together the rows that have the same values in the columns indicated in the group by list. In our example, we are grouping countries into subsets. As the subsets are created, DB2 calculates the average of each of those groups or subsets, in this case, by each country.

Manipulating Database Objects

When you combine vector functions and other elements, such as column names, scalar functions, or calculated columns, you must use the GROUP BY clause. In this case, you must include every element that is not a column function in the group by list. The only elements that can be omitted in the GROUP BY list are constant values.

The next SQL statement obtains a list that includes the average cut score and minimum test length for the DB2 Certification exams. We group this list by the type of exam as follows:

```
SELECT type, AVG(integer(cut_score)),
MIN(smallint(length))
    FROM test
    GROUP BY type
```

It is possible to sort the output of the previous example using an ORDER BY clause. Note that the ORDER BY clause should always be the last clause in an SQL statement.

On-line analytical processing (OLAP) applications use different levels of grouping within the same data. DB2 supports OLAP requirements implementing *super group* or aggregation features. OLAP-oriented grouping functions will be discussed in "Advanced SQL" on page 325.

Restricting the Use of Sets of Data

Up to now, we have discussed how to restrict output based on row conditions. With SQL, it is also possible to restrict that output using vector functions and the GROUP BY clause.

Suppose you want a list of all the test centers that have administered more than five DB2 Certification exams.

To make it easier to understand, let's first get the number of tests that have been taken in each test center.

```
SELECT tcid, count(*) FROM test_taken GROUP BY tcid
```

We use the COUNT vector function to get the total number of tests that have been taken in each test center. When you use an asterisk (*) with the COUNT function, you are indicating that you want the number of rows in a table that meet the criteria established in the SQL statement. In this example, we are grouping by tcid because we have a number of occurrences for all the test centers in the test_taken table. The test_taken table has an entry for every DB2 Certification exam that has been taken.

Finally, the output is restricted to only those test centers that have administered more than four exams.

```
SELECT tcid FROM test_taken
       GROUP BY tcid HAVING COUNT(*) > 4
```

This example introduces the HAVING clause. The HAVING clause is equivalent to the WHERE clause for groups and vector functions. The HAVING clause will restrict the result set to only the groups that meet the condition specified in it.

In our example, only the test centers that have administered more than four DB2 Certification exams will be displayed.

Eliminating Duplicates

When you execute a query, you might get duplicate rows in the answer set. The SQL language provides a special clause to remove the duplicate rows from your output.

The following SQL generates a list of names and phone numbers for all the candidates who have taken a test. In the following example, we eliminate the duplicate rows from our output list using the DISTINCT clause.

```
SELECT DISTINCT fname,wphone,hphone
       FROM candidate c,test_taken tt
       WHERE c.cid=tt.cid
```

The DISTINCT clause can also be used with the COUNT function. When you use DISTINCT inside a COUNT function, it will not count the duplicate entries for a particular column.

Let's say that you want to count how many different test centers have candidates registered.

```
SELECT COUNT(DISTINCT char(tcid)) FROM test_taken
```

This example provides the number of test centers that are registered in the test taken table. Remember that all the candidates who have registered for DB2 Certification exams are stored in this table.

Make sure that you understand the difference between COUNT(*) and COUNT(DISTINCT colname). They are very similar in syntax but differ in function.

Searching for String Patterns

SQL has a powerful predicate that allows you to search for patterns in character strings columns. This is the LIKE predicate.

Suppose you want to generate a list of the candidates whose first name starts with the letter G.

```
SELECT fname,lname,wphone,hphone FROM candidate
        WHERE fname LIKE'G%' ORDER BY lname,fname
```

In this query, we are using a *wildcard character* with the LIKE predicate.

In SQL, the percent character (%) is a substitute for zero or more characters. The search string (G%) can be substituted with names like George, Gary, Ginger, and so on (since the percent character can substitute zero or more characters, the search string can also be a single letter G).

The percent character can be used any place in the search string. It also can be used as many times as you need it. The percent sign is not case sensitive, so it can take the place of uppercase or lowercase letters. However, the constant characters included in your search string are case sensitive.

Another wildcard character used with the LIKE predicate is the underline character (_). This character substitutes one and only one character. The underline character can take the place of any character. However, the underline character cannot be substituted for an empty character.

The previous SQL can be modified to include all candidates' names and the telephone numbers for those candidates whose name has a lowercase letter "a" as its second letter.

```
SELECT fname,lname,wphone,hphone FROM candidate
          WHERE fname LIKE '_a%' ORDER BY lname,fname
```

This example uses two wildcard characters that work with the LIKE predicate. The search string, in this example, can include names, such as Paul, Gabriel, or Natalie. (The first character may be any character, the lowercase letter "a" is the second character in the string, and the string ends with any number of characters.)

Searching for Data in Ranges

SQL also offers us a RANGE operator. This operator is used to restrict rows that are in a particular range of values.

Consider the requirement to list those candidates whose scores in the DB2 Certification exam are between 60 and 75.

```
SELECT DISTINCT fname,lname,wphone,hphone
          FROM candidate c, test_taken tt
          WHERE c.cid=tt.cid
              AND integer (score) BETWEEN 60 AND 75
```

The BETWEEN predicate includes the values that you specify for searching your data. An important fact about the BETWEEN predicate is that it can work with character ranges as well.

In addition to the score requirement, this example modifies the SQL to include only those candidates whose last name begins with a letter between B and G.

```
SELECT DISTINCT fname,lname,wphone,hphone
          FROM candidate c, test_taken tt
          WHERE c.cid=tt.cid
              AND integer(score) BETWEEN 60 AND 75
              AND lname BETWEEN 'B' AND 'GZ'
```

In this example, the second BETWEEN predicate contains character values. We need to specify the GZ value to include all the possible names that start with the letter G. This was done assuming that the letter z is the last possible value in the alphabet.

Manipulating Database Objects

Searching for Null Values

NULL values represent an unknown value for a particular occurrence of an entity. We can use a NULL value in the cases where we don't know a particular value of a column.

Let's say that we want a list of all those candidates whose score is not yet input. This condition is represented with a NULL value.

```
SELECT fname,lname,wphone,hphone
          FROM candidate c, test_taken tt
          WHERE c.cid=tt.cid AND score IS NULL
```

The IS predicate is used to search for the NULL value in this example. Remember that the NULL value means "unknown." Because it has no particular value, it can't be compared with other values. You can't use conditional operands, such as equal (=), with null values.

Searching for Negative Conditions

The BETWEEN, IS, and LIKE predicates always look for the values that meet a particular condition. These predicates can also be used to look for values that don't meet a particular criterion.

The NOT predicate can be used to look for the opposite condition, combined with the LIKE, BETWEEN, and IS predicate, to accomplish negative searches as shown in the following example.

This example has a LIKE predicate combined with the NOT predicate. We want a list of those candidates whose last names do not start with the letter S.

```
SELECT DISTINCT fname,lname,wphone,hphone FROM candidate
      WHERE lname NOT LIKE 'S%'
   ORDER BY lname,fname
```

The next example has a BETWEEN predicate combined with the NOT predicate. We want the list of those candidates whose score, in any test, is not in the range 60 to 75.

```
SELECT DISTINCT fname,lname,wphone,hphone
        FROM candidate c, test_taken tt
        WHERE c.cid=tt.cid
        AND integer(score) NOT BETWEEN 60 and 75
```

In this example, the NOT predicate will exclude all the values that are in the range 60 to 75.

Negation can also be applied to the NULL value. This SQL produces a report that searches for those candidates that have a seat number assigned. This is expressed with a NOT NULL value.

```
SELECT DISTINCT fname,lname,wphone,hphone
      FROM candidate c, test_taken tt
      WHERE c.cid=tt.cid AND seat_no IS NOT NULL
```

Searching for a Set of Values

In SQL, it is possible to establish a restriction condition based on a set of values. Suppose that you need a list of the test centers that have candidates registered for the DB2 Fundamentals test and for the DB2 Application Development test. This can be queried with the following statement:

```
SELECT DISTINCT name,phone
    FROM test_center tc, test_taken tt
    WHERE tc.tcid=tt.tcid
    AND char(number) IN ('500','502')
```

The IN clause is used to denote a set of values. In this example, we are using a constant set of values. In this particular case, the SQL statement could also be written using the OR operator to restrict the test numbers.

You can also use the NOT predicate with the IN clause. In this case, the condition will be true when a value is not present in the set of values provided to the IN clause.

You can use as many values as you wish in the IN clause. However, there will be cases when the list of values is very long, and it would be better to retrieve them using another SQL statement.

Manipulating Database Objects

The IN predicate can also be used to define a set based on conditions. In this case, the IN predicate also accepts an SQL statement that defines the set of values. When you define the set of values using an SQL statement, the SQL statement that defines that set is called a sub-query.

Sub-Queries

A sub-query is an SQL statement that is used inside another SQL statement. Sub-queries can be used with the IN clause to specify the search arguments for an SQL statement.

Consider the difficulty of producing a report on the number of DB2 Certification exams if the name and number of the exams is unknown. The following SQL produces a report that includes all the test centers that have candidates registered for the DB2 Certification exams.

In the example, we'll use the word DB2 as the search string to find the numbers of the DB2 Certification program exams:

```
SELECT DISTINCT name,phone
   FROM test_center tc, test_taken tt
   WHERE tc.tcid=tt.tcid
   AND number IN
          (SELECT number FROM test
                WHERE name LIKE 'DB2%')
```

Fig. 6–11 *Using a sub-query*

In this example, the sub-query appears as part of the IN clause. In the sub-query, we are retrieving all the numbers for those tests that have the word DB2 in their name.

As you can see in the last example, the sub-query is a standard SQL statement. The only difference here is that the sub-query is used as a restriction condition. You will never see its output. We are only using the sub-query to create a list of values that will be used later by the outer SELECT statement.

The sub-query used in this example is known as an uncorrelated sub-query. An uncorrelated sub-query is one where the values retrieved by the sub-query are not directly related to the rows processed by the outer SELECT statement. A correlated sub-query is a query in which the sub-query references values of the outer SELECT.

In the next example, you want to count how many candidates are registered in each test center. This time you want to display the name of the center near the number of candidates. We use a correlated sub-query to accomplish this.

```
SELECT tc.name, count(*)
   FROM test_center tc,test t
   WHERE tc.tcid IN
      (SELECT tcid FROM test_taken tt
            WHERE tt.number=t.number)
   GROUP BY tc.name
```

Fig. 6–12 *Correlated sub-query*

Observe the WHERE clause in the sub-query in this example. It is making reference to a table that is listed in the outer FROM clause.

If you write this query as a uncorrelated sub-query, you will have different results. In this example, you need to use a correlated sub-query to be sure that all the rows of the test_taken table are counted. When you use an uncorrelated sub-query, you will only count one occurrence of the test number for each test center.

Note: You should understand the difference between sub-selects and sub-queries. Sub-selects are queries that do not include an ORDER BY clause, an UPDATE clause, or UNION operators. Sub-queries are to be used with the IN clause to specify the search arguments for an SQL statement as already described.

Quantified Predicates

A quantified predicate is used to compare a value or values with a collection of values. In Fig. 6–13, the partial syntax diagram for a quantified predicate is shown (please refer to the *DB2 UDB V7.1 SQL Reference* for the complete discussion). The right side of the expression is a fullselect.

A *fullselect* statement is a sub-select, a values-clause, or a number of both that are combined by set operators.

Manipulating
Database Objects

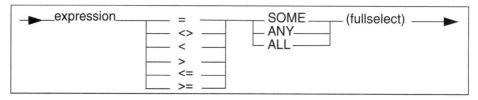

Fig. 6–13 *Quantified predicates*

Let's examine the use of a quantified predicate in a SELECT statement. First we look at the original queries:

```
SELECT cid, lname, fname FROM db2cert.candidate
```

```
CID LNAME       FNAME
--- ----------  --------
111 Wong        Bill
222 Baklarz     George
333 Visser      Susan
444 Sheffield   Glen
555 Stittle     Jim
666 Street      Kevin
777 Nicol       Bert
888 Zikopoulos  Paul

 8 record(s) selected.
```

Fig. 6–14 *A simple query (1)*

```
SELECT cid FROM db2cert.test_taken
```

```
CID
---
222
222
222
111
111
111
333
333
333

  9 record(s) selected.CID
```

Fig. 6–15 *A simple query (2)*

```
SELECT c.cid, lname, fname FROM db2cert.candidate c
   WHERE cid = SOME
        (SELECT tt.cid FROM db2cert.test_taken tt
            WHERE c.cid = tt.cid)
```

```
CID LNAME       FNAME
--- ---------- --------
111 Wong        Bill
222 Baklarz     George
333 Visser      Susan

  3 record(s) selected.
```

Fig. 6–16 *Using a quantified predicate in a SELECT statement*

A *quantified predicate* is used in Fig. 6–16 to find the test candidates who have taken or are scheduled to take a test. When SOME or ANY is specified for the fullselect statement, the predicate is true if the relationship is true for at least one value returned by the fullselect. The phrase ALL would result in all of the test candidate names being returned because the specified relationship is true for every value returned by the fullselect. The relationship cid = fullselect is true for all values returned by the fullselect because of the referential integrity constraints between our defined tables. It is impossible to have a cid value in the test_taken table that does not have a corresponding value in the candidate table.

Case Expressions

You can add some logic to your SQL statements and output using CASE expressions. Consider the generation of a list of those candidates who have passed the DB2 Fundamentals exam.

In the report, you want to print the score of the tests, but instead of printing the numeric score, you want to print a message. If the score is below the cut_score, you want to print Not Passed. If it is between the cut_score and 90, you want to print Passed, and if the score is above 90, you want to print Excellent. The following SQL statement using a CASE expression accomplishes this:

```
SELECT fname,lname,
      CASE
        WHEN integer(SCORE) < 65 THEN 'Not Passed'
        WHEN SCORE <= score(90) THEN 'Passed'
        ELSE
              'Excellent'
      END
    FROM candidate c, test_taken tt
    WHERE c.cid=tt.cid
        AND char(number)='500'
```

Fig. 6–17 *CASE expressions*

The SQL statement presented in Fig. 6–17 provides string messages based on the conditions of the CASE expression. In this example, the score column features a numeric value, but we are using it to produce a character string.

The order of the conditions for the CASE expression is very important. DB2 will process the first condition first, then the second, and so on. If you do not pay attention to the order in which the conditions are processed, you might be retrieving the same result for every row in your table. For example, if you coded the <= score(90) option before the < 65, all the data that is lower than 91, even 64 or 30, will display the message Passed.

 Note: You must use the end keyword to finish a CASE statement.

CASE expressions can also be used in places other than select lists. CASE expressions can be used inside functions and in the group list. Samples of these features will be presented in "Advanced SQL" on page 325.

Nested Table Expressions

A nested table expression is a special kind of sub-query. This sub-query is used in the FROM clause of an SQL statement. Nested table expressions will create local temporary tables that are only known in the SQL statement that defines them.

These sub-queries can be considered temporary views. You can use nested table expressions to select from a grouped table or to obtain the same results that you expect from a view.

Consider the problem of obtaining the maximum average score for the DB2 Certification program exams. To gather this result, you must first obtain the averages and then you must select the maximum value from that list.

Let's use a nested table expression to accomplish this request:

```
SELECT MAX(avg_score)
  FROM (
     SELECT number,
     avg(integer(score)) as avg_score
     FROM test_taken
     GROUP BY number
) AS averages
```

Fig. 6–18 *Using table expressions*

In this example, Fig. 6–18, the nested sub-select will create a temporary table that will be used by the outer SELECT to obtain the maximum average score. This temporary table is called averages.

The number column is included in the sub-query to be able to gather the average for each one of the exams. After the sub-query is completed, the outer SELECT will be able to obtain the maximum value of the averages calculated in the nested table expression.

An advantage of using nested table expressions over views is that nested table expressions exist only during the execution of the query, so you don't have to worry about their maintenance. They reduce contention over the system catalog tables, and since they are created at execution time, they can be defined using host variables.

Note: The TABLE clause can also be used to denote that the sub-query following it will create a temporary table. This keyword is also used to denote TABLE user-defined functions. Refer to "Advanced SQL" on page 325 for information about UDFs.

Scalar Fullselect

A scalar fullselect is a SELECT statement that returns only one value. This type of SELECT can be used in different parts of an SQL statement. It can be used in the select list or in the WHERE clause.

Scalar fullselects can be used to combine grouped information, such as averages or sums, with detailed information in a single query.

Occasionally, you may need to include row data in the report that includes information based on the entire table. For instance, you may want a report that shows the candidate's ID, score, the average score, and the maximum score for the DB2 Certification exams. This information cannot be gathered without the help of temporary tables or views. Let's see how the scalar fullselect can be used to assist in the retrieval of this data.

```
SELECT cid,number,score,
   (SELECT AVG(integer(score))
     FROM test_taken) AS AVG_Score,
   (SELECT MAX(integer(score))
     FROM test_taken) AS MAX_Score
 FROM test_taken
```

Fig. 6–19 *Combining detailed and aggregated information*

In the example shown in Fig. 6–19, we are using two scalar fullselects to retrieve the information about the aggregated data.

The first scalar fullselect calculates the average score and the second one calculates the maximum score for the DB2 Certification exams.

Observe how the SQL statements that produce the average and the maximum values are scalar fullselects. They are complete SQL statements that return only one value.

Now, let's extend this SQL to calculate the average and maximum scores for each one of the DB2 Certification exams.

To accomplish this request you need to use a correlated sub-select. This is because you must ensure that the SELECT statement returns only one value at a time.

The correlated sub-select will let you generate the average and maximum scores for each one of the DB2 Certification exams:

```
SELECT cid,number,score,
   (SELECT AVG(integer(score))
      FROM test_taken tt1
      WHERE tt1.number=tt.number
) AS AVG_Score,
   (SELECT MAX(integer(score))
      FROM test_taken tt2
      WHERE tt2.number=tt.number
) AS MAX_Score
FROM test_taken tt
```

Fig. 6–20 *Using a correlated scalar fullselect*

Examine the WHERE clauses in the Fig. 6–20 example. They both make reference to the table of the outer SELECT statement. The WHERE clauses are used to obtain a separate average and maximum value for each one of the test numbers in the test_taken table.

Now, let's use a scalar fullselect to create a list of those candidates who have a higher score than the average for the DB2 Fundamentals exam.

```
SELECT fname,lname,score
  FROM candidate c, test_taken tt
  WHERE c.cid=tt.cid
  AND integer(tt.score) > (SELECT AVG(integer(score))
                             FROM test_taken
                             WHERE number=test_id('500'))
```

Fig. 6–21 *Using a scalar fullselect in the WHERE clause*

In Fig. 6–21, the scalar fullselect is used in the WHERE clause. This scalar fullselect calculates the average score for the DB2 Fundamentals exam.

The value returned from the scalar fullselect is compared with the score of the candidate. In this way we retrieve those candidates whose score is higher than the average.

Common Table Expressions

A common table expression is a local temporary table that can be referenced many times in an SQL statement. However, this temporary table only exists for the duration of the SQL statement that defines it. A common table expression will provide many of the advantages of nested table expressions discussed earlier.

Every time that you reference a common table expression, the result will be the same. This means that the SQL statement that generates it will not be reprocessed each time the common table expression is referenced.

Consider a report that lists the candidates who have earned the highest score for each of the DB2 Certification program exams.

This can be accomplished using three common table expressions. Each of them corresponds to one of the DB2 Certification program exams. The common table expressions will be called MAX500, MAX501, and MAX502. They will contain the maximum score value for each one of the DB2 Certification program exams.

After calculating the maximum score for each one of the tests, we use those values to search for the candidates whose score is equal to the maximum score for a particular test. This will be accomplished by joining the score of each candidate with the maximum score of each one of the exams.

After the definition of a common table expression, you can use it in an SQL statement as any other table. An example is shown in Fig. 6–22.

```
WITH MAX500 AS
  (SELECT MAX(integer(score)) AS M500 FROM test_taken
  WHERE number=test_id('500')),
MAX501 AS
  (SELECT MAX(integer(score)) AS M501 FROM test_taken
  WHERE number=test_id('501')),
MAX502 AS
  (SELECT MAX(integer(score)) AS M502 FROM test_taken
  WHERE number=test_id('502'))

SELECT fname, lname, wphone
   FROM max500,max501,max502,candidate c, test_taken tt
   WHERE c.cid=tt.cid
   AND ((integer(score)=M500 and number=test_id('500'))
   OR (integer(score)=M501 and number=test_id('501'))
   OR (integer(score)=M502 and number=test_id('502')));
```

Fig. 6–22 *Using common table expressions*

The WITH clause is used to define a common table expression. The example shown in Fig. 6–22 defines three different common table expressions: MAX500, MAX501, and MAX502. Observe the commas that are used to separate each one of the common table expression definitions.

The common table expressions are used in the SQL statement that follows their definition. This SQL statement treats the common table expressions as if they were normal tables.

You can use a common table expression as many times as you wish. You can even create a common table expression based on a previously created common table expression. However, you can only use them in the SQL statement that defines them.

Set Operators

SQL offers a group of operators that are used to implement the relational operations of union (UNION operator), intersection (INTERSECT operator), and difference (EXCEPT operator).

Union

The UNION operation lets you combine the results of two or more different SQL statements into one answer set. You can combine many different tables or SQL statements using the UNION operator; the only restriction is that every table or SQL statement must have the same type, number, and order of columns.

Suppose you wanted to combine the minimum and maximum score for each of the DB2 Certification program exams and add a string constant that indicates which values are the maximum and minimum.

```
SELECT number,'Minimum:', MIN(integer(score))
  FROM test_taken
  GROUP BY number
UNION
SELECT number,'Maximum:', MAX(integer(score))
  FROM test_taken
  GROUP BY number
ORDER BY number,2
```

Fig. 6–23 *UNION operator*

The UNION operator shows you the results of two or more separate queries as a single one. In our example, the first query calculates the minimum score of the test_taken table. The the second query calculates the maximum score value. Both queries have the same type, order, and number of columns.

In Fig. 6–23, the two SQL statements are very similar. However, you can combine very different queries using the UNION operator. Just remember the restriction about the resulting rows.

The UNION operator removes duplicate rows from the resulting set. However, there will be times when you'll need to list all the rows processed by your SQL statements.

SQL provides you with an operator clause that allows you to keep all the rows involved in a UNION operation. This is the ALL clause. Let's create a list of all the first names and last names in our candidate table. In this example, shown in Fig. 6–24, we want all the first names that start with a letter G and all the last names for the candidates who have taken the DB2 Administration exam.

This example cannot be processed with an OR operator because we are not interested in the first names of those candidates who have taken the DB2 Administration exam. Since there can be a first name that is the same as a last name, we will use a UNION ALL operator to show all the rows.

```
SELECT fname FROM candidate
  WHERE fname like'G%'
UNION ALL
SELECT lname FROM candidate c,test_taken tt
  WHERE c.cid=tt.cid
  AND   char(number) = '501'
```

Fig. 6–24 *An example of UNION ALL*

Note: Always try to code a UNION ALL. Only code a UNION when duplicates are not desired. The UNION ALL offers better performance. However, you can't always substitute a UNION for a UNION ALL.

The UNION ALL operation provides us with a powerful mechanism, and as we will see when we discuss advanced SQL, it is required when writing recursive SQL.

Intersection (Intersect Operator)

The intersection set operation is implemented in DB2 using the INTERSECT operator. Using INTERSECT, we can find the elements that belong to two different answer sets.

For example, we want a list of all the candidate IDs that are present in the test_taken table and in the candidate table. This requirement can be seen as the intersection of the set *candidate IDs* and the set *candidates IDs present in test_taken.*

```
SELECT cid FROM candidate
  INTERSECT
SELECT cid FROM test_taken
```

Like the union operator, there is an INTERSECT ALL operator. If you use the INTERSECT ALL operator, the result set will return duplicate values, which is often desirable.

The SQL statement shown in this example is equivalent to a join operation between the candidate and test_taken tables using the DISTINCT clause in the select list.

Difference (Except Operator)

The difference set operation is the complementary set of an intersection between two sets. It is implemented in DB2 using the EXCEPT operator. Using a difference set operation, we can find out which elements of a resulting set are not present in another answer set.

This time, we want to know which candidate IDs are not present in the test_taken table. This is effectively saying, "Show me all the candidate IDs except those candidate IDs present in the test_taken table."

The query using the EXCEPT operator is shown in the following example:

```
SELECT cid FROM candidate
  EXCEPT
SELECT cid FROM test_taken
```

Manipulating Database Objects

The first part of the example retrieves all the candidate IDs. The second section of the query retrieves the candidate IDs present in the test_taken table. Finally, the EXCEPT operator performs the difference operation that filters those candidate IDs not present in the test_taken table. Without the EXCEPT operator, the query would have been more complicated. As with the other set operators, there is also an EXCEPT ALL operator that does not eliminate duplicates from the result.

Note: The columns in both select lists of a set operator, such as UNION, INTERSECT, and EXCEPT, must have the same column structure.

Data Modification

Up to now, we have discussed basic SELECT statements. The SELECT statement allows you to retrieve data from your database tables and assumes that data has been previously loaded into the tables. Now we will concentrate on getting data into the database tables using SQL. There are three main statements that can be used to add and change data stored in a DB2 database table. They are the INSERT, DELETE, and UPDATE SQL statements.

To perform these operations, you must have the required privileges on the tables being accessed. Usually, these privileges are more strictly enforced since they can allow the end-user to modify data records.

Inserting Data Records

To initially populate a DB2 table with data, the INSERT statement can be used to store one data record at a time. The statement can be targeted to insert data directly into a base table, or a view can be used instead. If a view is being used as the target, remember that it is the base table where the actual data is being stored.

Every row that is populated using the INSERT statement must adhere to table-check constraints, data type validation, dynamic (trigger) constraints, and referential integrity constraints. An SQL error will occur if any of these conditions are violated during the processing of the INSERT statement.

Note: Remember that you must have the necessary view or table privileges to perform an INSERT statement.

The first example is a simple INSERT statement. This statement will insert the data for the DB2 Data Propagation (#508) exam into the test table.

```
INSERT INTO db2cert.test
(number,name,type,cut_score,length,
 totaltaken,totalpassed) VALUES
('508','DB2 Data Propagation','P',NULL,90,0,0);
```

In this example, we specify all the column names and their corresponding values for this data record. Following the VALUES portion of the statement, we include all of the data values for this record.

In the VALUES clause, the number and order of the inserted elements must match the number and order of the column names defined in the INSERT statement. However, the order of the columns doesn't have to match the order in which they are defined in the table. For those columns that don't require a value, you can indicate null or default values. In this example, we are using the NULL value for the cut_score column.

 Note: The number of elements following the VALUES clause must match the number of names in the insert column list.

Depending on your column definition, the DEFAULT value can cause to be inserted a system-defined default, a user-defined default, or NULL. Be aware that if the column doesn't accept nulls (NOT NULL) and wasn't defined as WITH DEFAULT, you will receive an error message when using the DEFAULT value. This error is because the default value for those columns not using the WITH DEFAULT option is the NULL value.

When you want to insert values into all the columns of a table, you do not have to provide the column names in the INSERT statement. This example is shown next.

```
INSERT INTO db2cert.test VALUES
('508','DB2 Data Propagation','P',DEFAULT,90,79,11)
```

This method will only work if you specify a value for all the columns in a table. If you miss one of the columns of the table, DB2 will not allow you to insert the row into the table. The DEFAULT keyword used in this example will insert the default value for the cut_score column.

 Note: Remember, that depending on the column definition, the default value could be a user-defined default value, a system-defined default value, or NULL.

Inserting Data into Specific Columns

There are times when you need to add data to specific columns. Every column that is not included in the INSERT statement will receive its default value.

This operation can be accomplished only if the omitted columns accept nulls or have a default value definition. This means that you must specify a value for the columns defined as NOT NULL. This restriction excludes columns defined as NOT NULL WITH DEFAULT.

Let's insert a row into the test_taken table. In the following example, we will only insert data for the columns CID, TCID, NUMBER, and SEAT_NO.

```
INSERT INTO db2cert.test_taken
  (CID,TCID,NUMBER,SEAT_NO)
    VALUES('888','TR01','508','1')
```

Remember that columns defined using WITH DEFAULT that are not listed in the INSERT statement will receive the NULL value or a default value.

> **Note:** The test_taken table has some referential integrity with other tables. If you want to insert a record into a test_taken table, the appropriate values should be inserted into the other three tables in advance.

Inserting Multiple Rows

You can insert multiple rows into a table using a single INSERT statement. For instance, you may want to schedule a candidate for the DB2 Certification exams. This candidate will take all the exams on three different days:

```
INSERT INTO db2cert.test_taken
  (CID,TCID,NUMBER,DATE_TAKEN,SEAT_NO)
VALUES
  ('888','TR01','500','2000-06-04','1'),
  ('888','TR01','501','2000-07-11','2'),
  ('888','TR01','502','2000-11-08','1')
```

Fig. 6–25 *Multiple row INSERT statement*

In Fig. 6–25, we separate the values for different rows with a comma. When inserting multiple rows with a single statement, you have to consider that all the rows must have the same number, type, and order of columns. This means that you cannot insert values to one column in the first row and values to five columns in the last row.

Inserting a Set of Values

Using SQL, you can insert the result of a SELECT statement into the same or a different table. The SQL statement that generates the resulting set must follow these rules:

- The number of columns from the SELECT statement must equal the number of columns in the INSERT column list.
- The data type of each of the columns in the SELECT list must match the data type of those columns in the INSERT list.
- Column names can be omitted from the INSERT list only if values are inserted into all the columns in the table.
- Only columns defined to allow NULL or defined as NOT NULL WITH DEFAULT can be omitted from the INSERT list.

In some situations, it might be useful to create tables that are duplicates of others so that you can do multiple calculations against them. The next example uses a table called test_passed, which is a copy of the test_taken table. This new table will be used to extract the information about those candidates who have passed any of the DB2 Certification exams.

```
INSERT INTO db2cert.test_passed
 (cid,tcid,number,
 date_taken,start_time,finish_time,
 pass_fail,score,seat_no)

(SELECT cid,tcid,number,
        date_taken,start_time,finish_time,
        pass_fail,score,seat_no
 FROM db2cert.test_taken
   WHERE pass_fail='P')
```

Fig. 6–26 *Using a SELECT statement to insert values*

The select list used in the fullselect in Fig. 6–26 can also be substituted by a select asterisk (*). This is possible because the test_passed table has the same column structure as does the test_taken table. However, to keep this query isolated from future table modifications, it is recommended that you use the select list instead of the asterisk.

When you use a SELECT statement to insert data into a table, you must enclose it between parentheses. You can also use a table expression to insert values into a table or view using the INSERT clause.

Inserting Large Amounts of Data

Using the SELECT or VALUES statements to insert data into a table can be very useful. However, it is not recommended to load large amounts of data into a table using the INSERT statement as the transaction logging overhead can become unmanageable.

DB2 provides you with two utilities that are designed to move large amounts of data into a table. These utilities are IMPORT and LOAD and are described in "Maintaining Data" on page 451.

 Although not new to DB2 UDB V7.1, the NOT LOGGED INITIALLY option on table creation could improve your performance on high-volume inserts. This option tells DB2 not to log changes to the table during the current unit of work. Subsequent changes to this table will result in logging taking place. If future loads require that logging be turned off, the table can be placed back into a no-logging status with the command:
ALTER TABLE x ACTIVATE NOT LOGGED INITIALLY.
Before taking advantage of this feature, make sure you understand the recovery implications of logging being turned off during loads.

Updating Data Records

So far we have looked at the INSERT statement as a method of moving data into your DB2 table. You may wish to update only a column with values for a group of data records. There is an SQL UPDATE statement that can be used to specify the column and its new values. A table or a view can be referenced as the target for the UPDATE statement.

 Note: Remember that you must have the correct privileges in order to perform the UPDATE operation.

The UPDATE statement can be used in two forms:

- *Searched update*. This type of UPDATE statement is used to update one or more rows in a table. It requires a WHERE clause to establish the update condition (which rows are to be updated).
- *Positioned update*. This kind of UPDATE statement is always embedded into a program. It uses *cursors* to update the row where the cursor is positioned. As the cursor is repositioned using the FETCH statement, the target row for the UPDATE

statement changes.

We focus on searched updates in this chapter.

Similar to the INSERT statement, all of the database constraint mechanisms are enforced during an UPDATE statement. There can be specific update constraint triggers and referential integrity constraints that could be different from the insert constraints.

For example, the following is a transaction that updates candidate ID 888 exam day for the DB2 Fundamentals certification exam.

```
UPDATE db2cert.test_taken
  SET date_taken=date_taken + 3 days
  WHERE char(cid) ='888'
  AND number=test_id('500')
```

In this example, we are using an operation known as a *labeled duration* to add three days to the original date.

It is very important that you provide the proper WHERE clause to avoid updating unintended data records. In this example, we needed to specify the predicate number=test_id('500') to avoid changing the date for any of the other tests that the candidate can be scheduled for.

Note: DB2 labeled durations for data types include: YEARS, MONTHS, DAYS, HOURS, MINUTES, SECONDS, and MICROSECONDS.

The UPDATE statement can also be used with fullselects. In this case, the fullselect must return a row with exactly the same number of columns and column data types of the row that will be updated. Observe that this fullselect must return only one row.

Let's update a row using a SELECT statement to set the new value. Candidate ID 888 decides to take the DB2 Fundamentals test today in the test center located in Toronto, Canada.

```
UPDATE db2cert.test_taken
  SET (date_taken,tcid)=
      (SELECT current date,tcid FROM db2cert.test_center
          WHERE substr(city,1,7)='Toronto'
          AND country='Canada')
  WHERE CHAR(cid)= '888' AND number=test_id('500');
```

Fig. 6–27 *Using a row fullselect to update data*

In Fig. 6–27, we are updating two different columns in the same operation. These columns are indicated in the parentheses following the SET clause.

After indicating which columns are going to be updated, we use a SELECT statement to retrieve the current date (today) and the test center ID for the test center located in Toronto, Canada. Notice the last WHERE clause in the statement will restrict the rows that will be updated.

> **Note:** If you forget the update WHERE clause in a searched update, all of the data in your table will be updated.

The SQL statement that will update the date_taken and tcid columns is known as a row fullselect. This name is given because it returns only one row. Observe that the scalar fullselect can be considered a special case of a row fullselect.

> **Note:** CURRENT DATE is a DB2 special register that gives the system date. Others include: CURRENT TIME, CURRENT TIMESTAMP, and USER (the authid).

Updating Large Amounts of Data

There are times when you need to update a large number of rows of a particular table. This can be accomplished by issuing a searched update. However, this also could allocate a large amount of transactional log space. You can accomplish updates using positioned updates, where you can easily control the commit frequency.

Removing Data

There are many methods available to remove data from a DB2 database. To remove all of the data within a database, perform the DROP DATABASE command. This may remove more data than you intended because the entire database, including its configuration, will be physically removed.

It is also possible to remove data using the DROP TABLESPACE or DROP TABLE statements. These statements are usually only issued by the SYSADM or DBADM, since they will remove large amounts of data. If you wish to remove all of the data records from a table, it is easier and quicker to perform the DROP TABLE statement. If the table is dropped, it must be re-created before any data can be populated again in the table.

To remove a single data record or a group or records from a table, the DELETE statement should be used. The syntax of the DELETE statement is different from the SELECT or INSERT statements because columns cannot be selected, only rows can be deleted.

The DELETE statement can also be used with views. However, there are restrictions on the type of views that can be used within a DELETE statement.

Note: Remember that you must have the necessary privileges over a table to perform the DELETE operation.

In general, there are two kinds of DELETE statements:

- *Searched delete* - This DELETE statement is used to delete one or multiple rows from a table. It can use a WHERE clause to establish the delete condition.
- *Positioned delete* - This kind of DELETE operation is always embedded into a program. It uses *cursors* to delete the row where the cursor is positioned.

In this section we will focus on the searched delete.

Note: The following are provided to show you how to use the DELETE statement and are examples only.

The following SQL statement deletes candidates who don't have a telephone number loaded into the table. We will use a searched delete to accomplish this task.

```
DELETE FROM db2cert.candidate
 WHERE hphone IS NULL
 AND wphone IS NULL
```

This example uses a WHERE clause to delete the data that meets a specific criterion.

To verify the result of the DELETE statement, you can issue a SELECT statement with the same WHERE clause. If the DELETE was successful, the SELECT will return an empty set.

A delete can also become more sophisticated by using subselects. The next SQL statement deletes all the candidates who took the DB2 Certification exams in February of any given year.

```
DELETE FROM db2cert.candidate
 WHERE cid IN (SELECT cid FROM db2cert.test_taken
                WHERE MONTH(date_taken)=2)
```

In this example, we are using a sub-select to retrieve the cid values of the candidates who took a DB2 Certification exam in the month of February. This list will be used to search for the candidates we want to delete.

Deleting All the Rows in a Table

You can delete all the rows in a table if you don't specify a search condition in your DELETE statement. You must be aware of the implications of this type of statement. However, this is not the only way to delete all the rows in a table. You can also delete all the rows in a table if all the rows meet the search condition.

Deleting all the rows in a table by using a DELETE statement may not be the most efficient method. This kind of statement can consume a lot of log space when your tables are big.

 If a table has been created with the NOT LOGGED INITIALLY option, there is a way to delete all of the contents of the table without physically dropping it. Use the following command to tell DB2 to drop the contents of the records (without logging): ALTER TABLE x ACTIVATE NOT LOGGED INITIALLY WITH EMPTY TABLE. The advantage of deleting rows with this technique is that definitions relying on this table do not get dropped.

View Classification

Now that we have examined various SQL DML statements, let's take a closer look at views. We have already discussed creating views. Now we'll examine the different types of views.

Views are classified by the operations they allow. They can be:

- Deletable
- Updatable
- Insertable
- Read-only

The view type is established according to its update capabilities. The classification indicates the kind of SQL operation that is allowed while using the view.

The referential and check constraints are treated independently. They do not affect the view classification.

For example, you may not be able to insert a value into a table because of a referential constraint. If you create a view using that table, you also can't insert that value using the view. However, if the view satisfies all the rules for an insertable view, it will still be considered an insertable view. This is because the insert restriction is located on the base table, not on the view definition.

Deletable Views

Depending on how a view is defined, the view can be deletable. A deletable view is a view against which you can successfully issue a DELETE statement. There are a few rules that need to be followed for a view to be considered deletable:

- Each FROM clause of the outer fullselect identifies only one base table (with no OUTER clause), deletable view (with no OUTER clause), deletable nested table expression, or deletable common table expression.
- The outer fullselect doesn't use the VALUES clause.
- The outer fullselect doesn't use the GROUP BY or HAVING clauses.
- The outer fullselect doesn't include column functions in its select list.
- The outer fullselect doesn't use set operations (UNION, EXCEPT, or INTERSECT) with the exception of UNION ALL.
- The base tables in the operands of a UNION ALL must not be the same table, and each operand must be deletable.
- The select list of the outer fullselect does not include DISTINCT.

A view must meet all the rules listed above to be considered a deletable view.

```
CREATE VIEW deletable_view
  (tcid,cid,number,date_taken,start_time,seat_no,score)
AS
  SELECT tcid,cid,number,date_taken,
         start_time,seat_no,score
  FROM db2cert.test_taken
  WHERE tcid=center_id('TR01')
```

Fig. 6–28 *Example of a deletable view*

The view shown in Fig. 6–28 is deletable. It follows all the rules for a deletable view.

Updatable Views

An updatable view is a special case of a deletable view. A deletable view becomes an updatable view when at least one of its columns is updatable.

A column of a view is updatable when all of the following rules are true:

- The view is deletable.
- The column resolves to a column of a base table (not using a dereference operation) and the READ ONLY option is not specified.
- All the corresponding columns of the operands of a UNION ALL have exactly matching data types (including length or precision and scale) and matching default values if the fullselect of the view includes a UNION ALL.

```
CREATE VIEW updatable_view
  (tcid,cid,number,current_date,current_time,seat_no,score)
AS
  SELECT tcid,cid,number,CURRENT DATE,
                  CURRENT TIME,seat_no,score
  FROM db2cert.test_taken
  WHERE char(tcid)='TX01'
```

Fig. 6–29 *Example of an updatable view*

The view definition in Fig. 6–29 uses constant values that cannot be updated. However, the view is a deletable view and at least you can update one of its columns. Therefore, it is an updatable view.

Insertable Views

Insertable views allow you to insert rows using the view definition. A view is insertable when:

- All of its columns are updatable.
- The fullselect of the view definition doesn't include UNION ALL.

```
CREATE VIEW insertable_view
      (test_number,test_name,total_taken)
AS
SELECT number,name,totaltaken FROM db2cert.test
```

Fig. 6–30 *Example of an insertable view*

The view shown in Fig. 6–30 is an insertable view. However, an attempt to insert the view will fail. This is because there are columns in the base table that don't accept null values. Some of these columns are not present in the view definition. When you try to insert a value using the view, DB2 will try to insert a NULL into a NOT NULL column. This action is not permitted.

Note: Remember, the constraints defined on the base table are independent of the operations that can be performed using a view.

Read-Only Views

A read-only view is a nondeletable view. A view can be read-only if it is a view that doesn't comply with at least one of the rules for deletable views.

The READONLY column in the SYSCAT.VIEWS catalog view indicates a view is read-only (R).

Let's examine a read-only view:

```
CREATE VIEW read_only_view
   (name,work_phone,home_phone)
AS
SELECT DISTINCT fname,wphone,hphone
   FROM db2cert.candidate c, db2cert.test_taken tt
   WHERE c.cid=tt.cid
```

Fig. 6–31 *Example of a read-only view*

The view shown in Fig. 6–31 is not a deletable view as it uses the DISTINCT clause and the SQL statement involves more than one table.

Inoperative Views

A inoperative view is a view that is no longer available for SQL statements. A view becomes inoperative if:

- A privilege on which the view definition is dependent is revoked.
- An object, such as a table, alias, or function, on which the view definition is dependent is dropped.
- A view on which the view definition is dependent becomes inoperative.
- A view that is the super-view of the view definition (the sub-view) becomes inoperative.

Manipulating Database Objects

Summary

In this chapter, we have discussed the Data Manipulation Language (DML). DML has four primary statements: SELECT, UPDATE, INSERT, and DELETE. These statements enable all database object data manipulation.

The knowledge of basic SQL is mandatory for a DB2 database administrator and application developer. However, SQL is very powerful language, and the level of SQL will vary depending on the user's primary activity.

In this chapter, we talked about the basic functions of SQL statements, such as how to retrieve rows, how to sort the result set, how to restrict the result with some conditions, how to retrieve rows from more than one table at a time, how to add a row to a table, how to remove a record, how to change the value of the table, and so on. If you are a business analyst, you may expect more analytical, statistical information from DB2. DB2 supports very powerful SQL functions, such as OLAP, for various business needs. We'll talk about some advanced SQL in the next chapter.

Advanced SQL

- ◆ TRIGGERS
- ◆ RECURSIVE SQL
- ◆ OUTER JOIN
- ◆ OLAP
- ◆ CASE EXPRESSIONS
- ◆ TYPED TABLES
- ◆ SUMMARY TABLES

*T*his chapter will cover some very powerful features found in DB2's SQL. Features, such as triggers, recursion, outer join, OLAP features, and uses of the case expression, will be discussed. In addition, we will discuss structured types, typed tables, user-defined functions, and summary tables.

Triggers

A *trigger* is a set of actions that will be executed when a defined event occurs. The triggering events can be the following SQL statements:

- `INSERT`
- `UPDATE`
- `DELETE`

Triggers are defined for a specific table and once defined, a trigger is automatically active. A table can have multiple triggers defined for it, and if multiple triggers are defined for a given table, the order of trigger activation is based on the trigger creation timestamp (the order in which the triggers were created). Trigger definitions are stored in the system catalog tables. You can see them through these catalog views:

- `SYSCAT.TRIGGERS` - contains the trigger definition information; one row for each trigger defined
- `SYSCAT.TRIGDEP` - contains one row for every dependency of a trigger on some other object

Trigger Usage

Some of the uses of a trigger include:

- Data Validation - ensures that a new data value is within the proper range. This is similar to table-check constraints, but it is a more flexible data validation mechanism.
- Data Conditioning - implemented using triggers that fire before data record modification. This allows the new data value to be modified or conditioned to a predefined value.
- Data Integrity - can be used to ensure that cross-table dependencies are maintained. The triggered action could involve updating data records in related tables. This is similar to referential integrity, but it is a more flexible alternative.

Trigger Activation

A trigger can be defined to fire (be activated) in one of two ways:

- A *before trigger* will fire for each row in the set of affected rows before the triggering SQL statement executes. Therefore, the trigger body is seeing the new data values prior to their being inserted or updated into the table.

- An *after trigger* will fire for each row in the set of affected rows or after the statement has successfully completed (depending on the defined granularity). Therefore, the trigger body is seeing the table as being in a consistent state. (All transactions have been completed.)

Another important feature about triggers is that they can fire other triggers (or the same trigger) or other constraints. These are known as *cascading triggers*.

During the execution of a trigger, the new and old data values can be accessible to the trigger depending on the nature of the trigger (before or after).

By using triggers you can:

- Reduce the amount of application development and make development faster. Since triggers are stored in DB2 itself and are processed by DB2, you do not need to code the triggers or their actions into your applications.
- Provide a global environment for your business rules. Since the triggers only have to be defined once and then are stored in the database, they are available to all applications executing against the database.
- Reduce the maintenance of your applications. Again, since the trigger is handled by DB2 and is stored in the database itself, any changes to the trigger due to changes in your environment only have to occur in one not multiple applications.

The best method of understanding the usage of triggers is to see some in action. The DB2CERT database contains many relationships that can be maintained using triggers.

Trigger Example (After Trigger)

In Fig. 7–1, a trigger is defined to set the value of the PASS_FAIL column for each of the tests taken by a candidate. (Note that we add this column for this scenario.) The trigger has been given the name PassFail (no relationship with the column called PASS_FAIL). Once the trigger has been created, it is active.

The PassFail trigger is an AFTER, INSERT, and FOR EACH ROW trigger. Every time there is a row inserted into the test_taken table, this trigger will fire. The trigger body section will perform an UPDATE statement to set the value of the PASS_FAIL column for the newly inserted row. The column is populated with either the value P (representing a passing grade) or the value F (representing a failing grade).

> **Note:** Remember that a trigger defined against one table can modify other tables in the trigger body.

```
CREATE TRIGGER PassFail AFTER INSERT ON db2cert.test_taken
     REFERENCING NEW AS n
     FOR EACH ROW MODE DB2SQL
UPDATE db2cert.test_taken
SET PASS_FAIL =
          CASE
          WHEN n.score >=
              (SELECT cut_score FROM db2cert.test
                WHERE number = n.number)
               THEN'P'
          WHEN n.score <
              (SELECT cut_score FROM db2cert.test
                WHERE number = n.number)
               THEN'F'
          END
WHERE n.cid       = cid
  AND n.tcid      = tcid
  AND n.number    = number
  AND n.date_taken = date_taken
```

Fig. 7–1 *Creating an AFTER trigger*

Trigger Example (Before Trigger)

A before trigger will be activated before the trigger operation has completed. The triggering operation can be an INSERT, UPDATE, or DELETE statement. This type of trigger is very useful for three purposes: to condition data, to provide default values, or to enforce data value constraints dynamically.

There are three before trigger examples shown in Fig. 7–2 through Fig. 7–4 that are used in the DB2 Certification application.

All three of these triggers have been implemented to avoid seat conflicts for test candidates. The triggers will fire during an insert of each new candidate for a test.

```
CREATE TRIGGER pre9 NO CASCADE BEFORE
   INSERT ON db2cert.test_taken
      REFERENCING NEW AS n
      FOR EACH ROW MODE DB2SQL
      WHEN (n.start_time <'09:00:00')
   SIGNAL SQLSTATE'70003'
   ('Cannot assign seat before 09:00:00!')
```

Fig. 7–2 *Before trigger example (1)*

```
CREATE TRIGGER aft5 NO CASCADE BEFORE
   INSERT ON db2cert.test_taken
      REFERENCING NEW AS n
      FOR EACH ROW MODE DB2SQL
      WHEN (n.start_time +
            (SELECT SMALLINT(length) FROM db2cert.test
              WHERE number = n.number) MINUTES
                                        >'17:00:00')
   SIGNAL SQLSTATE'70004'
   ('Cannot assign seat after 17:00:00!')
```

Fig. 7–3 *Before trigger example (2)*

```
CREATE TRIGGER start NO CASCADE BEFORE
   INSERT ON db2cert.test_taken
      REFERENCING NEW AS n
      FOR EACH ROW MODE DB2SQL
      WHEN (
        EXISTS (SELECT cid FROM db2cert.test_taken
                WHERE seat_no   = n.seat_no    AND
                      tcid      = n.tcid       AND
                      date_taken = n.date_taken AND
                      n.start_time BETWEEN
                        start_time AND finish_time))
   SIGNAL SQLSTATE'70001'
   ('Start Time Conflict!')
```

Fig. 7–4 *Before trigger example (3)*

If the conditions are encountered, an SQL error will be flagged using the SQL function called SIGNAL. A different SQLSTATE value will be provided when the triggered conditions are encountered.

The pre9 trigger, shown in Fig. 7–2, is used to ensure that a test candidate is not scheduled to take a test before 9:00 a.m. The aft5 trigger is used to ensure that a test candidate is not scheduled to take a test after 5:00 p.m. The start trigger is used to avoid conflicts during a testing day.

Recursive SQL

A *recursive SQL* statement is one where an SQL statement repeatedly uses the resulting set to determine further results. This kind of SQL statement is built using a common table expression that make references to itself (i.e., it uses its own definition).

Such statements are useful to solve queries, such as hierarchical trees, routing airline flights, or bill-of-material types of queries.

Let's say that we have a table that indicates the distance between two cities. For this example, we are using the flights table. It contains information about the origin, destination, and distance between cities.

The table is shown in Fig. 7–5.

```
ORIGIN       DESTINATION DISTANCE
----------   ----------- -----------
Germany      New York        8000
Germany      Chicago         8700
Chicago      Austin          1300
New York     Houston         2100
Houston      Austin           300
New York     Chicago          950
Italy        New York       10000
Italy        Chicago        11000
Ireland      Chicago        10700
Chicago      Toronto          400
New York     Toronto          350
Mexico       Houston          770
```

Fig. 7–5 *Recursive SQL: Content of the flights table*

Our goal is to obtain a list with the distance and number of stops of all the destinations you can reach departing from Germany. We will create a recursive SQL statement to retrieve this information.

Let's first explain why this kind of query is resolved using recursive SQL. The table contains information about destinations and origins. After reaching one specific destination, this destination can be treated as an origin. This is where the recursion appears: The destination becomes an origin, and the next destination can become a new origin, and so on.

The way to resolve this query is by writing an SQL statement that, given an origin, will retrieve its destinations, then treat them as origins, obtain the new destinations, and so on.

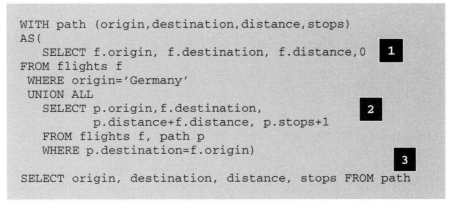

```
WITH path (origin,destination,distance,stops)
AS(
    SELECT f.origin, f.destination, f.distance,0    1
FROM flights f
  WHERE origin='Germany'
  UNION ALL
    SELECT p.origin,f.destination,                2
          p.distance+f.distance, p.stops+1
    FROM flights f, path p
    WHERE p.destination=f.origin)
                                                  3
SELECT origin, destination, distance, stops FROM path
```

Fig. 7–6 *Recursive SQL: Obtaining all the destinations from Germany*

As we have said before, recursion is built on common table expressions. In the recursive SQL example shown in Fig. 7–6, the common table expression is called path.

In **1** , we are obtaining the destinations that can be reached directly from Germany. In this case, the stops column is set to 0, because the flights are nonstop.

Then, in **2** , we are referencing the recently created common table expression path. In this part, we join the common table expression with the base table to create the recursion. This is where the destination becomes a new origin. We are also incrementing the distance and the number of stops. Observe that a UNION ALL clause is needed in the definition of a recursive query.

Finally, in **3** , we are retrieving all the possible routes accessible from Germany, the distance, and the number of stops.

The output of the recursive SQL statement is show in Fig. 7–7.

Advanced SQL

```
ORIGIN      DESTINATION  DISTANCE  STOPS
----------  -----------  --------  -----
SQL0347W The recursive common table expression "DB2.PATH"
may contain an infinite loop. SQLSTATE=01605

Germany     New York        8000       0
Germany     Chicago         8700       0
Germany     Houston        10100       1
Germany     Chicago         8950       1
Germany     Toronto         8350       1
Germany     Austin         10000       1
Germany     Toronto         9100       1
Germany     Austin         10400       2
Germany     Austin         10250       2
Germany     Toronto         9350       2
```

Fig. 7–7 *Recursive SQL: Destinations reached from Germany*

The SQL statement shown in Fig. 7–6 can run forever if there is a loop found in the flights table. When you are coding this kind of SQL statement, you must be aware of the possibility of infinite loops. To avoid an infinite loop, you can restrict the query using the number of stops.

Let's say that you are only interested in the routes that make less than five stops. You need to add the following restriction to the last SQL statement:

```
WHERE stops < 5
```

This condition can be used to avoid an infinite loop.

Now, let's create a more complex example based on the same idea. We want to obtain a list of the possible flights from Germany to Austin. This time, we want to obtain the flight route, the distance, and the number of stops.

As we can see from the output in Fig. 7–7, there are three different paths to reach Austin from Germany. Let's create the SQL statement that can tell us the complete path for each case.

```
WITH detail_path (origin,destination,route,distance,stops)
AS(
   SELECT f.origin, f.destination,
      VARCHAR(SUBSTR(f.origin,1,2),35),f.distance,0    1
      FROM flights f
      WHERE origin='Germany'
   UNION ALL
   SELECT p.origin,f.destination,
         route ||'>' || SUBSTR(p.destination,1,2),   2
         p.distance+f.distance, p.stops+1
      FROM flights f,detail_path p
      WHERE p.destination=f.origin
   )
                                                          3
SELECT route ||'>' || SUBSTR(destination,1,2),
      distance, stops
   FROM detail_path WHERE destination='Austin'
   ORDER BY distance
```

Fig. 7–8 *Recursive SQL: Obtaining routes from Germany to Austin*

The basics of the SQL statement in Fig. 7–8 are the same as the previous example. The difference is that now we are creating the route column. This column is created by extracting the first two characters of each visited airport on the way from Germany to Austin. The || (concatenation) operator is used to link each one of the cities visited to another.

In **1**, we are using the VARCHAR function to create a varchar column that will store all the cities visited in a specific path. This step will also add the origin city.

Then, in **2**, we are linking the route with each one of the intermediary cities visited.

Finally, in **3**, we link the final destination to the path. Also in this step, we specify the desired destination.

```
1                              DISTANCE   STOPS
----------------------- ----------- -----------
SQL0347W The recursive common table expression
"DB2.DETAIL_PATH" may contain an infinite loop.
SQLSTATE=01605

Ge>Ch>Au                       10000          1
Ge>Ne>Ch>Au                    10250          2
Ge>Ne>Ho>Au                    10400          2
```

Fig. 7–9 *Detailed path from Germany to Austin*

Outer Join

The join operation used most often is the one we have been using in the book exercises, which is known as an INNER JOIN. Now, we will talk about a different kind of join operation.

The result set of an inner join consists only of those matched rows that are present in both joined tables. What happens when we need to include those values that are present in one or another joined table, but not in both of them? This is the case when we need to use an OUTER JOIN operation. Outer joins are designed to generate an answer set that includes those values that are present in joined tables and those that are not. There are different kinds of outer joins as we will see.

Before getting into the details of the outer join, we will examine the explicit syntax used to code joins between tables. Let's start with an inner join coded with this syntax. The following join example produces an answer set containing the first name, the phone number, and the highest score for each candidate in the test_taken table.

```
SELECT fname, wphone, MAX(INTEGER(score))
  FROM db2cert.candidate c
      INNER JOIN db2cert.test_taken tt ON c.cid=tt.cid
GROUP BY fname, wphone
```

In this syntax, you indicate the tables that will be joined, along with the join operation, and the join columns that are required.

Observe the INNER JOIN operator in the example above. It belongs to the FROM clause of the statement. The INNER JOIN operator specifies that an inner join operation will be used for the statement. The keyword ON is used to specify the join conditions for the tables being joined. In our example, the join condition is based on the join columns, cid of the candidate table, and cid of the test_taken table.

The explicit join syntax also allows you to specify an outer join as we will see in the next sections.

Left Outer Join

A LEFT OUTER JOIN operation, also known as left join, produces an answer set that includes the matching values of both joined tables and those values only present in the left joined table. The left joined table is the one used in the left part of the LEFT OUTER JOIN operator when coding the join operation.

Advanced SQL

Note: You can also use LEFT JOIN to indicate a left outer join operation.

We have been requested to generate a report that includes the first name, the phone number, and the highest score for all the candidates present in the candidate table. If an inner join is used, as is shown in the last example, the report will only include data of those candidates present in the test_taken table.

The request could be solved using some SQL statements already discussed; however, the construction will be complex. We will use the left outer join to satisfy the request as the following example shows.

```
SELECT fname, wphone, MAX(INTEGER(score))
  FROM db2cert.candidate c
      LEFT OUTER JOIN db2cert.test_taken tt ON c.cid=tt.cid
  GROUP BY fname, wphone
```

Observe the syntax used to indicate a left outer join. The LEFT OUTER JOIN operator is used to indicate the left outer join operation. In this example, the answer set includes those candidates not present in the test_taken table. The MAX(INTEGER(score)) column will show nulls for those candidates.

Right Outer Join

A RIGHT OUTER JOIN operation, also known as right join, produces an answer set that includes the matching values of both joined tables and those values only present in the right joined table. The right joined table is the one used in the right part of the RIGHT OUTER JOIN operator when coding the join operation.

The example using a right outer join is shown below:

```
SELECT name, count(DISTINCT char(tt.cid))
    FROM db2cert.test_taken tt
      RIGHT OUTER JOIN db2cert.test t
      ON tt.number = t.number
    GROUP BY name
```

In this example, all test names present in the test table and the number of candidates who scheduled or took each test are requested. Notice there may be some tests for which no candidate was scheduled. You cannot report such tests using a inner join statement; however, you can do it using right outer join.

Full Outer Join

The `FULL OUTER JOIN` operation produces an answer set that includes the matching values of both joined tables and those values not present in one or the other of the tables.

To show a full outer join operation, we will create two sample tables: city and country. They show the relationship between a city and a country (`city` table) and a country and a continent (`country` table). The city table is designed to have countries that are not in the country table. The country table is also designed to have countries that are not in the city table. The contents of both tables are shown in Fig. 7–10 and Fig. 7–11.

```
CITY_NAME          COUNTRY_NAME
---------------    ---------------
Sidney             Australia
London             England
Dublin             Ireland
Firenze            Italy
Milano             Italy
Mexico             Mexico
Lima               Peru
Toronto            Canada
Vienna             Austria
Hannover           Germany
```

Fig. 7–10 *City table used in outer join*

```
COUNTRY_NAME      CONTINENT
---------------   ----------------------------
Australia         Australian Continent
England           European Continent
Ireland           European Continent
Italy             European Continent
Mexico            American Continent
Austria           European Continent
South Africa      African Continent
Spain             European Continent
```

Fig. 7–11 *Country table used in outer join*

We want to show all the countries, cities, and the continents that are in the tables. Therefore, we are using a full outer join as the following example shows:

```
SELECT ctry.continent, ctry.country_name,
       cty.country_name, cty.city_name
    FROM country ctry
         FULL OUTER JOIN
         city cty
         ON cty.country_name=ctry.country_name
    ORDER BY ctry.continent,
             cty.country_name,
             cty.city_name
```

Fig. 7–12 *Full outer join*

The result of the query is as follows:

```
CONTINENT                COUNTRY_NAME   COUNTRY_NAME   CITY_NAME
--------------------     ------------   ------------   ---------
African Continent        South Africa   -              -
American Continent       Mexico         Mexico         Mexico
Australian Continent     Australia      Australia      Sidney
European Continent       Austria        Austria        Vienna
European Continent       England        England        London
European Continent       Ireland        Ireland        Dublin
European Continent       Italy          Italy          Firenze
European Continent       Italy          Italy          Milano
European Continent       Spain          -              -
-                        -              Canada         Toronto
-                        -              Germany        Hannover
-                        -              Peru           Lima
```

Fig. 7–13 *Output of the full outer join*

As shown in Fig. 7–13, the rows that have a null value were added by the outer join operation. The `country_name` column is shown twice to see those countries present in the country table that are not present in the city table and vice versa.

Combining Outer Joins

Up to now we have discussed each outer join operation separately. Now, we will show a more complex example combining two outer joins in one single query. Let's display all the candidates and all the tests with their respective scores.

To create this query, we need two outer joins. The first outer join will obtain all candidates and their scores including candidates who did not schedule or take any tests. The second outer join will retrieve all the tests present in the test table even if no candidate scheduled or took those tests.

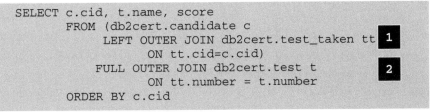

```
SELECT c.cid, t.name, score
    FROM (db2cert.candidate c
        LEFT OUTER JOIN db2cert.test_taken tt  1
            ON tt.cid=c.cid)
        FULL OUTER JOIN db2cert.test t          2
            ON tt.number = t.number
    ORDER BY c.cid
```

Fig. 7–14 *Two outer joins in one SQL statement*

The first outer join **1** is enclosed in parentheses. The parentheses are used for readability and to denote that the left outer join will be resolved first. This left outer join gathers all the candidate IDs. We only need a left outer join here. Because of referential integrity constraints, table `test_taken` can only have candidates present in the `candidate` table.

The second part is a full outer join **2**. With this outer join, we take all the tests taken by the candidates, the result of the left outer join, and join them with all the tests in the `test` table. We need a full outer join this time even though the `test_taken` table can only have test numbers that are present in the `test` table, because the left table of this outer join, which is the result of the first join, may include NULL values as a test number. The `test` table does not have null values, so we need to use a full outer join.

The output of the SQL statement is shown in Fig. 7–15.

Advanced SQL

```
CID NAME                                        SCORE
--- ------------------------------------------- -----------
111 DB2 Fundamentals                               65
111 DB2 Administration                             73
111 DB2 Application Development                     67
222 DB2 Fundamentals                               55
222 DB2 Application Development                     53
222 DB2 Application Development                     75
333 DB2 Fundamentals                               82
333 DB2 Administration                              -
333 DB2 Application Development                     92
444 -                                               -
555 -                                               -
666 -                                               -
777 -                                               -
888 -                                               -

 14 record(s) selected.
```

Fig. 7–15 *Result of two outer joins combined*

OLAP Features

Databases normally hold large amounts of data that can be updated, deleted, queried, and inserted on a daily basis. Databases in which data is constantly updated, deleted, and inserted are known as *Online Transaction Processing (OLTP)* systems. Databases that hold large amounts of data and do not have a heavy transaction work load but do have a large number of concurrent queries executing all the time, are known as *Decision Support Systems (DSS)*. Certain decision support systems have fewer queries, but each query can be very complex. These allow users to examine the data from different perspectives by performing *Online Analytical Processing (OLAP)*.

The functionality of the database is required to provide multidimensional views of relational data, without a significant performance effect. DB2 provides this capability, using a number of joining methods, SQL statements, and other database features. The next few sections explain the database technology found in DB2 that enhances the performance of OLAP queries.

STAR Schemas

The concept of a *STAR schema* is illustrated in Fig. 7–16. A business view of a highly normalized database often requires a number of attributes associated with one primary object. Each of these attributes is contained in separate tables.

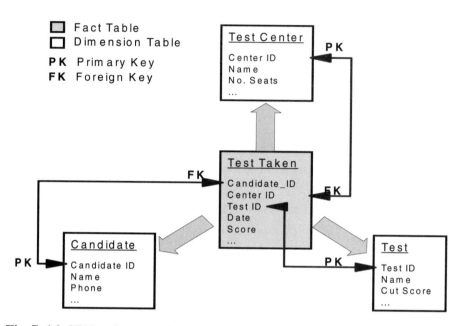

Fig. 7–16 *STAR schema in the DB2CERT database*

The following points are characteristic of a STAR schema design:

- There is a large Fact table that contains data relating to the Dimension tables. In Fig. 7–16, the Fact table is the test_taken table. It contains detailed information on each test taken, including exactly which test was taken, in which center the test was taken, and who took the test.
- There are a number of small Dimension tables that typically hold descriptive information about an entity that has a small number of rows. In Fig. 7–16, the Dimension tables are test, candidate, and test_center.
- The primary keys of the Dimension tables involved in the STAR schema supply foreign key entries in the Fact table. The concatenation of foreign keys from the Dimension tables usually forms a small subset of the Fact table. In Fig. 7–16, the foreign keys are Candidate ID, Center ID, and Test ID.

This approach allows as few attributes as possible to be stored in the Fact table. The benefit of this is that the Fact table is usually very large and therefore any data duplication in this table would be very costly in terms of storage and access times. If the DB2CERT database were used to store information on a university's entrance examinations, for example, the test_taken table could grow enormously.

OLAP schemas, such as the STAR schemas, are frequently used for large databases. These schemas make it very important to access the data in these databases in the optimal manner. Otherwise, the joins involved in the schemas may result in poor performance.

OLAP Indexes

A typical STAR schema includes a large number of indexes. This is due to the adhoc nature of queries in an OLAP environment. Such an environment is typically not subjected to constant insert or update activity and, therefore, does not have to suffer from significant performance degradation as a result of index maintenance.

The prime consideration of indexes in an OLAP environment is to facilitate the joining of tables and the ordering of output. This is particularly important for the fact table where multiple indexes are defined, especially on foreign key columns relating to the dimension tables. The benefit of multiple indexes in this environment is improved query performance against the fact table. The indexes defined on the tables could either be single-column or multicolumn indexes.

There are also certain issues to be considered when using multiple indexes in the OLAP environment. The first is that multiple indexes will require a certain amount of space, depending on the number of columns in each index and the size of the tables. The second is that there will be a significant one-time cost when building indexes, perhaps during a bulk load.

STAR Joins

A typical query against databases designed with the STAR schema would consist of multiple local predicates referencing values in the dimension tables and contain join predicates connecting the dimension tables to the fact table as shown in Fig. 7–17. These types of queries are called *STAR joins*.

In this example, we wish to find the average score of DB2 tests taken by Canadian citizens in the small test centers year by year. A STAR join query is difficult to execute efficiently, because no single join predicate reduces the cardinality of the fact rows significantly, although the combination of join predicates results in a small answer set. The more dimension tables involved in the join result, the more potential there is to plan an inefficient access path. To execute STAR join queries efficiently, multiple index access can be performed by the optimizer.

Advanced SQL

```
SELECT t.name, YEAR(tt.date_taken) AS year,
       AVG(integer(tt.score)) AS avgsc
FROM test t, test_taken tt, test_center tc,
     candidate c
WHERE c.cid = tt.cid          AND
      tc.tcid = tt.tcid       AND
      t.number = tt.number    AND
      t.name LIKE 'DB2%'      AND
      c.country='Canada'      AND
      tc.noseats < 10
GROUP BY t.name, YEAR(tt.date_taken);
```

Fig. 7–17 *STAR join*

Super Grouping

We will now discuss OLAP features known as *super grouping* functions. These functions are used to analyze data in multiple dimensions. The dimensions can be seen as different levels of aggregation over a set of tables. The term super grouping is used to describe OLAP features, because they allow the retrieval of multiple aggregation levels in one single pass of data.

Multiple Groups (Grouping Sets)

The GROUPING SETS specification in the GROUP BY clause is used to generate multiple aggregation groups in a single SQL statement. This feature is used to generate aggregated data based on different grouping criteria. Using GROUPING SETS, it is possible to calculate aggregations that would otherwise require a set operation, such as UNION, to put together the different aggregated answer sets.

Let's suppose we want to know the following:

- How may tests have been taken at the test centers?
- How many tests of each type have been taken in each test center?

To gather this information, we first need to count the tests taken grouped by test center and then count the tests taken in each test center. This requirement needs two different grouping sets, one grouped by test center and another grouped by test name and test center. See the following example and the result:

```
SELECT tt.tcid,t.name,count(*)
    FROM db2cert.test_taken tt, db2cert.test t
    WHERE tt.number=t.number
    GROUP BY
        GROUPING SETS (tt.tcid,(tt.tcid,t.name))
```

Fig. 7–18 *Grouping sets used in an SQL statement*

```
TCID NAME                                              3
---- --------------------------------------- -----------
TR01 -                                                 3
TX01 -                                                 6
TR01 DB2 Application Development                       2
TR01 DB2 Fundamentals                                 1
TX01 DB2 Administration                               2
TX01 DB2 Application Development                       2
TX01 DB2 Fundamentals                                 2

7 record(s) selected.
```

Fig. 7–19 *Result of grouping sets*

The GROUPING SETS specification calculates the first requirement, which is the number of tests taken at each test center, by listing the tcid column of the test_taken table. Then the second requirement, which is the number of tests by test center and test name, is calculated by listing tcid column of the test_taken table and name column of the test table. This second grouping is the same as if you coded a regular GROUP BY by using GROUP BY TT.TCID,T.NAME.

As seen in the result set shown in Fig. 7–19, the grouping sets can be formed by one or more columns.

Adding a Grand Total

Using the GROUPING SETS specification, you can add a grand total to your query. The example shown in Fig. 7–18 doesn't display the total of all tests taken at all test centers. This can be calculated by adding the grand total group to the grouping sets list.

As groups are created, null values are added to those columns that don't have a value in a particular group. In this way, the grand total row will show null values in all columns except for the grand total itself.

Let's see the next example. This one is similar to the example shown in Fig. 7–18. This time we are including a grand total group and converting the null-generated values to character strings using the `value` SQL function. In this example, if the first argument of the `value` function is null, the character string supplied as the second argument will be the result of the `value` function.

```
SELECT value(char(tt.tcid),'All'),
       value(t.name,'All Tests'),
       count(*)
 FROM db2cert.test_taken tt, db2cert.test t
 WHERE tt.number=t.number
 GROUP BY
    GROUPING SETS
        (tt.tcid,(tt.tcid,t.name),())
```

Fig. 7–20 *Grouping sets with a grand total*

```
1    2                                          3
---- ------------------------------------ -----------
All All Tests                                        9
TR01 All Tests                                       3
TX01 All Tests                                       6
TR01 DB2 Application Development                     2
TR01 DB2 Fundamentals                               1
TX01 DB2 Administration                             2
TX01 DB2 Application Development                     2
TX01 DB2 Fundamentals                               2

8 record(s) selected.
```

Fig. 7–21 *Result of grouping sets with a grand total*

The grand total group is specified with a pair of empty parentheses ( ) in the grouping set list.

Recognizing Group Added Null Values

There will be cases when the data used in a grouping function contains null values. In this case, is important to be able to distinguish between a null value and a group-generated null value.

DB2 provides the `GROUPING` function that identifies those null-generated values by giving them a value of 1.

Note: The GROUPING function returns only the values of 1 or 0. One (1) means that the null value was generated by DB2, and 0 means that the value was not generated by DB2.

Now, let's use the GROUPING function inside a CASE expression to differentiate between those groups with added null values and regular null values. To keep the query small, the example will only use the CASE expression for the tt.tcid column.

```
SELECT
    CASE                                              1
      WHEN GROUPING(tt.tcid)=1
            THEN 'All'
      WHEN GROUPING(tt.tcid)=0
            THEN char(tt.tcid)
      END,
      VALUE(t.name,'All Tests'),
      GROUPING(tt.tcid) AS grouped_tcid,             2
      GROUPING(t.name) AS grouped_name,
      COUNT(*)
  FROM db2cert.test_taken tt, db2cert.test t
  WHERE tt.number=t.number
  GROUP BY
        GROUPING SETS (tt.tcid,(t.name,tt.tcid),())
```

Fig. 7–22 *Using the grouping function to identify group added null*

```
1     2                              GROUPED_TCID   GROUPED_NAME 5
----  -----------------------------  ------------   ------------ ------
All   All Tests                          1              1          9
TR01  All Tests                          0              1          3
TX01  All Tests                          0              1          6
TR01  DB2 Application Development         0              0          2
TR01  DB2 Fundamentals                   0              0          1
TX01  DB2 Administration                 0              0          2
TX01  DB2 Application Development         0              0          2
TX01  DB2 Fundamentals                   0              0          2

8 record(s) selected.
```

Fig. 7–23 *The Result of the grouping function*

The case expression **1** , uses the GROUPING function over the tcid column. If a value of 1 is returned, then All will be printed. In our example, All indicates that the row contains a group-added null value. A null-generated value represents all the tests centers. If the GROUPING function returns a 0, it means that the value of the tcid column for that row was not generated by DB2.

The GROUPING functions shown in **2** will display a value of 1 or 0 depending on the value of the columns tt.tcid and t.name for a particular row. A value of 1 in GROUPING(tt.tcid) means that the row is a total grouped on the tcid column.

ROLLUP

The GROUPING SETS specification shown in the previous section allows you to create different levels of aggregation in one single pass of data. However, you need to specify each of the groups you want. There are cases when you need to create a report in which you require a total for each column you are grouping. Here is when a super group feature such as ROLLUP is required.

The ROLLUP grouping can generate various groups in one single pass. This will allow you to review different levels of aggregation as if you created a control break report.

Let's say that you need a report showing the following:

- How many tests have been taken by country?
- How many tests have been taken by country and test center?
- How many tests have been taken by country, test center, and test name?
- What is the total number of tests taken?

To solve this requirement, we will use the ROLLUP grouping, which will generate the aggregations requested. The SQL statement is shown in Fig. 7–24.

```
SELECT
  c.country,
  tt.tcid,
  substr(t.name,1,27) as test_name,
  count(*) as tests_taken
FROM db2cert.test_taken tt,db2cert.test t,db2cert.candidate c
WHERE tt.number=t.number AND tt.cid=c.cid
GROUP BY ROLLUP (c.country,tt.tcid,t.name)
ORDER BY c.country,tt.tcid,t.name
```

Fig. 7–24 *Using the ROLLUP operator*

The report generated allows you to roll up your information and drill down into your information. You can analyze the report from a grand-total level down to the country, test center, and test name.

```
COUNTRY        TCID  TEST_NAME                            TESTS_TAKEN
-------------  ----  -----------------------------------  ------------
Canada         TX01  DB2 Administration                             2
Canada         TX01  DB2 Application Development                     2
Canada         TX01  DB2 Fundamentals                               2
Canada         TX01  -                                              6
Canada         -     -                                              6
Germany        TR01  DB2 Application Development                     2
Germany        TR01  DB2 Fundamentals                               1
Germany        TR01  -                                              3
Germany        -     -                                              3
-              -     -                                              9

  10 record(s) selected.
```

Fig. 7–25 *The result of the ROLLUP operator*

Note: The ROLLUP operation is not commutative; the order in which you specify your groups is important. The resulting set of ROLLUP(COUNTRY, TCID, NAME) is different from ROLLUP(TCID, COUNTRY, NAME).

Super-group operations such as ROLLUP are built over the GROUPING SETS operation. The ROLLUP shown in Fig. 7–24 is equivalent to GROUPING SETS ((COUNTRY,TCID,NAME),(COUNTRY,TCID),COUNTRY, ()). This is why they are considered super-groups operations.

CUBE

From the answer set obtained by the ROLLUP operation shown in Fig. 7–24, there are some groups not present that can be useful. These groups include the number of tests taken only by test center or by test number.

The CUBE operation obtains all combinations of groups that can be formed in a grouping list. The groups, listed in the grouping list of a CUBE operation, will be permuted to calculate all the groups possible in that list. This creates all the aggregations needed to construct a cube of data.

The resulting cube can be sliced and diced in multiple dimensions to allow the users multidimensional analysis of data stored in DB2.

Now use the CUBE operation to generate the following groups:

- Tests taken by country
- Tests taken by test center
- Tests taken by test number
- All intermediate groups

You can write a statement as shown in Fig. 7–26.

```
SELECT c.country,tt.tcid,
       SUBSTR(t.name,1,27) AS test_name,
       COUNT(*) AS tests_taken
       FROM db2cert.test_taken tt,
            db2cert.test t,
            db2cert.candidate c
            WHERE tt.number=t.number
            AND    tt.cid=c.cid
             GROUP BY
                CUBE (c.country,tt.tcid,t.name)
                ORDER BY c.country,tt.tcid,t.name
```

Fig. 7–26 *Using the CUBE operator*

```
COUNTRY        TCID TEST_NAME                                   TESTS_TAKEN
-------------  ---- ------------------------------------------- -------------
Canada         TX01 DB2 Administration                                     2
Canada         TX01 DB2 Application Development                            2
Canada         TX01 DB2 Fundamentals                                       2
Canada         TX01 -                                                      6
Canada         -    DB2 Administration                                     2
Canada         -    DB2 Application Development                            2
Canada         -    DB2 Fundamentals                                       2
Canada         -    -                                                      6
Germany        TR01 DB2 Application Development                            2
Germany        TR01 DB2 Fundamentals                                       1
Germany        TR01 -                                                      3
Germany        -    DB2 Application Development                            2
Germany        -    DB2 Fundamentals                                       1
Germany        -    -                                                      3
-              TR01 DB2 Application Development                            2
-              TR01 DB2 Fundamentals                                       1
-              TR01 -                                                      3
-              TX01 DB2 Administration                                     2
-              TX01 DB2 Application Development                            2
-              TX01 DB2 Fundamentals                                       2
-              TX01 -                                                      6
-              -    DB2 Administration                                     2
-              -    DB2 Application Development                            4
-              -    DB2 Fundamentals                                       3
-              -    -                                                      9

 25 record(s) selected.
```

Fig. 7–27 *The result of the CUBE operator*

The CUBE operation shown in Fig. 7–26 generates eight different groups, including a grand total group. The number of groups generated by a CUBE operation is the result of the number of permutations that can be generated by the number of different groups listed in the grouping list.

The number of rows that super-group operations generate depends on the number of groups generated and the number of distinct values in each group.

The SQL statement shown in Fig. 7–26 can be written using the following GROUPING SETS:

```
GROUPING SETS ((COUNTRY,TCID,NAME),
               (COUNTRY,TCID),
               (COUNTRY,NAME),
               (TCID,NAME),
               (COUNTRY),
               (TCID),
               (NAME),
               ()
)
```

Fig. 7–28 *Grouping Sets generated by CUBE (COUNTRY, TCID, NAME)*

Moving Functions

DB2 contains a number of built-in functions that can help in the analysis of data. One type of calculation that is difficult to do in the relational model is one that is based on a "window" of data. For instance, you may want to know what the average of three sales is over a point in time. Column functions within DB2 (along with CUBE and ROLLUP) deal only with complete sets, not partial values.

Moving functions help to overcome this limitation with column functions. Along with the definition of a column function, a user can now supply a "window" specification to DB2 that defines how much data should be included as part of the calculation. For instance, Figure 7–29 shows a table with 10 values in it. These values could represent the sales of a store over 10 days. An AVG function applied to this data would give the average sales across all 10 days.

```
CREATE TABLE SALES (DAY INT, SALES INT);
INSERT INTO SALES VALUES (1,10),(2,14),(3,13),(4,15),
  (5,20),(6,14),(7,16),(8,17),(9,18),(10,9);

SELECT AVG(SALES) FROM SALES;

1
-----------
         14
```

Fig. 7–29 *Simple average calculation*

This AVG function could be modified to use a moving window. This is accomplished through the use of the OVER specification. Figure 7–30 shows the use of this function to calculate the moving 3-day average sales (1 day before and 1 day after).

```
SELECT DAY, AVG(SALES) OVER
   (ORDER BY DAY ROWS BETWEEN 1 PRECEDING AND 1 FOLLOWING)
   AS SMOOTH_VALUE FROM SALES;

DAY              SMOOTH_VALUE
-----------      -------------
          1               12
          2               12
          3               14
          4               16
          5               16
          6               16
          7               15
          8               17
          9               14
         10               13
```

Fig. 7–30 *Moving average calculation*

The moving average function gives a completely different picture from just doing an average against the column!

 Moving window calculations are a new feature to DB2 Version 7.1. The RANK function has also been improved in this release to allow more flexibility in the ranking calculations.

Advanced CASE Expressions

Up to now, we have been using the CASE expression in the select list of select statements. CASE expressions can also be used in other SQL statements, such as grouping lists, WHERE predicates, functions, and so on. We will review some of these uses in this section.

Using CASE Expressions to Group Values

As stated earlier, CASE expressions may be part of a grouping list. Being part of the grouping list can be used to rank data.

Suppose we want to know how many candidates have not passed the exams, how many have passed, and how many of them have an excellent score along with an average score for each classification. To solve this request, we will use a case expression in the select list and another one in the grouping list. The CASE expression used in the select list is used to rank the candidates. The CASE expression in the grouping list is used to create the groups based on the ranking defined in it.

```
SELECT number,
       CASE
           WHEN integer(SCORE) < 65 THEN 'Not Passed'
           WHEN SCORE < score(90)   THEN 'Passed'
           ELSE
              'Excellent'
       END as GROUPBY_CASE,
       COUNT(*) AS COUNT,
       AVG(integer(SCORE)) AS AVERAGE
       FROM db2cert.candidate c, db2cert.test_taken tt
       WHERE c.cid=tt.cid
       GROUP BY
          number,
          CASE
          WHEN integer(SCORE) < 65 THEN 'Not Passed'
          WHEN SCORE < score(90) THEN 'Passed'
          ELSE
             'Excellent'
          END
```

Fig. 7–31 *Grouping with CASE expressions*

Whenever you group using a CASE expression, the CASE expression in the grouping list must be exactly the same as the one used in the select list. What can be different is the use of the AS clause, because it is not permitted in the grouping list.

Using CASE Expressions in Functions

CASE expressions can be embedded as functions parameters. This allows you to pass different parameters to the function in a single pass of the data. Suppose that the `test_taken` table is very large and we have the following requirements:

- The number of tests taken with a score higher than 90
- The number of tests taken with a score of 90
- The number of tests taken with a score lower than 70
- The number of DB2 Fundamentals exams taken

Without the use of case expressions, this will require four different queries that will read the entire table. We want to do this in one single pass of the data, because the table is very large.

The query will use four count functions, each one evaluating different criteria using a CASE expression.

```
SELECT COUNT (CASE WHEN integer (score) > 90 then 1
                   ELSE null
             END) AS moregb90,
       COUNT (CASE WHEN integer (score) = 90 then 1
                   ELSE null
             END) AS equalgb90,
       COUNT (CASE WHEN integer (score) < 70 then 1
                   ELSE null
             END) AS minorgb70,
       COUNT (CASE WHEN number=test_id('500') then 1
                   ELSE null
             END) AS equalgb500
FROM db2cert.test_taken;
```

Fig. 7–32 *Using CASE expressions in functions*

This type of query may be useful when performing data inspection analysis. Notice that the four different requirements are solved in a single pass of the data.

The query was created using a different column function for each one of the conditions presented as a requirement. The conditions are evaluated in the case expression inside each function. When the condition evaluates true, it will return a value of 1 and the row will be counted. When the condition evaluates false, the case expression will return a null value and the row will not be counted.

Structured Types and Typed Tables

As mentioned in "Database Objects" on page 197, *user-defined structured types* are one of the data types in DB2 that allow you to create a structure that contains a sequence of named attributes, each of which has a data type. This structured type can be used as the type of a table or a view.

A table defined using a structured type is called a *typed table*, whereas a view defined using a structured type is called a *typed view*. A structured type can be a *sub-type* of another structured type, called a *super-type*. A sub-type inherits all attributes from its super-type and can be added to other attributes. A sub-type can be a super-type for other structured types. Therefore, you can create a hierarchy of structured types using this relationship between sub-type and super-type. Also, a hierarchy of typed tables can be created based on the structured type hierarchy. Structured types and typed tables enable you to configure a better model of business entities and relationships in the real world.

A structured type can be created by using the CREATE TYPE SQL statement. As discussed in "Database Objects" on page 197, a user-defined distinct type can also be created by a CREATE TYPE SQL statement, and it represents a column type of a table. For a user-defined structured type, you can call it a row type of a table. See Fig. 7–33 for an example.

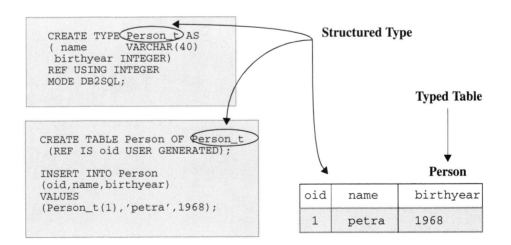

Fig. 7–33 *User-defined structured type*

In this example, a structured type Person_t is defined with two attributes, name and birthyear, and then a table Person is defined using the structured type.

Notice the table `Person` has `name` and `birthyear` columns that are defined by the `Person_t` type. The other column is called the *object identifier* (`OID`). Every typed table must have the `OID` column as its first column and the value of the `OID` column must be unique in the whole table hierarchy. The data type of the `OID` column is `REFERENCE`. Notice that the casting function `Person_t` is used to provide a value for the `OID` column in our example. The `OID` column will be talked about in greater detail later.

Creating Structured Types

A structured type supports a hierarchical structure. Therefore, a structured type can be created as a sub-type of another structured type (thereby inheriting the attributes of that type). Fig. 7–34 shows a simple structured type hierarchy. `Person_t` is defined as a `Root type` (not depending on other types) with two attributes, `name` and `birthyear`. `Emp_t` and `Student_t` are defined as sub-types of `Person_t`. Thus, `Emp_t` and `Student_t` inherit all attributes of `Person_t`. In addition, the structured type `Emp_t` and `Student_t` have several additional attributes that are specific to their particular types.

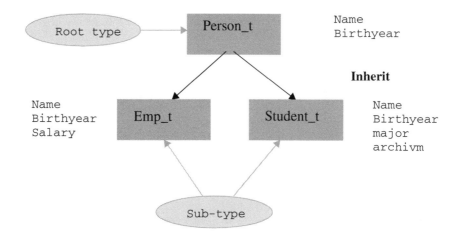

Fig. 7–34 *Hierarchy of structured types*

Let's see how we can define this structured type hierarchy. Look at the example shown in Fig. 7–35.

```
CREATE TYPE Person_t AS
  (Name VARCHAR(20),Birthyear SMALLINT)
    REF USING INTEGER
    MODE DB2SQL;

CREATE TYPE Emp_t UNDER Person_t
  AS (Salary INT)
  MODE DB2SQL;

CREATE TYPE Student_t UNDER Person_t
  AS (Major VARCHAR(10),
      Archivm DECIMAL(5,2))
  MODE DB2SQL;
```

Fig. 7–35 *Creating structured types and structured type hierarchies*

The AS clause provides the attribute definitions associated with the type. The UNDER clause specifies that the structured type is being defined as a sub-type of the specified super-type. In our example, the Emp_t type has Salary as its attribute. The Student_t type has Major and Archivm as its attributes. In addition, both have attributes Name and Birthyear, which are inherited from the Person_t type.

The REF USING clause is used when defining a root-type and specifies the built in data type used as the representation for the REFERENCE type of this structured type and all its sub-types. As seen in Fig. 7–33, a typed table must have the OID column, and a casting function is used when supplying a value for the OID column. This casting function casts the data type specified by the REF USING clause of the root type definition into the REFERENCE type. You can specify the following for the REFERENCE type: INTEGER, SMALLINT, BIGINT, DECIMAL, CHAR, VARCHAR, GRAPHIC, or VARGRAPHIC. The default type is VARCHAR(16) FOR BIT DATA.

Note: Successful execution of the CREATE TYPE statement also generates functions to cast between the REFERENCE type and its representation type (the built-in type specified by REF USING clause) and generates support for the comparison operators (=, <>, <, <=, >, and >=) for users with the REFERENCE type.

The MODE clause is used to specify the mode of the type. DB2SQL is the only value for MODE currently supported.

Altering Structured Types

The ALTER TYPE statement enables you to add or drop an attribute of an existing structured type. The following example shows the ALTER TYPE statements adding an attribute Tel to the Person_t type and dropping the attribute.

```
ALTER TYPE Person_t ADD ATTRIBUTE Tel CHAR(12);
ALTER TYPE Person_t DROP ATTRIBUTE Tel;
```

Note: The ALTER TYPE statement cannot be executed against a type if it, or one of its sub-types, is the type of an existing table.

Creating Typed Tables

A typed table is a table defined with a structured data type (refer to Fig. 7–33). Typed tables can have a hierarchy of structured types. A sub-table inherits all attributes of its super-table. All tables in an inherit relationship form a table hierarchy. A table that does not have a super-table in a hierarchy is called a *root-table*. In other words, a root-table is a table defined with the root-type of a type hierarchy.

A simple hierarchy of a typed table is shown in Fig. 7–36. You can see the two columns of the Person table are inherited by the Student table and the Emp table.

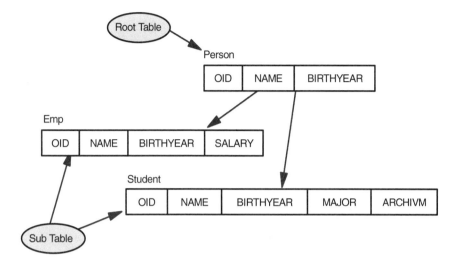

Fig. 7–36 *Hierarchy of typed tables*

Fig. 7–37 shows sample statements to create these typed tables. Typed tables are created using the CREATE TABLE statement.

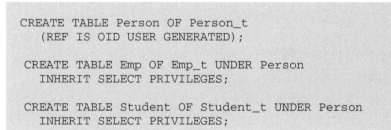

```
CREATE TABLE Person OF Person_t
   (REF IS OID USER GENERATED);

CREATE TABLE Emp OF Emp_t UNDER Person
   INHERIT SELECT PRIVILEGES;

CREATE TABLE Student OF Student_t UNDER Person
   INHERIT SELECT PRIVILEGES;
```

Fig. 7–37 *Create typed tables*

In our example, the Person table is the root-table, and the Emp table and the Student table are sub-tables. The Person table is defined to be of the structured type Person_t. This means that it has a column corresponding to each attribute of the structured type Person_t. The Emp table and the Student table inherit all attributes of the Person table.

As explained before, every typed table must have an OID column. The OID is defined at the root-table of a table hierarchy, and all sub-tables inherit the OID. The column name of the OID column is defined at the root-table of a table hierarchy using the REF IS clause. In our example, it is OID. Each row must have a unique value of OID in the whole hierarchy. The data type of the OID column is a system type REFERENCE.

The USER GENERATED clause indicates that the initial value for the OID column of each newly inserted row will be provided by the user when inserting a row. Once a row is inserted, the OID column cannot be updated.

The INHERIT SELECT PRIVILEGES clause means that any user or group holding SELECT privilege on the super table will be granted an equivalent privilege on the newly created sub-table. The definer of a sub-table is considered to be the grantor of this privilege.

Note: Within a typed table hierarchy, only one sub-table may exist of a particular sub-type.

Dropping Typed Tables

You can use a DROP TABLE statement to drop a typed table as well as a regular table. When you drop a typed table, you must make sure it does not have any sub-tables. If the typed table being dropped has sub-tables, the DROP TABLE statement will return an error.

Dropping a sub-table has the effect of deleting all the rows of the sub-table from the super-tables. Therefore, this may result in the activation of triggers or referential integrity constraints defined on the super-tables.

If you want to drop a whole table hierarchy, you can use the DROP TABLE HIERARCHY statement. Unlike dropping a single sub-table, dropping the table hierarchy does not result in the activation of triggers nor in referential integrity constraints of any tables in the hierarchy. The following example shows dropping the whole table hierarchy. You should specify the root table name of the table hierarchy.

```
DROP TABLE HIERARCHY Person
```

Note: You can use the DROP VIEW HIERARCHY statement to drop a total view hierarchy. The view hierarchy is explained later.

Inserting Rows into a Typed Table

Rows can be inserted into a typed table using an INSERT SQL statement. Examples of this are shown in Fig. 7–38.

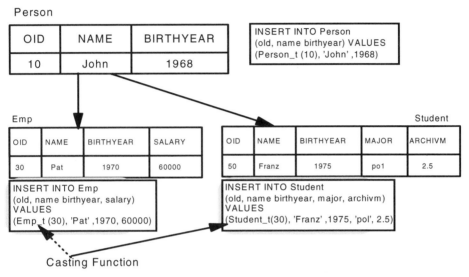

Fig. 7–38 *Inserting into a hierarchy of typed tables*

Notice that each INSERT statement uses a casting function for the value of the OID column. All OID values (of type REFERENCE) must be cast into the REFERENCE type of the table to which the value is being inserted. When you create a structured type, the casting function is created implicitly. The argument of the casing function should be of the built-in data type specified with the REF USING clause of the root type definition. The name of the casting function is the same as the underlying structured type, but optionally, you can specify another casting function name in the CREATE TYPE statement. See the *DB2 UDB V7.1 SQL Reference* manual for further details.

Selecting a Row from a Typed Table

When you issue a select statement for a typed table, the rows are returned from the target table and all of its sub-tables in the table hierarchy. Fig. 7–39 shows the SELECT statements against some typed tables. Each SELECT statement retrieves all columns and all rows from each table. Notice the select statement for the Person table returns not only the rows of the Person table but also the rows of the Emp table and Student table.

```
SELECT * FROM Person;

OID   NAME     BIRTHYEAR
----  ------   -----------
  10  John          1968
  30  Pat           1970
  50  Franz         1975

SELECT * FROM Emp;

OID   NAME     BIRTHYEAR     SALARY
----  ------   -----------   ---------
  30  Pat            1970       60000

SELECT * FROM Student;

OID   NAME     BIRTHYEAR   MAJOR   ARCHIVM
----  ------   -----------  ------  -------
  50  Franz          1975   POL         2.5
```

Fig. 7–39 *Issuing a SELECT statement against typed tables*

If you want to retrieve only rows of the `Person` table, you can use the `ONLY` clause for a select statement as follows:

```
SELECT * FROM ONLY(Person)
```

If you want to retrieve columns from not only the specified table but also its sub-tables, you can use the `OUTER` clause for a select statement as follows.

```
SELECT * FROM OUTER(Person)
```

The result is shown in Fig. 7–40 on page 363.

```
OID   NAME   BIRTHYEAR    SALARY    MAJOR   ARCHIVM
----  -----  -----------  --------  ------  ---------
  10  John          1968       - -                  -
  30  Pat           1970      60000 -               -
  50  Franz         1975         - Pol            2.5
```

Fig. 7–40 *Using the OUTER clause against a typed table*

Updating and Deleting Rows from Typed Tables

As in a regular table, you can use UPDATE and DELETE statements to update or delete rows of a typed table. Be aware that update and delete statements affect the target table and its sub-tables in a manner like a select statement. Let's take a look at some examples.

The first example changes the birthyear of a person whose OID is 10 to 1969. This statement will affect Person and its sub-tables (Emp and Student). Notice that a casting function, Emp_t, is used to cast the type INTEGER into the REFERENCE type.

```
UPDATE Person SET birthyear=1969 WHERE oid=Emp_t(10)
```

The next example deletes all rows from the Person table and its sub-tables (Emp and Student).

```
DELETE FROM Person
```

If you want to update or delete rows of a particular typed table only (and not its sub-tables), you can use the ONLY clause for an update or a delete statement, as the following example shows:

```
DELETE FROM ONLY(Person)
```

Physical Implementation of Typed Tables

The physical implementation of a typed table hierarchy is one table that holds all attributes of the tables in the table hierarchy. This table is called a *Hierarchy table* (H-Table). When a root-table is created, an H-Table is automatically created. Each time a sub-table having other columns different than its root table is created, the H-Table is altered and new columns are added. You can specify the name of the H-Table using the `HIERARCHY` option of the create table statement, but the default name is the root-table name followed by the suffix `_HIERARCHY`. This physical implementation has an advantage in performance and you can regard typed tables as if they are views defined for an H-Table. Fig. 7–41 shows a logical view of the typed table hierarchy and H-Table.

 Note: The H-Table cannot be manipulated with SQL statements.

Hierarchy Table

Person_Hierarchy

TYPE_ID	OID	NAME	BIRTHYEAR	SALARY	MAJOR	ARCHIVM
1035	10	John	1968	–	–	–
1037	30	Pat	1970	60000	–	–
1039	50	Franz	1975	–	pol	2.5

Fig. 7–41 *Logical view of a Hierarchy table (H-Table)*

The first column of an H-Table is the `TYPE_ID` column. Each value of this column specifies the structured type of the typed table to which this row was inserted.

Once a structured type and a typed table are defined, the DB2 system catalog tables hold their information. Let's peek into the system catalog tables through some system catalog views.

You can see the `ROWTYPESCHEMA` and the `ROWTYPENAME` column from the `SYSCAT.TABLES` view. These columns have the information to maintain typed tables. You can see each structured type through the `SYSCAT.DATATYPES` view as shown in Fig. 7–42. The values of the `SOURCENAME` column of the `SYSCAT.DATATYPES` catalog view is the name of the built-in type which was specified with the `REF USING` clause when creating the root type. You can see that `Emp_t` and `Student_t` inherit the attributes from their root-type, `Person_t`.

```
SELECT TYPENAME,SOURCENAME,METATYPE FROM SYSCAT.DATATYPES
```

```
TYPENAME              SOURCENAME           METATYPE
------------------    ------------------   --------
PERSON_T              INTEGER              R
EMP_T                 INTEGER              R
STUDENT_T            INTEGER              R
```

Fig. 7–42 *System catalog view information for typed tables*

In this example, only rows for structured types are extracted. The SOURCENAME column would be NULL, and the METATYPE column would have an S for built in data types. For user-defined distinct types, the METATYPE column would be T.

The SYSCAT.HIERARCHIES system catalog view contains the relationship between a sub-table and its immediate super-table, and between a sub-type and its immediate super-type. Fig. 7–43 shows some information from SYSCAT.HIERARCHIES.

```
SELECT METATYPE,SUB_NAME,SUPER_NAME, ROOT_NAME FROM
SYSCAT.HIERARCHIES;
```

```
METATYPE SUB_NAME     SUPER_NAME    ROOT_NAME
-------- -----------  ------------  -----------
R        EMP_T        PERSON_T      PERSON_T
R        STUDENT_T    PERSON_T      PERSON_T
U        EMP          PERSON        PERSON
U        STUDENT      PERSON        PERSON
```

Fig. 7–43 *System catalog view information for hierarchy relationships*

The METATYPE column of the SYSCAT.HIERARCHIES catalog view encodes the relationship type of the object as follows:

R - Between structured types

U - Between typed tables

W- Between typed views

Typed views are described later in this chapter.

Advanced SQL

Reference Columns

In a typed table definition, you can define columns as *reference columns* to another typed table. This referenced typed table is called a *target table*. A reference column holds values that correspond to OID values of the target table and clearly identify rows in the target tables. The data type of a reference column is REFERENCE, the same type as OID in the target table. The reference column is similar to a foreign key; however, the evaluation, like a foreign key, is not performed for operations such as insert, update, or delete.

Look at Fig. 7–44. This shows you a typed table, EMP, which has a reference column referring another typed table DEPT. This relationship is defined when the CREATE TABLE statement is executed and is called a *scope*.

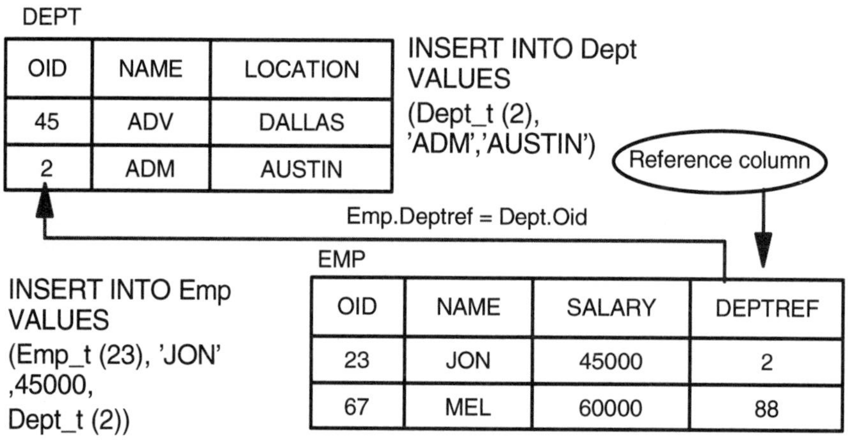

Fig. 7–44 *Reference column relationship*

As shown in Fig. 7–44, a reference column can have a value that the target table does not have. Notice the casting function Dept_t is used to provide a value for the reference column.

The reference column is defined through the CREATE TYPE and CREATE TABLE statements. Fig. 7–45 shows CREATE TYPE statements to set up a reference column, assuming the root type Person_t is already defined, as shown in Fig. 7–35 on page 357.

```
CREATE TYPE Dept_t AS (name CHAR(40),location CHAR(20))
 REF USING INTEGER MODE DB2SQL;

CREATE TYPE Emp_t UNDER Person_t
 AS (Salary INTEGER, Deptref REF(Dept_t)) MODE DB2SQL;
```

Fig. 7–45 *Create Type statement to define a reference column*

In our example, `Dept_t` is a root type of a different table hierarchy from the one to which `Emp_t` and `Person_t` belong. The definition of `Emp_t` supplies two attributes: one is `Salary`, which is of the `INTEGER` type, and the other is `Deptref`, which is of the `REFERENCE` type. `Deptref REF(Dept_t)` means that this attribute `Deptref` of `Emp_t` type is the reference type and the target of the reference is a row of the table whose row type is `Dept_t` or its sub-type.

You then need to create typed tables based on the structured types defined in Fig. 7–45. Fig. 7–46 shows the sample CREATE TABLE statements to define a reference column (define a scope). The second CREATE TABLE statement in this example creates a table with a reference column.

```
CREATE TABLE Dept OF Dept_t (REF IS Oid USER GENERATED);

CREATE TABLE Emp OF Emp_t UNDER Person
 INHERIT SELECT PRIVILEGES
 (Deptref WITH OPTIONS SCOPE Dept);
```

Fig. 7–46 *Create Table with a reference column*

In the CREATE TABLE statement, `Deptref WITH OPTIONS SCOPE Dept` means that the values in the column `Deptref` are pointing to rows in the table `Dept` or values in any sub-tables of the `Dept` table.

Dereference Operator

The *dereference operator* (->) returns the named column value of the target table or its sub-table from the row with the matching `OID` column. The following example shows a `SELECT` statement using the dereference operator.

```
SELECT E.name from emp E
   WHERE E.Deptref->location ='AUSTIN';
```

Advanced SQL

In this example, each `Deptref` column value is interrogated and checked. We check to see if the target table (`Dept` table) or its sub-table has a row whose `OID` value is the same. If such a row is found, the value of the `location` column is taken from that row and returned. That is how `Deptref->location` works. This predicate is true if the returned value is `AUSTIN`.

The `SELECT` statement above using the dereference operator (->) can be rewritten using a `JOIN` operation. The next example shows the equivalent SQL statement using a `JOIN` operation.

```
SELECT E.name from emp E, dept D
    WHERE E.deptref = D.oid
        AND D.location ='AUSTIN'
```

View Hierarchies

Typed views are views whose definition is based on structured types. You can create a view hierarchy with typed views as you would create a table hierarchy with typed tables. Fig. 7–47 shows the `CREATE VIEW` statements to define typed views. In our example, two typed views `Person_v` and `Emp_v` are created using the `Person_t` type and the `Emp_t` type. The `Person_v` view is defined as a root view of the view hierarchy and references all columns and rows of the `Person` table. The `Emp_v` view is defined as a sub-view of the `Person_v` view and references all columns and rows of the `Emp` table.

Notice that the `Person_v` definition uses the `ONLY` clause so that rows are selected from only the `Person` table. This is necessary because the `Person_v` view has a sub-view (`Emp_v`), and the `Person_v` view should not have rows that are assigned to the `Emp_v` view. Remember, it is not allowed to have duplicated `OID` values in the same view hierarchy.

The first `CREATE VIEW` statement will succeed even if `FROM Person` is used instead of `FROM ONLY(Person)`; however, you will get an error when creating the `Emp_v` view since all rows that conform to the full select of the `Emp_v` definition are referred to by the `Person_v` view. You do not need to use the `ONLY` clause for the `Emp_v` view because the `Emp_v` view does not have any sub-views.

```
CREATE VIEW Person_v OF Person_t MODE DB2SQL
  (REF IS Void USER GENERATED)
  AS SELECT Person_t(INTEGER(Oid)),Name,Birthyear
     FROM ONLY(Person);

CREATE VIEW Emp_v OF Emp_t MODE DB2SQL UNDER Person_v
  INHERIT SELECT PRIVILEGES
  AS SELECT Emp_t(INTEGER(Oid)),Name,Birthyear,Salary
     FROM Emp;
```

Fig. 7–47 *Create typed views*

SQL Functions for Typed Tables and Typed Views

You can use the following SQL functions for typed tables or typed views:

- DEREF (function)
- TYPE_ID (expression)
- TYPE_NAME (expression)
- TYPE_SCHEMA (expression)

The DEREF function returns the structured type of the argument. The argument can be the OID column or a reference column. The value that the DEREF function returns is also called a *dynamic data type*. This function can only be used on the left side of the TYPE predicate (explained later) or in the argument of the TYPE_ID, TYPE_NAME, or TYPE_SCHEMA functions. Let's look at each of the functions.

The TYPE_ID function returns the internal type identifier of the dynamic data type. The argument must be a structured type. The data type of the result of this function is an INTEGER. The following example shows an SQL statement using the TYPE_ID function. It retrieves the type identifier of each row and the person's name from the Person table.

```
SELECT TYPE_ID(DEREF(Oid)),name FROM Person
```

 Note: The values returned by the TYPE_ID function are not portable across databases. The type identifier may be different in each database even if the type schema and type name are the same.

The `TYPE_NAME` function returns the unqualified name of the dynamic data type. The argument must be a structured type. The data type of the result of the function is a `VARCHAR(18)`. The next example shows an SQL statement using the `TYPE_NAME` function. It retrieves the type name of each row (represented by `OID` values), `Name`, `Birthyear`, and the `Salary` from the table `Emp`.

```
SELECT TYPE_NAME(DEREF(Oid)),Name,Birthyear,Salary
     FROM Emp
```

The `TYPE_SCHEMA` function returns the schema name of the dynamic data type. The argument must be a structured type. The data type of the result of the function is a `VARCHAR(128)`. The next example shows an SQL statement using the `TYPE_SCHEMA` function. It retrieves the schema name of the dynamic type of each row (represented by `OID` values) and the `Name` from the table `Person`.

```
SELECT TYPE_SCHEMA(DEREF(Oid)),name FROM Person
```

TYPE Predicate

The `TYPE` predicate compares the type of an expression with one or more user-defined structured types. The `DEREF` function should be used whenever a `TYPE` predicate has an expression involving a reference type value. It evaluates whether the value that the `DEREF` function returns matches one or more candidates in the list. If there is a match, the result of the predicate is true. The next example shows an SQL statement using the `TYPE` predicate. It returns all attributes and rows whose `OID` type is `Person_t` and not a sub-type of `Person_t`.

```
SELECT * FROM Person
     WHERE DEREF(Oid) IS OF DYNAMIC TYPE (only Person_t);
```

You can leave out the keywords `DYNAMIC TYPE` and rewrite this example as follows:

```
SELECT * FROM Person
     WHERE DEREF(Oid) IS OF (only Person_t);
```

Considerations When Using Typed Tables and Views

Some considerations when using typed tables and views are:

- A primary key cannot be created on a sub-table (the primary key (OID) is inherited from the super table).
- An unique index cannot be created on a sub-table.
- A check constraint defined on a table automatically applies to all sub-tables of that table.
- The LOAD command is not supported.
- Replication is not supported.
- RUNSTATS, REORG, and REORGCHK can only be executed on a root-table.

Examples of a Typed Table Hierarchy

Now let's look at more examples of the user-defined structured type and typed table.

Assume you are building a data model of the people in a university. Each person has two base attributes, name and birth year. A person who works for the university is an employee. An employee belongs to a department and gets a salary. Therefore, salary and department are the attributes for an employee. A person who studies at the university is a student. A student majors in a subject and has an achievement record. Major and achievement are particular attributes for a student. A professor is working for the university, so he or she is an employee, but has a speciality. On the other hand, there are a lot of departments in an university. Each department has a manager, and the manager is working for the university as an employee.

The model of this example represents these relationships. Fig. 7–48 shows these relationships using structured types and a typed table hierarchy. There is a hierarchy whose root-type is Person_t. Emp_t and Student_t are the sub-types of Person_t, and Prof_t is a sub-type of Emp_t. There are two reference attributes, Mgr in Dept_t that points to Emp_t and Dept in Emp_t that points to Dept_t.

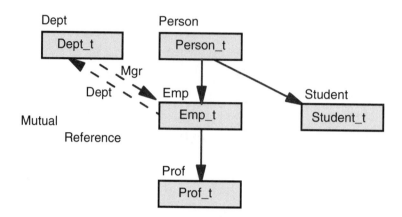

Fig. 7–48 *Example: Hierarchy of structured types and typed tables*

Dept_t and Emp_t reference each other. When you define two structured types referencing each other (mutual definition), you must create one of them first without the reference definition, and then add a reference attribute with the ALTER TYPE statement after the other type is created. This is because the referenced type should be defined in advance when a structured type is created with a reference.

In our example, the Emp_t type is created without a reference attribute first, and then the Dept_t type is created with the reference attribute Mgr, which refers the Emp_t type. Finally, the reference attribute Dept is added to the Emp_t type using an ALTER TYPE statement. See the SQL statements shown in Fig. 7–49.

```
CREATE TYPE Person_t AS
  (Name VARCHAR(20), Birthyear SMALLINT)
  REF USING INTEGER MODE DB2SQL;

CREATE TYPE Emp_t UNDER Person_t
  AS (Salary INT) MODE DB2SQL;

CREATE TYPE Student_t UNDER Person_t
  AS (Major CHAR(20), Archivm DECIMAL(5,2))
  MODE DB2SQL;

CREATE TYPE Dept_t AS
  (Name VARCHAR(20), Budget INT, Mgr REF(Emp_t))
  REF USING INTEGER MODE DB2SQL;

ALTER TYPE Emp_t ADD ATTRIBUTE Dept REF(Dept_t);

CREATE TYPE Prof_t UNDER Emp_t
  AS (Speciality VARCHAR(20)) MODE DB2SQL;
```

Fig. 7–49 *Example: Creating structured types*

Now let's create the table hierarchy. The table `Person`, which is created based on the `Person_t` type, is a root-table and has two sub-tables, `Emp` and `Student`. `Prof` is a sub-table of `Emp`. The table `Dept` has a scope of the reference column `Mgr`, which points to rows in the table `Emp`. The table `Emp` has a scope of the reference column `Dept`, which points to rows in the table `Dept`. Therefore, you should create the `Emp` table without a reference column, and then add a reference column after the `Dept` table is created. See the SQL statements shown Fig. 7–50.

Advanced SQL

```
CREATE TABLE Person OF Person_t
 (REF IS Oid USER GENERATED);

CREATE TABLE Emp OF Emp_t UNDER Person
 INHERIT SELECT PRIVILEGES;

CREATE TABLE Student OF Student_t UNDER Person
 INHERIT SELECT PRIVILEGES;

CREATE TABLE Dept OF Dept_t
 (REF IS Oid USER GENERATED, Mgr with options scope Emp);

ALTER TABLE Emp ALTER COLUMN Dept ADD SCOPE Dept;

CREATE TABLE Prof OF Prof_t UNDER Emp
      INHERIT SELECT PRIVILEGES;
```

Fig. 7–50 *Example: Creating typed tables*

The content of all the tables are shown in Fig. 7–51 (assuming these rows are previously inserted).

```
Person                              Dept
   OID    NAME    BIRTHYEAR            OID    NAME    BUDGET      MGR
------ ------- ----------          ------ -------- ----------- ----
       10 John        1968                10 math      300000    80
       20 Paul        1961                20 oec       500000    70
                                          30 headq    5000000    90
                                          40 itso     1000000    60


Emp

   OID    NAME    BIRTHYEAR  SALARY   DEPT
------ ------- ----------- -------- ------
       30 Pat         1970    60000     10
       40 Hitomi      1977    65000     20
       90 Lou            -        -      -
       50 Sam         1968    60000     40
       60 Uta         1961    95000     30


Student

  OID    NAME    BIRTHYEAR   MAJOR   ARCHIVM
------ -------- ----------- ------- -------
      100 Franzis     1975 pol       2.50
      110 Herb        1980 math      1.70


Prof

  OID    NAME    BIRTHYEAR   SALARY   DEPT  SPECIALITY
------ -------- ----------- -------- ------ ----------
       70 Rich        1941    90000     30 oec
       80 Herb        1962   120000     30 math
```

Fig. 7–51 *Example: Records that each typed table contains*

As already described, one hierarchy table (H-Table) is created for a table hierarchy. All columns and all rows of typed tables in a table hierarchy are stored in one hierarchy table. Let's look at the `Person_Hierarchy` table, which is the hierarchy table of our example, and see how a SELECT statement against typed tables is processed. Note that a hierarchy table cannot be directly manipulated by an SQL statement. See the following three examples. Each of them is a simple query from a typed table.

```
SELECT * FROM Person;

SELECT * FROM Emp;

SELECT * FROM OUTER(Emp);
```

The answer set is shown in Fig. 7–52. This figure shows the hierarchy table of our example and the answer set of the previous queries.

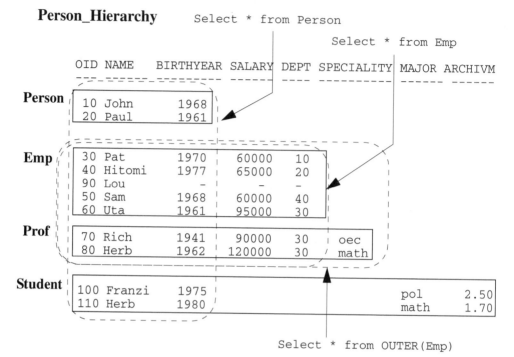

Fig. 7–52 *Example: Logical view of hierarchy tables (H-table)*

Note: Remember you cannot select rows directly from the hierarchy table.

Now let's look at other examples.

This example inserts an employee `Tetsu` with the `OID 200`, born in 1968, earning a $65,000 salary, and working in the `itso` department.

```
INSERT INTO Emp (Oid, Name, Birthyear, Salary, Dept)
  VALUES(Emp_t(200),'Tetsu',1968,65000,
         (SELECT Oid FROM Dept WHERE Name='itso'));
```

The next example selects all attributes of all employees born after 1970 who earn more than $50,000 a year.

```
SELECT * FROM emp WHERE birthyear > 1970 AND
   salary > 50000
```

The rows are retrieved from the `Emp` and `Prof` tables. The result is:

```
OID     NAME       BIRTHYEAR   SALARY     DEPT
------  ---------  ----------  ---------  ------
    40 Hitomi          1977      65000       20
```

The next example selects all persons who were born before 1965 who are either students or persons (excluding employees and professors).

```
SELECT * FROM Person WHERE Birthyear < 1965 AND
   DEREF(Oid) IS OF DYNAMIC TYPE (Student_t,ONLY Person_t)
```

This example uses the `TYPE` predicate, which compares a dynamic data type with a list of types. As already explained, the predicate is true if the dynamic type is specified in the list. In our example, `Student_t` and `Person_t` (with the keyword `ONLY`) are specified. Therefore, only rows whose data type is `Student_t`, its sub-types (although `Student_t` does not have any sub-types), or `Person_t` type are returned. The result is:

```
OID           NAME                      BIRTHYEAR
-----------   -----------------------   -----------
        20 Paul                             1961
```

Let's look at some reference column examples. Remember the `Dept` table and `Emp` table have a mutual reference relationship as shown in Fig. 7–53.

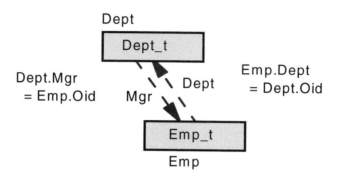

Fig. 7–53 *Reference column*

The next example finds the employee's name, salary, department name, and budget. It selects only the employees whose department's budget is greater than $500,000.

```
SELECT Name, Salary, Dept->Name, Dept->Budget FROM Emp
                        WHERE Dept->Budget > 500000";
```

Notice the department's name and the department's budget are retrieved from the Dept table, which is referenced by the reference column Dept of the Emp table and its sub-table, the Prof table. The result is as follows:

```
NAME      SALARY     NAME         BUDGET
--------  ---------  -----------  -----------
Sam         60000    itso           1000000
Uta         95000    headq          5000000
Rich        90000    headq          5000000
Herb       120000    headq          5000000
Tetsu       65000    itso           5000000
```

Summary Tables

A *summary table* is a table whose definition is based on the result of a query. As such, the summary table typically contains precomputed results based on the data existing in the table, or tables, on which its definition is based. If the DB2 optimizer determines that a dynamic query will run more efficiently against a summary table than the base table, the query executes against the summary table, and you obtain the result faster than you otherwise would.

The query rewrite function of the optimizer will access a summary table if it determines that the query can be answered by using the data in the summary table instead of accessing the base tables.

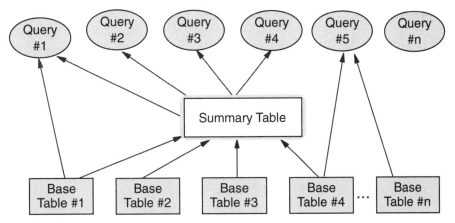

Fig. 7–54 *Summary table concept*

Note: Summary tables are only accessed for dynamic SQL.

Creating a Summary Table

A summary table can be created by a CREATE TABLE statement. Fig. 7–55 shows the CREATE TABLE statement to create a summary table.

```
CREATE SUMMARY TABLE Dept_group
  AS (SELECT Workdept,
             SUM(Salary) AS Salary,
             SUM(Bonus) AS Bonus
        FROM Employee GROUP BY Workdept)
    DATA INITIALLY DEFERRED
    REFRESH DEFERRED;
```

Fig. 7–55 *Create a summary table*

In this example, the keyword SUMMARY is used to indicate that this is a summary table; however, you can omit this keyword if you so choose. The keyword AS followed by a fullselect means that this is a summary table. The column attributes of the summary table are defined by this fullselect.

There are two options to update the data in the summary table, deferred refresh and immediate refresh. This is specified in the CREATE TABLE statement using REFRESH DEFERRED or REFRESH IMMEDIATE. The last example uses REFRESH DEFERRED, which means that the data in the table is refreshed when a REFRESH TABLE statement is executed. The data in the summary table reflects the result of the query at the time the REFRESH TABLE statement is executed. REFRESH IMMEDIATE means that the changes made to the underlying tables as part of a DELETE, INSERT, or UPDATE statement are cascaded to the summary table immediately.

The DATA INITIALLY DEFERRED clause indicates that data is not inserted into the table as part of the CREATE TABLE statement, and the REFRESH TABLE statement is the only way to populate the table.

 Note: After creating a summary table, the table is in check-pending state. The REFRESH TABLE statement or SET INTEGRITY statement with the IMMEDIATE CHECKED option enables you to get out of this check-pending state.

Fig. 7–56 shows a CREATE TABLE statement to create a summary table with the REFRESH IMMEDIATE option.

```
CREATE SUMMARY TABLE dept_group2
  AS (SELECT workdept,
              count(*) as reccount,
              SUM(salary) AS salary,
              SUM(bonus) AS bonus
       FROM employee GROUP BY workdept)
    DATA INITIALLY DEFERRED
    REFRESH IMMEDIATE;
```

Fig. 7–56 *Create a Summary table with the REFRESH IMMEDIATE option*

 Note: The summary table cannot be directly modified by the INSERT, UPDATE, or DELETE statements.

CURRENT REFRESH AGE Special Register

The CURRENT REFRESH AGE special register specifies a timestamp duration value with a data type of DECIMAL(20,6). This duration is the maximum duration, since a REFRESH TABLE statement has been processed on a deferred refresh summary table. It determines if a summary table can be used to optimize the processing of a query. The SET CURRENT REFRESH AGE statement enables you to change the value of the CURRENT REFRESH AGE special register. The value must be 0 or 99999999999999 (9999 years, 99 months, 99 days, 99 hours, 99 minutes, and 99 seconds).

- Zero (0) means that only summary tables defined with REFRESH IMMEDIATE may be used to optimize the processing of a query.
- 99999999999999 means that any summary tables defined with REFRESH DEFERRED or REFRESH IMMEDIATE may be used to optimize the processing of a query.

Note: The keyword ANY is shorthand for 99999999999999

The initial value of CURRENT REFRESH AGE is 0. If you want the DB2 optimizer to consider using the deferred refresh summary tables, you must set the CURRENT REFRESH AGE special register to ANY or 99999999999999 as follows:

```
SET CURRENT REFRESH AGE ANY
```

Advanced SQL

Considerations of Using Summary Tables

There are some considerations when you create a summary table. The fullselect of the summary table definition must not have following:

- References to a view (see *DB2 UDB V7.1 SQL Reference SQL Reference* for details), summary table, or typed table in any FROM clause
- Expressions that are a reference type or DATALINK type (or a distinct type based on these types)
- Functions that have an external action
- Functions that depend on physical characteristics (e.g., NODENUMBER, PARTITION)
- Table or view references to system objects (explain tables also should not be specified)

Other considerations you should be aware of include:

- The summary table does not support IMPORT or LOAD.
- A unique index cannot be created on a summary table.
- If the summary table is specified in the ALTER TABLE statement, the ALTER is limited to activating not logged initially, changing pctfree, locksize, append, or volatile.

Additionally, if you create a summary table with the REFRESH IMMEDIATE option, the following considerations exist:

- The fullselect in the summary table definition must be a sub-select and cannot include:
  - Functions that are not deterministic
  - Scalar full selects
  - Predicates with full selects
  - Special registers
- A GROUP BY clause must be included in the sub-select.
- The select list must have a COUNT(*) function (or COUNT_BIG(*)) and no DISTINCT.
- Only SUM (of not nullable columns), COUNT, or COUNT_BIG column functions are allowed in the select list (without DISTINCT) and other select list items must be included in the GROUP BY clause.
- All GROUP BY items must be included in the select list.
- No grouping sets are allowed (including CUBE and ROLLUP) or grouping on constants.
- A HAVING clause is not allowed.

System Catalog Information for Summary Tables

The system catalog tables maintain the information about summary tables as well as the usual tables. Here is the output of the LIST TABLES command. The value S in the type column indicates that this table is a summary table.

```
Table/View     Schema      Type Creation time
------------   ----------  ---- ---------------------------
DEPT_GROUP     AUSRES33    S    1999-04-19-16.21.48.826001
DEPT_GROUP2    AUSRES33    S    1999-04-19-16.21.48.756001
```

Fig. 7–57 *Output of LIST TABLES command showing summary tables*

Advanced SQL

Summary

In this chapter we have talked about very powerful SQL features, such as triggers, recursive SQL, outer joins, the OLAP functions, and case expressions. These SQL features that DB2 provides can reduce the amount of application development time and maintenance.

We have also discussed user-defined structured types. This is one of the capabilities that DB2 provides to manage the Object Relational Model. As explained in "Database Objects" on page 197, DB2 has implemented some Object Relational functions, Large Object (LOB) support, user-defined distinct types, user-defined functions, and so on. The concept of structured types and tables is very similar to object-oriented programming.

We have also introduced the summary table. The summary table is a physical table that contains precomputed results based on the data existing in the table, or tables, on which its definition is based. Many customers execute complex SQL to summarize the operational data for reporting or analysis purposes. These types of SQL often take a long time to provide the result. The summary table can be helpful in improving query performance.

C H A P T E R **8**

Concurrency

- ◆ CONCURRENCY
- ◆ ISOLATION LEVELS
- ◆ LOCKS
- ◆ LOCK CONVERSION
- ◆ LOCK ESCALATION
- ◆ LOCK WAIT

A database server acts as a central source of data access for a group of end-users. The number of end-users can vary from one to thousands. When many users access the same data source, some rules must be established for the reading, inserting, deleting, and updating of the data records to guarantee the integrity of the data.

The rules for data access are set by each application connected to a DB2 database and are established using two methods:

- Explicit control - Locking resources using an SQL statement or using a DB2 command
- Implicit control - Locking resources by specifying an *isolation level*

Some of the DB2 database resources, databases, table spaces, and tables can be explicitly controlled (for concurrency purposes). DB2 implicitly locks database resources at the row level. This can provide good concurrency and avoid resource conflicts. Record locking behavior is specified by isolation levels. We will examine the supported isolation levels and their locking semantics.

We will also examine the locks in DB2 and their behavior in an application environment. DB2 must also handle concurrency conflicts, including deadlocks, lock timeout, and resource contention. Some of the database configuration parameters affect the amount and type of locks acquired and the maximum length of time they are held by DB2 applications.

We will also examine concurrency problems that can occur in a multiuser environment. The concurrency examples are based on the `db2cert` certification testing application.

Concurrency

Data integrity is the primary concern in any database environment. The database server must guarantee the integrity of the data as it is modified. Every executable SQL statement that is issued is considered to be part of a *transaction*.

A transaction will contain at least one SQL statement. Multiple SQL statements can be grouped together and executed as a single transaction. Any data that has been accessed or modified by SQL statements will be tracked by DB2 and either permanently changed (committed), or returned to their original state (rolled back). This all-or-nothing behavior is known as *atomicity*. A transaction does not only guarantee atomicity, it also guarantees *persistency*. Persistency is provided through transactional logging. The log files are used to ensure that all committed transactions are physically applied to the database.

A transaction is started implicitly during the processing of the first SQL statement. The transaction is completed when a COMMIT or ROLLBACK statement has been issued, either explicitly or implicitly.

Note: The term *unit of work* is the same as *transaction*.

When the data has been permanently changed using the COMMIT or ROLLBACK statement, a point of consistency is established. A point of consistency is important because it is used during database crash recovery and roll forward recovery.

In a previous chapter, we discussed data access control. The GRANT and REVOKE statements can be used by users to provide and take away the ability to access tables, views, and packages. Once access control has been established, resource control must be considered. Concurrency problems can occur if resource control is not properly managed.

DB2 provides mechanisms to manage resource control. We discuss these mechanisms and strategies. The accuracy of the data is based on the correctness of the input and the extent to which data modification is controlled. The correctness of the input data needs to be monitored by the database administrator. DB2 provides some mechanisms to avoid incorrect data entry, including triggers, check constraints, and referential constraints.

We will discuss the control of data modification using transactions, examine some of the possible concurrency problems and the strategies that can be used to avoid them and examine some concurrency issues that need to be addressed by the db2cert application.

Concurrency Considerations

Database resource control requires the use of data modification rules. There are concurrency anomalies that we will consider when using the db2cert database application. They include:

- Lost update
- Uncommitted read
- Nonrepeatable read
- Phantom read

Lost Update Problem

A *lost update* problem occurs when the same data is retrieved by two test coordinators, both of whom change and save the data. The last successful change to the data will be kept, and the first change will be overwritten.

Here is an example. Suppose Shirley is a DB2 Universal Database Certification test candidate, and she wants to take the first DB2 exam. Shirley calls the testing center in Toronto. The test coordinator, Linda, gets the call. She looks at the availability of seats at the Toronto testing center for the date that Shirley wants. Linda's application screen is shown in Fig. 8–1. Linda notes that seat number 4 is available.

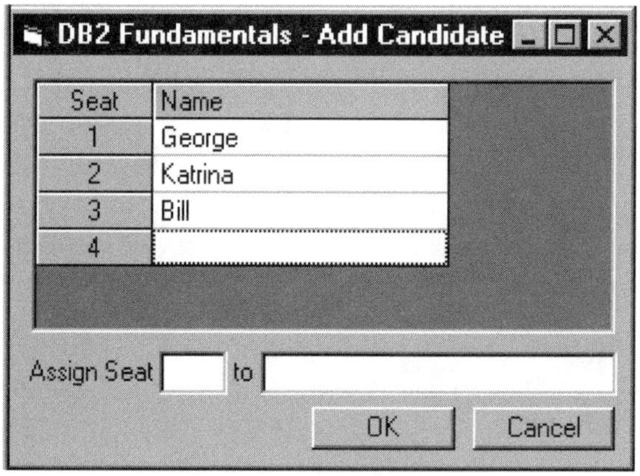

Fig. 8–1 *Available seats at Toronto testing center*

Shirley is not sure if she wants to take the test that day. Linda maintains her list of seats on the screen until Shirley decides if she will take the test on that day.

Meanwhile, Mike calls the testing center. Andrea, another test coordinator, takes Mike's call. Mike wants to take the same DB2 exam on the same day that Shirley has requested. Andrea checks the seat availability and obtains the same list as Linda. Andrea's screen is same as Linda's that is shown in Fig. 8–1.

The other test candidate, Shirley, decides to take the test and Linda assigns seat 4 to Shirley by clicking the OK button, as shown in Fig. 8–2.

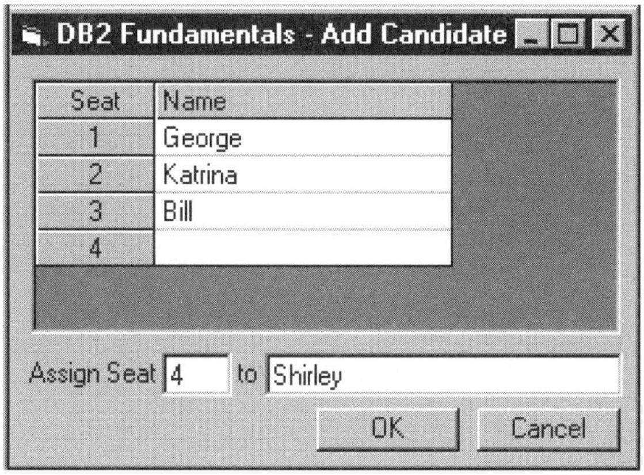

Fig. 8–2   *Linda assigns a seat to Shirley*

Andrea does not see that Linda has assigned seat 4 to Shirley, so she assigns the same seat to Mike. Remember, Andrea sees seat 4 as unassigned. The commit operation was successful for Andrea because no resource conflict was encountered.

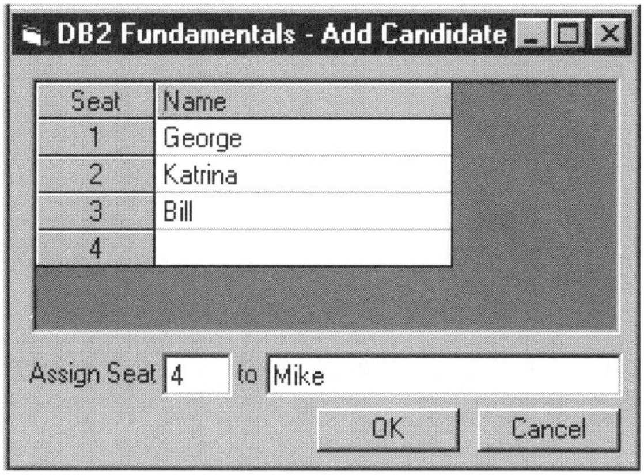

Fig. 8–3   *Andrea assigns a seat to Mike*

If the list of seats is refreshed (retrieved again), we see that seat 4 was assigned to Mike and the update made by Linda was overwritten. Fig. 8–4 shows the refreshed screen. On the day of the test, Shirley and Mike arrive at the testing center, and the database shows that Mike has a proper seat assignment. Shirley walks away unhappy and has to reschedule to take the exam another day.

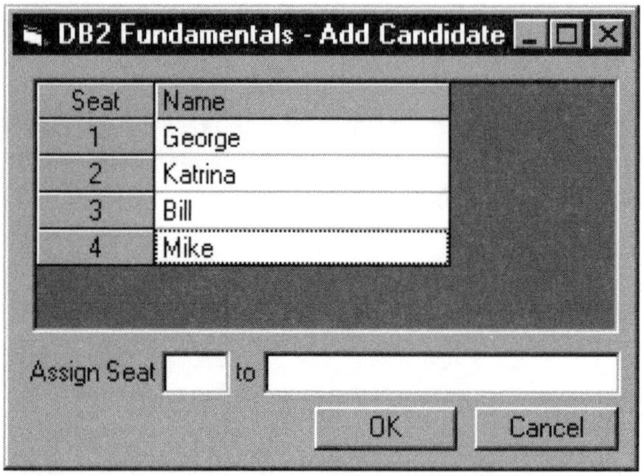

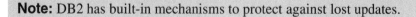

Fig. 8–4 *A refresh of the seat assignments*

What was the problem? To maintain the accuracy of the data, control mechanisms needed to be enforced. The goal of the database manager (DB2) is to avoid lost updates and guarantee the integrity of the data.

If table-level locking was used, then Linda's application would have restricted any update to the table. However, if Linda's application had update control for the table, then other test centers would not be able to assign seats since all test centers access the same table. Should only one test center coordinator be allowed to update data records for a given day? For some applications, this can be appropriate, but this does not provide a sufficient degree of concurrency for others.

The integrity of the database is not guaranteed in this example. An application has to lock the updated data to make it impossible for another application to overwrite the data. Record-level locking usually involves cursor processing.

Note: DB2 has built-in mechanisms to protect against lost updates.

Lost Update Solution

To avoid lost updates, control of each data record must be maintained by DB2. The control mechanism involves obtaining update control of all of the matching records or possible matching records for the query. This is known as *repeatable read*. See

"Repeatable Read" on page 397 for more details on establishing a repeatable read concurrency strategy.

The only explicit SQL control mechanism provided by DB2 is the LOCK TABLE statement. According to the design of the db2cert database, there is a table that represents all of the tests taken at all of the tests centers, the db2cert.test_taken table. If the application explicitly locked the table for update (known as EXCLU-SIVE mode), other test centers would not be allowed to update or even read any of the committed data in the table. If the application explicitly locked the table not for update (SHARE mode) other test centers would be allowed to read but not update the data.

Linda's application could have obtained a share lock on the test_taken table. The share lock would have prevented Andrea from successfully performing an UPDATE of the table (assignment of seat four to Mike). The table lock would remain in effect until Linda's application released the lock using the COMMIT or ROLLBACK statement.

An alternative method involves record or row-level locking. If Linda's application acquired record locks for seat 4, Andrea's update would have failed. You cannot explicitly acquire row-level locks using an SQL statement. See "Cursor Stability" on page 396 for more details on row-level locking.

Uncommitted Read

Linda's application locks the rows of unassigned seats and makes a temporary update to assign seat 4 to Shirley. Until Linda has committed or rolled back this update, no one else can update the record for seat 4. Fig. 8–5 shows the list retrieved by George. George has permission to read uncommitted changes, so he can see Shirley assigned to seat 4 instead of Mike.

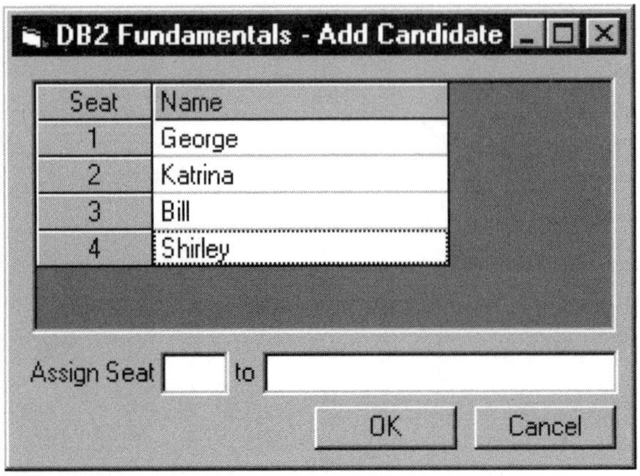

Fig. 8–5 *George retrieves uncommitted data*

If George were to reissue his query after Andrea assigned seat 4 to Mike, he would obtain a different result. This is known as an *uncommitted read* (dirty read).

Let's look at another example. The test center secretary runs a report to determine how many people will be tested in February. The following query is issued.

```
SELECT COUNT(*) FROM db2cert.test_taken
WHERE date_taken
BETWEEN ('2000-02-01') AND ('2000-02-28')
```

The result will include the temporary assigned seat. To avoid this behavior, the application should not be able to read uncommitted changes.

Nonrepeatable Read

A nonrepeatable read scenario can obtain a different result set within the same transaction. Uncommitted read applications do not guarantee a repeatable read.

Let's look at an example of a nonrepeatable read scenario. Suppose Shirley is going to take the certification exam. He asks Linda to check where (Toronto or Rockwood) he can take the exam. Linda sends a request to the database and retrieves the list of available seats in Toronto and Rockwood, as shown in Fig. 8–6.

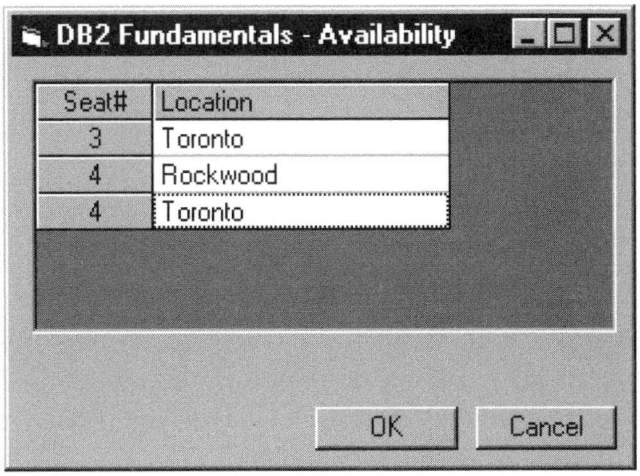

Fig. 8–6 *List of available seats (first query)*

In the meantime, Andrea has assigned and committed the last available seat in Rockwood to Mike. Shirley would like to take the test in Rockwood, so Linda attempts to assign the seat in Rockwood. The update fails, and when Linda refreshes her screen, the seat in Rockwood is no longer available. Linda's refreshed screen is shown in Fig. 8–7.

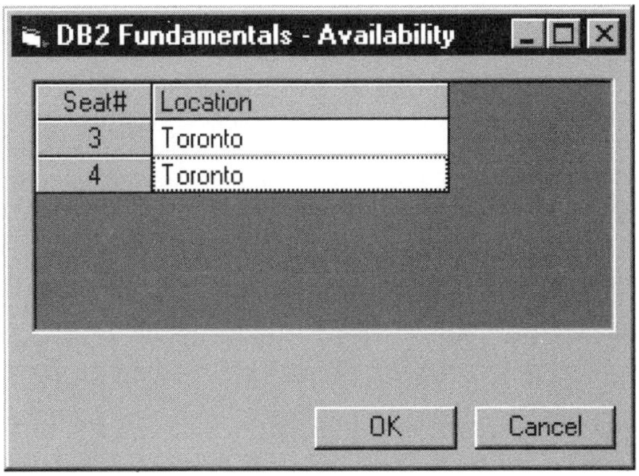

Fig. 8–7 *Linda's refreshed screen*

The application was coded to only lock the rows of data being updated. In this case, an exclusive lock was obtained by Andrea when she assigned the seat to Mike. This did not conflict with the locks held by Linda because she did not have that row locked. We are assuming that the row is only locked when it is chosen for update by the administrator.

To avoid this type of nonrepeatable read scenario, all of the retrieved data needs to be locked. If you want to guarantee that none of the selected data is modified, locking these rows is sufficient. This is known as read stability in DB2. If you would like to guarantee that the rows you have selected in getting this result will never change within the transaction, use repeatable read. This may require additional locking.

Phantom Read Problem

The *phantom read* phenomenon occurs if an application executes the same query twice; the second time the query is issued additional rows are returned. For many applications, this is an acceptable scenario. For example, if the query involved finding all of the available seats at a concert, then reissuing the query and obtaining a better seat selection is a desirable feature.

Let's take a look at our application again. Shirley wants to take the exam in Toronto or Rockwood. Linda requests the list of available seats for these locations, as shown in Fig. 8–8.

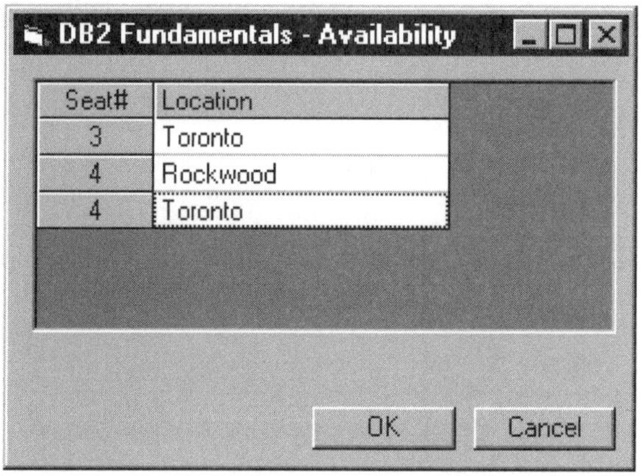

Fig. 8–8 *Available seats in Toronto and Rockwood (first query)*

Another test coordinator adds an additional seat to the Toronto testing site. Now it is possible to test five candidates in Toronto at the same time. If the query is issued again, Linda retrieves a different result set that includes five available seats. Although the application locked the previously retrieved rows, the application was able to add a new row to the result set, as shown in Fig. 8–9.

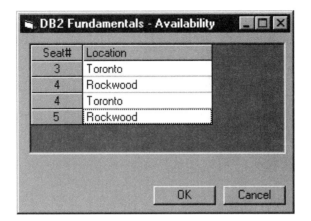

Fig. 8–9 *Linda's query (second query)*

Phantom Read Solution

Depending on the situation, a phantom read may be desirable. If you wish to avoid this behavior, the application has to lock all of the possible qualifying rows. This ensures that no other application can update, delete, or insert a row that would affect the result table. This is an important concept to understand.

Note: If DB2 needs to acquire locks for every row in the table to provide the required level of isolation, a table-level lock may be obtained instead of multiple row-level locks.

Isolation Levels

In the previous examples, we have seen some of the possible concurrency problems. DB2 Universal Database provides different levels of protection to isolate the data from each of the database applications while it is being accessed.

These levels of protection are known as isolation levels or locking strategies. The isolation levels supported by DB2 include:

- Uncommitted read
- Cursor stability
- Read stability
- Repeatable read

The isolation level is defined for embedded SQL statements during the binding of a package to a database using the ISOLATION option of the PREP or the BIND command. If no isolation level is specified, the default level of cursor stability is used.

If you are using the command line processor, you may change the isolation level using the CHANGE ISOLATION LEVEL command.

For DB2 Call Level Interface (DB2 CLI), you may change the isolation level as part of the DB2 CLI configuration (db2cli.ini) file.

Uncommitted Read

The Uncommitted Read (UR) isolation level, also known as dirty read, is the lowest level of isolation supported by DB2. It can be used to access uncommitted data changes of other applications. For example, an application using the uncommitted read isolation level will return all of the matching rows for a query, even if that data is in the process of being modified, and may not be committed to the database.

If you decide to use this isolation level, your application might access incorrect data. There will be very few locks held by uncommitted read transactions. Nonrepeatable read and phantom read phenomena are possible when this isolation level is being used.

Cursor Stability

The Cursor Stability (CS) isolation level locks any row on which the cursor is positioned during a unit of work. The lock on the row is held until the next row is fetched or the unit of work is terminated. If a row has been updated, the lock is held until the unit of work is terminated. A unit of work is terminated when either a COMMIT or ROLLBACK statement is executed.

An application using cursor stability cannot read uncommitted data. In addition, the application locks the row that has been currently fetched, and no other application can modify the contents of the current row.

If you decide to use this isolation level, your application will always read consistent data, but nonrepeatable read or phantom read situations are still possible.

Read Stability

The Read Stability (RS) isolation level locks those rows that are part of a result table. If you have a table containing 10,000 rows and the query returns 10 rows, then only 10 rows are locked.

An application using read stability cannot read uncommitted data. Instead of locking a single row, it locks all rows that are part of the result table. No other application can change or modify these rows.

If you decide to use this isolation level, your application will always get the same result if the query is executed more than once in a unit of work, though you may get additional phantom rows.

Repeatable Read

The Repeatable Read (RR) isolation level is the highest isolation level available in DB2. It locks all rows and application references within a unit of work. Locks are held on all rows processed to build the result set, no matter how large the result set. A table lock may be obtained instead depending on a number of factors.

An application using repeatable read cannot read uncommitted data of a concurrent application. If you decide to use this isolation level, none of the previous discussed situations (lost update, phantom read, or unrepeatable read) can occur in your application.

Choosing an Isolation Level

Choosing the proper isolation level is very important, because the isolation level influences not only the concurrency, but also the performance of the application. The more protection you have, the less concurrency is available.

Decide which concurrency problems are unacceptable for your application and then choose the isolation level that prevents these problems:

- Use the Uncommitted Read isolation level only if you use queries on read-only tables, or if you are using only SELECT statements and do not care whether you get uncommitted data from concurrent applications.

Concurrency

- Use the Cursor Stability isolation level when you want the maximum concurrency while seeing only committed data from concurrent applications.
- Use the Read Stability isolation level when your application operates in a concurrent environment. This means that qualified rows have to remain stable for the duration of the unit of work.
- Use the Repeatable Read isolation level if changes to your result set are unacceptable.

Locking

DB2 provides isolation levels to control concurrency. In most cases, you do not need to take direct action to establish locks. In general, locks are acquired implicitly by DB2 according to the semantics defined by the isolation level.

Lock Attributes

The resource being locked is called an object. The only objects you can explicitly lock are tables and table spaces. Implicit locks on other types of objects, such as rows, index keys, and sometimes tables, are acquired by DB2 according to the isolation level and processing situations. The object being locked represents the granularity of the lock.

> **Note:** The database itself can be locked if the CONNECT statement contains the clause IN EXCLUSIVE MODE. This will acquire an exclusive lock on the database and prevent any other users applications from connecting.

The length of time a lock is held is called the duration and is affected by the isolation level.

The access and rules that pertain to a lock are defined by the lock mode. Some lock modes are only used for locking table objects, while other lock modes are used for row objects. DB2 uses the following hierarchy of lockable database objects:

- Table spaces
- Tables
- Rows

The different modes of *table locks* are listed below in order of increasing control:

- IN (Intent None) - The owner of the lock can read any data, committed or noncommitted, in the table. Other applications can read or update the table.
- IS (Intent Share) - The owner of the lock can read any data in the table and obtains an S or NS lock on each row read. Other applications can read or update rows in the table.
- S (Share) - The owner of the lock can read any data in the table and will not obtain row locks. Other applications can read the table data.
- IX (Intent Exclusive) - The owner of the lock can read any data in the table if a U, S, NS, or X lock can be obtained on rows and also can change any data in the

table if an X lock can be obtained on rows. Other applications can both read and update table rows.

- SIX (Share with Intent Exclusive) -The owner of the lock can read any data in the table and change rows if it can obtain an X lock on the target row(s). Other applications can only read the table data.

- U (Update) - The owner of the lock can read any data in the table and can change data if an X lock on the table can be obtained prior to the update. Other applications can only read the table data.

- X (Exclusive) - The owner of the lock can read or update any data in the table. No row locks are obtained.Only other applications using the Uncommitted Read isolation level can read rows of the table.

- Z (Super exclusive) - No other application can access the table.

The different modes of *row locking* are listed below in order of increasing control over resources:

- NS (Next Key Share) -The row is being read by one application and can be read by concurrent applications. Held by applications using RS or CS isolation levels. It is compatible with the NX lock.

- S (Share) - The row is being read by one application and is available for *read-only* by concurrent applications.

- U (Update) - The row is being read by one application, which intends to update the data in this row. It is available for read-only by concurrent applications. Only one application can possess a U lock on a row. The lock owner will acquire X locks on the rows prior to update.

- NX (Next Key Exclusive) - This lock is acquired on the next row when a row is deleted from an index or inserted into an index in a table. The lock owner can read but not change the locked row.

- NW (Next Key Weak Exclusive) - This lock is acquired on the next row when a row is inserted into the index of a noncatalog table. The lock owner can read, but not change, the locked row. Only individual rows can be locked in NW mode. This is similar to X and NX locks except that it is compatible with the W and NS locks.

- X (Exclusive) - The row is being changed by one application and is not available for concurrent applications, except for those with uncommitted read isolation level. The lock owner can read and change data in the locked object.

- W (Weak Exclusive) - This lock is acquired on the row when a row is inserted into a noncatalog table. The lock owner can change the locked row. This lock is similar to a X lock except that it is compatible with the NW lock. Only uncommitted read applications can access the locked row.

The following table illustrates how all the lock modes work together (called *lock compatibility*). The table demonstrates whether one lock is compatible with another; **"no"** means the requesting application must wait for the lock to be released and "yes" means the lock can be granted.

Table 5–1 *Lock Type Compatibility*

State being Requested	State of Held Resource												
	none	IN	IS	NS	S	IX	SIX	U	NX	X	Z	NW	W
none	yes	yes	yes	yes	yes	yes	yes	yes	yes	yes	yes	yes	yes
IN	yes	yes	yes	yes	yes	yes	yes	yes	yes	yes	no	yes	yes
IS	yes	yes	yes	yes	yes	yes	yes	yes	no	no	no	no	no
NS	yes	yes	yes	yes	yes	no	no	yes	yes	no	no	yes	no
S	yes	yes	yes	yes	yes	no	no	yes	no	no	no	no	no
IX	yes	yes	yes	no	no	yes	no	no	no	no	no	no	no
SIX	yes	yes	yes	no	no	no	no	no	no	no	no	no	no
U	yes	yes	yes	yes	yes	no	no	no	no	no	no	no	no
NX	yes	yes	no	yes	no	no	no	no	no	no	no	no	no
X	yes	yes	no	no	no	no	no	no	no	no	no	no	no
Z	yes	no	no	no	no	no	no	no	no	no	no	no	no
NW	yes	yes	no	yes	no	no	no	no	no	no	no	no	yes
W	yes	yes	no	no	no	no	no	no	no	no	no	yes	no

Lock Conversion

If an application holds a lock on a data object, and the mode of access requires a more restrictive lock, the lock is converted to the more-restrictive lock. This process is known as *lock conversion*. During the lock conversion process, the more-restrictive lock may or may not be granted.

Let's look at an example of lock conversion. Assume that the application fetches a row from the test_taken table with the intent to update this row. The intent to update tells DB2 to acquire an update lock on the currently positioned row during the query processing.

The database manager holds an IX lock on the table and a U lock on the specified row. The SQL statements shown in Fig. 8–10 assign all test candidates currently scheduled to take the test at seat_no 1 to take the test at seat_no to 2.

When the update statement of our example is issued, the database manager holds an IX lock on the test_taken table and an X lock on the changed row.

```
SELECT * FROM db2cert.test_taken
WHERE seat_no = '1' AND date_taken = CURRENT DATE
FOR UPDATE OF seat_no;

UPDATE db2cert.test_taken
SET seat_no = '2'
WHERE seat_no = '1' AND date_taken = CURRENT DATE
```

Fig. 8–10 *Update a row - Lock conversion*

All the locks are released when your application terminates the unit of work with either a COMMIT or ROLLBACK.

The cursor stability isolation level was used in this example.

Note: When rows are being modified, an X lock is always required.

Lock Escalation

If your application changes many rows in one table, it may be better to have one lock on the entire table rather than many locks on each of the rows. DB2 requires memory for each lock; therefore, if a number of row locks can be replaced with a single table lock, the locking storage area can be used by other applications.

When DB2 converts the row locks to a table lock on your behalf, this is called *lock escalation*. DB2 will perform lock escalation to avoid resource problems by too many resources being held for the individual locks.

Note: Each DB2 lock consumes the same amount of memory.

Two database configuration parameters have a direct effect on lock escalation. They are:

- LOCKLIST - Defines the amount of memory allocated for the locks.
- MAXLOCKS - Defines the percentage of the total locklist permitted to be allocated to a single application.

There are two different situations for lock escalation:

- One application exceeds the percentage of the locklist as defined by the MAXLOCKS configuration parameter. The database manager will attempt to free memory by obtaining a table lock and releasing row locks for this application.
- Many applications connected to the database fill the locklist by acquiring a large number of locks. DB2 will attempt to free memory by obtaining a table lock and releasing row locks.

Also note that the isolation level used by the application has an effect on lock escalation:

- Cursor stability will acquire row level locks initially. If required, table level locks can be obtained. Usually, a very small number of locks are acquired by each cursor stability application since they only have to guarantee the integrity of the data in the current row.
- Read stability locks all rows in the original result set.
- Repeatable read may or may not obtain row locks on all rows read to determine the result set. If it does not, then a table lock will be obtain instead.

Lock Wait Behavior

What happens if one application requests to update a row that is already locked with an exclusive (X) lock? The application requesting the update will simply wait until the exclusive lock is released by the other application.

To ensure that the waiting application can continue without needed to wait indefinitely, the LOCKTIMEOUT configuration parameter can be set to define the length of the timeout period. The value is specified in seconds. By default, the lock timeout is disabled (set to a value of -1). This means the waiting application will not receive a timeout and will wait indefinitely.

Deadlock Behavior

In DB2, contention for locks by processes using the database can result in a deadlock situation.

Concurrency

A deadlock may occur in the following manner:

- Jon locks record 1.
- Finn locks record 5.
- Jon attempts to lock record 5, but waits since Finn already holds a lock on this record.
- Finn then tries to lock record 1, but waits since Jon already holds a lock on this record.

In this situation, both Jon and Finn will wait indefinitely for each other's locks until an external event causes one or both of them to ROLLBACK.

DB2 uses a background process, called the deadlock detector, to check for deadlocks. The process is activated periodically as determined by the DLCHKTIME parameter in the database configuration file. When activated it checks the lock system for deadlocks.

When the deadlock detector finds a deadlock situation, one of the deadlocked applications will receive an error code and the current unit of work for that application will be rolled back automatically by DB2. When the rollback is complete, the locks held by this chosen application are released, thereby allowing other applications to continue.

Lock Table Statement

You can use the LOCK TABLE statement to override the rules for acquiring initial lock modes. It locks the specified table until the unit of work is committed or rolled back. A table can be locked either in SHARE MODE or in EXCLUSIVE MODE.

When using the LOCK TABLE statement in SHARE MODE, no other application can update, delete, or insert data in the locked table. If you need a snapshot of a table that is frequently changed by concurrent applications, you can use this statement to lock the table for changes without using the repeatable read isolation level for your application.

The EXCLUSIVE MODE is more restrictive than SHARE MODE. It prevents concurrent applications from accessing the table for read, update, delete, and insert. If you want to update a large part of the table, you can use the LOCK TABLE statement in EXCLUSIVE MODE rather than locking each row.

LOCKSIZE parameter of ALTER TABLE statement

The default locking method for tables in DB2 is row locking. DB2 now provides you with the ability to override this default for a table by using the ALTER TABLE statement and the LOCKSIZE parameter.

The LOCKSIZE parameter allows you to specify the granularity of locking you wish DB2 to do for a particular table, either row or table level locking. For example, to change the default locking method for the test_taken table from row locking to table locking you would issue the following SQL statement:

```
ALTER TABLE db2cert.test_taken LOCKSIZE TABLE
```

Whenever an application requires a lock to access data in the table, an appropriate table level lock will be issued. It is important to realize that since all locks on the table are on the table level and not on the row level, it reduces the concurrency of applications accessing this table.

Concurrency

Summary

In this chapter, we have discussed some of the possible concurrency problems that can occur in a multiuser database environment. To protect the data as it is being modified, rules are established and the changes are grouped together in transactions.

The data updated by a transaction is either made permanent by the COMMIT statement or removed using the ROLLBACK statement. Each transaction is made up of one or more SQL statements. The rules of concurrent data access are determined by the isolation level, which are set for static and dynamic SQL application modules.

DB2 will implement the isolation level semantics of data access by implicitly acquiring locks on behalf of the applications. Applications can decide to lock a resource for EXCLUSIVE or SHARE mode. The only resource that can be directly locked using an SQL statement is a table. All row-level locks are acquired, according to the isolation level, by DB2.

If a requested lock is more restrictive, and another application already has the resource locked, a wait on the release of the lock will occur. The amount of time an application will wait is determined by a database configuration parameter known as LOCKTIMEOUT. The default amount of lock wait time is indefinite.

If multiple applications require access to data that is held by other applications, a deadlock scenario can occur. DB2 will detect the occurrence of any deadlocks and force one of the transactions to ROLLBACK. Every lock requested requires memory on the DB2 server. The amount of lock storage is configurable using the LOCKLIST and MAXLOCKS parameters.

P A R T   3

DB2 UDB Administration

CHAPTER 9

Data Storage Management

- ◆ PROCESSOR, MEMORY, DISK CONSIDERATIONS

- ◆ DB2 STORAGE MODEL

- ◆ TABLE SPACE DESIGN

- ◆ IMPLEMENTATION EXAMPLES

- ◆ MAINTENANCE

*B*eing able to efficiently store and quickly retrieve large amounts of data is one of the main functions of any relational database management system. The physical placement of the data can directly affect the query performance. It is the responsibility of the database administrator to understand the concepts of data placement and to create an appropriate physical database design.

Processor, Memory, and Disk Resources

Before looking at specific DB2 objects, you should consider the hardware that will be used to implement your DB2 system. Besides the minimum amount of processor, disk, and memory required to install the various DB2 components, how much of each component do you need to support your databases? Like most questions of this nature, the answer is: *it depends*.

Without adequate hardware resources, you will need to limit your performance expectations. No amount of tuning inside DB2 and/or the operating system can compensate for a hardware configuration that is lacking in processing power, hard disk capacity, or the amount of real memory.

On the other hand, if not enough attention is paid to configuring DB2 when there is enough hardware resource, your system may underperform.

Processors

DB2 can operate in the following hardware environments:

* Single partition on a single processor (uniprocessor).
* Single partition with multiple processors.
* Multiple partition configurations. These configurations are supported by the DB2 Universal Database Enterprise-Extended Edition products, which are beyond the scope of this publication. Refer to the *DB2 Universal Database Cluster Certification Guide* for a discussion of these products.

Single Partition on a Single Processor

The database in this environment serves the needs of a department or small office. A single processor system is restricted by the amount of disk-related processing the processor can handle. As workload increases, a single processor may become insufficient in processing user requests any faster, regardless of other additional components such as disk and memory that you may add to the system.

Single Partition with Multiple Processors

This environment is typically made up of several equally powerful processors within the same machine and is called a symmetric multiprocessor (SMP) system. Resources such as disk space and memory are shared. More disks and memory are found in this machine compared to the single-partition database, single processor environment.

This environment is easier to manage than multiple machines are since all components are physically contained in one machine. With multiple processors available, different database operations can be completed more quickly than with database operations assigned to only a single processor. DB2 can also divide the work of a single query among available processors to improve processing speed. Other database operations such as the LOAD, BACKUP, and RESTORE utilities, and the CREATE INDEX statement can take advantage of the multiple processors.

Parallel I/O operations are much more likely to occur in this environment, especially if data is spread out over multiple containers over multiple disk drives.

Memory

As previously mentioned, buffer pools are a very important tuning area in DB2 performance tuning. The way that you configure the system's real and virtual memory, DB2's internal memory usage, and the DB2 buffer pools will greatly influence the performance of the system.

Generally speaking, the more real memory, the better the overall performance. Balance this against the number of processors in the system. Not enough real memory will cause excessive paging in the operating system, which affects all applications, including DB2. The situation can arise where even though a page of DB2 data is sitting in the buffer pool, because the operating system does not have enough memory to keep that page in its real memory, it has to write it out to disk temporarily. This situation can have a severe performance effect on DB2.

Try to make the database server a dedicated machine. If DB2 has to share the machine with other applications, be aware of their memory requirements and factor that into how much memory is acquired for the machine.

Memory requirements are influenced by the number of concurrent users you will have. For example, in a Windows NT environment, it is recommended that for five concurrent users you start with 32 MB of memory, and for 25 concurrent users you start with 48 MB memory. Refer to the *DB2 UDB V7.1 Quick Beginnings* manual for the relevant operating system for further exact details for your release level.

Disk

The amount of disk required will ultimately depend on the amount of data that is required to be stored in your databases. Factors to be aware of in planning your hard disk configuration include:

- The capacity of the disks used. Sometimes it is better to use multiple disks of lower capacity so that greater degrees of parallel I/O operations can take place. The tradeoff to this approach is that additional hardware is required.
- The speed of disks used. Hard disk attributes such as latency and seek time affect the I/O performance. DB2's optimizer can make use of disk attributes in its calculation for the best access path.

- Compressed file systems can be used to hold DB2 table space containers when disk space is at a premium and/or when the performance requirements allow for the extra overhead incurred.
- If availability is a high priority issue you may want to mirror disks. If so this will double your disk requirements.

Performance and availability can be influenced by the hard disk controllers you use and how many disks are attached to the controller. By placing disks on separate controllers you can reduce the traffic going through the controllers, thereby reducing the contention for the disks.

DB2 Storage Model

The following data objects will be discussed:

- Buffer pool - allocates memory to DB2.
- Table space - logical layer between physical tables with data and the database.
- Table - represented by rows and columns. Several tables can reside in one table space.
- Container - allocates storage to a table space.

The DB2 storage model illustrates the relationship between tables, table spaces, databases, and a DB2 instance.

Buffer Pool

A *buffer pool* is an area of main memory allocated to the database manager to cache table and index data pages as they are read from disk or modified. The purpose of a buffer pool is to improve database system performance. The database manager decides when to bring data from disk into a buffer pool and when old data in a buffer pool is unlikely to be used in the short term and can be written back out to disk. Data can be accessed much faster from memory than from disk; therefore, the fewer times the database manager needs to read from or write to a disk, the better the performance. Multiple buffer pools can be created. The configuration of buffer pools is a very important tuning area, since you can reduce the delay caused by excessive physical I/O.

Note: On UNIX platforms, the creation of a DB2 database will create a default buffer pool called `IBMDEFAULTBP` of 1000 four-kilobyte pages. For other platforms, the buffer pool size is 250 four-kilobyte pages.

Table Spaces

One of the first tasks in setting up a relational database is mapping the logical database design to physical storage on your system. The object used to specify the physical location of data is known as a *table space*. A table space is used as a layer between the database and the container objects that hold the actual table data. A table space can contain more than one table.

As all DB2 tables reside in table spaces, this means you can control where table data is physically stored. This gives you the ability to create a physical database design to fit your particular environment. For example, you can choose slower disks to store less frequently accessed data.

Backup and recovery can be performed at the table space level. This will give you more granularity and control since you can back up or restore each table space individually.

There are two types of table spaces: System Managed Space and Database Managed Space.

SMS Table Spaces

In a *System Managed Space* (SMS) table space, the operating system's file system manager allocates and manages the space where the table is to be stored. This storage model typically consists of many files representing table objects, stored in the file system space. The user decides on the location of the files, DB2 controls their names, and the file system is responsible for managing them. Each container is a directory in the file space of the operating system.

DMS Table Spaces

In a *Database Managed Space* (DMS) table space, the database manager controls the storage space. The storage model consists of a limited number of devices, whose space is managed by DB2. The Database Administrator decides which devices to use, and DB2 manages the space on the devices. This type of table space is essentially an implementation of a special purpose file system designed to best meet the needs of the database manager. The table space definition includes a list of the devices or files belonging to the table space in which data can be stored. Each container is either a fixed size preallocated file or a physical device such as a disk.

Containers

A container is a physical storage device. It can be identified by a directory name, a device name, or a file name.

SMS   DMS

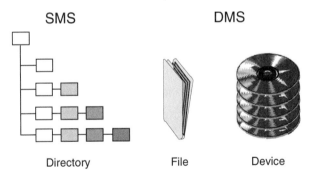

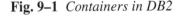

Directory   File   Device

Fig. 9–1 *Containers in DB2*

A container is assigned to a table space. All database and table data is assigned to table spaces. A table space's definitions and attributes are recorded in the database system catalog. Once a table space is created, you can then create tables within this table space. Details about containers can obtained by using the LIST TABLESPACE CONTAINERS command. A single table space can span many containers, but each container can belong to only one table space. Figure Fig. 9–2 shows an example of the relationship between tables and a table space within a database and the associated containers and disks.

Containers must reside on disks that are local; therefore resources such as LAN-redirected drives or NFS-mounted file systems cannot be used for table spaces.

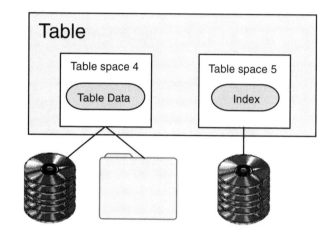

Fig. 9–2 *Table spaces and containers*

Directory Containers

Containers that are directory names are the only types of containers that can be used in SMS table spaces. An SMS table space can be defined with more than one container, each one of which could be mapped to a different physical disk to balance the I/O workload. DB2 will balance the amount data written to the multiple containers. It is very important to identify all the containers you want to use, since you cannot add or delete containers to an SMS table space after it has been created using the ALTER TABLESPACE statement.

The name for a directory container identifies an absolute or relative directory name. The directory named must not contain any files or subdirectories. The relative directory name is relative to the database directory. Refer to the CREATE TABLESPACE statement in the *DB2 UDB V7.1 SQL Reference* for more details.

Note: A table space container layout can be redefined during a restore of the table space. This is known as a *redirected restore*.

Device Containers

Device containers can be used only on AIX, Windows NT, and Solaris operating systems. In AIX and Solaris, the device is a logical volume with a *character special interface*. In Windows NT, it is an unformatted partition or a physical disk.

The device that the container is created on cannot be used in another table space. So when specifying the size of the container, make sure that all the space on the device is used because any unused space will be wasted. The amount space required can be specified in pages, kilobytes, megabytes, or gigabytes.

File Containers

File containers are files of preallocated size used by DMS table spaces. No operational differences exist between a file and a device. When defining the container name, you can use an absolute or relative file name. If any component of the directory name does not exist, it will be created by DB2. Similarly, if the file does not exist, it will be created and initialized to the specific size by DB2. The amount of space specified must exist when the table space is created. The amount space required can be specified in pages, kilobytes, megabytes, or gigabytes.

 Note: A container can only be added to a DMS table space. Containers cannot be added to an SMS table space with the ALTER TABLESPACE statement. You can add a container to an SMS table space during a *redirected restore* operation.

Table Space Design

In addition to defining whether a table space is SMS or DMS managed, there are several other parameters that may be specified during the CREATE TABLESPACE command. The major table space parameters include:

- REGULAR | TEMPORARY | LONG TABLESPACE - specifies the type of table space to be created; REGULAR will be selected if nothing is specified.
- MANAGED BY SYSEM | DATABASE USING - specifies SMS (SYSTEM) or DMS (DATABASE) table space; the containers are defined with the USING clause. For SMS table spaces, the container is a directory name. For DMS table spaces, a FILE or DEVICE container is specified and its size in PAGESIZE pages.
- PAGESIZE - allowable values for the page size of the table space: 4, 8, 16, or 32
- EXTENTSIZE - number of PAGESIZE pages that are written to a container before moving to the next container.
- PREFETCHSIZE - number of PAGESIZE pages read if prefetch is performed.
- BUFFERPOOL - name of buffer pool to be used for tables in this table space.
- OVERHEAD - number of milliseconds for the I/O controller to read a page (disk seek and latency time, default = 24.1).
- TRANSFERRATE - number of milliseconds to read one page into memory; this value is used by the optimizer in calculating I/O costs (default = 0.9).
- DROPPED TABLE RECOVERY ON | OFF - specifies if dropped tables in the table space can be recovered using the RECOVER TABLE ON option of the ROLL-FORWARD command.
- NODEGROUP - used to specify which nodegroup a table space will belong to in a clustered environment; the default assumes a nonclustered environment.
- NODE - in a clustered environment, this specifies the partition(s) on which the containers are created, the default assumes a single node (nonclustered) environment.

Some of the major table space parameters will now be reviewed in more detail.

Regular Table Space

Tables containing user data exist in one or many *regular* table spaces. By default, a table space called USERSPACE1 is created when the CREATE DATABASE command is executed. Indexes are also stored in regular table spaces. The system catalog tables exist in a regular table space as well. The default system catalog table space is called SYSCATSPACE. By default, both USERSPACE1 and SYSCATSPACE are created as SMSs, but can be defined as DMSs in the CREATE DATABASE command. While it is optional to use the USERSPACE1 table space (it is always created but may be dropped), it is mandatory to use SYSCATSPACE as the name of the table space holding the system catalog tables. The maximum size of a regular table space (including index data) depends on the page size used by the table space. For example, the maximum is 64 GB for 4 KB pages and 128 GB for 8 KB pages.

Long Table Space

Tables containing long field data or long object data, such as multimedia objects, exist in one or many *long* table spaces. Their use is optional, as long data can also reside in regular table spaces. Long table spaces must be DMSs. The maximum size of a long table space is 2 TB.

System Temporary Table Space

Temporary table spaces are used by the database manager during SQL operations for holding transient data such as immediate tables during sort operations, reorganizing tables, creating indexes, and joining tables. A database must have at least one temporary table space. By default, an SMS table space called TEMPSPACE1 is created when the database is created. It can be dropped after another temporary table space is created (one must always be in existence), and it can be called any legal table space name. The name TEMPSPACE1 does not have to be used. Temporary table spaces can be either SMSs or DMSs. The maximum size of a temporary table space is 2 TB.

> DB2 V7.1 supports system temporary table spaces and user temporary table spaces. A system temporary table space must exist for DB2 to operate properly. User temporary table spaces can be used to place temporary tables.

Extentsize

An *extent* is a unit of space within a container of a table space. Database objects are stored in pages within DB2 (except for LOBs and long varchars). These pages are grouped into allocation units called extents. The extent size is defined at the table space level. Once the extent size is established for the table space, it cannot be altered. A database configuration parameter DFT_EXTENT_SZ specifies the default extent size for all table spaces in the database. The range this value can take is from 2 to 256 pages; for example, 8 - 1024 KB for 4 KB pages or 16 - 2048 KB for 8 KB pages. This figure can be overridden by using the EXTENTSIZE parameter in the CREATE TABLESPACE statement. Although this parameter can be also specified in kilobytes or megabytes, DB2 ensures that the extent size is always a whole number of pages by taking the floor of the number of bytes divided by the page size.

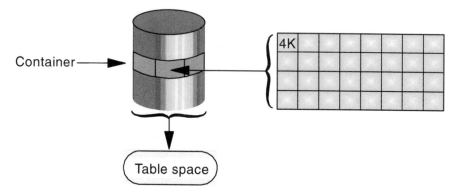

Fig. 9–3 *Extents and containers*

 Note: In addition to using extents for storing user data, extents are also used for space management within the table space.

Pagesize

Rows of DB2 table data are organized into blocks called *pages*. Pages can be four sizes: 4, 8, 16, and 32 KB. Table data pages do not contain the data for columns defined with LONG VARCHAR, LONG VARGRAPHIC, BLOB, CLOB, or DBCLOB data types.

In a page of table data, 76 bytes are reserved for DB2. The other 4020 bytes (8040 bytes for 8 KB pages) are available for user data, although no individual row can exceed 4005 bytes (8101 bytes for 8 KB pages) in length. The maximum number of columns in a table defined using a table space that uses 4 KB pages is 500; for 8, 16, and 32 KB pages, it is 1012 columns.

 Note: LOB and long field data can reside in table spaces of any page size.

Performance Considerations

The type and design of your table space determines the efficiency of the I/O performed against that table space. The following concepts are important in understanding how DB2 performs I/O operations:

Big-Block Reads

If several pages (usually an extent) are retrieved in a single request, then *big-block reads* have occurred. If rows that are in pages within the extent retrieved are used, another physical I/O will not be required, resulting in optimum performance.

Sequential Prefetching

Sequential prefetching is the ability of the database manager to read pages in advance of those pages being referenced by a query, in anticipation of being required by the query. This asynchronous retrieval can reduce execution times significantly.

You can control how aggressively the prefetching is performed by changing the PREFETCHSIZE parameter on the CREATE TABLESPACE statement. By default, this value is set to the DFT_PREFETCH_SZ database configuration parameter. This value represents how many pages will be read at a time when a prefetch request is triggered by DB2. By setting this value to a multiple of the extent size, multiple extents can be read in parallel. This function is even more effective when the containers for the table space are on separate hard disks.

> **Note:** On UNIX platforms, prefetching will create separate I/O processes. On Windows and OS/2, prefetching is accomplished using threads.

To enable prefetching, DB2 starts separate threads of control, known as *I/O servers*, to perform page reading. These I/O servers wait for requests for pages from database agents that manage the processing of all SQL requests. The first available I/O server will read the prefetch request from a queue and read the data into the buffer pool. Depending on the number of prefetch requests in the queue and the number of I/O servers configured by the NUM_IOSERVERS database configuration parameter, multiple I/O servers can be fetching data at the same time.

DB2 can monitor I/O activity in the system. If sequential page reading is occurring, DB2 will initiate prefetching requests. The function is called *sequential detection* and is implemented via the SEQDETECT database configuration parameter. By default, this parameter is set to YES. If set to NO, DB2 will only initiate sequential prefetching in a predetermined manner during query optimization for activities such as table sorts and scans where sets of contiguous pages of data are required during query processing.

Another form of prefetching that can occur regardless of the SEQDETECT parameter is *list prefetching*. This is when DB2 builds up a list of internal row identifiers that are required, usually after scanning an index, then sorts them into physical address sequence and starts scanning the table for the rows. Because DB2 knows beforehand which pages are required, it can retrieve them ahead of when the application needs them; thus, the time to retrieve the data is shortened significantly due to the asynchronous processing.

Page Cleaning

As pages are read and modified, they accumulate in the buffer pool. Whenever a page is read in, there must be a buffer pool page to read it into. If the buffer pool is full of modified pages, one of these modified pages must be written out to the disk before the new page can be read in. To prevent the buffer pool from becoming full, *page cleaner* tasks write out modified pages to guarantee the availability of buffer pool pages for use by read requests. This feature is implemented via the NUM_IOCLEANERS database configuration parameter.

The CHNGPGS_THRESH database configuration parameter specifies the level (percentage) of changed pages at which the page cleaner tasks will start. When started, they will build a list of the pages to write to disk. Once they have completed writing the pages to disk, they will become inactive again and wait for the next trigger to start. The default value for this parameter is 60%.

In addition to I/O considerations, there are also considerations relating to the use of the table space containers. These are detailed as follows.

Number of Extents Required

Five is the minimum number of extents required in a DMS table space:

- Three extents for overhead and control information
- Two extents for each table object (always assume one object)

Number of Pages Required

In a DMS table space, one page in every container is reserved for overhead, and the remaining pages will be used one extent at a time. Only full extents are used in the container, so for optimum space management, you can use the following formula to help determine the appropriate size to use when allocating a container size:

```
(extent size in pages * n) + 1
```

where `extent size` is the size of each extent for the table space and `n` is the number of extents you want to store in the container. Recall above that you need a minimum of five extents for a DMS table space.

Recall that with SMS table spaces, space is allocated by the operating system file system as required.

Striping

Given that a table space can span multiple containers, DB2 writes to each container in a *round robin* fashion, where an extent as it is filled with data is written to each container in turn. This is known as striping.

In an SMS table space, if any container becomes full, then the entire table space is considered full, and no more data can be added.

In a DMS table space, if a container becomes full, DB2 will continue to use space available in other containers.

In both cases, it is preferable that containers be designed so that they are of equal size on different physical drives to optimize space usage and DB2 parallel operations.

Using RAID Devices

If you plan to use RAID devices, here are some guidelines. For further information and details, please refer to the DB2 Administration Guide:

- Define one DMS container per RAID array.
- Make the extent size a multiple of the RAID stripe size.
- Make the container size and prefetch size a multiple of the extent size.
- Use the DB2 registry variable `DB2_STRIPED_CONTAINERS` to align extents to the RAID stripe size.
- Use the DB2 registry variable `DB2_PARALLEL_IO` to enable parallel disk I/O.

Device Containers Versus File Containers

For DMS table spaces, files can be less efficient than devices due to the runtime overhead of the filesystem. Files are useful when:

- Devices are not directly supported by operating system and/or DB2.
- A device is not available.
- Maximum performance is not required. By bypassing the file system layer, DB2 manages device containers directly, improving performance, whereas for files, DB2 interacts with the file system.
- Files can make use of the cache of a file system, whereas devices cannot. You may have to increase DB2 buffer pool resource to compensate for this when using device containers.
- You do not want the extra administrative overhead associated with setting up and maintaining devices. Note that a device can only support one container.

Some operating systems allow you to have physical devices greater than 2 GB in size. You should consider partitioning the physical device into multiple logical devices so that no container is bigger than the size allowed by the operating system.

Here are some considerations specific to the different supported operating systems:

- In Windows NT, a DMS table space can use devices. If you want to use an entire physical drive as a container, specify \\.\N, where N is the physical drive number. If you want to use a logical drive as a container, specify \\.\X:, where X is the logical drive letter. The drive must not be formatted. Other applications must not use these container locations.
- In AIX, create a volume group over the physical disks you are going to use for DB2 containers.
- On UNIX platforms, the creator of the logical volume must have write access to the character portion of the device container being used.
- In OS/2, a DMS table space can only use files as containers.

Multipage File Allocation

In an SMS table space, the associated file is extended one page at a time as the object grows. When inserting a large number of rows, some delay may result from waiting for the system to allocate another page. If you need improved insert perfor-mance, you can enable *multipage file allocation*. This allows the system to allocate or extend the file by more than one page at a time. It will allocate empty pages to fill up the last extent in all SMS table space containers (see the *DB2 UDB V7.1 Command Reference* for more information).

This facility is implemented by running the db2empfa utility and is indicated by the MULTIPAGE_ALLOC database configuration parameter.

Comparison of SMS and DMS Table Spaces

The following table compares the key features of SMS and DMS table spaces.

Table 9–1   *Characteristics of SMS and DMS User Table Spaces*

Characteristics	SMS	DMS
Can dynamically increase number of containers in table spaces	No	Yes
Can store index data for a table in a separate table space	No	Yes
Can store long data for a table in a separate table space	No	Yes
One table can span several table spaces	No	Yes
Space allocated only when needed	Yes	No
Table space can be placed on different disks	Yes	Yes
Extent size can be changed after creation	No	No

The Catalog Table Space

The DB2 system catalog is where DB2 keeps all its metadata about all the DB2 objects in the database. Previously we had mentioned that catalog table space is called SYSCATSPACE and that its definition occurs in the CREATE DATABASE command. The following are considerations when planning for the system catalog:

- The system catalog consists of many tables of varying sizes. In using a DMS table space, a minimum of two extents are allocated for each table object. Depending on the extent size chosen, a significant amount of allocated and unused space may result. If using a DMS table space, a small extent size (2 - 4 pages) should be chosen; otherwise, an SMS table space should be used.
- The catalog tables use large object data type columns. These columns are not kept in the buffer pool and are read from disk each time they are needed. By using an SMS table space or DMS table space with file containers, you can take advantage of the file system cache for LOB data types.
- As more DB2 objects are created, the size of the catalog will increase. If you use an SMS table space, you cannot add more containers. All you can do is use operating system functionality to increase the underlying file system size. If you use a DMS table space, you can add more containers.

Temporary Table Spaces

Temporary table spaces are important as they are DB2's work areas for placing intermediate tables as it determines the final result set of data in satisfying SQL queries. Therefore, a significant amount of activity takes place in temporary table spaces. Another important use is for intermediate storage during the REORG TABLE utility. Its use here is optional, as by default, DB2 will place the copy of the table in the same table space where the original table resides. Refer to the *DB2 Administration Guide* for more considerations about the `REORG TABLE` utility and temporary table spaces.

If a database has more than one temporary table space defined, temporary objects are allocated among the temporary table spaces in a round robin fashion. Each temporary table space must be large enough to accommodate the largest possible temporary table. An application may encounter a temporary table space full condition even though there is unused space in other temporary table spaces. It is recommended that just one temporary table space be defined for a database and that multiple containers on separate disks be used to improve performance.

Some guidelines for temporary table spaces are:

- Create one SMS temporary table space for every page size.
- Define the containers for these table spaces so that they share the same file system(s). This maximizes disk sharing and minimizes the total disk requirement. As each temporary table is created and deleted by DB2, the disk space used will be reclaimed.
- If you require the highest level of performance and can afford the dedicated disk space, consider using DMS for temporary table spaces. Although you will lose the benefits of flexibility that you have with SMS, you may benefit from the performance advantages of using DMS.

 Note: There must be at least one temporary table space for use by the database at all times.

Choosing an Extent Size

The extent size for a table space indicates the number of pages of table data that will be written to a container before data will be written to the next container. When selecting an extent size, you should consider the size and type of tables in the table space.

Space in DMS table spaces is allocated to a table an extent at a time. As the table is populated and an extent becomes full, a new extent is allocated. A table is made up of the following separate table objects:

- A DATA object - This is where the regular column data is stored.
- An INDEX object - All indexes defined on the table are stored here.
- A LONG FIELD object - If your table has one or more LONG columns, they are all stored here.

- Two LOB objects - If your table has one or more LOB columns, they are stored in these two table objects: one table object for the LOB data and a second table object for metadata describing the LOB data.

Each table object is stored separately, and each allocates new extents as needed. Each table object is also paired up with a metadata object called an *extent map*, which describes all the extents in the table space that belong to the table object. Space for extent maps is also allocated an extent at a time.

The initial allocation of space for a table is two extents for each table object. If you have many small tables in a table space, you may have a large amount of space allocated to store a relatively small amount of data. In such a case, you should specify a small extent size or use an SMS table space that allocates pages one at a time.

If, on the other hand, you have a very large table that has a high growth rate, and you are using a DMS table space with a small extent size, you could have unnecessary overhead related to the frequent allocation of additional extents.

In addition, the type of access to the tables should also be considered. Sequential scanning of tables, such as the type of SQL queries used in a data warehousing environment, will need to access a large percentage of rows in a table. In this type of workload, a larger extent size may be preferred to reduce the number of I/O operations DB2 has to perform. In addition, prefetching of data can also take place to reduce the time the application has to wait for DB2 to return data to it.

In contrast, an online transaction processing (OLTP) workload involves queries that access tables usually in a random manner, retrieving data by key values. In this case, a large extent would bring many data pages into the buffer pool that are not required by the application. In this case, a smaller extent size may be justified.

Long Field Data

For the data types of LONG VARCHAR and LONG VARGRAPHIC, 20 bytes are used for the descriptor that is kept in the table data row. For further information about how long field data is stored, see the *DB2 UDB V7.1 Administration Guide*.

Large Object Data

If a table has BLOB, CLOB, or DBCLOB data, in addition to the byte count (between 72 and 312 bytes) for the descriptor (in the table row), the data itself must be stored. This data is stored in two separate table objects that are structured differently than other data types.

LOB Data Objects

Data is stored in 64 MB areas that are broken up into segments whose sizes are a power of two times 1 KB. Hence these segments can be 1024 bytes, 2048 bytes, 4096 bytes, and so on, up to 64 MB.

To reduce the amount of disk space used by the LOB data, you can use the COM-PACT parameter in the lob-options-clause on the CREATE TABLE and ALTER TABLE statements. The COMPACT option minimizes the amount of disk space required by allowing the LOB data to be split into smaller segments so that it will use the smallest amount of space possible. This does not involve data compression but is simply using the minimum amount of space to the nearest 1 KB boundary. Without the COMPACT option, there is no attempt to reduce the space used to the nearest 1 KB boundary. Appending to LOB values stored using the COMPACT option may result in slower performance compared with appending LOB values for which the COMPACT option is not specified. The amount of free space contained in LOB data objects will be influenced by the amount of update and delete activity as well as the size of the LOB values being inserted.

LOB Allocation Objects

Allocation and free space information is stored in 4 KB allocation pages separated from the actual data. The number of these 4 KB pages is dependent on the amount of data, including unused space, allocated for the large object data. The overhead is calculated as follows: one 4 KB page for every 64 GB plus one 4 KB page for every 8 MB.

If character data is less than 4 KB in length, and it fits in the record with the rest of the data, the CHAR, GRAPHIC, VARCHAR, or VARGRAPHIC data types should be used instead of the large object data types.

Mapping Tables to Table Spaces

When determining how to map tables to table spaces in your design, consider the following:

- The *amount* of data. If your design involves tables with a small amount of data, consider using SMS table spaces for them. The effort in administering many small tables, each in their own DMS table space, would not be proportional to the benefit gained.

  It would be more prudent to concentrate on larger, more frequently accessed tables. Here you could justify placing each table in its own DMS table space.

- The *type* of data in the table. Historical data that is used infrequently and does not have a critical response time requirement can be placed on slower, less-expensive devices.

Conversely, the tables with fastest response time requirements should be assigned to the fastest devices available. In extreme cases, these table spaces could be given their own buffer pool.

Another approach is to group related tables together in table spaces. They may be related via referential integrity, triggers, or structured data types. Since the BACKUP and RESTORE utilities can work at the table space level, the related data between the tables can be relied on stay consistent and recoverable.

* Separating out index and long data components. By assigning the indexes for a table into a separate table space, the containers for this table space can be placed on different disks, thus reducing contention on the disks containing the actual table data. Indexes can then be given their own buffer pool to reduce index physical I/O.

Similarly, contention is also reduced by separating the long data from the other components. In addition, if long data is included with the regular data, it will take longer because of the extra I/O required to sequentially scan the table.

Data Storage Management

Implementation Examples

Now that we understand the characteristics of the DB2 storage objects we can implement them via the commands and SQL statements that create and delete them. For a detailed description of all the options available on the following commands and SQL statements, see the *DB2 UDB V7.1 Administration Guide*, the *DB2 UDB V7.1 SQL Reference* and the *DB2 UDB V7.1 Command Reference*.

Creating a Database

This is the simplest form of the CREATE DATABASE command. Note that this is a command and not an SQL statement.

```
CREATE DATABASE DB2CERT
```

The LIST TABLESPACES SHOW DETAIL command output below shows us the result of the above CREATE DATABASE command. Note that for this example, these commands are being executed in a Windows NT environment.

```
Tablespaces for Current Database

Tablespace ID                     = 0
Name                              = SYSCATSPACE
Type                              = System managed space
Contents                          = Any data
State                             = 0x0000
 Detailed explanation:
     Normal
Total pages                       = 975
Useable pages                     = 975
Used pages                        = 975
Free pages                        = Not applicable
High water mark (pages)           = Not applicable
Page size (bytes)                 = 4096
Extent size (pages)               = 32
Prefetch size (pages)             = 16
Number of containers              = 1

Tablespace ID                     = 1
Name                              = TEMPSPACE1
Type                              = System managed space
Contents                          = Temporary data
State                             = 0x0000
 Detailed explanation:
     Normal
Total pages                       = 1
Useable pages                     = 1
Used pages                        = 1
Free pages                        = Not applicable
High water mark (pages)           = Not applicable
Page size (bytes)                 = 4096
Extent size (pages)               = 32
Prefetch size (pages)             = 16
Number of containers              = 1

Tablespace ID                     = 2
Name                              = USERSPACE1
Type                              = System managed space
Contents                          = Any data
State                             = 0x0000
 Detailed explanation:
```

```
        Normal
 Total pages                        = 1
 Useable pages                      = 1
 Used pages                         = 1
 Free pages                         = Not applicable
 High water mark (pages)            = Not applicable
 Page size (bytes)                  = 4096
 Extent size (pages)                = 32
 Prefetch size (pages)              = 16
 Number of containers               = 1
```

Note how the default values have been applied. The three table spaces
SYSCATSPACE, TEMPSPACE1, and USERSPACE1 have been created as SMS table
spaces with an extent size of 32. The total page count for SYSCATSPACE is 975 at a
page size of 4 KB, which means the catalog by default occupies 3.9 MB. This will
grow as objects are created in the database. The other two table spaces have only
one page in them.

Let's look at a more complex example:

```
CREATE DATABASE DB2CERT
        DFT_EXTENT_SZ 4
        CATALOG TABLESPACE
                MANAGED BY DATABASE USING
                        (FILE'C:\CAT\CATALOG.DAT' 2000
                        ,FILE'D:\CAT\CATALOG.DAT' 2000)
                EXTENTSIZE 8
                PREFETCHSIZE 16
        TEMPORARY TABLESPACE
                MANAGED BY SYSTEM USING
                        ('C:\TEMPTS','D:\TEMPTS')
        USER TABLESPACE
                MANAGED BY DATABASE USING
                        (FILE'C:\TS\USERTS.DAT' 121)
                EXTENTSIZE 24
                 PREFETCHSIZE 48
```

Here we are asking DB2 to create a database with:

- A default extent size of four pages
- The system catalog table space as a DMS table space with two file containers,
  each with 2000 pages, 8-page extents, and prefetch size of 16 pages
- The temporary table space TEMPSPACE1 as an SMS table space with two containers
- The user table space USERSPACE1 as a DMS table space of one container, with
  121 pages, 24-page extents, and prefetch size of 48 pages

The output from LIST TABLESPACES SHOW DETAIL in this case is as follows:

```
                Tablespaces for Current Database
Tablespace ID                        = 0
Name                                 = SYSCATSPACE
Type                                 = Database managed space
Contents                             = Any data
State                                = 0x0000
 Detailed explanation:
    Normal
Total pages                          = 4000
Useable pages                        = 3984
Used pages                           = 2440
Free pages                           = 1544
High water mark (pages)              = 2440
Page size (bytes)                    = 4096
Extent size (pages)                  = 8
Prefetch size (pages)                = 16
Number of containers                 = 2

Tablespace ID                        = 1
Name                                 = TEMPSPACE1
Type                                 = System managed space
Contents                             = Temporary data
State                                = 0x0000
 Detailed explanation:
    Normal
Total pages                          = 2
Useable pages                        = 2
Used pages                           = 2
Free pages                           = Not applicable
High water mark (pages)              = Not applicable
Page size (bytes)                    = 4096
Extent size (pages)                  = 4
Prefetch size (pages)                = 16
Number of containers                 = 2

Tablespace ID                        = 2
Name                                 = USERSPACE1
Type                                 = Database managed space
Contents                             = Any data
State                                = 0x0000
 Detailed explanation:
    Normal
Total pages                          = 121
Useable pages                        = 120
Used pages                           = 72
Free pages                           = 48
High water mark (pages)              = 72
Page size (bytes)                    = 4096
Extent size (pages)                  = 24
Prefetch size (pages)                = 48
Number of containers                 = 1
```

Note how the number of usable pages in SYSCATSPACE is 3984. Because one page per container is required for overhead, this leaves 1999 pages available for use by extents.

Since the extent size is 8, this leaves a spare seven pages unable to be used for extents in each container because only full extents are used. Add to this the one mandatory page for overhead and you have a total of eight pages per container unusable. Therefore, 16 pages out of 4000 for the entire table space are unusable.

In the USERSPACE1 table space, note that the container size is 121. One page is used for overhead, leaving 120 pages usable. Three extents are also used for over-head, accounting for the used page count of 72. This leaves 48 pages (two extents) available free for user data. Given the extent size, this is minimum number of pages the container can be defined with.

The `LIST TABLESPACE CONTAINERS FOR 2 SHOW DETAIL` command produces the following output. Note that the table space ID that the command requires is for the table space `USERSPACE1`.

```
              Tablespace Containers for Tablespace 2

    Container ID                          = 0
    Name                                  = C:\TS\USERTS.DAT
    Type                                  = File
    Total pages                           = 121
    Useable pages                         = 120
    Accessible                            = Yes
```

Creating Buffer Pools

This statement creates a buffer pool of 2000 four-kilobyte pages (8 MB):

```
CREATE BUFFERPOOL BPCERT4K
    SIZE 2000
    PAGESIZE 4096
```

This statement creates a buffer pool of 1000 eight-kilobyte pages (8 MB):

```
CREATE BUFFERPOOL BPCERT8K
    SIZE 1000
    PAGESIZE 8192
```

A buffer pool with the same page size must exist before a table space with a non-4 KB page size can be created.

Creating Table Spaces

This is an example of how to define a table space that has a raw device container under Windows NT. In this case, we are using an unformatted logical drive.

```
CREATE TABLESPACE RAWTS
        PAGESIZE 4096
        MANAGED BY DATABASE USING
                (DEVICE'\\.\E:' 8001)
        EXTENTSIZE 8
        PREFETCHSIZE 16
        BUFFERPOOL BPCERT4K
```

This example uses the buffer pool created previously. The reports on the table space and container are:

```
Tablespace ID                       = 3
Name                                = RAWTS
Type                                = Database managed space
Contents                            = Any data
State                               = 0x0000
 Detailed explanation:
    Normal
Total pages                         = 8001
Useable pages                       = 8000
Used pages                          = 24
Free pages                          = 7976
High water mark (pages)             = 24
Page size (bytes)                   = 4096
Extent size (pages)                 = 8
Prefetch size (pages)               = 16
Number of containers                = 1


            Tablespace Containers for Tablespace 3

Container ID                        = 0
Name                                = \\.\E:
Type                                = Disk
Total pages                         = 8001
Useable pages                       = 8000
Accessible                          = Yes
```

Creating Tables

This example shows how a table and its indexes can be separated into separate table spaces. Both table spaces must be defined as DMS.

```
CREATE TABLE CERTTAB
        (COL1    CHAR(7) NOT NULL
         COL2    INTEGER NOT NULL)
         IN RAWTS INDEX IN USERSPACE1
```

Dropping Table Spaces

This example shows how to drop table spaces. More than one can be dropped at the same time. All objects defined in the table spaces will be implicitly dropped or invalidated. Containers that were created by DB2 are deleted.

```
DROP TABLESPACE RAWTS,USERSPACE1
```

Dropping Buffer Pools

This example shows how to drop buffer pools. Note that the default buffer pool IBMDEFAULTBP cannot be dropped. This command will fail if table spaces that use the buffer pool are still defined. Once dropped, the memory that the buffer pool used will not be released until the database is stopped.

```
DROP BUFFERPOOL BPCERT4K
```

Dropping a Database

A DB2 command (not an SQL statement) is used to drop a database. This completely deletes all objects in the database. All users must be disconnected from the database before this command can succeed.

```
DROP DATABASE DB2CERT
```

Creating Table Spaces Using the Control Center

Besides being able to execute the above statements via the command line processor or DB2 Command Center, you can also use the Control Center to create DB2 objects. Here is an example of creating the table space RAWTS, using the table space wizard.

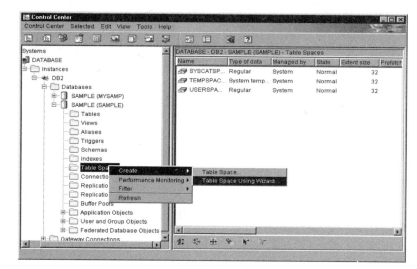

Fig. 9–4 *Control Center - Create Table Space Wizard*

When you enter the Create Table Space Wizard dialog, you must enter the name of
the table space and select the type and the space management options that you
require.

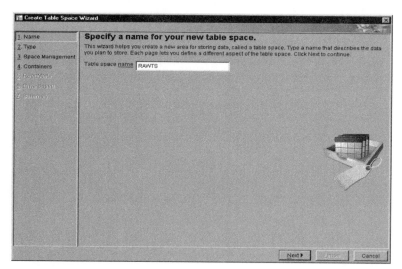

Fig. 9–5 *Create Table Space Wizard - Table space name*

After naming the table space, the table space type, either for data or indexes, needs
to be specified; also if the table space is a regular, long, or temporary table space.

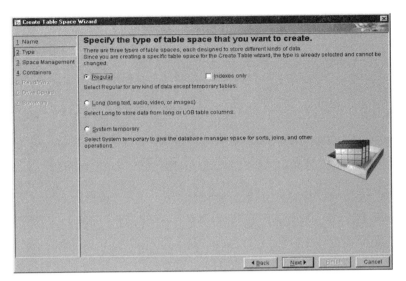

Fig. 9–6 *Create Table Space Wizard - Table space type*

The next decision is to specify whether the table space will be managed by the operating system (SMS) or the database (DMS).

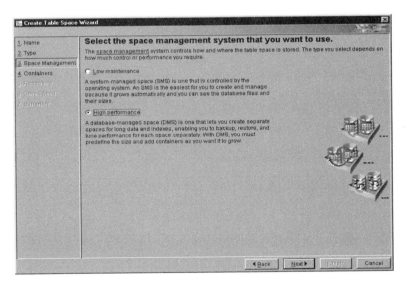

Fig. 9–7 *Create Table Space Wizard - Space management system*

By selecting **Add** on the next panel, a container can be defined for the table space.

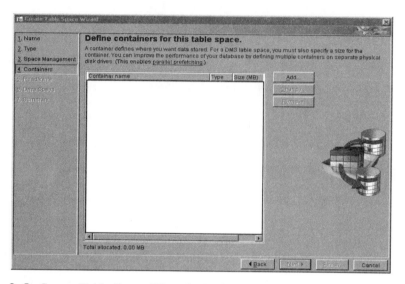

Fig. 9–8 *Create Table Space Wizard - Defining a container*

In this example, a file will be the container.

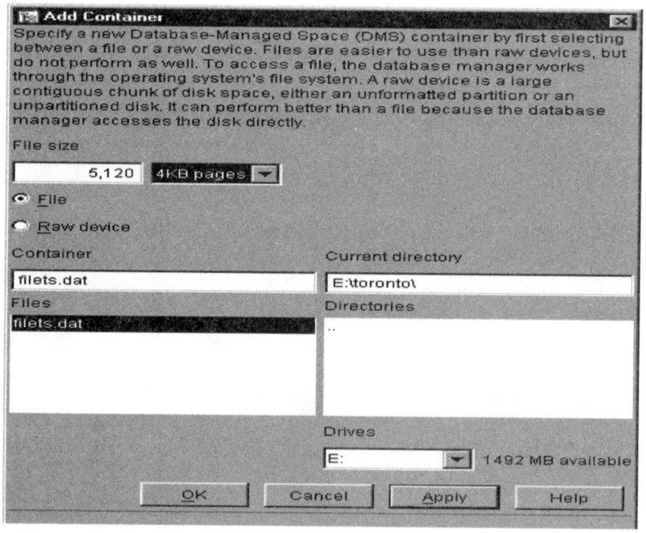

Fig. 9–9 *Adding a container*

The next panel allows extent and prefetch sizes to be specified.

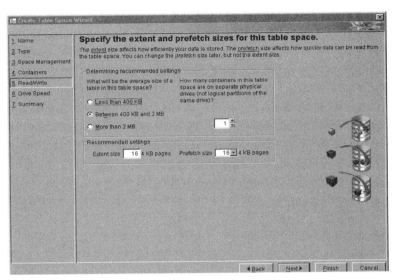

Fig. 9–10 *Create Table Space Wizard - Extent and prefetch size*

The next panel allows determines disk specifications that the optimizer will consider for optimizing data access.

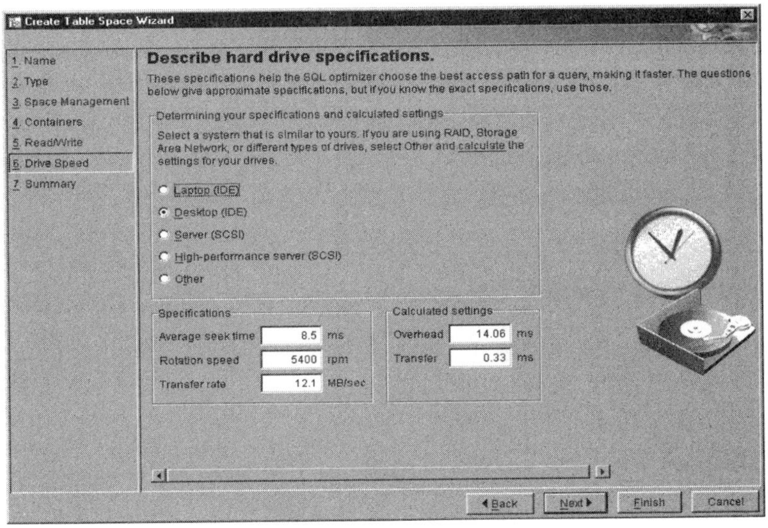

Fig. 9–11 *Create Table Space Wizard - Disk specifications*

The final panel summarizes the options specified for creating this table space.

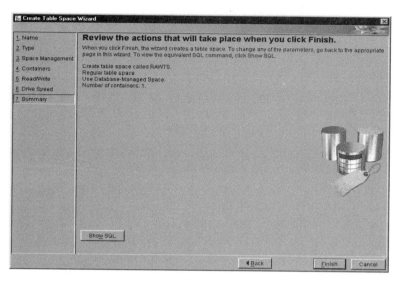

Fig. 9–12 *Create table space wizard - Summary*

One additional option is to select Show SQL, which gives the further option of saving the results to a script. As a DBA becomes more familiar with creating table spaces, the technique of submitting scripts will likely be less time consuming.

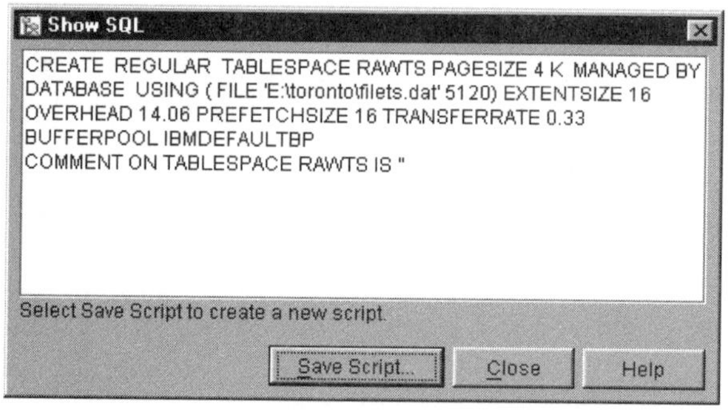

Fig. 9–13 *Show SQL for table space creation*

Table Space Maintenance

We have covered the creation of the DB2 storage objects to hold the database data. There are some additional commands and concepts to be aware of for maintaining them and monitoring changes in their size.

Database Files

The physical files that DB2 creates to support the database need to be protected from any direct access from outside of DB2.

- Do not make any direct changes to these files. They can only be accessed indirectly using the documented application programming interfaces (APIs) and by tools that implement those APIs.
- Do not remove or move these files.
- Using the security functions of the operating system, make sure all DB2 files and directories are secured. No one other than DB2 itself requires direct access to DB2 files and directories.
- The only supported means of backing up a database or table space is through the BACKUP API, including implementations of that API, such as those provided by the command line processor and Control Center.

Listing Table Spaces

To list basic or detailed information about table spaces, use the LIST TABLESPACES command. The syntax for this command is:

```
LIST TABLESPACES [SHOW DETAIL]
```

The basic information displayed by using this command is:

- Table space ID, the internal ID that DB2 uses for the table space
- Table space name
- Storage type (DMS or SMS)
- Table space type, which can be Regular (any data), Long, or Temporary
- State, a hexadecimal value indicating the current table space state

If the SHOW DETAIL option is used, the following additional details are normally shown:

- Total number of pages
- Number of usable pages
- Number of used pages
- Number of free pages
- High water mark (in pages)
- Page size (in bytes)
- Extent size (in bytes)
- Prefetch size (in pages)
- Extent size (in pages)
- Prefetch size (in pages)
- Number of containers

This information is important for informing you of how full the table spaces are and whether some action is required, such as adding new containers and running backups.

For examples of the output from this command, see the CREATE DATABASE command and the CREATE TABLESPACE statement in "Implementation Examples" on page 430.

Listing Table Space Containers

To list basic or detailed information about the table space containers for a specific table space, use the LIST TABLESPACE CONTAINERS command. The syntax for this command is:

```
LIST TABLESPACE CONTAINERS FOR tablespace_id [SHOW DETAIL]
```

The basic information displayed by using this command is:

- Container ID
- Container name
- Container type

When the SHOW DETAIL option is used the additional information shown is:

- Total number of pages
- Number of usable pages
- Accessible (yes or no)

Table Space States

DB2 maintains information about the states of table spaces and will not allow access using SQL (DML) statements if the table space is not in a *normal* state. Table space states are expressed in hexadecimal numbers. Sometimes, a table space can have more than one state associated with it. This will result in a combined hexadecimal number. There is a description of the state provided with the LIST TABLESPACES SHOW DETAIL command.

To view the table space state, issue the LIST TABLESPACES command and note the detailed explanation of the state. A table space is placed in a nonnormal state during load, backup, and recovery operations, or if placed in a quiesced condition via the QUIESCE TABLESPACE command. This command is not used very often by itself but is used by various DB2 utilities.

The LOAD command will place the table space in a LOAD PENDING state and leave the table space in this pending state until it has completed successfully. The RESTORE command will place the table space in ROLLFORWARD PENDING following a successful restore of the database. The table space will remain in this state until a successful ROLLFORWARD DATABASE command has been issued. The table space states are important to understand because if a table space is in any nonnormal state (not 0x0000) no SELECT, INSERT, UPDATE, or DELETE statements can be issued for any of the related table objects.

A list of some of the possible table space states follows:

- 0x0000 - Access to the table space is allowed (normal)
- 0x0001 - Quiesced share
- 0x0002 - Quiesced update
- 0x0004 - Quiesced exclusive
- 0x0008 - Load pending
- 0x0010 - Delete pending
- 0x0020 - Backup pending
- 0x0100 - Restore pending

For the further information about table space states, see the LIST TABLESPACES command in the *DB2 UDB V7.1 Command Reference*.

Note: If a container is not accessible, DB2 will place the associated table space in an OFFLINE state. Once the problem is resolved the ALTER TABLESPACE statement can be used with the SWITCH ONLINE option to make the table space available again.

System Catalog Information About Table Spaces

Table space information is kept in the SYSCAT.TABLESPACES catalog view. You are able to query this information using SQL. The layout of the view follows:

Table 9–2 *SYSCAT.TABLESPACES*

Column Name	Data Type	Nulls?	Description
TBSPACE	VARCHAR(18)		Name of table space
DEFINER	VARCHAR(128)		Authorization ID of table space definer
CREATE_TIME	TIMESTAMP		Creation time of table space
TBSPACEID	INTEGER		Internal table space identifier
TBSPACETYPE	CHAR(1)		The type of the table space: S = System managed space D = Database managed space
DATATYPE	CHAR(1)		Type of data that can be stored: A = All types of permanent data L = Long data only T = Temporary tables only
EXTENTSIZE	INTEGER		Size of extent, in pages of size PAGESIZE
PREFETCHSIZE	INTEGER		Number of pages of size PAGESIZE to be read when prefetch is performed
OVERHEAD	DOUBLE		Controller overhead and disk seek and latency time in milliseconds
TRANSFERRATE	DOUBLE		Time to read one page of size PAGESIZE into the buffer
PAGESIZE	INTEGER		Size (in bytes) of pages in the table space
NGNAME	VARCHAR(18)		Name of the nodegroup for the table space
BUFFERPOOLID	INTEGER		ID of buffer pool used by this table space (1 indicates default buffer pool)
DROP_RECOVERY	CHAR(1)		N = table is not recoverable after a DROP TABLE statement Y = table is recoverable after a DROP TABLE statement
REMARKS	VARCHAR(254)	Yes	User-provided comment

The following columns are of interest for table spaces from the SYSCAT.TABLES catalog view.

Table 9–3 *SYSCAT.TABLES*

Column Name	Data Type	Nulls?	Description
TBSPACEID	SMALLINT		Internal identifier of the primary table space of the table
TBSPACE	VARCHAR(18)	Yes	Name of primary table space for the table
INDEX_TBSPACE	VARCHAR(18)	Yes	Name of the table space that holds all indexes for the table
LONG_TBSPACE	VARCHAR(18)	Yes	Name of the table space that holds all long data for the table

Adding Containers to DMS Table Spaces

You can add a container to an existing table space to increase its storage capacity with the ALTER TABLESPACE statement. The contents of the table space are then rebalanced across all containers. Access to the table space is not restricted during the rebalancing. If you need to add more than one container, you should add them at the same time either in one ALTER TABLESPACE statement or within the same transaction to prevent DB2 from rebalancing the containers more than once.

You should check how full the containers are by using the LIST TABLESPACES and LIST TABLESPACE CONTAINERS commands. Adding new containers should be done before the existing containers are almost or completely full. The new space across all the containers is not available until the rebalance is complete.

Adding a container that is smaller than existing containers results in a uneven distribution of data. This can cause parallel I/O operations, such as prefetching data, to perform less efficiently than they otherwise could on containers of equal size.

Adding a New Container Using the CLP

This is an example of how to add another container, in this case, a file container to the table space that was created in an earlier example.

```
ALTER TABLESPACE RAWTS
     ADD (FILE'C:\TS\FILECON1.DAT' 8001)
     PREFETCHSIZE 32
     BUFFERPOOL IBMDEFAULTBP
```

Note how the ALTER TABLESPACE statement can be used to change the prefetch quantity and the buffer pool for the table space.

> **Note:** You can see the administrative activity performed against a table space including the addition of new containers using the LIST HISTORY command.

Adding a New Container Using the Control Center

Alternatively, you can also use the Control Center to add a container. In the list of table spaces, right-click on the table space you wish to alter.

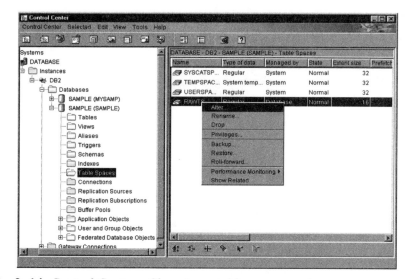

Fig. 9–14 *Control Center - Choosing a table space to alter*

The Alter Table Space panel is displayed:

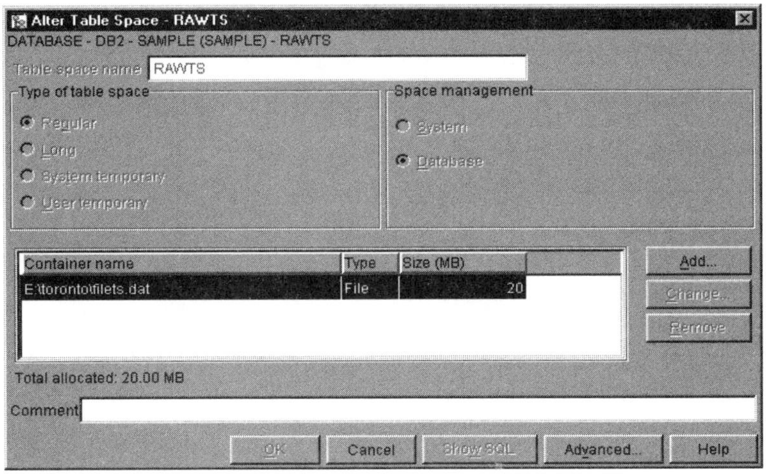

Alter Table Space - RAWTS ✕
DATABASE - DB2 - SAMPLE (SAMPLE) - RAWTS

Table space name RAWTS

Type of table space

- Regular
- Long
- System temporary
- User temporary

Space management

- System
- Database

Container name	Type	Size (MB)	
E:\toronto\filets.dat	File	20	

Add...
Change...
Remove

Total allocated: 20.00 MB

Comment

OK Cancel Show SQL Advanced... Help

Fig. 9–15 *Control Center - Altering a table space (1)*

Then click on **Add**. You can then enter the details of the new container. Options that cannot be changed have been grayed out.

Renaming a table space is a new option.

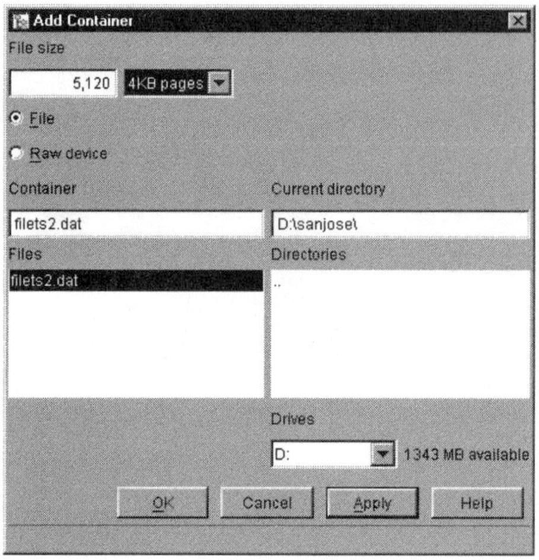

Fig. 9–16 *Control Center - Adding a container*

After defining the additional containers, the Alter Table Space panel displays the following:

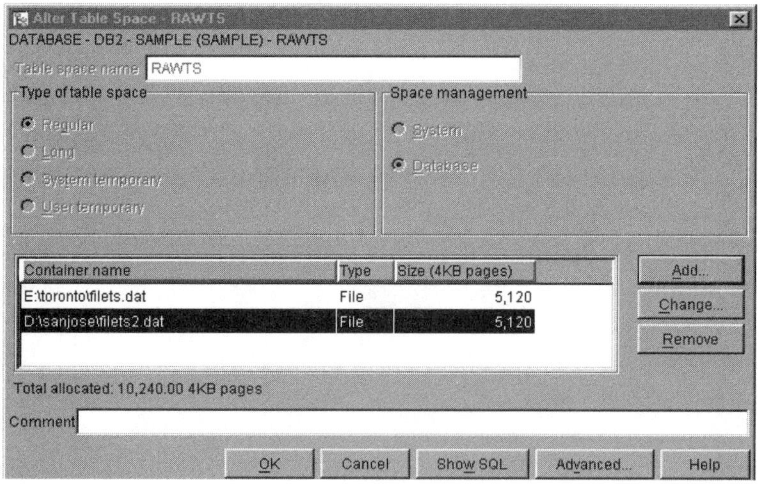

Fig. 9–17 *Control Center - Altering a table space (2)*

Select **OK** to add the container and DB2 will automatically rebalance the data across the containers.

Summary

This chapter discussed the physical placement of objects in DB2 databases. The types of objects discussed included:

- *Buffer pools* - Areas of main memory allocated to cache table and index data pages as they are being read or written to the hard disk.
- *Table spaces* - DB2 objects that isolate the logical definition of the table from the details of the physical storage. The storage types available are SMS (System Managed Space) and DMS (Database Managed Space). SMS is a storage model where space is acquired when needed. Its main benefit is its flexibility. DMS is preallocated storage space. Its main benefit is that it generally performs better than SMS. Regular table spaces can store any DB2 data. Optionally, indexes and long data can be placed in their own table spaces.
- *Containers* - Physical storage objects. They can be directories, files, or devices. Containers can be only assigned to one table space. Table spaces can consist of multiple containers.
- *Extents* - Units of space within a container. DB2 can use these units to transfer data between disk and buffer pools. Extents range in size from 2 to 256 pages. Once defined, the extent size for a table space cannot be changed.
- *Pages* - Blocks of storage that hold the rows of data. They can be either 4, 8, 16, or 32 KB in size. Buffer pool storage is divided into pages.
- *Large Object* (LOB) data is stored differently than other data types in DB2. LOB data objects are stored in 64 MB areas, broken up into segments. LOB allocation objects maintain allocation and free space information about large objects.

We discussed planning and design considerations for the DB2 physical environment:

- DB2 can operate in a single partition, single or multiple processor (SMP) environment. Multiple partition environments are covered by the DB2 Universal Database Enterprise-Extended Edition range of products.
- SMP systems have the capability of performing query and I/O operations in parallel.
- The way DB2 is configured to use the available memory resources is critical to its performance characteristics.
- Placing containers on separate disks gives DB2 the opportunity to perform parallel I/O operations by using sequential prefetching of pages.
- When a database is created, the system catalog table space SYSCATSPACE is created along with the temporary table space TEMPSPACE1 and user table space USERSPACE1.

- The choice of an extent size for a table space depends on factors such as the size and type of tables in the table space and the type of access to the tables.
- The mapping of tables to table spaces depends on factors such as the amount of data and the type of data in the table.

We then looked at how to implement, monitor, and change the objects via DB2 commands, SQL statements, and the Control Center.

CHAPTER **10**

Maintaining Data

- ◆ EXPORTING DATA
- ◆ IMPORTING DATA
- ◆ LOADING DATA
- ◆ REVIEW DATA PLACEMENT
- ◆ REORGANIZING DATA
- ◆ EXTRACTING STATISTICS

*I*n this chapter, the techniques of how to populate and extract DB2 data using the LOAD, IMPORT, and EXPORT utilities will be examined. The differences between these utilities will be examined along with the scenarios that would favor using one utility over another.

Additional maintenance topics will including examining the data and statistics of the database management system. Some of the utilities examined will include REORGCHK, REORG, RUNSTATS, and REBIND.

Moving Data

Whenever data is extracted or inserted into the database, particular care must be taken to check the format of the data. Sometimes a DBA may spend more time correcting the data format than actually inserting or extracting the data. To assist the DBA in this regard, DB2 supports various data formats for extraction and insertion. The formats include:

- DEL - delimited ASCII files
- ASC - fixed-length ASCII files
- PC/IXF - PC Integrated Exchange Format files
- WSF - Worksheet Format files

Delimited ASCII Files

This filetype, used extensively in Relational Database Management Systems (RDBMS) and other software packages, makes use of delimiters. A delimiter is a character that is used to identify the beginning or end of a data element. Some of the most important delimiters used in delimited ASCII (DEL) files include:

- *Character* delimiter - As the name suggests, this is used to mark the beginning and end of a character field. By default, DB2 uses the double quote (") character as a character delimiter. The DBA can optionally override this default and cause DB2 to make use of another character as the character delimiter.
- *Column* delimiter - This delimiter is used to mark the end of a field. The default column delimiter used is the comma (,) character, but the DBA may choose another character to use.
- *Row* delimiter - Used to mark the end of a record or row. DB2 assumes the new line character X'0A' (commonly used on UNIX operating systems to mark a new line) to be the row delimiter. On OS/2 and Windows NT, the carriage return/ linefeed characters X'0D0A' are used by DB2 as the row delimiter.

In DEL files, the rows are streamed into the file one after the other. They are separated with the *row delimiter*. The fields in the row are separated from one another by a *column delimiter.*

Character fields are encapsulated by two character delimiters.

Numeric fields are represented by their ASCII equivalent. A period (.) character is used to indicate the decimal point, if required. Float values are represented with the E notation, negative values with a leading minus (-) character, and positive values with a plus (+) sign.

To illustrate, a table named NAMES contains the following data:

Table 10–1 *Names Table*

EMP_NO	NAME	LASTNAME	DEPT_NO
10001	George	Baklarz	307
10002	Bill	Wong	204
10003	Beverly	Crusher	305

Assume the EMP_NO column is of type INTEGER and all the other columns are of a CHARACTER type. If the column delimiter is the comma (,), the row delimeter is the linefeed character and the character delimiter is the double quote (") character, a DEL file containing the data would consist of a datastream that looks like this:

```
10001,"George","Baklarz","307"
10002,"Bill","Wong","204"
10003,"Beverly","Crusher","305"
```

When choosing the column delimiter and the row delimiter of a DEL file, be careful not to use characters that are used in the datastream.

Non-Delimited ASCII Files

Non-delimited ASCII (ASC) files are sometimes referred to as fixed-length ASCII files. This file consists of a stream of ASCII characters of data values organized by row and column. Rows in the data stream are separated by a carriage return/line feed or new line character, and all column values are of fixed length. All variable-length character types are padded with blanks and represented using their maximum length. There are no column or character delimiters. Using the same example as above, an ASC file representing the data in the NAMES table would look like this:

```
10001George Baklarz307
10002Bill   Wong   204
10003BeverlyCrusher305
```

 Note: The columns are aligned in non-delimited ASCII files.

PC/IXF Files

PC Integrated Exchange Format (PC/IXF) files are used to move data among DB2 databases. For example, you can export a data file from a host database and use it as input to populate a table in a database on a DB2 server. In general, an IXF file consists of an unbroken sequence of variable-length records. Numeric values are stored as packed decimal or binary values, depending on the data type. Character values are stored in their ASCII representation, and only the used part of variable-length character types are stored. An IXF file also has the table definition stored within it along with the data.

> **Note:** If the host table contains packed fields, you will have to convert these fields before transferring the file to a DB2 database. To perform this conversion, create a view in the host database for all the columns that you require. A view automatically forms character fields out of the packed fields. From the view, you can export the required data as an IXF file.

IXF files cannot be edited by using a normal text editor.

An advantage of using this type of data file is that the table definition is included in the file, so a table and its indexes can be recreated and populated with this file format.

Worksheet Format Files

Lotus 1-2-3 and Symphony products use this type of file format to extract or import data. Although different releases have new added functions in their release-specific file types, the Worksheet Format (WSF) file type only uses a subset of this functionality accepted by most versions of these products. These files are not used to move data from one DB2 table to another.

Data Movement Utilities

A set of utilities is provided with DB2 to populate tables or to extract data from tables. These utilities enable you to easily move large amounts of data into or out of DB2 databases. The speed of these operations is very important. When working with large databases and tables, extracting or inserting new data may take a long time.

In this section, three DB2 utilities will be examined. The various options for each utility will be reviewed to explore their function and performance benefit. These utilities are:

- EXPORT
- IMPORT
- LOAD

The Export Utility

The EXPORT utility is used to extract data from a database table into a file. Data can be extracted into several different file formats, which can be used either by the IMPORT or LOAD utilities to populate tables. These files can also be used by other software products such as spreadsheets, word processors, and other RDBMSs to populate tables or generate reports.

You must already be connected to the database from which data is to be exported, and you must have SYSADM or DBADM authority, or CONTROL or SELECT privilege on the tables or views you access during the export.

To export all the data from a table NAMES into a file names.del of type DEL using all the default options, one would use the command:

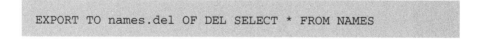

```
EXPORT TO names.del OF DEL SELECT * FROM NAMES
```

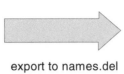

Names	
First_Name	**Last_Name**
George	Baklarz
Bill	Wong
Beverly	Crusher

export to names.del
of del
select * from names

names.del

"George","Baklarz"
"Bill","Wong"
"Beverly","Crusher"

Fig. 10–1 *Simple export*

Supported File Formats

The export utility allows the user to export data into one of three supported file types: IXF, DEL, or WSF.

To specify the file type, use the OF filetype clause. For example, data from the PRODUCT table can be exported to a file product.ixf of type IXF by using the command options (note that other options can also be specified):

```
EXPORT TO product.ixf OF IXF... SELECT... FROM product...
```

Although the ASC file type is not supported with the export command, the user can still generate a data file of type ASC by modifying the SELECT statement. For example, if two columns named FIRST_NAME defined as CHAR(10) and EMP_NO as CHAR(5) are to be exported to a file of type ASC, the user can specify the DEL file type and modify the select statement to:

```
EXPORT.. OF DEL.. SELECT first_name CONCAT emp_no FROM...
```

The output of the command is shown below:

```
"George     10001"
"Bill       10002"
"Beverly    10003"
```

When importing the data into a table, the column start position of the first column should be given as 2, thus ignoring the double quote (") character in the first position. Numeric values can be cast to a character type and then concatenated to the other columns.

Date Format Modification

For DEL and WSF files, the default format used for date values is *yyyymmdd*. The user has the option of changing the format to the ISO standard representation *yyyy-mm-dd* by specifying the DATEISO file type modifier with the EXPORT command:

```
EXPORT... MODIFIED BY DATEISO...
```

Delimiters Used with DEL Files

The default character delimiter is the double quote (") character. To override this, specify the CHARDEL file type modifier. For example, to use the asterisk (*) character as the character delimiter:

```
EXPORT... MODIFIED BY CHARDEL*
```

Note: The same character cannot be used for more than one delimiter in the file.

Handling Decimal Columns

When exporting to DEL files, decimal data types are exported with a decimal point (.) character. Leading and trailing zeros and a plus (+) or minus (-) sign are inserted before (or after) the value. For example, a value of 22.5 in a column named AMOUNT defined as DECIMAL(8,2) will be exported as:

```
+000022.50
```

To change the decimal point delimiter, specify the DECPT file type modifier:

```
EXPORT... MODIFIED BY DECPT^
```

The user can also change the way that positive decimal values are exported. By default, a plus (+) character is added in front of the value to identify it as a positive, value. By using the DECPLUSBLANK filetype modifier, no plus (+) will be added to positive values. Negative values are unaffected.

```
EXPORT... MODIFIED BY DECPLUSBLANK
```

Derived Column Names When Exporting

In some cases, the user may want to export data derived from one or more columns into a single column in the output file. For example, the SELECT statement may include a derived column defined as "Salary minus Deductions." In this case, a number will be generated and used as the name of the derived column. There are two ways to force the column to be renamed. You can do this for IXF and WSF type files only.

First, you can use the AS clause in the SELECT statement. In our example, "Salary minus Deductions" can be written as SALARY - DEDUCTIONS AS PAY. The name of the derived column will now be PAY.

```
EXPORT... SELECT SALARY - DEDUCTION AS PAY... FROM...
```

Alternatively, you can specify the METHOD N option followed by the names to be used for the columns, in the order in which they are selected. In our example, if the first column is the "Salary minus Deductions" column, the first name specified after the METHOD N option would be PAY:

```
EXPORT... METHOD N ('PAY',...)...
        SELECT salary - deduction,... FROM...
```

An IXF data file can be used to create a table in another database by using the table definition stored in the IXF file itself. By changing the names of the columns when exporting to the IXF file, the subsequent table can be created with the desired column names when the file is imported into the target database.

Capturing Error and Warning Messages

Use the MESSAGES option to specify a file that should be used to record all error and warning messages:

```
EXPORT... MESSAGES X:\Error_logs\Exports\Exp1.txt...
```

Exporting Large Object Data

When exporting tables that contain LOB data types, the user has two options of how the LOB values can be exported. The first 32 KB of LOB data can be included in the target file with the regular table data, or the LOB can be stored seperately, each LOB value in a file of its own. If the user decides on the first option, there are no extra parameters that need to be specified with the export command. However, only LOBs of 32 KB or less should be exported in this way. If a LOB value exceeds 32 KB in size, it will be truncated, and only the first 32 KB will be exported into the file.

For the export utility to export each LOB value to a seperate file, the user must specify where the files are to be put and what names are to be used. This is done by specifing three parameters:

- `LOBSINFILE` - A file type modifier, which when specified, informs the export utility that all LOB values are to be exported into separate files. If it is not specified, the export utility will ignore all other parameters related to exporting LOBs into separate files.
- `LOBS TO lob-path` specifies the path or paths where the LOB values will be exported as individual files. If the first path specified becomes full, the second will be used, and so on. When specifying the path name, make sure it ends with a "\" character for Windows- or OS/2-based systems or "/" for UNIX operating systems.
- `LOBFILE filename` tells the export utility what filename to use for the files. A three-digit number will be generated and added to the filename as an extension to ensure uniqueness.

In exporting LOB data from a table named `EMP_PHOTO` to a file named `emp_photo.del` and its LOB values to the directories `d:\lobdir1` and `d:\lobdir2` and the LOB filename to be used is `emp_photo_lob`, the `EXPORT` command would be written as follows:

```
EXPORT TO Emp_photo.del OF DEL LOBS TO
    D:\lobdir1\,D:\lobdir2\
    LOBFILE Emp_photo_lob... MODIFIED BY LOBSINFILE
 SELECT * FROM Emp_photo
```

Maintaining Data

The first LOB files exported would be named as follows:

```
d:\lobdir1\emp_photo_lob.001
d:\lobdir1\emp_photo_lob.002
d:\lobdir1\emp_photo_lob.003
.....and so on........
```

If the `d:\lobdir1` directory becomes full, the `d:\lobdir2` directory will be used.

Exporting Typed Tables

There are two ways in which data can be exported from typed tables. The first way is to treat the typed table as a normal table by using a SELECT statement.

For example, if a user wants to export rows from the EMPLOYEE table and no records from any subtables defined under it, then the ONLY option in the SELECT statement should be used:

```
EXPORT... SELECT... FROM ONLY(db2admin.Employee)...
```

If all the records in the EMPLOYEE table should be returned, including records from subtables under it, do not specify the ONLY option in the SELECT statement:

```
EXPORT... SELECT... FROM db2admin.Employee...
```

Another option is to export some or all tables in the hierarchy. The user needs to specify two things: all the subtables to export and the order in which they are to be exported. This order is referred to as the *traversal order*. Figure 10–2 shows a table hierarchy.

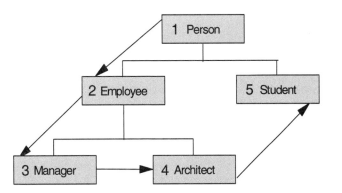

Fig. 10–2 *Exporting a table hierarchy - Traversal order*

The default traversal order starts from the highest table in the hierarchy – in our example, the PERSON table. The next table in the list can be either STUDENT or EMPLOYEE, depending on which of the two was created first. Assume that the EMPLOYEE table was created first. The next table in the list could be MANAGER or ARCHITECT; this is also dependent on which was created earlier. Assume the MANAGER table was created before the ARCHITECT table. There are no tables defined under MANAGER, so the ARCHITECT table will be the next table in the traversal order. Because the ARCHITECT table has no tables defined under it, the next in the list will be the STUDENT table.

It is important to realize that databases with the same table hierarchies may have two distinctly different default traversal orders. Make a note of the traversal order in which the tables in the hierarchy are exported because the same order must be used to import the tables.

To use the default traversal order, specify the subtable to start the export from after the STARTING option, in our case, the root table of the hierarchy, DB2ADMIN.PERSON:

```
EXPORT... HIERARCHY STARTING db2admin.Person
```

To specify another traversal order to use for the export, list the order of the tables instead of the STARTING table_name option. All subtables must be listed.

```
EXPORT... HIERARCHY (Person,Student,
    Employee,Architect,Manager)...
```

If rows are exported as part of a hierarchy, the first column in the output file will be a numeric value identifying the subtable to which the exported row belongs. The numeric value is derived from the position of the subtable in the traversal order list as defined with the EXPORT command, "1" being the first table in the list.

When exporting data as part of a hierarchy (or a result export for that matter), an optional WHERE clause also can be used to qualify the rows to export. For example, to export all data from the employees, managers, and architects working in the Sales Department, the following command could be used:

```
EXPORT... HIERARCHY STARTING Employee
   WHERE dept ='Sales'
```

Using the Control Center to Export a Table

The Control Center provides an easy interface to the EXPORT utility. To invoke it, select the table that needs to be exported and right-click on it. Select the **Export** option as shown in Fig. 10–3.

Once invoked, the user may specify the different options as discussed above. The Control Center will also be used to demonstrate EXPORT by showing how a user can export a table named PRODUCT to an DEL file. The output filename and message filename are selected as: d:\work\dba\data\product.del and d:\work\dba\data\product.msg.

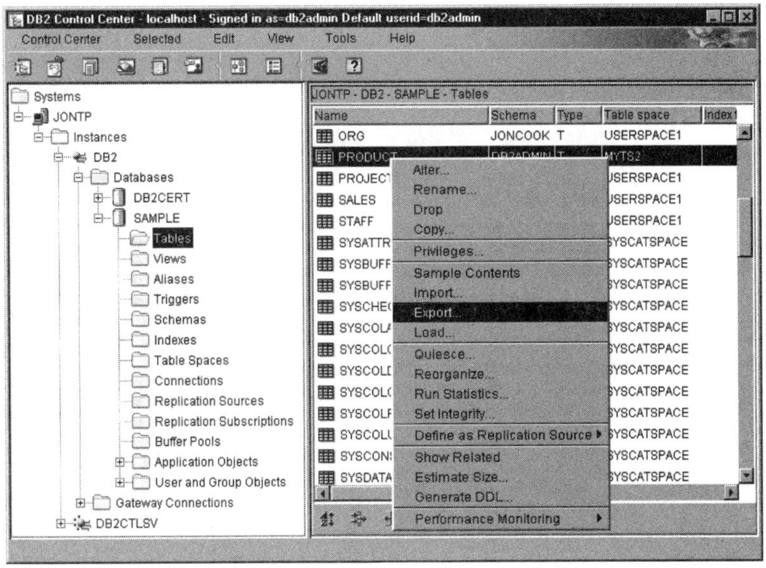

Fig. 10–3 *Invoking the EXPORT utility from the Control Center*

The Export Table notebook is displayed:

Fig. 10–4 *The EXPORT utility GUI in the Control Center*

As indicated by the SELECT statement in Fig. 10–4, all records and columns will be exported.

If the user chooses either DEL or WSF file types, modifiers specific to these file types may be specified by clicking on the **Options** button next to the file type. Fig. 10–5 shows the file type options that can be specified for DEL files.

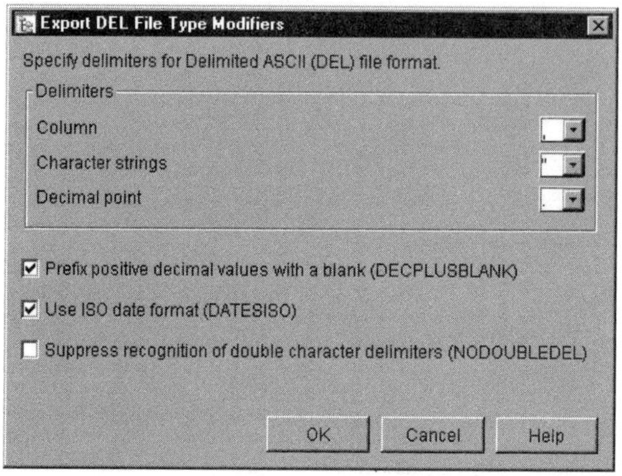

Fig. 10–5 *Changing the DEL EXPORT options in the control center*

The Columns tab (see Fig. 10–4) can be used to specify the column names to use in the exported file (IXF or WSF only). If not specified, the column names in the SELECT statement will be used.

If LOBs are to be exported into separate files, use the Large Objects tab to specify the paths and filenames to use.

Once all the information is captured in the relevant panels, the user may opt to run the EXPORT command by clicking on the **OK** button. Alternatively, the user may choose to look at the command that will be executed. Fig. 10–6 shows the command generated to export the PRODUCT table. The user may also choose to save the command to a script file to be executed at a later time.

```
Show Command                              [X]
EXPORT TO d:\\work\\dba\\data\\product.del OF DEL MODIFIED BY   coldel,
chardel' decpt. decplusblank datesiso MESSAGES
d:\\work\\dba\\data\\product.msg SELECT * FROM DB2ADMIN.PRODUCT




Select Save Script to create a new script.
              Close      Save Script...      Help
```

Fig. 10–6 *The EXPORT command generated*

EXPORT Considerations

The following information is required when exporting data:

- A SELECT statement (or hierarchy selection clause for typed tables) specifying the data to be exported
- The path and name of the file that will store the exported data
- The format the data will be written in (IXF, DEL, or WSF)

Note: An ASC filetype can be generated by concatenating and translating the columns in the SELECT statement.

The following information is optional when exporting data:

- A message filename
- A method that allows you to specify new column names when exporting to IXF or WSF files
- A file type modifier to specify additional formatting when creating DEL and WSF files
- Filenames and paths for exported LOB columns

Performance of the EXPORT Utility

When using the EXPORT utility, a DBA should make sure that the utility extracts the data efficiently. The SELECT statement used with this utility has the greatest effect on performance. There are some tools (like Visual Explain) available in DB2 that can be used to evaluate the performance of a SELECT statement.

The IMPORT Utility

The IMPORT utility inserts data from an input file into a table or view. You can either replace data or append data to the table or view if it already contains data.

With the IMPORT utility, you can specify how to add or replace the data into the target table. You must be connected to the database to use the utility, and if you want to import data into a new table using the CREATE option, you must have SYSADM or DBADM authorities or CREATETAB privilege for the database. To replace data in a table or view, you must have SYSADM or DBADM authorities or CONTROL privilege for the table or view. If you want to add data to an existing table or view, you must have SYSADM, DBADM, CONTROL (as above), or SELECT and INSERT privileges for the table or view.

> **Note:** If the existing table contains a primary key or unique constraint that is referenced by a foreign key in another table, data cannot be replaced, only appended.

Using the IMPORT Command

To import data from a file named names.del of type DEL into an empty table named NAMES using all the default options, use the following command:

```
IMPORT FROM Names.del OF DEL INSERT INTO Names
```

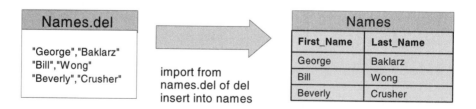

Fig. 10–7 *Simple import*

In this section, the use of the IMPORT command will be examined by looking at some of its most useful functions. Some of the options or parameters used with the IMPORT command are identical to the EXPORT command and will not be duplicated here. They are:

- The message file to use
- Changing column names using WSF and IXF files
- Delimiters used in DEL files
- Date formats to use
- Numeric data in the DEL files

File Types Supported

The file types supported are IXF, DEL, WSF, and ASC. To specify the file type, use the OF file-type clause. For example, a file named product.ixf of type IXF can be imported by using the command:

```
IMPORT FROM Product.ixf OF IXF...
```

The Import utility supports the following new format extensions: user-defined data and time formats, zoned decimal format, and preserves blanks in DEL format for char and varchar columns.

Creating Tables

When an IXF file is created using the EXPORT command, the table structure and definition is stored in it. The IMPORT utility can make use of the structure to recreate the table and its indexes. There are two ways to recreate the table. If the table already exists, it can be recreated by using the REPLACE_CREATE option. For example, if a table named PRODUCT exists and is to be recreated when importing new data, the IMPORT command can be invoked as follows. Note that this does not change the table definition – it only deletes all the data before doing the import. If the table does not exist and this option is used, the table will be created.

```
IMPORT FROM Product.ixf of IXF...
    REPLACE_CREATE INTO PRODUCT...
```

Note: If the PRODUCT table has a primary key defined that is referenced by another table's foreign key, the REPLACE_CREATE option can not be used.

If the PRODUCT table does not exist prior to the import, the CREATE option can be used to create it. For example:

```
IMPORT FROM Product.ixf of IXF...
   CREATE INTO Product...
```

When creating a table in this way, a user can also specify the table space in which it should be created. Optionally, the index and long table spaces can also be specified. For example, assume the source table PRODUCT has two indexes and contains long data. This example has a new table named PRODUCT created in an existing table space named DMS1 of type DMS, its indexes in table space INDEXDMS1 of type DMS, and its long data in table space LONG1 of type DMS. To accomplish this, the following statement would be issued on the command line:

```
IMPORT FROM Product.ixf OF IXF...
   CREATE INTO Product IN Dms1
   INDEX IN Indexdms1 LONG IN Long1
```

Appending Data

If the data in the source file is to be added to the data in the target table, the INSERT option should be used. For example, if the order of the columns in the exported file is the same as the order of the columns in the target table, the following command will insert the new records into the existing table named PRODUCT:

```
IMPORT... INSERT INTO Product
```

If the order of the columns in the source file is not the same as the order in which columns were specified when the table was created, then the order of the columns must be specified after the table name. For example, if the PRODUCT table has three columns named PROD_NO, PRICE, and DESCRIPTION in that order, and the source file contains the three columns in the order PRICE, PROD_NO, DESCRIPTION, the following command needs to be specified:

```
IMPORT... INSERT INTO Product(Price,Prod_no,Description)
```

Updating Existing Data and Inserting New Data

Sometimes a DBA receives a file that contains updated data for a table. Some of the records in the file do not exist in the target table, however, most do. Some of the existing data needs to be updated to reflect the new values. For example, the DBA receives a file named `product.del` that contains the new prices for some of the existing products as well as for new products. He cannot *insert* the new data because it contains records for some existing products nor can he *replace* the data because some of the valid product records do not exist in the table. The only option is to use the `INSERT_UPDATE` option of the `IMPORT` command. This will *insert* all the new records and *update* the existing data to reflect the new values.

The `IMPORT` utility uses the primary key and unique constraints defined on the table to determine if the row exists and whether it should be updated or inserted. In our example, the `PRODUCT` table has a primary key value defined as the product number (`PROD_NO`). In Fig. 10–8, four rows in the input file and three rows in the table before the import are shown.

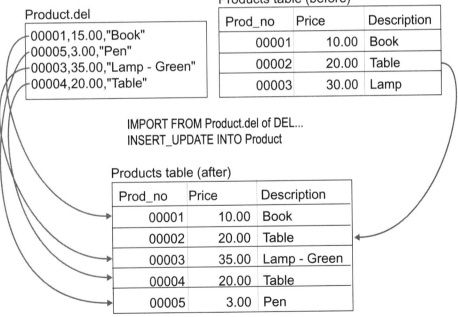

Fig. 10–8 *Using IMPORT with INSERT_UPDATE option*

The `IMPORT` statement is invoked with the `INSERT_UPDATE` option. The first row in the input file will cause the first row in the table to be updated. The reason for this is that the `PROD_NO` value supplied in the file matches an existing record in the table. As shown in the PRODUCTS table after the import, the value associated with the PRICE column has been updated to show the new price.

The second row in the input file has a PROD_NO value that does not exist in the PRODUCT table before the import. It is therefore treated as a new row that needs to be inserted into the table.

The third row updates both the description and the price of an existing row.

The fourth row in the input file is inserted as a new record because the PROD_NO value does not match an existing record in the table, even though the PRICE and DESCRIPTION do match an existing record in the table.

Replacing Data

To replace existing data in the table, you can specify the REPLACE option. This option is not valid if the table for which data needs to be replaced has a primary key that is referenced by a foreign key in another table. This is to enforce referential integrity. Assume that the PRODUCT table did not have any referential dependencies and that it is desired to replace the existing data in it with data provided in a file named product.ixf. The following would be specified with the IMPORT command:

```
IMPORT FROM Product.ixf OF IXF... REPLACE INTO Product
```

Forcing Intermediate Commits

By default, the IMPORT utility will only issue a commit at the end of a successful import. If the utility fails during its execution, all the changes to the table will be rolled back, so that it will seem as if the import never took place. The user may also direct the IMPORT utility to issue commit statements after a certain number of rows are successfully imported. If an error occurs during the import, only the changes in the data since the last commit will be rolled back.

To specify the frequency of such intermediate commit statements, use the COMMITCOUNT option followed by the number of rows to be imported before a COMMIT is issued. (For more details on using IMPORT and committing records, please refer to the *DB2 UDB V7.1 Command Reference.*) For example, if a COMMIT is to be issued after every 50 records processed from the input file, the following statement would be issued:

```
IMPORT... COMMITCOUNT 50...
```

Before and after the commit is executed, a message is written to the message file (if defined) or to the screen. The number of records read and committed are recorded in the message file. In the event of a failure, the DBA can find out how many records have been processed and which remaining ones have not been imported by looking at the message file.

All changes to data are logged in the transaction log files, and they have to stay active for as long as they contain records of uncommitted transactions. The amount of available active log file space can be limited; therefore, an import of a large file may fail if the COMMITCOUNT option is not used. In the case of a failure, all the changes may be rolled back or an automatic commit done based on the type of IMPORT being done (see the *DB2 UDB V7.1 Command Reference* for details). It is highly recommended that this option be used when importing data.

Restarting a Failed Import

If an IMPORT operation that did not have the COMMITCOUNT option specified fails, it can be reinvoked after fixing the problem that caused it to fail. The type of IMPORT being done will dictate the recovery needed.

If the IMPORT operation is invoked with the COMMITCOUNT option and subsequently fails, it can be reinvoked by using the RESTARTCOUNT option. This is used to tell the IMPORT utility to skip a certain number of records in the beginning of the file but to continue to import the remainder.

For example, a file named product.del was imported into a table named PROD-UCT by making use of the COMMITCOUNT 50 option. During the processing of the IMPORT command, the user accidently terminated the import session. This caused the import to fail half way through. The following extract is from the messages file:

```
SQL3109N The utility is beginning to load data from file
"Product.del".

SQL3221W...Begin COMMIT WORK. Input Record Count = "50".

SQL3222W...COMMIT of any database changes was successful.

SQL3221W...Begin COMMIT WORK. Input Record Count = "100".

SQL3222W...COMMIT of any database changes was successful.

SQL3005N Processing was interrupted.

SQL3110N The utility has completed processing. "100" rows were
read from the input file.
```

Maintaining Data

This shows that the first 100 records were committed. By reinvoking the IMPORT utility with the RESTARTCOUNT 100 option, the first 100 records found in the input file are skipped. Processing will continue starting with record 101 of the input file.

```
IMPORT FROM Product.del OF DEL...
    COMMITCOUNT 50 RESTARTCOUNT 100...
    INTO Product...
```

Importing ASC Files

When importing a file of type ASC, the IMPORT utility needs to be told where the column values start and end. The starting position and the ending position for all columns to be imported must be specified. This is done by making use of the METHOD L modifier. In Fig. 10–9, an input file of type ASC is shown. It consists of three columns that match the type and length of the three columns of the PRODUCT table. The first is the PROD_NO column, which is of type CHAR(5); the second is the PRICE column of type DECIMAL(8,2); and the last is DESCRIPTION of type VARCHAR(10). All blanks will be represented with the character "~".

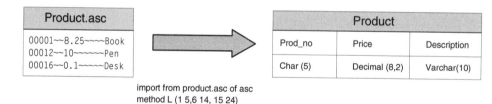

Fig. 10–9 *Import using METHOD L*

Selecting Columns to Import

Sometimes a data file contains more columns than is required by the target table. If the file is of type IXF or DEL, the column numbers can be used to import it by specifying the METHOD P option. For example, a DEL file contains record data in four columns, PROD_NO, PRICE, SUPPLIER, and DESCRIPTION. The target table PRODUCT only requires the columns PROD_NO, PRICE, and DESCRIPTION (columns 1, 2, and 4 of the input file). To import the data into the PRODUCT table, the following command can be used:

```
IMPORT FROM Product.del OF DEL... METHOD P (1,2,4)...
INTO Product(Prod_no,Price,Description)...
```

Importing Large Objects

LOBs can be exported as part of the table data in the exported file or as separate files. If the LOB data is in the same file as the rest of the table data, it can be imported without any extra parameters being specified with the IMPORT utility.

If the LOB values are exported into separate files, the IMPORT utility will need two things to be able to import: the directory or directories where the LOB files can be located and the file names of the LOB files.

Since the file names of the LOB files are stored in the exported file, the user does not need to specify them. To specify the source directory, use the LOBS FROM option followed by one or more directories that will serve as the source directories. Then specify the LOBSINFILE file-type modifier. If the LOBSINFILE modifier is not specified, the LOBS FROM option will be ignored.

For example, a table named EMP_PHOTO was exported to a file named emp_photo.del of type DEL, and its LOB files were exported with filenames emp_photo_lob.xxx into two directories. The emp_photo.del file is copied to another database server. The emp_photo_lob.xxx files in the first directory on the source database server are copied to the d:\lobdirA directory, and the emp_photo_lob.xxx files in the second directory are copied to the d:\lobdirB directory. To import the data into the EMPLOYEE_PHOTO table in the target database, the following options should be specified with the IMPORT command.

```
IMPORT FROM Emp_photo.del OF DEL
   LOBS FROM D:\LobdirA\,D:\LobdirB\
   MODIFIED BY LOBSINFILE... INTO Employee_photo...
```

 Note: When specifying the path, it must include the "\" character at the end for a Windows or OS/2 path or "/" when it is a UNIX path.

Maintaining Data

Importing Typed Tables

When importing data into a hierarchical structure, the user can specify the traversal order, which must match the order used when it was exported. It may be that the hierarchy structure at the destination differs from the one the data was exported from. For example, an extra table named TEMP_EMPLOYEES was created under the EMPLOYEE table as in our example. In this case, the default traversal order and the number and/or names of the tables are different than those in the original situation. The user can compensate for these differences by specifying a list of subtables to import into.

For example, an exported file contains the data associated with the EMPLOYEE and the MANAGER subtables only. The default traversal order can be used and imported with the command options:

```
IMPORT... (Employee,Manager)
   IN HIERARCHY STARTING Employee...
```

The traversal order could also be specified as:

```
IMPORT... (Employee,Manager)
   IN HIERARCHY (Employee,Manager)
```

If all the subtables named in the traversal order are to be imported, the ALL TABLES keyword could be used. In our example, this is only the EMPLOYEE and MANAGER tables:

```
IMPORT... ALL TABLES IN HIERARCHY (Employee,Manager)...
```

To import all tables including the EMPLOYEE table using the default traversal order, issue the command as follows:

```
IMPORT... ALL TABLES IN HIERARCHY STARTING Employee...
```

Invoking Import Using the Control Center

The IMPORT utility can also be invoked from the Control Center. Select the target table and click the right mouse button, then select the **Import** option. Fig. 10–10 shows the File tab of the Import Notebook. This next example will demonstrate the use of the Import Notebook.

The DBA is asked to import a file named d:\work\dba\data\product.del into an existing table named PRODUCT. The table is empty, so all the data in the DEL file has to be inserted. The DBA chooses the file d:\work\dba\data\product_imp.msg as the import message file. Since a large number of records are to be imported, the DBA decides to use a COMMITCOUNT option of 50 records to make sure the log files do not fill up. He also decides to use the COMPOUND=5 file type modifier. This will cause five records to be grouped together when inserted. It will improve the performance of the import.

Note: If one of the records in the compound group cannot be inserted, all will be rejected. Use this option if you know the data to be correct.

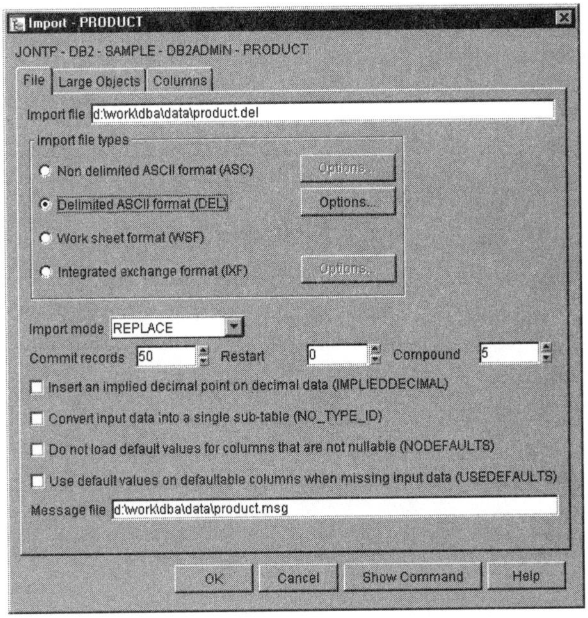

Fig. 10–10 *Import GUI in the control center*

Fig. 10–11 shows the file-type-specific options for DEL files. The DATESISO option has been selected, since the file was produced with this option.

Maintaining Data

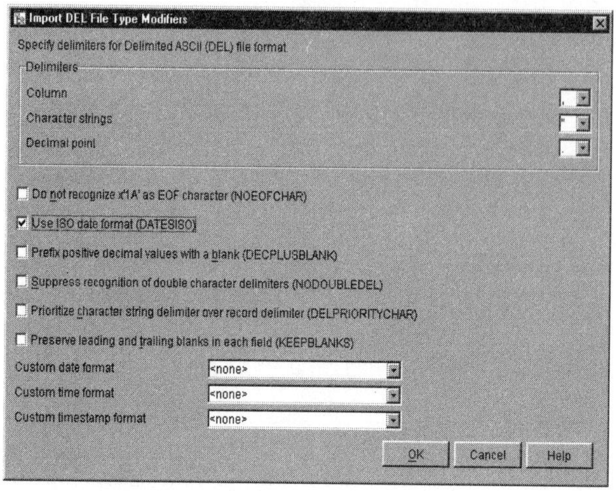

Fig. 10–11 *Import - Changing the DEL options in the Control Center*

The Columns tab can be used to specify which columns are present in the source file. The user can also use it to specify the order of the columns and new names to use if the file is an IXF file and if the table is to be created with the CREATE or REPLACE_CREATE options.

If LOBs are to be imported from separate files, use the Large Objects tab to specify the paths and file names to use.

Once all the information is captured in the relevant panels, the user may opt to run the IMPORT command by clicking on the **OK** button. Alternatively, the user may choose to look at the command that is to be executed. Fig. 10–12 shows the command generated to import the file into the PRODUCT table. The user may also choose to save the command to a script file to be executed at a later time.

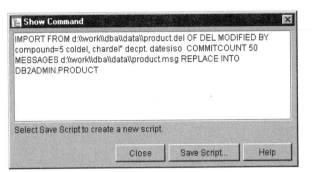

Fig. 10–12 *The IMPORT command generated*

IMPORT Considerations

The following information is required when importing data into a table or view:

- The path and the input file name where the data to import is stored.
- The name or alias of the table or view where the data is to be imported.
- The format of the data in the input file. This format can be IXF, DEL, ASC, or WSF.
- Whether the data in the input file is to be inserted, updated into the table, or view, or if the existing data is to be replaced.

You may also provide the following:

- A message file name
- The number of rows to insert before committing changes to the table
- The number of records in the file to skip before beginning the import
- The names of the columns within the table or view into which the data is inserted

> **Note:** The IMPORT utility will issue a COMMIT or a ROLLBACK statement, depending the success or failure of the import.

Examples of Using EXPORT and IMPORT

The first example shows how to export information from the PRODUCT table in the SALES database. Export to the file `product.ixf` with the output in IXF format:

```
EXPORT TO product.ixf OF IXF MESSAGES msgs.txt
   SELECT * FROM products
```

You must be connected to the database before you issue the command. To import the data into another database and create a table named PRODS in an existing tablespace named SMS1, the following command can be used:

```
IMPORT FROM product.ixf OF IXF
   COMMITCOUNT 50 MESSAGES product.msg
   CREATE INTO Prods IN SMS1
```

Note the use of the COMMITCOUNT option. This may prevent the log files from filling up.

In this second example, export all the data in a table hierarchy defined in the SALES database. The table hierarchy is defined as follows:

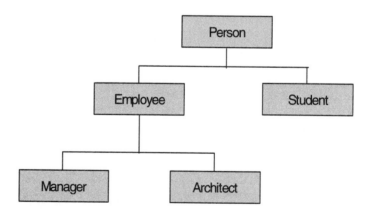

Fig. 10–13 *Table hierarchy of the Sales database*

Export the data to a DEL file named personh.del:

```
EXPORT TO personh.del OF DEL MESSAGES msgs.txt
   HIERARCHY STARTING person
```

A portion of the generated output file looks like this:

```
2,"y","Liezl        ","Blokker     ",28,"000054",90000,"b",,,,
2,"z","David        ","Walsh       ",45,"000145",120000,"b",,,,
2,"A","Pat          ","Turner      ",43,"000167",11000,"b",,,,
2,"B","Louise       ","Paterson    ",28,"000170",90000,"b",,,,
2,"C","Charles      ","Foster      ",34,"000301",100000,"b",,,,
```

Import the `personh.del` file into the entire PERSON hierarchy. Assuming all the tables in the hierarchy are all empty, use the INSERT command option. The command to issue is:

```
IMPORT FROM personh.del OF DEL
   COMMITCOUNT 50 MESSAGES personh.msg
   INSERT INTO ALL TABLES IN HIERARCHY STARTING person
```

Assume the import failed. The message file generated shows the following entries:

```
SQL3109N The utility is beginning to load data from file
"personh.del".
SQL3221W...Begin COMMIT WORK. Input Record Count = "50".
SQL3222W...COMMIT of any database changes was successful.
SQL3221W...Begin COMMIT WORK. Input Record Count = "100".
SQL3222W...COMMIT of any database changes was successful.
SQL3005N Processing was interrupted.
SQL3110N The utility has completed processing. "100" rows were
read from the input file.
```

The message file shows that 100 records were inserted into the table and committed. If one selected to restart the import, the first 100 rows need to be skipped. To do this the RESTARTCOUNT option is used. The following command will restart the import:

```
IMPORT FROM personh.del OF DEL
   COMMITCOUNT 50 RESTARTCOUNT 100
   MESSAGES personh.msg
   INSERT INTO ALL TABLES IN HIERARCHY STARTING person
```

The Load Utility

The LOAD utility, like the IMPORT utility, moves data supplied in an input file into a target table. Unlike the IMPORT utility, the target table *must* exist within the database prior to the start of the load process. The target table may be a new table that was created just before the load or an existing table to which data will be appended to or replaced. Indexes on the table may or may not already exist. The load process does not create new indexes – it only builds indexes that are already defined on the table.

To the DBA, the most important difference between the IMPORT and LOAD utilities relates to performance. The IMPORT utility inserts the data one row at a time. Each row inserted has to be checked for compliance with constraints (such as foreign key constraints or table check constraints). Changes are also logged in the log files.

The LOAD utility will insert data into a table much faster than will the IMPORT utility, because instead of inserting one row at a time, the LOAD utility will use the rows read from the input file to build pages which are then written directly into the database. Existing primary keys or unique indexes may be rebuilt after the data pages are inserted (rebuilt either totally or partially based on newly added data), and finally all the duplicate rows that do not comply with unique or primary key constraints are deleted from the table. During the load operation, individual records loaded are not logged in the log files.

The biggest disadvantage of the LOAD utility is that because the changes in the data are not logged, it cannot be rolled forward by using the log files. However, the LOAD utility can copy the source data, so it can be reloaded if required.

Before using the LOAD utility, the DBA must understand how it works, to exploit its performance benefits and to avoid any problems that may occur if it is used incorrectly.

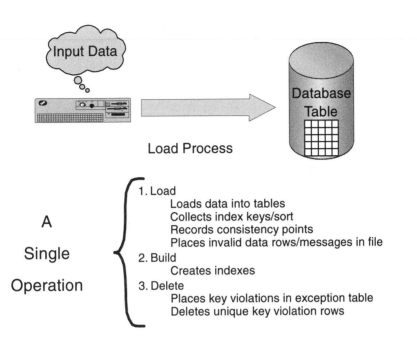

Fig. 10–14 *Three phases of load*

The three phases of the LOAD utility as shown in Fig. 10–14 will now be examined.

1. *Load* phase - Two things happen during the load phase: Data is stored in the table, and index keys are collected and sorted.

   When invoking the LOAD utility the DBA can specify how often it should generate points of consistency. A consistency point serves as a checkpoint to the LOAD utility. If the LOAD is interrupted during its execution, it can be restarted and will continue from the last consistency point. As part of taking a consistency point, the LOAD utility will write a message to the message file stating how many records have been loaded. This can then be used by the DBA to monitor the progress of the LOAD utility.

    The input file to be loaded can now reside on the remote client instead of on the database server.

2. *Build* phase - During the build phase, indexes are created based on the index keys collected in the load phase. If a failure occurs during the build phase and the LOAD utility is restarted (with the RESTART option), it will restart from the beginning of the build phase.

3. *Delete* Phase - During the delete phase, all rows that have violated a unique or primary key constraint are deleted and copied to an exception table (if it is specified when the LOAD utility is invoked). Only these two constraint types are checked. If a failure occurs during the delete phase and the LOAD utility is restarted, it will do so from the beginning of the delete phase.

When input rows are rejected, messages are generated in the message file.

All phases of the load process are part of one operation that is completed only after all three phases complete successfully. The LOAD utility will generate messages during the progress of each phase. Should a failure occur during one of the phases, these messages can assist the DBA in problem analysis and resolution.

If the utility is to replace an existing table (using the REPLACE option), the user must have SYSADM, DBADM, or LOAD authority or INSERT privilege and DELETE privilege on the table.

The new LOAD authority allows users to load tables without requiring SYSADM or DBADM authority to be granted.

The LOAD utility can receive as input a file, device, or pipe in one of the following formats: IXF, DEL, or ASC.

The LOAD utility supports the new format extensions, user-defined data and time formats, and zoned decimal format, and preserves blanks in DEL format for char and varchar columns.

Replacing Data in an Existing Table

By using the REPLACE option, the LOAD utility will delete all the data in an existing table before loading the new data. It will not recreate the table. For example, if a file named Product.ixf contains data that should replace the data in an existing table named PRODUCT, the user would use the following command:

```
LOAD FROM Product.ixf OF IXF... REPLACE INTO PRODUCT...
```

Inserting New Data into an Existing Table

By using the INSERT option with the LOAD command, all data in the input file will be inserted as new data into an existing table. For example, to load the table named PRODUCT by inserting the data contained in Product.ixf, the user would specify the following command:

```
LOAD FROM Product.ixf OF IXF... INSERT INTO PRODUCT...
```

Terminating a Load Operation

Sometimes it is necessary to terminate a load process; for example, the user is loading the wrong file, or the LOAD utility was invoked with the wrong options. To terminate the interrupted load operation, the user has to invoke the LOAD utility again, using the exact options it was invoked with the first time, but replacing the INSERT or REPLACE option with the TERMINATE option. For example, if the LOAD utility was invoked with the following options and then interrupted:

```
LOAD FROM Product.del OF DEL SAVECOUNT 500
   INSERT INTO Product
```

The load operation can be terminated by replacing the INSERT option with TERMINATE:

```
LOAD FROM Product.del OF DEL SAVECOUNT 500
   TERMINATE INTO Product
```

In the case of the original load being invoked with the INSERT option, all the new records loaded into the table will be deleted, and the state of the table will be the same as it was before the LOAD utility was invoked.

If the original load was invoked with the REPLACE command option, all the records in the table, old and new, will be deleted.

Generating Consistency Points

The user may choose to generate consistency points during the load operation. During the generation of consistency points, all internal buffers are flushed to disk. A record is also written to the message file. These consistency points are used to monitor the progress of the LOAD utility and to restart a failed load.

 Note: The generation of a consistency point has some performance overhead.

To specify the frequency with which the consistency points should be generated, use the SAVECOUNT command option followed by the number of rows to load between consistency points. For example, if roughly 500 rows should be loaded between consistency points, the following option should be used with the LOAD command:

```
LOAD FROM... SAVECOUNT 500...
```

Although the user specifies the number of rows with this option, it is converted internally to the number of pages on which that number of rows will fit. It is then rounded up to the nearest extent.

Restarting a Failed Load

If the load operation should fail, the DBA should look at the message file and error logs to determine the reason for the failure. Once the problem has been identified and fixed, the user can than reinvoke the LOAD utility with the RESTART command option. Care should be taken to reinvoke it with the same options as the first invocation, replacing the INSERT or REPLACE command option with the RESTART command option.

If the load failed during the load phase and consistency points were generated, it will restart the load phase from the last consistency point.

If the load failed in the build or delete phases, it will restart from the beginning of the phase in question.

Limiting the Number of Rows To Load

Sometimes the DBA may want to load only part of the data file, for example, to test the load options without loading all the data. When invoking the LOAD utility, the ROWCOUNT command option can be used to specify the number of records to load from the beginning of the file.

Forcing the Load to Fail on Warnings

In some cases, all the rows in the input file *must* be loaded into the target table, for example, an account table at a bank. If even a single record is not loaded correctly, this could cause a problem. To specify that the load should fail if one or more warnings are generated, use the following option when invoking the LOAD utility:

```
LOAD FROM... WARNINGCOUNT 1...
```

If the load fails because of the WARNINGCOUNT option, it can be restarted by using the RESTART option.

Preventing Generation of Warning Messages

If the user is not interested in warning messages about rejected rows, he can suppress them by using the NOROWWARNINGS file type modifier to specify that they should not be recorded. This can enhance the performance of the LOAD utility if large amounts of row warning messages would otherwise be generated.

Specifying a File For Rejected Rows

Rows that are not formatted correctly may be rejected by the LOAD utility and not be loaded. For example, if a row has a character value where the load expects a numeric or date value, it will not be loaded. These rows can be placed separately, from the other records, in a file by specifying the DUMPFILE file type modifier. This option is only valid for DEL and ASC filetypes. For example:

```
LOAD FROM... OF DEL... MODIFIED BY DUMPFILE=C:\dump.del..
```

Using an Exception Table

A user-defined exception table can be used to store rows that do not comply with unique or primary key constraints. Using an exception table is an optional parameter of the LOAD command. However, if an exception table is not specified with the LOAD utility, any rows that violate unique constraints will be discarded without any chance of recovering or altering them.

The exception table definition is very similar to the target table definition. The first n columns match exactly the column names and data types of the target table. The $n + 1$ column is an optional column, which if defined must be of data type TIMESTAMP. The $n + 2$ column is also an optional column. It can only be created if the TIMESTAMP column $n + 1$ precedes it. It should be defined as type CLOB of 32 KB or larger. This is to be used as a message column. It stores information about the particular constraint that caused the rejection of the row (Fig. 10–15).

Target Table

Name CHAR(20)	Age INT	Serial_num CHAR(3)	Salary INT	Department CHAR(25)
Bill	26	105	30000	Toy
Shirley	31	83	45000	Shoe
George	28	214	39000	Shoe
Katrina	35	251	55000	Toy
Dana	10	317	85000	Shoe

Valid exception table 1

Name CHAR(20)	Age INT	Serial_num CHAR(3)	Salary INT	Department CHAR(25)	Timestamp TIMESTAMP

Valid exception table 2

Name CHAR(20)	Age INT	Serial_num CHAR(3)	Salary INT	Department CHAR(25)	Timestamp TIMESTAMP	Description CLOB(32k)

Fig. 10–15 *Exception table definition*

Building Indexes

During the build phase, the indexes that existed prior to the load can be rebuilt. The user can define the method to be used for the rebuild. There are four options available:

- *Rebuild* - This option will force all indexes to be recreated independent of the type of load, INSERT or REPLACE.
- *Incremental* - This will allow the LOAD utility to use the data in the existing indexes and add the new data to them when the load is invoked with the INSERT option. This is useful if the amount of data loaded into the table is small compared with the existing data.
- *Deferred* - This option will prevent the LOAD utility from rebuilding indexes; instead, the indexes will be flagged as needing a refresh. They will subsequently be rebuilt upon the first access to the table or when the database is restarted. The value specified for the INDEXREC parameter in the database configuration file is used to determine when the indexes are recreated. This option is not supported

for tables that have a primary key index or unique indexes defined, since they need to be used for checking for duplicates.

- *Autoselect* - Will allow the LOAD utility to choose between the REBUILD and INCREMENTAL options.

For example, if a table named PRODUCT has two indexes defined and no unique or primary key constraints, and the LOAD utility is used to replace all existing data, the following options specified with the LOAD command will allow the index build to be deferred:

```
LOAD FROM... INDEXING MODE DEFERRED...
    REPLACE INTO Product...
```

If the DBA needs to add some data to the PRODUCT table immediately after the load completes, the following options can be used to rebuild the indexes:

```
LOAD FROM... INDEXING MODE REBUILD...
    INSERT INTO Product...
```

When using consecutive load operations on the same table, the index build should be deferred until the last LOAD is performed on the table.

Leaving Free Space

The LOAD utility provides the functionality to leave some free space on the pages created during the load for both index and data pages. It can also format some additional pages and leave them empty. This space can then be used for subsequent inserts into the table or indexes. The file type modifiers used to do this are:

- PAGEFREESPACE - Indicates the percentage free space to leave at the end of each data page
- INDEXFREESPACE - Indicates the percentage free space to leave at the end of each index page
- TOTALFREESPACE - Indicates the number of empty pages to be added to the table as a percentage of the total number of used pages

For example, if you want to load a table named PERSON by replacing all the existing data, leaving 20% of each data page empty, 20% of each index page empty, and ensuring that 15% of the total number of used pages are to be empty pages at the end of the table, use the following options:

Maintaining Data

```
LOAD FROM... MODIFIED BY PAGEFREESPACE 20
    INDEXFREESPACE 20 TOTALFREESPACE 15...
    INTO Person...
```

Generating Statistics

The LOAD utility can be used to generate statistics associated with the table and or indexes. These statistics are used by the optimizer to determine the most efficient way in which an SQL statement should be executed. The user can also specify how detailed the statistics should be for tables and/or indexes if they use the REPLACE load option. Table 10–2 shows the different combinations of statistics that can be generated for tables and indexes.

Table 10–2 *Load - Generating Statistics*

	Max Table Stats	Min Table Stats	No Table Stats
Max Index Stats	YES WITH DISTRIBUTION AND DETAILED INDEXES ALL	YES AND DETAILED INDEXES ALL	YES FOR DETAILED INDEXES ALL
Min Index Stats	YES WITH DISTRIBUTION AND INDEXES ALL	YES AND INDEXES ALL	YES FOR INDEXES ALL
No Index Stats	YES WITH DISTRIBUTION	YES	NO

For example, if you require the maximum detail of statistics to be generated for both indexes and the associated table, use the following options:

```
LOAD FROM... STATISTICS YES WITH DISTRIBUTION AND
DETAILED INDEXES ALL...
```

If minimal statistics need to be generated for both indexes and the associated table, use the following options:

```
LOAD FROM... STATISTICS YES AND INDEXES ALL...
```

For in-depth statistics on the table only:

```
LOAD FROM... STATISTICS YES WITH DISTRIBUTION...
```

If no statistics should be generated, use the following option:

```
LOAD FROM... STATISTICS NO...
```

Locking the Table After the Load Has Completed

The user may specify the HOLD QUIESCE option when invoking the LOAD command. This will lock the table spaces that are being used to store the table, its indexes, and long data for administrative use only after the load has completed.

To reset the lock on the table spaces involved in the load of a table named PRODUCT, use the following command:

```
QUIESCE TABLESPACES FOR TABLE Product RESET
```

Bear in mind that the QUIESCE state is retained for a user and the connection is used to lock the table space. If the connection is reset, the user should reestablish a connection with the database and quiesce the table space again before it can be reset with the command shown above.

Specifying a Temporary Directory

The LOAD utility uses a subdirectory in the directory where the database is created to store temporary files. These files are deleted after successful completion of the LOAD command. The user may specify a directory to use as the temporary directory. Specifying a directory on a separate device where the data is read from and written to may increase the performance of the LOAD utility.

```
LOAD FROM... TEMPFILES PATH E:\tempdir...
```

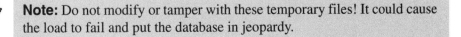

Note: Do not modify or tamper with these temporary files! It could cause the load to fail and put the database in jeopardy.

Loading Large Object Files

The same considerations that apply to the `IMPORT` utility apply to the `LOAD` utility. See "Importing Large Objects" on page 473. The parameter names and specification are also the same.

Performance Considerations

The `LOAD` command has a number of performance-related options. Some of these options are:

- `COPY YES/NO`
- `NONRECOVERABLE`
- `FASTPARSE`
- `ANYORDER`
- `DATA BUFFER`
- `CPU_PARALLELISM`
- `DISK_PARALLELISM`

These options are now examined in more detail.

Copy Yes/No and Nonrecoverable

During the load process, no logging of changes is done. This means that a user cannot perform roll-forward recovery for the load operation using the `RESTORE` and `ROLLFORWARD` commands. The user can choose to make the table recoverable but at the expense of performance.

The `LOAD` utility provides three ways in which the performance and recoverability can be balanced. The options are:

- *Nonrecoverable* - This option is used to ensure the table space is not set to a backup-pending state after the table is loaded nor does a copy of the data have to be made. Users can therefore access the table and the new data immediately after the load has completed. Following the load, no changes to the table data will be logged. If a previous backup of the database is restored and rolled forward past the load operation, the table will be marked as invalid. There is *no* recovery from this state. The only operation allowed is for the table to be dropped. A nonrecoverable load is useful when loading large read-only tables. You could also load multiple tables into a table space with the nonrecoverable option. Then, once the last table has been loaded, you can back up the database or the table spaces in which the table, its indexes, and long data reside.

- *Copy No* - (Default) If this option is specified and archival logging is enabled for the database, the table space in which the table resides will be placed in backup-pending state after the load. The table space will not be accessible until a database or table space backup is made. Since the `LOAD` utility's changes to the data are not logged, taking a backup of the table space or database is required to be able to recover it in the event of damage after the load operation has completed.

- *Copy Yes* - If YES is specified for the COPY option and archival logging is enabled for the database, a copy of the changes caused by the load process will be saved to tape, directory, or ADSM server, and the table spaces will not be left in backup-pending state. This option does not apply to a database that uses circular logging and is thus nonrecoverable. If database damage occurs just after the load operation has completed, an existing backup can be restored and rolled forward (assuming archival logging is used).

Fastparse

This is a file type modifier that can be used to reduce the amount of data checking. It should only be used if the data is known to be correct. Since IXF files can only contain the data in the correct format, this parameter may not improve the performance of the LOAD when IXF file types are used. If DEL or ASC files are used, the LOAD utility may perform faster.

Anyorder

If the SAVECOUNT option is not used, this parameter will allow the LOAD utility to load the data into the table without having to respect the order in which the data appears in the input file. If the data in the input file is ordered according to a clustering index, then this option may not be a very good choice because it will affect the performance of a subsequent REORG operation. When used, this file type modifier may improve the performance of the LOAD utility, particularly in SMP systems (and the CPU_PARALLELISM option is > 1).

Data Buffer

Specifies the amount of memory in 4 KB pages allocated from the Utility Heap to be used as an internal load buffer. If not specified, a calculated default will be used that takes into consideration the size allocated in the Utility heap and the characteristics of the table being loaded. Specifying a large buffer size may improve the performance of the load.

CPU_parallelism

This option should be used on SMP machines to indicate how many processes or threads should be used to parse, convert, or format the data. If no value is specified, a default is calculated based on the number of CPUs on the machine. The data is loaded using the order that it appears in the input file. Choosing the correct value may considerably improve the performance of the LOAD utility if it runs on an SMP machine.

Disk_parallelism

This option specifies the number of processes or threads to use for writing data to disk. The default value is calculated based on the number of containers specified for all the table spaces in which objects for the table are stored and other table characteristics.

Other LOAD options and file type modifiers that may affect the performance include:

- *Norowwarnings* - If specified, this will usually improve the performance.
- *Savecount* - The larger amount of records loaded before a consistency point, the better for performance.
- *Statistics* - The less statistics generated, the better the performance. However, the combined runtime for the LOAD and the RUNSTATS utilities is very often longer than using the LOAD utility to generate the statistics.

Using the Load Utility from the Control Center

You invoke the LOAD utility in much the same way as the IMPORT and EXPORT utilities. Use the Control Center and select the target table to be loaded. Click the right mouse button and select the **Load** option.

Once invoked, the user can specify all the options available on the command line. The use of the Control Center approach will be demonstrated by an example.

The DBA wants to load a file named sales.ixf into a table named SALES, replacing all the data currently in the table. After invoking the Load GUI, the DBA uses the File tab to add the fully qualified path name of the source file as shown in Fig. 10–16.

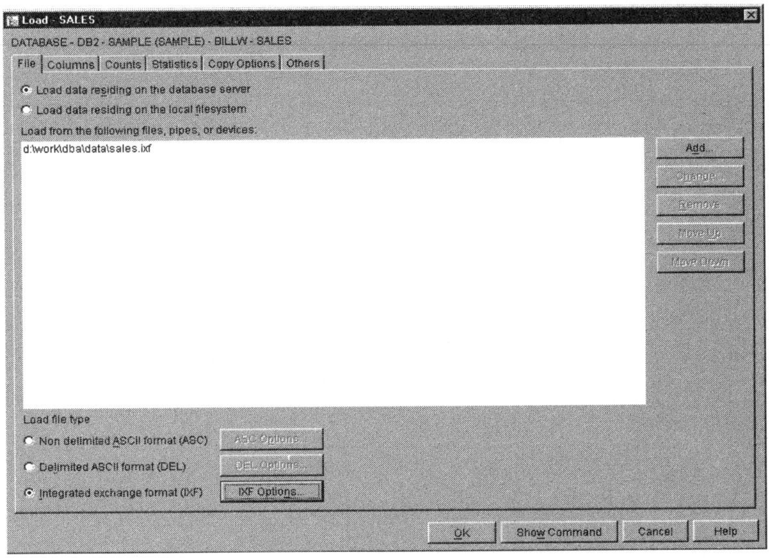

Fig. 10–16 *LOAD from Control Center - File specification*

The DBA then selects the file type IXF and clicks on the **IXF Options** button.

The Load utility now supports loading data from a remote client.

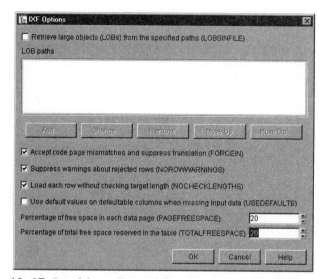

Fig. 10–17 *Load from Control Center - IXF input file options*

Figure 10–17 shows the options that were selected.

Since the file was generated by another DB2 server, the DBA decides to use the FORCEIN, NOROWWARNINGS, and NOCHECKLENGTHS options. This may increase the performance of the load. He also chooses to leave some free space on the loaded pages of the table and to add some empty preformatted pages to the table. This may improve the performance of subsequent INSERT and UPDATE SQL statements.

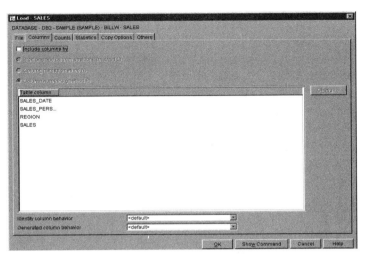

Fig. 10–18 *Load from Control Center - Columns tab*

The Columns tab as shown in Fig. 10–18 is used to specify whether and how you want the columns from the data files loaded into the table columns.

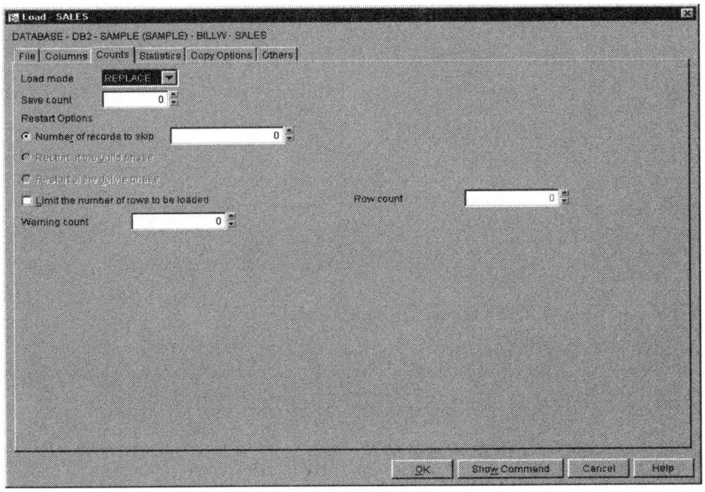

Fig. 10–19 *Load from Control Center - Counts tab*

The Counts tab as shown in Fig. 10–19 can be used to specify the type of load command operation (INSERT, REPLACE, TERMINATE, RESTART). In our case, the data in the SALES table needs to be replaced. The DBA can also specify the number of rows from the beginning of the file to be loaded (ROWCOUNT), the maximum number of row warnings be allowed before the load fails (WARNINGCOUNT), and the

Maintaining Data

number of rows to load between generation of consistency points (SAVECOUNT). In our case, none of these options are set.

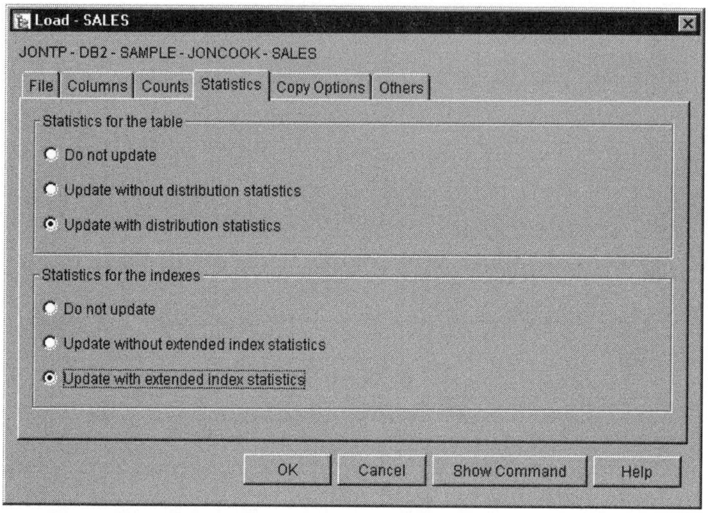

Fig. 10–20 *Load from Control Center - Statistics tab*

The DBA decided to let the LOAD utility generate in-depth statistics for both the indexes and the table. Figure 10–20 shows how this can be specified on the Statistics tab.

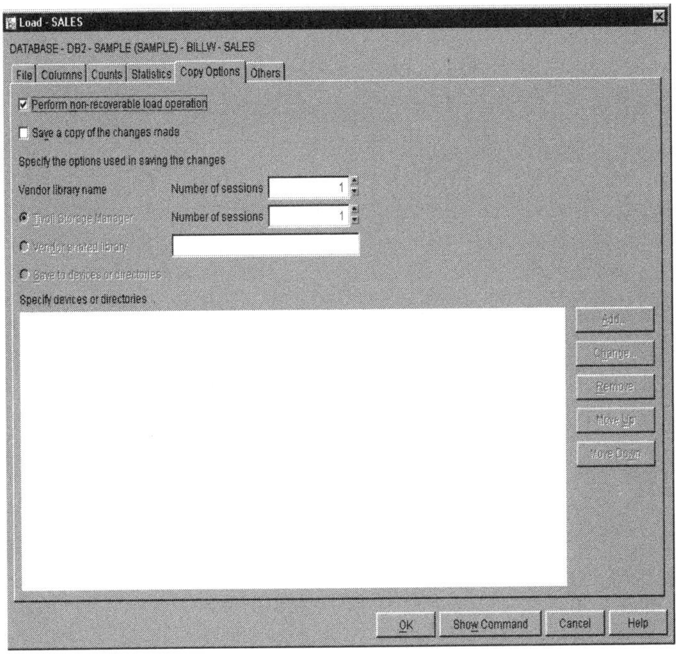

Fig. 10–21 *Load from Control Center - Copy options tab*

The Copy Options tab, as shown in Fig. 10–21, is used to specify the recoverability options to be used with the LOAD command. If "Save a copy of the changes made" is specified, the user can define the location of the copied data. In our case, the NONRECOVERABLE command option is used.

Load - SALES
DATABASE - DB2 - SAMPLE (SAMPLE) - BILLW - SALES
File
Columns
Counts
Statistics
Copy Options
Others
Temporary directories used during index creation
Add...
Change...
Remove
Move Up
Move Down
Leave the table in quiesced state after load
Preservation of source data order is not required
Skip the header verification code
Data buffer in 4K pages
Sort buffer in 4K pages
Degree of CPU parallelism
Degree of disk parallelism
Percentage of free space to be left on index pages
10
Message file
c:\messages\sales.msg
Temporary control file
c:\tempfiles\sales_remote
Exception table schema
BILLW
Name
OK
Show Command
Cancel
Help

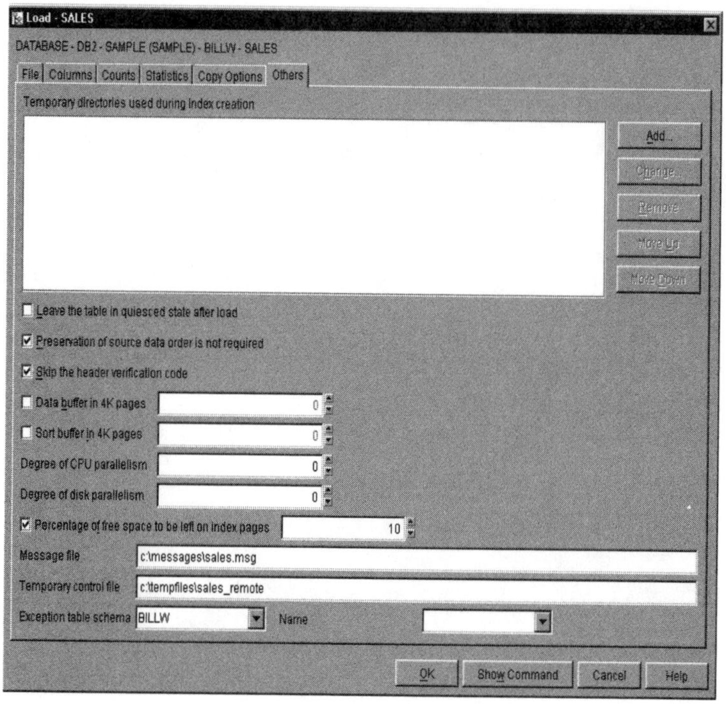

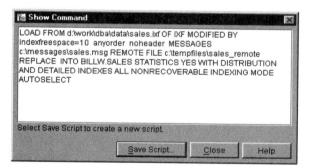

Fig. 10–22 *Load from Control Center - Others tab*

Finally, the Others tab as shown in Fig. 10–22 can be used to specify a few remaining options. After specifying all the relevant parameters and options for the LOAD, the user can display the command that will be executed by clicking on the **Show Command** button. Fig. 10–23 shows the generated command.

Show Command
LOAD FROM d:\work\dba\data\sales.ixf OF IXF MODIFIED BY
indexfreespace=10 anyorder noheader MESSAGES
c:\messages\sales.msg REMOTE FILE c:\tempfiles\sales_remote
REPLACE INTO BILLW.SALES STATISTICS YES WITH DISTRIBUTION
AND DETAILED INDEXES ALL NONRECOVERABLE INDEXING MODE
AUTOSELECT
Select Save Script to create a new script.
Save Script...
Close
Help

Fig. 10–23 *LOAD from Control Center - Generated command*

The user can choose to save the command as a script to be invoked at a later time.

After Load Has Finished

The LOAD utility can put the table space in which the target table resides in one of three pending states or can set the table to a pending state. If this happens, users cannot access the tables in the table space or access the table itself.

To query the state of a table space, use the LIST TABLESPACES command as described in "Data Storage Management" on page 409. The states that the LOAD utility can put the table space into are as follows:

Load Pending

The table space is put into this state during the load and build phases. If the load operation fails during one of these two phases, the table space will be left in the load-pending state. The DBA can get more information about the failure by looking at the messages file.

To remove the load-pending state, the user can do one of the following:

* Correct the problem indicated in the message file and reinvoke the LOAD utility using the exact same options, replacing the INSERT or REPLACE option with the RESTART option. This will restart the load operation starting with the phase that failed, or at the last consistency point if it failed in the load phase, and the SAVECOUNT option was specified with the LOAD command.

* Choose to redo a LOAD with the REPLACE option if the REPLACE option was specified with the first invocation of the utility.

* If the problem could not be resolved, the TERMINATE option can be used to *roll back* the load operation. If the LOAD command was originally invoked with the REPLACE option, all the data that existed in the table prior to its invocation will be lost and the table left empty. If it was invoked with the INSERT option, all the new data will be deleted from the table, and the old data will be unaffected. The table is returned to the state it was in before the LOAD utility was invoked.

* The DBA may also opt to drop the table space(s) and recreate.

* Restoring a backup of the table space and not rolling forward or rolling forward to a point prior to LOAD utility's invocation would also remove the pending state and allow users to access the tables.

Delete Pending

During the delete phase of the load, the unique constraints defined on the table are checked and the violating rows are deleted. To be able to do this, the LOAD utility puts the table space (in which the target table is located) in a delete-pending state. If the LOAD operation fails during this phase, the delete-pending state will remain on the table space.

Backup Pending

If a table is loaded with the COPY NO command option and archival logging is switched on, the table spaces involved in the load operation will be put in a BACKUP PENDING state.

This state forces the user to take a backup of the database or table space the target table resides in. This is done to ensure that if needed, the table can be recovered.

If the LOAD utility was invoked with the NONRECOVERABLE or COPY YES command options, the table space will not be put in a backup-pending state. It is recommended that the DBA take a backup of the table space or database as soon as possible if NONRECOVERABLE is used. If not, the DBA will *not* be able to recover it by restoring a older backup and then rolling forward using the log files. If this is attempted, the table will be flagged as invalid. The only operation that can be performed is to drop the table.

Table in Check Pending

The load utility can also put the *table* in check-pending state. This state occurs if constraints other than primary key and unique constraints are defined on the target table. They include the following:

- *Foreign key* constraints - Used to enforce referential integrity.
- *Check* constraints - User-defined constraints. Normally used to check for valid data ranges on columns.
- *Summary* table involved in the scenario - if this table is used to refresh a summary table that has the REFRESH IMMEDIATE option set.

The state of a table is recorded in the SYSCAT.TABLES catalog view. To find the state associated with a table, issue the following select statement:

```
select tabshema,tabname,status, const_checked from
syscat.tables where
tabname='MYTAB' and tabschema='MYSCHEMA'
```

The status column is of type CHAR and indicates the state the table is in. Valid values for it are:

- C - Check pending
- N - Normal
- X - Inoperative view

The CONST_CHECKED column is of type CHAR(32). The first character denotes the status of the foreign key constraints, character two denotes the status of the check constraints, and character five denotes the status of the summary table refresh. Valid values for these states are:

- Y - Checked by the system.
- N - Not checked. This is a check-pending state.
- U - Checked by the user.
- W - Was in the state "U" before it was placed in this state. This is also a check-pending state.

The select statement can be rewritten to eliminate all the unnecessary information returned by the previous one:

```
SELECT TABSCHEMA AS Schema,
       TABNAME AS Name,
       STATUS AS State,
       SUBSTR(CONST_CHECKED,1,1) AS Foreign_Keys,
       SUBSTR(CONST_CHECKED,2,1) AS Check_Constraints,
       SUBSTR(CONST_CHECKED,5,1) AS Summary_Tables
  FROM SYSCAT.TABLES
    WHERE TABNAME='MYTAB' AND TABSCHEMA='MYSCHEMA'
```

To remove the check-pending state on the table, the SET INTEGRITY statement can be used. The usage of this statement is discussed in "The SET INTEGRITY Statement" on page 505.

The DBA can check for records that could not be loaded because of formatting or NULL value violations by looking in the dump file (as specified with the MODI-FIED BY DUMPFILE option). In addition, the exception table (if specified) can be queried to find records that were rejected because of duplicate values. The remote file can be queried by using the LOAD QUERY command. It contains information about the number of rows read, rejected, and loaded, as well as any error or warning messages generated by the LOAD utility. In the event of failure, an SQL error code with a short description will be returned. Also, the db2diag.log file can be checked. It can give useful information about the sequence of events that preceded the failure.

The LOAD QUERY Command

The LOAD QUERY command is used to interrogate a LOAD operation and generate a report on its progress. The user may direct it to summarize or to display the difference or delta since the last invocation.

Maintaining Data

Load Query Syntax

The syntax of the LOAD QUERY command is provided to add to the discussion of the command. Figure 10–24 shows the syntax diagram.

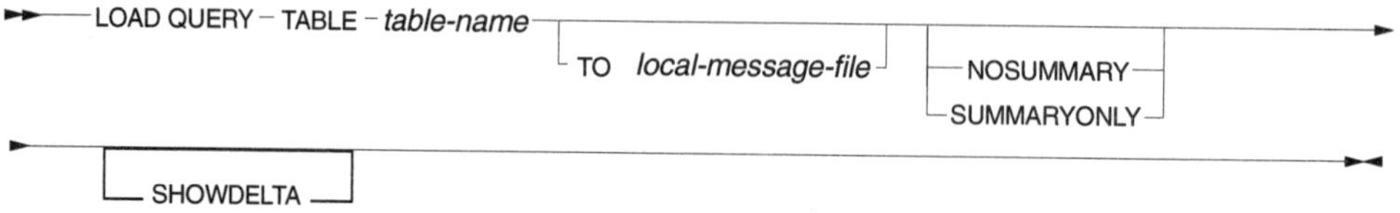

Fig. 10–24 *The LOAD QUERY command*

The explanation of the options are as follows:

- table-name - The name of the table that is being loaded.
- TO local-message-file - The name of a file on the server (where the LOAD is executed). The load query report will be output to this file. This cannot be the same file as the message file specified in the LOAD command. If the file specified exists, all new output will be appended to it.
- NOSUMMARY - Indicates that no summary information should be generated.
- SUMMARYONLY - Will generate summary information about the number of records read, loaded, rejected, and so on.
- SHOWDELTA - Will cause only the new information since the last invocation of LOAD QUERY to be displayed.

Using Load Query and LOAD

Here is an example of using the LOAD QUERY command.

In this example, a load will be performed on a table named SALES from a file named sales.del with the character delimiter (*) and the column delimiter (|). New data will be added to the table.

There are two summary tables defined on the SALES table. The first is a summary table on the sales per employee, and the second is defined to summarize the sales per product. The first, EMP_SALES, is defined with the option REFRESH DEFERRED, and the second, PROD_SALES, is defined with the option REFRESH IMMEDIATE.

The SALES table also has a foreign key constraint defined that references the PRODUCT table. It also has a check constraint defined on the AMOUNT column. This constraint ensures that any row inserted or updated in the table has an amount that is greater than zero. Figure 10–25 shows the relationships between these tables:

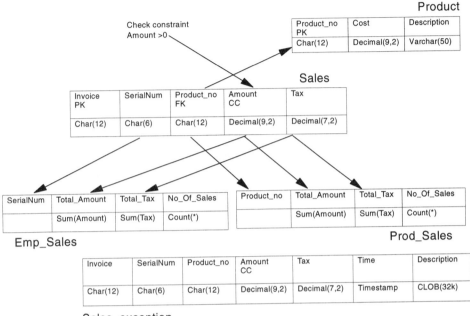

Product

Product_no PK	Cost	Description
Char(12)	Decimal(9,2)	Varchar(50)

Check constraint
Amount >0

Sales

Invoice PK	SerialNum	Product_no FK	Amount CC	Tax
Char(12)	Char(6)	Char(12)	Decimal(9,2)	Decimal(7,2)

SerialNum	Total_Amount	Total_Tax	No_Of_Sales
	Sum(Amount)	Sum(Tax)	Count(*)

Emp_Sales

Product_no	Total_Amount	Total_Tax	No_Of_Sales
	Sum(Amount)	Sum(Tax)	Count(*)

Prod_Sales

Invoice	SerialNum	Product_no	Amount CC	Tax	Time	Description
Char(12)	Char(6)	Char(12)	Decimal(9,2)	Decimal(7,2)	Timestamp	CLOB(32k)

Sales_exception

Fig. 10–25 *The SALES table dependencies*

After evaluating the information, the DBA decided to load the SALES table with the following options:

```
LOAD FROM Sales.del OF DEL
   MODIFIED BY COLDEL| CHARDEL*
   SAVECOUNT 100
   MESSAGES msgs.txt
   TEMPFILES PATH d:\temp
   INSERT INTO Sales FOR EXCEPTION Sales_exception
   STATISTICS YES AND INDEXES ALL
   COPY NO
   CPU_PARALLELISM 4
   DISK_PARALLELISM 3
   INDEXING MODE INCREMENTAL
```

The LOAD utility will move all the duplicate rows to the exception table SALES_EXCEPTION during the delete phase.

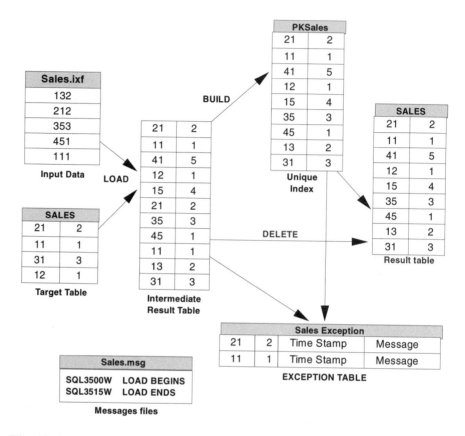

Fig. 10–26 *Loading the SALES table*

It will not make a copy of the data loaded during the load, but it will force the user to take a backup of the table space(s) involved.

During the load of the SALES table, the DBA decided to monitor the load progress using the following command. He would be able to query this file to determine the status of the LOAD at that time.

```
LOAD QUERY TABLE Sales TO D:\messages\load\Sales.msg
```

After loading the data into the SALES table, the DBA attempts to issue an INSERT statement on the SALES table. It fails with the following error message:

```
DB21034E The command was processed as an SQL statement because
it was not a valid Command Line Processor command. During SQL
processing it returned:
SQL0290N Table space access is not allowed. SQLSTATE=55039
```

This indicates that the table space is in a backup-pending state. The reason for this is the DBA specified the COPY NO option. After taking a backup of the table space, the DBA attempts to select data from the table. This time it fails with the following error message:

```
SQL0668N Operation not allowed when the underlying table (or a
dependent table) is in the Check Pending state. SQLSTATE=57016
```

This error occurs because the table is in check-pending state. To verify this, the DBA executes the following SQL statement:

```
SELECT TABNAME,STATUS FROM SYSCAT.TABLES
    WHERE TABNAME='SALES'
```

The result set:

```
TABNAME                     STATUS
------------------------    ------
SALES                       C
```

Recovery from this state by using the SET INTEGRITY statement will be examined in the next section.

The SET INTEGRITY Statement

The integrity or validity of data in a database is of crucial importance. It is difficult to ensure the validity of data being inserted into a database; many RDBMS products, however, including DB2, provide the ability to define some rule-based constraints or checks that can be incorporated into the database. In DB2, the following checks can be used to minimize the risk of inserting incorrect data into a table:

- The fields in a row are checked to see if they conform to the data type and length of the columns with which they are associated. For example, the value "g553g" does not match a column data type of DECIMAL, and therefore the row will be rejected, thus ensuring the validity of the data in the database.
- If a *primary key* constraint has been defined on a table, then each row in the table must have a unique value in the column or columns that collectively form

the primary key. If a row is inserted with the same key as an existing one, the new row will be rejected.

- If a *unique* constraint has been defined on a table, each row in the table must comply with this constraint by having a unique value or combination of values that make up the unique key.

- If a *foreign key* constraint has been defined, each row in the table must have a value in the foreign key column or columns that matches a primary key of a row in the parent table. In some cases, a null value may be acceptable if the column or columns defined as part of the foreign key are also defined as nullable.

- If a *check* constraint has been defined on a column, each row must comply with the constraint. For example, a check constraint on a salary column of an employee table may prevent an application or user from inserting a new employee record or row for which the salary is less than zero. Any row inserted into the table that has a salary value of less than zero will be rejected, thus minimizing the risk of inserting incorrect data into the table.

In most cases, the enforcing of these rules or constraints is done automatically. For instance, whenever a row is inserted, updated, imported, or loaded, the following will always be checked:

- Validity of the data format and length
- Primary key values
- Unique constraints

Whenever a row is inserted, updated, or imported, the following checks will also be checked or executed:

- Compliance with foreign key constraints
- Compliance with check constraints
- Updating of summary tables defined with IMMEDIATE CHECKED option

The second list above is *not* checked or executed when data is *loaded* into a table. Because it is not checked, the validity of the data remains in doubt until such time as the data is checked and found to be consistent. For this reason, DB2 restricts access to the table by placing it in a check-pending state. This prevents the data in the table from being accessed and indicates that explicit checking of the data is required.

A table might also be placed into this state if a new constraint is defined on the table, and the checking of the constraint is not performed immediately. This is done because there is no guarantee that the existing rows in the table comply with the new constraint.

The validity of the existing data in a table can be checked by using one of these statements:

- SET INTEGRITY (also known as SET CONSTRAINTS)
- REFRESH TABLE

The SET INTEGRITY statement can be used to do the following:

- *Set* a table to check-pending state and mark one or more of the following as *not* checked: check constraints, foreign key constraints, and the refreshing of refresh immediate summary tables.

  By marking any one of the above as *not* checked, the table is set to check-pending state. Primary key and unique key constraint checking cannot be turned off and will still be enforced. Because the table is set to the check-pending state, access to the table data is restricted.

- *Reset* the check-pending state of a table by *checking* all or some of the following constraints: check constraints, foreign key constraints, and the refreshing of refresh immediate summary tables.

- *Reset* a check-pending state by *marking* any of the following constraints as checked: check constraints, foreign key constraints, and the refreshing of refresh immediate summary tables.

  The actual checking of the constraints will not be done. This is referred to as deferred checking.

The REFRESH TABLE statement can be used on summary tables only. It will update the data in the summary table by making use of the current data in the table that it is derived from.

If existing data is to be checked, the user can specify that it should be done incrementally. This means that only the data that has been added to the table since checking has turned off has to be checked.

> **Note:** The SET INTEGRITY statement can also be used in a Data Links environment. For more information, see the *DB2 UDB V7.1 SQL Reference.*

The following example is a continuation of the LOAD example in "Using Load Query and LOAD" on page 502. In the previous example, after the LOAD completed, the table space was in a backup-pending state. After a backup was made, a SELECT statement failed with the following error message:

```
SQL0668N Operation not allowed when the underlying table (or a
dependent table) is in the Check Pending state. SQLSTATE=57016
```

This message indicates that the table is in a check-pending state. As mentioned before, this pending state can occur on tables that have foreign key constraints or check constraints defined. Use the following statement to find the reason for the check-pending state on the SALES table.

```
SELECT TABSCHEMA AS Schema,
       TABNAME AS Name,
       STATUS AS State,
       SUBSTR(CONST_CHECKED,1,1) AS Foreign_Keys,
       SUBSTR(CONST_CHECKED,2,1) AS Check_Constraints,
       SUBSTR(CONST_CHECKED,5,1) AS Summary_Tables
FROM SYSCAT.TABLES
   WHERE TABNAME='SALES' AND TABSCHEMA='DB2ADMIN'
```

The result is shown below. The value "C" in the STATUS column indicates that the table is in a check-pending state.

```
SCHEMA    NAME      STATE FOREIGN_KEYS CHECK_CONSTRAINTS SUMMARY_TABLES
--------- --------- ----- ------------ ----------------- --------------
DB2ADMIN  SALES     C     N            N                 Y
```

The "N" shown in the output indicates the reason for the check-pending state. In our case it is because one or more constraints have not been checked. To remove the check-pending state on the table, use the SET INTEGRITY statement:

```
SET INTEGRITY FOR Sales IMMEDIATE CHECKED
    FOR EXCEPTION IN Sales USE Sales_Exception
```

The statement generates the following message:

```
SQL3602W Check data processing found constraint violations and
moved them into the exception table. SQLSTATE-01603
```

At this point, the table should now be accessible.

Using Set Integrity from the Control Center

The SET INTEGRITY statement can also be executed from the Control Center. To do so, right-click on the table in question and choose the **Set Integrity** option. Fig. 10–27 illustrates how you can choose the constraint checking options.

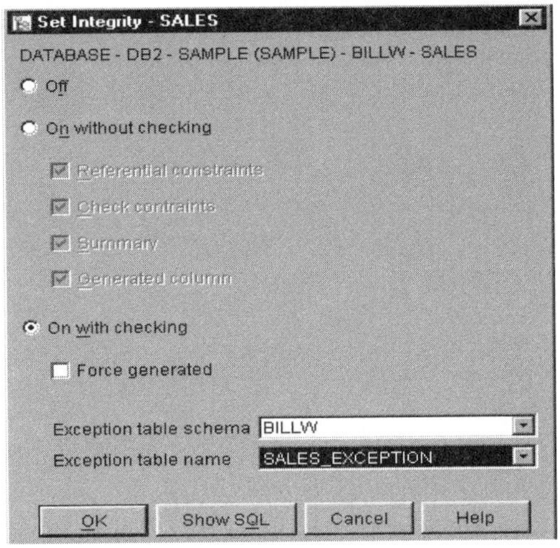

Fig. 10–27 *Set Integrity from the Control Center*

During the execution of the SET INTEGRITY statement, all the rows that do not comply with either of the two constraints defined on the SALES table will be copied to the SALES_EXCEPTION exception table. This exception table can also be used during the LOAD operation.

Fig. 10–28 shows how a foreign key constraint defined on the SALES table is evaluated. All the rows in the SALES table that refer to a nonexistent value in the PRODUCT table will be deleted from the SALES table and copied to the exception table. The same process will be used to delete the rows in the SALES table that do not comply with the check constraint defined on the table. Copies of these rows will also be placed in the SALES_EXCEPTION table.

After completion of the SET INTEGRITY operation, the user can query the message column (if defined) in the SALES_EXCEPTION table to determine the reason a given row was rejected. These rows can then be modified and reinserted into the SALES table at a later time.

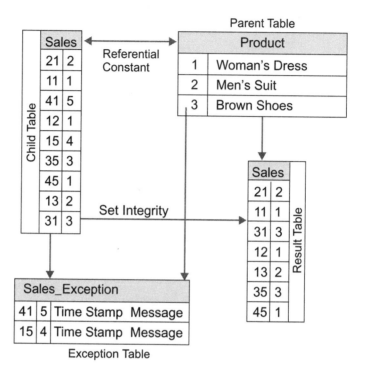

Fig. 10–28 *SET INTEGRITY and the use of the exception table*

The DB2MOVE Utility

The DB2MOVE utility can be used to move data between different DB2 databases that may reside on different servers. It is very useful when a large number of tables need to be copied from one database to another. The utility can run in one of three modes: EXPORT, IMPORT, or LOAD.

When running in the *export* mode, it will use the EXPORT utility to export data from the table or tables specified into data files of type IXF. It will also produce a file named db2move.1st that records all the names of the tables exported and the file names produced when they were exported. It will also produce various message files that record any errors or warning messages generated during the execution of the utility.

If the DB2MOVE utility is executed in *import* mode, the IMPORT utility will be used to import data files of type IXF into a given database. It will attempt to read the db2move.1st file to find the link between the file names of the data files and the table names into which the data must be imported.

In the *load* mode, the input files specified in the db2move.lst file will be loaded into the tables using the LOAD utility.

Here is the syntax of the DB2MOVE utility:

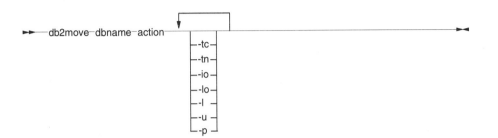

Where:

- dbname - The name of the database.
- action - Valid actions are IMPORT, EXPORT, or LOAD
- -tc - Followed by one or more creator IDs separated by a comma. The "*" may be used as a wildcard character. If this option is not used, the default behavior of this utility is to work with all the creator IDs.
- -tn - Flag only valid if used with the EXPORT action. If specified, it should be followed by one or more (maximum ten) table names separated by commas.
- -io - Flag used to specify the import action to take. If specified, it should be followed by any one of the following options: INSERT, INSERT_UPDATE, REPLACE, CREATE, or REPLACE_CREATE. If not specified when the IMPORT action is specified, the option REPLACE_CREATE will be used as the default.
- -lo - Flag used to specify the load option to use. Valid options are INSERT and REPLACE. If not specified when the LOAD action is specified, INSERT will be used as the default load option.
- -l - Specify the absolute path names for the directories to be used when importing, exporting, or loading LOB values into or from separate files. If specified with the EXPORT action, the directories will be cleared before the LOBs are exported to files in the directory or directories.
- -u - Followed by a userid that is to be used to run the utility. If not specified, the userid of the logged-on user will be used to execute the utility.
- -p - Followed by the password to be used to authenticate the userid that is used when executing the utility.

Here is an example of using the DB2MOVE utility:

An existing database, DB2CERT, needs to be copied to a new database on another server. The new database name is NEWCERT. The user has not defined any tables in the new database and plans to do this using the DB2MOVE utility. To export all the tables in the DB2CERT database, the user uses the following command:

```
db2move db2cert export
```

This produces the following files:

- EXPORT.out - The results of the EXPORT action
- db2move.lst - A file containing a list of file names and the table names they originate from
- tabnnn.ixf - The IXF files containing the data from the tables
- tabnnn.msg - The messages file associated with the export operation on each table

The user now wants to recreate the database structure in the NEWCERT database and populate it with the data in the IXF files. The following command can now be used:

```
db2move newcert import -io REPLACE_CREATE
```

The use of the -io option is not required in our case because the default option is REPLACE_CREATE.

The files used as input by the utility are:

- db2move.lst - The list file containing the table names and file names of the data files for the tables
- tabnnn.ixf - The actual data files of type IXF

The output files of this operation are:

- IMPORT.out - This file contains a summary of the results of the individual import operations.
- tabnnn.msg - These files contains error and warning messages generated during the import of the various files.

The DB2LOOK Utility

The DB2LOOK utility can be used to do one of three tasks. It can generate a report of database statistics. This report file can be a postscript, LaTeX, or a normal text file. (LaTeX, like HTML, is a markup language used to represent documents.)

DB2LOOK can also be used extract statistics and/or the Data Definition Language (DDL) statements for the creation of tables, indexes, views, and so on that are needed to generate a Command Line Processor (CLP) script file used to recreate database objects and/or to update the statistics.

Why is it useful? If an application developer needs access to a database that is the same as the production database except for the data it contains, the DB2LOOK utility can be used to extract the DDL and statistics into a script. This script can then be used to create a "development" database and update the statistics without actually copying the production data to the development database. An application programer can now use the development database for testing code. In addition, performance evaluation can be undertaken using utilities like Visual Explain, which use the database statistics to report on how an SQL statement will be executed and give an indication of its likely performance.

The syntax of the command is as follows:

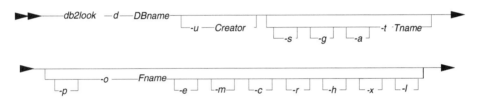

Where:

- -d DBname - The name of the database must be specified. This is not optional.
- -u Creator - If specified, only information about objects created by the Creator will be extracted.
- -a - Option will allow information to be extracted for all objects in the database. If neither -u or -a is specified, the USER environment variable is used. When using Windows NT, no default value is specified for this environment variable, in which case a SET USER=XXXX statement can be used prior to the invocation of the utility to set the USER environment variable.
- -s - Flag will cause the utility to format the output to LaTeX file and then convert it to a postscript file. This requires LaTeX software to be installed.
- -g - Flag is similar to the -s option. The difference is a graph that will be created to show fetch page pairs for indices. This requires LaTeX and Gnuplot software to be installed.
- -p - If specified, this flag will cause the information extracted to be formatted as a plain text file.
- -o filename - Specifies the file name that is to be used for the output files. The extension need not be specified. If the output file is a LaTeX file, the tex exten-

sion will be used. If the output file is a postscript file, `ps` will be used, and if it is a text file, then `txt` will be used. If the utility is used to generate a CLP script file, no extension will be added to the file name.

- `-e` - Flag will inform the utility to extract the necessary DDL statements to recreate some objects in the database, including tables, indexes, views, and triggers.
- `-l` - Option indicate that DDL statements for the creation of table spaces, buffer pools and nodegroups.
- `-x` - Should be used to extract various GRANT statements used to duplicate the authorization aspects of the database and the objects in it.
- `-m` - If this flag is specified, the utility will run in mimic mode. It will generate a text file that contains all the SQL statements required to update the statistics in the updatable catalog views of a target database to reflect that of the source database.
- `-c` - Flag indicates to the utility that no COMMIT, CONNECT, or CONNECT RESET statements should be generated in the output file. This flag is ignored if the `-m` flag is not specified.
- `-r` - Flag will cause the utility to not execute the RUNSTATS command prior to the extraction of statistics from the catalog.
- `-i userid` - Specifies the userid to use when running the DB2LOOK utility against a remote database.
- `-w password` - Specifies the password to use when running the DB2LOOK utility against a remote database.

Here is an example of using the DB2LOOK command:

A production database named DB2CERT exists on a server that is exclusively used for production. Application programmers that develop applications that use the DB2CERT database require access to a database that has the same structure as the one in production. The DBA decides to extract the DDL script from the DB2CERT database to use it to build a database named NEWCERT on the server that is to be used for development only. The command the DBA uses to extract the DDL is:

```
db2look -d db2cert -a -o db2cert.ddl -e -x -l
```

The DBA edits the `db2cert.ddl` file, replaces DB2CERT with NEWCERT in the CONNECT statement and executes the following command:

```
db2 -tvf db2cert.ddl
```

The Control Center allows a user-friendly method to invoke the DB2LOOK utility. Simply right-click the mouse on the required database object and select the **Generate DDL** option (Fig. 10–29).

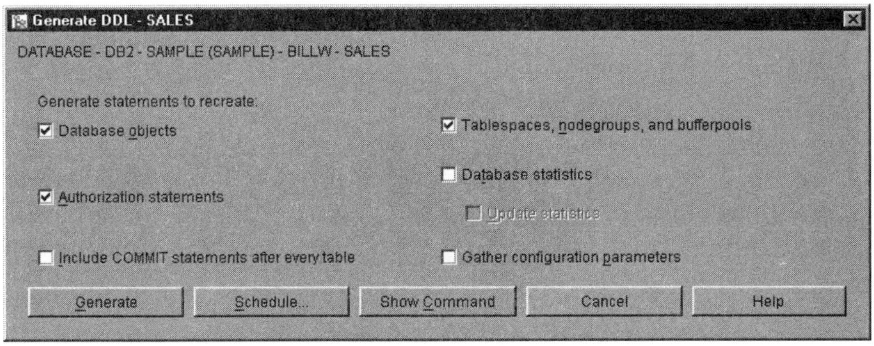

Fig. 10–29 *The Generate DDL GUI for a table from the Control Center*

Executing DB2LOOK from the Control Center

The DB2LOOK utility can be invoked remotely, so the user does not specify the output file name in which the output will be stored. Instead, the user can look at the script file produced by invoking the Script Center to view and edit the script, as shown in Figure 10–30.

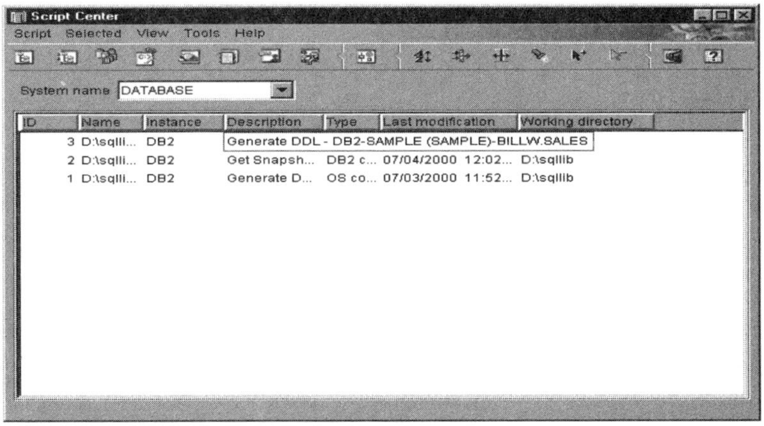

Fig. 10–30 *The Script Center listing the DB2LOOK output script*

To edit the script file containing the DB2LOOK command, select the script in the Script Center and double-click on it. The user can now further customize the script by editing the DB2LOOK command, as shown in Fig. 10–31.

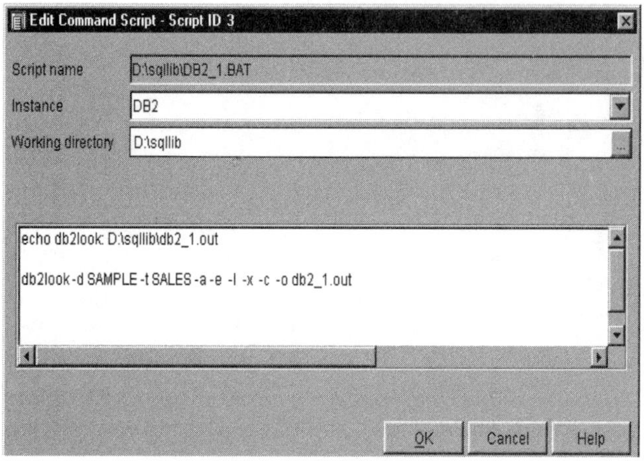

Fig. 10–31 *The DB2LOOK script produced*

Data Maintenance

The physical distribution of the data stored in tables has a significant effect on the performance of applications using those tables. The way the data is stored in a table is affected by the update, insert, and delete operations on the table. For example, a delete operation may leave empty pages of data that may not be reused later. Also, updates to variable-length columns may result in the new column value not fitting in the same data page. This can cause the row to be moved to a different page and so produce internal gaps or unused space in the table. As a consequence, DB2 may have to read more physical pages to retrieve the information required by the application.

These scenarios are almost unavoidable. However, as the database administrator, you can use the data maintenance commands provided in DB2 to optimize the physical distribution of the data stored in your tables.

There are three related utilities or commands that can help you organize the data in your tables. These are:

* REORGCHK
* REORG
* RUNSTATS

Analyzing Data's Physical Organization

It has been discussed that certain SQL operations may produce internal gaps in tables. So the question you may ask is how can you determine the physical organization of your tables or indexes? How can you know how much space is currently being used and how much is free?

Questions like these can be answered by using the REORGCHK utility. This utility is used to analyze the system catalog tables and gather information about the physical organization of your tables and indexes. The user has the option of using the current information in the catalog or to make the REORGCHK utility update the information before using it.

With the information collected from the system catalog tables, the REORGCHK utility displays the space allocation characteristics of the tables and indexes. The utility uses six formulas to help you decide if your tables and indexes require physical reorganization.

These formulas are general recommendations that show the relationship between the allocated space and the space that is being used for the data in your tables. Three formulas are used for tables, and three are used for indexes.

It is recommended that you establish a data maintenance policy to ensure that the data in your table is stored as efficiently as possible. If you don't, you may discover that your applications start to experience degradation in performance. This may be caused by the poor physical organization of your data, so before this happens, do preventive maintenance on your tables.

The following is an example of using the REORGCHK utility. This utility will be executed against the table DB2CERT.CANDIDATE.

```
REORGCHK UPDATE STATISTICS ON TABLE db2cert.candidate
```

The output of the REORGCHK utility is shown here:

```
Doing RUNSTATS....


Table statistics:

F1: 100*OVERFLOW/CARD < 5
F2: TSIZE / ((FPAGES-1) * (TABLEPAGESIZE-76)) > 70
F3: 100*NPAGES/FPAGES > 80

CREATOR    NAME                CARD    OV    NP    FP    TSIZE  F1  F2 F3 REORG
------------------------------------------------------------------------------
DB2CERT CANDIDATE                8     0     1     1       72   0   - 100 ---
------------------------------------------------------------------------------

Index statistics:

F4: CLUSTERRATIO or normalized CLUSTERFACTOR > 80
F5: 100*(KEYS*(ISIZE+10)+(CARD-KEYS)*4) / (NLEAF*INDEXPAGESIZE) > 50
F6: (100-PCTFREE) * (INDEXPAGESIZE-96) / (ISIZE+12) ** (NLEVELS-2) * (INDEXPAGES
IZE-96) / (KEYS * (ISIZE+8) + (CARD-KEYS) * 4) < 100

CREATOR  NAME              CARD LEAF LVLS ISIZE   KEYS   F4    F5  F6 REORG
------------------------------------------------------------------------------
Table: DB2CERT.CANDIDATE
SYSIBM   SQL970812225853720   8    1    1     9      8  100    -    - ---
------------------------------------------------------------------------------

CLUSTERRATIO or normalized CLUSTERFACTOR (F4) will indicate REORG is necessary
for indexes that are not in the same sequence as the base table. When multiple
indexes are defined on a table, one or more indexes may be flagged as needing
REORG. Specify the most important index for REORG sequencing.
```

The output of REORGCHK is divided into two sections. The first section shows the table statistics and formulas. The second section displays information about the table's indexes and associated formulas.

Interpreting the Output from REORGCHK

The REORGCHK utility uses six formulas that may help you decide whether a table requires reorganization. An explanation of the elements that are used to calculate these formulas are examined in this section:

```
Table statistics:

F1: 100*OVERFLOW/CARD < 5
F2: 100*TSIZE / ((FPAGES-1) * TABLEPAGESIZE) > 70
```

```
F3: 100*NPAGES/FPAGES > 80

CREATOR   NAME            CARD    OV    NP    FP    TSIZE  F1  F2 F3 REORG
-------------------------------------------------------------------------
DB2CERT CANDIDATE           8     0     1     1       72   0   -  100 ---
-------------------------------------------------------------------------
```

- CREATOR - Column indicates the schema to which the table belongs. Remember that the authorization ID of the creator of an object is used as the default schema.
- NAME - Column indicates the name of the table for which the REORGCHK utility has been run. REORGCHK can check a set of tables at one time.
- CARD - Indicates the number of data rows in the base table.
- OV (OVERFLOW) - The overflow indicator. It indicates the number of overflow rows. An overflow may occur when a new column is added to a table or when a variable-length value increases its size.
- NP (NPAGES)- Indicates the total number of pages that contain data.
- FP (FPAGES) - Indicates the total number of pages allocated to the table.
- TSIZE - Indicates the table size in bytes. This value is calculated from the result of multiplying the number of rows in the table times the average row length.
- TABLEPAGESIZE - Indicates the page size of the table space in which the table resides.
- REORG - Column has a separate indicator for each one of the first three formulas. A hyphen (-) indicates that reorganization is not recommended. An asterisk (*) indicates that reorganization is recommended.

The formulas F1, F2, and F3 provide guidelines for table reorganization. The formulas are shown in the REORGCHK output.

- *F1* works with the number of overflow rows. It recommends a table reorganization if 5% or more of the total number of rows are overflow rows.
- *F2* works with the free or unused space. It recommends a table reorganization if the table size (TSIZE) is less than or equal to 70% the size of the total space allocated to the table. In other words, it recommends to reorganize a table when more than 30% of the allocated space is unused.
- *F3* works with free pages. It recommends a table reorganization when more than 20% of the pages in a table are free. A page is considered free when it contains no rows.

Whenever the formulas find that table reorganization is needed an asterisk will be shown in the REORG column of the output.

Maintaining Data

For example, if the overflow rows of a table exceed the recommended value, the REORG column will look like this:

```
REORG
-----
*--
```

Remember, these values are only general guidelines. You may use your own thresholds. However, most of the time, you will find these values adequate for your environment.

Another part of REORGCHK involves interpreting the output gathered from indexes. To do this, some information about the structure of indexes is needed. Indexes in DB2 are created using a B+ tree structure. These data structures provide an efficient search method to locate the entry values of an index. The logical structure of a DB2 index is shown in Fig. 10–32:

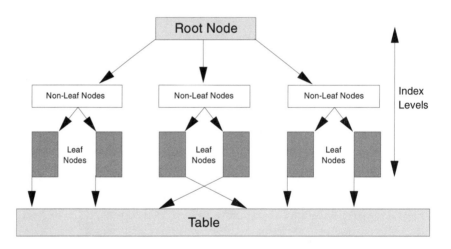

Fig. 10–32 *DB2 index structure*

An index can have several levels. The fewer levels an index has, the more quickly DB2 can access the table or data pages. The index shown in Fig. 10–32 has two levels. Here is a review of the REORGCHK index information.

```
F4: CLUSTERRATIO or normalized CLUSTERFACTOR > 80
F5: 100*(KEYS*(ISIZE+10)+(CARD-KEYS)*4) / (NLEAF*INDEXPAGESIZE) > 50
F6: (100-PCTFREE) * (INDEXPAGESIZE-96) / (ISIZE+12) ** (NLEVELS-2) *
    (INDEXPAGESIZE-96) / (KEYS * (ISIZE+8) + (CARD-KEYS) * 4) < 100
```

CREATOR	NAME	CARD	LEAF	LVLS	ISIZE	KEYS	F4	F5	F6	REORG
Table: DB2CERT.CANDIDATE										
SYSIBM	SQL970812225853720	8	1	1	9	8	100	-	-	---

- CREATOR - Column indicates the schema to which the index belongs. Remember that the creator of an object is used as the default schema.
- NAME - Column indicates the name of the index. REORGCHK is only specified at the table level. It will show statistics about all the indexes of a table. The information is also collected for system-defined indexes, such as primary key indexes.
- CARD - Indicates the number of rows in the associated base table.
- LEAF - Indicates the number of leaf nodes of the index.
- LVLS (LEVELS) - Indicates the total number of levels of the index.
- ISIZE - Index size calculated from the average column length of the key columns.
- INDEXPAGESIZE - Page size of the table space in which the table indexes reside.
- KEYS - Indicates the number of unique index entries.
- PCTFREE - Percentage of each index page to leave as free space.
- REORG - Column has a separate indicator for each one of the index formulas. An asterisk indicates that reorganization is recommended, and a hyphen indicates that the reorganization is not recommended.

The formulas F4, F5, and F6 provides guidelines for index reorganization. The formulas are shown in the REORGCHK output.

- *F4* indicates the CLUSTERRATIO or normalized CLUSTERFACTOR. This ratio shows the percentage of data rows that are stored in same physical sequence as the index.
- *F5* calculates space reserved for index entries. Less than 50% of the space allocated for the index should be empty.
- *F6* measures the usage of the index pages. The number of index pages should be more than 90% of the total entries that NLEVELS can handle.

Whenever the formulas find that an table reorganization is needed, an asterisk will be shown in the REORG column of the output.

For example, if the CLUSTERRATIO of an index is below the recommended level, the REORG column will appear as:

```
REORG
-----
*--
```

Note: The REORGCHK utility is an analysis tool provided with DB2. To reorganize your tables, you must use the REORG utility.

REORGCHK Options

You can use the CURRENT STATISTICS option of the REORGCHK utility to use the statistics in the system catalog tables at that time. For example, to analyze the current statistics of table DB2CERT.TEST_TAKEN:

```
REORGCHK CURRENT STATISTICS ON TABLE db2cert.test_taken
```

To review the current statistics of all the tables in a database, including the system catalog and user tables:

```
REORGCHK CURRENT STATISTICS ON TABLE ALL
```

You can also verify the organization of the system catalog tables using the SYSTEM option. Alternatively, you can select all the tables under the current user schema name by specifying the USER keyword:

```
REORGCHK CURRENT STATISTICS ON TABLE SYSTEM
```

If you don't specify the CURRENT STATISTICS parameter, REORGCHK will call the RUNSTATS utility.

> **Note:** REORGCHK cannot be run from the Control Center. You can use the Command Center to run the REORGCHK command and to capture the output for analysis.

Table Reorganization

After using the REORGCHK utility, you may find the physical reorganization of a table necessary. This reorganization is done using the REORG command.

> **Note:** To use the REORG command, you must have one of the following authorities: SYSADM, SYSCTRL, SYSMAINT, DBADM, or CONTROL privilege on the table.

The REORG utility will delete all the unused space and write the table and index data in contiguous pages. With the help of an index, it can also be used to place the data rows in the same physical sequence as the index. These actions can be used to increase the CLUSTERRATIO of the selected index.

Assume that, after running the REORGCHK utility, you find that it is necessary to reorganize the DB2CERT.TEST_TAKEN table.

This command will reorganize the DB2CERT.TEST_TAKEN table and all of its indexes, but will *not* put the data in any specific order.

```
REORG TABLE db2cert.test_taken
```

 Note: When using REORG, it is mandatory to use the fully qualified name of the table.

Using an Index to Reorganize a Table

With the help of an index, REORG will put the table data in the same physical order as the selected index is. This operation can help improve the response time in the execution of your applications. This is because the data pages of the table will be placed in sequential order according to an index key. This will help DB2 find the data in contiguous space and in the desired order, reducing the seek time needed to read the data.

If DB2 finds an index with a very high cluster ratio, it may use it to avoid a sort, thus improving the performance of applications that require sort operations.

When your tables have only one index, it is recommended to reorganize the table using that index. If your table has more than one index defined on it, you should select the most frequently used index for that table.

As an example, assume that the table DB2CERT.TEST_CENTER has an index called BY_COUNTRY and that most of the queries that use the table are grouped by country. Therefore, you might want to reorganize the DB2CERT.TEST_CENTER table using the BY_COUNTRY index.

The REORG command is as follows:

```
REORG TABLE db2cert.test_center INDEX BY_COUNTRY
```

The INDEX option tells the REORG utility to use the specified index to reorganize the table. After the REORG command has completed, the physical organization of the table should match the order of the selected index. In this way, the key columns will be found sequentially in the table.

In Fig. 10–33, the *high* cluster ratio index was used to REORG the table shown. The *low* cluster ratio index is shown to emphasize the difference between using and not using an index to perform the reorganization.

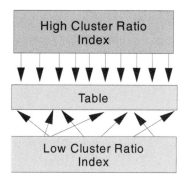

Fig. 10–33 *Cluster ratio*

The arrows in Fig. 10–33 illustrate the position of the index keys in the table. In a high cluster ratio index, the keys will be in sequential order. In a low cluster ratio index, the keys will be distributed throughout the table.

A *clustering index* defined on the table may assist DB2 in keeping future data in a clustered index order by trying to insert new rows physically close to the rows for which the key values of the index are in the same range. You can only have one clustering index for a table.

After reorganizing a table using the index option, DB2 will not force the subsequent inserts or updates to match the physical organization of the table. You may wish to run the REORG utility on a regular basis.

Using a Temporary Table Space for Reorganization

While REORG is executing, it creates temporary files (or tables) in the table space where the table resides. You can specify a different table space for the REORG utility. If you want to have control over the location of these tables, you need to specify the USE option.

If the page size of the table space where the table being reorganized resides is 8 KB for instance and you want to use the USE option, the table space specified with this option must have the same page size of 8 KB.

In this example, the temporary tables created during the processing of the REORG utility will be placed in the temporary table space, TEMPSPACE1.

```
REORG TABLE db2cert.test_center INDEX BY_COUNTRY USE
tempspace1
```

Note: In the event of a failure, do *not* delete the temporary files created by REORG. DB2 will need them for recovery purposes.

In addition to using the REORG utility, an index may be created with the MINPCTUSED option to enable an online reorganization of only the index. This parameter indicates the minimum acceptable amount of space used on index pages. If the deletion of records leads to the deletion of index entries on a page in the index and the percentage space used on the index page is less than the MINPCTUSED value, then DB2 may merge two pages, marking one as completely empty. This will impove the performance of the index. The empty page will not be deleted, however; therefore, the size of the index file (SMS) or storage used by the index (DMS) will be unaffected. To delete the empty page and reduce the amount of storage space used, the user must explicitly reorganize the table.

Note: On-line index reorganizing will take place automatically, so the DBA does not have to execute an explicit command.

Using the REORG Utility from the Control Center

You can also REORG a table from the Control Center by right-clicking on the table and selecting **Reorganize**. Fig. 10–34 gives an example of how a temporary table space and index to use for the REORG is specified.

Fig. 10–34 *Reorganize Table from the Control Center*

The user has the option to see the command that is generated and to save it or schedule it for later execution (Fig. 10–35):

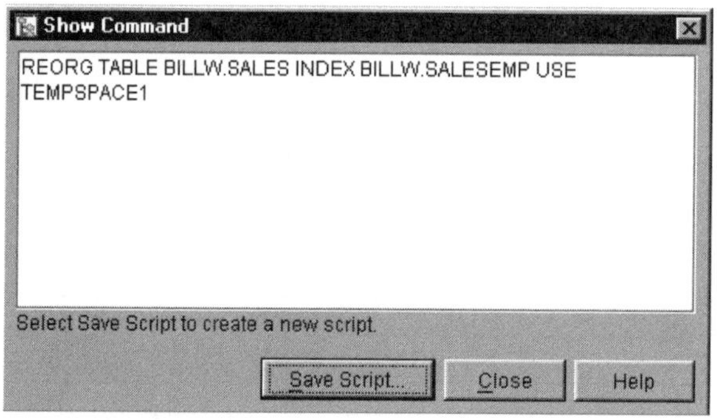

Fig. 10–35 *REORG command generated*

Recommended Actions After Reorganizing a Table

Table reorganization may help to improve the performance of your applications. There are some additional steps that you should follow. These actions will allow your existing applications to benefit from the table reorganization:

1. Use the RUNSTATS command on the tables and their indexes. This will provide the optimizer with the updated information about the new physical organization of each table and its indexes.

2. Use the REBIND utility on the packages that access the reorganized table. This will allow your applications to take advantage of any changes selected by the optimizer to improve the access strategy of your SQL statements.

Generating Statistics

The system catalog tables contain information about columns, tables, and indexes. They contain such information as the number of rows in a table, the use of space by a table or index, and the number of different values in a column.

However, this information is not kept current. It has to be generated by a utility called RUNSTATS.

The statistics collected by the RUNSTATS utility can be used in two ways: to display the physical organization of the data and to provide information that the DB2 optimizer needs to select the best access path for executing SQL statements.

To have efficient access paths to data, current statistics must exist that reflect the actual state of your tables, columns, and indexes. Whenever a dynamic SQL statement is issued, the DB2 optimizer reads the system catalog tables to review the available indexes, the size of each table, the characteristics of a column, and other information to select the best access path for executing the query.

If the statistics do not reflect the current state of the tables, the DB2 optimizer will not have the correct information to make the best choice in selecting an access path to execute your query. This becomes more crucial as the complexity of the SQL statements increases. When only one table is accessed without indexes, there are fewer choices available to the optimizer. However, when the SQL statement involves several tables, each one with one or more indexes, the number of choices available to the optimizer increases dramatically.

Choosing the correct access path can reduce the response time considerably. Depending on the size of the tables, the indexes available, and other considerations, the selected access path can affect the response time, which varies from minutes to hours. You may also want to consider the physical and logical design in your database.

The next step in improving performance involves the use of the RUNSTATS utility.

It is recommended to you execute RUNSTATS on a frequent basis on tables that have a large number of updates, inserts, or deletes. For tables with a great deal of insert or delete activity, you may decide to run statistics after a fixed period of time or after the insert or delete activity.

Note: It is recommended to use the RUNSTATS utility after a REORG of a table.

An important feature of DB2 is that it allows you to reorganize and use the RUNSTATS utility on the system catalog tables. This feature of DB2 can improve the access plans generated when querying the system catalog tables. DB2 may access these tables when you issue an SQL statement, even though you are referencing only user tables. Therefore, it is very important to have current statistics on the system catalog tables.

Maintaining Data

Using the RUNSTATS Utility

To use the RUNSTATS utility you must have one of the following authorities: SYSADM, SYSCTRL, SYSMAINT, or DBADM or have CONTROL privilege on the table.

Suppose you are the database administrator and have noticed that every time your decision support system tries to resolve a user request, it takes a considerable amount of time before data is retrieved. You decide to investigate by using the RUNSTATS utility on some of the system catalog tables. This example will use the SYSIBM.SYSCOLUMNS table:

```
RUNSTATS ON TABLE SYSIBM.SYSCOLUMNS
```

The RUNSTATS utility does not produce any output. You can only see its results by querying the system catalog tables.

Here is some of the data updated by RUNSTATS:

```
TABSCHEMA TABNAME              CARD        NPAGES      FPAGES      OVERFLOW
--------- ------------------   ----------- ----------- ----------- -----------
SYSIBM    SYSCOLUMNS                   927          32          32           1
SYSIBM    SYSTABLES                    -1          -1          -1          -1
```

This output was obtained by selecting all the columns of the SYSSTAT.TABLES catalog view. The -1 (negative one) value indicates that there are no statistics available for that object. The columns of the SYSSTAT.TABLES view have the same meaning as those of the REORGCHK utility:

* CARD - Indicates the number of data rows in the table
* NPAGES - Indicates the total number of pages that contain data
* FPAGES - Indicates the total number of pages that have been allocated to the table
* OVERFLOW - Indicates the number of overflow rows

Identifying Updated Statistics

It is not difficult to identify the absence of available statistics for a specific object. The -1 (negative one) value in the statistical information columns indicates this state. However, it is also important to identify the time of the last update of the object's statistics.

When you perform RUNSTATS on an object, the utility records the timestamp of its execution in the system catalog tables. Depending on the type of object, you can find the timestamp information in SYSCAT.TABLES or SYSCAT.INDEXES. In both views, the information is stored in the STATS_TIME column.

Old statistics may also affect the access path selection. They can mislead the optimizer to choose a improper access plan for an SQL statement.

Having current statistics is the best way to help the optimizer choose the best access path for a particular SQL statement.

Collecting Statistics for Tables and Indexes

It is possible to perform RUNSTATS on a table and all of its indexes at the same time. This is shown in the following command:

```
RUNSTATS ON TABLE db2cert.test_taken AND INDEXES ALL
```

The REORGCHK utility executes the command shown above when it calls the RUNSTATS utility. The INDEXES ALL option indicates that statistics for all the indexes of a table are required. The AND option specifies that you want statistics for the table and the indexes.

Collecting Statistics for Indexes Only

After creating a new index on a table, you may find it useful to gather statistics only for the indexes of that table. If table statistics have never been generated, then this command will generate both table and index statistics; otherwise, only index statistics will be generated.

```
RUNSTATS ON TABLE db2cert.test_taken FOR INDEXES ALL
```

Collecting Distribution Statistics on Table Columns

There may be some columns in which the values are not distributed in a uniform manner or in which the values are concentrated in a particular range.

This kind of nonuniform distribution of data may mislead the optimizer when choosing the most appropriate access method. However, the RUNSTATS utility provides the ability to show this non-uniform distribution to the optimizer. This may improve the access plans for such tables.

In this example, suppose that 75% of the DB2 certification program exams are taken in one testing center and the other 25% are distributed in other testing centers. This nonuniform distribution of values is stored in the DB2CERT.TEST_TAKEN table.

The following command can be used to collect distribution statistics:

```
RUNSTATS ON TABLE db2cert.test_taken WITH DISTRIBUTION
```

The WITH DISTRIBUTION option is used to instruct DB2 to collect data about the distribution of values for the columns in a table. This option is related to three database configuration parameters: NUM_FREQVALUES, NUM_QUANTILES, and STAT_HEAP_SZ. These parameters will limit the action of the WITH DISTRIBUTION option.

- NUM_FREQVALUES - Indicates the number of most frequent values that DB2 will collect. For example, if it is set to 10, only information for the 10 most frequent values will be obtained.
- NUM_QUANTILES - Indicates the number of quantiles that DB2 will look for. This is the amount of information DB2 retains about the distribution of values for columns in the table.
- STAT_HEAP_SZ - Indicates how much memory DB2 uses for collecting these statistics.

This procedure is demanding, and it is not recommended for all your tables. Only tables presenting a high volume of nonuniform values are candidates for this option.

Collecting Detailed Information About Indexes

It is possible to collect data that will give more information about an index, in this example, information on the indexes of the table DB2CERT.TEST_TAKEN:

```
RUNSTATS ON TABLE db2cert.test_taken FOR DETAILED
INDEXES ALL
```

The DETAILED option is used to gather this information. The statistics collected are stored in the CLUSTERFACTOR and PAGE_FETCH_PAIRS columns of the SYSIBM.SYSINDEXES system catalog table.

This option generates statistics similar to the CLUSTERRATIO. However, CLUSTERFACTOR and PAGE_FETCH_PAIRS provide a more accurate measurement of the relationship between the index and the data pages. These two values can give the optimizer a more detailed way to model the I/O operations and select a better access path for an SQL statement. The DETAILED option is also affected by the STAT_HEAP_SZ database parameter.

Access to Tables During RUNSTATS

The RUNSTATS utility allows applications different types of access to the table being analyzed:

- CHANGE - Other applications have read/write access to the table.
- REFERENCE - Other applications have read-only access to the table.

You specify this level of access (also known as the *share level*) using the SHRLEVEL option in the RUNSTATS command. For example, while executing RUNSTATS on the CANDIDATE table, you could prevent other applications from writing to the table by using the following command:

```
RUNSTATS ON TABLE db2cert.candidate SHRLEVEL REFERENCE
```

The default level of access allowed to other applications during a RUNSTATS is CHANGE.

Recommended Actions After RUNSTATS

Now that the system catalog tables have been updated, you should perform the following procedures. This will give your applications the benefit of the recently collected statistics about your tables.

- Do a REBIND on the packages that access the reorganized table. This will provide your applications with any changes selected by the DB2 optimizer to improve the access strategy for your SQL statements.
- Dynamic SQL statements will experience immediate benefits from the execution of the RUNSTATS utility. Packages in this situation do not need to be rebound.

Collecting Statistics from the Control Center

By right-clicking on a table in the Control Center, you can click on **Runstats** and update the table's statistics through the graphical interface. You can specify what statistics you would like to collect for both the table and the indexes on that table. Fig. 10–36 shows a RUNSTATS against the SALES table. The Extended Index Statistics option is identical to the DETAILED INDEXES parameter in the RUNSTATS command.

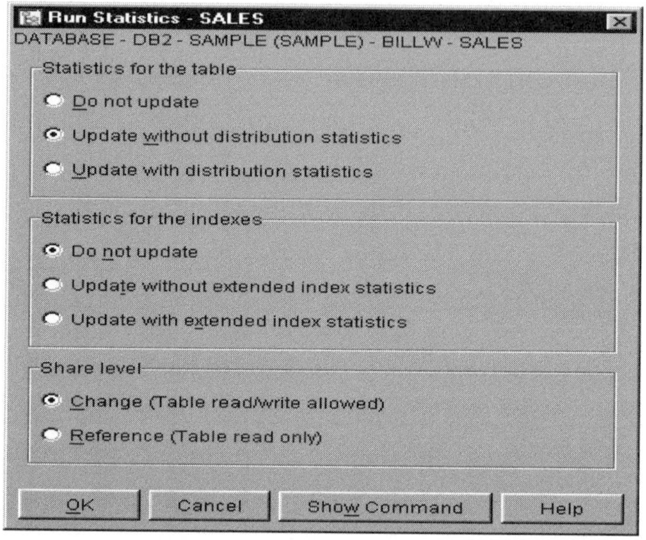

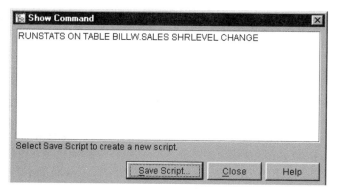

Fig. 10–36 *RUNSTATS from the Control Center*

The user has the option to review the command generated and to save or schedule it to be executed at a later time. Fig. 10–37 shows the command generated:

Fig. 10–37 *RUNSTATS command generated*

The Rebind Utility

The REBIND utility provides the ability to recreate a package with the information available in the system catalog tables. This may allow your embedded SQL applications to use a different access path selected by the optimizer.

The REBIND utility is recommended after doing REORG or RUNSTATS. The DB2 SQL optimizer will use the new organization and recently collected statistics to generate an access path. This access path may be better suited to the new physical organization of your data.

For example, suppose you have an application called db2cert that uses the table DB2CERT.TEST_TAKEN. You have just created a new index for the table, and you need to use REBIND so that the db2cert application can try to use the new index for data access.

```
REBIND db2cert
```

If you made significant changes to your database and updated all the statistics, you might want to recreate the packages for *all* applications that use the database. In this scenario, you might want to use the db2rbind tool. The db2rbind tool allows you to do an explicit rebind of all packages that are currently in the SYSCAT.PACKAGES catalog view. The following command rebinds all packages in the DB2CERT database, and logs the results to db2rbind.log.

```
db2rbind db2cert /l db2rbind.log
```

Data Maintenance Process

As shown in Fig. 10–38, the data mainenance process starts with the RUNSTATS and REORGCHK utilities. The REORGCHK utility can execute the RUNSTATS utility at the same time. However, it is recommended to call RUNSTATS separately, so you can control the utility's options and customize it for your environment.

After performing RUNSTATS, the REORGCHK utility reviews the statistics collected, applies six formulas, and then gives recommendations about whether a REORG is needed.

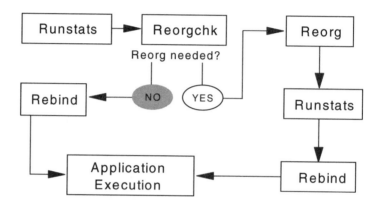

Fig. 10–38 *The data maintenance process*

If reorganization is recommended, use the REORG utility on the selected objects and then do RUNSTATS and REBIND. You must perform a REBIND on any packages affected by the above operations, so they can take advantage of the benefits of the new physical organization and updated statistics. After performing subsequent update, insert, and delete operations, as part of the data maintenance process, repeat by first executing the RUNSTATS utility.

Establish a routine for RUNSTATS and the REBIND processes. Updated statistics will give you precise information about your database state.

Modeling a Production Environment

You can use the SYSSTAT schema to update system catalog statistical information. You can enter values for statistics such as table cardinality, column distribution, or index cluster ratio. In doing so, you will be able to model different volumes of data on test databases.

This is useful when you want to be sure that the access plans your applications use in your production environment are the same as those in your development environment. The access paths selected by the optimizer in each environment may differ because of different data volumes.

By updating the SYSSTAT views, you will be able to provide the optimizer with the same environment found in different databases. The update procedure is performed using the SQL UPDATE statement.

There are five updatable views under the SYSSTAT schema. These views are:

- SYSSTAT.TABLES
- SYSSTAT.COLUMNS
- SYSSTAT.INDEXES
- SYSSTAT.COLDIST
- SYSSTAT.FUNCTIONS

These catalog views can be used to provide a "what-if" analysis for your database applications. For example, you can increase the cardinality of a table or the cluster ratio of an index.

You can use the REBIND utility to model the behavior of your static SQL applications in the "what-if" analysis process. You can create or drop an index and then use the REBIND utility to see how the access plan is affected.

As a general recommendation, only update the SYSSTAT schema view in a development environment.

Maintaining Data

Summary

This chapter has dealt with the issues of data movement, organization, and placement in your database. Various utilities in DB2 Universal Database that move data into database tables and to extract data from tables have been reviewed. These included the EXPORT, IMPORT, and LOAD utilities. Included in this discussion was a summary of the various file types allowed by DB2. The numerous options provided with these commands give you flexibility in their use. All the utilities can be invoked in a command line type environment. Also, you can use the DB2 Control Center to graphically initiate these processes.

Having data in your tables is only the first step. The utilities and commands in DB2 that allow you to perform data maintenance on your environment were also reviewed. This included analysis of data in tables and indexes with the REORGCHK utility, physically changing the organization of your table and index data using the REORG command, and how to update the statistics of table and index data using the RUNSTATS command.

An important component of the data maintenance process is ensuring that your applications are aware of the updated statistics in your environment. To this end, the REBIND command was examined in detail.

Database Recovery

- LOG FILES
- LOGGING
- BACKUP
- RESTORE
- ROLLFORWARD
- RECOVERY

*O*ne of the fundamental functions of any database management system is the ability to recover from events that would lead to the integrity of the database being compromised. DB2 is no different in this regard and has a number of features and functions available to help you manage your environment and ensure that you can perform adequate recovery of your data.

In this chapter, the concept of logging in a relational database system as it relates to the recovery of a database will be discussed. In addition, the major utilities involved in the area of database recovery, BACKUP and RESTORE, will be reviewed.

Database Recovery Concepts

While DB2 has mechanisms to provide automatic recovery from situations that threaten the integrity of its databases, it cannot cater to all situations, especially unforeseen external events. While it is impossible to cover every possible scenario, careful planning can ensure that recovery is possible for the majority of situations with minimum loss of data.

Some situations you should consider are:

- System outage - The operating system fails due to a hardware or software problem. An interruption to the power supply also falls under this category.
- Transaction failure - A transaction fails before completion. What happens to changes made to the database before the point of failure?
- Media failure - A disk drive failure causes a partial or complete loss of data on the disk.
- Disaster - A wide range of nontrivial damage to more than just a single component of the system. The facility at which the system is located suffers damage that impacts the system's operation.

Unit of Work

To ensure consistency of the data in a database, it is often necessary for applications to apply a number of changes together as a unit. This is called a *unit of work*. A unit of work is a recoverable sequence of operations within an application process. It is the basic mechanism that an application uses to ensure database integrity. At any time, an application process has a single unit of work, but the life of an application process may involve many units of work.

Transaction

Units of work are also known as *transactions*. Any application that successfully connects to a database automatically starts a transaction. The application must end the transaction by issuing a COMMIT or a ROLLBACK statement. The COMMIT statement tells the database manager to apply all database changes (inserts, updates, deletes, creates, alters, grants, revokes) to the database at once. The ROLLBACK statement tells the database manager not to apply the changes but to return the affected rows back to their state before the beginning of the transaction.

Types of Recovery

Recovery can be one of the following: crash, version, or roll-forward. Each type will now be examined.

Crash Recovery

Crash recovery protects a database from being left in an inconsistent or unusable state. Units of work against the database can be interrupted unexpectedly. For example, should a power failure occur before all of the changes that are part of a unit of work are completed and committed, the database will be left in an inconsistent state.

The database is made consistent again by undoing the uncommitted transactions. The RESTART DATABASE command initiates this function. If the AUTORESTART database configuration parameter is set to ON (which is the default), the first connection to the database after a failure will imitate the RESTART DATABASE.

Version Recovery

Version recovery allows for the restoration of a previous version or image of the database that was made using the BACKUP command.

Restoration of the database will rebuild the entire database using a backup of the database made at some point in time earlier. A backup of the database allows you to restore a database to a state identical to the time when the backup was made. Every unit of work from the time of the backup to the end of the log files is lost. (These can be recovered using roll-forward recovery.)

The version recovery method requires a full database backup for each version you may want to restore in the future. Table spaces can also be backed up and restored using the version recovery technique. DB2 supports version recovery by default.

Roll-Forward Recovery

This technique extends the version recovery by using full database backups in conjunction with log files to provide the capability of restoring a database or selected table spaces to a particular point in time.

By using a full database backup as a baseline, if all the log files are available covering the time period from the time of the backup to the current time, you can choose to have DB2 apply all the units of work for any or all table spaces in the database, up to any time within the time period covered by the logs.

Roll-forward recovery is specified at a database level in DB2 and has to be explicitly enabled.

Database Recovery

Note: The catalog table space SYSCATSPACE, when used in table space roll-forward recovery, *must* be rolled forward to the end of the logs. It can be rolled forward to a point in time as part of database roll-forward recovery.

Recovery Strategies

Some of the factors to consider when formulating a recovery strategy include:

- Will the database be recoverable or nonrecoverable?
- How near to the time of failure will you need to recover the database (the point of recovery)?
- How much time can be spent recovering the database?
- How large a window do you have for all recovery activities?
- What storage resources are available for storing backups and log files?

In general, a database maintenance and recovery strategy should ensure that all information is available when it is required for database recovery. In addition, you should include elements that reduce the likelihood and impact of database failure.

Recoverable and Nonrecoverable Databases

Recoverable databases in DB2 are distinguished by the LOGRETAIN and/or USEREXIT database configuration parameters being enabled. This means that crash, version, *and* roll-forward recovery techniques are available for use.

Nonrecoverable databases *do not* support roll-forward recovery.

The decision whether a database should be recoverable depends on factors such as:

- If the database is query only, then there will be no units of work in the log, therefore the database may not need to be recoverable.
- If there is little volatility in the database (that is, few changes to the data) and the data can be recreated easily, then you may wish to consider not having your database recoverable.
- Databases that have data that is not easily recreated should be made recoverable.
- If there is a lot of update activity, a recoverable database should be considered.

Online and Offline Access

When performing the various database recovery activities, the database can be considered *offline* or *online*.

Online means that other applications can connect to the database during the operation being performed. Conversely, offline means that no other application can use the database while the operation is in progress.

Offline and online are not available for all recovery activities.

Use of Log Files

All DB2 databases have logs associated with them. These logs keep a record of all changes made to database objects and data. All the changes are first written to log buffers in memory before being flushed to the log files on disk at COMMIT time.

For example, in case of a mishap such as power failure, the log files would be used to bring the database back to a consistent state. All units of work would be re-applied using the log files, and then all uncommitted units of work would be rolled back.

Log files have a predefined, configurable size. Therefore, when one log file is filled, logging continues in another log file.

Fig. 11–1 shows how multiple log files are being used to manage concurrent transactions. The top part of the diagram represents the evolution of three user processes (1 - 3) accessing the same database. The boxes represent database changes such as inserts or updates. The life of every transaction is also depicted (A - F). The lower-middle section of the diagram shows how the database changes are synchronously recorded in the log files (x,y). The letter in each box indicates the transaction to which the database change belongs.

Note: DB2 uses a write-ahead-logging scheme to ensure data integrity by having any updates, deletes, or inserts of data written first to the log files. At a later time, these changes are then written to the relational database.

When a COMMIT is issued, the log buffer containing the transaction is written to disk. This is represented by the arrows and the small wavy lines. Transaction E is never written to disk because it ends with a ROLLBACK statement. When log file x runs out of room to store the first database change of transaction D, the logging process switches to log file y. Log file x remains active until all transaction C changes are written to the database disk files. The period of time during which log file x remains active after logging is switched to log file y is represented by the hexagon.

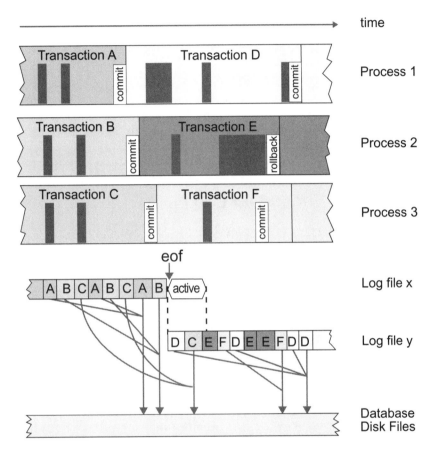

Fig. 11–1 *Transaction log file use*

Log Buffers

Before being written to the log files, log records are firstly written into buffers. The size of these buffers range from 4 to 512 four-kilobyte pages, with the default setting of eight pages. The database configuration parameter that defines the size of the log buffer is called LOGBUFSZ. The memory is allocated from an area called the database heap, whose size is controlled by the database configuration parameter DBHEAP.

The log records are written to disk when one of the following occurs:

- A transaction commits or a group of transactions commit, as defined by the MINCOMMIT database configuration parameter.
- The log buffer is full.
- As a result of some other *internal* database manager event.

Buffering the log records will result in more-efficient logging file I/O because the log records will be written to disk less frequently, and more log records will be written to the log files at each I/O. If there is considerable logging activity in the system, increase the size of the log buffers to improve performance.

Primary and Secondary Log Files

There are two types of log files: primary and secondary.

- *Primary* log files establish a fixed amount of storage allocated to the recovery log files. These files are preallocated during the first connection to the database. The database configuration parameter LOGPRIMARY determines the number of primary log files created of a size specified by the LOGFILSIZ database configuration parameter.

- *Secondary* log files are allocated one at a time as needed (up to the value of the database configuration parameter LOGSECOND) when the primary log files become full. The size of secondary log files is also specified by the LOGFILSIZ database configuration parameter.

  When all secondary log files become full, a log-full error condition occurs, and the entire unit of work is rolled back.

  One recommendation is to use secondary log files for databases that have periodic needs for large amounts of log space. For example, an application that is run once a month may require log space beyond that provided by the primary log files.

> **Note:** The default value of LOGFILSIZ is 1000 pages for UNIX-based versions of DB2. For other versions of DB2, the value is 250 pages. The page size is always 4 KB.

Types of Logging

There are two types of logging that can occur in DB2: circular and archival.

- *Circular logging* supports nonrecoverable databases. This type of logging uses active log files only (see below for details). Primary and secondary log files are used as described above. When a log file has had all of its transactions committed or rolled back, then it can be reused. Roll-forward recovery is not possible with this logging method, whereas crash recovery and version recovery are available. This is the default logging method when a DB2 database is created.

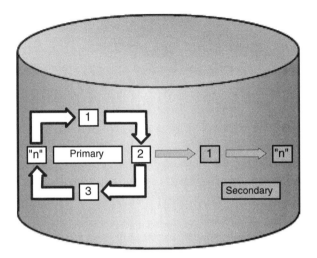

Fig. 11–2 *Circular logging*

The circular logging method is shown in Fig. 11–2.

- *Archival logging* is where log files are archived when they become inactive. Archival logging is not the default logging method. It is the only method that will allow you to support roll-forward recovery and implement recoverable databases. There are three types of log files associated with this method, shown in Fig. 11–3.

Database Recovery

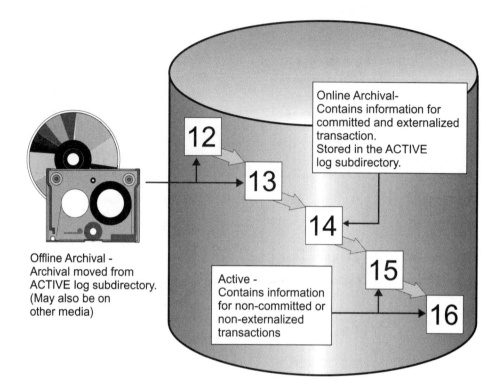

Fig. 11–3 *Archival logging*

Log files can be classified as follows:

- *Active* - Indicated by numbers 15 and 16. These files contain information related to units of work that have not yet been committed (or rolled back). They also contain information about transactions that have been committed but whose changes have not yet been written to the database files.

  Active log files are used by crash recovery to prevent a failure from leaving the database in an inconsistent state. The RESTART DATABASE situation (for crash recovery) and ROLLFORWARD command (for point-in-time recovery or recovery to the end of the logs) use the active logs to reapply or roll back units of work if necessary to bring the database to a point of consistency.

- *Online Archived* - Indicated by number 14. When all changes in the active log are no longer needed for normal processing, the log is closed and becomes an archived log.

  These files contain information related to completed transactions no longer required for restart recovery. They are called *online* because they reside in the same subdirectory as the active log files.

- *Offline Archived* - Indicated by numbers 12 and 13. These log files have been moved from the active log file directory. The method of moving these files could be a manual or automated process such as that invoked by a user exit. Archived log files can be placed offline simply by moving them to another directory or storing them on tape or other medium. They can also be managed by an external storage manager such as IBM's ADSM products.

Two database configuration parameters, LOGRETAIN and USEREXIT, allow you to configure a database for archival logging.

When the LOGRETAIN database configuration parameter is enabled, log files are not deleted when they become inactive. When the USEREXIT database configuration parameter is enabled, DB2 will call the user exit program when a log file is ready for archiving. The database name, path of the log file, and several other parameters are passed to the program.

> **Note:** The default setting for LOGRETAIN and USEREXIT is NO; thus circular logging is the default.

Roll-forward recovery can use online archived logs, offline archived logs, and active logs to rebuild a database or table space either at the end of the logs or at a specific point in time. The roll-forward function achieves this by reapplying committed units of work that are found in the archived and active logs to the restored database.

> **Note:** The current log file path is indicated by the database configuration parameter LOGPATH. When a database is created, the log files are placed under the default database directory. The NEWLOGPATH database configuration parameter is used to change the log file location.

Log File Usage

There are some considerations to bear in mind in relation to the use of log files. These considerations are as follows.

Erasing Logs

If an active log is erased, the database becomes unusable and must be restored before it can be used again.

If an archive log is erased, you will only be able to roll-forward changes up to the first log erased.

It is critical that all log files be protected by the security subsystem of the operating system. Other than the process of moving archive logs out of the log path directory, no other user or application other than DB2 has any need to access the log files.

Using the Not Logged Initially Option

The NOT LOGGED INITIALLY option exists for the CREATE TABLE and ALTER TABLE statements. When this option is used, no loggable activity within the unit of work that creates or alters the table or activates this option at a later time is logged. This is an advantage when inserting or updating a large amount of data into a table for the first time. This option is also suitable for work tables where data can be easily recreated.

The advantage of this option is the improvement in performance due to the absence of logging overhead; the disadvantage is the lack of recoverability of the unit of work.

Logging Using Raw Devices

Normally, log files use the standard operating system file systems to support their implementation (e.g., NTFS for Windows, JFS for AIX).

In addition to the standard file systems, you can use raw devices for logging. By using raw devices, you can avoid the overhead of using the file system, and therefore logging performance should be improved. This support is available on the Windows, AIX, and Solaris operating systems.

This involves using an unformatted hard disk partition (Windows) or a raw logical volume (AIX). The database configuration parameter NEWLOGPATH is set to point to the raw device.

Some considerations for using raw devices for logging are:

- Primary log files (extents) are still used according to the LOGPRIMARY and LOGFILSIZ database configuration parameters. The amount of space in the raw device must be at least (LOGPRIMARY * (LOGFILSIZ + 2)) + 1) pages of 4 KB each.
- Secondary log files are not used. You may have to increase the number and/or size of primary log files to compensate for this.

Refer to the *DB2 UDB V7.1 Administration Guide* for more details about logging using raw devices.

Version Recovery Using Backup and Restore

Version recovery is implemented using the BACKUP and RESTORE commands. These two commands will now be examined in greater detail.

Backing Up a Database

The BACKUP command can be invoked from the Command Line Processor, Command Center, application programming interface, or Control Center.

Before taking a backup, consider the following:

- You must have SYSADM, SYSCTRL, or SYSMAINT authority to invoke BACKUP.
- The database may be local or remote. The backup itself remains on the database server.
- The BACKUP command can interface with an external storage manager such as ADSM to directly manage the backup.
- BACKUP can directly send its output to tape via the operating system (except on OS/2, where a user exit program is required to back up to tape).
- BACKUP can directly send its output to disk on all platforms.
- Multiple backup files may be created to contain the backed-up data from the database.

When you invoke the BACKUP command, you should be aware of the following:

- DB2 must be started.
- The database must be in a normal or backup-pending state.
- When using the BACKUP utility, refer to the database name by its alias. In most cases this will be the same name as the database.
- You can run the backup in online mode via the ONLINE parameter or in offline mode, which is the default. Online mode allows other applications to remain connected to the database and do active work while the backup is proceeding. Alternately, for an offline backup, only the backup job itself may be connected to the database.

  For online mode, the database must be recoverable; that is, archive logging must be enabled. When running in online mode, DB2 attempts to acquire S (share) locks on tables with LOBs (large objects). This might result in failures running the utility due to applications connected to the database holding incompatible locks.

In addition, consider the following to improve the backup performance:

- The value of the PARALLELISM parameter. Using this parameter can reduce the amount of time required to complete the backup. It defines the number of processes or threads that are started to read data from the database. Each process or thread is assigned to back up a specific table space. When it completes backing up the table space, it requests another. Increasing the value requires additional processor and memory resources. The default value is one.

- The backup buffer size and number of buffers. If you use multiple buffers and I/O channels, you should use at least twice as many buffers as channels to ensure that the channels do not have to wait for data. The size of the buffers should ideally be a multiple of the table space extent size. If you have differing extent sizes, choose a multiple of the largest extent size. If the buffer size if not specified the value is taken from the database manager configuration parameter BACKBUFSZ, which by default is 1024 (4 KB) pages.

Backup Images Created by Backup

Backup images are created at the target specified when the BACKUP utility is invoked:

- In the directory for disk backups
- At the device specified for tape backups
- At an external storage manager server
- Through an user exit (OS/2 backup to tape)

The *recovery history file* is updated automatically with summary information whenever you carry out a backup of a database. This information is useful when tracking the backup history of a database. Other utilities' activities are also recorded in this file.

In UNIX-based environments, the file name(s) created on disk will consist of a concatenation of the following information, separated by periods; on other platforms, a four-level subdirectory tree structure is used:

- *Database alias* - A one to eight character database alias name that was supplied when the backup command was invoked.
- *Type* - Type of backup taken, where: "0" is for full database, "3" is for table space.
- *Instance name* - A one to eight character name of the instance.
- *Node number* - The node number.
- *Catalog node number* - The node number of the database's catalog node.
- *Time stamp* - A 14-character representation of the date and time the backup was performed. The timestamp is in the format yyyymmddhhnnss, where:
    yyyy is the year (1995 to 9999), mm is the month (01 to 12),
    dd is the day of the month (01 to 31), hh is the hour (00 to 23),
    nn is the minutes (00 to 59), ss is the seconds (00 to 59).
- *Sequence number* - A three-digit sequence number used as a file extension.

In UNIX-based operating systems, the format would appear as:

```
DB_alias.Type.Inst.nodennnn.catnnnn.timestamp.seq_num
```

For example, a database named STAFF in the DB601 instance is backed up to disk as a file named:

```
STAFF.0.DB601.NODE0000.CATN0000.20000715120112.001
```

On Windows and OS/2 operating systems, the format appears as:

```
DB_alias.Type\Inst\nodennnn\catnnnn\yyyymmdd\hhmmss.seq_num
```

For example, a database called DB2CERT in instance DB2 is backed up to disk as a file named:

```
D:\DB2CERT.0\DB2\NODE0000\CATN0000\20000715\122229.001
```

For tape-directed output, file names are not created; however, the above information is stored in the backup header for verification purposes.

Examples of Using Backup

You can run the BACKUP command from the DB2 Command Line Processor or DB2 Command Center. For example:

```
BACKUP DATABASE DB2CERT TO C:\DBBACKUP
```

This command backs up the database DB2CERT to the C:\DBBACKUP directory on a Windows system. The other parameters take their default values.

```
BACKUP DATABASE DB2CERT TO /dev/rmt0
       WITH 2 BUFFERS
       BUFFER 512
       PARALLELISM 2
```

This command backs up the database DB2CERT to a tape device on an AIX system. Two buffers of 512 (4 KB) pages each are allocated. Two parallel tasks are used to backup in parallel.

You can also use the Control Center in invoke a backup. After right-clicking on the database you wish to back up, select the Backup Database option, as shown in Fig. 11–4:

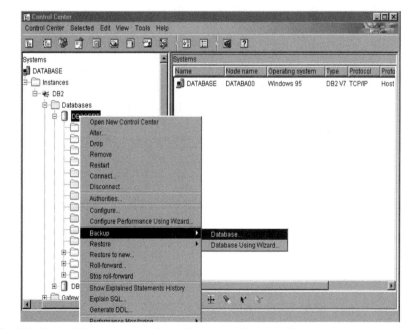

Fig. 11–4 *Backing up a database from the Control Center*

The Backup Database panel is displayed:

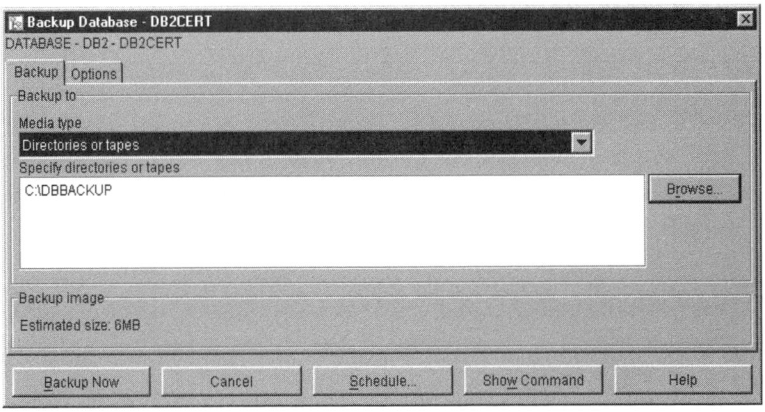

Fig. 11–5 *Backup database - Backup panel*

Here you specify where you want the backup image to reside and the media type. An estimate of the size of the backup image is provided. Click on **Browse** to select the target directories or devices.

By clicking on the **Options** tab, the following window is displayed:

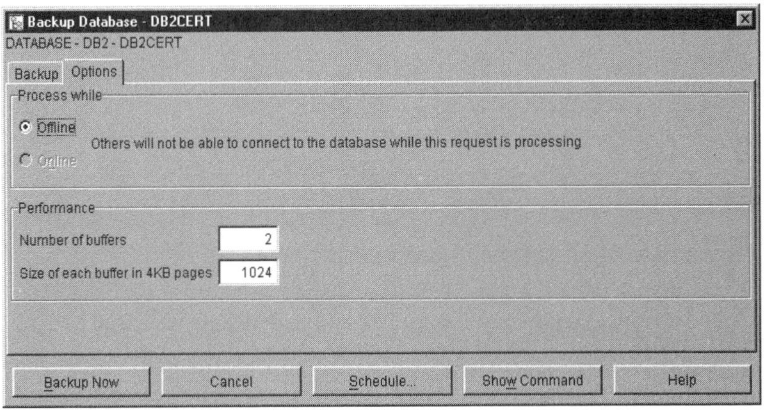

Fig. 11–6 *Backup database - Options*

Here you can choose whether to perform the backup in online or offline mode. In addition, the number of backup buffers and the backup buffer size can be specified.

Click on **Backup Now** to initiate the backup. This is done by submitting a job via the Control Center.

In addition, you can schedule the backup to run at a set frequency by clicking on **Schedule** or you can show the SQL Command and then save it as a script to be

Database Recovery

invoked at a later time. These are features of the Control Center and are not available through other DB2 tools.

From these panels, you can use the **Show Command** button to see the DB2 command used to do the work on your behalf.

If you wish to have DB2 guide you through the backup process and make recommendations, you can invoke the **Backup Database Using Wizard** option from the Control Center.

In both cases, you can monitor and view the results of running the BACKUP command through the Journal, which can be invoked from the Control Center.

After an online backup is complete, DB2 will close the current active log. This operational enhancement makes it easier to ensure that the online backup has the necessary archived logs for recovery.

Restoring a Database

The RESTORE command can be invoked from the Command Line Processor, Command Center, application programming interface, or Control Center.

Before performing a restore, consider the following:

- You must have SYSADM, SYSCTRL, or SYSMAINT authority to perform a RESTORE to an existing database and SYSADM or SYSCTRL if performing a RESTORE to an new database.
- You can only use this command if the database has been previously backed up with the BACKUP command.
- The RESTORE command can interface with an external storage manager such as ADSM to directly use a backup image managed by the external storage manager.
- RESTORE requires an exclusive connection to the database; no applications can be running against the database when the utility is started. Once it starts, it prevents other applications from accessing the database until the restore is completed.
- The database may be local or remote.

When you invoke the RESTORE command, you should be aware of the following:

- DB2 must be started.
- You can restore to a new or an existing database.

- You can run the restore in online mode via the ONLINE parameter for table space restores only.
- The TAKEN AT parameter requires the timestamp for the backup. If there is more than one backup image in the same directory, this parameter is required. The timestamp can be exactly as it was displayed after the completion of a successful backup, that is, the format yyyymmddhhnnss. It can also be a partial timestamp as long as it is not ambiguous in identifying a backup image. If this parameter is not specified when using ADSM, the latest the backup image is used for restoration.

In addition, consider the following to improve the performance of RESTORE:

- The value of the PARALLELISM parameter. Using this parameter can reduce the amount of time required to complete the restore. It defines the number of processes or threads that started for restore processing. The default value is one.

- Increasing the restore buffer size and number of buffers. You can improve the performance of RESTORE by increasing the restore buffer size (BUFFER parameter) and number of buffers (WITH n BUFFERS parameter).

  The minimum value for the BUFFER parameter is 16 pages; the default value is 1024 pages. If a buffer size of 0 is specified, the value in the database manager configuration parameter RESTBUFSZ will be used and must be set to 16. The specified value is compared with the value specified during the backup.The actual restore buffer size will be an even multiple of the backup buffer size, which is equal to or greater than the backup buffer size.

  For example, if a backup buffer size of 1024 pages was specified and an attempt made to restore this backup with a buffer size of 16 pages, the actual restore buffer size would be 1024. If the specified restore buffer size were 2049, the actual restore buffer size would be 2048.

> **Note:** If a failure occurs during a database restore, the database will not be useable until a successful restore is completed.

Examples of Using Restore

You can run the RESTORE command from the Command Line Processor or Command Center. For example:

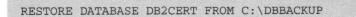

```
RESTORE DATABASE DB2CERT FROM C:\DBBACKUP
```

This command restores the database DB2CERT from the C:\DBBACKUP directory on a Windows system. The other parameters use their default values. This may leave the database in a roll-forward pending state that requires the ROLLFORWARD command be executed before the database can be accessed.

```
RESTORE DATABASE DB2CERT FROM C:\DBBACKUP
        WITHOUT ROLLING FORWARD
        WITHOUT PROMPTING
```

The above RESTORE command eliminates the requirement for the ROLLFORWARD command to be executed. The ROLLFORWARD command is discussed in greater detail later in this chapter in "Rolling Forward Databases and Table Spaces" on page 567.

The WITHOUT PROMPTING option specifies that the restore will run unattended and any actions that normally require user intervention will instead return an error message.

```
RESTORE DATABASE DB2CERT FROM C:\DBBACKUP
        INTO NEWDB
        WITH 2 BUFFERS
        BUFFER 512
        WITHOUT ROLLING FORWARD
```

The above command restores the database into a new database called NEWDB and assigns two restore buffers of 512 pages each.

You can also use the Control Center to invoke a restore. After right-clicking on the database you wish to restore, select the Restore Database option, as shown in Fig. 11–7. The example below allows us to restore to an existing database.

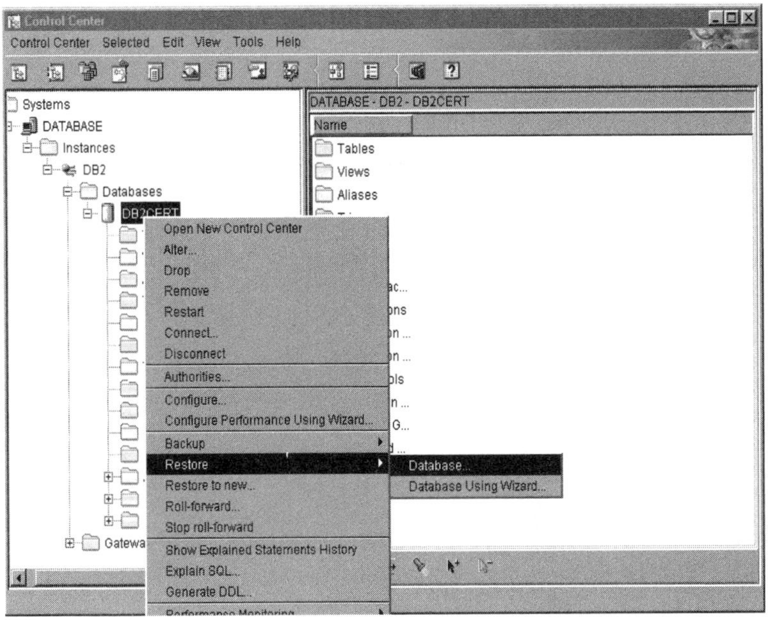

Fig. 11–7 *Restoring a database using the Control Center*

The Restore Database panel is displayed:

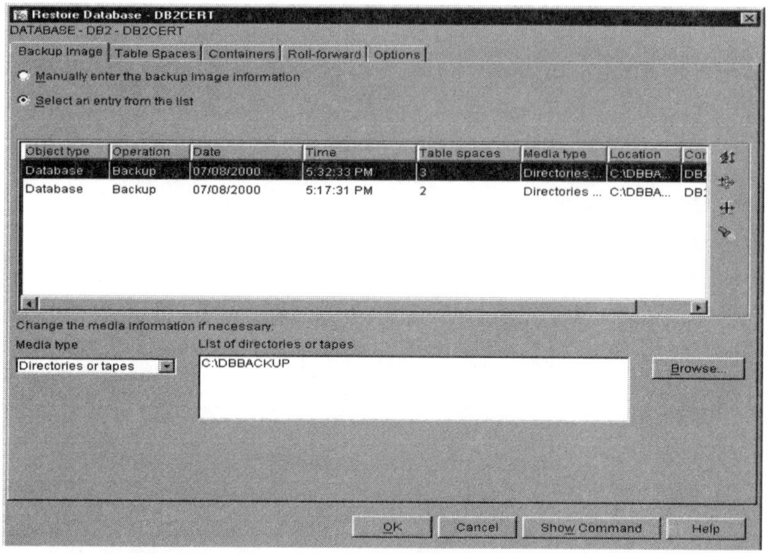

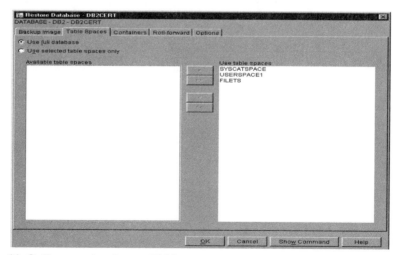

Fig. 11–8 *Restore database - Backup image*

First you determine which backup image you use wish to use for the restore operation, as shown above.

Fig. 11–9 *Restore database - Table spaces*

The Table Spaces tab (Fig. 11–9) allows you to specify which table spaces out of the backup image you want to restore or whether it is a full database restore.

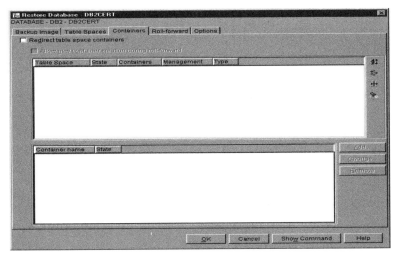

Fig. 11–10 *Restore database - Containers*

The Containers tab (Fig. 11–10) allows you to redefine the containers that a table space uses. You should only do this if you want to change the containers from those defined in the backup image. This is known as a *redirected restore*.

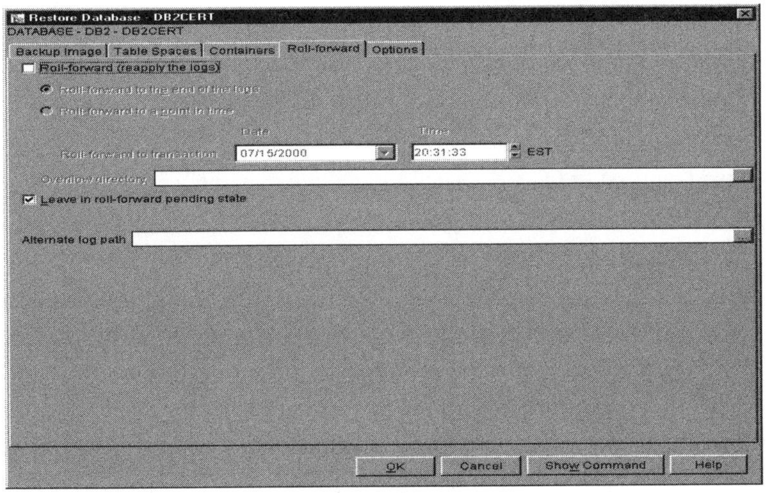

Fig. 11–11 *Restore database - Roll-forward*

The Roll-forward tab (Fig. 11–11) gives you options for not rolling forward or rolling forward to a point in time. This dialog can invoke the RESTORE, ROLLFORWARD, and SET TABLESPACE CONTAINER commands as part of its output.

As indicated earlier with the BACKUP command, you can press the **Show Command** button to see the DB2 command that will be issued on your behalf from the Control Center. The Journal can then be used to monitor the execution and the results of the command that was issued.

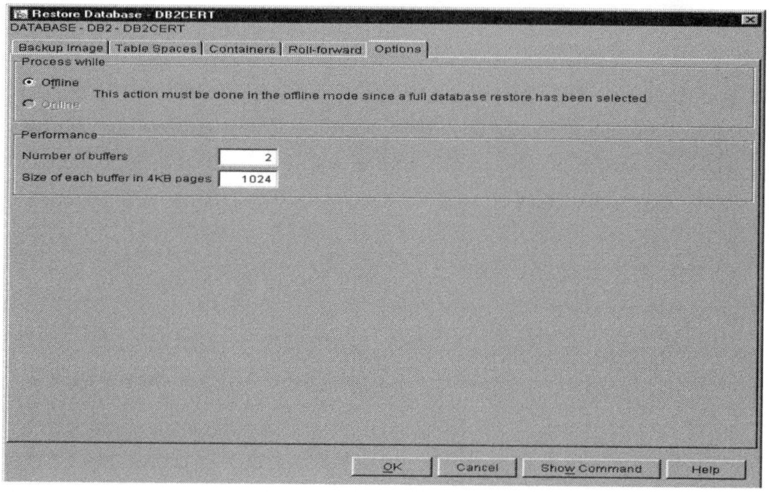

Fig. 11–12 *Restore database - Options*

Finally, the Options tab (Fig. 11–12) lets you set the buffer-related parameters of restore and whether the restore is performed offline or online. Online processing has a requirement that the database be recoverable.

As with the Backup command, you have the option of invoking the **Restore Database Using Wizard** panel from the Control Center.

Redefining Table Space Containers During Restore

During a backup of a database, a record is kept of all the table space containers in use by the table spaces being backed up. During a restore, all containers listed in the backup are checked to see if they currently exist and are accessible. If one or more of the containers is inaccessible for any other reason, the restore will fail. To allow a restore in such a case, the redirecting of table space containers is supported during the restore. This support includes the adding, changing, or removing of table space containers.

There are cases in which you want to restore, even though the containers listed in the backup do not exist on the system. An example of such a case is where you wish to recover from a disaster on a system other than that from which the backup was taken. The new system may not have the necessary containers defined.

To allow a restore in this case, the redirecting of table space containers at the time of the restore to alternate containers is supported.

In both cases, the process of restoring and redefining containers is called a *redirected restore.*

Note: A redirected restore can also be useful for backing up a production database at the primary site to a database at a designated backup site, which will typically be configured with less resources, such as the amount of disk available for containers.

As shown previously, you can use the restore dialog in the Control Center to perform a redirected restore or use the Command Center or Command Line Processor.

Here is an example of a redirected restore from a command line interface:

```
RESTORE DATABASE DB2CERT FROM C:\DBBACKUP
        INTO NEWDB
        REDIRECT
        WITHOUT ROLLING FORWARD
```

The above command requests that the DB2CERT database be restored into a new database called NEWDB. However, since DB2CERT has table spaces with specific SMS and DMS containers and containers cannot be shared by databases, new containers for the new database must be defined. The RESTORE utility returns the following messages:

```
SQL1277N Restore has detected that one or more table space
containers are inaccessible, or has set their state to
'storage must be defined'.
DB20000I The RESTORE DATABASE command completed
successfully.
```

To list the containers to be redefined, issue the LIST TABLESPACES command, which produces the following output. Note that from the previous RESTORE command, you are connected to the NEWDB database, with restricted functionality.

```
                    Tablespaces for Current Database
     Tablespace ID                              = 0
     Name                                       = SYSCATSPACE
     Type                                       = Database managed space
     Contents                                   = Any data
     State                                      = 0x2001100
        Detailed explanation:
           Restore pending
           Storage must be defined
           Storage may be defined

     Tablespace ID                              = 1
     Name                                       = TEMPSPACE1
     Type                                       = System managed space
     Contents                                   = Temporary data
     State                                      = 0x2001100
        Detailed explanation:
           Restore pending
           Storage must be defined
           Storage may be defined

     Tablespace ID                              = 2
     Name                                       = USERSPACE1
     Type                                       = Database managed space
     Contents                                   = Any data
     State                                      = 0x2001100
        Detailed explanation:
           Restore pending
           Storage must be defined
           Storage may be defined

     Tablespace ID                              = 3
     Name                                       = FILETS
     Type                                       = Database managed space
     Contents                                   = Any data
     State                                      = 0x2001100
        Detailed explanation:
           Restore pending
           Storage must be defined
           Storage may be defined
```

Note that all the table spaces are in the "Storage must be defined" state. To continue, define new containers for all the table spaces using the SET TABLESPACE CONTAINERS command as follows:

```
SET TABLESPACE CONTAINERS FOR 0
    USING (FILE "d:\newdb\cat.dat" 5000)

SET TABLESPACE CONTAINERS FOR 1
    USING (PATH "d:\newdb2")

SET TABLESPACE CONTAINERS FOR 2
    USING (FILE "d:\newdb\user.dat" 1000)

SET TABLESPACE CONTAINERS FOR 3
    USING (FILE "d:\newdb\newdb.dat" 1000)
```

Now that the containers are defined, continue the redirected restore with the following statement:

```
RESTORE DATABASE DB2CERT CONTINUE
```

This completes the redirected restore. Note that table spaces that were SMS and ones that were DMS must stay with their respective storage types during the redirection.

You should also be aware of the following considerations when using redirected restores:

- Directory and file containers are automatically created if they do not exist. No redirection is necessary unless the containers are inaccessible for some other reason. DB2 does not automatically create device containers.
- The ability to perform container redirection on any restore provides considerable flexibility in managing table space containers. For example, even though DB2 does not directly support adding containers to SMS table spaces, you could accomplish this by simply specifying an additional container on a redirected restore. Similarly, you could move a DMS table space from file containers to device containers.

Restoring to an Existing Database

DB2 uses *database seeds* to determine the database that a given database backup was created from. A database seed is an unique identifier of a database that remains constant for the life of the database. This seed is assigned by DB2 when the database is first created.

When restoring to an existing database, the following functions are performed:

- Delete table, index, long field, and large object contents for the existing database and replace them with the contents from the backup.
- Replace table space entries for each table space being restored.
- Retain the recovery history file unless the existing one is damaged, in which case it will be replaced with the one from the backup image.
- Retain the authentication for the existing database.
- Retain the database directories for the existing database that define where the database resides and how it is cataloged.

Certain functions depend on the database seed. When the database seeds are different:

- Delete the logs associated with the existing database.
- Copy the database configuration file from the backup.
- Change the database configuration file to indicate that the default log file path should be used for logging.

When the database seeds are the same:

- Retain the current database configuration file, unless it is damaged.
- Delete the logs if the image is of a nonrecoverable database.
- The LOGPATH parameter from the database configuration file in the backup is used to set the log file directory path.

Restoring to a New Database

When restoring to a new database, the following functions are performed:

- Create a new database, using the database name and alias that was specified by the target database alias. If not specified, a database with the name and alias of the source database alias will be created.
- Restore the database configuration file from the backup.
- Modify the database configuration file to indicate that the default log file path should be used for logging.
- Restore the authentication type from the backup.
- Restore the recovery history file for the database.

Roll-Forward Recovery

Roll-forward recovery enables *recoverable* databases. When enabled, in addition to what can be performed for version recovery, the following can be performed:

- Recovery at an individual table space level
- Point in time recovery using the ROLLFORWARD command
- Online processing of BACKUP and RESTORE commands

As previously mentioned, roll-forward recovery is enabled by enabling either or both the LOGRETAIN or USEREXIT database configuration parameters. When roll-forward recovery is enabled, the database goes into backup-pending state, which requires that a full database backup be taken before the database can be used.

Backing Up a Database

The points made here are in addition to the considerations discussed in the version recovery section earlier in this chapter.

Before taking a backup, consider the following:

- By using the TABLESPACE option of the BACKUP command, you can back up individual table spaces. This can reduce the overall time it takes to back up the database by backing up only the more volatile table spaces. The PARALLELISM parameter can also used to back up multiple table spaces in parallel.
- A table space backup and a table space restore cannot be run at the same time, even if the backup and restore are working on different table spaces.
- If you have the index or large object components of a table in different table spaces, the set of table spaces encompassing the entire table should be backed up together to ensure a consistent point of recovery.

When you invoke the BACKUP command, you should be aware of the following point in addition to the points made in the version recovery discussion:

- The database or table spaces must be in a normal or backup-pending state for BACKUP to function.

Example of Backing Up at the Table Space Level

You can run the BACKUP command from the Command Line Processor or Command Center. The same function can also be done graphically from the Control Center. For example, using the Command Line Processor:

```
BACKUP DATABASE DB2CERT
        TABLESPACE (SYSCATSPACE,FILETS) TO C:\DBBACKUP
```

Database Recovery

This command backs up the catalog table space SYSCATSPACE and user table space FILETS in the DB2CERT database to the C:\DBBACKUP directory on a Windows system. Default values are used for the other parameters.

Restoring a Database

The points made here are in addition to the considerations discussed under version recovery.

Before performing a restore, consider the following:

- You can restore a backup copy of a full database or table space backup to an existing database. The backup image may differ from the existing database in its alias name, database name, or its database seed.
- Databases restores can be in offline mode only.
- Table spaces can be restored in offline or online mode. While in online mode, connections to the database can be made. This is advantageous in the case of table space restoration when other table spaces can still be used concurrently while the restore is executing.
- A database enabled for roll-forward recovery must be rolled forward after it is restored unless the WITHOUT ROLLING FORWARD option is used. However, this option cannot be used if the backup was taken with the ONLINE option or if the backup image is of table spaces only.
- Even though the restore and roll-forward are separate functions, your recovery strategy may have restore as the first phase of a complete roll-forward recovery of a database. After a successful restore, a database that was configured for roll-forward recovery at the time the backup was taken enters a roll-forward-pending state, being unusable until the ROLLFORWARD command has been run successfully.
- When the ROLLFORWARD command is issued, if the database is in roll-forward-pending status, the database is rolled forward. If the database is not in roll-forward-pending status, but the table spaces are, when you issue the ROLLFORWARD command and specify a list of table spaces, only those table spaces are rolled forward. If you do not specify a list, all table spaces that are in roll-forward-pending status are rolled forward.
- Another database RESTORE is not allowed when the roll-forward process is running.
- You can only restore a table space if the table space currently exists and is the *same* table space. This means it must have the same name and has not been dropped and recreated between taking the backup image and restoration.
- You cannot use a table space backup image to restore the table space to a different database.

- If you have the index or large object components of a table in different table spaces, the set of table spaces encompassing the entire table should be restored together to ensure a consistent point of recovery.
- You can restore selected table spaces from a full database backup image. All log files associated with the table space must exist from the time the backup was created.

Example of Restoring at the Table Space Level

You can run the RESTORE command from the Command Line Processor or Command Center. Of course, the same function can also be done from the Control Center. From the Command Line Processor, for example:

```
RESTORE DATABASE DB2CERT
        TABLESPACE (FILETS) ONLINE FROM C:\DBBACKUP
```

This command restores the table space FILETS in database DB2CERT from the C:\DBBACKUP directory in online mode on a Windows system. Connections can still be made to the database. Default values are used for the other parameters. This command will leave the table space in a roll-forward-pending state, which requires that the ROLLFORWARD command be executed before the table space can be accessed.

Rolling Forward Databases and Table Spaces

The ROLLFORWARD command can be invoked from the Command Line Processor, application programming interface (API), or Control Center.

Before performing a roll-forward, consider the following:

- You must have SYSADM, SYSCTRL, or SYSMAINT authority to invoke ROLLFORWARD.
- The database may be local or remote.
- The database must be recoverable.
- A database must be restored successfully (using the RESTORE command) before it can be rolled forward.
- A table space, besides being restored, can also be put into roll-forward-pending state from a media error or some other unexpected event.
- A database roll-forward runs in offline mode. The database is not available for use until the roll-forward completes. Online roll-forward for table spaces is available, except for the catalog table space SYSCATSPACE, which requires an offline roll-forward. Other table spaces are available for use during online roll-forward.

- You can use any backup image that you have as long as you have the necessary log files to cover the period you wish to roll-forward.
- Frequent backups reduce the execution time of ROLLFORWARD, as less log data has to be read between the time of the backup and the recovery point.

Generally, the sequence of commands when invoking ROLLFORWARD is as follows:

- Issue the ROLLFORWARD command without the STOP/COMPLETE option.
- Issue the ROLLFORWARD command with the QUERY STATUS option. The QUERY STATUS option can indicate that log file(s) may be missing if the point in time returned is earlier than expected for rolling forward to the end of the log.
- Issue the ROLLFORWARD command with the STOP/COMPLETE option. After this command is invoked, it is not possible to roll forward additional changes.

When you invoke the ROLLFORWARD command, you should be aware of the following:

- If you need to cancel a roll-forward operation, you can use ROLLFORWARD with the CANCEL option. This places the database into restore-pending state, whether or not a roll-forward is in progress against the database.
- If you issue ROLLFORWARD with the CANCEL option and specify a list of table spaces that are in roll-forward pending state, they are put in restore-pending state.
- You cannot use ROLLFORWARD with the CANCEL option to cancel a roll-forward operation that is running. You can only use it to cancel a roll-forward operation that completed but did not have a ROLLFORWARD STOP issued for it or for a roll-forward operation that failed before completing.
- A log uses a timestamp associated with the completion of a unit of work. The timestamp in the logs uses Coordinated Universal Time (UTC). The format is yyyy-mm-dd-hh.mm.ss.nnnnnn (year, month, day, hour, minutes, seconds, microseconds). When you want to roll-forward to a point in time, you have to specify the time in UTC, as opposed to the timestamp used in backups, which uses the local time.
- If you are rolling forward one or many table spaces to a point in time, you must roll-forward at least to the minimum recovery time, which is the last update to the system catalogs for the table spaces. The minimum recovery time is shown in the output of the LIST TABLESPACES SHOW DETAIL command.

Table Space States During Roll-Forward

Different states are associated with a table space to indicate its current status:

- A table space will be placed in *roll-forward-pending* state after restoration or following an I/O error. The table space must be rolled forward to remove the roll-forward-pending state. If the cause was an I/O error, this situation must be corrected before doing a roll-forward.
- A table space will be placed in *roll-forward-in-progress* state when a roll-forward operation is in progress on that table space. The state remains until roll-forward operations are completed successfully. If the STOP/COMPLETE option was not used on a point in time recovery, the table space will also stay in this state.
- A table space will be placed in the *restore-pending* state after a ROLLFORWARD with CANCEL option or an unrecoverable error occurs in the execution of ROLLFORWARD. The table space must be restored and rolled forward again.
- A table space will be placed in the *backup-pending* state after a ROLLFORWARD to a point in time or after a LOAD NO COPY operation. The table space must be backed up before it can be used.

Examples of Rolling Forward

You can run the **ROLLFORWARD** command from the Command Line Processor or Command Center. For example:

```
ROLLFORWARD DATABASE DB2CERT
            TO END OF LOGS
            OVERFLOW LOG PATH (C:\LOGS)
```

This command rolls forward the DB2CERT database that was in roll-forward-pending status from the RESTORE command. The roll-forward will be performed to the end of the logs, which means that it will reapply all units of work in the logs up to the last unit of work in all online archive log files. This does not mean that the roll-forward will process up to the current time. For example, if there is a problem with the availability of the most recent active log, the command will still succeed. Use the QUERY STATUS option to ensure that the latest unit of work is at the expected time and that the log files were processed as expected.

The directory where the log files are kept (as listed in the database configuration parameter LOGPATH) is used by ROLLFORWARD to find active and online archive logs. The OVERFLOW LOG PATH parameter specifies the directory where offline archive log files are kept so that ROLLFORWARD can use them for reapplying units of work.

```
ROLLFORWARD DATABASE DB2CERT
        TO END OF LOGS AND COMPLETE
        TABLESPACE (FILETS) ONLINE
```

This command rolls forward the FILETS table space that is in roll-forward-pending status from the RESTORE command. The ONLINE parameter allows concurrent access to other table spaces. The AND COMPLETE parameter instructs DB2 to complete the rolling forward, roll back any incomplete units of work, and to enable the database to become available for general use by turning off the roll-forward-pending state.

```
ROLLFORWARD DATABASE DB2CERT
        QUERY STATUS
```

This command lists the log files that DB2 has rolled forward, the next archive file required, and the timestamp (in UTC) of the last committed transaction since roll-forward processing began. The information returned contains the following:

- Rollforward status - The status may be database or table space roll-forward pending, database or table space roll-forward in progress, database or table space roll-forward processing stop, or no roll-forward pending.
- Next log file to be read - A string containing the name of the next required log file.
- Log files processed - A string containing the names of the processed log files that are no longer needed for recovery and that can be removed from the directory.
- Last committed transaction - A string containing a timestamp in ISO format (yyyy-mm-dd-hh.mm.ss). This timestamp marks the last transaction committed after the completion of roll-forward recovery. The timestamp applies to the database. For table space roll-forward, it is the time tamp of the last transaction committed to the database.

Here is sample output of the QUERY STATUS option:

```
                    Rollforward Status

    Input database alias            = db2cert
    Number of nodes returned status = 1
    Node number                     = 0
    Rollforward status              = DB working
```

```
Next log file to be read           = S0000019.LOG
Log files processed                = S0000014.LOG - S0000018.LOG
Last committed transaction         = 2000-07-15-00.09.51.000000
```

Note the status is DB working, meaning that this is a database roll-forward and that it is still in progress, as the STOP/COMPLETE option has not been specified.

```
ROLLFORWARD DATABASE DB2CERT
            COMPLETE
```

This command stops the rolling forward of log records and completes the roll-forward recovery process by rolling back any incomplete transactions and turning off the roll-forward-pending state of the database. This allows access to the database or table spaces that have been rolled forward. The keywords STOP and COMPLETE are equivalent. When rolling table spaces forward to a point in time, the table spaces are placed in backup-pending state.

Here is output of the QUERY STATUS option:

```
                Rollforward Status

Input database alias               = db2cert
Number of nodes returned status    = 1
Node number                        = 0
Rollforward status                 = not pending
Next log file to be read           =
Log files processed                = S0000014.LOG - S0000018.LOG
Last committed transaction         = 2000-07-15-00.09.51.000000
```

Note that the status has now changed to not pending.

```
ROLLFORWARD DATABASE DB2CERT
            TO 2000-07-24-00.00.00.000000
            TABLESPACE (FILETS) ONLINE
```

This command rolls forward the FILETS table space to a particular point in time. Note that the roll-forward time is UTC, regardless of the local time.

Here is the output of the QUERY STATUS option (which is produced by default as a function of the above command):

Database Recovery

```
                    Rollforward Status

Input database alias                = db2cert
Number of nodes returned status     = 1
Node number                         = 0
Rollforward status                  = TBS working
Next log file to be read            =
Log files processed                 = -
Last committed transaction          = 2000-07-15-00.09.51.000000
```

Note that the status has now changed to TBS working, as this is a table space roll-forward. You can keep rolling forward past the nominated time, as there are still units of work that could be applied (note the "Last committed transaction" time is later than the requested point in time) or issue the ROLLFORWARD command with the COMPLETE option to roll back incomplete units of work and make the table space available for general use.

You can also use the Control Center to invoke a roll-forward. After right-clicking on the database you wish to roll-forward and selecting the **Roll-forward** option, the Roll-Forward panel is displayed (Fig. 11–13). You will not be able to enter this panel unless the database is in roll-forward-pending state.

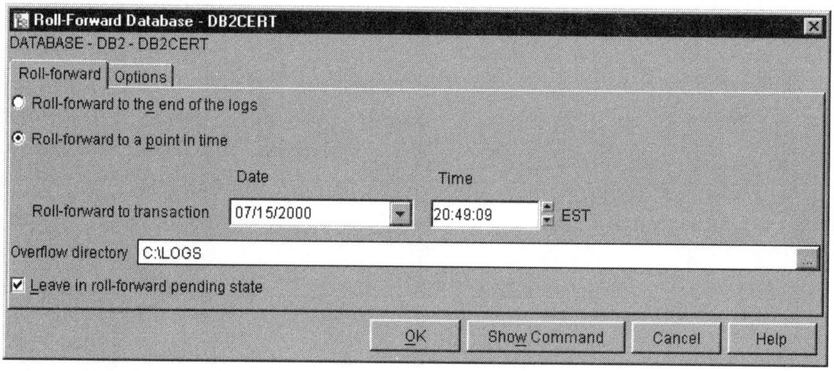

Fig. 11–13 *Control Center - Roll-forward database*

In this panel, you can see options for end of log recovery, point in time recovery, the overflow log path, and the leave in roll-forward-pending state (equivalent to the STOP/COMPLETE option). In the Options tab, you can choose whether the processing should be offline or online. Clicking on **OK** will submit a Control Center job to perform the roll-forward.

You can press the **Show Command** button to see the command issued by DB2. In addition, you can monitor the execution of the command (and see the results) in the Journal.

Managing Log Files

In this section, aspects of log file management will be reviewed, such as how log files are named and how to avoid losing them.

Log File Naming Scheme

Log file names are of the format Snnnnnnn.LOG, where nnnnnnn is a seven-digit number ranging from 0000000 to 9999999. When a database is first created, logs starting from S0000000.LOG are created.

DB2 restarts the log file numbering sequence at S0000000.LOG under the following conditions:

- When the database configuration file is changed to enable archive logging
- When the database configuration file is changed to disable archive logging
- When the log file sequence wraps, that is after log S9999999.LOG is used

When the ROLLFORWARD command has been run and you have issued the STOP/COMPLETE option successfully, the last log used is truncated and logging begins with the next sequential log. Any log in the log path directory with a sequence number greater than the last log used by ROLLFORWARD is reused. You can make a copy of the old logs and place them in a different directory if you want to be able to reexecute the ROLLFORWARD command using the old logs.

> DB2 V7.1 allows the database administrator to force the archive of a log on demand. This allows greater flexibility in managing log files, especially in situations that support offsite recovery.

Log File Placement for Recovery

DB2 ensures that an incorrect log is not applied during roll-forward recovery, but it cannot detect the location of the required logs.

If you moved log files to a location other than specified by the LOGPATH database configuration parameter, use the OVERFLOW LOG PATH parameter of the ROLLFORWARD command to specify the path for DB2 to search.

If you are rolling forward changes in a database or table space and ROLLFORWARD cannot find the next log, then ROLLFORWARD stops and returns the next log name in the SQL Communications Area (SQLCA).

If you change the log path directory via the NEWLOGPATH database configuration parameter, any existing archive logs are unaffected and do not get moved to the new path. You must keep track of the location of these logs.

Database Recovery

Losing Logs

Log files can be erased in the following ways:

- Dropping a database erases all logs in the current log path directory. You may need to back these logs up for any future restoration purposes.
- As noted previously, when recovering to a point in time, log files chronologically past the point in time are reused. If you need to restore again past the point in time used earlier, you cannot do so because the logs were reused. You must back up the original set of logs to a different location and copy them back for the restoration.
- If you change the log path directory and then remove the subdirectory or erase any logs in that subdirectory requested by DB2 in the log path, DB2 will look for logs in the default log path (SQLOGDIR) when the database is opened. If the logs are not found, the database will enter a backup-pending state.
- If you lose the log containing the point in time of the end of the online backup and you are rolling forward the corresponding restored image, the database will not be useable. To make the database usable, you must restore the database from a different backup and all its associated logs.

Prune Logfile Command

This command will delete all log files created prior to a nominated log file. It will only do so from the active log path, so if any log files have been moved to another path they will not be considered by this command. For example:

```
PRUNE LOGFILE PRIOR TO S0000100.LOG
```

This command will delete all log files in the active log path up to and including S0000099.LOG.

 DB2 V7.1 has increased the log size from 4 GB to 32 GB, allowing for even larger amounts of work to be executed within a transaction.

Other Recovery Considerations

Additional considerations related to recovery will be covered here, such as the time taken to recover a database, the recovery history file, and how to recover dropped tables.

Recovery Time Required

The time required to recover a database is composed of:

- The time required to complete the restore of the backup.
- If the database is recoverable, the time it takes to roll-forward through the logs.

When formulating a recovery plan, you should plan a sufficient amount of time for your business operations to be affected while the database is being recovered.

Testing your overall recovery plan will assist you in determining whether the time required to recover the database is reasonable given your business requirements. Following each test, you may want to increase the frequency with which you take a backup. If roll-forward recovery is part of the strategy, this will reduce the number of logs that are archived between backups and reduce the time taken in rolling forward through the units of work.

Storage Considerations For Log Files

To prevent a media failure from destroying a database and your ability to rebuild it, you should keep the database backup, the database logs, and the database itself on other devices. Use the LOGPATH database configuration parameter to move the logs to a new device once the database is created.

Because the log files can occupy a large amount of disk space, if you plan on using roll-forward-recovery, you have to plan how to manage the archive logs. You can:

- Dedicate enough space in the database log path directory to retain the logs
- Manually copy the archive logs to a storage device or directory other than the database log path directory
- Use a user exit program to copy the logs to another storage device

When using disk mirroring of the log files, you need to account for twice the amount of disk storage.

The Quiesce Command

You can issue the QUIESCE TABLESPACES FOR TABLE command to create a point of consistency that can be used for subsequent roll-forward recovery. When you quiesce table spaces for a table, the request will wait (through locking) for all running transactions that are accessing objects in the table spaces to complete, at the same time blocking new requests against the table spaces. When the quiesce request is granted, all outstanding transactions are already completed (committed or rolled back), and the table spaces are in a consistent state. You can look in the recovery history file to find quiesce points and check whether they are past the minimum recovery time to determine a desirable time to stop the roll-forward.

```
QUIESCE TABLESPACES FOR TABLE DB2CERT.EMPLOYEE SHARE
```

In the example above, when the quiesce share request is received, the transaction requests intent share locks for the table spaces and one for the table.
When the transaction obtains the locks, the state of the table spaces is changed to QUIESCED SHARE. The state is granted to the quiescer only if there is no conflicting state held by other users.

The table cannot be changed while the table spaces for the table are in QUIESCED SHARE state. Other share mode requests to the table and table spaces will be allowed. When the unit of work commits or rolls back, the locks are released, but the table spaces for the table remain in QUIESCED SHARE state until the state is explicitly reset by issuing the following command:

```
QUIESCE TABLESPACES FOR TABLE DB2CERT.EMPLOYEE RESET
```

The QUIESCE command can be invoked from the Command Line Processor, Command Center, or application programming interface.

The Recovery History File

A recovery history file is created with each database and is automatically updated whenever there is a:

- BACKUP of a database or table space
- RESTORE of a database or table space
- ROLLFORWARD of a database or table space
- ALTER of a table space
- QUIESCE of a table space
- DROP of a table
- LOAD of a table
- REORG of a table
- Updating of table statistics in the catalog via RUNSTATS

You can use the summarized backup information in this file to recover all or part of the database to a point in time. The information in the file includes:

- The part of the database that was copied and the copy procedure
- The time that the copy was made
- The location of the copy
- The last time a restore was done

Every backup operation includes a copy of the recovery history file. The file is linked to the database, so when a database is dropped, the file is deleted.

If the current database is unusable and the file is damaged or deleted, an option in the RESTORE command allows only the recovery history file to be restored.

The file is managed with the PRUNE HISTORY command. Entries in the file earlier than a specified date and time can be deleted with this command.

The LIST HISTORY command reports on information in the recovery history file. For example:

```
LIST HISTORY ALL FOR DB2CERT
```

This command produces this sample output:

```
                    List History File for db2cert
 Number of matching file entries = 45


 Op Obj Timestamp+Sequence Type Dev Earliest Log Current Log Backup ID
 -- --- ------------------ ---- --- ----------- ----------- ------------
 B D 20000715120004001   F    D S0000000.LOG S0000000.LOG
 ---------------------------------------------------------------------
 Contains 3     tablespace(s):

 00001 SYSCATSPACE
 00002 USERSPACE1
 00003 FILETS
 ---------------------------------------------------------------------
    Comment: DB2 BACKUP DB2CERT OFFLINE
 Start Time: 20000715120004
   End Time: 20000715120034
 ---------------------------------------------------------------------
 00001 Location: d:\temp\DB2CERT.0\DB2\NODE0000\CATN0000\20000715


 Op Obj Timestamp+Sequence Type Dev Earliest Log Current Log Backup ID
 -- --- ------------------ ---- --- ----------- ----------- ------------
 R D 20000715120335001   F    D                          20000715120004
 ---------------------------------------------------------------------
 Contains 3     tablespace(s):

 00001 SYSCATSPACE
 00002 USERSPACE1
 00003 FILETS
 ---------------------------------------------------------------------
    Comment: DB2 RESTORE DB2CERT WITH RF
```

```
Start Time: 20000715120335
  End Time: 20000715120352
----------------------------------------------------------------------
00002 Location: d:\temp\DB2CERT.0\DB2\NODE0000\CATN0000\20000715
```

Here is a backup and restore event displayed. Note that the full name and path of the backup is shown.

For further details on the contents of the recovery history file, please refer to the *DB2 UDB V7.1 Command Reference* and the *DB2 UDB V7.1 Administration Guide*.

Tables Related to Other Tables

If you want to roll-forward a table space to a point in time and a table in the table space participates in a referential constraint with another table in another table space, you should roll-forward both table spaces to the same point in time; otherwise, both tables will be placed into check-pending state.

Similarly, for an underlying table for a summary table that is in another table space or vice versa, you should roll-forward both table spaces to the same point in time; otherwise, the summary table is placed into check pending state.

When tables affect other tables via triggers, you should consider backing up and recovering the related table spaces together as well keeping the same consistency points and therefore the integrity of the data. The updates to the database as a result of triggers *firing* will still occur during roll-forward processing.

Dropped Table Recovery

Tables that have been accidentally dropped can be recovered using the following technique:

Prior to the table being accidentally dropped:

- Use the CREATE or ALTER TABLESPACE statement with the DROPPED TABLE RECOVERY ON option. DB2 will write additional log and recovery history file entries to support recovery of dropped tables.

When a table has been dropped and needs to be recovered, do the following:

- Extract the DDL from the recovery history file using the LIST HISTORY DROPPED TABLES command. This will provide you with not only the list of tables that have been dropped but also the statements needed to recreate them.
- Restore a database or table space from a backup image. Of course, this image must have coexisted before the table was dropped.
- roll-forward the database or table space using the RECOVER DROPPED TABLE option. This option requires you to specify both a tableid and an export direc-

tory. The `tableid` is taken from the LIST HISTORY command, and the export directory is the directory where DB2 will place an export file of the data for the dropped table.

* Recreate the table with the extracted DDL from the history file.
* Import the recovered data.

This technique should only be used on regular table spaces.

Reorganization of Tables

If you reorganize a table, you should back up the affected table spaces after the operation completes. If you later issue the roll forward command and you did not back up, you will have to roll forward through the entire REORG operation.

Large Objects

If a table contains long field or large object (LOB) columns, you should consider placing this data into a separate table space. With the amount of time and disk space potentially required to back up LOB data, by putting it in a separate table space, you can decide to back it up at a lower frequency than the regular table spaces.

You can also choose not to log LOB columns when creating or altering tables, which will also save log file space. This is feasible if the LOB data is easily recreatable.

Offline and Online Table Space States

During database start-up/activation, DB2 checks to make sure that all of the table space containers are accessible.

If a container is not accessible, the table space will be placed into an *offline* state in addition to the other recovery states it may have, such as back-up-pending, restore-pending, roll-forward-pending, and so on. So a table space may have a state of, for example, BACKUP PENDING + OFFLINE.

To get a table space back into an *online* state after resolving the container problem:

* Disconnect all applications and reconnect to or activate the database.
* If the database still has applications connected to it, use the ALTER TABLESPACE statement with the SWITCH ONLINE option.

The table space can also be dropped while in an *offline* state.

If the container problem cannot be resolved, to restart the database cleanly so that there are no errors, use the RESTART DATABASE command with the DROP PENDING TABLESPACES option. This will instruct DB2 to start the database successfully, even though the list of supplied table spaces are in error. Once the database is started, the only operation that can be performed on those table spaces that cannot be recovered is to drop them.

DB2 High Availability Support

DB2 supports high availability functionality, where in the event that one machine running a DB2 instance fails, another machine automatically takes over the processing for the failed machine.

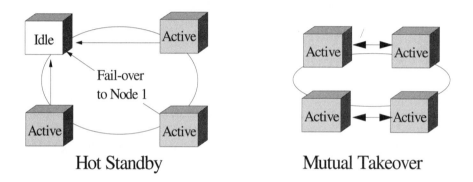

Fig. 11–14 *High availability scenarios*

For example, on AIX, this support uses and is enabled by the High Availability Cluster Multi-Processing (HACMP) product. HACMP provides increased availability through clusters of processors that share resources such as disks or network access. If one processor fails, another in the cluster can substitute for the failed one. Additional high-availability programs are available depending on the operating environment.

A brief description of the hot standby and mutual takeover modes follows.

- *Hot standby* - Active processors are being actively used to run the DB2 instance and a DB2 server is in standby mode ready to take over the instance if there is an operating system or hardware failure involving the first processor.

- *Mutual takeover* - The various processors are either used to run separate DB2 instances or used to run a DB2 instance while another processor is used to run DB2 applications. If there is an operating system or hardware failure on one of the processors, the other processor takes over the tasks of the failing processor. Once the failover is complete, the remaining processor is doing the work of both processors.

Summary

This chapter discussed concepts and facilities of DB2 recovery. These included:

- *Unit of work* - A recoverable sequence of operations within an application process. This could involve one or many SQL statements depending upon the business logic required. Either all the SQL covering the unit of work gets applied or none of it. This is also known as a *transaction*.

There are three kinds of recovery to consider:

- *Crash recovery* - Protects the database from being left in an inconsistent or unusable state. Unexpected interruptions that leave incomplete units of work are handled by crash recovery, which rolls back the changes made by uncommitted transactions.
- *Version recovery* - Allows the restoration of a database from a backup image taken at an earlier point in time. Table spaces can also be version recovered.
- *Roll-forward recovery* - Extends version recovery by using full database backups in conjunction with log files to provide the capability of recovering to any point in time covered by the log files.

Recoverable databases support crash, version, and roll-forward recovery. DB2 supports recoverable databases by allowing the LOGRETAIN and/or USEREXIT database configuration parameters. Nonrecoverable databases support crash and version recovery. DB2 implements this type of database by not allowing the use of the above two parameters.

Offline access to the database means that access to the database is in exclusive mode; no one else can connect to the database. Online access means that other applications can concurrently connect to the database when the particular operation is being performed.

Primary log files establish a fixed, preallocated amount of storage to the recovery log files. Enough disk space for the primary log files must be allocated before the database is connected to. Secondary log files are used when the primary log files become full and are allocated one at a time when required.

There are two kinds of logging supported by DB2:

- *Circular logging* - Supports nonrecoverable databases, as primary log files are reused in a circular manner.
- *Archival logging* - Supports recoverable databases by archiving logs once they have been written to; that is, log files are not reused.

Log files can be characterized as one of the following:

Database Recovery

- *Active log files* - The log files written to by DB2 that support crash recovery.
- *Archive log files* - The log files that have been written to by DB2 and are no longer needed to support crash recovery. Online archive log files reside in the active log path directory. Offline archive log files do no reside in the active log path directory. They can be moved manually or by an external storage management product.

The following DB2 commands enable the recoverability of databases:

- The BACKUP command creates images of databases or table spaces that are used for restoration purposes.
- The RESTORE command takes the backup images created by the BACKUP command and restores databases or table spaces.
- The ROLLFORWARD command supports roll-forward recovery by reapplying units of work captured in the log up to the nominated point in time that roll-forward recovery stops.
- The QUIESCE command establishes a point of consistency for related table spaces that can be used in roll-forward operations later on. It does this by taking locks on tables which ensures that no other application can update the tables being quiesced.

To improve the availability of DB2, you can use high availability products such as HACMP on AIX to implement hot standby and mutual takeover modes. This allows automatic switching of DB2 operations to a backup machine if the primary machine fails without interruption to operations. This can significantly improve the operational availability of DB2.

Monitoring and Tuning

- ◆ PLANNING
- ◆ DB2 ARCHITECTURE OVERVIEW
- ◆ DATABASE MONITORING
- ◆ SQL MONITORING
- ◆ TUNING CONFIGURATION PARAMETERS
- ◆ PROBLEM DETERMINATION

Understanding the performance of the DB2 database management system, its databases, and active applications in a dynamic environment requires monitoring. This means that a database administrator should gather information regarding the usage of the database. An application programmer may also require SQL statement execution information. Gathering database information using DB2's monitoring facilities and information regarding SQL statement processing will be discussed.

In this chapter, the various DB2 facilities for the monitoring and gathering of information that is input into the tuning process will be reviewed. The *Explain Facility*, *Snapshot Monitor*, and *Event Monitor* are the main tools used to monitor DB2 databases and SQL statements.

These tools may be used to perform the following tasks:

- Understand user and application activity within DB2
- Better understand how an SQL statement is processed
- Determine the sources and causes of problems
- Tune configuration parameters
- Improve database and application performance

Elements of Performance

Performance is the way a computer system behaves given a particular work load. Performance is measured through one or more of the system's response time, throughput, and availability. It is affected by:

- The resources available
- How well the resources are utilized

Performance tuning should be undertaken when you want to improve the cost-benefit ratio of your system. Specific situations include:

- You want to process a larger, more demanding work load without increasing processing costs that may include having to acquire additional hardware.
- Obtaining faster system response time, or higher throughput, without increasing processing costs.
- Reducing processing costs without negatively affecting service to the client(s).

Translating performance from technical terms to economic terms is difficult. Performance tuning costs money through labor and machine resources, so the cost of tuning must be weighed against the benefits tuning may or may not deliver.

Some of these benefits, including less resource usage and the ability to add more users to the system, are tangible, whereas other benefits, such as increased customer satisfaction, are less tangible from a monetary perspective.

Tuning Guidelines

The following guidelines should be considered in developing an overall approach to performance tuning:

Remember the Law of Diminishing Returns

Your greatest performance benefits usually come from your initial efforts. Further changes generally produce smaller and smaller benefits and require greater effort.

Do Not Tune Just for the Sake of Tuning

Tune to relieve identified constraints. If you tune resources that are not the primary cause of performance problems, this can have little or no effect on response time until you have relieved the major constraints, and it can actually make subsequent tuning work more difficult. If there is any significant improvement potential, it lies in improving the performance of the resources that are major factors in the response time.

Consider the Whole System

You can never tune one parameter or system in isolation. Before you make any adjustments, consider how it will affect the system as a whole.

Change One Parameter at a Time

Do not change more than one performance tuning parameter at a time. Even if you are sure that all the changes will be beneficial, you will have no way of evaluating how much each change has contributed. You also cannot effectively judge the trade-off you have made by changing more than one parameter at a time. Every time you adjust a parameter to improve one area, you almost always affect at least one other area that may not have been considered.

Measure and Reconfigure by Levels

For the same reasons that you should change only one parameter at a time, tune one level of your system at a time. You can use the following list of levels within a system as a guide:

- Hardware
- Operating system
- Application server and requester
- Database
- SQL statements
- Application programs

Check for Hardware and Software Problems

Some performance problems may be corrected by applying service to your hardware, your software, or to both. Do not spend excessive time monitoring and tuning your system when simply applying service may be the solution to the problem.

Understand the Problem Before Upgrading Hardware

Even if it seems that an additional storage or processor resource could immediately improve performance, take the time to understand where the bottlenecks are. You may spend money on additional disk storage only to find that you do not have the processor resource to exploit it.

Put Fall Back Procedures in Place Before You Start Tuning

Because changes are being made to an existing system, you must be prepared to back out those changes out if they do not have the desired effect or have a negative effect on the system.

Performance Improvement Process

Monitoring and tuning a database and its applications should be performed using the following basic process:

- Establish performance indicators.
- Define performance objectives.
- Develop a performance monitoring plan.
- Implement the plan.
- Analyze the measurements. Determine if the objectives have been met. If so, consider reducing the number of measurements to keep to a minimum the amount of resource consumed for monitoring.
- Determine the major constraints in the system.
- Decide where you can afford to make trade-offs and which resources can bear an additional load. Most tuning activities involve trade-offs among system resources and various elements of performance.
- Adjust the configuration of the system. If you think that it is feasible to change more than one tuning option, implement one at a time.
- Based on the results, start another iteration of the monitoring cycle.

You may want to follow the above process for periodic monitoring or when significant changes occur to the system and/or work load taken on by the system.

How Much Can a System Be Tuned?

There are limits to how much you can improve the efficiency of a system. Consider how much time and money you should spend on improving system performance and how much the spending of additional time and money will help the users of the system.

Your system may perform adequately without any tuning at all, but it probably will not perform to its potential. Each database is unique. As soon as you develop your own database and applications for it, investigate the tuning parameters available and learn how you can customize their settings to reflect your situation. In some circumstances, there will only be a small benefit from tuning a system. In most circumstances, however, the benefit may be significant.

There are wizards are available from the DB2 Control Center that assist in tuning the database parameters. The performance Configuration Wizard can be found by clicking the right mouse button on the database you want to tune.

If your system encounters performance bottlenecks, it is likely that tuning will be effective. If you are close to the performance limits, and you increase the number of users on the system by about 10%, the response time may rise by much more

Monitoring and Tuning

than 10%. In this situation, you will need to determine how to counterbalance this degradation in performance by tuning your system. However, there is a point beyond which tuning cannot help. At that point, you should consider revising your goals and expectations within that environment. Or you should change your system environment by considering more disk storage, faster/additional processors, additional memory, or faster networking solutions.

A Less-Formal Approach

If you do not have enough time to set performance objectives and to monitor and tune in a comprehensive manner, you can address performance by listening to your users. Find out if they are having performance-related problems. You can usually locate the problem or determine where to start looking for the problem by asking a few simple questions. For example, you can ask your users:

- What do you mean by slow response? Is it 10% slower than you expect it to be or ten times slower?
- When did you notice the problem? Is it recent or has it always been there?
- Do you know of other users who are complaining of the same problem? Are those complaining one or two individuals or a whole group?
- Are the problems you are experiencing related to a specific transaction or application program?
- Do your problems appear during regular periods, such as at lunch hour, or are they continuous?

DB2 Architecture Overview

To understand performance and what can be monitored, a brief overview of DB2 from an architectural perspective will be presented. The architectural components that will be examined include:

- Process model
- DB2 memory usage
- SQL compiler/optimizer

Process Model

The process model or server architecture for DB2 is known as an *n-n process model*. The main feature of this architecture is its ability to ensure database integrity. It isolates all database applications from critical database resources. These resources include database control blocks and critical database files.

During the database connection process, a DB2 coordinating agent is assigned to each database application. Each DB2 agent works on behalf of the database application and handles all of the SQL requests. The application and database agents communicate using Inter-Process Communication (IPC) techniques (such as message queues, shared memory, and semaphores). DB2 coordinating agents work with DB2 subagents if intra-partition parallelism is enabled.

> **Note:** The DB2 agents are *threads* in Windows and OS/2 and *processes* in UNIX operating systems.

This architecture provides a firewall to protect the database resources from an errant application.

Fenced/Not Fenced Resources

A database stored procedure is a dynamically loadable library that can be invoked from a database application by using the `CALL` statement. The library is stored on the DB2 database server, and it can execute as a *fenced* resource or a *not fenced* resource. A fenced resource is one that executes in a separate process from the database agent. A not fenced resource will execute in the same process as the database agent.

> **Note:** A DB2 stored procedure is also called a Dynamic Application Remote Interface (*DARI*) process.

Monitoring and Tuning

A not fenced resource will have better performance than a fenced resource since there is less interprocess communication overhead. However, a not fenced resource can overwrite DB2 control blocks if it is not well tested.

 Note: User-defined functions (UDFs) can also be defined to execute as a fenced or unfenced (not fenced) resource.

Query Parallelism

In Chapter 1, the scalability options of how DB2 can grow from a small uniprocessor machine to a massively parallel system was briefly discussed. There are certain elements inside DB2 that take advantage of hardware parallelism in addition to the benefits of a multitasking operating system. The exploitation of parallelism has significant performance benefits for queries against DB2 as well as other administrative tasks.

There are two types of query parallelism: *inter-query* parallelism and *intra-query* parallelism.

- *Inter-query* parallelism refers to the ability of multiple applications to query a database at the same time. Each query will execute independently of the others, but DB2 will execute all of them at the same time. DB2 has always supported this type of parallelism.
- *Intra-query* parallelism refers to the processing of parts of a single query at the same time using either *intra-partition* parallelism or *inter-partition* parallelism or both. With intra-query parallelism, one single complex query can be taken by the DB2 optimizer and split into pieces that can be executed in parallel.

Intra-Partition Parallelism

Intra-partition parallelism refers to the ability to break up a query into multiple parts. This type of parallelism subdivides what is usually considered a single database operation such as index creation, database load, or SQL queries into multiple parts, many or all of which can be executed in parallel within a single database partition. Intra-partition parallelism is best suited to take advantage of the symmetric multiprocessor (SMP) system. See Fig. 12–1.

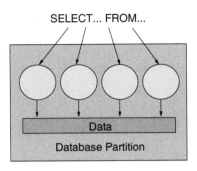

Fig. 12–1 *Intra-partition parallelism*

Fig. 12–1 shows a query broken into four pieces that can be executed in parallel, with the results returned more quickly than if the query were run in a serial fashion. To utilize intra-partition parallelism, you need to configure the database appropriately. You can choose the degree of parallelism or let the system do it for you. The degree of parallelism is the number of pieces of a query that execute in parallel. It will be discussed later in this section.

Inter-Partition Parallelism

Inter-partition parallelism refers to the ability to break up a query into multiple parts across multiple partitions of a partitioned database on one machine or multiple machines. The query is performed in parallel. Inter-partition parallelism is best suited to take advantage of the massively parallel processing (MPP) system. See Fig. 12–2.

Monitoring and Tuning

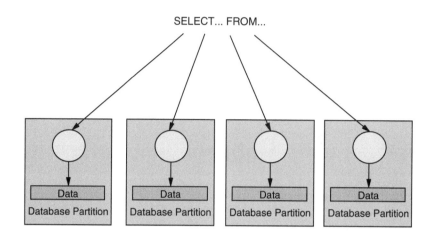

Fig. 12–2 *Inter-partition parallelism*

Fig. 12–2 shows a query broken into four pieces that can be executed in parallel, with the results returned more quickly than if the query were run in a serial fashion in a single partition. The degree of parallelism is largely determined by the number of partitions you create and how you define your nodegroups. DB2 Enterprise-Extended Edition (EEE) needs to be installed to enable the inter-partition parallelism as well as combining intra-partition and inter-partition parallelism. This product is covered in detail in the *DB2 Cluster Certification Guide*.

Subsection Piece (SSP) of Intra-Partition Parallelism

In a parallel environment, the DB2 optimizer considers access plans that do not run a complete query but break the query down into different parts (also called *query decomposition*). The DB2 optimizer considers different groupings of operators that can be sent to different processes or threads to be executed. The parts are called Subsection Pieces (SSPs) with one SQL statement consisting of one or many subsection pieces.

 Note: The use of subsection pieces or SSPs will only be considered by the optimizer if intra-partition parallelism is enabled.

A subsection piece is a sequence of one or more database operators belonging to the same SQL query that, when executed, completes the processing part of that query. A subsection piece must be executed in one DB2 process or thread. A subsection piece may receive data from other DB2 subsection pieces or feed data to another subsection piece or return data to the user. Subsection pieces can be cloned or duplicated by the optimizer to speed up the processing.

DB2 provides the capability to change the *degree of parallelism*. The degree of parallelism limits the number of SSPs a query can be broken down into.

The optimizer handles all of this behind the scenes; therefore, users do not need to change anything in their applications to utilize SMP parallelism other than setting the intra-parallel database manager configuration parameter to yes and setting the degree of parallelism >1. Users can explicitly set the degree of parallelism for the DB2 instance, the application, or the statement. In addition, if a section is built by the optimizer with a specific degree of parallelism, it will be reduced if the instance default degree of parallelism is lower.

When breaking a query into multiple SSPs, the optimizer will also determine if the SSPs will work on the same data or if the data can be partitioned among the SSPs. In determining the optimal way to split the section into SSPs and to partition the data, the optimizer will be mainly influenced by the degree of parallelism and the cardinality of the data.

In an SMP environment, the SSPs will be duplicates or clones of each other. DB2 will then execute the SSPs in parallel and return the results faster than if the query were run on one processor. Each SSP copy will work on a subset of the data. As determined by the optimizer, this subset may be based on the data values or on equal divisions of the data based on the number of rows.

Note: If the degree of parallelism is set to a value >1, the number of SSPs created is equal to that value.

DB2 Memory Usage

Database activity involves disk access (I/O) and memory access (CPU). Each of the DB2 configuration parameters affects either the memory or disk resources. Because disk access is much slower than memory access is, the key database performance tuning objective is to decrease the amount of disk activity. If you are able to eliminate I/O wait time, the database requests are CPU bound, and increasing performance would then require faster CPUs or multiple CPUs.

Monitoring and Tuning

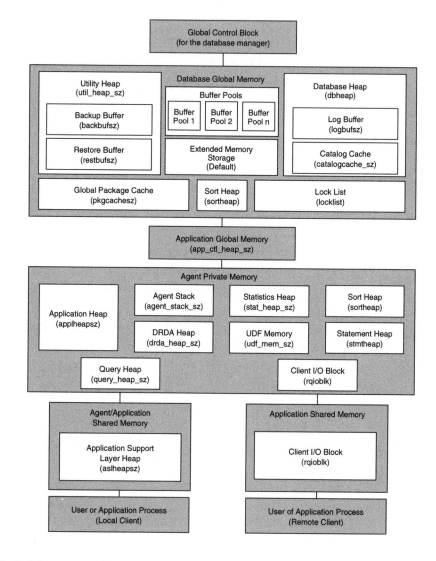

Fig. 12–3 *Memory used by DB2*

Fig. 12–3 shows the relationship of the various configurable memory parameters. Memory is allocated on the server or the client. The number of memory segments allocated for the Database Global Memory depends on the number of currently active databases.

Each DB2 application has an associated DB2 *coordinating agent*. The database agent accesses the database resources on behalf of the application. Therefore, there are tuning parameters that adjust resource usage of the database agent. The Agent Private Memory exists for each agent, and the size is determined by the values of the following parameters:

- Application heap size (`applheapsz`)
- Sort heap size (`sortheap`)
- Statement heap size (`stmtheap`)
- Statistics heap size (`stat_heap_sz`)
- Query heap size (`query_heap_sz`)
- DRDA heap size (`drda_heap_sz`)
- UDF shared memory set size (`udf_mem_sz`)
- Agent stack size (`agent_stack_sz`)

If intra-partition parallelism is enabled by setting the intra-parallel database manager configuration parameter to yes, which is the default value in an SMP environment, the coordinating agent distributes database requests to *subagents*, and these agents perform the requests for the application. Once the coordinating agent is created, it handles all database requests on behalf of its application by coordinating the subagents that perform requests on the database.

The application control heap is used as a global work area for all the agents (coordinating and subordinate) working for the application. The database parameter is `APP_CTL_HEAP_SZ`.

The memory area, known as application shared memory, is used to determine the amount of memory used to communicate between the application and its DB2 coordinating agent. Record blocking occurs within this memory area. The DBM parameter is `ASLHEAPSZ`.

SQL Compiler Overview

The SQL compiler performs a number of tasks during the creation of the compiled form of the SQL statements. These phases are described below and are also shown in Fig. 12–4 on page 597. As you can see in this figure, the representation of the query is stored in an internal in-memory structure known as the *Query Graph Model*.

- Parse query - The first task of the SQL compiler is to analyze the SQL query to validate the syntax. If any syntax errors are detected, the SQL compiler stops processing, and the appropriate SQL error is returned to the application attempting to compile the SQL statement. When parsing is complete, an internal representation of the query is created.
- Check Semantics - The second task of the compiler is to further validate the SQL statement by checking to ensure that the parts of the statement make sense

Monitoring and Tuning

given the other parts, for example, ensuring that the data types of the columns input into scalar functions are correct for those functions.

Also during this stage, the compiler adds the behavioral semantics to the query graph model, such as the effects of referential constraints, table check constraints, triggers, and views.

- Rewrite query - The SQL compiler uses global semantics provided in the query graph model to transform the query into a form that can be optimized more easily. For example, the compiler might move a predicate, altering the level at which it is applied, in an attempt to improve query performance. This particular process is called *general predicate pushdown*.

  Any changes made to the query are rewritten back to the query graph model.

- Optimize access plan - The SQL optimizer portion of the SQL compiler uses the query graph model as input and generates many alternative execution plans for satisfying the user's request. It estimates the execution cost of each alternative plan using the statistics for tables, indexes, columns, and functions, and chooses the plan with the smallest estimated execution cost.

  The optimizer uses the query graph model to analyze the query semantics and to obtain information about a wide variety of factors, including indexes, base tables, derived tables, subqueries, correlation, and recursion.

  The output from this step of the SQL compiler is an access plan. The access plan provides the basis for the information captured in the *explain tables*. The information used to generate the access plan can be captured with an *explain snapshot*.

- Generate executable code - The final step of the SQL compiler uses the access plan and the query graph model to create an executable access plan, or section, for the query. This code generation step uses information from the query graph model to avoid repetitive execution of expressions that only need to be computed once for a query. Examples for which this optimization is possible include code page conversions and the use of host variables.

Information about access plans for static SQL is stored in the system catalog tables. When the package is executed, DB2 will use the information stored in the system catalog tables to determine how to access the data and provide results for the query. It is this information that is used by the db2expln tool.

It is recommended that the RUNSTATS command be done periodically on tables used in queries where good performance is desired. The optimizer will then be better equipped with relevant statistical information on the nature of the data. If the RUNSTATS command is not run, or the optimizer determines that RUNSTATS was run on empty or near-empty tables, the optimizer may either use defaults or attempt to derive certain statistics based on the number of file pages used to store the table on disk.

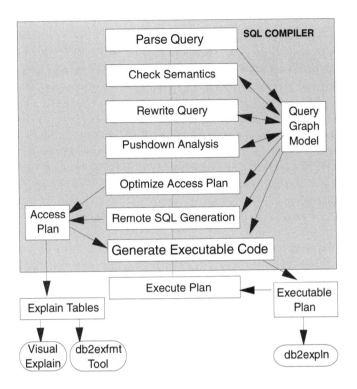

Fig. 12–4 *Steps performed by SQL compiler*

Explain information must be captured before you can review it using one of DB2's explain tools. You can decide to capture detailed information regarding the access plan. While the query is being compiled, the information can be captured into a file or special tables known as explain tables.

DB2 Sorting Methods

When an SQL query requires the data to be returned in a defined sequence or order, the result may or may not require sorting. DB2 will attempt to perform the ordering through index usage. If an index cannot be used, the sort will occur. A sort involves two steps:

1. A sort phase

2. Return of the results of the sort phase

How the sort is handled within these two steps results in different categories or types by which the sort can be described. When considering the sort phase, the sort can be categorized as *overflowed* or *nonoverflowed*. When considering the return of the results of the sort phase, the sort can be categorized as *piped* or *non-piped*.

Overflowed and Nonoverflowed

If the information being sorted cannot fit entirely into the sort heap (a block of memory that is allocated each time a sort is performed), it overflows into temporary database tables. Sorts that do not overflow always perform better than those that do.

Piped and Non-Piped

If sorted information can return directly without requiring a temporary table to store a final, sorted list of data, it is referred to as a piped sort. If the sorted information requires a temporary table to be returned, it is referred to as a non-piped sort. A piped sort always performs better than a non-piped sort.

The DB2 optimizer will determine if a nonoverflowed sort can be performed and if a piped sort can be performed by comparing the expected result set with the value of the SORTHEAP database configuration parameter, and so forth.

 Note: To obtain an ordered result set, a sort is not always required. If an index scan is the access method used, then the data is already in the order of the index, and sorting is not required.

Database Monitoring

There are various methods to obtain the required monitoring information. These methods involve using the following DB2 facilities: *Explain Facility*, *Snapshot Monitor*, and *Event Monitor*. The following is a description of the information provided by the Explain Facility and the database monitors:

- Choose the Snapshot or Event Monitor if you want to gather data about DB2's operation, performance, and the applications using it. This data is maintained as DB2 runs and can provide important performance and troubleshooting information.

- Choose the Explain Facility if you want to analyze the access plan for an SQL statement or a group of SQL statements.

This chapter will give you information to decide which of the existing facilities is the best for your needs. It shows how to capture data using the Explain Facility, the Snapshot Monitor, the Event Monitor, and the graphical Performance Monitor and how to interpret the collected information.

This chapter also gives you information on how to diagnose problems in DB2 applications, ODBC applications, and also in DB2 databases.

Obtaining Database Access Information

The first step in the database monitoring process is defining your objectives. Defining the objectives is very important in selecting the best facility to meet your requirements. An objective can be:

- Understanding how a given query will be optimized in a specific environment. For example, there is a query used in an application that does not perform well.
- Understanding how applications use database manager resources at a specific point of time. For example, database concurrency is reduced if a specific application is started.
- Understanding which database manager events have occurred when running applications. For example, you notice a degradation in overall performance when certain applications are run.

Database Monitors

DB2 monitors are used to collect detailed resource usage information. Monitoring activity may be performed from a DB2 client or a DB2 server. The monitor interface can be invoked using CLP commands, graphical Performance Monitors, or monitoring APIs. DB2 provides different kinds of monitoring, which differ in the way monitoring data is gathered. The two ways of monitoring are:

Monitoring and Tuning

- *Snapshot Monitoring* - Provides information regarding database activity at a specific point in time. It is a picture of the current state of DB2 activity. The amount of data returned to the user when a snapshot is taken is determined using monitor switches. These switches can be set at the instance or application level.
- *Event Monitoring* - Records the occurrence of specific milestones of DB2 events. This can allow you to collect information about transient events, including deadlocks, connections, and SQL statements.

The two monitoring options are discussed in the following pages.

Snapshot Monitoring

The Snapshot Monitor provides cumulative information in the form of counters. These counters can be reset. The snapshot information is provided in special data structures that can be examined by the application issuing the snapshot.

The amount of data returned by the Snapshot Monitor is set according to switches. The monitor switches, along with the information they provide, are displayed in the following table.

Table 12–1 *Data Returned by the Snapshot Monitor*

Group	Information Provided	Monitor Switch	DBM Parameter
Sorts	Number of heaps used, overflows, sorts performance	SORT	DFT_MON_SORT
Locks	Number of locks held, number of deadlocks	LOCK	DFT_MON_LOCK
Tables	Measure activity (rows read, rows written)	TABLE	DFT_MON_TABLE
Bufferpools	Number of reads and writes, time taken	BUFFERPOOL	DFT_MON_BUFPOOL
Unit of work	Start times, end times, completion status	UOW	DFT_MON_UOW
SQL statements	Start time, stop time, statement identification	STATEMENT	DFT_MON_STMT

The monitor switches can be turned on and off at the instance (DBM configuration) level or at the application level (using the UPDATE MONITOR SWITCHES command). There is also base information provided by the Snapshot Monitor that is gathered regardless of the monitor switches settings.

Setting the instance configuration parameters for monitor switches will affect all databases within the instance. Every application connecting to a database will inherit the default switches set within the DBM configuration.

 Note: DB2 Snapshot Monitors can only be used by users having SYSADM, SYSCTRL, or SYSMAINT authority. Event Monitors require SYSADM or DBADM authority.

For example, to capture detailed information about SQL statements executing in DB2, the appropriate monitor switches must be turned on. The commands are:

```
UPDATE DBM CONFIGURATION USING DFT_MON_STMT ON
```

You can alternatively use this command:

```
UPDATE MONITOR SWITCHES USING STATEMENT ON
```

The UPDATE DBM CONFIGURATION command will modify the database manager configuration. Therefore, SQL statement information will be captured for applications accessing all databases within the instance.

 Note: When you change the value of the database manager configuration parameters, you usually need to stop and start the instance to make those changes effective; however, the changes of the default monitor switches will be effective immediately. Therefore, you don't need to stop and start the instance.

On the other hand, the UPDATE MONITOR SWITCHES command will only capture SQL statements for the application that activated the switch. (In this example, the application is the command line processor.)

 Note: Even if none of the switches are turned on, there will be some basic information captured by the Snapshot Monitor.

Monitoring and Tuning

Viewing Snapshot Monitor Data

When a monitor switch is turned on, the monitor data starts being collected. To view the monitor data, a *snapshot* must be taken.

 Note: There is a minor performance effect when the data is recorded. Issuing the snapshot has additional performance overhead.

A snapshot is requested using the DB2 command GET SNAPSHOT. This command can be executed in different ways. It can be executed within the Command Center GUI tool, embedded in an application using the appropriate API, executed from the Command Center or CLP, or executed by the Performance Monitor.

The graphical Performance Monitor is integrated into the Control Center GUI tool. Before the output of the Snapshot Monitor is examined, how the snapshot information is captured will be discussed. Use the Command Center interface to capture database monitor snapshots. While taking a snapshot, it is possible to define a particular area of interest.

There are different levels of monitoring used with the Snapshot Monitor. These levels allow you to focus your analysis in a particular area of interest.

The following Snapshot Monitor levels are available:

- *Database manager* - Captures information for an active instance
- *Database* - Captures database(s) information
- *Application* - Captures application(s) information
- *Bufferpools* - Captures buffer pool activity information
- *Table space* - Captures information for table spaces within a database
- *Table* - Captures information for tables within a database
- *Lock* - Captures information for locks held by applications against a database
- *Dynamic SQL* - Captures point-in-time statement information from the SQL statement cache for the database

Snapshot Monitor switches and levels are combined to provide different monitoring information when taking a snapshot. The two are very closely related. If the proper monitor switch is not turned on, the snapshot level used may not return any data.

As said before, the GET SNAPSHOT command is used to review the Snapshot Monitor data.

To gather lock information for the Certification database, execute the following DB2 command from the Command Center:

```
GET SNAPSHOT FOR LOCKS ON db2cert
```

The output of the snapshot is displayed in the Command Center Results window. It is a good idea to save the output to a file for analysis purposes.

The output of the SNAPSHOT FOR LOCKS command is shown in Fig. 12–5. If you want detailed information about locks, as shown in Fig. 12–5, you must turn on the Lock Monitor Switch.

Analyzing the snapshot, you can see that the first application (application ID *LOCAL.db2cert.000613040452) is in Lock-Wait status. It is attempting to acquire a row lock on a row having an X lock held by the second application (application ID *LOCAL.db2cert.000613145839). To release the lock, the application holding it must complete its transaction using a COMMIT or ROLLBACK statement.

Note: The LOCKTIMEOUT database configuration parameter controls the maximum time that an application should wait in Lock-Wait status. Its default value is to wait until the locked resource is available.

```
                    Database Lock Snapshot

Database name                          = DB2CERT
Database path                          = /db2db/db2cert/NODE0000/SQL00001/
Input database alias                   = DB2CERT
Locks held                             = 19
Applications currently connected       = 3
Agents currently waiting on locks      = 1
Snapshot timestamp                     = 06-13-2000 10:26:33.523028

Application handle                     = 0
Application ID                         = *LOCAL.db2cert.000613040452
Sequence number                        = 0001
Application name                       = db2bp_r
Authorization ID                       = DB2CERT
Application status                     = Lock-wait
Status change time                     = Not Collected
Application code page                  = 819
Locks held                            = 7
Total wait time (ms)                   = 502724

   Subsection waiting for lock         = 0
   ID of agent holding lock            = 1
   Application ID holding lock         = *LOCAL.db2cert.000613145839
   Lock object type                    = Row
   Lock mode                           = Exclusive Lock (X)
   Name of tablespace holding lock     = USERSPACE1
   Schema of table holding lock        = DB2CERT
   Name of table holding lock          = CANDIDATE
   Lock wait start timestamp           = 06-13-2000 10:18:10.799239

Object Name Object Type Tablespace Name Table Schema Table Name   Mode Status
----------- ----------- --------------- ------------ ------------ ---- --------
30          Table       USERSPACE1      DB2CERT      CANDIDATE    IS   Granted
0           Internal                                              S    Granted
20          Row         SYSCATSPACE     SYSIBM       SYSDATATYPES S    Granted
22          Table       SYSCATSPACE     SYSIBM       SYSDATATYPES IS   Granted
2313        Row         SYSCATSPACE     SYSIBM       SYSTABLES    S    Granted
2           Table       SYSCATSPACE     SYSIBM       SYSTABLES    IS   Granted
0           Internal                                              S    Granted

Application handle                     = 1
Application ID                         = *LOCAL.db2cert.000613145839
Sequence number                        = 0001
Application name                       = db2bp_r
Authorization ID                       = DB2CERT
Application status                     = UOW Waiting
Status change time                     = Not Collected
Application code page                  = 819
Locks held                            = 12
Total wait time (ms)                   = 0

Object Name Object Type Tablespace Name Table Schema Table Name   Mode Status
----------- ----------- --------------- ------------ ------------ ---- ------
11          Row         USERSPACE1      DB2CERT      CANDIDATE    X    Granted
10          Row         USERSPACE1      DB2CERT      CANDIDATE    X    Granted
9           Row         USERSPACE1      DB2CERT      CANDIDATE    X    Granted
8           Row         USERSPACE1      DB2CERT      CANDIDATE    X    Granted
7           Row         USERSPACE1      DB2CERT      CANDIDATE    X    Granted
```

Fig. 12–5 *Output of GET SNAPSHOT for locks on DB2CERT*

The information provided by the Snapshot Monitor is a valuable resource to solve many problems. At the time of the snapshot shown in Fig. 12–5, there was a concurrency problem in the database. Therefore, the LOCKS monitoring level was used to analyze the database activity.

The information from APPLICATIONS Snapshot Monitor level as shown in Fig. 12–6 was taken using the following command:

```
GET SNAPSHOT FOR APPLICATIONS ON db2cert
```

```
                  Application Snapshot

Application handle                        = 1
Application status                        = Lock-wait
Status change time                        = Not Collected
Application code page                      = 819
Application country code                   = 1
DUOW correlation token                     = *LOCAL.db2cert.000613040432
Application name                          = db2bp_r
Application ID                            = *LOCAL.db2cert.000613040452
Sequence number                          = 0001
Connection request start timestamp         = 06-13-2000 23:04:52.725918
Connect request completion timestamp       = 06-13-2000 23:04:53.355324
Application idle time                      = Not Collected
Authorization ID                          = DB2CERT
Execution ID                             = db2cert
Configuration NNAME of client              =
Client database manager product ID         = SQL06010
Process ID of client application           = 24030
Platform of client application             = AIX
Communication protocol of client           = Local Client
Database name                            = DB2CERT
Database path                            = /db2db/db2cert/NODE0000/SQL00001/
Client database alias                     = db2cert
Input database alias                      = DB2CERT
Last reset timestamp                      =
Snapshot timestamp                        = 06-13-2000 13:52:55.373922
......
Locks held by application                  = 8
Lock escalations                          = 0
Exclusive lock escalations                 = 0
Number of Lock Timeouts since connected    = 0
Total time UOW waited on locks (ms)        = Not Collected
......
Number of SQL requests since last commit   = 38
Commit statements                        = 43
Rollback statements                       = 5
Dynamic SQL statements attempted           = 486
Static SQL statements attempted            = 48
Failed statement operations                = 6
Select SQL statements executed             = 38
Update/Insert/Delete statements executed   = 2
DDL statements executed                    = 6
.......
Internal rollbacks due to deadlock         = 0
Rows deleted                             = 0
Rows inserted                            = 18
Rows updated                             = 0
```

Fig. 12–6 *Partial output of Get Snapshot for applications command*

The snapshot provides detailed data about the activity of applications. In this example, only a portion of the output is shown. Using this snapshot, you can see application activity, such as how may rows have been read, updated, or deleted by an application. To obtain more information regarding database objects shown in an application snapshot, such as tables or locks, the appropriate monitor switches and monitoring levels should be used.

To review a table level snapshot, issue the following command:

```
GET SNAPSHOT FOR TABLES ON db2cert
```

The output from the table level snapshot is shown in Fig. 12–7. By using a table snapshot, further information can be obtained, such as which table has the most activity in the database.

```
              Table Snapshot

First database connect timestamp      = 06-13-2000 23:04:52.725918

Last reset timestamp                  =
Snapshot timestamp                    = 06-13-2000 14:21:13.529358
Database name                         = DB2CERT
Database path                         = /db2db/db2cert/NODE0000/SQL00001/
Input database alias                  = DB2CERT
Number of accessed tables             = 6

Table Schema     Table Name     Table Type    Rows    Written    Rows Read  Overflows
---------------  ------------   -----------   -------  ---------  ---------- --------
SYSIBM           SYSFUNCTIONS   Catalog          0        4          0          0
SYSIBM           SYSTABLES      Catalog          0        8          0          0
SYSIBM           SYSPLAN        Catalog          0        2          0          0
SYSIBM           SYSDBAUTH      Catalog          0        4          0          0
DB2CERT          CANDIDATE      User            24       48          0          0
SYSIBM           SYSDATATYPES   Catalog          0        8          0          0
```

Fig. 12–7 *GET SNAPSHOT for tables on the db2cert database*

 Note: To collect the snapshot information shown in Fig. 12–7, the TABLE monitor switch must be set to ON.

The table snapshot output shows different tables being accessed. In our example, user and catalog tables were accessed. Catalog tables are used by DB2 for different activities, such as checking the authorizations granted to the user requesting an SQL statement, reviewing distinct types used, and so on.

The snapshots that have been presented show data related to DB2 logical objects, such as tables, locks, and applications. Snapshots can be used to provide information related to the physical database environment, such as disk activity and memory usage. This kind of information is gathered using a table space level snapshot using the command below. Partial output follows in Figure 12–8.

```
GET SNAPSHOT FOR TABLESPACES ON db2cert
```

```
                    Tablespace Snapshot

First database connect timestamp        = 06-13-2000 14:59:55.061853
Last reset timestamp                    =
Snapshot timestamp                      = 06-13-2000 15:04:20.450507
Database name                           = DB2CERT
Database path                           = /db2db/db2cert/NODE0000/SQL00001/
Input database alias                    = DB2CERT
Number of accessed tablespaces          = 3

Tablespace name                         = SYSCATSPACE
  Data pages copied to extended storage    = 0
  Index pages copied to extended storage   = 0
  Data pages copied from extended storage  = 0
  Index pages copied from extended storage = 0
  Buffer pool data logical reads        = 33
  Buffer pool data physical reads       = 9
  Asynchronous pool data page reads     = 0
  Buffer pool data writes               = 0
  Asynchronous pool data page writes    = 0
  Buffer pool index logical reads       = 71
  Buffer pool index physical reads      = 23
  Asynchronous pool index page reads    = 0
  Buffer pool index writes              = 0
  Asynchronous pool index page writes   = 0
  Total buffer pool read time (ms)      = 399
  Total buffer pool write time (ms)     = 0
  Total elapsed asynchronous read time  = 0
  Total elapsed asynchronous write time = 0
  Asynchronous read requests            = 0

  Direct reads                          = 40
  Direct writes                         = 0
  Direct read requests                  = 8
  Direct write requests                 = 0
  Direct reads elapsed time (ms)        = 97
  Direct write elapsed time (ms)        = 0
  Number of files closed                = 0
.....
Tablespace name                         = USERSPACE1

  Data pages copied to extended storage    = 0
  Index pages copied to extended storage   = 0
  Data pages copied from extended storage  = 0
  Index pages copied from extended storage = 0
  Buffer pool data logical reads        = 32
  Buffer pool data physical reads       = 4
  Asynchronous pool data page reads     = 0
  Buffer pool data writes               = 0
  Asynchronous pool data page writes    = 0
  Buffer pool index logical reads       = 20
  Buffer pool index physical reads      = 10
  Asynchronous pool index page reads    = 0
  Buffer pool index writes              = 0
  Asynchronous pool index page writes   = 0
  Total buffer pool read time (ms)      = 132
  Total buffer pool write time (ms)     = 0
  Total elapsed asynchronous read time  = 0
  Total elapsed asynchronous write time = 0
  Asynchronous read requests            = 0

  Direct reads                          = 576
```

Fig. 12–8 *Partial output of GET SNAPSHOT for table spaces on DB2CERT*

The snapshot in Fig. 12–8 is organized according to the I/O and buffer pool activity for each table space. The data captured shows different counters representing time (expressed in milliseconds) or times that a different activity has occurred. Along with the table space information, this monitor level shows information about the buffer pool usage. Buffer pool information is only gathered if the BUFFERPOOL monitor switch is turned on.

Any I/O prefetching activity is shown as asynchronous reads, and any buffer pool asynchronous page cleaning is shown as asynchronous writes. The term direct read/write corresponds to synchronous reads or writes.

Reviewing the Snapshot Monitor Switch Status

At any time, you can determine the current settings of database monitor switches by issuing the following command:

```
GET MONITOR SWITCHES
```

The switch states are shown in Fig. 12–9. The timestamps correspond to the last time the switches were reset or turned on.

```
                    Monitor Recording Switches

Buffer Pool Activity Information  (BUFFERPOOL) = OFF
Lock Information                        (LOCK) = ON  06-12-2000 15:01:22.624422
Sorting Information                     (SORT) = OFF
SQL Statement Information          (STATEMENT) = ON  06-12-2000 15:01:27.155032
Table Activity Information             (TABLE) = ON  06-12-2000 15:01:09.482143
Unit of Work Information                 (UOW) = ON  06-12-2000 15:01:15.340116
```

Fig. 12–9 *Monitor switch settings*

The monitor switch settings for an application are shown in Fig. 12–9. If you want to know the instance settings for the monitor switches, use the following command:

```
GET DBM MONITOR SWITCHES
```

Resetting the Snapshot Monitor Switches

As demonstrated, the data returned by a Snapshot Monitor is based primarily on counters. These counters are associated with a monitor switch.

Monitor switches are initialized or reset when one of the following occurs:

- Application level monitoring is used, and the application connects to the database.

- Database level monitoring is used, and the first application connects.
- Table level monitoring is used, and the table is first accessed.
- Table space level monitoring is used, and the table space is first accessed.
- Issuing the RESET MONITOR command.
- Turning on a particular monitor switch.

Monitor switches can be reset at any time by issuing the command:

```
RESET MONITOR FOR DATABASE db2cert
```

Resetting the monitor switches effectively starts all of the counters at zero, and further snapshots are based on the new counter values.

To reset the monitor switches for all databases within an instance, the RESET MONITOR ALL command should be used.

Note: Every application has its own copy of the snapshot monitor values. Reseting the monitor switches only affects the counters of the application that issues the reset.

Event Monitoring

While Snapshot Monitoring records the state of database activity when the snapshot is taken, an Event Monitor records the database activity when an *event* or *transition* occurs. Some database activities that need to be monitored cannot be easily captured using the Snapshot Monitor. These activities include deadlock scenarios. When a deadlock occurs, DB2 will resolve the deadlock by issuing a ROLLBACK for one of the transactions. Information regarding the deadlock event cannot be easily captured using the Snapshot Monitor because the deadlock was probably resolved before a snapshot could be taken.

Event Monitors are created using SQL Data Definition Language (DDL) like other database objects. Event Monitors can be turned on or off much like the Snapshot Monitor switches.

Note: SYSADM or DBADM authority is required to create an Event Monitor.

Monitoring and Tuning

When an Event Monitor is created, the type of event to be monitored must be stated. The Event Monitor can monitor the following events:

- *Database* - Records an event record when the last application disconnects from the database.
- *Tables* - Records an event record for each active table when the last application disconnects from the database. An active table is a table that has changed since the first connection to the database.
- *Deadlocks* - Records an event record for each deadlock event.
- *Tablespaces* - Records an event record for each active table space when the last application disconnects from the database.
- *Bufferpools* - Records an event record for buffer pools when the last application disconnects from the database.
- *Connections* - Records an event record for each database connection event when an application disconnects from a database.
- *Statements* - Records an event record for every SQL statement issued by an application (dynamic and static).
- *Transactions* - Records an event record for every transaction when it completes (COMMIT or ROLLBACK statement).

As shown above, many types of event monitors generate an event record when the last application is disconnected. However, you can use the FLUSH EVENT MONITOR command to write out current database monitor values for all active monitor types associated with a particular event monitor.

```
FLUSH EVENT MONITOR evmon_name
```

The event records written out by this command are noted in the Event Monitor log with *a partial record identifier.* You should be aware that flushing out the Event Monitor will not cause the Event Monitor values to be reset. This means that the Event Monitor record that would have been generated if no flush were performed will still be generated when the normal monitor event is triggered.

Note: Event Monitors can be created using either using SQL or the db2emcrt GUI tool. This is discussed in more detail below.

The output of an Event Monitor is stored in a directory or in a named pipe. The existence of the pipe or the file will be verified when the Event Monitor is activated. If the target location for an Event Monitor is a named pipe, then it is the responsibility of the application to promptly read the data from the pipe. If the target for an Event Monitor is a directory, then the stream of data will be written to a series of files. The files are sequentially numbered and have a file extension of "evt" (e.g., `00000000.evt` and `00000001.evt`). The maximum size and number of Event Monitor files is specified when the monitor is defined.

> **Note:** An Event Monitor will turn itself off if the defined file space has been exceeded.

Creating Event Monitors

As mentioned, Event Monitors are database objects created using SQL DDL statements. The `db2emcrt` GUI tool can also be used to create event monitors. In this example, a deadlock Event Monitor will be created to store its event records in the "`/eventmonitors/deadlock/evmon1`" directory. The SQL method will be used to do this.

> **Note:** The Event Monitor output directory will not be created by DB2. It must be created by the database administrator, and the instance owner must be able to write to the specified directory.

The following SQL statement creates an Event Monitor. In our example, the Event Monitor is called `evmon1`.

```
CREATE EVENT MONITOR evmon1 FOR DEADLOCKS
WRITE TO FILE '/eventmonitors/deadlock/evmon1'
MAXFILES 3 MAXFILESIZE 1000
```

This Event Monitor is defined to allocate up to three files, each 4 MB in size, for a total monitor storage area of 12 MB. Other Event Monitor options include specifying the size of the write buffer, synchronous (BLOCKED) writes, asynchronous (UNBLOCKED) writes, APPEND the Event Monitor data to existing records, or REPLACE the Event Monitor data in the directory when the monitor is activated.

Monitoring and Tuning

The following two system catalog tables are used to store Event Monitor definitions:

- SYSCAT.EVENTMONITORS - Contains a record for each Event Monitor, including the current state of the Event Monitor.
- SYSCAT.EVENTS - Contains a record for each event being monitored. A single Event Monitor can be defined to monitor multiple events (e.g., DEADLOCKS and STATEMENTS).

Event Monitors can be defined to monitor many different types of database activities. A filter can also be specified for an Event Monitor, which can be based on the APPL_ID, AUTH_ID, or APPL_NAME (e.g., AUTH_ID='DB2CERT', APPL_NAME='PROGRAM1').

Note: There is no limit in the number of defined Event Monitors, but a maximum of 32 Event Monitors can be active per DB2 instance at a time.

Starting and Stopping Event Monitors

An Event Monitor must be active in order to collect the monitoring data. Once the Event Monitor has been defined using the CREATE EVENT MONITOR statement, it must be activated. The following statement is used to activate an Event Monitor.

```
SET EVENT MONITOR evmon1 STATE = 1
```

When the Event Monitor has been activated, Event Monitor records are written to the files contained in the defined directory or pipe (such as /eventmonitors/deadlocks/evmon1 in our example).

An Event Monitor can be started automatically each time the database is started using the AUTOSTART option. This option is specified at creation time.

Note: The GUI tool db2emcrt allows you to create and start an Event Monitor in the one operation. It also allows you to stop the monitor.

To turn off an Event Monitor, the SET EVENT MONITOR STATE statement is once again used:

```
SET EVENT MONITOR evmon1 STATE = 0
```

Turning off an Event Monitor will also flush all of its contents.

Even when an Event Monitor has been turned off, it is still defined in the system catalog tables. However, it is not recording monitor information.

To determine if an Event Monitor is active or inactive, use the SQL function EVENT_MON_STATE or view the status in the GUI panel of db2emcrt. The EVENT_MON_STATE function returns a value of "1" if the Event Monitor is active and "0" if the monitor is not active.

A sample SQL statement using the EVENT_MON_STATE function to query the state of the evmon1 Event Monitor is as follows:

```
SELECT evmonname, EVENT_MON_STATE(evmonname)
FROM SYSCAT.EVENTMONITORS WHERE evmonname = 'EVMON1'
```

Removing an Event Monitor

Just like other database objects, Event Monitors can be dropped from the database. Removing the definition will remove the associated rows in the SYSCAT.EVENTMONITORS and SYSCAT.EVENTS system catalog views. An example of removing the evmon1 Event Monitor is as follows:

```
DROP EVENT MONITOR evmon1
```

Event Monitor Records

Event Monitor files cannot be analyzed directly. An application must be used. There are a few alternatives provided by DB2 for analyzing Event Monitor data that will be discussed. First some of the Event Monitor records will be examined.

To ensure that all of the event records have been written to disk (some may be buffered), simply turn the Event Monitor off. You can also use the BUFFER option of FLUSH EVENT MONITOR command as follows:

```
FLUSH EVENT MONITOR evmon1 BUFFER
```

It forces the Event Monitor buffers to be written out. The FLUSH EVENT MONITOR command with the BUFFER option does not generate a partial record. Only the data already present in the Event Monitor buffers are written out.

Event monitoring is similar to tracing since each event is recorded as it occurs, and it is appended to the event record log files. An Event Monitor file will contain a number of event records covering event types including:

- Connections
- SQL statements
- Transactions
- Deadlocks
- Buffer pool events
- Table space events
- Table events

If an Event Monitor is monitoring database, table space, or table events, it will write complete event records when the last application using the database disconnects. As already explained, you can use the FLUSH EVENT MONITOR command to record the partial event records.

Analyzing Event Monitor Output

There are three utilities available to analyze Event Monitor data:

- *db2evmon* - A text-based tool that will read the event records and generate a report.
- *db2eva* - A GUI tool that can be invoked from a command line.
- *db2emcrt* - Another GUI tool allowing you to view reports graphically and much more. This can be invoked either from the command line by issuing the db2emcrt command or from the DB2 folder (if available on your platform) as the **Event Monitor** entry.

In this section, the db2evmon utility program is reviewed. The db2eva GUI tool will be discussed later in the chapter. The graphical utility called db2emcrt will not be discussed here and is left for the reader to explore.

A deadlock situation will now be created to demonstrate the Event Monitor. To do this, you need two DB2 Command Center windows with the AUTOCOMMIT feature turned off. Don't forget to make sure you have created an event monitor for DEADLOCKS and activate it. Here are the steps to create a deadlock situation:

- In the first window, issue: LOCK TABLE TEST_TAKEN IN SHARE MODE
- In the second window, issue: LOCK TABLE TEST IN SHARE MODE
- Back in the first window, issue: LOCK TABLE TEST IN EXCLUSIVE MODE
- Back in the second window, issue: LOCK TABLE TEST_TAKEN IN EXCLUSIVE MODE

These steps will generate a deadlock situation that will be resolved by DB2. The data captured by the deadlock Event Monitor evmon1 will now be analyzed.

To generate the Event Monitor report for the evmon1 monitor, issue the following command indicating where the event monitor files are located:

```
db2evmon -path /eventmonitors/deadlock/evmon1
```

or

```
db2evmon -db db2cert -evm evmon1
```

The -path option of the db2evmon command is used to indicate the path where the Event Monitor files reside.

> **Note:** It is a good idea to name the directories used for Event Monitor files using the type of Event Monitor (deadlock) and its name (evmon1).

The output of the db2evmon utility will be displayed on the screen by default. It is best to redirect the output to a file for analysis. A portion of the Event Monitor output for the evmon1 Event Monitor as shown in Fig. 12–10 will now be examined.

```
------------------------------------------------------------------------
                            EVENT LOG HEADER
    Event Monitor name: EVMON1
    Server Product ID: SQL07010
    Version of event monitor data: 6
    Byte order: LITTLE ENDIAN
    Number of nodes in db2 instance: 1
    Codepage of database: 1252
    Country code of database: 1
    Server instance name: DB2
------------------------------------------------------------------------


------------------------------------------------------------------------
    Database Name: DB2CERT
    Database Path: H:\DB2\NODE0000\SQL00002\
    First connection timestamp: 07-17-2000 20:31:35.953271
    Event Monitor Start time:   07-17-2000 20:51:50.622910
------------------------------------------------------------------------

8) Deadlock Event ...
    Number of applications deadlocked: 2
    Deadlock detection time: 07-17-2000 20:53:39.275268
    Rolled back Appl Id: : *LOCAL.DB2.000718012735
    Rolled back Appl seq number: : 0001

9) Deadlocked Connection ...
    Appl Id: *LOCAL.DB2.000718012735
    Appl Seq number: 0001
    Appl Id of connection holding the lock: *LOCAL.DB2.000718012741
    Seq. no. of connection holding the lock: 0001
    Lock wait start time: 07-17-2000 20:53:29.893465
    Requesting lock as part of escalation: FALSE
    Deadlock detection time: 07-17-2000 20:53:39.275268
    Table of lock waited on      : TEST_TAKEN
    Schema of lock waited on     : DB2CERT
    Tablespace of lock waited on : USERSPACE1
    Type of lock: Table
    Mode of lock: S
    Mode application requested on lock: X
    Node lock occured on: 0
    Lock object name: 5
    Application Handle: 11

10) Deadlocked Connection ...
    Appl Id: *LOCAL.DB2.000718012741
    Appl Seq number: 0001
    Appl Id of connection holding the lock: *LOCAL.DB2.000718012735
    Seq. no. of connection holding the lock: 0001
    Lock wait start time: 07-17-2000 20:53:23.737501
    Requesting lock as part of escalation: FALSE
    Deadlock detection time: 07-17-2000 20:53:39.275268
    Table of lock waited on      : TEST
    Schema of lock waited on     : DB2CERT
    Tablespace of lock waited on : USERSPACE1
    Type of lock: Table
    Mode of lock: S
    Mode application requested on lock: X
    Node lock occured on: 0
    Lock object name: 3
    Application Handle: 12
```

Fig. 12–10 *Deadlock event monitor records*

In Fig. 12–10, a deadlock event record and two deadlock connection event records
are shown. The information identifies the two applications involved in the deadlock and the reason for the deadlock.

In this example, the deadlock involves two shared locks: one on the DB2CERT.TEST_TAKEN table and the other on the DB2CERT.TEST table. The Event Monitor shows the ID of the application that was rolled back and the time when the deadlock occurred.

Using an Event Monitor to capture deadlock information is just one of its uses. For example, you can monitor every SQL statement issued against a database or every SQL statement issued by a particular application.

Visual Performance Monitors

The steps involved in obtaining Snapshot and Event Monitor data has been reviewed. DB2 provides graphical interfaces that allow you to analyze and gather monitoring data for the Snapshot and Event Monitors. These tools are:

- *Event Analyzer* - Allows you to analyze the Event Monitor files
- *Performance Monitor* - Allows you to analyze and view graphical representations of the Snapshot Monitor

Event Analyzer/Monitor

The Event Analyzer is the graphical equivalent to the db2evmon tool that was reviewed in previous sections.

The Event Analyzer displays the Event Monitor records that have been previously collected. To invoke the Event Analyzer, execute the db2eva command. If you are working on a Windows or OS/2 machine, you can select the **Event Analyzer** icon in the DB2 folder.

The window shown in Fig. 12–11 appears. Enter the path where the Event Monitor files reside and also select the database.

Monitoring and
Tuning

Fig. 12–11 *Event Analyzer initial window*

Click **OK** after entering the path and the database name. Then you will see the window as shown in Fig. 12–12. It displays the time frames when the Event Monitor, which used the specified path, has been active.

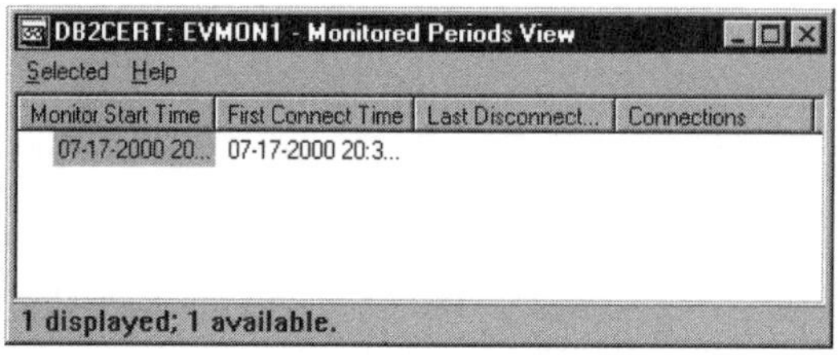

Fig. 12–12 *Monitored periods view of an event monitor*

From the Monitored Periods View window, as shown in Fig. 12–12, you can analyze the event records for a specific time frame when the Event Monitor was active. Right-click on the desired time period to bring up a pop-up menu. From the pop-up menu, you should select the event to analyze. In this example, select the **DEADLOCK** event. This is shown in Fig. 12–13.

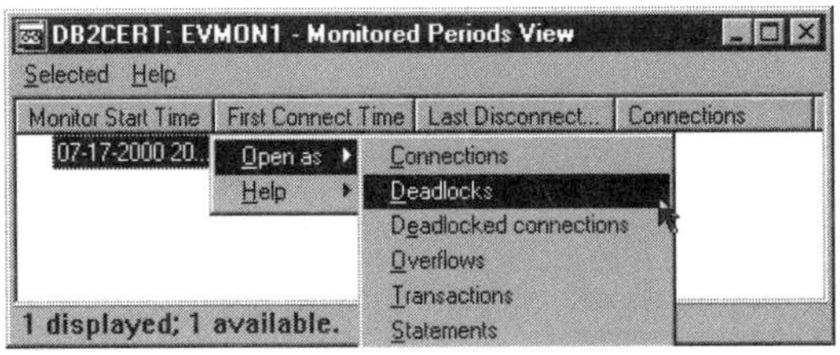

Fig. 12–13 *Selecting the deadlock event for a particular period of time*

After selecting the deadlock Event Monitor, notice the information in the Deadlocks View window as shown in Fig. 12–14.

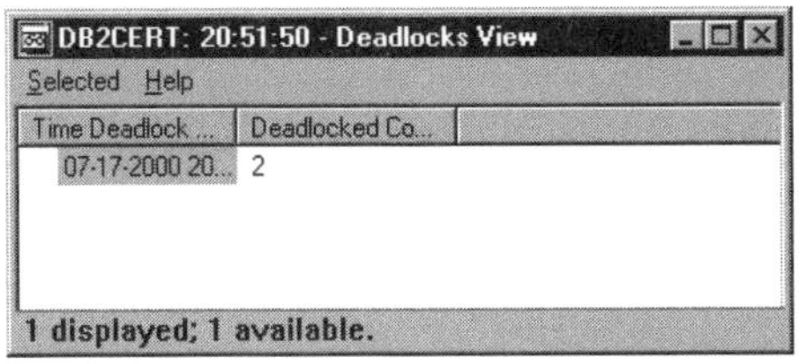

Fig. 12–14 *Deadlock event view*

The Deadlocks View window indicates that a deadlock was detected. Right-clicking the selected item will display the next level of detail.

Fig. 12–14 displayed two connections that caused the deadlock. Right-click and select **Open as Deadlocked Connections**. The Deadlocked Connections window is shown in Fig. 12–15.

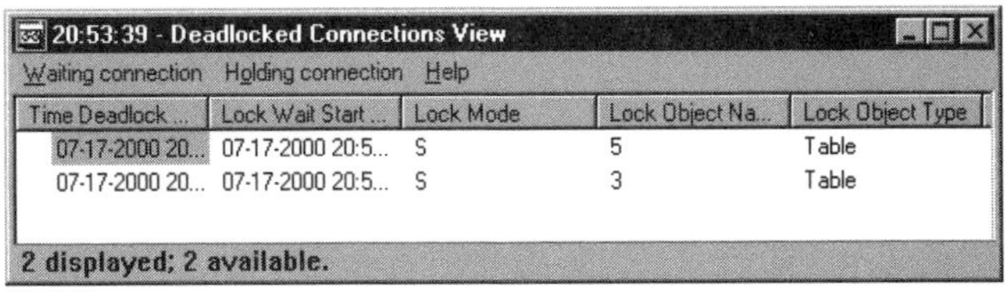

Fig. 12–15 *Deadlocked Connections view*

If you want additional information on the connection, select the **Open as → Data Elements** option from the Waiting or Holding connection menus. Fig. 12–16 shows the data available on the Waiting connection of the deadlock.

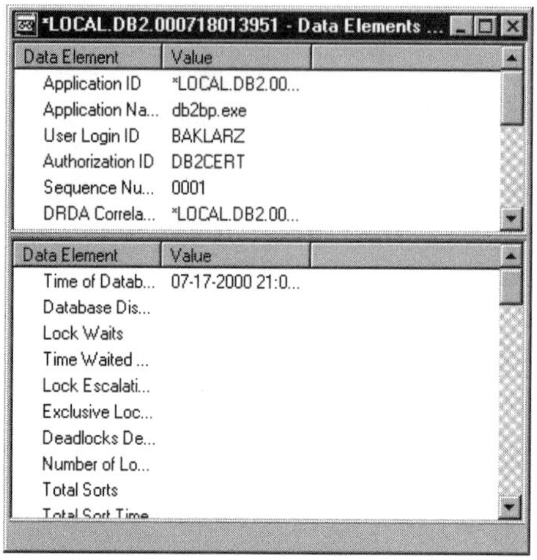

Fig. 12–16 *Waiting connection deadlock data*

The Event Analyzer will only display previously captured data. Therefore, there is no overhead in using the Event Analyzer as there is with the Snapshot Monitor. The Event Analyzer may not contain the desired information as it can only display the event records that have been previously captured. For example, if you select **Open as Statements** and no statement information was defined for the Event Monitor, the display will not contain SQL statement information.

To start the Event Analyzer, select the **Event Analyzer** icon from the DB2 folder. You can also select the **Event Monitor** icon from the DB2 folder. It brings up an initial window that prompts you to enter the database name. You will then see the window as shown in Fig. 12–17.

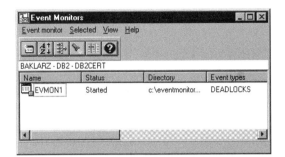

Fig. 12–17 *Event Monitor window*

You can see all Event Monitors defined in the database. Right-clicking one of them and selecting **View Event Monitor files** brings up the same windows as shown in Fig. 12–12 on page 618.

Performance Monitor

The Performance Monitor is a graphical utility that can be used to display snapshot information at predefined intervals (the default interval is 30 seconds). It can monitor DB2 objects, such as instances, databases, table spaces, tables, or connections. The information from the Performance Monitor can be used to:

- Detect performance problems
- Tune databases for optimum performance
- Analyze performance trends
- Analyze the performance of database applications
- Prevent problems from occurring

The Performance Monitor is initiated from the Control Center interface.

Note: On the Windows platform, the DB2 Performance Monitor is closely integrated with the Windows Performance Monitor so that it can be used to monitor DB2 activity in the Windows environment.

When an object is being monitored, the color of the icon appears green, yellow, or red to indicate the status of the monitor. The colors represent the severity of the problems as defined by the thresholds that you have set. Green signifies that the monitor is running and everything is fine. Yellow is a warning and signifies that the monitor is reaching the thresholds that you have set. Red indicates an alarm and that the monitor has reached the threshold.

Monitoring and Tuning

You use the Performance Monitor when you need to monitor an existing problem or when you want to observe the performance of your system. It lets you take a snapshot of database activity and performance data at a point in time. These snapshots are used for comparisons over time. Each point on the performance graph represents a data value.

Performance monitoring in DB2 can be done using the predefined monitors provided when DB2 is installed, or you can copy and modify them to meet your requirements. Use the predefined monitors to learn about performance monitoring and to create your own monitors by copying a predefined monitor and adding or removing performance variables from your own monitors. The predefined monitors that are supplied with DB2 include:

- *Monitoring Capacity* - Used to get information on system capacity. This monitor can be checked on a regular basis to see the overall usage of your system over time.
- *Sort* - Used to ensure that your sort heap and sort heap threshold parameters are set correctly. This monitor should be run when you first start your system, in peak periods of activity, or as applications change.
- *Locking* - Used to determine how much locking is occurring in your system and whether your lock list parameters are appropriately set.
- *Cache* - Used to optimize cache usage. By monitoring these values during peak periods, you can determine if you need to increase the size of the cache.
- *Deadlocks* - Used to determine whether your applications are getting into deadlocks.
- *Prefetchers* - Used to determine whether you have enough prefetchers defined for the system.
- *Disk Performance* - Used to watch input and output. This monitor contains performance variables that focus on disk performance at the database and table space levels.
- *Global Memory* - Used to watch application memory use.
- *Long Running Query* - Used to help determine why a query is taking a long time to complete.

To see a list of available monitors, from the Control Center, click the right mouse button on the **Systems** folder and select **List Monitors** from the pop-up menu. The List Monitors window opens as shown in Fig. 12–18.

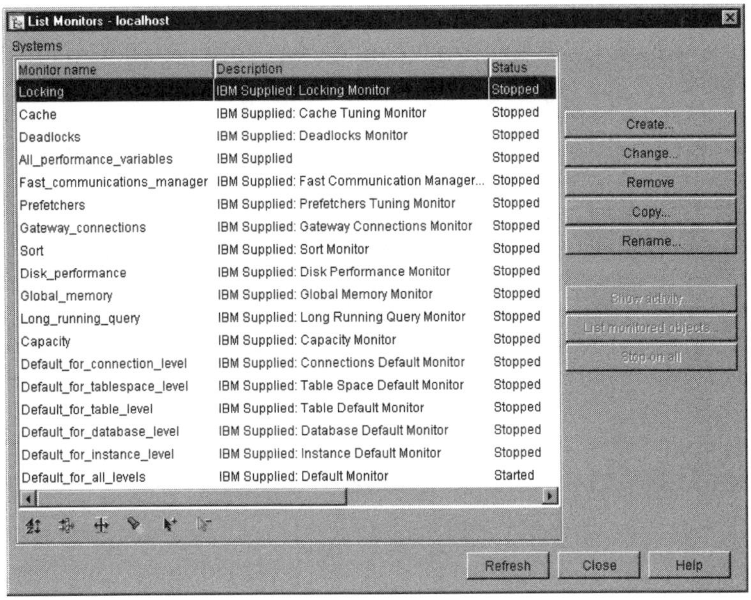

Fig. 12–18 *List performance monitors window*

Fig. 12–18 shows the predefined monitors. The right side of the window contains buttons that allow you to perform various tasks on the monitors. You can create, change, remove, copy, or rename monitors listed in this window. However, regarding a predefined monitor, you cannot change its name, equation, or text description. What you can do with a predefined monitor is change its threshold values, change alert actions, or copy it.

One of the predefined monitors will be examined and modified to meet our requirements. Select a monitor from the List Monitor window, click the **Copy** button, and enter the new monitor name in the copy window. You will see the new monitor name in the List Monitors window. Then select the new monitor and click the **Change** button. This will bring up the Change Monitor window.

Fig. 12–19 shows the Change Monitor window. In our example, the new monitor was copied from the Default_for_database_level monitor that is one of the predefined monitors. This was saved as the Database_New monitor.

Monitoring and Tuning

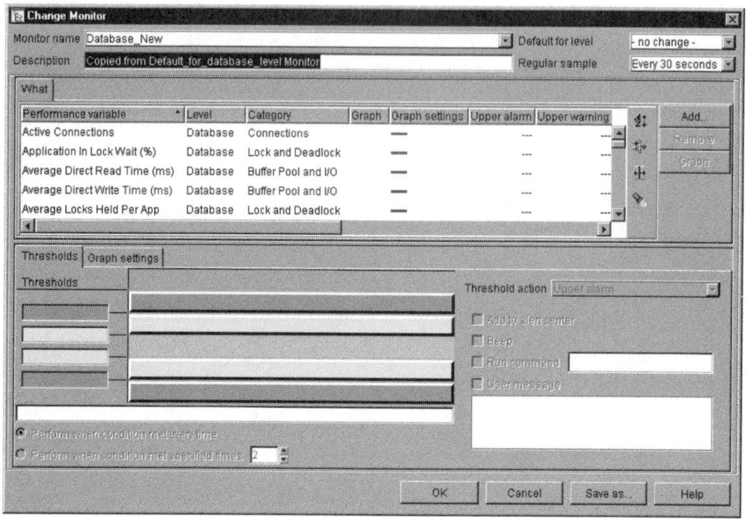

Fig. 12–19 *Change performance monitor window*

This window shows the performance variables that the monitor includes. If you want to add more performance variables to this monitor, click the **Add** button. All available performance variables are displayed, and you can select from there (see Fig. 12–20).

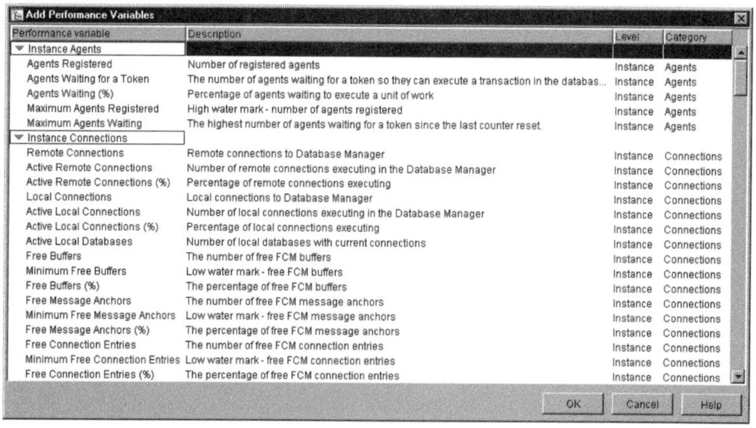

Fig. 12–20 *Add Performance Variables for a performance monitor*

The lower side of the window (Fig. 12–19) shows the graph settings. You can see whether each performance variable is displayed in the graph. You can also set the thresholds for each variable. You should define the warning and alarm zone borders for the selected performance variables.

When you define a threshold, you can set how DB2 responds when the value exceeds this threshold. The possible responses are:

- Adding an entry to the Alert Center
- Issuing a warning beep
- Have a program or script start
- Have a message sent to the user by bringing up a pop-up window

The database object DB2CERT will be monitored using the Database_New monitor, which is copied from the predefined Default_for_database_level monitor. Right-click the DB2CERT database icon, then select **Performance monitoring** and **Start Monitor**. This brings up the Start monitor window as shown in Fig. 12–21. Select the monitor you want to start (in our example, Database_New) and click **OK**. In the Control Center window, the icon of the database object DB2CERT that is being monitored will appear green. As explained before, the colors represent the severity of the problems as defined by the thresholds that you have set. Green signifies that the monitor is running and everything is fine.

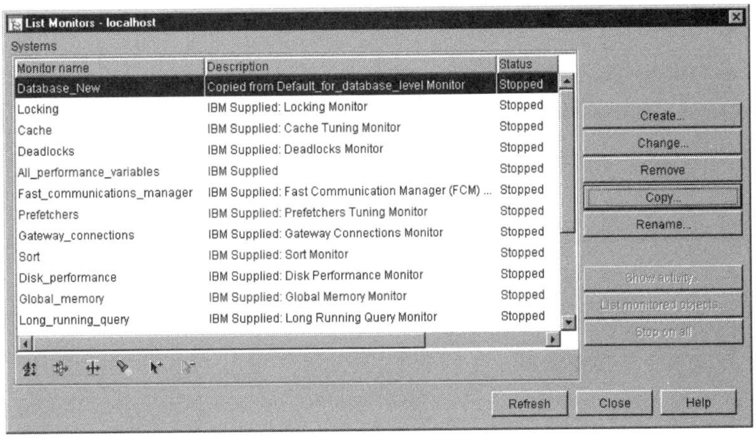

Fig. 12–21 *Start monitor window*

Note: Only one monitor can be active at a time per instance.

You can specify which monitor is used as the default monitor for the instance level, the database level, the table space level, the table level, and the connection level. If you want to change the database level default monitor, for example, right-click the **Databases** folder in the Control Center, select **Performance monitoring** and

Change default monitor, and then select a monitor from the displayed monitors that you want to specify as the default.

> **Note:** You can also change the default monitor by changing the value of *Default for level* field in the Change Monitor window.

When you start a performance monitor, you can select the monitor from the Start Monitor window as shown in Fig. 12–21 and also define it as the default monitor in advance and start it. To start the database level default monitor, right-click on a database object, then select **Performance monitoring** and **Start default monitor**.

Once monitoring has started, the information the Performance Monitor is gathering can be displayed. To see the information that the Database_New monitor has been collecting, right-click the DB2CERT database icon, select **Performance monitoring** and **Show monitor activity**. The Show Monitor window is shown in Fig. 12–22.

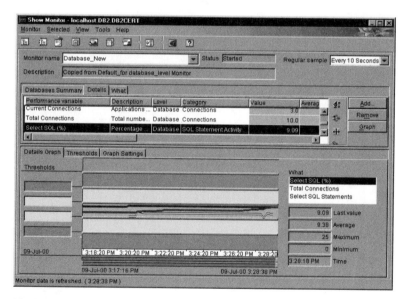

Fig. 12–22 *Show Monitor window*

This window displays the values of all the performance variables monitored. In Fig. 12–22, the upper side of the window displays the detailed data of each performance variable. You can also display the summary data or the description of each performance variable by clicking the **Database summary** tag or the **What** tag.

In the lower side of the window, the values of performance variables can be graphed over time to record gradual performance changes or to compare one performance variable with another. The graph is drawn based on the threshold you defined. If the value of the performance variable is between the upper warning value and the lower warning value, the graph is drawn in the green band. In this example, Total Connections and SQL activity are displayed. Each performance variable has thresholds, and if the value exceeds the threshold, an entry is added to the Alert Center.

When the Performance Monitor places an entry in the Alert Center, the Alert Center only displays where the alert took place. To see what values have exceeded thresholds, you must click on the relevant entry to look at the Performance Details. The entries in the Alert Center will be erased when the value of the performance variable is out from the warning or alert zone.

DB2 Governor

When monitoring DB2, you can detect where bottlenecks are occurring in the system, where certain types of database activity are occurring, and if DB2 is using all the server's resources to their full extent. You can also analyze the behavior of database applications to see if certain applications are more resource intensive than others. However, if an application is resource intensive or is stopping other applications from obtaining resources, the DBA must first detect the application using monitoring techniques and then change the behavior of the application or explicitly force the application off the system.

The *DB2 Governor* is a server application that performs such checking automatically. The governor can also force an application that is deemed to be using too many resources on the server. (Please note that you can also use the FORCE APPLICATIONS command of DB2 to force an application or all applications off of the instance. Please refer to the *DB2 UDB V7.1 Command Reference* for further details on this command.)

The governor collects statistics about applications running against a database. It then checks these statistics against rules that have been specified for that database. Such rules might include:

- Increase the priority of application *X* so that it always completes quickly.
- Slow down a subset of applications, namely *A*, *B*, and *C*.
- Don't let any unit of work run for more than 15 minutes.

The governor then enforces these rules by changing the parameters for the specified applications or by forcing the application off the system. You start and stop the DB2 Governor the same way you might start and stop monitoring DB2. For example, using a governor configuration file (which contains the governor rules) called

Monitoring and Tuning

`mygov.cfg`, you can start the governor monitoring the DB2CERT database using the `db2gov` utility at the operating system command prompt.

```
db2gov START DB2CERT mygov.cfg gov.log
```

The file that was specified, `gov.log`, is where the DB2 Governor will log any actions it takes. You can then stop the governor running against the DB2CERT database.

```
db2gov STOP DB2CERT
```

You can have multiple instances of the DB2 Governor running against multiple databases. The DB2 Governor does incur a performance impact when running against a DB2 database because it collects statistics and monitors the activity of database applications at regular intervals. You can examine the logs generated by the DB2 Governor using the `db2govlg` tool.

SQL Monitoring

If you want to know how a query will be executed by DB2, you must analyze its *access plan*, which is the method for retrieving data from a specific table. The explain facilities will provide information about how DB2 accesses the data to resolve the SQL statements.

Before describing the capabilities and features of the explain facilities, you should understand at a high level how SQL statements are processed by the DB2 database engine. Each SQL statement is analyzed by DB2, and then it is determined how to process the statement during a static bind or when executed dynamically. The method used to retrieve data from tables is called the *access plan*.

The component within DB2 that determines the access plan to be used is known as the optimizer. During the static preparation of an SQL statement, the SQL compiler is called on to generate an access plan. The access plan contains the data access strategy including index usage, sort methods, locking semantics, and join methods. The executable form of the SQL statement is stored in the system catalog tables when a BIND command is executed (assuming a deferred binding method). This is called a *package*.

> **Note:** The method for retrieving data from a specific table, such as whether indexes are used, is called the access path. The access plan involves a set of access paths.

Sometimes, the complete statement is not known at application development time. In this case, the compiler is invoked during program execution to generate an access plan for the query that can be used by the database manager to access the data. Such an SQL statement is called a dynamic SQL statement. The access plans for a dynamic SQL statement are not stored in the system catalogs. They are temporarily stored in memory (known as the global package cache). The compiler will not be invoked if the access plans for the dynamic SQL statements already exist in the package cache.

Explain Tables

DB2 uses explain tables to store access plan information so that users can see the decisions the optimizer has made. These tables are called:

- EXPLAIN_ARGUMENT - Represents the unique characteristics for each individual operator.

- EXPLAIN_INSTANCE - Main control table for all explain information. Each row of data in the explain tables is explicitly linked to one unique row in this table. Basic information about the source of the SQL statements being explained and environment information is kept in this table.
- EXPLAIN_OBJECT - Contains data objects required by the access plan generated to satisfy the SQL statement.
- EXPLAIN_OPERATOR - Contains all the operators needed to satisfy the SQL statement.
- EXPLAIN_PREDICATE - Identifies which predicates are applied by a specific operator.
- EXPLAIN_STATEMENT - Contains the text of the SQL statement in two forms. The original version entered by the user is stored in addition to the re-written version that is the result of the compilation process.
- EXPLAIN_STREAM - This table represents the input and output data streams between individual operators and data objects. The data objects themselves are represented in the EXPLAIN_OBJECT table. The operators involved in a data stream are represented in the EXPLAIN_OPERATOR table.

The explain tables have to be created before any explain information can be gathered. The CLP input file, called EXPLAIN.DDL, located in the misc directory of the SQLLIB directory, contains the definition of the explain tables. To create the explain tables, you can connect to the database and use the following command:

```
db2 -tvf EXPLAIN.DDL
```

 Note: Explain tables are created the first time you use Visual Explain.

Gathering Explain Data

There are different kinds of explain data that can be collected. They differ in the explain table columns that will be populated. The explain data options are:

- EXPLAIN - Captures detailed information of the access plan and stores the information in the explain tables. No snapshot information is stored.
- EXPLAIN SNAPSHOT - Captures the current internal representation of an SQL query and related information. The snapshot information is stored in the SNAPSHOT column of the EXPLAIN_STATEMENT table.

Not all explain tools require the same kind of explain data. Some tools use the data captured using the EXPLAIN option and others, such as Visual Explain, require snapshot data.

After creating the explain tables, you can start capturing the explain data that will populate them. Not all SQL statements can be explained. The explainable SQL statements include: SELECT, SELECT INTO, UPDATE, INSERT, DELETE, VALUES, and VALUES INTO statements.

Depending on the number of SQL statements or kind of application you want to explain, you should use different methods. These methods include the following:

- EXPLAIN statement - Gathers explain data for an SQL statement
- CURRENT EXPLAIN MODE special register - Specifies the gathering of explain data for dynamic SQL statements
- CURRENT EXPLAIN SNAPSHOT special register - Specifies the gathering of explain snapshot data for dynamic SQL statements
- BIND options - Specify the gathering of explain data for static and/or dynamic embedded SQL statements in a package

Each of these methods will be examined in turn.

EXPLAIN Statement

The EXPLAIN statement is useful when you want to gather explain information for a single dynamic SQL statement. The EXPLAIN statement can be invoked either from the Command Line Processor, Command Center, or from within an application.

You can control the amount of explain information that the EXPLAIN statement will store in the explain tables. The default is to only capture regular explain table information and not the snapshot information. If you wish to modify this behavior, use the following EXPLAIN statement options:

- WITH SNAPSHOT- Captures explain and explain snapshot data into the explain tables.

Monitoring and Tuning

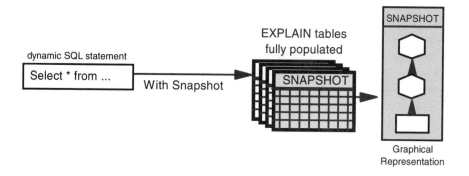

- `FOR SNAPSHOT` - Only captures the explain snapshot information. No other explain information is captured other than that normally found in the `EXPLAIN_INSTANCE` and `EXPLAIN_STATEMENT` tables.

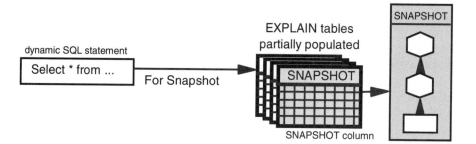

The default case is used when no other explain option is specified. In the default case, the `EXPLAIN` statement will only gather the explain data. No explain snapshot data is captured.

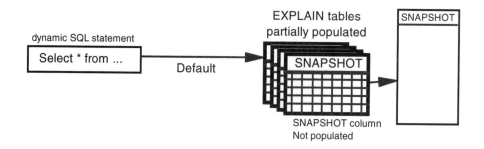

To issue the EXPLAIN statement, the user must have INSERT privilege on the explain tables.

 Note: The SQL statement being explained using the EXPLAIN statement will not be executed; only the explain data is captured.

An example of gathering access plan information using the EXPLAIN statement will now be examined. The explain statement is shown below. This example collects all the available explain information for the explain tables.

```
EXPLAIN ALL WITH SNAPSHOT FOR "SELECT * FROM candidate"
```

 Note: Instead of the keyword ALL, used in our example, the keywords PLAN and PLAN SELECTION can be used. Your EXPLAIN statement must include one of them.

The EXPLAIN statement shown in the last example populates a number of explain tables including the SNAPSHOT column of the EXPLAIN_STATEMENT table.

The SNAPSHOT_TAKEN column in the EXPLAIN_INSTANCE table indicates the existence of a Visual Explain snapshot for each explained statement.

The EXPLAIN statement can also be embedded in an application that populates the explain tables. Once the explain tables are populated, they can be queried. Special operators can be examined to determine if the ideal access plan was used for the query.

Explain Special Register

Another way to collect explain information is to use the explain special registers. There are two special registers used by DB2 for gathering explain information for dynamic SQL statements. These registers can be set interactively, or they can be used in a dynamic embedded SQL program. The values of special registers are modified using the SET statement.

The special registers are:

- CURRENT EXPLAIN MODE - Used to populate only the explain data. No snapshot will be taken.

- CURRENT EXPLAIN SNAPSHOT - Used to capture only the explain snapshot data.

The following statements are used to set the value of the explain special registers:

```
SET CURRENT EXPLAIN MODE       option
SET CURRENT EXPLAIN SNAPSHOT option
```

The explain registers options are:

- NO - No explain information is captured for dynamic SQL statements.
- YES - Explain tables or snapshot information will be populated for dynamic SQL statements while executing the SQL statement, and the result is returned.
- EXPLAIN - Explain tables or snapshot information will be populated for dynamic SQL statements without executing the SQL statement. Use this state to obtain explain information without executing the SQL statement.

The following two options are for the CURRENT EXPLAIN MODE register only. They will be illustrated in the section that discusses the Index Advisor.

- RECOMMEND INDEXES
- EVALUATE INDEXES

Note: Once you have set a register to YES or EXPLAIN, any subsequent dynamic SQL statements will be explained until the register is reset to NO.

Explain BIND Options

The BIND command is discussed in "Development Considerations" on page 691. However, in this section, the bind options related to the explain information will be reviewed.

There are two explain BIND options that can be specified: EXPLAIN and EXPLSNAP. The EXPLSNAP option collects explain snapshot information. If you want to view the access plan using Visual Explain, you use the EXPLSNAP option. The EXPLAIN option only populates the explain information without including a snapshot.

Note: Explain snapshots cannot be performed for DRDA application-servers.

Fig. 12–23 shows options of the BIND command and the explain tables that are populated when the options are used.

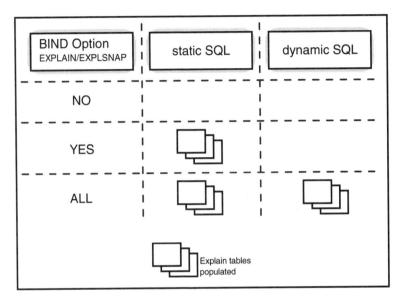

BIND Option EXPLAIN/EXPLSNAP	static SQL	dynamic SQL
NO		
YES	▢	
ALL	▢	▢

▢ Explain tables populated

Fig. 12–23 *Using the EXPLAIN or EXPLSNAP option for BIND command*

Explain data using a bind option will now be captured.

```
BIND checkid.bnd EXPLSNAP ALL
```

In this example, the explain snapshot information will be populated for all of the static SQL statements defined in the checkid.bnd package. Because the ALL option was specified, the dynamic SQL statements issued during package execution will also have explain snapshot information gathered at run time.

The method of obtaining explain information during binds is useful for an administrator to determine the access plans of static or dynamic statements executed from packages.

To examine the access plan data for individual dynamic SQL statements, the special register technique is an easier method to use.

Using the Explain Report Tools to Gather and Analyze Explain Data

There are alternative methods of gathering explain data that is stored in a report rather than in the explain tables. They are the *dynexpln* tool and the *db2expln* tool.

The db2expln tool describes the access plan selected for static SQL statements in the packages stored in the system catalog tables, and the dynexpln tool describes the access plan selected for dynamic SQL statements. It creates a static package for the statements and then uses the db2expln tool to describe them.

The explain output of both utility programs is stored in a readable report file. The explain report tools are useful as quick and easy methods for gathering access plan information.

Examining Explain Data

Once the explain data has been stored in the explain tables, it can be queried or displayed using Visual Explain or other explain tools. How to use Visual Explain and analyze access plan data will now be reviewed.

Visual Explain

Visual Explain is a Graphical User Interface (GUI) utility that gives the database administrator or application developer the ability to examine the access plan determined by the optimizer. Visual Explain can only be used with access plans explained using the snapshot option.

Visual Explain can be used to analyze previously generated explain snapshots or to gather explain data and explain dynamic SQL statements. If the explain tables have not been created when you start Visual Explain, it will create them for you. You can invoke Visual Explain from either the Command Center or Control Center.

From the Control Center interface, right-click the database where your explain snapshots are stored. You will notice that there is an option called **Show Explained Statements History,** as shown in Fig. 12–24.

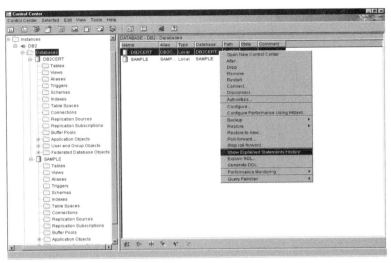

Fig. 12–24 *DB2 Control Center - Accessing Visual Explain*

The **Explain SQL...** option, also shown in Fig. 12–24, allows you to gather explain data and show the graphical representation of a dynamic SQL statement. This is the easiest way to explain a single SQL statement.

Once the Explained Statement History window has been opened, all of the explained statements will be listed as shown in Fig. 12–25. Because it can be customized to your environment, the displayed information may differ. In Fig. 12–25, the total costs and the SQL statements are shown.

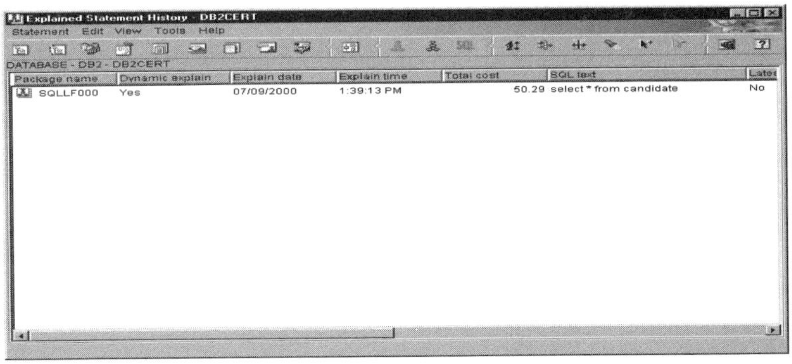

Fig. 12–25 *Customized display of Explained Statement History panel*

To examine an access plan in detail, simply double-click the explained statement or highlight the entry of interest and use the panel menu to select **Statement → Show access plan** on the Explained Statement History window.

All of the explain statements will be displayed in the Explained Statement History list, but only the explained statements with EXPLAIN SNAPSHOT information can be examined using Visual Explain.

 Note: The Explain SQL option on the Control Center or the Command Center are useful to explain a single dynamic SQL statement.

You can add comments to the explain snapshots listed in the Explained Statement History window. To add a comment describing a query, highlight the entry and then select **Statement → Change**. This option can be used to provide a query tag, which can be used to help track the explain snapshot information. You may also wish to remove explain snapshots. The snapshots can be removed from the explain tables by selecting **Statement → Remove** after highlighting the entry to be removed.

The Visual Explain output displays a hierarchical graph representing the components of an SQL statement. Each part of the query is represented as a graphical object. These objects are known as *nodes*. There are two basic types of nodes:

- *OPERATOR* nodes indicate an action that is performed on a group of data.
- *OPERAND* nodes show the database objects on which an operator action takes place. An operand is an object that the operators act on. These database objects are usually tables and indexes.

There are many operators that can be used by the DB2 optimizer to determine the best access plan. Some of the operators used by Visual Explain are shown in Fig. 12–26.

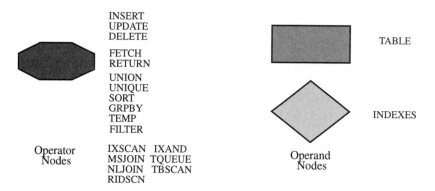

Fig. 12–26 *Operators and operands displayed in Visual Explain*

These operators indicate how data is accessed (IXSCAN, TBSCAN, RIDSCN, IXAND), how tables are joined internally (MSJOIN, NLJOIN), and other factors, such as if a sort will be required (SORT). More information about the operators can be found using Visual Explain Online Help.

The objects shown in a Visual Explain graphic output are connected by arrows showing the flow of data from one node to another. The end of an access plan is always a RETURN operator.

The access plan shown in Fig. 12–27 is a simple SQL statement: SELECT * FROM DB2CERT.CANDIDATE. In this example, there are two operators and a single operand. The operand is the DB2CERT.CANDIDATE table, and the operators include a table scan (TBSCAN) and a RETURN operator.

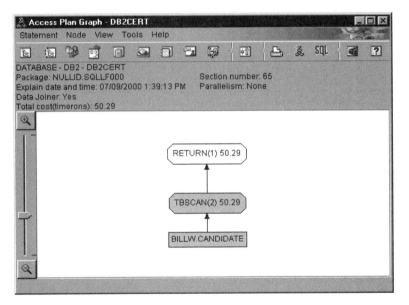

Fig. 12–27 *Visual Explain: Graphical access plan for SQL statement*

Generating explain data for an SQL statement is the only way to analyze the access plan determined by the DB2 optimizer.

Each node, shown in an access plan graph, has detailed information that can be accessed by double-clicking the node or by choosing the **Show details** option from the **Node** menu item.

To display the details of the table scan operation, select the **TBSCAN** operator node and then select **Show details** from the **Node** menu item. The information about the TBSCAN operation, shown in the access plan, is displayed in Fig. 12–28.

Monitoring and Tuning

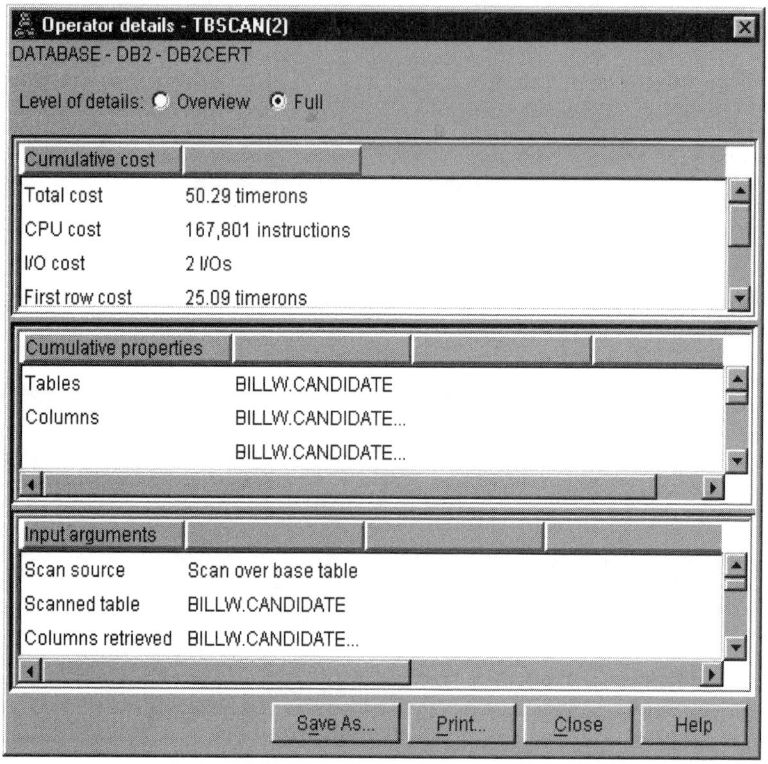

Fig. 12–28 *Visual Explain: Operator details*

This window contains several different sections:

- Cumulative costs - Contains information about the estimated cumulative costs calculated using the statistics stored in the system catalog tables.
- Cumulative properties - Contains information about the table, columns, and so forth used to satisfy the query.
- Input arguments - Contains information about the input arguments that affect the behavior of the operator.

It is also possible to examine the detailed information about the operands. Select a operand node and then select **Show statistics** from the **Node** menu item.
Fig. 12–29 shows operand details for the db2cert.candidate table.

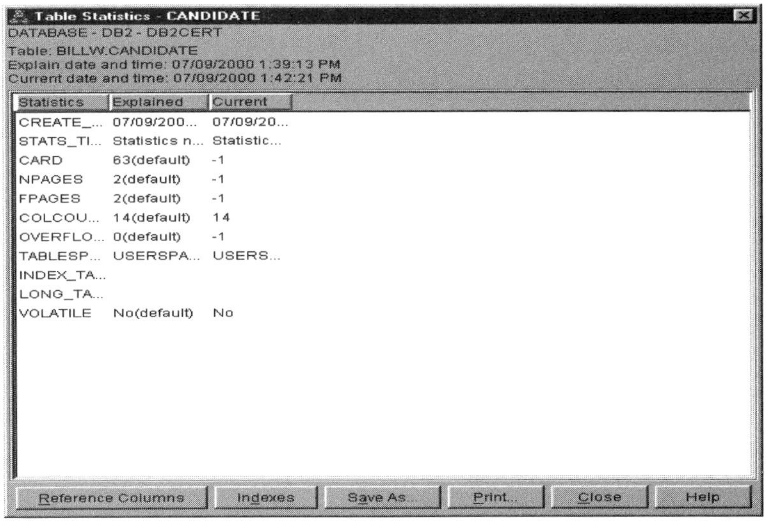

Fig. 12–29 *Visual Explain: Detailed statistics information for an operand*

Detailed information for operand nodes shows the table or index statistics, including table space information, the number of columns, and the number of rows in the object. Fig. 12–29 shows the explained and current statistics from the system catalog tables. These statistics are used by the DB2 optimizer to determine the access plan. Fig. 12–29 shows that there were no statistics gathered for the DB2CERT.CANDIDATE table.

When the optimizer has no statistics to work with for a table, or if the statistics for a table indicate that the cardinality of the table is relatively small, then the optimizer itself will attempt to calculate the cardinality of the table. The optimizer does this by using certain factors, including the average column length of the table and the number of pages used by the table.

Current statistics are the key to good access plans. If DB2 is not aware of the characteristics of objects involved in a query, it may not be able to generate a good access plan. To ensure the latest statistics are available for the optimizer, a DB2 utility must be used. This utility is called RUNSTATS. Here is an example of gathering statistics for the DB2CERT.CANDIDATE table.

```
RUNSTATS ON TABLE DB2CERT.CANDIDATE
              WITH DISTRIBUTION AND DETAILED INDEXES ALL
```

Statistics for the DB2CERT.CANDIDATE table are stored in the system catalog tables. After running the RUNSTATS utility, rebind the packages against the database and re-explain the SQL statement. You will note that the values for the current statistics have changed, and probably the total cost of the access plan generated would change too. Fig. 12–30 shows that the updated DB2CERT.CANDIDATE statistics have changed.

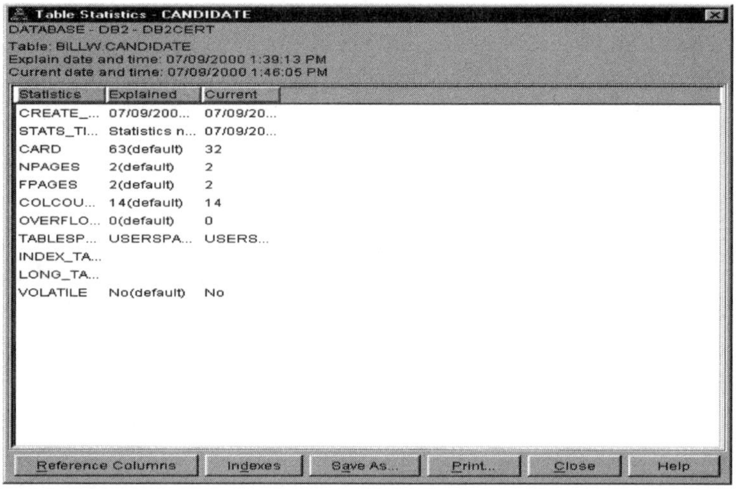

Fig. 12–30 *Visual Explain: Table statistics after RUNSTATS*

When determining the access plan for dynamic SQL statements, the DB2 optimizer always uses the current statistics. For a static SQL statement, DB2 uses the statistics available at BIND time (when the package was created). To ensure that current statistics are used with static SQL statements that were compiled before the statistics were updated, the packages must be recreated. This can be accomplished using the REBIND command.

In Fig. 12–31, the total cost for the SQL statements is not the same in both cases. They differ because different statistics were used by DB2 when the explain snapshot was captured.

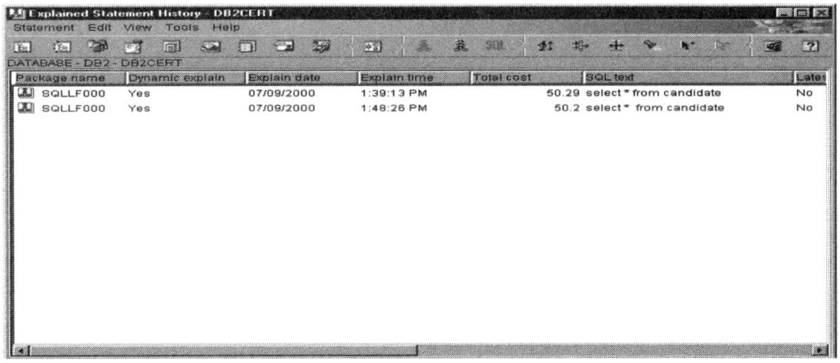

Fig. 12–31 *Visual Explain: List of explained statements*

In our example, the difference of the total cost of the explained queries is very small. This is because the DB2 optimizer estimates some statistics for tables if the statistics have not been gathered. Therefore, the default statistics were quite close to the actual statistics, hence, the similar total costs. The statistics are estimated based on the number of pages in the tables, row length, and so on. Due to the dynamic nature of databases, the estimated, or catalog, statistics may be very different than what the database really looks like. In these cases, the access plan chosen by DB2 may be inefficient.

Please refer to "Maintaining Data" on page 451 for detailed information about the RUNSTATS and REBIND commands.

Note: Updated statistics are always needed and become critical as your SQL statements grow in complexity.

Visual Explain can be used to see the decisions that the optimizer made for sorting. In Fig. 12–32, you can see that an index was used to provide the ordered result from the DB2CERT.CANDIDATE table.

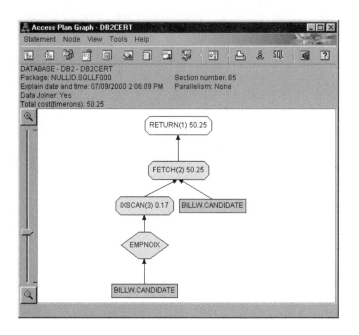

Fig. 12–32 *Sort request satisfied by an index*

The sort heap is used for each application sort request. The DB2 optimizer may decide to attempt to perform a nonoverflowed piped sort. However, if there is not enough available memory to allocate another sort heap at run time, then the sort may be performed using a temporary table instead.

There is a database manager parameter that is used to control the total amount of memory allocated for sorting on the DB2 server. The parameter is called SHEAPTHRES. The SHEAPTHRES parameter should be set to the maximum amount of memory for all sort heaps allowed to be allocated at any given time.

As already explained, if intra-partition parallelism is enabled, a sort operations can be processed in parallel, and it can be a private sort or a shared sort, which uses memory from two different memory sources. The size of the shared sort memory area is statically predetermined (and not preallocated) at the time of the first connection to a database based on the value of SHEAPTHRES. The size of the private sort memory area is unrestricted.

The SHEAPTHRES parameter is used differently for private and shared sorts.

For private sorts, this parameter is an instance-wide soft limit on the total amount of memory that can be consumed by private sorts at any given time. When the total private-sort memory consumption for an instance reaches this limit, the memory allocated for additional incoming private-sort requests will be considerably reduced.

For shared sorts, this parameter is a database-wide hard limit on the total amount of memory consumed by shared sorts at any given time. When this limit is reached, no further shared-sort memory requests will be allowed (until the total shared-sort memory consumption falls below the limit specified by SHEAPTHRES).

The Visual Explain output shown in Fig. 12–33 shows a sort operator. If the detailed information for the sort operator is displayed, the type of sort and the columns involved are shown. Accompanying Performance Monitor information could be used to determine if the sort operation was piped or non-piped. Note that there are two relational table scan operators. The first table scan is reading the base table DB2CERT.CANDIDATE, and the second table scan is reading from a temporary sort table.

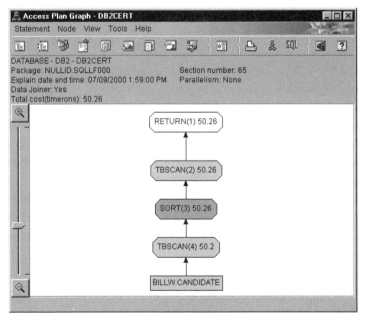

Fig. 12–33 *Visual Explain with sort operator*

There are a number of sorting-related performance variables that can be monitored using the DB2 Performance Monitor. These parameters include:

- *Percentage of overflowed sorts* - This variable can be monitored to determine if the optimizer is attempting to use a sort heap and fails. If the percentage is high, consider increasing the sortheap and/or sheapthres values.

- *Percentage of piped sorts accepted* - This variable can be monitored to determine if piped sorts are being chosen but not accepted by the optimizer. If the percentage is low, consider increasing the `sortheap` and/or `sheapthres`.

As with the buffer pool allocation, it is important to allocate as much memory as possible to the sort heap (and set the threshold accordingly) without over-allocating memory and causing memory paging to occur.

Guidelines on Using Explain Output

There are a number of ways in which analyzing the explain data can help you to tune your queries and environment. For example:

- *Are indexes being used?* Creating appropriate indexes can have a significant benefit on performance. Using the explain output, you can determine if the indexes you have created to help a specific set of queries are being used. In the explain output, you should look for index usage in the following areas:
  - Join Predicates
  - Local Predicates
  - GROUP BY clauses
  - ORDER BY clauses
  - The select list

You can also use the Explain Facility to evaluate whether a different index can be used instead of an existing index or no index at all. After creating a new index, collect statistics for that index using the RUNSTATS command and recompile your query. Over time, you may notice, through the explain data, that instead of an index scan, a table scan is now being used. This can result from a change in the clustering of the table data. If the index that was previously being used now has a low cluster ratio, you want to:

- Reorganize your table to cluster the data according to that index.
- Use the RUNSTATS command to update the catalog statistics.
- Recompile the query (bind or rebind).
- Reexamine the explain output to determine whether reorganizing the table has affected the access plan.
- *Is the type of access appropriate for the application?* You can analyze the explain output and look for types of access to the data that, as a rule, are not optimal for the type of application being executed. For example:

Online Transaction Processing (OLTP) Queries

OLTP applications are prime candidates to use index scans with range-delimiting predicates because they tend to return only a few rows that are qualified using an equality predicate against a key column. If your OLTP queries are using a table scan, you may want to analyze the explain data to determine the reasons why an index scan was not used.

Read-Only Queries

The search criteria for a *read-only* type query may be vague causing a large number of rows to qualify. If the user usually looks only at a few screens of the output data, she may want to try to ensure that the entire answer set need not be computed before some results are returned. In this case, the goals of the user are different from the basic operating principle of the optimizer, which attempts to minimize resource consumption for the entire query, not just the first few screens of data.

For example, if the explain output shows that both merge scan join and sort operators were used in the access plan, the entire answer set will be materialized in a temporary table before any rows are returned to the application. In this case, you can attempt to change the access plan by using the OPTIMIZE FOR clause on the SELECT statement. In this way, the optimizer can attempt to choose an access plan that does not produce the entire answer set in a temporary table before returning the first rows to the application.

Index Advisor Facility

The *Index Advisor* is a management tool that provides assistance in the designing of indexes on tables. It is useful in the following situations:

- Finding the best indexes for a problem query
- Finding the best indexes for a set of queries (work load) subject to resource limits that are optionally applied
- Testing out an index on a work load without having to create the index

There are two concepts associated with this facility: *work load* and *virtual indexes*.

A work load is a set of SQL statements (SELECT, INSERT, UPDATE, DELETE) that DB2 has to process over a given period of time. The information in the work load is concerned with the type and frequency of the SQL statements over a given period of time. The index advisor uses this work load information in conjunction with the database information to recommend indexes. The goal of the advising engine is to minimize the total work load cost.

Virtual indexes are indexes that do not exist in the current database schema. These indexes could be either recommendations that the facility has made or indexes that are being proposed to create but wish to model the effect using the advisor facility.

Monitoring and Tuning

The advisor facility uses two tables that are extensions to the EXPLAIN tables:

- ADVISE_WORKLOAD –This table is where you describe the work load to be considered. Each row in the table represents an SQL statement and is described by an associated frequency. There is an identifier called WORKLOAD_NAME for each work load that is a field in the table. All SQL statements that are part of the same work load, should have the same WORKLOAD_NAME.

- ADVISE_INDEX - This table stores information about recommended indexes. Information is placed into this table by the SQL compiler, the Index Wizard, the db2advis tool (index advisor), or manually using SQL statements.

By setting the CURRENT EXPLAIN MODE special register to RECOMMEND INDEXES, the ADVISE_INDEX table will be populated when the EXPLAIN function is invoked.

When the CURRENT EXPLAIN MODE special register is set to EVALUATE INDEXES, the ADVISE_INDEX table will be used as input into the EXPLAIN process, reading the virtual index definitions and using them in the EXPLAIN process as if they were real indexes.

The Index Advisor can be invoked using the db2advis utility or by invoking the index creation wizard from the Control Center.

Configuring Database Resources

Monitoring database activity should be performed with a purpose in mind. The purpose of monitoring may be to achieve greater concurrency or to reduce the amount of disk access wait time. Another key purpose of monitoring database activity is to provide input for configuring various DB2 (instance) and database parameters to optimize memory utilization and increase performance.

Some of the key DBM and DB configuration parameters and how they relate to each other will be examined. Some of these parameters are used to determine the size of the memory allocated for each DB2 instance, database, or application.

One of the most important factors affecting database performance is the size of each buffer pool in the database. When you create or alter a buffer pool, you have to set the size of each one. If you set the size to minus 1, then the default size is used, which is specified by the BUFFPAGE parameter in the database configuration file. Each buffer pool is the data cache between the applications and the physical disk. You can place your data in separate buffer pools by specifying a buffer pool for a particular table space. Also, it is possible for multiple table spaces to use one buffer pool.

If there were no buffer pools, then all database activity would result in disk access. If the size of each buffer pool is too small, the buffer pool hit ratio will be low, and the applications will wait for disk access activity to satisfy SQL queries. If one or more buffer pools are too large, memory on the server may be wasted. If the total amount of space used by all buffer pools is larger than the physical memory available on the server, then operating system paging (disk activity) will occur. Accessing a buffer pool that has been paged out to disk is inefficient.

If you create your own buffer pools in addition to the default buffer pool IBMDEFAULTBP, you must be careful how you allocate space for each one. There is no point in allocating a large buffer pool to a table space containing a large number of small, rarely used tables and a small buffer pool to a table space containing a large, frequently accessed table. The size of buffer pools should reflect the size of tables in the table space and how frequently they are updated or queried.

The DB2 optimizer will utilize the different buffer pools to achieve the best query performance. There is a parameter that provides the optimizer with information regarding the average number of active applications (AVG_APPLS). This parameter is used by the optimizer to determine how much of each buffer pool may be used for each application.

Another memory block shared at the database level is called the database heap (DBHEAP). There is one database heap per database, and the database manager uses it on behalf of all applications connected to the database. It contains control block information for tables, indexes, table spaces, buffer pools, and so forth.

There are many I/O caches that can be configured, including a log file cache (LOGBUFSZ) and a system catalog table cache (CATALOGCACHE_SZ). The log buffer is used as a buffer for writing log records to disk. Every transaction involves writing multiple log records. To optimize disk write performance, the writes are buffered in memory and periodically flushed to disk. The catalog cache is used to store the system catalog tables in memory. As an SQL statement is compiled or referenced, the database object information needs to be verified. If the information is in memory, then there is no need to perform disk activity to access the data. The package cache (PCKCACHESZ) is used to reduce the need to reload access plans (sections) of a package. This caching can improve performance when the same section is used multiple times within a program.

Note: The access plans are cached for static and dynamic SQL statements in the package cache.

Record blocking is a distributed caching technique used to send a group of records across the network to the client instead of a single record at a time. The decrease in network traffic increases application performance and allows for better network throughput. The records are blocked by DB2 according to the cursor type and bind parameter. If the optimizer decides to return the query output in blocks, the amount of data in each block is determined by the ASLHEAPSZ parameter.

The application heap (APPLHEAPSZ) contains a number of memory blocks that are used by DB2 to handle requests for each application.

The sort heap (SORTHEAP) determines the maximum number of memory pages that can be used for each sort. The sort heap area is allocated in the agent private memory if intra-partition parallelism is disabled. However, if intra-partition parallelism is enabled, a sort operation is processed in parallel, and the sort heap area is allocated in the agent private memory or the database global memory depending on which type of sort, a *private sort* or a *shared sort*, is performned. For a private sort, a sort heap area is allocated independently for each parallel agent in the private agent memory. For a shared sort, a sort heap area is allocated in the database global memory, and each parallel agent shares this sort heap. The SORTHEAP parameter is used by the optimizer to determine if the sorting can be performed in memory or on disk. DB2 will always attempt to perform the sort in memory.

The sheapthres parameter is used to control the amount of memory that can be allocated for sort heaps in a DB2 server.

One of the key performance parameters that affects the amount of memory used on the DB2 server as a data cache (database level) will now be modified. The default buffer pool size can be updated to 2 MB using the following command:

```
UPDATE DB CFG FOR db2cert USING BUFFPAGE 500
```

Allocating at least half of the physical memory on a machine to buffer pool space is usually a good starting point when adjusting the size of buffer pools. This assumes a dedicated DB2 database server and a single database active at any given time. For example, to effectively use a database server with 40 MB of RAM, the total size of all the buffer pools could amount to 20 or 25 MB.

Any modification to the database configuration file will not be effective until all applications using the database are disconnected. The subsequent database connection will use the new database configuration parameters. If you change the DBM (instance) configuration parameters, the new values will not be effective until the instance has been stopped and restarted.

The size of the memory used to perform record blocking will now be modified. The memory area used for record blocking is known as the application support layer heap (ASLHEAPSZ). The following command would set the record blocking to be 200 KB in size (the units are 4 KB).

```
UPDATE DATABASE MANAGER CONFIGURATION USING ASLHEAPSZ 50
```

Any changes to the database manager configuration will not take effect until the instance is stopped and restarted except default database monitor switch parameters, such as DFT_MON_BUFPOOL, DFT_MON_LOCK, DFT_MON_SORT, DFT_MON_TABLE, DFT_MON_UOW, and DFT_MON_STMT.

In this example, when the instance is restarted, records will be sent across the network from the DB2 server to the application in 200 KB blocks (likely more than a single row). If the average row length were 1 KB, then 200 records would be returned in a single block of data (assuming more than 200 records are in the final result table).

 Note: Record blocking occurs for remote and local DB2 client applications.

DB2 Universal Database also provides graphical tools that enable you to configure DB2 easily. The Performance Wizard is a tool that asks you to define what you want to use the database for: to define size requirements and certain country specific information. Then, using your input as a guideline, the Wizard tunes certain parameters to better fit your needs in DB2. Right-click on a database icon in the Control Center window and select Configure using Wizard. This will bring up the Configure Performance Wizard window as shown in Fig. 12–34.

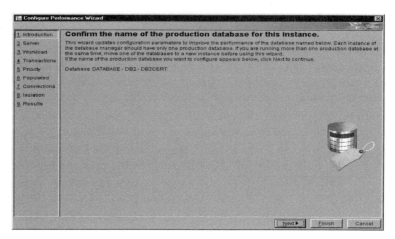

Fig. 12–34 *Configure Performance Wizard*

The various tabs in the Wizard panel indicate the range of questions that the Wizard might ask. Once the Wizard has been filled in, you can go to the Results panel and see the new values of the parameters. In complex environments, the Wizard may not be able to make all the changes that are needed, so you may want to review the different parameters to see what has been changed and left unchanged. Fig. 12–35 gives an idea of what the Results panel might look like. You do not need to apply the changes immediately in the Wizard. Instead, you can save a command to make the result come into effect as a script file, which can be run later from the Script Center.

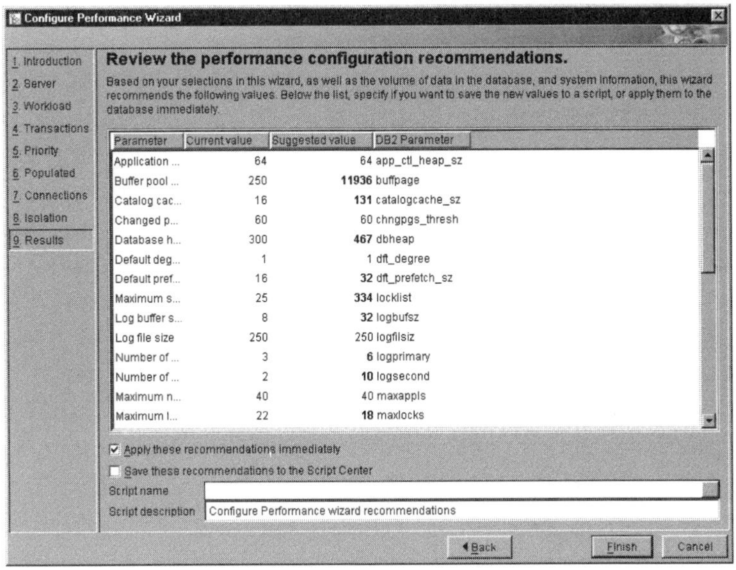

Fig. 12–35 *Configure Performance Wizard - Results panel*

The second tool provided by DB2 is a graphical view of the database manager and database configuration files. Using the Control Center, you can configure either the database manager or each database, using online help to guide you along.
Fig. 12–36 shows how you can configure the DB2CERT database from the Control Center. The configuration tool also provides hints for each database configuration parameter.

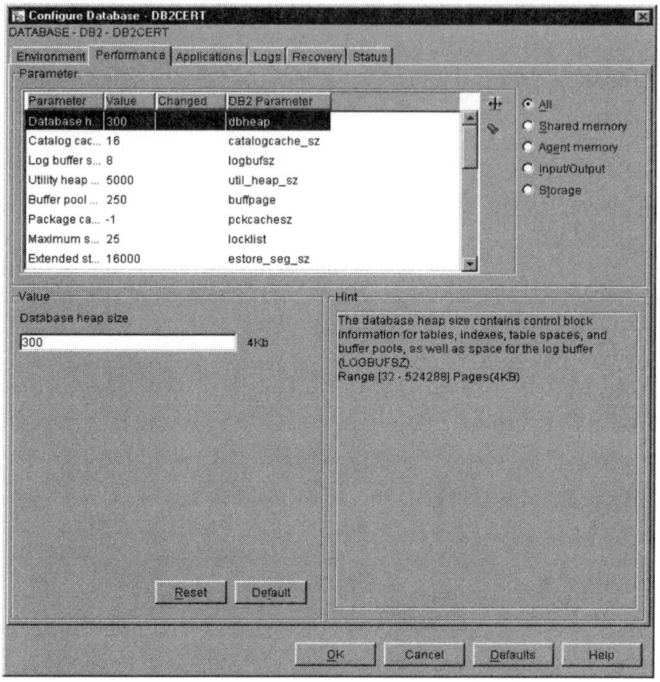

Fig. 12–36 *Configure database using Control Center*

Configuring Intra-Partition Parallelism

Intra-partition parallelism in DB2 can be enabled using the INTRA_PARALLEL DBM configuration parameter. To enable intra-partition parallelism in DB2, you would issue the following command:

```
UPDATE DBM CFG USING INTRA_PARALLEL YES
```

Note: The default value for the INTRA_PARALLEL parameter is YES in an SMP machine and NO in a uniprocessor machine.

If the degree of parallelism is set to ANY, then the optimizer will decide the degree of parallelism for each SQL query. For instance, on a four-way SMP machine, a simple insert statement will gain no advantage from being run in parallel across the CPUs, so using the ANY setting will result in this type of statement running on only one CPU (a degree of parallelism of 1).

Setting the DBM configuration parameter MAX_QUERYDEGREE to 2 in a uni-processor machine environment could improve I/O performance slightly. This is because the uni-processor may not have to wait for input or output tasks to complete before working on a new query, thus improving the performance of I/O bound applications.

Embedded SQL applications and CLI applications can override the default degree of parallelism with various options. The following table gives a brief overview of the parameters and options that can enable parallelism in DB2

Table 12–1 *DB2 Parallelism Parameters*

Parameter	Values
INTRA_PARALLEL (Database Manager Configuration)	• YES/NO. • Defaults to NO on uni-processor machine. • Defaults to YES on SMP machine. • If changed, packages already bound will automatically be rebound at next execution.
MAX_QUERYDEGREE (Database Manager Configuration)	• 1-32767, ANY. • Defaults to ANY - Allows optimizer to choose degree of parallelism based on cost. • No SQL executed on a database in this instance can use a degree of parallelism higher than this value.
DFT_DEGREE (Database Configuration)	• 1-32767, ANY. • Defaults to 1 (no parallelism). • Provides the default value for: • CURRENT DEGREE special register. • DEGREE bind option. • Maximum for any SQL in this database.
CURRENT DEGREE (Special Register)	• 1-32767, ANY. • Sets degree of parallelism for dynamic SQL. • Defaults to DFT_DEGREE.
DEGREE (precompile or bind option)	• 1-32767, ANY. • Sets degree of parallelism for static SQL. • Defaults to DFT_DEGREE. • To change: PREP STATIC.SQL DEGREE 2.

Monitoring and Tuning

Table 12–1 *DB2 Parallelism Parameters (Continued)*

Parameter	Values
RUNTIME DEGREE (SET RUNTIME DEGREE command)	<ul><li>1-32767, ANY.</li><li>Sets degree of parallelism for running applications.</li><li>To change (setting degree to 4 for the application whose handler number is 100): SET RUNTIME DEGREE FOR (100) to 4</li><li>Only affects queries issued after SET RUNTIME is executed.</li></ul>
DB2DEGREE (CLI configuration file)	<ul><li>1-32767, ANY.</li><li>Default is 1.</li><li>Sets degree of parallelism for CLI applications.</li><li>CLI application issues a SET CURRENT DEGREE statement after database connection.</li></ul>

The maximum query degree of parallelism for an active application is specified using the SET RUNTIME DEGREE command. The application can set its own runtime degree of parallelism by using the SET CURRENT DEGREE statement. The actual runtime degree used is the lower of:

* MAX_QUERYDEGREE DBM configuration parameter
* Application runtime degree
* SQL statement compilation degree

More information on parallelism support in DB2 Universal Database can be found in the *DB2 UDB V7.1 Administration Guide*

Performance Tuning Scenario

A straightforward DB2 performance tuning scenario will now be examined. A database application user telephones you because he or she has observed that around 2:00 p.m every day the application is much slower than at other times. The response is slow, and sometimes the user has to wait to obtain database requests.

You assume that this problem occurs because there are many applications accessing the database around 2:00 p.m. So, you decide to use the Performance Monitor to gather information from that time frame. The first resources you decide to monitor are the buffer pool activity and the number of lock escalations. You will obtain this information if snapshots are captured before, during, and after 2:00 p.m and the output compared. Snapshots are taken every 30 seconds for a period of time.

You notice that the buffer pool hit ratio decreases below 50 percent, the number of lock escalations increases, and the average lock wait time is increasing around 2:00 p.m.

You decide to capture a snapshot of the currently active applications for the DB2CERT database. The DB2 command LIST APPLICATIONS, as shown below, is actually a database monitor snapshot for applications. You can also list and force off applications using the Control Center.

```
LIST APPLICATIONS FOR DATABASE db2cert
```

The LIST APPLICATIONS command will list all of the currently active applications connected to the database as shown below.

```
Auth Id   Application     Appl.    Application Id                    DB        # of
          Name            Handle                                    Name      Agents
-------   -------------   ------   ----------------------------     -------   -------
DB2CERT   db2bp_r         51       *LOCAL.db2cert.000621152850      DB2CERT   1
DB2CERT   DB2CC.EXE       53       09030177.0449.000621153153       DB2CERT   1
DB2CERT   DB2BP.EXE       58       09030177.044F.000621154423       DB2CERT   1
RNICOL    db2bp.exe       59       09030173.04D5.000621154801       DB2CERT   1
RNICOL    db2bp.exe       60       09030173.04D7.000621154834       DB2CERT   1
DB2USER   DB2CERT2.EXE    61       09030180.04E3.000621154925       DB2CERT   1
```

Fig. 12–37 *Output of LIST APPLICATIONS command*

You note that DB2USER, the user who was complaining about performance, was using the DB2CERT2 application shown as the last line in the output.

Taking snapshots based on locks for each of the other applications, you note that the DB2USER user has a large number of row locks allocated and is using most of the locking memory as defined by the LOCKLIST database parameter.

Snapshots are then taken based on statements for the APPL_ID
*LOCAL.db2cert.000621152850. It is discovered that the application is performing a large number of inserts on the TEST table.

You decide to increase the amount of memory allocated for locks because lock escalation occurs when an application starts exhausting the available lock list.

The lock memory is defined in the database configuration file. The value can be modified using the CLP, the Command Center, or the Control Center. The CLP command to obtain the current database configuration settings is:

```
GET DATABASE CONFIGURATION FOR db2cert
```

Some of the important database configuration parameters are shown in Fig. 12–38. The first step for resolving the locking problem is to increase the size of the LOCKLIST and the value for MAXLOCKS. You can issue the following CLP command to perform the update:

```
UPDATE DB CFG FOR db2cert USING LOCKLIST 250 MAXLOCKS 30
```

```
Degree of parallelism                       (DFT_DEGREE) = 1
Default query optimization class          (DFT_QUERYOPT) = 5
Database heap (4KB)                            (DBHEAP) = 1200
Catalog cache size (4KB)                (CATALOGCACHE_SZ) = 64
Log buffer size (4KB)                        (LOGBUFSZ) = 8
Utilities heap size (4KB)               (UTIL_HEAP_SZ) = 5000
Buffer pool size (4KB)                       (BUFFPAGE) = 1000
Extended storage segments size (4KB)     (ESTORE_SEG_SZ) = 16000
Number of extended storage segments   (NUM_ESTORE_SEGS) = 0
Max storage for lock list (4KB)              (LOCKLIST) = 100

Max appl. control heap size (4KB)       (APP_CTL_HEAP_SZ) = 128

Sort list heap (4KB)                         (SORTHEAP) = 256
SQL statement heap (4KB)                     (STMTHEAP) = 2048
Default application heap (4KB)              (APPLHEAPSZ) = 128
Package cache size (4KB)                    (PCKCACHESZ) = (MAXAPPLS*8)
Statistics heap size (4KB)                (STAT_HEAP_SZ) = 4384
Percent. of lock lists per application       (MAXLOCKS) = 10

Changed pages threshold                  (CHNGPGS_THRESH) = 60
Number of asynchronous page cleaners     (NUM_IOCLEANERS) = 1
Number of I/O servers                     (NUM_IOSERVERS) = 3
Sequential detect flag                       (SEQDETECT) = YES
Max number of active applications            (MAXAPPLS) = 40
Average number of active applications        (AVG_APPLS) = 1
Group commit count                          (MINCOMMIT) = 1

Max DB files open per application             (MAXFILOP) = 6
```

Fig. 12–38 *Database configuration parameters*

You may also decide to change the average number of active applications to match the database activity. The AVG_APPLS parameter will affect the usage of each buffer pool as determined by the optimizer. Since there were only five applications using the database according to the LIST APPLICATIONS command, set the value to 8 (allow a few extra connections). The following CLP command will modify the AVG_APPLS parameter:

```
UPDATE DB CFG FOR db2cert USING AVG_APPLS 8
```

After all these modifications, you should create new application packages (to create new access plans for any static SQL). Use the REBIND command to update the package information. You can also use the db2rbind utility to take care of this.

Now you should verify that the changes were beneficial. In this example, you should determine whether the lock escalations occur the next day and verify that the user (db2user) is obtaining acceptable response time. Remember that some performance problems must be addressed within the application or the database design itself.

Monitoring and Tuning

Diagnostics and Problem Determination

DB2 Universal Database offers a range of tools that can be used to determine the cause of problems or errors in the DB2 system. Common problems include:

- Operating-system-specific
- Hardware- or I/O-specific
- Application-specific
- Communications-specific

In a complex environment, such as a distributed V7.1 DB2 database system or a high-volume OLTP database system, there is a possibility that problems could occur. You need tools to analyze anything that might be characterized as an error. In more serious cases, you may want to determine the cause of a system crash. This kind of troubleshooting needs to be done as quickly and efficiently as possible.

Error Messages and SQL Codes

DB2 Universal Database has a large number of error codes that explain the possible problems within the database system. This means DB2 can report on problems within a database but also on problems within any of the tools and functions that are supplied with DB2.

These messages are divided into a few different categories. Each message has an error code associated with it. The three-letter prefix of the error code dictates what category the error code falls under:

- ASN - DB2 Replication Support messages
- CCA - Client Configuration Assistant messages
- CLI - ODBC/CLI application messages
- DBA - Control Center or DBA Utility messages
- DBI - DB2 Installation messages
- DB2 - CLP or Command Center messages
- DWC - Data Warehouse Center messages
- FLG - Information Catalog Manager messages
- GSE - Spatial Extender messages
- SAT - DB2 Satellite Edition messages
- SPM - Syncpoint Manager messages
- SQJ - DB2 embedded SQL in Java (SQLJ) messages
- SQL - SQL messages

Because the DB2 environment can be complex, there are a large number of error messages. During installation and setup of DB2, administrators may encounter some DBI, DBA, and CCA messages as they become accustomed to the new system. Another example might be users running ad hoc queries against a DB2 database. They could receive SQL errors because of inaccurate SQL syntax or because they were not granted access to certain tables. If you have the specific code associated with an error, you can view the error message text in two ways: first, by consulting the *DB2 Messages Reference*, which details all the error codes in DB2; Second, by querying the code using the CLP or Command Center:

```
DB2 ? SQL0818
```

If an SQL statement fails, you receive an SQL error code as well as an SQLSTATE code. The SQLSTATE code is a standard code based on the ISO/ANSI SQL92 standard. It is unchanged across all the members of the DB2 Family, including RDBMSs on host systems. The SQL error codes may be unique to DB2 Universal Database for UNIX, Windows, and OS/2.

The SQL codes can be in two formats: a negative code (or in the format SQLxxxxN) or positive code (or in the format SQLxxxxW). The *negative* codes signify SQL *errors*, and the *positive* codes signify SQL *warnings* (a zero SQL code means that the SQL completed successfully).

Sometimes the SQL codes contain reason codes within the error message text. These reason codes usually provide more detailed information to supplement the message text. Some examples of reason codes include operating system return codes and communications protocol return codes. The *DB2 UDB V7.1 Messages Reference* provides some detail on common return codes. Sometimes, however, it may be necessary to consult other system documentation.

When using the Administration tools that come with DB2, the Journal records any messages that are returned to the user. For example, if you try to use the Control Center to access the DB2CERT database while an offline backup is in progress, a pop-up dialog box will inform you that the database is in use. This message is then recorded in the Journal. Fig. 12–39 gives an example of the messages logged by the Journal.

Monitoring and Tuning

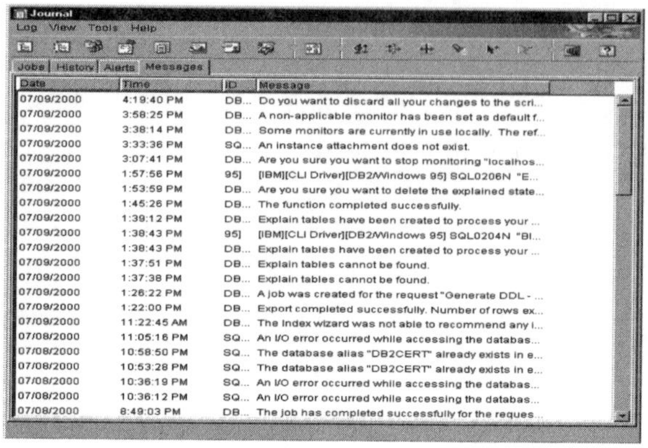

Fig. 12–39 *Messages in the journal*

Diagnostic and Service Logs

DB2 will allow you to log most administrative tasks within the system. There are diagnostic log files for each DB2 instance, a diagnostic log for the Administration Tools that come with DB2, a report log for the DB2 Governor, and logs to document DB2 installation. The focus will be on the diagnostic logs for each DB2 instance (including Administration Server instances).

DB2 will not log any Data Definition Language (DDL) statements or Data Manipulation Language (DML) statements. DB2 *will* log different administrative tasks, such as activating databases, backing up databases, starting and stopping DB2, or starting DB2 communications support.

These kinds of messages, when logged by DB2, are known as *informational* messages. However, in a troubleshooting scenario, the messages that you will be looking for are *error* and *warning* messages. This is also known as *First Failure Data Capture (FFDC)* information. FFDC information is diagnostic information about an error that is captured automatically by DB2 when the error occurs. This information includes:

- db2diag.log - This is the primary diagnostic log for DB2 and should be the first point of reference for the administrator whenever unexpected errors occur. The DIAGLEVEL parameter dictates exactly how much information is logged in the file (see below).
- db2alert.log - If an error is determined by DB2 to be an alert, then an entry is made in the db2alert.log file and to the operating system logs. An alert is an error notification when a *severe* error occurs. Alerts can also trigger SNMP traps.
- Dump files - Sometimes, when a DB2 process or thread fails and signals an error, it will also log extra information in external binary dump files. These files

are more-or-less unreadable and are intended for DB2 Customer Service personnel.

- Trap files - DB2 creates a trap file if an operating system trap/segmentation violation/exception occurs.

> **Note:** Alerts written to the db2alert.log are *not* the same as alerts logged in the Alert Center or Journal, which are warnings generated by the DB2 Snapshot Monitor. Alerts written to the db2alert.log are notifications of severe system errors.

The FFDC information is logged in the directory specified by the DIAGPATH database manager configuration parameter. FFDC information is logged separately for each DB2 instance and is logged for both DB2 Server instances and DB2 Administration Server instances. The default DIAGPATH value is null at instance creation time. By default, the diagnostic files are written to the instance directory (in the db2dump subdirectory in UNIX platforms).

The DIAGPATH parameter is a database manager configuration parameter, so you could change it in the Control Center by right-clicking on the appropriate instance and clicking on **Configure**. You could also use the CLP or Command Center:

```
UPDATE DBM CFG USING DIAGPATH 'C:\NEWDIAGPATH'
```

The level of diagnostic information, DIAGLEVEL, is also a database manager configuration parameter. The DIAGLEVEL parameter can be set to the following values:

- 0 - No diagnostic data (not recommended)
- 1 - Severe errors only
- 2 - All errors (severe and not severe)
- 3 - All errors and warnings (default)
- 4 - All errors, warnings, informational messages, and other internal diagnostic information

The default DIAGLEVEL is usually sufficient for normal DB2 operation. However, during the initial set-up of DB2, or when errors are occurring, the DIAGLEVEL could be updated to 4 in order to gather as much information as possible:

```
UPDATE DBM CFG USING DIAGLEVEL 4
```

Monitoring and Tuning

Inside The DB2DIAG.LOG

The information in the db2diag.log is easy to read, but it can be difficult to interpret certain pieces of data, such as hexadecimal dumps and internal DB2 codes. The db2diag.log is an ASCII file with a series of message entries. Each message entry includes:

- A timestamp for the entry
- The location reporting the error, either a DB2 application, DB2 tool, or even a DB2 function inside the database manager
- A diagnostic message, with the prefix DIA, explaining the error
- Supporting data, such as SQLCA data structures and pointers to other FFDC information

The following example excerpt describes the header of an entry in the db2diag.log file that allows you to interpret the contents more easily.

```
2000-06-05-14.38.03.576271  ▮1  Instance:db2inst1  ▮2  Node:000  ▮3
PID:45698(db2sysc.exe)  ▮4  ID: 372 Appid:*LOCAL.db2inst1.000605193714  ▮5
buffer_pool_services  ▮6  sqlbSMSDirectWrite  ▮7  Probe:99  ▮8  Database:DB2CERT      ▮9

SMS Tablespace 2(USERSPACE1) is full.  Detected on Container 0.
```

1 Timestamp of error.

2 Instance in which the error occurred.

3 Database partition number in which error occurred (applicable in a partitioned database environment). In a nonpartitioned database environment, the node number will always be 000.

4 Process ID - More applicable in a UNIX environment with separate processes. The process ID will then allow you to identify what process returned the error. In OS/2 and Windows environments, however, DB2 operates with multiple threads and, therefore, the process ID will usually identify the main executable.

5 Application ID - Identifies the application for which the process is working. To gather more information about the application, you can use the LIST APPLICATIONS command or use the Snapshot Monitor.

6 The component in DB2 that is writing the message.

7 The name of the function providing the message.

8 Location of the reported internal error.

9 The database in which the error occurred.

The message text of this db2diag.log entry is easy to read in this example, so the error is simple to interpret. However, Fig. 12–40 gives a good idea of some of the less-intuitive errors logged. In this example, DB2 was loading data into a table when the SMS table space filled up and halted the load.

```
2000-06-05-14.38.03.576271   Instance:db2inst1   Node:000
PID:45698(db2sysc.exe)   TID:372 Appid:*LOCAL.db2inst1.000605193714
buffer_pool_services  sqlbSMSDirectWrite   Probe:99   Database:DB2CERT

SMS Tablespace 2(USERSPACE1) is full. Detected on Container 0.

2000-06-05-14.38.03.967437   Instance:db2inst1   Node:000
PID:45698(db2sysc.exe)   Appid:*LOCAL.db2inst1.000605193714
buffer_pool_services  sqlbSMSDirectWrite   Probe:825   Database:DB2CERT
DIA3612C Disk was full.

ZRC=FFFFD60C

2000-06-05-14.38.04.322180   Instance:db2inst1   Node:000
PID:45698(db2sysc.exe)   Appid:*LOCAL.db2inst1.000605193714
buffer_pool_services  sqlbSMSDirectWrite   Probe:825   Database:DB2CERT

 Obj={pool:2;obj:2;type:0} State=x27 Page=4533 Cont=0 Offset=4533 Blk-
Size=12

Data Title:SQLB_OBJECT_DESC PID:45698 Node:000
0002 0002 0002 0002 0000 0000 0000 0000        ...............
0000 007d 2636 0000 0000 0000 0000 0000        ...}&6..........
0000 0000 0000 0001 0000 0027 0000 0000        ...........'....
0000 0000 0000 0000 0000 0001 4001 e424        ...........@.ä$
400c c030 0000 0000                            @.À0....
```

Fig. 12–40 *Example of db2diag.log file*

In the second entry of the db2diag.log, there is an error code with a "DIA" prefix. The DIA error codes are accompanied with an error text that explains the reason for the error. However, in this example, it is accompanied by an internal DB2 return code (FFFFD60C). Usually this return code is accompanied by a ZRC= keyword or a DiagData keyword. The section below, *Interpreting DB2 Internal Return Codes*, explains how to interpret such hexadecimal values. The third entry in the db2diag.log file is a hexadecimal dump of a data structure in DB2, which does not provide any information for our purposes but might be of interest to DB2 Customer Service.

Interpreting DB2 Internal Return Codes

The db2diag.log file often has return codes of the format FFFF???? or ????FFFF, where ???? is a four-character hexadecimal value. The *DB2 Troubleshooting Guide* contains an appendix that interprets the return codes. Using the previous example, take our return code (FFFFD60C) and look in the *DB2 Troubleshooting Guide:* D60C means Disk full. This is known already because the internal return code was preceded by an error message. However, sometimes the only error output written to the db2diag.log is the internal return code.

However, if the return code were in the format ????FFFF, some manipulation of the value would be required to get the actual return code. This manipulation is called byte reversal, and all that is required is to read the return code backwards, byte by byte (a byte in hexadecimal is represented by two alphanumeric characters). For example, if a 0AD5FFFF return code in the db2diag.log was found, with no other DIA errors, a byte reversal on the code would be necessary to determine what the error was. 0AD5FFFF byte-reversed becomes FFFFD50A. This return code, according to the *DB2 Troubleshooting Guide*, means Lock list full.

Tracing Problems in DB2 Universal Database

Sometimes problems occur in DB2 or applications using DB2, and the FFDC information is not sufficient to determine the source of the problem. At this point, DB2 Customer Service may ask the DBA to run traces against the application, against the CLI/ODBC driver (if the application is using ODBC), or against DB2 Universal Database itself.

Tracing or debugging the DB2 application is primarily a task for the application developer who created the program. DB2 embedded SQL programs provide extensive error-reporting functions using the SQLCA structure. This allows application developers to monitor their code executing against DB2.

IBM provides utilities to help the DBA in scenarios where tracing must be performed against DB2 or against the DB2 ODBC driver. The output that these tools dump is not for the DBA to decipher but rather for either the CLI/ODBC application developer or DB2 Customer Service.

To trace an ODBC Application, all that is required is that you switch tracing on and specify a file for the trace output. You can use the Client Configuration Assistant to do this. Select an ODBC data source in the Client Configuration Assistant window and click **Properties**. This will bring up the Database properties windows. Click the **Setting** button in the CLI/ODBC field and then click the **Advanced** button in the CLI/ODBC setting window. You will see the CLI/ODBC Advanced settings window as shown in Fig. 12–41. (The Service tab is selected in this example.)

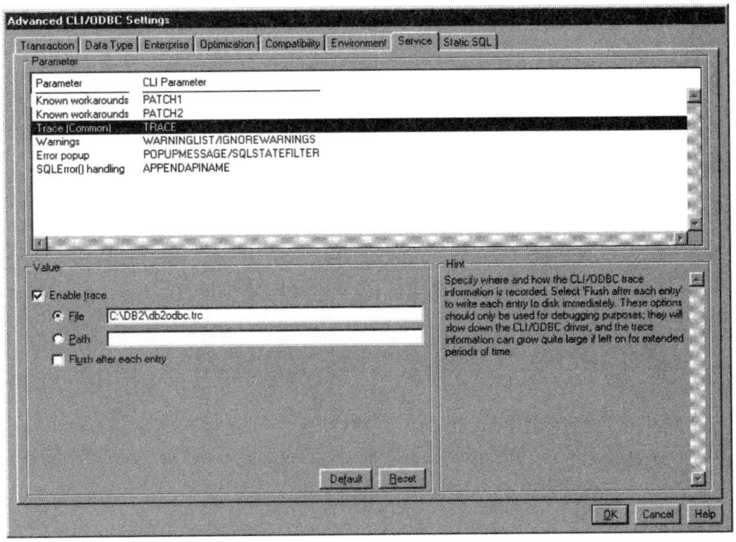

Fig. 12–41 *CLI/ODBC tracing setup from the CCA*

The interface gives you tips on each parameter. You can switch on tracing, specifying a file name to write to or a directory to which multiple files will be written. You can also specify that whenever the trace gathers new data, it should be written immediately to disk using the TRACEFLUSH option. These options can also be specified without using the CCA by editing the DB2CLI.INI file and adding the following section:

```
[COMMON]
TRACE=1
TRACEFILENAME=C:\SQLLIB\DB2ODBC.TRC
TRACEFLUSH=0
```

The output from the DB2 CLI/ODBC trace is a sequence of CLI/ODBC API calls. Fig. 12–42 gives an example of what the ODBC trace output would look like. In this example, the trace captures an unsuccessful connect to a DB2 database.

Monitoring and Tuning

```
Build Date: %E% - Product: QDB2/NT (5) - Driver Version: 06.01.0000

SQLAllocHandle( fHandleType=SQL_HANDLE_ENV, hInput=0:0, phOutput=&12d1d5c
)

SQLAllocHandle( phOutput=0:1 )
    <--- SQL_SUCCESS    Time elapsed - +1.000000E-002 seconds

SQLSetEnvAttr( hEnv=0:1, fAttribute=SQL_ATTR_ODBC_VERSION,
vParam=2,cbParam=0)
    ---> Time elapsed - +0.000000E+000 seconds

SQLSetEnvAttr( )
    <--- SQL_SUCCESS    Time elapsed - +0.000000E+000 seconds

SQLAllocHandle( fHandleType=SQL_HANDLE_DBC, hInput=0:1, phOutput=&12d1d4c
)
    ---> Time elapsed - +0.000000E+000 seconds

SQLAllocHandle( phOutput=0:1 )
    <--- SQL_SUCCESS    Time elapsed - +0.000000E+000 seconds

SQLGetInfo( hDbc=0:1, fInfoType=SQL_DRIVER_ODBC_VER, rgbInfoV-
alue=&12d1e30, cbInfoValueMax=12, pcbInfoValue=&128324 )
    ---> Time elapsed - +0.000000E+000 seconds

SQLGetInfo( rgbInfoValue="03.00", pcbInfoValue=5 )
    <--- SQL_SUCCESS    Time elapsed - +0.000000E+000 seconds

SQLDriverConnect( hDbc=0:1, hwnd=11:1402, szConnStrIn="DSN=DB2CERT;",
cbConnStrIn=-3, szConnStrOut=&12d1e50, cbConnStrOutMax=256, pcb-
ConnStrOut=&129130, fDriverCompletion=SQL_DRIVER_COMPLETE_REQUIRED )
    ---> Time elapsed - +0.000000E+000 seconds
( DBMS NAME="DB2/NT", Version="06.01.0000", Fixpack="0x21010104" )
( StmtOut="SET CURRENT DEGREE 'ANY'" )
( COMMIT=0 )

SQLDriverConnect(
szConnStrOut="DSN=DB2CERT;UID=tetsuya;PWD=******;DB2DEGREE=ANY;LOBMAXCOLUM
NSIZE=1048575;LONGDATACOMPAT=1;DBALIAS=DB2CERT;PATCH1=131072;", pcb-
ConnStrOut=121 )
    <--- SQL_SUCCESS    Time elapsed - +1.502000E+000 seconds
( DSN="DB2CERT" )
( UID="tetsuya" )
( PWD="******" )
( DB2DEGREE="ANY" )
( LOBMAXCOLUMNSIZE="1048575" )
( LONGDATACOMPAT="1" )
( DBALIAS="DB2CERT" )
( PATCH1="131072" )
```

Fig. 12–42 *Example of a CLI/ODBC trace*

Note: Tracing a CLI/ODBC application will slow down the application's performance considerably. Also, a large amount of data is written to the output trace file and may use up a large amount of disk space.

There are some other diagnostic parameters that you can use to gather more information: `AppendAPIName` and `PopUpMessage`. When these parameters are switched on, the CLI/ODBC driver will present the user with dialog boxes monitoring the progress of the CLI/ODBC application. These parameters can be set using the Client Configuration Assistant or again by adding the following entries to the [COMMON] section of the DB2CLI.INI:

```
[COMMON]
APPENDAPINAME=1
POPUPMESSAGE=1
```

Tracing against DB2 itself is somewhat similar to CLI/ODBC tracing. You specify where you want the trace output to go and then turn on tracing. Tracing also has a significant performance impact on DB2. However, you have some flexibility when tracing inside DB2. You can filter what you want to monitor. You can specify how large a memory buffer you wish to use to hold trace information. You can specify how many DB2 errors the trace retains. Tracing against DB2 can be started with the **db2trc** command. You have to specify certain options to gather the trace information. You take a DB2 trace in four steps:

- Switch on tracing (`db2trc on`).
- Dump the trace output (`db2trc dump`).
- Switch off tracing (`db2trc off`).
- Format the trace output (`db2trc flw` or `db2trc fmt`).

Using the `flw` option, you can specify that you would like the trace output formatted in order of DB2 thread/process. Using the `fmt` option, you can specify that you want the trace output formatted in chronological order. When switching on tracing, you can specify some additional options:

- `-m` - Mask the particular record types you wish to trace.
- `-e` - Specify a limit to the number of DB2 errors retained by the trace.
- `-r` - Specify a limit to the size of trace records.
- `-s` or `-f` - Specify whether the trace output should be held in shared memory or written directly to a file.
- `-l` or `-i` - Specify the size of the memory buffer in which the trace output is stored. The `-l` option will retain the last records of the trace. The `-i` option will retain the initial records.

Monitoring and Tuning

The following example switches on tracing using the db2trc command and specifies a 4 MB buffer for tracing and uses the defaults for everything else (the defaults capture all trace information; do not set any limits and trace to memory):

```
db2trc on -l 4000000
```

After you have used the db2trc dump command and the db2trc off command, you can format the trace output. You execute the db2trc fmt command, for example:

```
C:\SQLLIB\BIN> db2trc fmt mytrace.dmp mytrace.out
  Trace wrapped       :YES
  Size of trace       :3996054 bytes
  Records in trace     :39450
  Records formatted     :39450
```

Fig. 12–43 *db2trc command*

A trace is wrapped when the trace fills up the memory buffer allocated to it (in this example, 4 MB) and begins overwriting the beginning of the buffer again. It is important that you specify a large enough buffer size for tracing. This is to avoid a scenario in which trace wrapping overwrites the important error information you are trying to capture.

A trace file formatted with the db2trc fmt command might look something like the excerpt in Fig. 12–44.

```
14719    DB2 fnc_retcode    SW- query graph        sqlnq_ftb::new (1.33.60.55)
         pid 138; tid 117; cpid 139; time 7951153; trace_point 254
         return_code = 000000 = 0

14720    DB2 fnc_entry     SW- query graph        sqlnq_ftb::sqlnq_ftb (1.30.60.56)
         pid 138; tid 117; cpid 139; time 7951153; trace_point 0
         called_from 0081F618

14721    DB2 cei_entry      oper_system_services sqlogmblk (1.20.15.82)
         pid 138; tid 117; cpid 139; time 7951153; trace_point 0
         called_from 10047AE9

14722    DB2 cei_data      oper_system_services sqlogmblk (1.25.15.82)
         pid 138; tid 117; cpid 139; time 7951153; trace_point 1
         4c05 9601 8c00 0000 0000 0000        L...........
```

Fig. 12–44 *Example of DB2 trace records*

For more information on tracing in DB2 Universal Database, please refer to the *DB2 Troubleshooting Guide*.

Troubleshooting Information

Extensive information on problem determination in DB2 can be found in the *DB2 Troubleshooting Guide*. Also, there are a number of readme files, technical hints and tips, as well as online DB2 publications available in the DB2 Technical Library on the World Wide Web. The DB2 Technical Library is located at:

```
http://www.software.ibm.com/data/db2/library
```

Monitoring and Tuning

Summary

Understanding the DB2 database environment is an important part of any database administrator's job. To gain this understanding, there are various facilities that can be used.

There are two types of monitors available to analyze the database activity. They are called the Snapshot Monitor and the Event Monitor. A Snapshot Monitor provides point-in-time information regarding resource usage. Many of the elements returned from a snapshot are counters and high-water marks. An Event Monitor is defined through a GUI db2emcrt or by using a DDL statement. Once activated, the monitored events will be written to disk or to a named pipe.

Graphical monitoring tools are provided with DB2 Universal Database. The graphical Performance Monitor uses the Snapshot Monitor API to gather database activity and display the activity as a graph or in detailed format. The Event Analyzer is a graphical interface to help analyze the collected Event Monitor records.

The DB2 optimizer is one of the most advanced in the relational database industry. The optimizer will generate an access plan during query compilation. Access plans are stored in the system catalog tables for static SQL applications. Access plans for dynamic SQL statements are generated at query execution time and stored in memory.

To gain an understanding of the access plan (strategy) chosen by the DB2 optimizer, the Explain Facility may be used. The Explain Facility will populate relational tables with detailed information for the SQL statements. These tables can then be queried to determine the plan information regarding index usage and other database resources. There is a snapshot column in the explain tables that is used to store a graphical representation of the access plan. This graphical version of the plan can be examined using Visual Explain.

In this chapter, the topics of record blocking, sorting, database parameter tuning, and database parallelism were also discussed

Diagnostics and problem determination information is provided in DB2. This information comes in the form of SQLCODE, and SQLSTATE codes, DB2DIAG.LOG entries, CLI/ODBC and DB2 traces, and other First Failure Data Capture (FFDC) information.

PART 4

Developing Applications

13

Application Development Overview

- ◆ DEVELOPMENT ENVIRONMENT
- ◆ PROGRAMMING INTERFACES

Applications represent the interface to the database, and as a DB2 Universal Database administrator, you may have to provide support to developers when they write applications that access the database. DB2 does not have its own programming language. Instead, it allows data to be manipulated using interfaces that pass SQL statements. It also provides an Application Programming Interface for managing and administering the database.

A DB2 application can perform specific queries or process well-defined transactions. An application that performs transaction processing is sometimes referred to as an Online Transaction Processing (OLTP) application. An application that performs ad hoc queries is sometimes referred to as a Decision Support System (DSS) or Online Analytical Processing (OLTP) application. DB2 can be used as the database server for both types of applications.

In this chapter, we will explore the DB2 application development environment, become familiar with many of the options available for developing DB2 applications, and examine some common features of DB2 applications.

DB2 Application Development Environment

You can develop applications at a DB2 server or a client. You can develop and test applications that run on one operating system and access databases on the same or a different operating system. For example, you can create an application that runs on the Windows operating system but accesses a database on a UNIX platform such as AIX. Once you have developed your applications, you can distribute them to other systems, where they can be executed using the DB2 runtime client component that is included in all DB2 products.

To supplement or extend client applications, DB2 programming can also involve development of components that run on the server either as parts of the database manager or as separate modules.

Software Requirements

Before developing applications for DB2, the following products need to be installed and configured:

- Non-DB2 application development utilities, including a compiler or interpreter
- DB2 Universal Database, installed locally or remotely
- DB2 Developer's Edition including the Application Development client

Non-DB2 Application Development Utilities

DB2 allows for application development through a variety of programming languages and third-party application development tools. You must ensure that the proper programming tools and products are installed on each of the development machines. For example, if you are planning to develop an application using a programming language like C, C++, COBOL, or FORTRAN, you need to have the appropriate compilers for creating application modules such as executables and libraries. For Java programs, you need the Java Development Kit (JDK). To develop REXX applications, you need to have REXX support installed, which includes a runtime interpreter. Third-party or ODBC application development environments such as Lotus Approach and Microsoft Visual Basic have their own requirements.

Because each compiler or development tool has different attributes, you may need to configure it for use with DB2. Instructions for setting up development tools and a list of supported compilers is provided in the *DB2 UDB V7.1 Application Building Guide.*

DB2 Universal Database

The database server can either be installed on the same system where the application is being developed or on a remote machine. Generally, if the database is to be accessed by a single developer, it may as well reside on the same system where the application is being developed. When many developers need to access a database, a common database server may be more suitable.

Most of the time, the database location for development purposes is chosen based on convenience and may not be its final location. This is because location and platform of the database server has little influence over the application development process on the client. For example, if the database were moved from a development platform of DB2 on Windows NT to a production platform of DB2 on AIX, it is unlikely that the application would require any changes. However, you may need to bind the application to the new database. We will discuss the bind process in more detail later.

DB2 provides a sample database that you require for running the supplied sample programs. The sample database can be created using the db2sampl command or through the First Steps tools found in the DB2 folder. You may use the sample database for development purposes or choose to create a customized database. A database can be created using the Control Center, Command Center, Command Line Processor (CLP) or a script. A database can only be created by a user with SYSADM or SYSCTRL privileges. Upon creating the database, the user who created the database will be the DBADM (by default). This user can then grant privileges to other users who can create database objects and populate them with data to be used for development purposes.

Once you have successfully created a database and all of its objects, you should verify that your environment has been set up properly by establishing a connection to the database. You can test the connection to the database using the DB2 CLP, Command Center, Client Configuration Assistant, or the Control Center.

DB2 Application Development Client (DB2 ADC)

The DB2 ADC provides tools (such as precompilers) and required files (such as DB2 library and header files) needed to develop applications that access DB2 databases using an embedded SQL or DB2 CLI interface. It also contains sample programs that use all of the supported DB2 programming interfaces. The DB2 ADC comes as part of the DB2 Developer's Edition products.

The Personal Developer's Edition (PDE) product provides for the application development needs of a single user on Windows 32-bit operating systems, Linux, and OS/2. The DB2 Universal Developer's Edition (UDE) provides for the application development needs of one or more users on all DB2-supported platforms. When there are multiple developers in the development environment, additional licenses permit developers to share the programming libraries and pre-compilers.

The DB2 ADC is unique for each *client* development platform. For example, suppose you have been asked to develop an embedded SQL application that would allow a Windows user to access a DB2 database on an AIX server. The user needs a Windows application. You would require the DB2 Software Developer's Kit for Windows NT to develop the application.

You do not need the DB2 Software Developer's Kit for developing JDBC programs. Developing applications through many end-user and ODBC tools also does not require the DB2 SDK.

DB2 Programming Interfaces

There are many programming methods available to a DB2 application developer. These include:

- Embedded SQL - Static and dynamic
- Call Level Interface (CLI), Open Database Connectivity (ODBC)
- Java Interfaces - JDBC, SQLJ
- Native DB2 Application Programming Interfaces (APIs)
- Microsoft Data Objects - ADO, RDO, DAO
- Other interfaces, third-party, and ODBC end-user tools

Why are there so many different programming methods? Each programming method has its unique advantages. We will examine each of the methods and provide examples of their advantages and disadvantages.

Embedded SQL

Structured Query Language (SQL) is the database interface language used to access and manipulate data in DB2 databases. You can embed SQL statements in your applications, enabling them to perform any task supported by SQL, such as retrieving or storing data.

An application in which you embed SQL statements is called a host program. A programming language that you compile, and in which you embed SQL statements, is called a host language. The program and language are defined this way because they host or accommodate SQL statements. Using DB2, you can code your embedded SQL applications in the C/C++, COBOL, FORTRAN, Java (SQLJ), and REXX programming languages.

There are two types of embedded SQL statements: static and dynamic. These are discussed in the following sections.

Static Embedded SQL

Static SQL statements are ones in which the SQL statement type and the database objects accessed by the statement, such as column names, are known prior to running the application. The only unknowns are the data values the statement is searching for or modifying. The database objects being accessed must exist when a static embedded application module is bound to the database. The development process involves the combination of SQL with a third-generation programming language. When the embedded SQL program is executed, it uses predefined SQL statements that have been bound to the database as application packages. Thus, the access plan to data is retained in the database in a ready-to-execute package.

There are many performance benefits to having ready-to-execute database logic stored within the database. Static embedded SQL programs have the least runtime overhead of all the DB2 programming methods and execute faster. The package is in a form that is understood by the database server. However, as you might have guessed already, this method of developing applications is not the most flexible because every SQL statement that the end-user executes needs to be known and understood during the development process.

The transactions are grouped into packages and stored in the database. The SQL statements are embedded within programming modules. The programming modules, which contain embedded SQL statements, must be precompiled. The modified programming modules, created by the precompiler, are then compiled and linked to create the application. During the precompile phase, the SQL statements are analyzed and packages are created. We will examine all of the steps for creating static embedded DB2 applications in the next chapter.

Static applications for DB2 can be coded using C/C++, Java, COBOL, or FORTRAN. DB2 provides support for static SQL statements in Java programs using the SQLJ (Embedded SQL for Java) standard. REXX cannot be used for static SQL.

Generally, static statements are well suited for high-performance applications with predefined transactions. A reservation system is a good example of such an application.

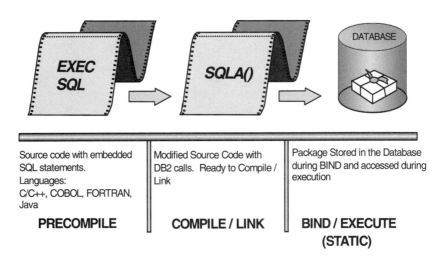

Fig. 13–1 *SQL statements prepared during application development*

Advantages

- Ready-to-use packages may be optimal for faster execution
- Use programming skills in COBOL, C/C++, or FORTRAN

Disadvantages

- Must define SQL statements during development
- Requires precompiling

Dynamic Embedded SQL

Dynamic SQL statements are those statements that your application builds and executes at runtime. An interactive application that prompts the end-user for key parts of an SQL statement, such as the names of the tables and columns to be searched, is a good example of dynamic SQL. The application builds the SQL statement while it is running and then submits the statement for processing.

Dynamic embedded SQL, as shown in Fig. 13–2 on page 682, still requires the precompile, compile, and link phases of application development. The binding or selection of the most effective data access plan is performed at program execution time, as the SQL statements are *dynamically prepared*. Choosing the access path at program execution time has some advantages and some drawbacks.

The database objects being accessed must exist when a static embedded application module is bound to the database. Dynamic embedded SQL modules do not require that these database objects exist when the application is precompiled. However, the database objects must exist at runtime.

An embedded static SQL programming module will have its data access method determined during the static bind phase, using the database statistics available at bind time. An embedded dynamic SQL programming module will have its data access method determined during the statement preparation and will utilize the database statistics available at query execution time.

Therefore, there is no need to rebind dynamic embedded SQL programming modules to the database following a collection of database statistics. The database statistics are collected when the RUNSTATS command is issued. The results are stored in the system catalog tables. There is, of course, a query execution time overhead to choose the access path, since each dynamically prepared SQL statement must be optimized.

In Fig. 13–2, the development steps for embedded dynamic SQL program modules are shown. Using embedding dynamic SQL statements does not remove the precompile phase of development, but it does provide the execution of dynamic SQL statements.

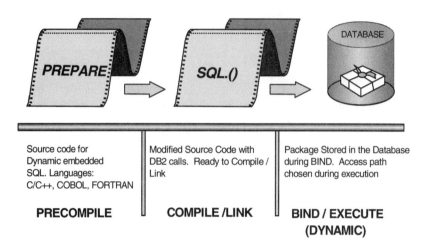

Source code for Dynamic embedded SQL. Languages: C/C++, COBOL, FORTRAN	Modified Source Code with DB2 calls. Ready to Compile / Link	Package Stored in the Database during BIND. Access path chosen during execution
PRECOMPILE	**COMPILE /LINK**	**BIND / EXECUTE (DYNAMIC)**

Fig. 13–2 *SQL statements prepared during application execution*

Generally, dynamic SQL statements are well suited for applications that run against a rapidly changing database where transactions need to be specified at runtime. An interactive query interface is a good example of such an application.

Advantages

- Current database statistics are used for each SQL statement.
- Database objects do not have to exist before runtime.
- They are more flexible than static SQL statements.

Disadvantages

- Since queries are optimized at runtime, they may take more time to execute.

Call Level Interface and ODBC

The DB2 Call Level Interface (CLI) is a programming interface that your C and C++ applications can use to access DB2 databases. DB2 CLI is based on the Microsoft Open Database Connectivity Standard (ODBC) specification and the X/Open and ISO Call Level Interface standards. Because DB2 CLI is based on industry standards, application programmers who are already familiar with these database interfaces may benefit from a shorter learning curve. Many ODBC applications can be used with DB2 without any modifications. Likewise, a CLI application is easily ported to other database servers.

DB2 CLI is a dynamic SQL application development environment. However, instead of embedding the SQL statements, your application passes dynamic SQL statements as function arguments to the database using C/C++ Application Programming Interfaces (APIs) provided with DB2. The necessary data structures used to communicate between the database and the application are allocated transparently by DB2.

Because the SQL statements are issued through direct API calls, CLI programs are not precompiled. Also, CLI applications use common access packages provided with DB2; hence, there is no need to bind the program modules separately. You only need to bind the DB2 CLI packages once to each database you want to access using any DB2 CLI or ODBC applications on a client.

Many differences exist between developing an embedded SQL application module and developing a CLI module. Since an application is usually composed of a number of program modules, the modules can use different DB2 programming techniques. It can be beneficial to use different DB2 programming interfaces in a single application.

The CLI application development environment is shown in Fig. 13–3.

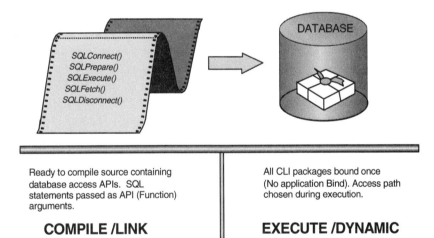

Ready to compile source containing database access APIs. SQL statements passed as API (Function) arguments.

All CLI packages bound once (No application Bind). Access path chosen during execution.

COMPILE /LINK   **EXECUTE /DYNAMIC**

Fig. 13–3 *Application development using CLI or ODBC*

Advantages

- Precompiler *not* required
- Binding an application package to the database *not* required
- Current database statistics used
- Can store and retrieve sets of data
- Can use scrollable and updatable cursors
- Easy porting to other database platforms

Disadvantages

- Must have C/C++ programming skills
- Dynamic binding can result in slower query execution

Java Interfaces (JDBC and SQLJ)

DB2 provides support for many different types of Java programs including applets, applications, servlets, and advanced DB2 server-side features. Java programs that access and manipulate DB2 databases can use the Java Database Connectivity (JDBC) API and Embedded SQL for Java (SQLJ) standard. Both of these are vendor-neutral SQL interfaces that provide data access to your application through standardized Java methods. The greatest benefit of using Java regardless of the database interface is its *write once, run anywhere* capability, allowing the same Java program to be distributed and executed on various operating platforms in a heterogeneous environment. And since the two Java database interfaces supported by DB2 are industry open standards, you have the added benefit of using your Java program against a variety of database vendors.

For JDBC programs, your Java code passes *dynamic* SQL to a JDBC driver that comes with DB2. DB2 executes the SQL statements through JDBC APIs and the results are passed back to your Java code. JDBC is similar to DB2 CLI because JDBC uses dynamic SQL and you do not have to precompile or bind a JDBC program.

With DB2 SQLJ support, you can build and run SQLJ programs that contain *static* embedded SQL statements. Since your SQLJ program contains static SQL, you need to perform steps similar to precompiling and binding. Before you can compile an SQLJ source file, you must translate it with the SQLJ translator to create native Java source code. After translation, you need to create the DB2 packages using the DB2 for Java profile customizer (`db2profc`). Mechanisms contained within SQLJ rely on JDBC for many tasks like establishing connections.

Choosing between SQLJ and JDBC for your Java program involves many of the same considerations and tradeoffs as for static versus dynamic embedded SQL in other languages. SQLJ may be beneficial because static SQL can be faster. Java programs containing embedded SQL can also be subjected to static analysis of SQL statements for the purposes of syntax checking, type checking, and schema validation. On the other hand, not all data objects to be accessed may be known before execution, requiring JDBC for dynamic SQL. A Java programmer can create a powerful application by including both static and dynamic constructs with ease since SQLJ shares environment and state information with JDBC.

Table 13-1 *Differences Between JDBC and SQLJ*

JDBC	SQLJ
SQL via API calls	SQL is embedded
Dynamic SQL	Static SQL
Precompiling not required	Translate SQLJ and create packages

Advantages

Java programs written for DB2 offer:

- Increased portability to other database systems and operating platforms
- Easy access to databases across the Internet from multiple client platforms
- Representation of the NULL state built into Java types
- Object-oriented application development and data access model

Disadvantages

- Must have Java programming skills
- Can be slower since Java is interpreted

Native DB2 APIs

DB2 supplies native Application Programming Interfaces (APIs), which can be used to directly manipulate DB2 instances and databases. They are also called administrative or database manager APIs. Some tasks, such as performing a backup of a database, must be coded using these APIs. There is no method of embedding an SQL statement to perform this operation because the BACKUP DATABASE command is not part of SQL.

The DB2 APIs are provided in many programming languages, including C/C++, COBOL, and FORTRAN. Information is exchanged between the application and database using special data structures. If the source program module contains only DB2 APIs, there is no need to precompile, and a database package is not created.

The native DB2 APIs are not directly used for coding SQL statements on their own. The native APIs rely on embedded SQL or CLI to perform OLAP/OLTP and are generally used in conjunction with these interfaces to provide administrative or database management functions. For example, the function `sqlaintp()` is commonly used to retrieve the complete text for a DB2 error message, so an embedded SQL application can then display the error message to the end-user. The DB2 APIs are grouped by functional category (see Table 13–2). For details on using these APIs, see the *DB2 UDB V7.1 API Reference*.

Table 13–2 *Types of Native (Administrative) DB2 APIs*

Backup/Recovery	Database Monitoring
Database Control	Operational Utilities
Database Manager Control	Data Utilities
Database Directory Management	General Application Programming
Client/Server Directory Management	Application Preparation
Network Support	Remote Server Utilities
Database Configuration	Table Space Management
Node and Nodegroup management	

Advantages

- Enables advanced features of DB2 (e.g., table space administration)
- No precompiling or binding required

Disadvantages

- Requires host language compiler/linker
- Can be more difficult to implement
- Cannot issue SQL statements
- Not easily ported to other database servers

Microsoft Data Objects (DAO, RDO, ADO, OLE-DB)

You can write Microsoft Visual Basic and Microsoft Visual C++ applications that conform to the Data Access Object (DAO) and Remote Data Object (RDO) specifications. These applications interface with DB2 using DB2's ODBC (CLI) driver. DB2 also supports ActiveX Data Object (ADO) applications via the OLE:ODBC bridge, or a native OLE DB driver for DB2.

ActiveX Data Objects (ADO) allow you to write an application to access and manipulate data through an OLE DB provider. The OLE DB API was designed by Microsoft to allow data access to a much broader set of data providers than are available through ODBC. The primary benefits of ADO are high speed, ease of use, low memory overhead, and a small disk footprint.

Remote Data Objects (RDO) provide an information model for accessing remote data sources through ODBC. RDO offers a set of objects that make it easy to connect to a database, execute queries and stored procedures, manipulate results, and commit changes to the server. It is specifically designed to access remote ODBC relational data sources and makes it easier to use ODBC without complex application code. It is a primary means of accessing a relational database that is exposed with an ODBC driver.

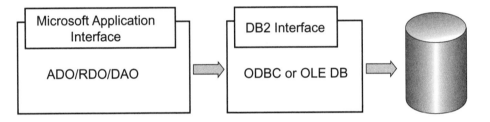

Fig. 13–5 *Applications using Microsoft data objects*

Microsoft Visual Basic is a widely used tool that permits development of rich featured applications using a variety of data access models including ADO, DAO, and RDO.

Advantage

• Provide standardized programming model independent of data source

Disadvantage

• Data objects available on Microsoft Windows platforms only

Other Interfaces and Tools

There are numerous third-party application building tools and end-user applications that interface with DB2 using one or more programming methods described previously. However, many of these tools and applications provide their own front-end data access methods, making the underlying interface to the database transparent to application developers and end-users. This can provide a simpler alternative to developing applications than using a high-level programming language.

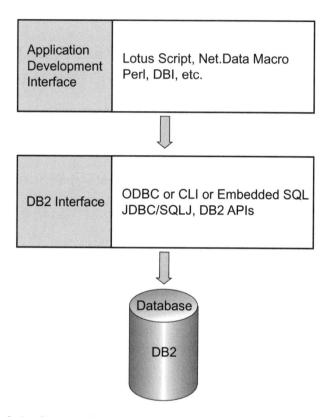

Fig. 13–6 *Application development using other interfaces*

ODBC Tools

There might be cases where you need to perform a basic task, such as querying the database, developing reports, and analyzing data. ODBC end-user tools such as Lotus Approach and Microsoft Access assist in creating applications to perform these tasks. With Lotus Approach, you can develop applications using LotusScript, a full-featured, object-oriented programming language that comes with a wide array of objects, events, methods, and properties, along with a built-in program editor.

Net.Data

Net.Data enables development of Web applications for Internet and intranet access to DB2 data. It provides an intermediary interface between the Web server and DB2 client code, allowing end-users to access DB2 using just their Web browsers on their workstations. It can run on the Web server machine as a common gateway interface (CGI) application or exploit Web server interfaces (APIs) and FastCGI to provide better performance. Net.Data supports client-side processing as well as server-side processing with languages such as Java, REXX, Perl, and C++. It provides conditional logic and a rich macro language. Net.Data uses CLI as the default back-end for connecting to DB2. Besides DB2, it also supports access to other data sources such as Oracle, Sybase, DRDA-enabled data sources, and ODBC data sources, as well as flat file and Web registry data.

DB2 and Net.Data form an integral part of IBM Websphere Commerce Suite, a product that enables Internet commerce and Web-based shopping activities in a secure and robust manner.

Perl DBI

Perl DBI is an application programming interface that provides database access for the Perl language. Like ODBC, Perl DBI provides a standardized database interface independent of the actual database being used. DB2 supports the Perl Database Interface (DBI) specification for data access through the DBD::DB2 driver. This driver works in conjunction with the DBI to access DB2 via CLI. The ability to access DB2 from a Perl environment is particularly useful for database testing and maintenance scripts on UNIX platforms and Windows NT. Perl applications are also commonly used for writing CGI scripts for Web access.

Each of the third-party products mentioned in this section has its own benefits and drawbacks. Some common features are described below.

Advantages

- Quick access to data using a simple or graphical interface
- Faster way for developing relatively simple applications
- Development skills reusable with other data sources
- Provide abstraction over low-level data access details

Disadvantages

- Sometimes unsuitable for complex applications
- May not be able to access certain DB2 features and functions

Summary

DB2 supports applications on a wide variety of operating platforms and numerous methods of coding the applications.

Applications can contain embedded SQL or be coded using standard APIs like CLI, ODBC, and JDBC. Applications can also be developed using other interfaces such as Perl DBI and ActiveX Data Objects. There are many IBM and non-IBM products like Net.Data and Visual Basic, and end-user tools such as Lotus Approach and Microsoft Access, which make the process of application development faster and easier.

Depending on the type of application, one or more programming techniques can be used. DB2 allows applications to be developed that use many popular programming languages including C/C++, COBOL, FORTRAN, Java, and REXX. The DB2 Software Developer's Kit (SDK) included with DB2 Personal Developer's Edition (PDE) and DB2 Universal Developer's Edition (UDE) provides support for developing DB2 applications using these programming languages.

In this chapter, we also examined the main tasks involved in coding a DB2 application as well as the usage of schemas and aliases with respect to accessing database objects from a program.

14

Development Considerations

- ◆ PACKAGES
- ◆ BINDING
- ◆ CLI & ODBC SETTINGS
- ◆ JDBC & SQLJ SETTINGS
- ◆ SQL STORED PROCEDURE BUILDER

*E*mbedded SQL programming was introduced in the previous chapter. Even though many of the alternatives to embedded SQL programming offer faster and easier ways to develop applications, it is nevertheless useful to understand and know how to program using embedded SQL. Static statements offer great performance benefits and are only possible through embedded SQL. If you are migrating applications from mainframes such as S/390 or using COBOL, you may prefer embedded SQL.

A precompiler for a variety of programming languages is provided with the DB2 Development Kits (Personal and Universal). The precompiler is used to convert embedded SQL statements into a series of Application Programming Interface (API) requests (as was discussed in the previous chapter).

Embedded SQL Overview

Fig. 14–1 on page 693 illustrates the steps involved in building an embedded SQL application. These are as follows:

1. Create source files that contain programs with embedded SQL statements.

2. Connect to a database, then precompile each source file.

   The precompiler converts the SQL statements in each source file into DB2 run-time API calls to the database manager. The precompiler also produces an access package in the database and, optionally, a bind file, if you specify that you want one created. We will discuss packages and bind files in the following sections.

3. Compile the modified source files (and other files without SQL statements) using the host language compiler.

4. Link the object files with the DB2 and host language libraries to produce an executable program.

5. Bind the bind file to create the access package if this was not already done at precompile time or if a different database is to be accessed.

6. Run the application. The application accesses the database using the access plan in the package.

Creating Packages

A *package* is a database object that contains optimized SQL statements. A *package* corresponds to a single source programming module and, *sections* corresponds to the SQL statements contained in the source program module.

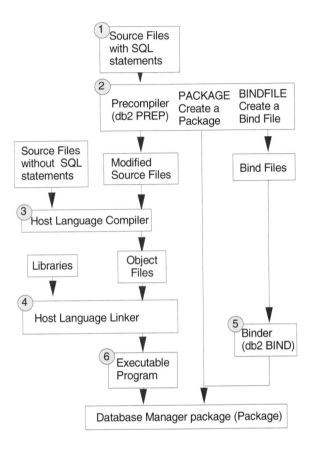

Fig. 14–1 *Process for creating embedded SQL applications*

A programming module that contains embedded *static* SQL statements requires precompiling, during which time the precompiler generates a package (by default). This package contains a number of sections that correspond to embedded SQL statements. A section is the compiled form of an SQL statement. While every section corresponds to one statement, every statement does not necessarily have a section. An optimized *access plan* will be stored in the section. The package can be stored directly in the database, or the data needed to create a package can be stored in a bind file. Creating a bind file and bind it in a separate step is known as *deferred binding*.

A program module that contains embedded *dynamic* SQL statements has an associated package and sections, but in this case, the sections are used as placeholders for the SQL statement that will be dynamically prepared. There are no access plans stored in the sections because they are in embedded static SQL modules.

Like views and tables, packages have an associated schema name. The fully qualified name of a package is SCHEMA-NAME.PACKAGE-NAME.

In most cases, application developers use deferred binding. Deferred binding requires a two-step process:

1. Creating a bind file (which contains information to create a package)

2. Binding the package bind file to the database

Let's examine these steps. First, we need to create a bind file. The bind file is generated by the precompiler when the appropriate option is specified. The precompiler can be invoked with the PREP or PRECOMPILE command using the Command Center or the Command Line Processor (CLP).

The precompiler input is always a source programming module with embedded SQL statements. Each DB2-supported programming language has its own precompiler provided with the DB2 Software Developer's Kit. The file extension of the source program module is used to determine which precompiler (e.g., C, C++, COBOL, FORTRAN) will be invoked.

In Table 14–1, the input host language source file extensions and the modified source file output extensions are provided. The examples in this book are written in C. Therefore, the embedded SQL program files are named program-name.sqc, and the precompiler output files are named program-name.c. The name of the source module is important, because the precompiler will use this as the name of the package unless otherwise specified.

Table 14–1 *Precompile File Extensions*

Host Language	File Extension (Input - Source)	File Extension (Output - Modified Source)
C	.sqc	.c
C++ (case sensitive - AIX)	.sqC	.C
C++ (case insensitive - OS/2, Windows)	.sqx	.cxx
COBOL - Use TARGET and/or OUTPUT options to use other extensions	.sqb	.cbl
FORTRAN (UNIX)	.sqf	.f
FORTRAN (OS/2, Windows)	.sqf	.for

If you issue these DB2 commands/statements:

```
connect to db2cert user db2cert using db2
precompile prog1.sqc
connect reset
```

then you would create an application package called DB2CERT.PROG1 in the DB2CERT database. This package would contain a lot of information about the embedded SQL statements, apart from the host variable values required to execute the embedded SQL statements that are contained in the file prog1.sqc. There are additional steps required before you have an executable application. All database objects specifically referenced (tables, views, etc.) must exist during the precompile phase because in this example deferred binding is not being used. The other inconvenient aspect of not creating a separate bind file is that the entire database would need to be provided, along with the application to the end-user, since the package only exists in the database. The data needed to create the package is not contained in a separate bind file in this example.

Let's look at an example of deferred binding with the DB2 commands/statements:

```
connect to db2cert user db2cert using db2
precompile prog1.sqc bindfile
connect reset
```

This example demonstrates the use of the precompiler option BINDFILE. This option is used to generate an output file that contains all of the data needed to create the package for the source module. By using this option, this data is stored in a file called prog1.bnd. You can change the name of the output bind file, but in this example, we did not rename the bind file. To avoid confusion between source program modules, bind files, and package names, try to avoid renaming any of these objects. If you want to create the package using a different name, use the option PACKAGE USING <PACKAGE-NAME>. If you want to create the package using a different schema name, use the option COLLECTION <SCHEMA-NAME>.

The name of the package is determined when the prog1.bnd file is bound to the database. If the same user were to bind this package, the name of the package would be DB2CERT.PROG1. If the database objects do not exist during precompile, only warnings will be generated, and the bind file is created. (Object existence and authentication SQL codes are treated as warnings instead of as errors.) The BIND command verifies the existence and access privileges of database objects and will only be successful once the required objects are present.

 Note: Database objects referenced in embedded static SQL programs must exist in the database during package creation (PRECOMPILE without BINDFILE option or BIND).

For each source program module containing embedded static SQL statements, a corresponding package must exist in the database. Assume that we are creating an application that accesses two different DB2 databases. The objects referenced in the application must exist in the database for the package to be created success-fully. Therefore, we will develop the application using two different program mod-ules. Each program module or source file represents a database package. If we keep the SQL statements for each database in separate packages, the bind will be suc-cessful. We can then compile and link the program modules together into a single executable.

Any PRECOMPILE error messages will be reported to the display or to a message file. The error message file can be specified using the MESSAGES option when issu-ing the PRECOMPILE command. It is recommended to send the messages to an out-put file so you can examine the file to determine the cause of the errors. Errors during precompile could include invalid host variable definitions and incorrect SQL statements.

When precompiling, you can also determine whether the SQL embedded in the program conforms to different syntaxes and standards. For example, you can check to see if the application works against DB2 for OS/390, or is ISO/ANS SQL92 compliant. This is done using the LANGLEVEL, SQLFLAG, and SQLRULES options when precompiling the program.

It is important to remember that an embedded dynamic SQL programming module does have associated packages but does *not* contain access plans or executable sec-tions. For example, suppose an SQL program contains four static SQL statements and two dynamic SQL statements in a single source module. There would be four SQL sections (each with an access plan) created and stored in the database within a single package.

Binding Applications

The most common method of binding in application development is *deferred binding*. When deferred binding is used, the information about the SQL statements is stored in the bind file created by the precompile process. This bind file must be bound against the database to create a package. Once the package exists in the database, there is no longer any need to bind the application.

The SQL statements from the bind file are examined during the bind process, and the current database statistics are used to determine the best method of data access. At this point, an access plan is chosen by the DB2 optimizer. This access plan is then stored in the database system catalog tables. An access plan is *only* created for static embedded SQL statements. Embedded dynamic SQL statements have a package and a section number assigned, but there is *no* access plan created until the statement is executed.

The bind process needs to be performed following each successful precompile of the application source modules. When the bind file is created, a timestamp is stored in the package. The timestamp is sometimes referred to as a *consistency token*. This same timestamp is also stored in the database when the bind is completed and is used to ensure that the resulting application executes the proper SQL statement.

The modified source module (output from the precompile) will attempt to execute the SQL statements by package name and section number. If the required package and section are not found, the following message will be returned:

```
SQL0805N Package "pkgschema.pkgname" was not found.
SQLSTATE=51002
```

The SQLERROR(CONTINUE) and VALIDATE(RUN) bind options, in previous releases only available with DB2 Universal Database for OS/390, are now available for the DB2 Universal Database family. This allows you to port your DB2 Universal Database for OS/390 applications that make use of these options to the rest of the DB2 Universal Database family.

If the required package and section exist in the database system catalogs, the timestamp is then checked. If the timestamp in the application executable does not

Development
Considerations

match the timestamp stored in the system catalog tables in the database, the following message is returned:

```
SQL0818N A timestamp conflict occurred.
SQLSTATE=51003
```

Authorization Considerations for Static SQL

If the package does not yet exist in the database, the user who issues the BIND must have BINDADD authority for the database or be a member of a group that has this authority. The user must also have one of these privileges: IMPLICIT_SCHEMA on the database (if the schema name of the package does not exist) or CREATEIN on the schema (if the schema name does already exist). The person who binds the package by default becomes the package owner, unless the OWNER keyword is specified during the BIND. In addition, since static statements execute with privileges of the package owner authorization ID, that userid must also have the proper privileges for all of the referenced objects in the SQL statements referenced in the bind file information. These privileges must be explicitly granted to the user binding the packages or to PUBLIC. If the privileges are granted to a group of which the user is a member but are not granted explicitly to the user, the bind will fail.

Unqualified database objects in embedded static SQL programs are by default qualified with the userid of the package owner. Alternatively, you may specify the QUALIFER keyword during the BIND to indicate the qualifier name for unqualified objects in static SQL statements. Table 14–2 summarizes the behavioral characteristics of static SQL with respect to authorization ID used for statements and the qualifier for unqualified database objects depending on whether the OWNER and QUALIFIER options are used during the BIND:

Table 14–2 *Static SQL - Authorization and Qualifier Summary*

BIND Keyword	Authorization ID	Qualification Value for Unqualified Objects
OWNER and QUALIFIER NOT specified	ID of the user binding the package	ID of the user binding the package
OWNER specified	ID of the user specified in OWNER bind option	ID of the user specified in OWNER bind option
QUALIFIER specified	ID of the user binding the package	ID of the user specified in the QUALIFIER bind option

Table 14–2 *Static SQL - Authorization and Qualifier Summary (Continued)*

BIND Keyword	Authorization ID	Qualification Value for Unqualified Objects
OWNER and QUALIFIER specified	ID of the user specified in OWNER bind option	ID of the user specified in the QUALIFIER bind option

Once the package exists in the database, any person with EXECUTE privilege on the package can issue any of the SQL statements contained in the package, even if the individual does not have explicit privilege on the database object. This is a feature of embedded static SQL program modules. It allows end-users access to a portion of data contained in a table without defining a view or column-level privileges.

Authorization Considerations for Dynamic SQL

Unlike static SQL, dynamically prepared statements can be made to execute under the authorization ID of either the user that binds the package (the package owner) or the user who executes the application, depending on which option is used for the DYNAMICRULES keyword during the bind.

Under DYNAMICRULES RUN (the default), the person who runs a dynamic SQL application must have the privileges necessary to issue each SQL statement (it specifies that the authorization ID of the user executing the package is to be used) as well as the EXECUTE privilege on the package. The privileges may be granted to the user's authorization ID, to any group of which the user is a member, or to PUBLIC. With DYNAMICRULES RUN, the person binding the application only needs the BINDADD authority on the database, if the program contains no static SQL.

When using the DYNAMICRULES BIND option, authorizations and privileges required are similar to static SQL. That is, the user that binds a dynamic SQL application (the authorization ID of the package owner) must have BINDADD authority as well as the privileges necessary to perform all the dynamic and static SQL statements in the application. The user that runs the application inherits the privileges associated with the package owner authorization ID and therefore only needs the EXECUTE privilege on the package.

Note: If you bind packages with DYNAMICRULES BIND, and have SYSADM or DBADM authority or any authorities that the user of the package should not receive, consider explicitly specifying OWNER to designate a different authorization ID. This prevents the package from automatically inheriting SYSADM, DBADM, or other unnecessary privileges on dynamic SQL statements from the userid that binds the application.

Development Considerations

The authorization ID privileges and qualifier values used for DYNAMICRULES RUN and BIND options are summarized in Table 14–3:

Table 14–3 *Dynamic SQL - Authorization and Qualifier Summary*

DYNAMICRULES Option	Authorization ID	Qualification Value for Unqualified Objects
RUN (default)	ID of user executing package	Owner's authorization ID whether or not the owner is explicitly specified. It can be superseded by the CURRENT SCHEMA special register.
BIND	The implicit or explicit value of OWNER bind option	The implicit or explicit value of the QUALIFIER bind option.

Examining Packages and Timestamps

We have briefly discussed packages and timestamps. Let's examine how we can verify that the bind file and the packages in the database match. When the BIND command is successful, a single entry in the system catalog view SYSCAT.PACKAGES is created. There are a number of columns defined for this table. We will not go into a complete explanation here, but let's look at the timestamp column. The timestamp associated with a package is actually stored in the column named UNIQUE_ID. If you were to successfully issue the command:

```
bind db2look.bnd messages msg1.out
```

the SYSCAT.PACKAGES view would have a new entry for this bind file with the package name DB2LOOK and the package schema as your authorization user ID. Any error or warning messages would be written to the file called msg1.out. To examine the timestamp contained in the db2look.bnd file, there is a utility provided with DB2 called db2bfd.

Here is an example of the output of the db2bfd tool:

```
db2look.bnd:  Header Contents

Element name        Description                       Value
---------------     ----------------------------      ------------------
bind_id             Bind file identifier              :BINDV610:
header1             Bind file header length           :4024:
relno               Bind file release number          :0x600:
application         Access package name               :DB2LOOK :
timestamp           Access package timestamp          :yAQPCTFP: 1999/05/19 02:15:16:50
creator             Bind file creator                 :DB2ADMIN  :
endian              Bit representation                :L: Little Endian (Intel)
```

```
sqlda_doubled     Indicates if SQLDA doubled        :1:
insert            DB2/PE buffered inserts           :0:
max_sect          Highest section number used       :57:
num_hostvars      Number of host variables          :214:
num_stmt          Number of SQL statements          :265:
statements        Offset of SQL statements          :4024:
declarel          Size of data declarations         :7417:
declare           Offset of data declarations       :63268:
prep_id           Userid that created bindfile      :DB2ADMIN  :
date_value        Date/Time format                  :0: Default (Default)
stds_value        Standards Compliance Level        :0: SAA (Default)
isol_value        Isolation option                  :2: Uncommitted Read (Defined)
blck_value        Record blocking option            :1: Block All (Defined)
sqler_value       SQLERROR option                   :0: (Defined)
level_value       Level option                      : : (Defined)
colid_value       Collection ID option              : : (Defined)
vrsn_value        Version option                    : : (Default)
owner_value       Package owner option              : : (Default)
qual_value        Default Qualifier option          : : (Default)
text_value        Text option                       : : (Default)
vldte_value       Validate option                   :1: (Default)
expln_value       Explain option                    :0: (Default)
actn_value        Action option                     :1: (Default)
rver_value        REPLVER option                    : : (Default)
retn_value        Retain option                     :1: (Default)
rlse_value        Release option                    :0: (Default)
dgr_value         Degree of I/O parallelism         :1: (Default)
str_value         String delimiter option           :0: (Default)
decd_value        Decimal delimiter option          :0: (Default)
csub_value        Character subtype option          :0: (Default)
ccsids_value      Single byte CCSID option          :8: (Default)
ccsidm_value      Mixed byte CCSID option           :892424789: (Default)
ccsidg_value      Double byte CCSID option          :0: (Default)
decprc_value      Decimal precision option          :25722880: (Default)
dynrul_value      Dynamic rules option              :0: (Default)
insert_value      DB2/PE buffered inserts           :0: (Default)
explsnap_value    Explain snapshot                  :0: (Default)
funcpath_value    UDF function path                 : : (Default)
sqlwarn_value     SQL warnings                      :1: (Default)
queryopt_value    Query optimization                :5: (Default)
cnulreqd_value    C Null required option            :1: (Default)
generic_value     Generic option                    : : (Default)
defprep_value     Deferred prepare option           : : (Not Used)
trfgrp_value      Transform group option            : : (Not Used)
```

Note that the timestamp is encoded as yAQPCTFP and the decoded timestamp is also shown. This timestamp is the exact time when the PRECOMPILE command was used to generate the bind file.

To confirm that this bind file (db2look.bnd) has been bound to the database, issue this SQL statement once connected to the database:

```
select pkgschema, pkgname, unique_id
from syscat.packages
where pkgname = 'DB2LOOK'
```

The output of this SQL statement should contain a single row result with a UNIQUE_ID matching the bind file, as shown here:

```
PKGSCHEMA   PKGNAME  UNIQUE_ID
---------   -------  ---------
DB2ADMIN    DB2LOOK  yAQPCTFP
```

The `UNIQUE_ID` contained in the bind file matches this value. Therefore, you know that this bind file has been successfully bound to the database.

Binding Utilities

The CLP is a dynamic SQL application that is provided with DB2. The packages associated with the utilities, like the DB2 CLP, are included in the `sqllib` directory, in the `bnd` subdirectory.

The bind files associated with the DB2 CLP and utilities are found in a list file called `db2ubind.1st`.

Specifically, the bind files associated with the DB2 CLP are: `db2clpcs.bnd`, `db2clprr.bnd`, `db2clpur.bnd`, `db2clprs.bnd`, and `db2clpnc.bnd`.

 Note: Each of the CLP bind files is created with different isolation levels. This allows a user the ability to change the isolation level when using the CLP utility, using the `CHANGE ISOLATION LEVEL` command.

These bind files must have been bound to the database you wish to access using the DB2 Command Center, the DB2 CLP or the Client Configuration Assistant (CCA).

 Note: To bind the DB2 utilities (e.g., `CLP`, `IMPORT`, `EXPORT`) issue the command: `bind @db2ubind.1st blocking all`.

To bind a number of packages using a single `BIND` command, add the "@" character in front of the source filename. When this character is encountered, DB2 will assume that the file contains a list of bind files and is not a bind file itself.

Blocking

Record blocking is a feature of DB2 Universal Database that reduces data access time across networks when an application is retrieving a large amount of data. The record blocking is based on cursor type and the amount of storage allocated on the DB2 server to perform record blocking. Cursors are used in applications to manipulate multirow result sets from a DB2 server.

The DBM configuration parameter known as ASLHEAPSZ specifies the amount of memory used to buffer data on the server for applications requesting multiple data records. For applications executing on remote clients, the buffer is specified by the DBM configuration parameter known as RQRIOBLK.

You can think of record blocking as data retrieval caching. The record blocking options are described in Fig. 14–4. Usually, you would specify BLOCKING ALL for applications that perform many queries. An *ambiguous cursor* is a cursor that has been defined without any reference to its intended usage in an SQL statement. As we will see, all cursors are defined using a SELECT statement. They are used in a SELECT, DELETE, or UPDATE statement.

The default blocking option for static embedded applications is BLOCKING UNAMBIG. The default blocking option for CLI applications and the CLP is BLOCKING ALL.

Table 14–4 *Record Blocking Options*

BLOCKING <option>	Record Blocking Behavior
UNAMBIG	All cursors except those specified as FOR UPDATE are blocked.
ALL	Ambiguous cursor are blocked.
NO	No cursors are blocked.

Record blocking affects the way you, as an application developer, declare your cursors within your application. The more specific you are with your cursor declaration, the more likely DB2 will use record blocking appropriately. If record blocking is enabled, the cache is allocated when the cursor is opened. It is deallocated when the cursor is closed. Therefore, to avoid wasting memory resources on the server, avoid keeping cursors open if they are no longer required.

Note: All cursors used for dynamic SQL statements are assumed to be ambiguous.

Support for CLI and ODBC Programming

We have been discussing static and dynamic SQL statement processing by embedding the SQL statements in an application module. A precompile or preparation stage is required to map these SQL statements to DB2 API calls. We are required to manipulate SQLDA data structures to handle dynamic SQL. This can become quite complex and, more importantly, are not easily ported to various database vendors. An alternative method of developing database applications using callable SQL interfaces has become a popular technique of creating powerful yet highly portable applications.

A callable SQL interface involves invoking APIs (also referred to as functions or function calls in this chapter) that allow the developer to access database information directly; therefore, there is no need for precompiling the application and there is no database-specific language to learn. One such callable SQL interface is Microsoft's Open Database Connectivity (ODBC). There are slightly different callable SQL interface standards known as Call Level Interface (CLI) as defined by groups such as X/Open and ISO.

DB2 has its own CLI which is based on the X/Open, ISO, and ODBC standards. The focus of the discussion here will be application development using DB2 CLI. We will also cover ODBC briefly but will not go into too much detail because the two standards are very similar.

All of the SQL statements are dynamically prepared and executed using CLI or ODBC. The programming techniques and runtime environment for CLI are quite different than those for embedded SQL. We will discuss many of these differences.

Embedded Dynamic Versus Call Level Interface

Developing an application using CLI is different than using embedded SQL techniques. So before we examine how to code CLI applications, let's examine some of the key differences.

The DB2 CLI environment is different from embedded SQL in the following ways:

- No explicit cursors are required.
- There is no precompile stage.
- No application level packages created. There is a set of CLI packages that is bound once for all CLI applications.
- No COMMIT/ROLLBACK statement is used to control transaction processing. An API called SQLEndTran() is used to commit or rollback a transaction.
- No SQLDA data structure is required.

- No SQLCA data structure is used because the errors are analyzed using SQLSTATES and return codes though special error-handling APIs.
- No host variables are used in SQL statements; parameter markers are used instead.

The differences listed above are important to understand before attempting to develop CLI applications. There are some unique features provided with CLI that are not available in an embedded SQL environment including:

- Manipulation of multiple rows of data at a time (array fetch/insert)
- The ability to have bidirectional (scrollable) cursors
- Easier to query the system catalog tables because there are predefined APIs to query system catalog table resources

ODBC Versus CLI

The ODBC and CLI standards overlap in many areas. They are both based on a set of APIs that access data sources using programs written in the C/C++ programming language. The initial ODBC standard was based on an early version of the X/Open CLI standard, and they have evolved over the years.

The ODBC standard is based on levels of conformance. The DB2 ODBC driver currently conforms to level 2 of ODBC 2.0 and level 1 of ODBC 3.0. It also supports some ODBC 3.0 level 2 functions. As the ODBC standard continues to evolve, so may DB2's ODBC conformance.

The DB2 product provides both a CLI driver and an ODBC driver. In the CLI environment, the application communicates directly with the CLI driver. In an ODBC environment, the ODBC Driver Manager provides the interface to the application. It also dynamically loads the ODBC driver for the necessary database server that the application connects to. It is the driver that implements the ODBC function set, with the exception of some extended functions implemented by the Driver Manager. Fig. 14–2 illustrates the relationship between the application and DB2 in both the ODBC and CLI environments.

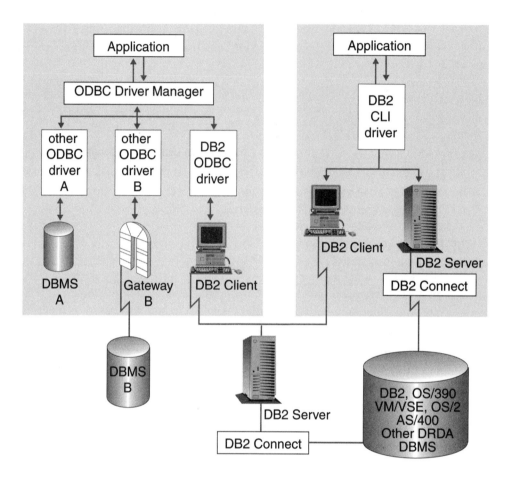

Fig. 14–2 *DB2 CLI versus ODBC*

A DB2 CLI application does not require the ODBC driver or the ODBC driver manager to operate. The advantage of coding an ODBC application is the ease of portability. Also, the application can access more than one database vendor product. Therefore, you could develop an application that accesses data from multiple database vendor products quite simply with the ODBC interface. The DB2 CLI driver can only access DB2 Family data sources.

> **Note:** The installation of the ODBC driver is *only* required if ODBC applications are being executed. To run CLI applications, only the DB2 runtime client needs to be installed. It includes the DB2 CLI driver.

Setting Up the CLI Environment

There are several steps involved in setting up a DB2 CLI environment. All of the CLI APIs are contained in a static library. These are the names of the libraries on the various DB2 development operating systems:

- The DB2 CLI library on OS/2 and Windows platforms is called db2cli.lib.
- The DB2 CLI library on UNIX platforms is called libdb2.a or libdb2.so.

Before we attempt to develop an application, we must ensure that the following steps have been performed successfully:

- The DB2 Software Developer's Kit must be installed.
- The database being accessed is cataloged properly. If the database is remote, a node must also be cataloged.
- DB2 CLI bind files must be bound to the database.
- Configure the CLI environment using the Client Configuration Assistant or edit the db2cli.ini file directly. It is important to remember to examine the CLI environment settings in the db2cli.ini file or by using the Client Configuration Assistant. These settings affect the execution behavior of all CLI applications executing on the system.

CLI Bind Files

The bind files required for CLI applications will be automatically bound when the first CLI application connects to the database. If CLI applications from multiple systems connect to a database, the CLI packages from each client platform and unique build level (fixpak level) need to be bound to the database. The bind may not be successful if the user does not have BINDADD authority on the database. Therefore, the database administrator may be required to bind the necessary bind files manually using the DB2 BIND command or the Client Configuration Assistant (CCA). Each of the supported DB2 servers use different bind files (Table 14–5).

Table 14–5 *CLI Bind List Files*

Bind File	DB2 Server
db2cli.lst	DB2 Universal Database (OS/2, Windows, UNIX)
ddcsvm.lst	DB2 for VM (SQL/DS)
ddcsvse.lst	DB2 for VSE (SQL/DS)
ddcsmvs.lst	DB2 for OS/390 (MVS/ESA)
ddcs400.lst	DB2 for OS/400

For example, to manually bind the CLI packages from a DB2 Command Window on Windows NT against a DB2 for AIX database, you would issue the following command after connecting to the database:

```
DB2 BIND @db2cli.lst MESSAGES db2cli.msg GRANT PUBLIC
```

Likewise, if the DB2 database resides on S/390, you could use this command:

```
DB2 BIND @ddcsmvs.lst BLOCKING ALL SQLERROR CONTINUE
MESSAGES mvsbind.msg GRANT PUBLIC
```

Configuring CLI

Usually it is not necessary to modify the DB2 CLI configuration file (db2cli.ini). It is important to understand that the file exists and may require small modifications. Some of the reasons for modifying the CLI configuration file include:

- Increase CLI application performance
- Change default CLI behavior
- Enable workarounds for specific applications

The db2cli.ini file is located in the sqllib/cfg directory of the instance owner in UNIX environments, in the sqllib directory for OS/2 and Windows 32-bit operating systems, or the sqllib/win directory for 16-bit Windows environments.

```
; Comment Goes Here
[DB2CERT]
CURSORHOLD=0
TNXISOLATION=4
DEFERREDPREPARE=1
DB2DEGREE=4
PATCH1=2
```

Fig. 14–3 *Example db2cli.ini configuration*

An example db2cli.ini file is shown in Fig. 14–3. There are many more options that can be specified in the CLI configuration file, but these options were selected because they can dramatically affect an application's execution environment. The keywords and values shown here may not be applicable to your environment.

The first line is a comment about this section of the file. Multiple databases may be configured in this file. The second line contains the database alias name in brackets, [DB2CERT]. The DB2CERT database can still be accessed from a DB2 CLI application without an entry in the db2cli.ini file, but if there is no section for the DB2CERT database, all of the default values for the parameters will be used. This may not be desirable.

The five lines below the database name contain keywords and corresponding values. The supported keywords are defined in the DB2 *V7.1 Call Level Interface Guide and Reference,* but let's examine the keywords defined in Fig. 14–3 and explain them in Table 14–6.

Table 14–6 *Configuring a DB2 CLI Environment*

Keyword	Meaning
CURSORHOLD	0 = cursor no hold (the cursors are destroyed when the transaction is committed) 1 = cursor hold (default) The default value of this keyword is 1. This means that the cursors are maintained across units of work. This is quite different from embedded SQL since all cursors exhibit the cursor without hold behavior unless the DECLARE CURSOR statement includes the phrase WITH HOLD.
TXNISOLATION	1 - Uncommitted Read 2 - Cursor Stability (default) 4 - Read Stability 8 - Repeatable Read 32 - No Commit (DB2 for OS/400 only) This keyword identifies the isolation level used for concurrency.

Development Considerations

Table 14–6   *Configuring a DB2 CLI Environment (Continued)*

Keyword	Meaning
DEFERREDPREPARE	0 = Deferred Prepare is not used. 1 = Deferred Prepare is used (default). Defers sending the PREPARE request until the corresponding execute request is issued. The two requests are then combined into one command/reply flow (instead of two) to minimize network flow and to improve performance.
DB2DEGREE	0-32767/ANY (Default is 0) Sets the degree of parallelism for the execution of SQL statements.
PATCH1 PATCH2	The keywords Patch1 and Patch2 are used for work-arounds to known problems when using certain applications or environments. In our example, we used PATCH1=4 to map timestamp values to date values. To use multiple Patch1 values, simply add the values together to form the keyword value. For example, if you want the patches 1, 4, and 8, then specify PATCH1=13. Unlike PATCH1, to specify multiple patches for PATCH2, the values are specified in a comma delimited string, for example PATCH2="7,15".

The DB2 CCA or ODBC Administrator Tool on Windows and OS/2 platforms allows you to configure the CLI environment without editing the `db2cli.ini` file directly. The interface is easy to use and explains each parameter that can be modified:

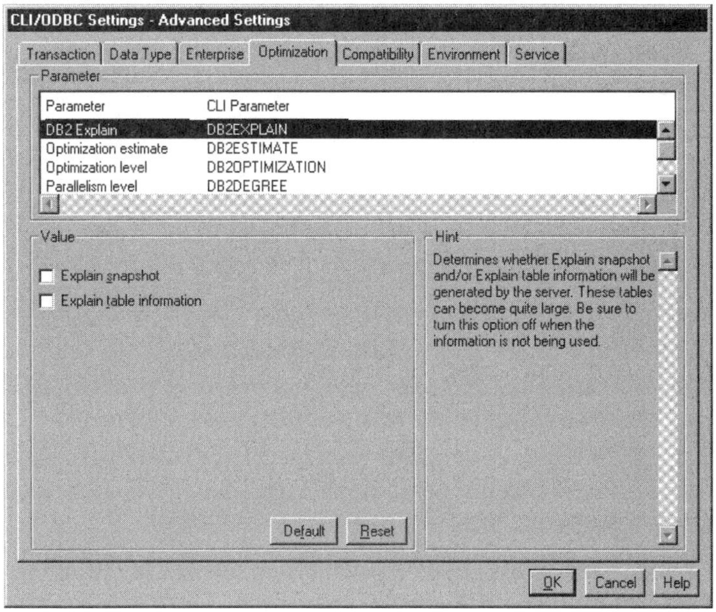

Fig. 14–4 *CLI/ODBC settings panel in the Client Configuration Assistant*

Accessing a DB2 Database via ODBC

To access a DB2 database from ODBC, the following are required on the DB2 client where the ODBC application executes:

- DB2 runtime client or server must be installed. If the database is on a remote DB2 system, it should be cataloged correctly and be accessible for connecting to.
- The ODBC Driver Manager must be installed.
- An ODBC driver for DB2 must be installed and registered with the ODBC driver manager.
- The DB2 database must be registered as an ODBC data source with the driver manager.

There must be an ODBC driver manager installed on the computer where the ODBC application has been installed. For all Microsoft operating systems, the ODBC driver manager is provided by Microsoft.

The IBM DB2 ODBC driver or another ODBC driver for DB2 must be installed and registered. The Microsoft ODBC driver manager and the DB2 ODBC driver are automatically installed on Windows 32-bit platforms during DB2 installation as long as the ODBC component, highlighted by default, is not unchecked. The DB2 ODBC driver is also registered with the driver manager during installation of DB2 on Windows platforms. On Windows platforms, you can run the Microsoft ODBC Administrator from the Control Panel to verify that "IBM DB2 ODBC Driver" is shown in the list. On UNIX platforms, the DB2 ODBC driver and databases available through it are specified using .odbc.ini and .odbcinst.ini files in the home directory of the user running the ODBC application.

The database must be identified to the ODBC driver manager as an available data source. The data source can be made available to all users of the system (a system data source) or only to the current user (a user data source). On Windows, you can register the data source with the driver manager using the CCA, as shown in Fig. 14–5. Databases configured though the CCA are selected as system ODBC data sources by default, unless you explicitly uncheck the selection. For non-Windows platforms, this is accomplished by using the appropriate ODBC Administration tool or by configuring the driver manager manually.

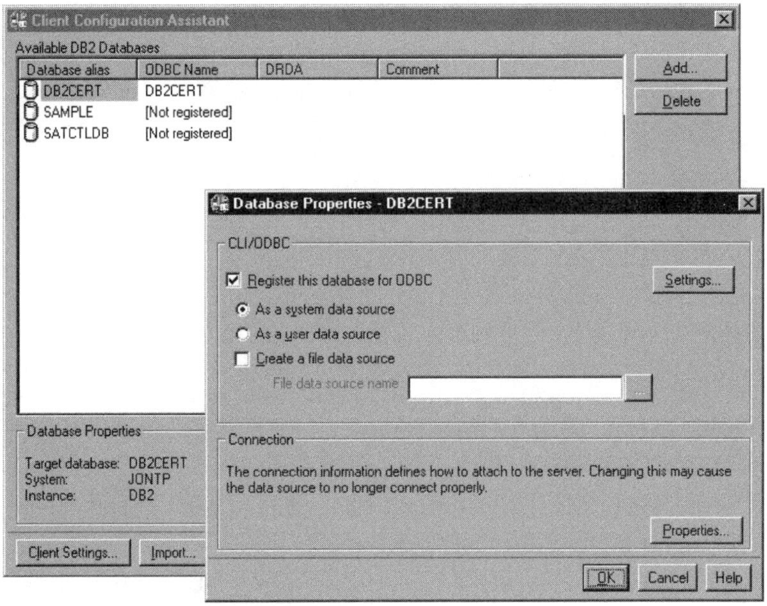

Fig. 14–5 *Database properties*

ODBC Development Considerations

For ODBC application development, you must obtain an ODBC Software Development Kit.

The steps of binding of CLI packages and customizing CLI using db2cli.ini or CCA are also applicable to ODBC applications that will access DB2 data sources. These steps are performed in the same way as for CLI applications.

Support For Java Programming

DB2 supports many types of Java programs. Applets and applications are two main types of Java programs. Before explaining how to code applets and applications for DB2, let's first examine these two types.

Java applications rely on the DB2 client code to connect to the DB2 database. You start your application from the desktop or command line, like any other application. The DB2 JDBC driver handles the JDBC API calls from your application.These calls to the DB2 JDBC driver are translated to DB2 CLI calls via Java native methods.The JDBC driver uses the CLI driver on the client to communicate the requests to the server, receives the results, and passes them to the Java application. Thus an application requires at least the DB2 runtime client code to be installed where the application executes.

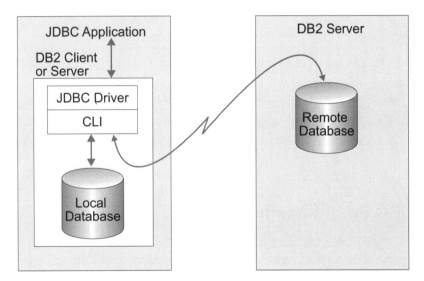

Fig. 14–6 *Java applications for DB2*

Java applets do not require any DB2 client code to be installed on the system where they execute. You need only a Java-enabled Web browser on the client machine to run your applet. Typically, you would embed the applet in a HyperText Markup Language (HTML) page. When you load your HTML page, the browser downloads the Java applet to your machine, which then downloads the Java class files and DB2's JDBC driver. When your applet calls the JDBC API to connect to DB2, the JDBC driver establishes a separate network connection with a DB2 JDBC applet server residing on the Web server. The JDBC server communicates with the database via the DB2 CLI driver and sends the results back to the client through the separate connection.

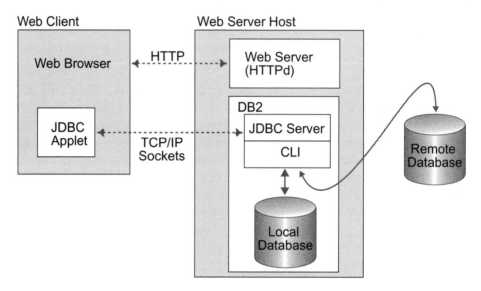

Fig. 14–7 *Java applets for DB2*

DB2 also supports user-defined functions and stored procedures written in Java.

Java programs that access DB2 databases can do so using JDBC or SQLJ interfaces. The JDBC API allows you to write Java programs that make dynamic SQL calls to databases. SQLJ extends JDBC to support embedded static SQL. The next few sections deal with coding Java programs for DB2 using JDBC and SQLJ.

JDBC Programming

If your DB2 application or applet uses JDBC, you need to familiarize yourself with the JDBC specification and understand how to call JDBC APIs to access a database and manipulate data in that database. Here we introduce some commonly used terms and constructs to help you better understand JDBC programs for DB2.

DB2's JDBC Drivers

DB2 JDBC drivers are installed during the installation of DB2 client or server code. DB2 provides an *app* driver: COM.ibm.db2.jdbc.app.DB2Driver. You would use this driver for *applications* that run on machines where DB2 (client or server) is installed. DB2 also comes with a *net* driver: COM.ibm.db2.jdbc.net.DB2Driver. You would use this driver when your Java program executes on a machine that does not have DB2 installed, that is, for running applets. The class files for the drivers are packaged in db2java.zip.

The JDBC classes are found in the java.sql package.

SQLJ Programming

SQLJ source files contain embedded static SQL statements. Even though we covered static embedded SQL in the previous chapter, we will discuss Embedded SQL for Java (SQLJ) separately in this section. This is because Java differs from the traditional host languages like C and also because SQLJ uses JDBC as a foundation for such tasks as connecting to databases and handling SQL errors.

SQLJ programs use JDBC as the runtime interface with DB2; however, any static SQL statements require the application packages to exist in the database before executing the programs. The interaction between SQLJ programs and DB2 is shown in Fig. 14–8.

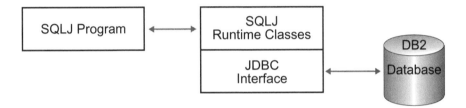

Fig. 14–8 *SQLJ's interface with DB2*

Because SQLJ applications and applets access the database through DB2's JDBC support, they require the JDBC classes (java.sql.*), and DB2's JDBC driver classes contained in db2java.zip. The SQLJ translator that replaces embedded SQL statements in the SQLJ program uses classes in sqlj.zip (in the sqllib/java directory). However, the interfaces and classes in sqlj.zip are not required for executing the program. To execute SQLJ programs, the SQLJ runtime classes (sqllib/java/runtime.zip) are needed to authenticate and execute any SQL packages that were bound to the database at the precompiling and binding stage.

Stored Procedure Builder

DB2 comes with a Stored Procedure Builder (SPB), a graphical application to aid in rapid development of stored procedures. SPB provides a single development environment that supports the entire DB2 family ranging from the workstation to System/390.

SPB comes with design assistants that guide you through basic design patterns, help you create SQL queries, and estimate the performance cost of invoking a stored procedure. Stored procedures created with SPB are implemented with Java, and all database connections are managed using Java Database Connectivity (JDBC). SQL statements can be specified using JDBC, SQLJ, or the SQL Procedure Language. Once you develop the basic SQL structure using SPB, if you have highly sophisticated stored procedure logic you can use your editor to modify the stored procedure.

Note: The DB2 SPB assists you with creating the part of the stored procedure that runs on the database server. You must write the client application separately.

SPB provides an easy-to-use development environment for creating, installing, and testing stored procedures so that you can focus on creating your stored procedure logic rather than on the details of registering, building, and installing stored procedures on a DB2 server. Since the SPB helps you create stored procedures in Java, they are highly portable among operating systems. The SQL Procedure Language is also portable among all members of the DB2 Family.

A sample of the Stored Procedure builder is found in Figure 14–9.

The SQL Procedure Language is new to DB2 UDB Version 7.1. This stored procedure language is based on an SQL standard and simplifies their development. Developers familiar with programming languages such as Visual Basic will find this language easy to learn.

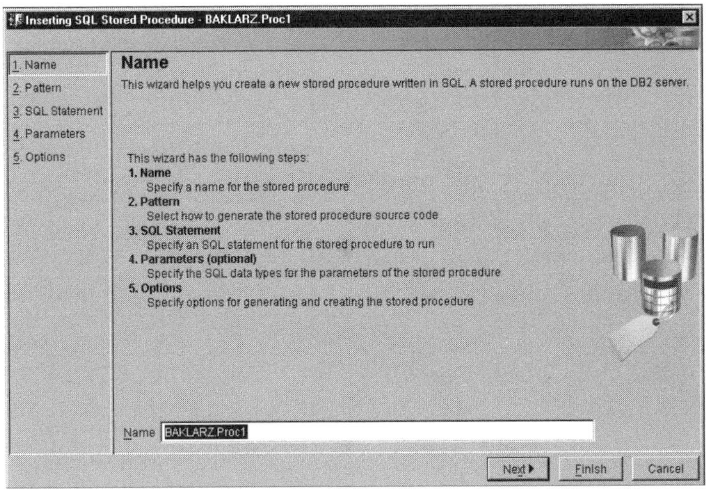

Fig. 14–9 *Stored Procedure builder*

Summary

The process of creating static embedded SQL program modules was discussed in this chapter. By embedding SQL statements into a programming language, we can manipulate the data contained in a DB2 database. The programming modules containing the SQL statements must be converted from SQL statements to DB2 library APIs. This step is known as the precompilation step, since it is always performed before the programming module is compiled and linked.

Development SQL

- ◆ USER-DEFINED FUNCTIONS
- ◆ USER-DEFINED STRUCTURED DATATYPES
- ◆ SYNONYM AND ALIAS
- ◆ COMMIT AND ROLLBACK

*T*his chapter will cover some of the additional SQL features that are included in DB2 that are primarily intended for developers. User-defined functions (UDFs) and user-defined structured datatypes can be used for enhancing the functions and datatypes available in DB2. SYNONYM, ALIAS, COMMIT, and ROLLBACK are used within programs for controlling the access to objects and determining changes in the database.

User-Defined Functions

User-defined functions (UDFs) form the basis of *Object-Relational* extensions to the SQL language along with user-defined types (UDTs) and LOBs. Fundamentally, a database function is a relationship between a set of input data values and a result value. DB2 Universal Database comes with many built-in functions; however, it is possible to create your own column, scalar, and table functions.

There are three types of functions:

- Column
- Scalar
- Table

Column functions take in a set of data values and derive a single result. For example, to determine the average score of all tests taken:

```
SELECT AVG(SCORE) FROM TEST_TAKEN
```

Column functions such as AVG, SUM, and COUNT are detailed in the *DB2 UDB V7.1 SQL Reference*.

Scalar functions take in one value and return another value. For example, to look at all tests taken since 1996:

```
SELECT * FROM TEST_TAKEN
        WHERE YEAR(DATE_TAKEN) > 1996
```

The third type of function, a table function, can only be used in the FROM clause of an SQL statement. It returns columns of a table, resembling a regular created table.

There are a large number of functions built-in to DB2 and can be found in the *DB2 UDB V7.1 SQL Reference*.

In DB2, you can create your own functions (which can be scalar or table functions). A UDF can be written in a high-level programming language such as C, C++, or Java or you can use a single SQL statement.

You can also create a user-defined function based on another UDF or built-in function. This concept is similar to *overloading* classes in object-oriented programming. This is called a *sourced* function. A UDF that you write from scratch is called an *external* function.

> **Note:** In a Windows environment, as part of the Microsoft Object Linking and Embedding (OLE) architecture, DB2 can act as an OLE Automation Controller. Through this mechanism, DB2 can invoke methods of OLE automation objects as external UDFs.

External UDFs, once written and generated as dynamically loadable libraries or classes, must be registered with the database. The `congrat` function shown in Fig. 15–1 is registered using the CREATE FUNCTION statement.

```
CREATE FUNCTION congrat(VARCHAR(30),VARCHAR(40))
       RETURNS CLOB(1K)
       EXTERNAL NAME 'congrat.a!congrat'
       LANGUAGE C
       PARAMETER STYLE DB2SQL
       DETERMINISTIC
       FENCED
       NO SQL
       NO EXTERNAL ACTION
       DISALLOW PARALLEL;
```

Fig. 15–1 *Registering a user-defined function*

Sourced UDFs are registered in the same way, simply by specifying the *parent* source function. This example allows us to create an AVG function for the SCORE data type:

```
CREATE FUNCTION AVG (SCORE)
       RETURNS SCORE
       SOURCE  SYSIBM.AVG(DECIMAL);
```

These CREATE FUNCTION statements place an entry for each UDF in the view SYSCAT.FUNCTIONS. You can view the UDFs registered with the database in the Control Center.

Development SQL

With DB2, you can also create a third type of user-defined function called a *table function*. A table function is a UDF that returns a table to the SQL statement that calls it. This means that a table function can only be referenced in the FROM clause of a SELECT statement. The table function provides a means of including external data in SQL queries. Table functions can read non-DB2 data, for instance, a file on the operating system or over the World Wide Web, tabularize it, and return the data to DB2 as a relational table that can subsequently be treated like any other relational table. For example, the appform table function in the next example takes in a candidate application form, processes it, and returns the data in an appropriate format to be inserted in the CANDIDATE table (except for the candidate ID, which is generated):

```
CREATE FUNCTION appform(VARCHAR(30))
RETURNS TABLE (LNAME VARCHAR(30),FNAME VARCHAR(30),
               INITIAL CHAR(1), HPHONE PHONE,
               WPHONE PHONE, STREETNO VARCHAR(8),
               STREETNAME VARCHAR(20),
               CITY VARCHAR(20),
               PROV_STATE VARCHAR(30),
               CODE CHAR(6), COUNTRY VARCHAR(20))
EXTERNAL NAME 'tbudf!appform'
LANGUAGE C
PARAMETER STYLE DB2SQL
NO SQL
DETERMINISTIC
NO EXTERNAL ACTION
FINAL CALL
DISALLOW PARALLEL
CARDINALITY 20;
```

Fig. 15–2 *User-defined table function - appform*

If we wanted to insert a new candidate into the CANDIDATE table based on his or her application form, we could use the following SELECT statement:

```
INSERT INTO CANDIDATE
   SELECT SUBSTR(GENERATE_UNIQUE(),1,9) AS CID,
          LNAME, FNAME, INITIAL,
          HPHONE, WPHONE,
          STREETNO, STREETNAME, CITY,
          PROV_STATE, CODE, COUNTRY
   FROM appform('D:\DOCS\NEWFORM.TXT');
```

> **Note:** DB2 also provides table functions for accessing data from OLE
> DB providers. This allows you to incorporate data into your DB2 database
> or application from a wide variety of relational and non-relational data
> sources including Oracle, Microsoft SQL Server, and Microsoft Access.

User-defined functions are like any other database object in DB2, meaning that
each UDF has a schema name associated with it. Ideally, each UDF is fully qualified when it is called. However, this can be quite difficult and can limit the flexibility of SQL queries. The alternative is to use the special register CURRENT
FUNCTION PATH. DB2 uses this path to resolve unqualified function references.
The path in this case is not a list of directories, but a list of schema names such as
"SYSIBM", "SYSFUN" or "DB2CERT". SYSFUN is the schema used for built-in UDFs.
Note that the authorities needed to create UDFs are the same as those required to
create stored procedures.

For more information on the various types of UDFs and the parameters used in the
CREATE FUNCTION statement, please refer to the *DB2 UDB V7.1 Application
Development Guide.*

SQL-Bodied Scalar Functions

The previous examples referred to user-defined functions and table functions that
used a programming language such as C, C++, or Java to create the logic associated with the function. An alternative method of creating these functions is through
the use of SQL statements.

```
CREATE FUNCTION BONUS(salary int, bonus_percent int)
  RETURNS INT
  LANGUAGE SQL CONTAINS SQL
  RETURN
    (
    salary * bonus_percent / 100
    );
```

Fig. 15–3 *User-defined function - BONUS*

The CREATE FUNCTION statement allows the use of a single SQL statement to calculate the value to be returned. The BONUS function takes the salary value and cal-

culates the bonus based on a percentage rate. This function could now be used in an SQL statement to calculate the bonus for an employee:

```
VALUES bonus(30000,10);

1
-----------
        3000
```

Fig. 15–4 *Using the BONUS function*

This function could be used anywhere in an SQL statement where a normal function could be used. Figure 15–5 illustrates how the BONUS function could be used as part of an INSERT statement.

```
UPDATE EMPLOYEE
   SET BONUS_PAY = BONUS(EMPLOYEE.SALARY, 10);
```

Fig. 15–5 *Advanced use of the BONUS function*

The body of the function can only consist of one SQL statement and no form of logic is allowed. However, the SQL language does include the CASE statement, so this can allow for a limited form of logic. The BONUS function is modified in Figure 15–6 to return different bonus values depending on the salary level.

```
CREATE FUNCTION BONUS(salary int, bonus_percent int)
   RETURNS INT
   LANGUAGE SQL CONTAINS SQL
   RETURN
   (
   CASE
      WHEN salary <= 20000 then salary / bonus_percent
      WHEN salary <= 30000 then salary / bonus_percent / 2
      WHEN salary <= 40000 then salary / bonus_percent / 4
      ELSE 0
   END
   );
```

Fig. 15–6 *BONUS function - Additional logic*

The following SQL shows the result from four different salary values:

```
VALUES BONUS(20000,10), BONUS(30000,10), BONUS(40000,10),
BONUS(50000,10);

1
-----------
       2000
       1500
       1000
          0
```

Fig. 15–7 *Using the BONUS function*

SQL-Bodied Table Functions

User-defined table functions can also be written using a single SQL statement. This gives the user the capability of creating a table UDF without the need to write a program in C, C++, or Java.

The table UDF can only access database tables as part of the definition, so it is not as flexible as an external UDF. The example in Fig. 15–8 creates a table UDF that returns records from the TEST_TAKEN table where the test scores are between two values.

```
CREATE FUNCTION GET_MARKS(
     begin_range INT,
     end_range   INT)
   RETURNS TABLE(cid     CANDIDATE_ID,
                 number TEST_ID,
                 score   SCORE)
   LANGUAGE SQL READS SQL DATA
   RETURN
     SELECT CID, NUMBER, SCORE FROM TEST_TAKEN
        WHERE
             SCORE BETWEEN SCORE(begin_range) AND
                          SCORE(end_range);
```

Fig. 15–8 *GET_MARKS table function*

Note the extensive use of user-defined types in this example. The function takes two SCORE arguments that represent the range of marks that we want to retrieve from the table. This table function can now be used as part of a select statement. The SQL in Fig. 15–9 retrieves the list of candidates who scored between 60 and 70 percent on their test.

```
SELECT * FROM TABLE(GET_MARKS(60,70)) AS MARKS

CID NUMBER SCORE
--- ------ -----------
111 500              65
111 502              67
```

Fig. 15–9 *GET_MARKS table function usage*

In order to use the table function, the SQL statement must make use of the TABLE clause with the table function imbedded within it. In addition, the resulting table must be named with the AS clause.

The table that is returned via the table function can also have additional SQL predicates applied to it. For instance, the SQL could have been modified to only return those marks for test number 500:

```
SELECT * FROM TABLE(GET_MARKS(60,70)) AS MARKS
   WHERE NUMBER = TEST_ID('500');

CID NUMBER SCORE
--- ------ -----------
111 500              65
111 502              67
```

Fig. 15–10 *GET_MARKS table function usage with additional logic*

The table UDF can be used in situations where the developer wants to dynamically control the rows being returned to a user. A view definition could have been created to return information about the TEST_TAKEN table, but the definition would have been static. For instance, the following view definition would return exactly the same result:

```
CREATE VIEW GET_MARKS AS (
   SELECT CID, NUMBER, SCORE FROM TEST_TAKEN
      WHERE
            SCORE BETWEEN SCORE(60) AND
                          SCORE(70));
```

Fig. 15–11 *GET_MARKS as a VIEW*

However, it will only return the scores between 60 and 70. In contrast, the table UDF can use variables to change the rows that are returned.

More information on user-defined table definitions can be found in the *DB2 UDB V7.1 SQL Reference* and how to develop these functions using a high-level language are found in the *DB2 UDB V7.1 Application Development Guide*.

 User-defined functions and user-defined table functions were introduced to DB2 in a prior release. However, the ability to use SQL statements to define the actual function or table function are new in DB2 UDB Version 7.1.

Development SQL

Structured Datatypes

Structured datatypes (or sometimes referred to as abstract datatypes) is extended to table definitions in DB2 UDB Version 7.1. The structured datatype is similar to the typed tables discussed in "Advanced SQL" on page 325. However, these datatypes are used within the definition of the table itself, rather than being used to define tables.

For instance, our db2cert database contained information about the candidates taking the test. The original definition for the table is shown in Figure 15–12.

```
CREATE TABLE CANDIDATE
  (CID          CANDIDATE_ID    NOT NULL,
   LNAME        VARCHAR(10)     NOT NULL,
   FNAME        VARCHAR(8)      NOT NULL,
   INITIAL      CHAR(1),
   HPHONE       PHONE,
   WPHONE       PHONE,
   STREETNO     VARCHAR(8),
   STREETNAME   VARCHAR(15)     NOT NULL,
   CITY         VARCHAR(10)     NOT NULL,
   PROV_STATE   VARCHAR(10)     NOT NULL,
   CODE         CHAR(6)         NOT NULL,
   COUNTRY      VARCHAR(10)     NOT NULL,
   CERT_DBA     CHAR(1) NOT NULL WITH DEFAULT,
   CERT_APP     CHAR(1) NOT NULL WITH DEFAULT,
   PRIMARY KEY (CID)
);
```

Fig. 15–12 *Table definition for the CANDIDATE table*

A number of UDTs were used in the definition of this table. For instance, a UDT called CANDIDATE_ID was created to represent a unique identifier for this individual. Further down the table definition, a number of fields were created for storing the address information of the candidate in the table. These multiple fields could be combined into one structured datatype definition as shown in Figure 15–13.

```
CREATE TYPE ADDRESS_TYPE AS
 (
 STREETNO        VARCHAR(8),
 STREETNAME      VARCHAR(15),
 CITY            VARCHAR(10),
 PROV_STATE      VARCHAR(10),
 CODE            CHAR(6),
 COUNTRY         VARCHAR(10)
 )
 MODE DB2SQL WITH FUNCTION ACCESS INSTANTIABLE;
```

Fig. 15–13 *Creating structured datatype*

Now that the definition has been created, we can use it as part of the table creation:

```
CREATE TABLE CANDIDATE
 (CID           CANDIDATE_ID    NOT NULL,
 LNAME          VARCHAR(10)     NOT NULL,
 FNAME          VARCHAR(8)      NOT NULL,
 INITIAL        CHAR(1),
 HPHONE         PHONE,
 WPHONE         PHONE,
 ADDRESS        ADDRESS_TYPE NOT NULL,
 CERT_DBA       CHAR(1) NOT NULL WITH DEFAULT,
 CERT_APP       CHAR(1) NOT NULL WITH DEFAULT,
 PRIMARY KEY (CID))
```

Fig. 15–14 *Creating CANDIDATE table with the address structure*

The use of structured datatypes can help simplify the definitions of tables that have many common elements. This will also make it much easier to develop applications that use object-oriented techniques. Your structured datatypes can contain other structured datatypes as well as UDTs within them.

There are a number of administrative changes that you need to be aware of when using these datatypes in the definition of the table. The first change is how elements are inserted into a table. The relational model always assumes that a column contains one value. Because of this restriction, a number of new operators were required to allow structures to be inserted into tables. For instance, the INSERT command needs to know how to insert a structure.

To illustrate the use of these new operators, we will create a new table with a structured datatype of COMPENSATION.

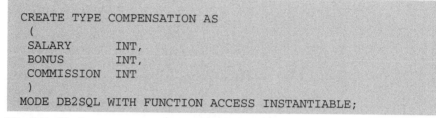

Fig. 15–15 *Creating COMPENSATION datatype*

The COMPENSATION structure contains three elements that make up a person's pay. This structure will be used in the creation of an EMPLOYEE table.

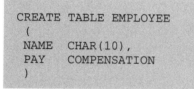

Fig. 15–16 *Creating EMPLOYEE table with COMPENSATION datatype*

At this point we need to insert some information into the EMPLOYEE table. To insert values into the PAY column, we use the COMPENSATION constructor (similar to a casting function):

```
INSERT INTO EMPLOYEE VALUES (
'Shirley',
COMPENSATION()..SALARY(30000)..BONUS(1000)..COMMISSION(3000)
)
```

Fig. 15–17 *Inserting a structure into the EMPLOYEE table*

The COMPENSATION constructor indicates to DB2 that the fields following it make up part of the structure and the double-dot ".." notation combines the elements. The values needed to be cast as a COMPENSATION type since the PAY column is defined as a COMPENSATION type.

Fortunately for the developer, you can also generate a PAY SQL-bodied function that makes the syntax more readable.

```
CREATE FUNCTION PAY(A INT, B INT, C INT)
  RETURNS COMPENSATION
  LANGUAGE SQL
  RETURN(
    COMPENSATION()..SALARY(A)..BONUS(B)..COMMISSION(C)
  );
```

Fig. 15–18 *Creating PAY constructor*

Now the SQL for inserting the structure can be simplified:

```
INSERT INTO EMPLOYEE VALUES
(
'Katrina',PAY(40000,2000,6000)
)
```

Fig. 15–19 *Using PAY function to insert a structure*

After the data has been inserted into the table, you must use the ".." notation to extract the individual elements of the structure. When you define your structured datatype, DB2 generates a number of functions that allow you to extract the values without using the double-dot notation. The two statements found in Figure 15–20 generate identical results:

```
SELECT NAME, PAY..SALARY, PAY..BONUS, PAY..COMMISSION
  FROM EMPLOYEE;

SELECT NAME, SALARY(PAY), BONUS(PAY), COMMISSION(PAY)
  FROM EMPLOYEE;

NAME        2            3            4
---------- ------------ ------------ ------------
SHIRLEY          30000         1000         3000
KATRINA          40000         2000         6000
```

Fig. 15–20 *Selecting information from the EMPLOYEE table*

When displaying structures, DB2 does not generate column names as in the case of regular column types. The user must supply column names through the use of the AS keyword in the SELECT list.

The structure elements can also be used in the where clause and in any part of the SQL that uses column information. For instance, the previous SQL could be modified to return only those employees who have a salary >= 30000 and a bonus and commission that do not exceed 5000 in value.

```
SELECT NAME, PAY..SALARY, PAY..BONUS, PAY..COMMISSION
  FROM EMPLOYEE
WHERE
  SALARY(PAY) >= 30000 AND
  (BONUS(PAY) + PAY..COMMISSION <= 5000);

NAME             2               3               4
----------  ------------  ------------  ------------
SHIRLEY          30000           1000           3000
```

Fig. 15–21 *Selecting information from the EMPLOYEE table with logic*

Figure 15–21 illustrates the use of the double-dot notation and the casting functions against the same structure.

Finally, the developer or DBA needs to create some transform functions for DB2 so that it can handle SELECT commands that do not explicitly name the columns in the select list. The following SQL statement will generate an error:

```
SELECT * FROM EMPLOYEE;

SQL20015N  A TRANSFORM GROUP "DB2_PROGRAM" IS NOT DEFINED
  FOR DATA TYPE "DB2CERT.COMPENSATION".  SQLSTATE=42741
```

Fig. 15–22 *Error when selecting without column names*

DB2 does not know how to represent the PAY structure found within the EMPLOYEE table. In order to make a SELECT * work, two steps need to be taken. First, a UDF needs to be created that returns the contents of the structure as one value. This value must be a simple type, not a structure. For instance, we could create a function that returns the value of each field in the PAY structure as a string of values. The SQL in Figure 15–23 returns the PAY structure as a character string.

```
CREATE FUNCTION SHOW_PAY (P COMPENSATION)
    RETURNS VARCHAR(25)
    LANGUAGE SQL
    RETURN '(' ||
            RTRIM(CHAR(P..SALARY)) || ',' ||
            RTRIM(CHAR(P..BONUS)) || ',' ||
            RTRIM(CHAR(P..COMMISSION)) ||')' ;

SELECT NAME, SHOW_PAY(PAY) FROM EMPLOYEE;

NAME        2
----------  -------------------------
SHIRLEY     (30000,1000,3000)
KATRINA     (40000,2000,6000)
```

Fig. 15–23 *SHOW_PAY function for displaying PAY column*

After this function is defined, we need to create a transform for this column so that DB2 knows how to handle it in a select statement.

```
CREATE TRANSFORM FOR COMPENSATION
    DB2_PROGRAM
    ( FROM SQL WITH FUNCTION SHOW_PAY(COMPENSATION)) ;
```

Fig. 15–24 *Transform function for COMPENSATION type*

Once the transform is defined, the PAY column can be used in a select list without worrying about the structure underneath.

```
SELECT * FROM EMPLOYEE;

NAME        PAY
----------  -------------------------
SHIRLEY     (30000,1000,3000)
KATRINA     (40000,2000,6000)
```

Fig. 15–25 *Transform function for COMPENSATION type*

Since the PAY column can now be represented as a single value, DB2 places the column heading at the top of the results.

Development SQL

When creating transforms for columns, the developer or DBA should understand how a user would interpret the column. The transform function that was defined previously represents the PAY column as a character string. This may seem odd to a user who expects to see a single value being returned from the database. A more-intuitive definition would be to have the SHOW_PAY function calculate the actual employee PAY by summing the columns together. The SQL in Figure 15–26 creates a function that returns the sum of the three PAY elements.

```
CREATE FUNCTION SHOW_PAY (P COMPENSATION)
    RETURNS INT
    LANGUAGE SQL
    RETURN P..SALARY + P..BONUS + P..COMMISSION ;

SELECT NAME, SHOW_PAY(PAY) FROM EMPLOYEE;

NAME            2
----------  ----------
SHIRLEY         34000
KATRINA         48000

SELECT * FROM EMPLOYEE;

NAME        PAY
----------  ----------
SHIRLEY         34000
KATRINA         48000
```

Fig. 15–26 *Alternative function for displaying PAY column*

The advantage of creating a function like SHOW_PAY that returns a single value is that it can now be used in a regular SQL statement to select records based on the total pay of the individual. For instance, the following SQL statement will return only those employees who have a total pay greater than 45000.

```
SELECT * FROM EMPLOYEE
    WHERE SHOW_PAY(PAY) > 45000;

NAME        PAY
----------  ----------
KATRINA         48000
```

Fig. 15–27 *Alternative function for displaying PAY column*

User-defined structured datatypes and user-defined functions are powerful features within DB2. A development group can create common structures and routines to be used within the database. That can lead to better control of data definitions as well as to encourage more code reuse through the use of UDFs.

 User-defined structured types were originally introduced in DB2 for use with typed tables. Version 7.1 extended this capability to column definitions within tables.

Schemas and Aliases

In this section, we will discuss two database objects, schemas and aliases, which have not been discussed in detail in the previous chapters.

Schema

A schema is a database entity that represents a collection of named objects within a DB2 database. The schema name is actually part of the fully qualified name of the object being accessed. When database objects are being defined using the SQL CREATE <db object> statement, a qualifier or schema-name should be provided in the name of the database object.

Schemas may be explicitly created using the CREATE SCHEMA statement with a one user specified as the owner. If the user Bert wanted to create tables with a schema called DB2, the DBADM could use the Control Center to create the schema for Bert or use the following statement. Since Bert owns the schema, he can create objects within the schema.

```
create schema db2 authorization bert
```

Schema names are associated with many database objects, including tables, views, indexes, and packages. For application development purposes, the table, view, and package objects are of primary interest because indexes cannot be directly referenced in SQL DML statements (INSERT, UPDATE, DELETE). If the creator of a database object does not include the schema name in the database object definition, then the object will be created using the creator's authorization ID (assuming IMPLICIT_SCHEMA has not been revoked for the creator).

For example, assume that a user called Mark created a table using the statement: CREATE TABLE TABLE1 (C1 CHAR(3)). The complete name of the database object would be `MARK.TABLE1`, and the application would have to specify the entire name.

> **Note:** Avoid using unqualified table or view names in SQL statements.

In Fig. 15–28, the schema for the table called `TEST` is `DB2CERT`. If you refer to this table in an embedded SQL application, you should reference the table using its fully qualified name, `DB2CERT.TEST`. Failure to include the schema name can result in unexpected behavior.

In an embedded SQL application, unqualified database objects are qualified with the authorization ID of the person who performed the `BIND` command to bind the application package to the database. In a dynamic SQL application, unqualified database objects are qualified with the authorization ID of the person who is executing the statement. This difference is a major consideration during application development because it affects the required data access privileges.

The fully qualified name of a database object must be unique within the database. Thus, from the previous example, another table can exist with the name `TEST`, if the schema name is something other than `DB2CERT`.

```
create table db2cert.test (
    number      test_id      not null,
    name        varchar(30)  not null,
    type        char(1)      not null,
    avgscore    score        not null,
    cutscore    score        not null,
    length      minutes      not null,
    totaltaken  integer      not null,
    totalpassed integer      not null,
    constraint primary key(number))
```

Fig. 15–28 *Creating a table specifying a schema*

Alias

An alias can be used to refer to a table within the database. If an application contains SQL statements that access tables based on an alias, then the alias can be defined to represent different tables without modifying the application. An alias can be created for a table or another alias.

For example, assume a user named Dana created a table called `PRICES`, and a user named Austin created a table called `PRICES`. These tables reside in the same database and are named `DANA.PRICES` and `AUSTIN.PRICES`. Suppose you are asked to develop an application that would access both of these tables and produce summary reports. Also assume that you are using an embedded SQL technique. Your application would require two sets of queries, one for each schema name: DANA and AUSTIN. This is not a good programming technique and is prone to error. For instance, if you find a problem with one of the SQL statements, you may forget to make the corresponding change in the statement that accesses the other table. An alias can be used as the target table name for the SQL statements in your application. If the referenced object in your application is an alias, it can be defined to represent the table DANA.PRICES or AUSTIN.PRICES.

Let's create the alias objects that could be used in the example scenario.

```
create alias db2cert.prices for dana.prices
or
create alias db2cert.prices for austin.prices
```

The application could be developed referencing the table object as DB2CERT.PRICES. The application would then access whichever table has been defined as the source for the DB2CERT.PRICES alias. There can only be one definition for the DB2CERT.PRICES alias at any given time within the database. You could not create the DB2CERT.PRICES alias twice, for example. However, the same alias name could be used in different databases.

Another example of using aliases involves creating multiple aliases for the same source table or view. Assume that the database object was called DB2CERT.PRICES, and we wanted to allow the users Andrew and Geoff to issue the following SQL statement from the CLP:

```
select * from prices
```

The SELECT statement did not explicitly qualify the table name by using the table's schema name. Since the CLP interface is an embedded dynamic SQL interface, the table is implicitly qualified with the current authorization IDs. The target table for this query would be ANDREW.PRICES and GEOFF.PRICES. These are two different tables. However, the goal of the SELECT statement was to access the data in the DB2CERT.PRICES table. Create two aliases to provide the desired results:

```
create alias andrew.prices for db2cert.prices
create alias geoff.prices for db2cert.prices
```

Development
SQL

If you were not the user Andrew, and you tried to create the alias ANDREW.PRICES, you would require CREATE_IN authority in the schema ANDREW or DBADM or SYSADM authority to create the alias ANDREW.PRICES in the schema. Once you create the alias ANDREW.PRICES, the privileges on the referenced table or view (in this case, DB2CERT.PRICES) are used to determine if access is granted to users on ANDREW.PRICES.

COMMIT and ROLLBACK

A program must establish a connection to the target database server before it can run any executable SQL statements. This connection identifies both the authorization ID of the user who is running the program and the name of the database server against which the program is run. After the connection has been established, the program can issue SQL statements that manipulate data (SELECT, INSERT, UPDATE, or DELETE), define and maintain database objects (CREATE, ALTER, or DROP), and initiate control operations (GRANT, REVOKE, COMMIT, or ROLLBACK). These statements are considered as parts of a transaction. A transaction is a sequence of SQL statements (possibly with intervening program logic) that the database manager treats as a whole. An alternative term that is often used for transaction is unit of work. To ensure the consistency of data at the transaction level, the system makes sure that either all operations within a transaction are completed or none are completed.

A transaction begins implicitly with the first executable SQL statement and ends with either a COMMIT or a ROLLBACK statement or when the program ends. In some DB2 programming interfaces, you do not issue the COMMIT or ROLLBACK SQL statements explicitly, but instead employ APIs or object methods to end transactions that result in a commit or a rollback. A commit makes the changes performed during the current transaction permanent, and a rollback restores the data to the state it was in prior to beginning the transaction.

To properly end a program, it must perform these steps:

- End the current transaction (if one is in progress) by explicitly issuing either a COMMIT statement or a ROLLBACK statement.
- Release the connection to the database server by using the CONNECT RESET statement or the appropriate function or method for your programming interface.
- Clean up resources used by the program. For example, free any temporary storage.

Developers can also create intermediate SAVEPOINTS within their SQL so that they can selectively ROLLBACK to a prior point in their code. This feature allows for greater flexibility when working with modular code and stored procedures.

SAVEPOINTS are new to DB2 UDB Version 7.1 and are used primarily with stored procedures.

Summary

In this chapter, we have examined additional SQL features used in DB2 application development.

User-defined functions allow a developer to extend the types of functions used within DB2 and allow for the sharing of common routines between users and application developers.

User-defined structured datatypes can be used to create common structures in database tables and allow for tighter control of datatypes in table definitions.

Schemas and aliases can be used to simplify application development and to reduce confusion when accessing objects in a database.

Finally, the Commit and Rollback commands provide a way of ensuring transaction integrity within the database.

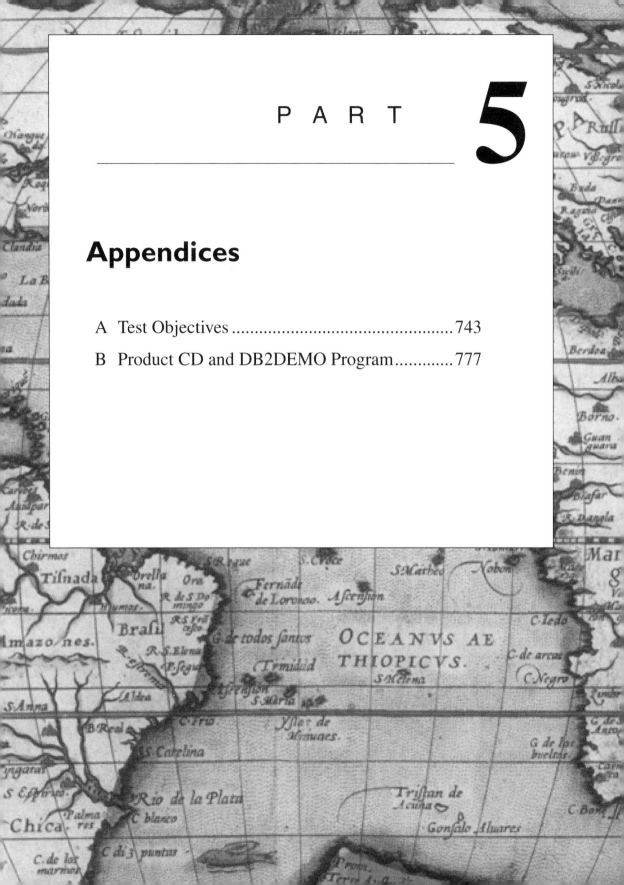

PART 5

Appendices

DB2 UDB V7.1
Certification Test Objectives

This appendix provides the test objectives for the following exams:

- DB2 Family Fundamentals (512)
- DB2 for OS/2, Windows, and UNIX Database Administration (513)

There are sample questions for these tests located at the end of each chapter. Where appropriate, there are exercises provided at the end of each of the chapters.

Detailed information on the IBM Professional Certification program including the DB2 Universal Database certification exams can be found at: http://www.ibm.com/certify.

Experience with DB2 Universal Database Version 7.1 is the best route to preparing for the DB2 UDB V7.1 certification exams. This certification guide is intended to be used alongside your day-to-day use of DB2 UDB V7.1 while preparing for the exams.

DB2 Family Fundamentals (512)

IBM certification in DB2 UDB 7.1 Fundamentals requires an in-depth knowledge of basic SQL, DML, DDL, and an understanding of Database Objects (tables, views, etc.). Further, a basic understanding of the concepts and features of DCL, database creation, data types, stored procedures, programming, components and packaging (SDK, EEE, etc.), protocols supported, installation of products, GUI tools, CLP, basic isolation levels, and import/export is required.

Below are listed the primary objectives which the DB2 UDB V7.1 Fundamentals exam covers. These objectives are listed here to assist you in your preparation for the DB2 UDB V7.1 Fundamentals exam, which is a critical component toward any DB2 UDB V7.1 certification.

To prepare for this exam, Chapters 1 - 8 should be completed. This will give you a good base toward your exam preparation and together with your experience with DB2 UDB V7.1, should prepare you for the DB2 UDB V7.1 Fundamentals (512) test.

I. Installation and Planning

- Ability to install DB2 Universal Database, DB2 Clients & Developers Edition
- Knowledge of and ability to use the DB2 UDB GUI Tools and CLP
- Knowledge of concepts of Datawarehouse and OLAP Issues
- Knowledge of JAVA prerequisites for the Control Center
- Knowledge of new tools

II. Security and Instances

- Ability to describe the functionality of the Administration Server Instance (DAS)
- Ability to provide users with authority on DB objects

III. Creating and Accessing DB2 Databases

- Ability to create DB2 database
- Ability to catalog a remote database or local database or DRDA
- Ability to use the DB2 GUI tools to create, access and manipulate DB2 objects
- Ability to create and access basic DB2 objects

IV. SQL Usage

- Ability to start/end a unit of work
- Given a DDL SQL statement, knowledge to identify results
- Given a DML SQL statement, knowledge to identify results
- Given a DCL SQL statement, knowledge to identify results
- Ability to use SQL to SELECT data from tables
- Ability to use SQL to SORT or GROUP data
- Ability to use SQL to UPDATE, DELETE, or INSERT data
- Knowledge to identify the affect of a COMMIT or ROLLBACK statement
- Knowledge to identify the scope of a COMMIT or ROLLBACK

V. Database Objects

- Ability to demonstrate usage of DB2 data types
- Given a situation, ability to create table
- Given a situation, knowledge to identify when referential constraints are used
- Knowledge to identify methods of data validation
- Knowledge to identify characteristics of a table, view, or index
- Knowledge of concepts of extenders

VI. Database Concurrency

- Knowledge to identify factors that influence locking
- Ability to list the objects that locks can be obtained on
- Knowledge to identify scope of different types of DB2 locks
- Knowledge to identify factors affecting amount of locks that are used
- Knowledge to identify factors affecting the type of locks obtained
- Given a situation, knowledge to identify the isolation levels that should be used

DB2 for OS/2, Windows, and UNIX Database Administration (513)

The certification role of IBM Certified Solutions Expert - DB2 UDB V7.1 Database Administration for UNIX, Windows, and OS/2 requires an in-depth knowledge of DB2 UDB Data Movement, Recovery, Utilities, Configuration, and Authorization and Privileges.

Listed below are the primary objective coverage areas in the DB2 UDB V7.1 Database Administration test, which is required to obtain this certification role. They are listed here to assist you in your preparation toward this certification.

To prepare for this exam, Chapters 9 - 12 should be completed. A good knowledge of the material covered in Chapter 1 - 8 is also required. This will give you a good base toward your exam preparation and together with your significant experience with DB2 UDB V7.1, should prepare you for the DB2 for OS/2, Windows, and UNIX Database Administration (513) test.

I. DB2 Server Management

- Ability to configure/manage DB2 instances (e.g., scope)
- Knowledge of and manage DB2 groups and users
- Knowledge of how to differentiate database security levels
- Ability to set user/group access to database objects using GRANT/REVOKE
- Ability to force users/applications off of DB2
- Ability to configure client/server connectivity for a given protocol
- Ability to schedule jobs
- Ability to configure client server connectivity using DISCOVERY

II. Data Placement

- Ability to create a database
- Skill in discussing the use of schemas
- Ability to differentiate between DMS and SMS table spaces
- Skill in discussing the various table space states
- Ability to separate the storage of a table's data and indexes
- Knowledge of how to choose the correct number of containers
- Ability to create and manipulate the various DB2 objects

III. Database Access

- Ability to create DB2 scripts
- Ability to create and manage indexes on tables
- Knowledge of how to choose the type of index (clustering, unique, primary key)
- Ability to create RI constraints on tables
- Ability to create views on tables
- Skill in examining the contents of the System Catalog tables
- Ability to use GUI Tools to access DB objects
- Knowledge of how to enforce data uniqueness
- Knowledge of ways to generate DDL
- Ability to join tables in different databases

IV. Monitoring DB2 Activity

- Ability to obtain/modify database manager configuration information
- Ability to obtain/modify database configuration information
- Ability to capture EXPLAIN/VISUAL EXPLAIN information
- Skill in analyzing EXPLAIN/VISUAL EXPLAIN information (sortheap, buffpage, degree)
- Knowledge of the uses of query patroller
- Ability to obtain and modify registry values
- Ability to capture snapshots
- Skill in analyzing snapshots
- Ability to create and manipulate event monitors
- Skill in analyzing event monitor output
- Ability to analyze journal information
- Ability to configure alerts

V. DB2 Utilities

- Ability to use EXPORT utility to extract data from a table
- Ability to use IMPORT utility to insert data into a table
- Ability to use the LOAD utility to insert data into a table
- Knowledge to identify when to use IMPORT versus LOAD
- Ability to use the REORG, REORGCHK, and RUNSTATS utilities
- Ability to use DB2move

VI. Database Recovery and Maintenance

- Ability to perform database-level and table space level BACKUP and RESTORE
- Knowledge to identify and explain issues on index creation/recreation
- Knowledge of logging concepts
- Ability to configure and monitor user exit
- Knowledge of recovery policies

VII. Problem Determination

- Skill in interpreting basic information in the DB2DIAG.LOG file

Sample Questions (Fundamentals - Exam 512)

1. A client application on OS/390 must access a DB2 server on Unix, Windows, or OS/2. At a minimum, which of the following is required to be the DB2 server machine?

    A. DB2 Connect Enterprise Edition

    B. DB2 Universal Database Enterprise Edition

    C. DB2 Connect and DB2 Universal Database Workgroup Edition

    D. DB2 Connect and DB2 Universal Database Enterprise Edition

2. Which of the following products is required to be installed in order to build an application on AIX that will access a DB2 UDB for OS/390 database?

    A. DB2 Connect Personal Edition

    B. DB2 Personal Developer's Edition

    C. DB2 Universal Developer's Edition

    D. DB2 Universal Database Workgroup Edition

3. Which of the following tools can be used to catalog a database?

    A. Journal

    B. Alert Center

    C. License Center

    D. Client Configuration Assistant

4. Which of the following utilities would you run to order data and reclaim space from deleted rows in a table:

    A. reorg

    B. db2look

    C. db2move

    D. runstats

5. Which of the following processes is NOT performed by DB2 Warehouse Manager?

    A. Query

    B. Loading

    C. Extraction

    D. Transformation

6. Which of the following DB2 components allows reference to Oracle and DB2 databases in a single query?

    A. DB2 Query Patroller

    B. DB2 Warehouse Manager

    C. DB2 Relational Connect

    D. DB2 Connect Enterprise Edition

7. The purpose of the USE privilege is to:

    A. query data in a table

    B. load data into a table

    C. create tables within a table space

    D. create table spaces within a database

8. Which of the following database authorities is required to create packages in a database?

    A. BINDADD

    B. CREATETAB

    C. CREATEPKG

    D. PACKAGEADD

9. Which two of the following authorities can create a database?

    A. DBADM

    B. SYSADM

    C. DBCTRL

    D. SYSCTRL

    E. SYSMAINT

10. Cataloging a remote database is:

    A. Performed on a PC or UNIX machine to identify the server the DB2 database manager is on

    B. Performed on a PC or UNIX machine to identify the DB2 database to users and applications

    C. Never performed in DB2, as only one database per node is allowed, so cataloging a node automatically catalogs the database at that node

    D. Performed on a PC or UNIX machine to open the catalogs in the DB2 database and present a user with a list of all accessible tables in that database

11. CREATE DISTINCT TYPE kph AS INTEGER WITH COMPARISONS
CREATE DISTINCT TYPE mph AS INTEGER WITH COMPARISONS
CREATE TABLE speed_limits

    (route_num   SMALLINT,
     canada_sl   KPH NOT NULL,
     us_sl   MPH NOT NULL)

Which of the following is a valid query?

A. SELECT route_num FROM speed_limits WHERE canada_sl > 80

B. SELECT route_num FROM speed_limits WHERE canada_sl > kph

C. SELECT route_num FROM speed_limits WHERE canada_sl > us_sl

D. SELECT route_num FROM speed_limits WHERE canada_sl > kph(80)

12. Given the tables:

```
COUNTRY
ID NAME                PERSON CITIES
1  Argentina           1      10
2  Canada              2      20
3  Cuba                2      10
4  Germany             1      0
5  France              7      5


STAFF
ID LASTNAME
1  Jones
2  Smith
```

The statement:

INSERT INTO staff SELECT person, 'Greyson' FROM country WHERE person > 1

will insert how many rows into the STAFF table?

A. 0

B. 1

C. 2

D. 3

13. Which of the following statements eliminates all but one of each set of duplicate rows in the final result table?

A. `SELECT UNIQUE * FROM t1`

B. `SELECT DISTINCT * FROM t1`

C. `SELECT * FROM DISTINCT T1`

D. `SELECT UNIQUE (*) FROM t1`

E. `SELECT DISTINCT (*) FROM t1`

14. Given the following table definition and SQL statements:

```
CREATE TABLE table1 (col1 INT, col2 CHAR(40), col3 INT)
GRANT INSERT, UPDATE, SELECT, REFERENCES ON TABLE table1 TO
USER usera
```

Which of the following SQL statements will revoke privileges for user USERA on COL1 and COL2?

A. `REVOKE UPDATE ON TABLE table1 FROM USER usera`

B. `REVOKE ALL PRIVILEGES ON TABLE table1 FROM USER usera`

C. `REVOKE ALL PRIVILEGES ON TABLE table1 COLUMNS (col1, col2) FROM USERA`

D. `REVOKE REFERENCES ON TABLE table1 COLUMNS (col1, col2) FROM USER usera`

15. Given the two table definitions:

```
ORG
    deptnumb        INTEGER
    deptname        CHAR(30)
    manager         INTEGER
    division        CHAR(30)
    location        CHAR(30)

STAFF
    id              INTEGER
    name            CHAR(30)
    dept            INTEGER
    job             CHAR(20)
    years           INTEGER
    salary          DECIMAL(10,2)
    comm            DECIMAL(10,2)
```

Which of the following statements will display each department, alphabetically by name, and the name of the manager of the department?

A. SELECT a.deptname, b.name FROM org a, staff b WHERE
   a.manager=b.id

B. SELECT a.deptname, b.name FROM org a, staff b WHERE
   b.manager=a.id

C. SELECT a.deptname, b.name FROM org a, staff b WHERE
   a.manager=b.id GROUP BY a.deptname, b.name

D. SELECT a.deptname, b.name FROM org a, staff b, WHERE
   b.manager=a.id GROUP BY a.deptname, b.name

16. Given the following tables:

```
NAMES
Name                    Number
Wayne Gretzky           99
Jaromir Jagr            68
Bobby Orr               4
Bobby Hull              23
Brett Hull              16
Mario Lemieux           66
Steve Yzerman           19
Claude Lemieux          19
Mark Messier            11
Mats Sundin             13

POINTS
Name                    Points
Wayne Gretzky           244
Jaromir Jagr            168
Bobby Orr               129
Bobby Hull              93
Brett Hull              121
Mario Lemieux           189

PIM
Name                    PIM
Mats Sundin             14
Jaromir Jagr            18
Bobby Orr               12
Mark Messier            32
Brett Hull              66
Mario Lemieux           23
Joe Sakic               94
```

Which of the following statements will display the player's names, numbers, points, and PIM for all players with an entry in all three tables?

A. `SELECT names.name, names.number, points.points, pim.pim FROM names INNER JOIN points ON names.name=points.name INNER JOIN pim ON pim.name=names.name`

B. `SELECT names.name, names.number, points.points, pim.pim FROM names OUTER JOIN points ON names.name=points.name OUTER JOIN pim ON pim.name=names.name`

C. `SELECT names.name, names.number, points.points, pim.pim FROM names LEFT OUTER JOIN points ON names.name=points.name LEFT OUTER JOIN pim ON pim.name=names.name`

D. `SELECT names.name, names.number, points.points, pim.pim FROM names RIGHT OUTER JOIN points ON names.name=points.name RIGHT OUTER JOIN pim ON pim.name=names.name`

17. Given the following table definitions:

```
DEPARTMENT
    deptno              CHAR(3)
    deptname            CHAR(30)
    mgrno               INTEGER
    admrdept            CHAR(3)

EMPLOYEE
    empno               INTEGER
    firstname           CHAR(30)
    midinit             CHAR
    lastname            CHAR(30)
    workdept            CHAR(3)
```

Which of the following statements will list every employee's number and last name with the employee number and last name of their manager, including employees without a manager?

A. `SELECT e.empno, e.lastname, m.empno, m.lastname`
   `FROM employee e LEFT INNER JOIN department INNER JOIN`
   `employee m ON mgrno = m.empno ON e.workdept = deptno`

B. `SELECT e.empno, e.lastname, m.empno, m.lastname,`
   `FROM employee e LEFT OUTER JOIN department INNER JOIN`
   `employee m ON mgrno = m.empno ON e.workdept = deptno`

C. `SELECT e.empno, e.lastname, m.empno, m.lastname`
   `FROM employee e RIGHT OUTER JOIN department INNER JOIN`
   `employee m ON mgrno = m.empno ON e.workdept = deptno`

D. `SELECT e.empno, e.lastname, m.empno, m.lastname`
   `FROM employee e RIGHT INNER JOIN department INNER JOIN`
   `employee m ON mgrno = m.empno ON e.workdept = deptno`

18. Given the table:

```
STAFF
ID LASTNAME
1  Jones
2  Smith
```

When issuing the query "`SELECT * FROM staff`", the row return order will be based on which of the following?

A. An ambiguous order

B. The primary key order

C. The order that the rows were inserted into the table

D. The values for the ID column, then the LASTNAME column

19. Given the table:

```
STAFF
ID LASTNAME
1  Jones
2  Smith
3  <null>
```

Which of the following statements removes all rows from the table where there is a NULL value for LASTNAME?

A. DELETE FROM staff WHERE lastname IS NULL

B. DELETE FROM staff WHERE lastname = 'NULL'

C. DELETE ALL FROM staff WHERE lastname IS NULL

D. DELETE ALL FROM staff WHERE lastname = 'NULL'

20. Given the tables:

```
COUNTRY
  ID NAME              PERSON   CITIES
  1  Argentina         1        10
  2  Canada            2        20
  3  Cuba              2        10
  4  Germany           1        0
  5  France            7        5

STAFF
  ID LASTNAME
  1  Jones
  2  Smith
```

Which of the following statements removes the rows from the COUNTRY table that have PERSONS in the STAFF table?

A. DELETE FROM country WHERE id IN (SELECT id FROM staff)

B. DELETE FROM country WHERE id IN (SELECT person FROM staff)

C. DELETE FROM country WHERE person IN (SELECT id FROM staff)

D. DELETE FROM country WHERE person IN (SELECT person FROM staff)

21. STOCK TABLE has the following columns definitions:

```
type          CHAR(1)
status        CHAR(1)
quantity      INTEGER
price         DEC(7,2)
```

Items are indicated to be out of stock by setting STATUS to NULL and QUANTITY and PRICE to zero. Which of the following statements updates the STOCK table to indicate that all the items except for those with TYPE of "S" are temporarily out of stock?

A. `UPDATE stock SET status='NULL', quantity=0, price=0 WHERE type <> 'S'`

B. `UPDATE stock SET (status, quantity, price) = (NULL, 0, 0) WHERE type <> 'S'`

C. `UPDATE stock SET (status, quantity, price) = ('NULL', 0, 0) WHERE type <>'S'`

D. `UPDATE stock SET status = NULL, SET quantity=0, SET price = 0 WHERE type <>'S'`

22. Given successfully executed embedded SQL:

```
INSERT INTO staff VALUES (1, 'Colbert', 'Dorchester', 1)
COMMIT
INSERT INTO staff VALUES (6, 'Anders', 'Cary', 6)
INSERT INTO staff VALUES (3, 'Gaylord', 'Geneva', 8)
ROLLBACK WORK
```

Which of the following indicates the number of new rows that would be in the STAFF table?

A. 0

B. 1

C. 2

D. 3

23. Given, `CREATE TABLE t1 (c1 CHAR(4) NOT NULL)`. Which of the following can be inserted into this table?

A. 4

B. NULL

C. "abc"

D. "abcde"

24. Which of the following DDL statements creates a table where employee IDs are unique?

A. `CREATE TABLE t1 (employid INTEGER)`

B. `CREATE TABLE t1 (employid UNIQUE INTEGER)`

C. `CREATE TABLE t1 (employid INTEGER NOT NULL)`

D. `CREATE TABLE t1 (employid INTEGER NOT NULL, primary key (employid))`

25. Given the transaction:

```
"CREATE TABLE t1 (id INTEGER,CONSTRAINT chkid
     CHECK (id<100))"
"INSERT INTO t1 VALUES (100)"
"COMMIT"
```

Which of the following results from the transaction?

A. The row is inserted with a NULL value.

B. The row is inserted with a value of 100.

C. The row insertion with a value of 100 is rejected.

D. The trigger called chkid is fired to validate the data.

26. Which of the following delete rules will not allow a row to be deleted from the parent table if a row with the corresponding key value still exists in the child table?

A. `DELETE`

B. `CASCADE`

C. `RESTRICT`

D. `SET NULL`

27. If a table is defined with a check constraint for one or more columns, which of the following will perform the data validation after the table is loaded with the load utility?

A. Reorg

B. Check

C. Runstats

D. Image Copy

E. Set Constraints

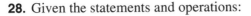

28. Given the statements and operations:

```
"CREATE TABLE t1 (c1 CHAR(1))"
```

Six rows are inserted with values of: a, b, c, d, e, and f

```
"SET CONSTRAINTS FOR t1 OFF"
"ALTER TABLE t1 ADD CONSTRAINT con1 CHECK (c1 ='a')"
"SET CONSTRAINTS FOR t1 IMMEDIATE CHECKED
     FOR EXCEPTION IN t1 USE t1exp"
```

Which of the following describes what happens to the rows with values of b, c, d, e, and f?

A. Deleted from T1 only

B. Deleted from T1 and written into the t1exp file

C. Deleted from T1 and inserted into the table t1exp

D. Deleted from T1 and written into the db2diag.log file

E. Deleted from T1 and inserted into the table syscat.checks

29. A declared temporary table is used for which of the following purposes:

A. Backup purposes

B. Storing intermediate results

C. Staging area for the load utility

D. Sharing result sets between applications

30. Given the statement:

```
CREATE VIEW v1 AS SELECT c1 FROM t1 WHERE c1='a'
WITH CHECK OPTION
```

Which of the following SQL statements will insert data into the table?

A. INSERT INTO v1 VALUES (a)

B. INSERT INTO v1 VALUES (b)

C. INSERT INTO v1 VALUES ('b')

D. INSERT INTO v1 VALUES ('a')

E. INSERT INTO v1 VALUES ('ab')

31. Which of the following products can be used to store image data in a DB2 database?

A. Net.Data

B. Net Search

C. DB2 AVI Extenders

D. DB2 XML Extenders

E. DB2 Text Extenders

32. For which of the following database objects can locks NOT be obtained?

A. A row

B. A table

C. A column

D. An index key

33. An update lock gets released by an application using the repeatable read isolation level during which of the following?

A. If the cursor accessing the row is closed

B. If the transaction issues a ROLLBACK statement

C. If the cursor accessing the row is moved to the next row

D. If the transaction changes are made via an UPDATE statement

34. Which of the following isolation levels is most likely to acquire a table level lock during an index scan?

A. Read Stability

B. Repeatable Read

C. Cursor Stability

D. Uncommitted Read

35. Which of the following processing can occur for a unit of work using an isolation level of Uncommitted Read and scanning through the table more than once within the unit of work?

A. Access uncommitted changes made by other processes

B. Update uncommitted changes made by other processes

C. Update rows of a return set and have those updates changed by other processes from one scan to the next

D. Update rows of a return set and have those updates committed by other processes from one scan to the next

36. Which of the following releases a lock by an application using the cursor stability isolation level?

  A. If the cursor accessing the row is moved to the next row

  B. If the cursor accessing the row is used to update the row

  C. If the application's current row is deleted by the application

  D. If the application's current row needs to be updated by another application

37. Given the requirement of providing a read-only database, applications accessing the database should be run with which of the following isolation levels to allow for the most read concurrency?

  A. Read stability

  B. Repeatable read

  C. Cursor stability

  D. Uncommitted read

Sample Questions (Administration - Exam 513)

1. Given the following Node 1 entry:

   ```
   Node name    = DB2SERV
   Comment      = My TCPIP connection
   Protocol     = TCPIP
   Hostname     = db2inst1
   Service name = db2svce
   ```

   Which of the following commands must be executed before updating the DBM configuration for this instance?

   A. ATTACH TO db2serv

   B. ATTACH TO db2inst1

   C. CONNECT TO db2serv

   D. CONNECT TO db2inst1

2. Two databases, DATA1 and DATA2, will reside in different instances on the same DB2 UDB server. Which of the following actions provides a user with SYSADM authority on DATA1, but no SYSADM authority on DATA2?

   A. GRANT SYSADM to the user on DATA1

   B. REVOKE SYSADM from the user on DATA2

   C. Specify different SYSADM groups for the instances

   D. Specify different SYSADM groups for the databases

3. Which two of the following authority levels can reduce the RUNTIME DEGREE of parallelism for an active application?

   A. DBADM

   B. DBCTRL

   C. SYSADM

   D. DBMAINT

   E. SYSCTRL

   F. SYSMAINT

4. Given the statement:

```
GRANT UPDATE ON table1 TO user1 WITH GRANT OPTION
```

Which of the following privileges can user1 grant to user2?

A. DBADM on DATABASE to user2

B. INSERT on TABLE table1 to user2

C. SELECT on TABLE table1 to user2

D. UPDATE on TABLE table1 to user2

5. Which of the following actions is required before forcing a user off of a remote database?

A. Catalog the remote database

B. Quiesce the remote database

C. Connect to the remote database

D. Attach to the remote DB2 instance

E. Update DB2INSTANCE environment variable

6. Which two of the following steps are required to set up a DB2 server to allow remote client access using APPC and TCP/IP?

A. Update the DBM configuration

B. Catalog the client workstation

C. Set the DB2COMM registry variable

D. Create a DB2 instance for each protocol

E. Update the DB configuration for each database

7. Which two of the following are required to schedule jobs?

A. DBADM authority at the DAS instance

B. SYSADM authority at the DAS instance

C. SYSMAINT authority at the DAS instance

D. Supply your userid and password when you schedule the job

E. Set the time on the server and client to be in the same time zone

8. Which two of the following must be done to allow DB2 databases to be automatically detected by DB2 clients?

    A. Run the Client Configuration Assistant at the database server

    B. Set AUTHENTICATION=CLIENT in the database manager configuration

    C. Ensure the database configuration parameter DISCOVER_DB is set to ENABLE

    D. Ensure the database manager configuration parameter DISCOVER is set to ENABLE

    E. Ensure the database manager configuration parameter DISCOVER_INST is set to ENABLE

9. Given the statement:

    ```
    "CREATE DATABASE payroll"
    ```

    Which of the following indicates the number of table spaces that are created?

    A. 0

    B. 1

    C. 2

    D. 3

    E. 4

10. Given the command:

    ```
    CREATE DATABASE inventory
    CATALOG TABLESPACE
        MANAGED BY SYSTEM USING ('path1','path2')
        EXTENTSIZE 16 PREFETCHSIZE 32
    USER TABLESPACE
        MANAGED BY SYSTEM USING ('patha')
    TEMPORARY TABLESPACE
        MANAGED BY DATABASE USING ( FILE 'filea' 1000 )
    WITH "EXTENTSIZE 10"
    ```

    Which of the following indicates the extent size for the system catalog table space?

    A. 10

    B. 16

    C. 32

    D. 1000

11. Which of the following schemas contain the views that are used to update statistical information used by the optimizer?

A. SYSCAT

B. SYSIBM

C. SYSOPT

D. SYSSTAT

12. Given a table space creation statement that does not indicate the size of its containers, which of the following table spaces types was created by DB2?

A. DMS

B. LOB

C. SMS

D. LONG

E. INDEX

13. Which of the following must be used when storing regular table data in one table space and index data in another table space?

A. Two DMS tablespaces using files

B. Two SMS tablespaces using files

C. Two SMS tablespaces using directories

D. Two DMS tablespaces using directories

14. Which of the following table space creation statements enables container space to be allocated as required?

A. CREATE TABLESPACE TS1 MANAGED BY SYSTEM USING ('D:\CONTAIN3', 'G:\CONTAIN4')

B. CREATE INCREMENTAL TABLESPACE TS1 MANAGED BY DATABASE USING (DEVICE '/dev/rdev11' 24000)

C. CREATE TABLESPACE TS1 MANAGED BY DATABASE USING (DEVICE '/dev/rdev23' 150000) EXTENTSIZE 1

D. CREATE INCREMENTAL TABLESPACE TS1 MANAGED BY SYSTEM USING ('D:\CONTAIN1', 'G:\CONTAIN2') EXTENTSIZE 1

15. Given the following statement:

```
CREATE TYPE Emp_type AS
( Serialno            Char(6)
Name                  Varchar(32)
Address               Varchar(100)
Salary                Integer
Photo                 Blob(1M))
MODE DB2SQL
```

Which of the following statement stubs must be used to create a table with this definition?

A. `CREATE TABLE StateEmp OF Emp_type...`

B. `CREATE TABLE StateEmp OF TYPE Emp_type...`

C. `CREATE TABLE StateEmp WITH TYPE Emp_type...`

D. `CREATE TABLE StateEmp USING TYPE Emp_type...`

16. The following create index command is issued:

```
CREATE UNIQUE INDEX IX1 ON TABLE1 (org asc, date1 desc)
INCLUDE (title) ALLOW REVERSE SCANS
```

Which of the following are TRUE?

A. Index IX1 will support forward index scans

B. Index IX1 will support reverse index scans

C. Columns org, date1, and title enforce uniqueness

D. Columns org, date1, and title are included in the index

17. Given the table definitions:

```
ID.PC                          ID.EMPLOYEES
serial_num       INT           employee_num   INT NOT NULL PRIMARY KEY
model_num        INT           employee_name  CHAR(20)
owner_id         INT
```

and the query:

```
SELECT employee_name, serial_num
FROM id.employees, id.pc
WHERE owner_id = employee_num
```

Creating an index on which of the following will speed up this query?

A. owner_id

B. serial_num

C. employee_num

D. employee_name

18. Given the following tables:

```
TEST_TAKEN
TestName                    CHAR(50) NOT NULL
TestNumber                  INTEGER NOT NULL
TestScore                   INTEGER NOT NULL
CandidateID                 INTEGER NOT NULL

CANDIDATE_DB2
CandidateName               CHAR(20) NOT NULL
CandidateID                 INTEGER NOT NULL
Address                     CHAR(100) NOT NULL
CandidatePhoto              BLOB(1M)
```

And the following information:

- Candidate IDs are unique
- A query that returns all addresses of individuals who have taken a DB2 test

While reading a minimum number of physical pages, an optimizer needs to consider the index to scan over all rows of the table data. Which of the following indexes must be created?

A. Primary key on candidate_db2 (CandidateID)

B. Unique clustered index on test_taken (CandidateName)

C. Unique index on test_taken (CandidateID, TestNumber)

D. Unique index on candidate_db2 (CandidateID, CandidateName)

E. Unique clustered index on candidate_db2 (Candidate ID, CandidateName)

19. Given the table definitions:

```
CREATE TABLE id.pc
(serial_num INT NOT NULL PRIMARY KEY,
   model_num INT NOT NULL,
   owner_id INT,
   FOREIGN KEY (owner_id)
   REFERENCES id.employees ON DELETE SET NULL)
CREATE TABLE id.employees
   (employee_num INT NOT NULL PRIMARY KEY,
   employee_name  CHAR(20))
```

and the statement:

```
DELETE FROM id.employees WHERE employee_num = 12345
```

Which of the following occurs to data in the id.pc table?

A. All rows where owner_id was 12345 are deleted.

B. All rows where owner_id was 12345, owner_id is not null.

C. All rows where owner_id was 12345, the owner_id is null.

D. All rows where owner_id was 12345 are placed in an exception table.

20. Which of the following will occur when a view is created on a DB2 table?

A. Memory usage is reduced.

B. Data access time is increased.

C. Data access control is increased.

D. Query compilation time is reduced.

21. In which of the following are the definitions of the tables stored in a DB2 database?

A. The system catalogs

B. The DB2DIAG.LOG file

C. The recovery history file

D. The database configuration

22. Which of the following tools will allow users to schedule batch updates to their table(s)?

A. Journal

B. Command Center

C. Script Center

D. Control Center

23. Given the following:

```
CREATE TABLE tab1 (col1 INT CONSTRAINT notnul CHECK(col1 IS
NOT NULL), col2 CHAR(10))
```

Which of the following will enforce uniqueness of col1, which currently does not contain duplicate values?

A. Create primary key on col1

B. Create unique index on col1

C. Create a cluster index on col1

D. Create unique constraint on col1

24. How can an existing trigger's behavior be modified, if at all?

A. Use ALTER TABLE.

B. Use an ALTER TRIGGER statement.

C. Use the Modify tab in the Control Center against the TRIGGERS object.

D. The trigger cannot be modified. It must be dropped and recreated with the desired syntax to modify its behavior.

25. Which of the following enables joining tables in heterogeneous databases with DB2's Federated Database function:

A. The join columns in the two tables must have exactly the same data type.

B. The only join permitted with heterogeneous databases is a cartesian product, so join columns are not required.

C. The user or DBA may have to override some mappings of data types from the non-DB2 database to a different DB2 data type for the join to succeed.

D. The Federated database feature will automatically map all data type values in the non-DB2 database to the closest DB2 data type so the join keys match.

26. In which of the following is the size of the buffer used during an online backup defined?

A. DB2_BACKUPSZ registry variable

B. DBM configuration of database instance

C. DBM.INI file for the database instance

D. DB configuration for database being backed up

27. Which of the following enables archival logging?

   A. Allocating the database primary logs

   B. Setting the LOGPATH database parameter

   C. Setting the LOGSECOND database parameter

   D. Setting the LOGRETAIN database parameter

28. Which of the following will capture static SQL explain snapshots for an application?

   A. The EXPLAIN YES bind option

   B. The EXPLSNAP YES bind option

   C. The SET CURRENT EXPLAIN SNAPSHOT YES statement

   D. The SET CURRENT EXPLAIN SNAPSHOT EXPLAIN statement

29. Which of the following is designated by a Visual Explain Access Plan Graph TQUEUE (table queue) symbol?

   A. Sort operation

   B. Merge scan join

   C. Nested loop join

   D. Index scan operation

   E. Intra-query parallelism

30. Which of the following in Visual Explain output indicates that intra-partition parallelism is being used in the access strategy?

   A. Sort table queues

   B. Local table queue

   C. Remote table queue

   D. Look-ahead table queue

31. To govern users of DB2 with a graphical view, you would use which of the following?

   A. The DB2 Monitor

   B. The DB2 Governor

   C. The Command Center

   D. The DB2 Query Patroller

32. If a DB2 environment variable is set in multiple places, which of the following is the correct search order?

   A. Session Environment Variables, DB2 Global-Level Registry Profile, DB2 Instance-Level Registry Profile

   B. Session Environment Variables, DB2 Instance-Level Registry Profile, DB2 Global-Level Registry Profile

   C. DB2 Instance-Level Registry Profile, DB2 Global-Level Registry Profile, Session Environment Variables

   D. DB2 Global-Level Registry Profile, DB2 Instance-Level Registry Profile, Session Environment Variables

33. Snapshot monitoring accumulates the number of times a deadlock is detected. Which of the following commands will initialize the deadlocks detected value to zero?

   A. `RESET MONITOR ALL`

   B. `UPDATE MONITOR FOR ALL`

   C. `INITIALIZE MONITOR ALL`

   D. `RESET MONITOR USING LOCK OFF`

   E. `UPDATE MONITOR USING LOCK OFF`

   F. `INITIALIZE MONITOR USING LOCK OFF`

34. Given the following scenario:

```
GET SNAPSHOT FOR ALL DATABASES
Database Snapshot
Database name                        = SAMPLE
.....   Sort overflows               = 18
```

Which of the following actions will NOT reduce sort overflows?

   A. Create an index

   B. Increase sort heap size

   C. Reorganize sorted tables

   D. Update statistics on sorted tables

   E. Decrease number of concurrent users

35. When event monitor output is channeled to a named pipe, which of the following is the correct order for processing of the named piped?

   A. Create pipe, Open pipe, Read pipe, Activate monitor, Deactivate monitor, Close pipe, Delete pipe

   B. Create pipe, Open pipe, Activate monitor, Read pipe, Deactivate monitor, Close pipe, Delete pipe

   C. Create pipe, Open pipe, Activate monitor, Deactivate monitor, Read pipe, Close pipe, Delete pipe

   D. Create pipe, Activate monitor, Open pipe, Read pipe, Close pipe, Deactivate monitor, Delete pipe

36. From the Journal, which of the following can reschedule a job to execute at a later time?

   A. Messages page

   B. Job History page

   C. Pending Jobs page

   D. Running Jobs page

37. Which of the following must be performed to specify when the Alert Center Window should surface on a desktop?

   A. Open the Alert Center page of the Journal

   B. Open the Alert Center page of the Script Center

   C. Open the Alert Center page of the Command Center

   D. Open the Alert Center page of the Event Analyzer

   E. Open the Alert Center page of the Tools Settings notebook

38. Which of the following file formats allows for the creation of a table during import?

   A. ASC

   B. IXF

   C. MDB

   D. TXT

   E. WSF

39. Which of the following DB2 utilities can insert data into a DRDA host database?

   A. LOAD

   B. EXPORT

   C. IMPORT

   D. UPLOAD

   E. FORCEIN

40. Which of the following DB2 UDB utilities provides the fastest method of adding large amounts of data to a table?

   A. LOAD

   B. APPEND

   C. IMPORT

   D. UPLOAD

   E. FASTLOAD

41. Which of the following DB2 utilities can add data to a table with a primary key defined and have all rows that violate the primary key constraint stored in an exception table?

   A. LOAD

   B. FORCE

   C. EXPORT

   D. IMPORT

   E. UPLOAD

42. Having just completed a reorganization of a DB2 table, which two of the following steps should be completed to improve query performance?

   A. Run statistics on the table

   B. Update the database configuration

   C. Reorganize each index on the table

   D. Drop and recreate each index on the table

   E. Rebind any packages that access the table

43. Which of the following must be used to move a DB2 database from Windows NT to Linux?

   A. Backup the database on Windows NT and restore it on Linux

   B. Use Relational Connect to move the data using INSERT statements with subselects

   C. Use db2move to automate exporting the tables on Windows NT and LOADing them on Linux

   D. Use db2look with the -e option to capture the DDL and data for each table in a format that can be imported to DB2 on Linux

44. A database sample exists in the instance prod1 on workstation work2. Workstation work1 has cataloged the remote node n2 for work2 and database sample at this node. Which of the following will backup the database sample from workstation work1?

   A. BACKUP DATABASE sample REMOTE prod1

   B. ATTACH TO n2; BACKUP DATABASE sample

   C. ATTACH TO prod1; BACKUP DATABASE sample

   D. CONNECT TO sample; BACKUP DATABASE sample

45. Which of the following is the minimum authority required to perform a restore to a new database?

   A. DBADM

   B. SYSADM

   C. SYSCTRL

   D. SYSMAINT

46. Immediately following the creation of an index on a table to improve query performance, which of the following SQL requests is adversely affected by the additional index?

   A. FETCH

   B. SELECT

   C. CONNECT

   D. PREPARE

47. Online index reorganization is the ability to reclaim index free space after deletion of an index key. Which of the following options gives an index this capability?

   A. `CREATE INDEX .... ONLINE`

   B. `CREATE INDEX .... RECLAIM`

   C. `CREATE INDEX .... MINPCTUSED`

   D. `CREATE INDEX .... REORGSPACE`

48. Which of the following must be ensured prior to a redirected restore of a database?

   A. All containers in the redirected restore have been untagged.

   B. The redirected restore is not on the same instance as the original database.

   C. The redirected restore does have the same container names as the original database.

   D. The output from a "list tablespaces is obtained which shows detail" and "list tablespace containers".

49. Which of the following DB2DIAG.LOG level will produce the most information written to the DB2DIAG.LOG?

   A. 1

   B. 2

   C. 3

   D. 4

   E. 5

50. The location of the DB2DIAG.LOG file is specified in which of the following?

   A. db2.ini file

   B. DB2 registry

   C. Database directory

   D. Database configuration

   E. Database manager configuration

Answers

Fundamentals - Exam 512

1.	B	2.	C	3.	D	4.	A	5.	A
6.	C	7.	C	8.	A	9.	B/D	10.	B
11.	D	12.	D	13.	B	14.	B	15.	C
16.	A	17.	B	18.	A	19.	A	20.	C
21.	B	22.	B	23.	C	24.	D	25.	C
26.	C	27.	E	28.	C	29.	B	30.	D
31.	C	32.	C	33.	B	34.	B	35.	A
36.	A	37.	D						

Administration - Exam 513

1.	A	2.	C	3.	C/E	4.	D	5.	D
6.	A/C	7.	B/D	8.	C/E	9.	D	10.	B
11.	D	12.	C	13.	A	14.	A	15.	A
16.	C	17.	A	18.	E	19.	C	20.	C
21.	A	22.	C	23.	B	24.	D	25.	C
26.	B	27.	D	28.	B	29.	E	30.	B
31.	D	32.	B	33.	A	34.	C	35.	B
36.	C	37.	E	38.	B	39.	C	40.	A
41.	A	42.	A/E	43.	C	44.	B	45.	C
46.	D	47.	C	48.	D	49.	D	50.	E

CD-ROM Installation

The accompanying CD-ROM contains a copy of DB2 UDB Personal Edition V7.1 for Windows. This product is provided in "Try and Buy" mode. Once the product has been installed, it will continue to operate for 90 days. To use this software past the 90-day period requires a DB2 license, which is not provided. To install DB2 for Windows, perform the following steps:

- Insert CD-ROM.
- From File Manager: Execute X:\SETUP.EXE (where X is the drive letter of your CD drive).

If you are installing on a Windows NT workstation, you must be an administrator. This username must belong to the Administrators group and must comply with SQL naming standards.

DB2DEMO

The DB2DEMO program is included on the CD-ROM. To install this program, perform the following steps after installing the DB2 database program:

- Insert CD-ROM.
- Copy the file DEMOINST.EXE from the CD-ROM to a temporary directory on your machine
- From File Manager: Execute Y:\DEMOINST.EXE (where Y is the drive letter and directory where the DEMOINST.EXE file is located)
- From File Manager: Execute Y:\SETUP.EXE (where Y is the drive letter and directory where the DEMOINST.EXE file was placed)

This will install the DB2DEMO program which will allow you to demonstrate and use the various SQL features of DB2. One of the shortcuts created in the DB2DEMO folder is the DB2 UDB V7 Certification Examples icon. By clicking on this icon, you will be able to try out many of the features found within the Certification Guide. Help for this product can be found from within the product itself, or by using a browser to view the INDEX.HTM file in the DB2DEMO directory that was created as part of the installation process.

Index

Index

Index

Index